Fodor's

THE AMALFI COAST, CAPRI & NAPLES

6th Edition

New York, Toronto, London, Sydney, Auckland

Eugene Fodor:
The Spy Who Loved Travel

As Fodor's celebrates our 75th anniversary, we are honoring the colorful and adventurous life of Eugene Fodor, who revolutionized guidebook publishing in 1936 with his first book, *On the Continent, The Entertaining Travel Annual.*

Eugene Fodor's life seemed to leap off the pages of a great spy novel. Born in Hungary, he spoke six languages and graduated from the Sorbonne and the London School of Economics. During World War II he joined the Office of Strategic Services, the budding spy agency for the United States. He commanded the team that went behind enemy lines to liberate Prague, and recommended to Generals Eisenhower, Bradley, and Patton that Allied troops move to the capital city. After the war, Fodor worked as a spy in Austria, posing as a U.S. diplomat.

In 1949 Eugene Fodor—with the help of the CIA—established Fodor's Modern Guides. He was passionate about travel and wanted to bring his insider's knowledge of Europe to a new generation of sophisticated Americans who wanted to explore and seek out experiences beyond their borders. Among his innovations were annual updates, consulting local experts, and including cultural and historical perspectives and an emphasis on people—not just sites. As Fodor described it, "The main interest and enjoyment of foreign travel lies not only in 'the sites,' . . . .but in contact with people whose customs, habits, and general outlook are different from your own."

Eugene Fodor died in 1991, but his legacy, Fodor's Travel, continues. It is now one of the world's largest and most trusted brands in travel information, covering more than 600 destinations worldwide in guidebooks, on Fodors.com, and in ebooks and iPhone apps. Technology and the accessibility of travel may be changing, but Eugene Fodor's unique storytelling skills and reporting style are behind every word of today's Fodor's guides.

Our editors and writers continue to embrace Eugene Fodor's vision of building personal relationships through travel. We invite you to join the Fodor's community at fodors.com/community and share your experiences with like-minded travelers. Tell us when we're right. Tell us when we're wrong. And share fantastic travel secrets that aren't yet in Fodor's. Together, we will continue to deepen our understanding of our world.

Happy 75th Anniversary, Fodor's! Here's to many more.

Tim Jarrell, Publisher

FODOR'S THE AMALFI COAST, CAPRI & NAPLES

Editor: Robert I. C. Fisher

Writers: Martin Wilmot Bennett, Fergal Kavanagh, Fiorella Squillante

Production Editor: Jennifer DePrima
Maps & Illustrations: *cartographers;* Bob Blake, Rebecca Baer, *map editors;* William Wu, *information graphics*
Design: Fabrizio La Rocca, *creative director;* Guido Caroti, *art director;* Tina Malaney, Nora Rosansky, Chie Ushio, *designers;* Melanie Marin, *associate director of photography*
Cover Photo: (Positano, Amalfi Coast) Günter Gräfenhain/fototeca 9x12
Production Manager: Angela L. McLean

SPECIAL SALES

This book is available at special discounts for bulk purchases for sales promotions or premiums. Special editions, including personalized covers, excerpts of existing books, and corporate imprints, can be created in large quantities for special needs. For more information, write to Special Markets/Premium Sales, 1745 Broadway, MD 6-2, New York, NY 10019, or e-mail specialmarkets@randomhouse.com.

AN IMPORTANT TIP & AN INVITATION

Although all prices, opening times, and other details in this book are based on information supplied to us at press time, changes occur all the time in the travel world, and Fodor's cannot accept responsibility for facts that become outdated or for inadvertent errors or omissions. So **always confirm information when it matters,** especially if you're making a detour to visit a specific place. Your experiences—positive and negative—matter to us. If we have missed or misstated something, **please write to us.** Share your opinion instantly through our online feedback center at fodors.com/contact-us.

PRINTED IN SINGAPORE

10 9 8 7 6 5 4 3 2

CONTENTS

About This Book 7

**1 EXPERIENCE THE AMALFI COAST,
    CAPRI & NAPLES 9**

What's Where 10

Campania Planner 12

Campania Today 14

Top Attractions 16

Top Experiences 18

Quintessential Campania 20

Making the Most of Your Euros . .22

2 THE AMALFI COAST 23

Welcome to The Amalfi Coast . . .24

The Amalfi Coast Planner 26

Shore to Please 28

Positano to Conca Dei Marini . . .31

Amalfi: First of the
Sea Republics 62

Ravello to Paestum 78

3 CAPRI, ISCHIA, AND PROCIDA 97

Welcome to Capri,
Ischia, and Procida 98

Capri, Ischia, and Procida
Planner 100

Capri Is for Walkers 102

Capri: A Siren Landscape 105

Ischia: The Seaside Cure 144

Procida: Island of Contrasts . . .158

**4 SORRENTO AND THE
    SORRENTINE PENINSULA . . . 163**

Welcome to Sorrento and
the Sorrentine Peninsula 164

Sorrento Planner 166

Getting Around 168

Campania's Wine Renaissance . .170

Sorrento 173

Fodor's Features

Buckle Up for the Amalfi Drive 39

Capri by Boat 119

Ancient Pompeii:
Tomb of a Civilization 215

Going for Baroque 256

Walking Spacanapoli 275

An Appetite for Naples 307

Sant'Agnello to Marina del
Cantone 186

5 THE BAY OF NAPLES 193

Welcome to The Bay of
Naples 194

The Bay of Naples Planner 196

Campania's Ancient Treasures . .198

Vesuvius and Environs 201

Pompeii: City of Vesuvius 213

West of Naples: The Phlegrean
Fields 225

6 NAPLES 237

Welcome to Naples 238

Naples Planner 240

Campania's Seafood Bounty . . .242

Toledo: The Monumental City
Center 248

CONTENTS

The Vomero to the
Lungomare. 263

Spaccanapoli: The Soul of
Naples 272

Museo Archeologico Nazionale
to Porta Capuano 292

Town and Country: La Sanità
to Capodimonte 299

Where to Eat 302

Where to Stay. 326

Nightlife and the Arts 337

Shopping. 342

ITALIAN VOCABULARY 349

TRAVEL SMART 354

Getting Here and Around. 355

Essentials 364

INDEX 382

ABOUT OUR WRITERS 392

MAPS

The Amalfi Coast 32

Positano. 36

Amalfi 65

Ravello 80

Capri. 109

Ischia 145

Sorrento. 176

The Sorrentine Peninsula 184

East of Naples: Vesuvius
and Environs 203

West of Naples: The Phlegrean
Fields 227

Toledo 249

Vomero and Lungomare 266

Spaccanapoli. 273

Museo Archeologico Nazionale to
Capodimonte. 296

Where to Eat and Stay in
Naples. 314

ABOUT THIS BOOK

Our Ratings

Sometimes you find terrific travel experiences and sometimes they just find you. But usually the burden is on you to select the right combination of experiences. That's where our ratings come in.

As travelers we've all discovered a place so wonderful that its worthiness is obvious. And sometimes that place is so experiential that superlatives don't do it justice: you just have to be there to know. These sights, properties, and experiences get our highest rating, **Fodor's Choice**, indicated by orange stars throughout this book.

Black stars highlight sights and properties we deem **Highly Recommended**, places that our writers, editors, and readers praise again and again for consistency and excellence.

By default, there's another category: any place we include in this book is by definition worth your time, unless we say otherwise. And we will.

Disagree with any of our choices? Care to nominate a place or suggest that we rate one more highly? Visit our feedback center at www.fodors.com/contact-us.

Budget Well

Hotel and restaurant price categories from ¢ to $$$$ are defined in the opening pages of each chapter. For attractions, we always give standard adult admission fees; reductions are usually available for children, students, and senior citizens. Want to pay with plastic? **AE, DC, MC, V** following restaurant and hotel listings indicate if American Express, Diners Club, MasterCard, and Visa are accepted.

Restaurants

Unless we state otherwise, restaurants are open for lunch and dinner daily. We mention dress only when there's a specific requirement and reservations only when they're essential or not accepted—it's always best to book ahead.

Hotels

Hotels have private bath, phone, TV, and air-conditioning. We indicate whether they operate on the European Plan (EP, meaning without meals), Breakfast Plan (BP, with a full breakfast), Modified American Plan (MAP, with breakfast and dinner) or American Plan (AP, including all meals). We always list facilities but not whether you'll be charged an extra fee to use them, so when pricing accommodations, find out what's included.

Listings		**Hotels & Restaurants**	**Outdoors**
★ Fodor's Choice	✎ E-mail	🏨 Hotel	🏌 Golf
★ Highly recommended	✉ Admission fee	➡ Number of rooms	⚠ Camping
⊠ Physical address	☺ Open/closed times	⚴ Facilities	**Other**
✛ Directions or Map coordinates	Ⓜ Metro stations	⍲ Meal plans	☺ Family-friendly
🕮 Mailing address	▭ No credit cards	✕ Restaurant	⇨ See also
🖼 Telephone		⍣ Reservations	⊠ Branch address
🗎 Fax		🏛 Dress code	☞ Take note
⊕ On the Web		⤢ Smoking	
		🍴 Meal plans	

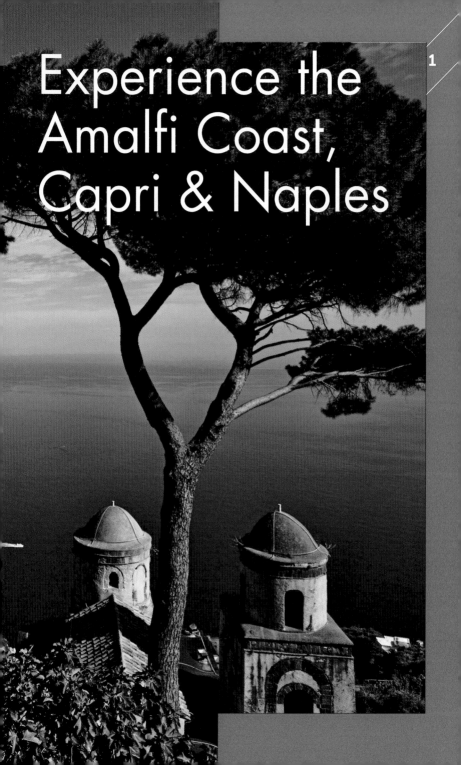

Experience the Amalfi Coast, Capri & Naples

WHAT'S WHERE

The following numbers refer to chapters.

1 The Amalfi Coast. One of the most achingly beautiful places on Earth, this corner of Campania tantalizes, almost beyond bearing, the visitor who can stay but a day or three. South of Sorrento you espy the spectacularly scenic Amalfi Coast, traversed by a road that must have a thousand turns, each with a view more stunning than the last. Here, sunbaked towns compete to win nature's beauty contest. They include **Positano**, the world's most photographed fishing village; **Amalfi**, adorned with the coast's grandest cathedral; and sky-high **Ravello**, perched 1,500 feet over the famously blue Bay of Salerno.

2 Capri, Ischia, and Procida. History's hedonists have long luxuriated on Campania's islands. The most famous, rocky **Capri**, mixes natural beauty and *dolce vita* glamour. In summer, the day-trippers are legion, but even crowds don't spoil the charm. Twice the size of Capri, **Ischia** has Campania's most beautiful white-sand beaches and great spas and springs. Nearby **Procida** is a rugged island with houses so multi-hued that you'll be reaching for your paintbrush.

3 Sorrento and the Sorrentine Peninsula. A Belle Epoque treasure, with picturesque alleyways, palm-shaded cafés, and "queen-for-a-day" grand hotels, **Sorrento** has one of the world's most charming old towns, and a peninsula perfect for escaping the madding crowds.

4 The Bay of Naples. East of Naples lie **Pompeii** and **Herculaneum**, the most completely preserved cities of classical antiquity, along with **Vesuvius**, which buried them in ash and mud in AD 79. West of Naples is a fabled region, one where Nero and Hadrian had summer villas, Virgil composed his poetry, and the Apostle Paul landed to spread the gospel. Track their footsteps in ancient **Baia** and **Cumae**.

5 Naples. Perhaps the most operatic city in the world, Napoli can seduce you one moment and exasperate you the next: it's lush, chaotic, friendly, scary, amusing, confounding, and very beautiful. Unfolding like a pop-up book of history, the city's canyon-like streets are packed with people, cafés, pizzerias, great museums, and an amazing number of Norman and baroque churches.

CAMPANIA PLANNER

When to Go

In April, May, and early June, southern Italy is at its best—the weather is generally pleasant and flowers are in bloom. Easter is a busy time for most tourist destinations; if you're traveling then, have lodging reserved in advance. In May the ocean water is warm enough for swimming, and beaches are uncrowded.

Temperatures can be torrid in summer, making it a less-than-ideal time to visit. The archaeological sites swarm with visitors, and the islands and Amalfi Coast resorts are crowded. If you seek a beach, keep in mind that during August all of Italy flocks to the shores.

From late September through early November you'll find gentle, warm weather, and acres of beach space; swimming temperatures last through October. Watch the clock, however, as the days get shorter. At most archaeological sites you're rounded up two hours before sunset—but by then most crowds have departed, so afternoon is still a good time to see Pompeii and Herculaneum.

Early winter is relatively mild, but later in the season cold fronts can arrive and stay for days. In resort destinations, many hotels, restaurants, and other facilities close from November until around Easter.

Getting Here

Major gateways to Italy are Rome's Aeroporto Leonardo da Vinci, better known as **Fiumicino** (FCO), and Milan's **Aeroporto Malpensa** (MIL). To fly into most other Italian cities you need to make connections at Fiumicino and Malpensa or another European airport.

Located just 8 km (5 mi) outside Naples, **Aeroporto Capodichino** (NAP) serves the Campania region. It handles domestic and international flights, including several flights daily between Naples and Rome (flight time 45 minutes). In Rome you can also take the airport train to Termini station and catch a train to Naples. It typically takes about an hour to get from the airport to the station, and the trip from Rome to Naples is around 90 minutes.

Italy's airports are not known for being new, fun, or efficient. Security measures, including random baggage inspection and bomb-sniffing dogs, may seem daunting, but they don't pose any problems for the average traveler. *For further information about getting into the region, see the Travel Smart chapter at the end of this book.*

What to Pack

In summer stick with light clothing, but toss in a sweater in case of cool evenings, especially if you're headed for the islands. Sunglasses, a hat, and sunblock are essential. In winter, bring a coat, gloves, hat, and scarf. Winter weather is milder than in the northern and central United States, but central heating isn't always reliable. Bring comfortable walking shoes in any season.

As a rule, Italians dress well. They do not usually wear shorts. Men aren't required to wear ties or jackets anywhere except in the most formal restaurants, but are expected to look reasonably sharp—and they do. A certain modesty (no bare shoulders or knees) is expected in churches, and strictly enforced in many.

If you stay in budget hotels, **take your own soap.** Many such hotels do not provide it or give guests only one tiny bar per room. Washcloths, also, are rarely provided even in three- and four-star hotels.

Restaurants: The Basics

A meal in Italy has traditionally consisted of five courses, and every menu you encounter will still be organized along this five-course plan:

First up is the *antipasto* (appetizer), often consisting of cured meats or marinated vegetables. Next to appear is the *primo*, usually pasta or soup, and after that the *secondo*, a meat or fish course with, perhaps, a *contorno* (vegetable dish) on the side. A simple *dolce* (dessert) rounds out the meal.

This, you've probably noticed, is a lot of food. Italians have noticed as well—a full, five-course meal is an indulgence usually reserved for special occasions. Instead, restaurant meals are a mix-and-match affair: you might order a primo and a secondo, or an antipasto and a primo, or a secondo and a contorno.

The crucial rule of restaurant dining is that you should order at least two courses. It's a common mistake for tourists to order only a secondo, thinking they're getting a "main course" complete with side dishes. What they wind up with is one lonely piece of meat.

Hotels: The Basics

Hotels in Italy are usually well maintained (especially if they've earned our recommendation in this book), but in some respects they won't match what you find at comparably priced U.S. lodgings. Keep the following points in mind as you set your expectations, and you're likely to have a good experience:

■ First and foremost, rooms are usually smaller, particularly in cities. If you're truly cramped, ask for another room, but don't expect things to be spacious.

■ A "double bed" is commonly two singles pushed together.

■ In the bathroom, tubs are not a given—request one if it's essential. In budget places, showers sometimes use a drain in the middle of the bathroom floor. Washcloths are a rarity.

■ Most hotels have satellite TV, but there are fewer channels than in the United States, and only one or two will be in English.

■ Don't expect wall-to-wall carpeting. Particularly outside the cities, tile floors are the norm.

Speaking the Language

Because Naples and the surrounding resort areas see many English-speaking tourists, in restaurants and hotels you're bound to find someone with a rudimentary understanding of English. On the other hand, if you're fluent in Italian you still may not be able to follow conversations heard on the street; locals often use dialect that even fellow Italians have a hard time deciphering. But locals speak standard Italian as well, so you can still benefit from knowledge of the language.

Italy from Behind the Wheel

Having a car in Italian cities is almost always a liability—nowhere more so than in Naples. In the towns of the Amalfi Coast parking is hard to come by, and on the islands of the bay, car access is very limited. In short, you're usually better off not renting a car in this part of the country. If you do get one, be aware that Italians tend to be aggressive drivers—expect tailgating and high-risk passing. Your best response is to stick to a safety-first approach; the *autostrada* is one place where you don't want to "go native." On the upside, Italy's roads are well maintained. Note that wearing a seat belt and having your lights on at all times are required by law.

CAMPANIA TODAY

. . . is losing its distinctive character.

First put on the map by 19th-century Grand Tour travelers, the Amalfi Coast has recently come under assault by international hotel chains. One by one, its richly atmospheric hotels, veritable time machines that offer sepia-toned dreams of the past have been given way to grotesque face-lifts, all in the name of progress. This is especially tragic in that last outpost of old-world refinement, Ravello.

First, the Palazzo Sesso was Las Vegasized by Richard Branson with the addition of hot tubs on the roof, glass elevators, and roaring fountains with *Playboy* Mansion statuary. Then the Orient-Express luxury chain eviscerated the magical Hotel Caruso-Belvedere, trading its antiques and lace-trimmed ambience for dreary rattan sofas seen from Kansas to Katmandu, beige-on-beige cocktail lounges, and, almost prosecutable, destroying the fabled medieval Belvedere Window, seen on a 1,001 travel posters, by encasing it alive within a plastic Lucite wall.

Next up was the Hotel Cappuccini Convento in Amalfi, which once delighted Longfellow and Wagner, dukes and duchesses. Now, contempo furniture and art, supermodern facilities, and other high-rolling luxuries have displaced the royal sense of civility this hotel used to have.

Happily, there are still some hotels left on the *Costiera Divina* that retain the patina of the past—but hurry!

. . . remains distinctly different from the north.

Southern Italy is slap bang in the middle of the Mediterranean, so it's no wonder that it has experienced invasions and migrations for millennia, many of which have left their mark culturally, linguistically, and architecturally.

The southerners, despite the homogenizing influences of television and education, really *are* different from Italians farther north. Under an ostensibly sociable and more expressive exterior, they are more guarded when dealing with strangers, less at home with foreign languages, and more oriented toward the family than the community. The trappings of affluence, like cars and scooters, become essential status symbols here, which in part explains why Naples is congested and noisy.

. . . has issues when it comes to local politics.

Politics tends to be clientalistic in large swaths of the south. In this climate of mutual back scratching and with unemployment rates (13.6%) twice the national average, the main preoccupation for many voters is *il posto fisso* (a steady job).

Votes are all too often cast for the politician who promises opportunities for career advancement—or lucrative contracts—preferably in the public sector. Over the years, this approach has insured inefficiencies, if not outright corruption.

. . . endures national political upheaval.

The political landscape in Italy as a whole is less stable than in any other industrialized nation. The country has had a new government an average of about once a year since the end of World War II, and hopes are slim that the situation will change much in the near future.

This virtual turnstile outside the prime minister's office takes a toll on Italy in any number of ways: economic growth is slow in part because businesses are continually adapting to new sets of government policies, and polls show that rank-and-file Italians are increasingly cynical about their political institutions. As a result, they're much less likely to trust in or depend upon the government than neighbors elsewhere in Europe do.

. . . has its economic ups and downs.

While the north has developed relatively rapidly in the past 50 years, the Italian entrepreneurial spirit in the south struggles to make good. Despite a pool of relatively cheap, willing labor, foreign investment across the entire south is merely one-tenth of that going to the northern region of Lombardy alone.

The discrepancy can be attributed in large part to the stifling presence of organized crime. Each major region has its own criminal association: in Naples, it's the *Camorra*. The system creates add-on costs at many levels, especially in retail.

It is not all bad news though. Southern Italy has woken up to its major asset, its remarkable cultural and natural heritage. UNESCO lists 14 World Heritage Sites in southern Italy alone, while the last decade has seen the creation of several national parks, marine parks, and regional nature preserves. Environmental and cultural associations have mushroomed as locals increasingly perceive the importance of preserving across the generations.

In general, the small average farm size in the south (5.8 hectares, under 15 acres) has helped preserve a pleasing mosaic of habitats in the interior. Landscape and product diversity has been aided by the promotion of traditionally grown products by the European Union and its PDO (Protected Designation of Origin) project.

. . . lives with the black market.

Nobody knows how big Italy's black-market economy is, though experts all agree it's massive. Estimates place it at anywhere from a fourth to a half of the official, legal economy.

Put another way, if the highest estimates are correct, Italy's black-market economy is about as large as the entire economy of Mexico or India. If the black-market figures were added to Italy's official GDP, the country would leapfrog France, the U.K., and China to become the world's fourth-largest economy.

The presence of the black market isn't obvious to the casual observer, but whenever a customer is not given a printed receipt in a store or restaurant, tobacco without a tax seal is bought from a street seller, or a product or service is exchanged for another product or service, that means the transaction goes unrecorded, unreported, and untaxed.

. . . misses the lira.

Italy was among a dozen European Union countries that switched to the euro currency at the start of 2002. For many Italians, the change was not a welcome one.

In day-to-day conversations, the euro is blamed for higher prices and for the handing over of more control of the Italian economy to bureaucrats in Brussels, the seat of the European government.

The most common complaint is that many vendors simply took the old prices in *lire* and erased three zeros, meaning something that used to cost 1,000 lire (around 0.52 euro) now costs one euro.

Many Italians still value purchases in their beloved lira. Years after the switch, it is still common to hear someone in the midst of a negotiation argue the price in the now-dead currency, "Eight euros? But that's 16,000 lire!"

TOP ATTRACTIONS

Spaccanapoli, Naples

(A) To learn why people fall in love with Naples, stroll down this arrow-straight road through the heart of the city. It's all here: gorgeous churches, café-lined piazzas, colorful shops, and, most of all, the exuberant Neapolitans, engaged in the drama of their daily lives. (⇨ *Chapter 6*)

Museo Archeologico Nazionale, Naples

The National Archaeological Museum has arguably the world's finest collection of classical artifacts. The most impressive finds from Pompeii and Herculaneum—everything from sculpture to carbonized fruit—are on display; a visit before heading to the ruins makes the experience significantly richer. (⇨ *Chapter 6*)

Pio Monte Misercordia, Naples

(B) Among the many impressive churches in Naples, this one bears special mention for its altar painting, Caravaggio's *Seven Acts of Mercy*, the city's most heralded artwork. (⇨ *Chapter 6*)

Sorrento

(C) Sorrento's old town quarter is one of the most romantic places in Italy—be sure to dine in front of the Sedile Dominova, a 16th-century frescoed loggia that is a colorful backdrop for caffè and serenading waiters warbling "Come Back to Sorrento." (⇨ *Chapter 4*)

The Ruins around Vesuvius

(D) This may be the closest you'll ever get to time travel. Thanks to Vesuvius blowing its top in AD 79, the towns at its base were carpeted in fallout and preserved for posterity. Allow a good half day to look round bustling Pompeii or the more compact, less busy Herculaneum. For the best Roman frescoes, head to the Villa of Oplontis between the two ancient cities. (⇨ *Chapter 5*)

La Piazzetta, Capri

(E) Sitting in one of the cafés on this main square, watching the world go by, is a classic Capri experience. It's at its best in the evening, when day-trippers have departed and locals make an appearance. (⇨ *Chapter 3*)

Villa San Michele, Capri

(G) Emperor Tiberius himself would have been impressed by this antique-rich 19th-century villa. Make a wish while standing on the Sphinx Parapet; here, high atop Anacapri, it feels as if anything is possible. (⇨ *Chapter 3*)

The Amalfi Drive

(G) The road along the Amalfi Coast combines the thrills of a roller-coaster ride with some of the most spectacular views anywhere. If you're taking a car, you'll need a confident driver who can keep his eyes on the road. Go by bus if you want a seasoned pro behind the wheel. (⇨ *Chapter 2*)

Belvedere of Infinity, Villa Cimbrone, Ravello

(F) This sky-kissing terrace, set amid gorgeous gardens and overlooking the bluest bay in the world, is the high point, in more ways than one, of any trip to the Amalfi Coast. (⇨ *Chapter 2*)

Positano

(H) Whitewashed houses cascade down to the azure sea in this remarkable village, described by the artist Paul Klee as "The only place in the world conceived on a vertical rather than a horizontal axis." (⇨ *Chapter 2*)

The Temples of Paestum

(I) These are some of the best-preserved ancient Greek monuments found anywhere (including Greece). Paestum's remoteness from the main tourist routes means it's seldom overrun by crowds. The best times to absorb the grandeur of the three temples are daybreak and dusk. (⇨ *Chapter 2*)

TOP EXPERIENCES

Il Dolce Far Niente

"The sweetness of doing nothing" has long been an art form in Italy—particularly in southern Italy. This is a place where life's pleasures are warmly celebrated, not guiltily indulged.

Of course, doing "nothing" doesn't really mean nothing.

It means doing things differently: lingering over a glass of wine for the better part of an evening as you watch the sun slowly set; savoring a slow and flirtatious evening *passeggiata* along the main street of a little town; and making a commitment—however temporary—to thinking that there is nowhere that you have to be next, and no other time than the magical present.

Along the Amalfi Coast, it's easy to achieve such a state of mind. No matter where you choose to situate yourself, you can hardly go wrong: there's quiet little Ravello, stunningly positioned on a hilltop lookout; the vertical fishing village of Positano, where a tranquil sunset is a balm to the soul; and Amalfi with its Moorish passageways and other hints of a long, multicultural history.

On Capri the pace picks up a little, and in Naples a lot, but there's still a sense of taking life's pleasures where you find them. The sense of enjoyment is, fortunately, infectious.

Simply Fabulous Food

It's no wonder *la cucina Napolitano* has won the hearts (and stomachs) of millions: the rich volcanic soil and fertile waters surrounding the city provide abundant and varied seafood, Vesuvian wines, vine-ripe tomatoes, and luscious fruits. This food is simple and earthy, at once wholesome and sensual, as sophisticated in its purity as the most complex cuisine, as inspired as the great art and architecture born out of the same culture.

Like Michelangelo freeing the prisoners that dwelt within the stone, chefs in Campania seem intuitively to seek out the essence of what they are preparing—exhibit 1 being that Neapolitan delight, pizza.

It's worth noting that in Campania, as in much of Italy, the most revered (and most expensive) restaurants are often found in the countryside or in small, remote towns. These are places for food pilgrimages, where you can escape the city and indulge in a long, opulent meal free from distractions.

A notable example is Don Alfonso 1890, the region's most famous temple of fine dining, located in the mountainside village of Sant'Agata on the Sorrentine Peninsula.

Neapolitan Baroque

Of the numerous artistic styles on display in Naples, none suits the city's temperament better than the baroque—the style that came to the fore in the 17th century and continued in the 18th century under the Bourbon kings.

In a city of volcanic passions, the flagrantly emotional, floridly luxurious baroque—a style that seems perpetually on the point of bursting its bonds—found immediate favor.

With untrammeled individualism given full play, the results, visible throughout the city center today, are dramatic, dynamic, and sometimes wonderfully showy.

Like the city itself, the decorative scheme is diffuse and disjunctive, with little effort to organize everything into an easily understood scheme.

Taking to the Water

Despite its miles of beautiful coast, Campania's beaches can be disappointing—most are small stretches of coarse sand. That doesn't mean you shouldn't pack your swimsuit, but leave any Caribbean-inspired expectations behind.

The area around Positano has good beach-going options: Spiaggia Grande (the main beach) is pleasant; a little farther west, Spiaggia di Fornillo gets better; and you can go by boat to the remote Spiaggia di Laurito for a leisurely day of swimming and lunching on seafood.

On Ischia, the best sandy beach is at Citara, south of Forio, and on Capri you can take a dip in the waters around the famous Faraglioni rock formation.

Your may not be won over by the sand, but the water itself is spectacular, with infinite varieties of blue shimmering in the sun, turning transparent in the coves. And you may have as much fun on the water as in it. In particular, boating around Capri is a classic experience, allowing you to see sights that are either remote or entirely inaccessible by land.

Edenic Gardens

"What nature gives you makes you rich," they say in Campania. One look at Capri's perfectly tonsured palm trees, Sorrento's frangipani, and Amalfi's lemon trees laden with golden fruit, and you know what they mean.

So it's not surprising to learn that one of the major joys of this region is the abundance of spectacular gardens. Many of the most celebrated gardens were created by English green thumbs, such as the 18th-century "romantic" garden planted by Sir William Hamilton (and his Lady Emma) at the royal palace of Caserta, the 19th-century medieval-style garden designed by Sir Francis Reid at Ravello's Villa Rufolo, and Lord Grimthorpe's relentlessly picturesque paradise created in the early 20th century at Ravello's Villa Cimbrone. When it comes to gardens, Campania is *incomparabilo*.

The Glories of Spring

In April and May, *all* of Campania seems like a garden. Wherever you look—roadsides, archaeological sites, public gardens, even along railroad tracks— you're likely to see a dazzling array of natural colors.

From seemingly untended fields of scarlet poppies, to overflowing flower boxes on the streets of Naples, to the yellow umbels of giant fennel on Capri, this is the Mediterranean at its most explosive. Come back in June and much of the tapestry will have faded, with plants dispersing their seeds for next year's show.

Stepping Back in Time

The regions to the west and east of Naples are two of the world's greatest treasure troves of Greek and Roman antiquity.

Quick to appreciate the sybaritic possibilities of Campania Felix—"happy land"—the ancient Romans built palatial country residences and luxurious resorts.

Although the finest art relics have been moved to the Museo Archeologico in Naples, there's still plenty to see at the original ancient sites.

The most famous, rightly, is Pompeii, but it's well worthwhile to check out some of the many other notable locations, including Baia, pleasure spot of the Roman emperors; Lake Averno, legendary entrance to Hades; Oplontis, perhaps once home to Mr. and Mrs. Nero; and Cumae, where from her cave the famous Sibyl announced to kings and emperors her portents of the future.

QUINTESSENTIAL CAMPANIA

Il Caffè (Coffee)

The Italian day begins and ends with coffee, and more cups of coffee punctuate the time in between. To live like the Italians do, drink as they drink, standing at the counter or sitting at an outdoor table of the corner bar. (In Italy, a "bar" is a coffee bar.)

A primer: *caffè* means coffee, and Italian standard issue is what Americans call espresso—short, strong, and usually taken very sweet. *Cappuccino* is a foamy half-and-half of espresso and steamed milk; cocoa powder *(cacao)* on top is acceptable, cinnamon is not.

If you're thinking of having a cappuccino for dessert, think again—Italians drink only caffè or caffè *macchiato* (with a spot of steamed milk) after lunchtime. Confused? Homesick? Order caffè *americano* for a reasonable facsimile of good old filtered joe.

Il Calcio (Soccer)

Imagine the most rabid American football fans—the ones who paint their faces on game day and sleep in pajamas emblazoned with the logo of their favorite team. Throw in a dose of melodrama along the lines of a tear-jerking soap opera. Ratchet up the intensity by a factor of 10, and you'll start to get a sense of how Italians feel about their national game, soccer—known in the mother tongue as *calcio*. On Sunday afternoons throughout the long September-to-May season, stadiums are packed throughout Italy.

Those who don't get to games in person tend to congregate around television sets in restaurants and bars, rooting for the home team with a passion that feels like a last vestige of the days when the country was a series of warring medieval city-states. How calcio mania affects your stay in Italy depends on how eager you are to get involved. At the very least, you may

If you want to get a sense of contemporary Italian culture and indulge in some of its pleasures, start by familiarizing yourself with the rituals of daily life. These are a few highlights—things you can take part in with relative ease.

notice an eerie Sunday-afternoon quiet on the city streets, or erratic restaurant service around the same time, accompanied by cheers and groans from a neighboring room.

If you want a memorable, truly Italian experience, attend a game yourself. Availability of tickets may depend on the current fortunes of the local team, but they often can be acquired with help from your hotel concierge.

Il Gelato (Ice Cream)

During warmer months, *gelato*—the Italian equivalent of ice cream—is a national obsession. It's considered a snack rather than a dessert, bought at stands and shops in piazzas and on street corners, and consumed on foot, usually at a leisurely stroll (⇨ *see La Passeggiata, below*).

Gelato is softer, less creamy, and more intensely flavored than its American counterpart. It comes in simple flavors that capture the essence of the main ingredient.

(You won't find Chunky Monkey or Cookies 'n' Cream.)

Standard choices include pistachio, *nocciola* (hazelnut), caffè, and numerous fresh-fruit varieties. Quality varies; the surest sign that you've hit on a good spot is a line at the counter.

La Passeggiata (Strolling)

A favorite Italian pastime is the *passeggiata* (literally, the promenade). In the late afternoon and early evening, especially on weekends, couples, families, and packs of teenagers stroll the main streets and piazzas of Italy's towns.

It's a ritual of exchanged news and gossip, window-shopping, flirting, and gelato eating that adds up to a uniquely Italian experience. To join in, simply hit the streets for a bit of wandering. You may feel more like an observer than a participant, until you realize that observing is what la passeggiata is all about.

MAKING THE MOST OF YOUR EUROS

Below are suggestions for ways to save money on your trip, courtesy of the Travel Talk Forums at Fodors.com.

Transportation

"Don't hire a tour, take the train to Pompeii, or stay on it to Sorrento and take the bus down the coast." —JoanneH

Food and Drink

"Book a hotel room with a mini-refrigerator—you can keep tap water cold to save on buying bottled water constantly. You can also buy great food from the markets or small shops to have picnics in your room. If you aren't a foodie and don't care about having all your meals in a sit-down restaurant you can really save a lot this way. Many people mention picnics as a way to save on food cost, but having the flexibility that a small refrigerator in the room allows can make a big difference." —isabel

"Bars always have two different prices: If you have your coffee at the counter, it's cheaper than when a waiter serves it at a table (*servizio al tavolo*)." —quokka

"Visit wine fill-up shops in Italy; get table wine from the cask for 2–3 euros a liter. In Rome we would get them filled at the Testaccio market . . . I will usually ask at the local bar where I go for my coffee." —susanna

"If you aren't hungry, skip to *secondo*—the 'second course.' Rarely do Italians eat a *primo e secondo* when they go out." —glittergirl

Sights

"You really don't realize how much money you spend on museums, places of interest, tours, etc., since it's 'six euros here,' 'ten euros there,' until you add them all up or worse yet, see the total on the credit card bill when you return home. When people ask me what I want for Christmas/ my birthday, I ask them to purchase my tickets for specific sights/tours online, print them out and give those to me for presents. I just inform them the days that I will be there and give them the Web sites. It's easy for them and saves me money." —goferfan512

"Always visit the tourist offices and get the free guides for what is going on." —gotkids

Shopping

"So many travelers, especially during the first couple of trips to Europe, feel the need to buy souvenirs for so many people back home. I quit doing that ages ago. Even if you buy inexpensive items if you feel you have too many people to buy for (example, if I buy this for Trisha I must buy something for Joyce) etc., it can be surprising how all the items can add up. And often, although people think it is nice to be remembered, it was not their trip so the souvenirs really do not mean that much to them and often just adds to the 'stuff' they already have in their homes." —LoveItaly

Lodging

"When looking up lodging, I mostly check the official Web sites of the cities I want to visit or Italian websites aimed for Italians tourists. I've been able to find very good deals on inexpensive and wonderful B&B's or hotels that I haven't been able to find on regular foreign-tourist-oriented Web sites or book guides." —Castellanese

"Go off-season—March or November have better air prices and also accommodations, particularly if you stay in apartments, which you can rent for much less off-season (and plan some meals in-house—make the noon meal your biggest of the day, then have a small dinner in the apartment)." —bobthenavigator

The Amalfi Coast

WORD OF MOUTH

"The Amalfi Coast can be a beguiling place of exceptional natural beauty, fun-loving hedonism, and a hint of Italy's ancient Greek antecedents. It is this part of Italy that breaks everybody's heart, and everybody longs to return to: the mozzarella, the pasta, the lemons, the blue of the sea, the friendly people."

—zeppole

WELCOME TO THE AMALFI COAST

TOP REASONS TO GO

★ **A world made of stairs:** Built like a steep amphitheater, Positano may very well be the best triathlon training ground imaginable. The town's only job is to look enchanting—and it does that very well.

★ **Amalfi, city of the sea doges:** Offering a dazzling layer cake of civilizations—Norman, Saracen, and Arab-Sicilian—this medieval city is so picturesque it will practically click your camera for you.

★ **Furore, art in the hills:** This "town that doesn't exist," with no discernible center, is perched between the sea and sky and decorated with murals by local and international artists.

★ **Villa Cimbrone, Ravello:** No one should miss the spellbinding gardens of this villa and its Belvedere of Infinity, set like an eagle's nest 1,500 feet over the sea.

★ **Grecian glory:** Paestum has three sublime temples sitting side by side—some of the best preserved of ancient architectural monuments anywhere (including Greece).

1 Positano to Conca dei Marini. Emerging from Sorrento's peninsula, the Amalfi Drive wriggles its way 5 mi south to Positano, the seaside village that, brilliantly two-faced, moves between luxe-sophisticated and beachcomber-casual. Sheltered by Monte Comune (which keeps the town warm in the winter and cool in the summer), Positano's three districts—the Sponda Lower Town, the central Mulini area, and the Chiesa Nuovo Upper Town—are all connected by endless staircases offering views well worth the blistered feet. Farther south along the Amalfi Drive is picturesque Praiano; the adorable anchorage-lido of Marina di Praia; a tchotchke hamlet called Furore; and Conca dei Marini, noted for its Emerald Grotto and gorgeous Santa Maria della Neve harbor.

2 Amalfi. Nestled between the green Valle dei Mulini and the blue Gulf of Salerno, Amalfi is threaded with Moorish rambling passages that suggest the Oriental caravansary of romance, testimony to the city's Norman and Arab-Sicilian past. A great medieval maritime republic, the city's former glory is best seen in its fantastic cathedral. The transportation hub of the coast, Amalfi's waterfront Piazza Flavio Gioia serves as the terminus for SITA's major bus routes.

3 Ravello to Paestum. Just beyond the Valley of the Dragon lies Ravello, perched "closer to the sky than the sea" atop Monte Cereto and set over the breathtaking Bay of Salerno. Famed for its medieval gardens (one of which inspired Wagner) and its bluer-than-blue vistas, this mountain aerie is one of the most beautiful towns in Italy. Return to earth along the Amalfi Drive past modern Maiori to Cetara's quaint fishmen's beach. Leapfrog over chaotic Salerno to the Cilento Coast where Paestum's legendary Greek temples make a rousing finale to any trip.

GETTING ORIENTED

With a thrill every 100 yards and a photo-op at nearly every bend, the Costiera Amalfitana is about the most satisfying 30 mi of coastline to be found in tourist Europe. Winding its way south of Sorrento, its Amalfi Drive—the "road of a 1,001 turns"—threads a string of towns that glisten like pearls in a necklace. Locals dare you to conjure up places that are as lovely as Positano, Amalfi, and Ravello, even in your imagination.

THE AMALFI COAST PLANNER

Making the Most of Your Time

The Amalfi Coast is laid out in the easiest possible way for touring—it kicks off in Positano and then heads down the coastline for 19 km (12 mi) to Amalfi, with innumerable towns set along the main coastal drive. If a once-over of the coast's most fascinating sights is enough, three days will allow you to see Positano, Amalfi, and Ravello—the absolute musts.

However, a practical minimum for an overview of the splendors to be found here, visiting also Paestum and smaller village treasures along the coast (such as Furore, Conca dei Marini, or Cetara), is five days.

If staying in one place is a priority, and you will not be going exploring, start by picking a favorite base (obvious candidates are Positano, Amalfi, and Ravello), but it's best to arrange for at least two of these overnight destinations.

Finding a Place to Stay

Most lodgings in this part of Campania have been owned by the same families for generations, and whether the owner is plain mama-and-papa or an heir to a ducal line, personality is evident. Along with local management may come quirks, even in the fanciest establishments.

But the 21st century has finally wrought change, and with it, numerous 19th-century cliff-side villas and palazzi, with their big gardens and grand staircases, huge baths and tile floors, have been transformed into luxury hotels. Three landmark hotels of Ravello—the Villa Cimbrone, Palazzo Sasso, and the Caruso—have all been newly outfitted with the most luxurious mod-cons, as has Amalfi's iconic Cappuccini Convento. Happily, you don't need to be a millionaire to enjoy comfy lodgings along the Costa Divina: there are many "cheaper" options; the quote marks are used because many of these places cost more than €100 a night, due to their prime real estate overlooking the sea, but there are also plenty of bargains, such as the Albergo Sant'Andrea, where €50 buys you a single room overlooking the million-euro view of Amalfi's Duomo steps.

When booking, note that a few hotels *require* half or even full board, usually with a minimum stay of two or three nights. Some hotels have minimum stays for the peak periods of July and August and around holidays. If you're traveling by car and reserving rooms in advance, ask about parking fees. Many guests staying in Positano and Amalfi suffer a nasty shock when they find they have to pay up to €20 per day. Porterage is run by cooperatives, not by hotels, in central Positano (☎ *089/811496* ⊕ *www. positanoporter.it*) and Amalfi, and is another extra charge to be factored in.

WHAT IT COSTS (IN EUROS)

	¢	$	$$	$$$	$$$$
Restaurants	under €20	€20–€30	€30–€45	€45–€65	over €65
Hotels	under €75	€75–€125	€125–€200	€200–€300	over €300

Restaurant prices are for a first course (*primo*), second course (*secondo*), and dessert (*dolce*). Hotel prices are for two people in a standard double room in high season, including tax and service.

Boat Travel

The **Metro del Mare** (☎ 199/600700 ⊕ www.metrodelmare.net) connects the northern ports of Bacoli and Pozzuoli to Naples and from there goes to Sorrento, Positano, Amalfi, and beyond. Services run in the summer months; check the Web site or the Naples daily paper, *Il Mattino,* for timetables.

To get to smaller towns make arrangements with private boat companies or independent fishermen recommended by the tourist office or your hotel.

Ferries operated by **Travelmar** (☎ 089/872950 ⊕ www.travelmar.it) and **Linee Marittime Partenopee** (☎ 089/227979 ⊕ www.consorziolmp.it) cover the region. Tickets can be purchased at booths on piers and docks.

Car Travel

Running between the Sorrentine peninsula and Salerno, Strada Statale 163 (or State Highway 163), the Amalfi Drive, can be reached from Naples via the A3 Autostrada to Castellammare di Stabia, then linked to Sorrento via Statale 145.

When driving round-trip, many choose to go only in one direction on the seaside road, going the other way via the inland highway threading the mountains. If you do drive, be prepared to pay exorbitant parking fees (and to consider yourself lucky when you find a parking space).

There's much to be said for traveling the Amalfi Drive by bus. *For more on the subject, see the feature "Buckle Up for the Amalfi Drive" in this chapter.*

Train Travel

The towns of the Amalfi Coast aren't directly accessible by train. You can go by train to Sorrento or Salerno and then use bus service from there. The **Circumvesuviana railway** (☎ 800/181313 ⊕ www.vesuviana.it), which runs along the curve of the Bay of Naples from Naples to Sorrento, runs approximately every half hour.

The state railway train stops in Salerno on the Milan–Reggio Calabria line. The station here is a good starting point for buses to the Amalfi Coast.

Bus Travel

Most travelers tour the Amalfi Drive by bus. **SITA buses** (⊕ www.sitabus.it) make the trip over 30 times daily between 6 am and 10 pm (festival, Sunday, and bank holiday schedules vary from weekday schedule).

Major bus stops from Sorrento are: Sant'Agnello, Piano di Sorrento, Meta, Positano (at Chiesa Nuova then at Sponda), Praiano, Conca dei Marini, and then Amalfi. SITA bus drivers will stop anywhere on the main route as long as you inform them of your destination when boarding.

Tickets are called Unico Costiera, and cost from €2.45 for 45 minutes to €18 for three days. They must be purchased in advance and inserted in the time-stamp machine when you enter the bus. Ticket vendors can be found in caffè, bars, and newsstands. *For more about bus travel along the coast, see the feature "Buckle Up for the Amalfi Drive" in this chapter.*

SHORE TO PLEASE
THE AMALFI COAST'S BEST BEACHES

Have beach, will travel? If sun and fun are at the top of your agenda, remember that the Amalfi Coast is famed for its dramatically scenic beaches.

Above: Life's a beach in the quaint town of Cetara. Opposite top: Is Positano Italy's most picturesque beach? Opposite bottom: Warmed by the sun, waters on this coast are mildest in December.

Considering the natural splendor of this region, it's no surprise that it flaunts some of the most spectacularly beautiful beaches in the world.

Crystal lagoons lapped by emerald green water; vertiginous cliffs hallowed out with fairy grottoes; white, sun-baked villages dripping with flowers: all these create real Italian wet dreams.

The larger masterpieces, like Positano, are easily accessible but the magic often lies in finding treasures hidden among the cliffs, such as Vallone di Furore, a tiny beach below a tchotchke of a village.

Sun beds and umbrellas cost plenty—usually €7–€10. Operators in Positano and Amalfi can ferry you to smaller beaches—prices depend on whether it's a drop-off (and pick up!) or a full-day excursion with light lunch.

GOOD TO KNOW

The terrain below sea level is as steep as the land above—a boon for good swimmers—but this means caution needs to be taken with kids. Get to beaches early, as the sun dips behind the coast's high hills and cliffs (or only hits up a beach) in midafternoon—for the full low-down, check out Roberto Pellecchia's *100 Beaches of the Amalfi Coast*, at bookstores in the area or *www. spiaggecostieraamalfitana. it).*

POSITANO

Positano was the only beach on the coast to be awarded a Bandiera Blu (Blue Flag) in 2010, recognition of its water quality, safety, and services offered. The Spiaggia Grande (large beach) has the glorious, rainbow-hued backdrop of the town, but for a more informal atmosphere surrounded by lush vegetation, follow the Via Positanesi d'America to the Fornillo beach. Almost 300 meters long, its position between the medieval Trasita and Clavel Towers made it a favorite of Pablo Picasso.

CONCA DEI MARINI

With its wonderful patches of emerald set in a blue-glass lagoon, Conca dei Marini's harbor is one of the most enchanting visions on the coast. Descend (and later ascend!) the *scalinatelle* past the Borgo Marinaro houses (a colony for off-duty celebrities) and down to the harbor of Santa Maria della Neve, set with caffès and a little chapel that seems to bless the picture-perfect beach.

The Capo di Conca, landmarked by its giant Saracen Tower, protects bathers from the western winds. Here, it is the water that compels: infinite shades of aquamarine, lapis, and amethyst shimmering in sunshine, glowing silver in moonlight, and becoming transparent in the rocky coves.

SANTA CROCE

Named for the ruins of a chapel found in the beach's grotto, the rocky beach of Santa Croce is about 400 steps down from the village of Vettica Minore, west of Amalfi. Paradise for swimmers, the water is crystal-clear and the surrounding coast is studded with emerald grottos—stronger swimmers can admire a natural arch in the rock, about 150 meters west (locals say that kissing your *bella* while swimming underneath ensures everlasting love). With a delightful restaurant and sunbeds on offer, this is the perfect beach experience.

CETARA

On Cetara's picturesque marina, the beach of this town is landmarked with a spectacular medieval Norman tower. With blue-and-white boats lying on the sand, anchovy-fishing boats in the harbor, and children playing in the adjacent park, the beach is a hive of activity—stretch out your towel and enjoy the buzz. The water here is clean, and the lido has a cool bar and sun beds for rent. The sun shines here until late afternoon, so if hunger strikes, try the fried anchovies in the Cuopperia on the marina—served in paper cones, this is local fast food.

Updated
by Fergal
Kavanagh

One of the most gigglingly gorgeous places on Earth, this corner of Campania tantalizes, almost beyond bearing, the visitor who can stay but a day or two. Poets and millionaires have long journeyed here to see and sense its legendary sights: perfect, precariously perched Positano (a claim that is more than alliteration); Amalfi, a shimmering medieval city; romantic mountain-high Ravello; and ancient Paestum, with its three legendary Greek temples.

Today, the coast's scenic sorcery makes this a top destination, drawing visitors from all over the world, who agree with UNESCO's 1997 decision to make this a World Heritage Center. This entire area is also a honeymoon Shangri-la—it is arguably the most divinely sensual 48-km (30-mi) stretch of water, land, and habitation on Earth.

Legends abound, but the Greeks were early colonizers at Paestum to the south, and Romans fled their own sacked empire in the 4th century to settle the steep coastal ridge now called the Lattari Mountains (because of the milk, or latte, produced there). Despite frequent incursions by covetous Lombards, Saracens, and other hopefuls, the medieval Maritime Republic of Amalfi maintained its domination of the seas and coast until the Normans began their conquest of southern Italy in the 11th century. By 1300, Naples, the capital of the Angevin Kingdom, had become the dominant ruler of the region and remained so until Italy unified in the mid-19th century.

By the late 19th century tourism had blossomed, giving rise to the creation of the two-lane Amalfi Drive, what has come to be called the "Divina Costiera." A thousand or so gorgeous vistas appear along these almost 40 km (25 mi), stretching from just outside Sorrento to Vietri, coursing over deep ravines and bays of turquoise-to-sapphire water, spreading past tunnels and timeless villages.

The justly famed jewels along this coastal necklace are Positano, Amalfi, and Ravello, but today's traveler will find the satellite baguettes—including Conca dei Marini, Furore, Atrani, Scala, and Cetara—just as sparkling. The top towns along the Amalfi Drive may fill up in high season with tour buses, but in the countryside not much seems to have changed since the Middle Ages: mountains are still terraced and farmed for citrus, olives, wine, and dairy; and the sea is dotted with the gentle reds, whites, and blues of fishermen's boats. Vertiginously high villages, dominated by the spires of *chiese* (churches), are crammed with houses on, into, above, and below hillsides to the bay; crossed by mule paths; and navigated by flights of steps called *scalinatelle* often leading to outlooks and belvederes that take your breath away—in more ways than one. Songs have been composed about these serpentine stone steps, and they may come to haunt your dreams as well; some *costieri* (natives of the coast) count them one by one to get to sleep.

Semitough realities lurk behind the scenic splendor of the Divina Costiera, most notably the extremes of driving (potentially dangerous, although accidents are reassuringly rare), the endless steps, and virtually nonexistent parking. Furthermore, it often rains in spring, parts of the hills burn dry in summer, museums are few, and until you adjust, people seem to talk at maximum decibels. So what? For a precious little time, you are in a land of unmarred beauty.

POSITANO TO CONCA DEI MARINI

As you head past the Sorrentine Peninsula and onto the coastal Amalfi Drive, we trust you are not driving your own car. If you are, you will have to make the trip later, with someone else driving, in order to properly enjoy one of the world's most beautiful scenic roads, because it is likewise a tortuous road, writhing its way along a coast that wriggles past caverns, little inlets, cliffs, and gardens, curving sharply every 20 feet. So save your nerves and tempers by leaving your cars behind and get ready to savor this stretch of the Amalfi Drive, between Positano and the city of Amalfi. Indecently beautiful, the Costiera Amalfitana remains the scenic showstopper of the entire Campania.

POSITANO

56 km (35 mi) southeast of Naples, 16 km (10 mi) east of Sorrento.

The first town on the Amalfi Drive is, to many travelers, the best: Positano. People head for this most popular of Amalfi Coast destinations, which is set in a natural amphitheater, as though to a hit play. The show does not disappoint.

GETTING HERE AND AROUND

By car, take the SS163 (Amalfitana) from outside Sorrento or Salerno. By SITA bus from Sorrento–Amalfi, summer ferries from Naples–Amalfi–Salerno. Purchase tickets prior to boarding at a Tabaccheria (newsstand). The SITA bus stops here are at Chiesa Nuova and Sponda. SITA buses pass through Positano every 40 minutes or so in both directions, departing from Amalfi or Sorrento 6:30 am–10 pm.

The Amalfi Coast

KEY
Ferry Lines

0   3 mi
0   3 km

Coperchia
Capezzano
Paestum →
Salerno
S. Pietro
Pregiato
18
Vietri sul Mare
A3
Cava de Tirreni
Monte Campinola
Monte Finestra
Campinola
Cetara Beach
163
Monte dell'Avocata
Cetara
Erchie
Capo d'Orso
Golfo di Salerno
Ponte Primario
Vecite
Maiori
Maiori Beach
Minori Beach
Coast
Cesarano
Ravello see detail map
Minori
Atrani
163
Amalfi see detail map
Santa Croce Beach
Amalfi
Corbara
S. Antonio Abate
Monte Cerreto
S. Lorenzo
Scala
Pogerola
Lone
Vettica
Conca dei Marini
Conca dei Marini Beach
Capo di Conca
The Tyrrhenian Sea
Casola de Napoli
Monte Cervigliano
Campora
S. Lazzaro
Furore
Marina di Furore
LATTARI
Pianillo
Agerola
Bomberano
S. Ichele
Marina di Praia
Praiano
Capo Sottile
Piazza
Franche
366
MONTE
Nocelle
Laurito
Vettica Maggiore
M. Coppola
Fontana
Montepertuso
Castellammare di Stabia
145
163
Monte Faito
Monte Sant'Michele
Positano Beach
Positano see detail map
Moiano
Monte Creasuolo
269
163
P. Germano
TO CAPRI, NAPLES AND SORRENTO
A3

The ferry and hydrofoil ticket office is beside the Spiaggia Grande; ferries to Amalfi, Sorrento, and Capri are available at the dock under Via Positanesi d'America, near the public beach in the center of town.

Local Flavio Gioia orange buses regularly ply even the smallest roads and make more stops than the SITA buses. Look for the ceramic sign and wait there. The local orange bus frequently plies the one-and-only one-way Via Pasitea, hairpinning from Transita to Piazza dei Mulini then up to the mountains and back, making a loop through the town every half hour. The taxi rank is at the top of Via dei Mulini. Service on most Flavio Gioia routes begins at 7:30 and ends at midnight; departures are usually every half hour on the main lines.

VISITOR INFORMATION

In Positano, the **Azienda Autonoma Soggiorno e Turismo** (⊠ *Via del Saracino 4, Positano* ☎ *089/875067* ⊕ *www.aziendaturismopositano.it*) is open weekdays 8:30–2:30, and June to September, it remains open until 8 pm, as well as Sunday mornings.

EXPLORING

When John Steinbeck stayed here in 1953, he wrote that it was difficult to consider tourism an industry because "there are not enough [tourists]." Alas, there are more than enough now. What Steinbeck wrote, however, still applies: "Positano bites deep. It is a dream place that isn't quite real when you are there and becomes beckoningly real after you have gone."

The most photographed fishing village in the world, this fabled locale is home to some 4,000 *Positanesi*, who are joined daily by hordes arriving from Capri, Sorrento, and Amalfi, eager to celebrate the fact that Positano is, impossibly, there. The town clings to the Monti Lattari and has been called by artist Paul Klee "the only place in the world conceived on a vertical rather than a horizontal axis." Its arcaded, cubist buildings, set in tiers up the mountainside, reflect the sky in dawn-color walls: rose, peach, purple, some tinted the ivory of sunrise's drifting clouds. In fact, the colors on these Saracen-inspired dwellings may have originally served to help returning fishermen spot their own digs in an instant.

It may have started with bread. Roman Emperor Tiberius, son of poison-happy Livia, sent his three-oar boat to a mill in Positano, understandably afraid that his neighbors on Capri would poison him. The (now modernized) mill still grinds healthful flour, but Positano is now more than just a grocery stop. Its name could be a corruption of the Greek "Poseidon," or derived from a man named Posides, who owned villas here during the time of Claudius; or even from Roman freedmen, called the Posdii. The most popular theory is that the name "Positano" comes from Pestano (or Pesitano), a 9th-century town by a Benedictine abbey near Montepertuso, built by refugees of Paestum to the south, whose homes had been ransacked by the Saracens.

Pisa sacked the area in 1268, but when an elaborate defensive system of watchtowers was in place, Positano once again prospered, briefly rivaling Amalfi. As a fiefdom of Neapolitan families until the end of the 17th century, Positano produced silk and, later, canvas goods, but decline began again in the late 18th century. With the coming of the steamship

Found just down the street from the Lower Town bus stop, this copy of Pompeii's famed bronze faun welcomes visitors to someone's house, and to all Positano.

in the mid-19th century, some three-fourths of the town's 8,000 citizens emigrated to America—mostly to New York—and it eventually regressed into a backwater fishing village. That is, until artists and intellectuals, and then travelers, rediscovered its prodigious charms in the 20th century, especially after World War II; Picasso, Stravinsky, Diaghilev, Olivier, Steinbeck, Klee—even Lenin—were just an inkling of this town's talented fans. Lemons, grapes, olives, fish, resort gear, and, of course, tourism keep it going, but despite its shimmery sophistication and overwrought popularity, Positano's chief export remains its most precious commodity: beauty.

Most car travelers leave their wheels either in one of the few free parking spaces on the upper Sorrento–Amalfi main road or in one of the scarce and pricey garages a few minutes' walk from the beach if their hotel doesn't provide parking. The best bet for day-trippers is to get to Positano early enough so that space is still available. Even those arriving in Positano by SITA bus should get a morning start, as traffic on the Amalfi Drive grows combustible by noon. The bus has two main stops in Positano: Transita, or Upper Town—near the large church of Santa Maria delle Grazie, or Chiesa Nuova—and Sponda, closer to the Lower Town, to the east of the main beach. A word of advice: Make sure you have some comfortable walking shoes and that your back and legs are strong enough to negotiate those picturesque, but daunting and ladderlike *scalinatelle*. In the center of town, where no buses can go, you're on your own from Piazza dei Mulini: Make a left turn onto the pedestrianized, boutique-flanked Via dei Mulini to head down to the

Palazzo Murat, Santa Maria Assunta, and the beach—one of the most charming walks of the coast—to begin your explorations.

NEED A BREAK? If you want to catch your breath after a bus ride to Positano, take a quick time-out for an espresso, a slice of *Positanese* (a chocolate cake as delectable as its namesake), or a fresh-fruit iced granita; check out **Bar-Pasticceria La Zagara** (✉ *Via dei Mulini 8* ☎ *089/875964*). Deservedly famous for its lemon profiteroles as much as for its tree-lined terrace, suspended on a wooden platform above the Lower Town, Zagara is ideal for morning coffee, predinner aperitivo, or postdinner digestivo.

TOP ATTRACTIONS

Fodor'sChoice
★ **Palazzo Murat.** Past a bevy of resort boutiques, amble down Via dei Mulini to find the prettiest garden in Positano—the 18th-century courtyard of the Palazzo Murat, named for Joachim Murat, who sensibly chose the palazzo as his summer residence. This was where Murat, designated by his brother-in-law Napoléon as King of Naples in 1808, came to forget the demands of power and led the simple life. Simple may not be the right word—this "palace" looks as if it was airlifted in from the heart of Naples and seems all the grander next to the adjacent low-lying houses and harbor beach. Built in the early 18th century, the palazzo is replete with soaring limestone walls, shell sconces, and wrought-iron balconies (in summer, adorned with waterfalls of incredible bougainvillea flowers). Since Murat was one of Europe's leading style setters, Neapolitan baroque suited him perfectly, and he is unlikely to have filed complaints about the views from the palazzo (now a hotel). ✉ *Via dei Mulini 23* ☎ *089/875177* ⊕ *www.palazzomurat.it.*

★ **Santa Maria Assunta.** At the bottom of Via dei Mulini is the Chiesa Madre, or parish church of Santa Maria Assunta, its green-and-yellow majolica dome, topped by a perky cupola, visible from just about anywhere in town. Built on the site of the former Benedictine abbey of St. Vito, the 13th-century Romanesque structure was almost completely rebuilt in the 18th century. The last piece of the ancient mosaic floor can be seen under glass behind the altar. Note the carved wooden Christ, a masterpiece of devotional religious art, with its bathetic face and bloodied knees, on view in the chapel to the left of the altar. Above the altar is a Byzantine 13th-century wooden painting of Madonna with Child, popularly, although erroneously, known as the Black Virgin, carried to the main beach every August 15 to celebrate the Feast of the Assumption. Legend claims that the painting was once stolen by Saracen pirates, who, fleeing in a raging storm, heard a voice from on high, *Posa, Posa*—"Put it down, put it down." When they placed the painting on the beach near the church, the storm calmed down, as did the Saracens. Positano was saved, and the town's name was established (yet again). Embedded over the doorway of the church's bell tower, set across the tiny piazza, is a medieval bas-relief of fishes, a fox, and a Pistrice—the mythical half-fox, half-fish sea monster, which supposedly characterizes the town's mixture of mountainous and marine activities. This is one of the few relics of the medieval abbey of St. Vito. The newly opened Oratorio houses historic statues from the Sacristy, while renovations to the

Palazzo Murat **1**

Santa Maria
Assunta **2**

Spaggia
Grande **3**

Via Positanesi
d'America **4**

Crypt have unearthed ancient (1st century) Roman columns. ✉ *Piazza Flavio Gioia* ☎ *089/875480* ⊕ *www.chiesapositano.com* ✉ *€2, Crypt* ⊙ *Church daily 8–noon, 4–9, Crypt daily 9:30–1, 4:30–8.*

Spaggia Grande. The walkway from the Piazza Flavio Gioia leads down to the Spaggia Grande, or main beach, bordered by an esplanade and some of Positano's best restaurants. Surrounded by the spectacular amphitheater of houses and villas that leapfrog up the hillsides of Monte Commune and Monte Sant'Angelo, this remains one of the most picturesque beaches in the world. Although it faces stiff competition from Positano's Spaggia di Fornillo beach, which is a far bigger and whiter strand of sand (find it hidden behind the bends of Via Positanesi d'America, which is set to the right side of the Spaggia Grande as you look out to the sea), the Spaggia Grande wins the beauty contest hands down.

WORTH NOTING

Fodor's Choice
★ **Via Positanesi d'America.** From the right-hand border of the Spaggia Grande beach, a tiny road that is the loveliest seaside walkway on the entire coast, rises up and borders the cliffs leading to the Fornillo beach. It's named for the town's large number of emigrants in the 19th century, as Positano virtually survived during World War II thanks to the money and packages these emigrants sent home from America. Halfway up the path you can find the Torre Trasìta, the most distinctive of Positano's

three coastline defense towers, which define the edges of Positano in various states of repair. The Trasìta—now a residence occasionally available for summer rental—was one of the defense towers used to warn of pirate raids. Beyond the tower is Lo Guarracino, a stunningly idyllic, arbor-covered restaurant. As you continue along the Via Positanesi d'America, you'll pass a tiny inlet and an emerald cove before the large Spaggia di Fornillo beach

comes into view. Once you've explored Positano top to bottom (or vice versa), you may want to head heavenward and visit two villages perched directly over Positano high in the crags of the Lattari Mountains.

NEED A BREAK?

Up at the top of the town, Bar Internazionale (⊠ *Via G. Marconi 306* ☎ *089/875434*) is more than just a place to wait for the bus (being opposite the main SITA bus stop—you can also buy tickets here). As a meeting place for locals and visitors alike, it's a happy spot where you can read newspapers from several countries while mulling over a fine creamy cappuccino.

WHERE TO EAT

$$
SOUTHERN ITALIAN

✕**Chez Black.** A local institution, allegedly nicknamed after owner Salvatore Russo's eternal tan, this nautically themed place cannot be beaten for its location (right on the Spiaggia Grande) or as a great spot for people-watching. Regular visitors include Denzel Washington, who was best man at Salvatore's son's wedding. Despite catering to the day-tripping coachloads, the friendly staff will guide you through their specialties, including *zuppa di pesce* (fish soup) and *spaghetti con ricci di mare* (sea urchins), served in a large metal urchin. Start with their *aperitivo*, the *grotta dello smeraldo*—gin, lemon, and crème de menthe. ⊠ *Via del Brigantino 19* ☎ *089/875036* ⊕ *www.chezblack.it* ⊟ *AE, DC, MC, V* ⊘ *Closed Nov.–Feb.*

$
SOUTHERN ITALIAN

✕**Da Adolfo.** Several coves away from the Spiaggia Grande, on a little beach where pirates used to build and launch their boats, this laid-back trattoria has been a favorite Positano landmark for more than 40 years. The pirates are long gone, but their descendants now ferry you free to the private cove, round-trip from Positano (look for the boat with the red fish on the mast named for the restaurant—it leaves every half hour in the morning; you can also make a steep descent from the main coastal road off the hamlet of Laurito). Sit under a straw canopy on a wooden terrace to enjoy *totani con patate* (squid and potatoes with garlic and oil), then sip white wine with peaches until sundown. Some diners even swim here—so bathing suits are just fine. It gets busy here, so it may be best to ask your hotel to reserve, since personal reservations are often not honored. ⊠ *Spiaggia di Laurito* ☎ *089/875022* ⊕ *www.daadolfo. com* ⚛ *Reservations essential* ⊟ *AE, DC, MC, V* ⊘ *Closed Oct.–Apr.*

$$$ **✕ La Cambusa.** The two bronze lions guarding the steps leading up to
SOUTHERN this "pantry" right off Spiaggia Grande are not actually part of the
ITALIAN restaurant, but aptly guide you to this safe haven for tasty local cuisine
for 40-plus years. Linguine with mussels and fresh fish with potatoes
and tomato sauce are among the favorites, while English sashimi chef
Andy Reid prepares raw salmon, tuna, and prawns in Asian style with
a Mediterranean twist. Owners Baldo and Danielle are well known
around town for maintaining high standards even during the hectic
summer season. The outdoor dining terrace, framed by a hand-painted
batik, holds pride of place directly above the entrance to the Spiaggia
Grande. ⊠ *Piazza Amerigo Vespucci 4* ☎ *089/875432* ▭ *AE, DC, MC,
V* ☉ *Closed Wed. in Nov.–Mar.*

$$ **✕ La Pergola.** Occupying a prime piece of real estate near dead center
SOUTHERN on the Spaggia Grande beach, this arbor-covered seating area offers a
ITALIAN truly idyllic (though festive, due to the happy crowds) setting. Often
confused with the equally good Buca di Bacco upstairs, until the 1970s
it functioned as a dance club. Dining here is just as seductive, with seafood unsurprisingly being the main fare—be sure to try the *scialatielli
ai frutti di mare* or sea bass in *acqua pazza*—while pizza is also served.
The chicken breast with fries is another great way to carb up for an
afternoon under the beach umbrella. Open until midnight, there's plenty
of time to digest before trying their *dolci* (desserts) and ice cream made
in their own *pasticceria,* Il Vicoletto on Via Sariceno. ⊠ *Via del Brig-
antino 35* ☎ *089/811461* ⊕ *www.bucapositano.it* ▭ *AE, DC, MC, V*
☉ *Closed Jan. 7–Feb.*

$–$$ **✕ Lo Guarracino.** Enjoy a setting to make you fall in love, or rekindle it
SOUTHERN (be careful who you sit with)—this partly arbor-covered, perched-on-
ITALIAN a-cleft aerie is about the most idyllic place to enjoy your lemon pasta
Fodor's Choice and glass of vino as you watch the yachts come and go. Set a few steps
★ above Positano's prettiest seaside path, the terrace vista takes in the
cliffs, the sea, Li Galli islands, Spiaggia Fornillo, and Torre Clavel. The
supercharming backroom arbor, covered with thick, twining vines and
set with little tables covered in cloths that match the tint of the bay, is
the place to sit. Fine fish specialties are top delights on the menu. In
fact, the day's catch is often cooked, with potatoes, in the wood-fired
pizza oven (adorned with an icon of Saint Francesco di Paola, patron
saint of bakers, renamed here Saint Pizza), giving it a distinct flavor.
⊠ *Via Positanesi d'America 12* ☎ *089/875794* ⊕ *www.loguarracino.net*
▭ *AE, MC, V* ☉ *Closed Jan.–Mar.*

$$ **✕ O' Capurale.** Even though *o' capurale* ("the corporal") himself no
SOUTHERN longer runs the place, his eponymous restaurant is still a great find in
ITALIAN the crowded center of Positano. Positano is about easy-come elegance,
★ and this dining spot sums it all up. Graced with a coved ceiling adorned
with a colorful Fauvist-style fresco, the dining room is filled with happy,
stylish diners, literally unwinding before your eyes, thanks to the deli-
cious, serious food (veal cutlet in white wine, fresh pasta with mussels
and pumpkin, or rockfish *all'acqua pazza* with a few tomatoes and
garlic are favorites) and lovely setting. Alfresco diners walk downstairs
to choose the tables on the backstreet with a charmingly framed view of

Continued on page 44

BUCKLE UP FOR THE AMALFI DRIVE

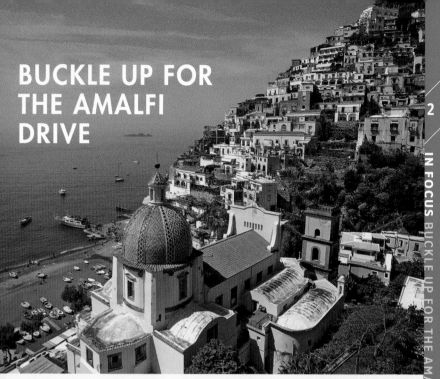

The vertical village of Positano

If travelers do nothing else along this coast, they have to experience the Amalfi Drive, a cliff-hugging stretch of road that tests their faith in civil engineering. One of the most beautiful coastal drives in the world, this roller-coastal "route of 1,001 bends" offers views that are drop-dead breathtaking—literally, it sometimes seems.

When visitors to the Amalfi Coast take the spectacular 50-minute bus ride along the sea and begin to note the bus soaring and banking along the cliff-side concrete ribbon, they may well wonder if the driver has a hankering to mature his insurance policy. As the road wiggles in and out hundreds of feet above the water (while it's still there—landslides, you know), the Mario Andretti at the wheel seems to shift into juggernaut speed. Bottles begin to roll around on the floor and a lady takes out her rosary. With car-chase determination, the driver negotiates a whiplash twist in the road. Terrifying though some switchbacks are, what meets travelers' eyes (when they can bear to open them) is breath-stopping beautiful: bays of turquoise-to-sapphire water, timeless cliff-top villages, vertiginous pinnacles of rock. As the bus finally pulls into Amalfi, passengers congratulate themselves on surviving the ride of their life.

POSITANO TO CONCA DEI MARINI

Positano

POSITANO The most beautiful vertical village in the world suffered from its confined space, so when it grew, it grew up the mountainside.

LATTARI MOUNTAINS

Pianillo

VETTICA MAGGIORE More priceless than any landscape painting in the National Gallery is the panorama you get from Vettica's seaside piazza and its San Gennaro church.

Mount
▲ Tre Galli

366

Bomerano

Positano

163

TO
SORRENTO &
SANT'AGATA
SUI DUE GOLFI

MARINA DI PRAIA
Wedged between two soaring cliffs is this adorable harbor, crammed with dollhouse-issue chapel, restaurant, and beach.

FERRY TO
CAPRI

TO
I GALLI ISLANDS

FERRY TO
AMALFI

Punta S. Pietro

163

I GALLI ISLANDS Nicknamed "The Birds"—owing to their formation—these three (still private) islets off the Positano coast were famed as Homer's Home of the Sirens and, more recently, as Rudolf Nureyev's last residence.

Vettica Maggiore

Marina
di Praia

T. di Grado

Praiano

Capo Sottile

Tyrrhenian

A GUIDE TO THE DRIVE

Statale (Highway) 163—the Amalfi Drive, as we call it—was hewn from the lip of the Lattari Mountains and completed in 1852, varying from 50 feet to 400 feet above the bay. You can thank Ferdinand, the Bourbon king of the Two Sicilies, for commissioning it, and Luigi Giordano for designing this seemingly improbable engineering feat. A thousand or so gorgeous vistas appear along these almost 40 km (25 mi), stretching from just out-

side Sorrento to Vietri. John Steinbeck once joked that the Amalfi Drive "is carefully designed to be a little narrower than two cars side by side" so the going can be a little tense: the slender two lanes hovering over the sheer drops sometimes seem impossible to maneuver by auto, let alone by buses and trucks.

Many travelers arrive from Sorrento, just to the north, connecting to the coast through Sant'Agata sui Due Golfi on

San Genarro church, Maggiore

Hotel San Pietro, Positano

Pontone

VALLONE DI FURORE
This tchotchke of a fishermen's village comprises a mere handful of pastel-hue houses and is set in the coast's only "fjord."

Pogerola

Atrani

EMERALD GROTTO
The Amalfi Coast's version of Capri's Blue Grotto, the Grotta dello Smeraldo is a spectacle of stalactites and Harry Winston-esque color.

Amalfi   T. di Amalfi

163

S. Lazzaro

FERRY TO
POSITANO

FERRY TO
SALERNO

Vettica Minore

Furore

CONCA DEI MARINI
Retreat of the rich and famous, this village sprawls up a mountainside dotted with villas and churches—but you'll use up all your flash card just photographing its storybook harbor.

366

Conca dei Marini

Mola

Il Furore   163

S. Pancrazio

Punto Varo   Grotta dello Smeraldo

Copo di Conca

S e a

0   1 mi

0   1 km

the Statale 145—the Strada del Nastro Azzurro (Blue Ribbon Road), whose nickname aptly describes its width, and the color at your alternating right and left. The white-knuckle part, or, as some call it, the Via Smeraldo (Emerald Road), begins as the road connects back to Statale 163, threading through coastal ridges at Colli di S. Pietro, and continuing to wend its way around the Vallone di Positano. From ravine to ravine, Positano then begins to beckon out your window, appearing and disappearing like a flirtatious coquette. Just east of Positano, at Punta San Pietro, Statale 163 again winds sharply around valleys, deep ravines, and precipices, affording more stunning ridge views. Past Praiano, the Furore gorge is crossed by viaduct. From here on to Amalfi, the ridges soften just a bit.

CHICKEN?

If you think a road is just for getting from here to there, the Amalfi Drive is not for you. So if you want to leapfrog over all the thrills, opt for the high mountain pass called the Valico di Chiunzi, easily reached via the A3 Naples–Salerno Autostrada from the exit at Angri.

AMALFI TO CETARA

Villa Rufolo, Ravello

RAVELLO Suspended between sky and sea, this ritzy hilltop village—home to a famous annual music festival—is noted for its spectacular gardens and bluer-than-blue vistas.

Minori

Maiori

Ravello

Scala

Torre Mezza Capo

Torre Paradiso

Torre Normanna

ATRANI Lined with piggy-backed houses and threaded by corkscrew staircases, this stage set of a medieval town revolves around a picture-perfect piazza.

Torre dello Scappariello

Castiglione

Amalfi

Atrani

163

T. di Amalfi

AMALFI The largest town of the Costiera Amalfitana, this is a must-do because of its spectacular Arab-Sicilian cathedral and its impossibly romantic souk-like streets and endless Scalinatelle steps.

FERRY TO SALERNO

FERRY TO POSITANO

DOING THE DRIVE BY CAR

With countless twists and turns, the Amalfi Drive succeeds in making every driver into a Gran Turismo pro. In fact, at times you may feel you've entered the Amalfi Indy: The natives joke that the English complete the "course" in two hours, the Italians in a half hour. The drive is studded with stops built off the roadside for you to pull into safely and experience what your passengers are oohing and ahhing about. The round reflecting mirrors set along major curves in the road intend to show if others are coming around a bend, but honk before narrow curves to let oncoming traffic know about you, and listen for honks from oncoming curves. Buses and trucks will sometimes require you to back up; if there's a standoff, take it in stride, as it goes on all the time. At various points on the drive, stewards will stop larger vehicles so that cars can pass. Note that the road inevitably is closed some days due to landslides.

Villa Cimbrone, Ravello　　　　Atrani　　　　Cetara

MARINA DI ERCHIE
All the scenic magic of the coast is distilled here on a beach framed by a Norman tower and a 10th-century Benedictine abbey.

CETARA The waterfront cafés here still serve up the anchovies once so prized by the Roman emperors. Reserve an alfresco table and let it all soak in. This is why you came to Italy.

Mount Dell'Avvocata

Mount Della Rena

TO VIETRI

163

Cetara

163

Torre di Cesare

Torre di Badia

Mount Piano

Marina di Erchie

Capo d'Orso

Torre di Tummolo

T y r r h e n i a n　 S e a

0　　　　　　　1 mi
0　　　　　　　1 km

DOING THE DRIVE BY BUS

There's one main reason why you should forget the car and opt for taking one of the convenient and inexpensive SITA buses that travel the route (usually once an hour: *see* www.sitabus.it): The view is much better, thanks to the mighty elevation of bus seats, which allows you to drink in mountain-meets-sea vistas, often missed in a car because of the highway's low stone barrier. The best views can be yours if you sit on the sea side of the bus (on your right as you board the bus if you're starting in Sorrento, on your left if you begin in Amalfi). The trip between Sorrento and Amalfi generally takes 80 minutes. Buses make regular stops at all the main destinations: happily, the driver will stop anywhere on the main route as long as you inform him of your destination, be it hotel or fork in the road, when boarding. Note that buses fill up in the summer months, and the locals aren't usually orderly when it comes to making a line.

CLOSE UP

Rules for the Amalfi Drive

As submitted by Az to the Forums at ⊕ www.fodors.com:

1. Don't look down.

2. Don't look up.

3. Don't look—it's easier that way.

4. Forget about camels not passing through the eye of a needle.

5. Timidity will get you nowhere—literally.

6. The solid center line in the middle of the road is merely a suggestion.

7. Whoever gets to a lane first has the right of way—it doesn't matter whose side the lane is on.

8. Traffic mirrors are put there so that you can see what you are about to hit head on.

9. Tour buses will back up. (This one is true; they don't want a fender bender that will upset the itinerary of all their passengers.)

10. Garbage trucks won't back up.

11. Motorcyclists are fearless.

12. Pedestrians are fearlesser.

13. Five headlights coming toward you equal two cars plus one motorcycle, or one car plus three motorcycles, or five motorcycles, all equally probable.

14. The probability of an accident is very low; at 40 mph around a hairpin curve 1,000 feet above the sea everyone pays attention. (Same is true for the Autostrada: at 130 mph, nobody's attention wanders.)

15. Have plenty of limoncello on hand at the end of a day spent driving the coast.

Rosenatti, another Forums user, added the following coda:

"If the large, orderly group of people approaching your car from the opposite direction looks like a marching band, this is because it is a marching band. No, it will not turn around."

the beach. ⊠ Via Saracino 7 ☎ 089/875374 ⊕ www.ocapuralepositano. it ▤ AE, DC, MC, V ☉ Closed Nov.–Feb.

$ ✕ **Pupetto.** A simple place at the end of the Fornillo beach, the Pupetto's
SOUTHERN main feature is its long terrace, stretching almost the length of the beach
ITALIAN and partly set under heavily perfumed lemon trees. Opt for the excellent grilled fish, best followed by the homemade limoncello. To get there from the upper town, take the elevator from the Hotel Vittorio. The restaurant is part of a hotel with spacious guest rooms in pastel shades—most have lovely views of the sea. ⊠ Via Fornillo 37 ☎ 089/875087 ⊕ www.hotelpupetto.it ▤ AE, DC, MC, V ☉ Closed Nov.–Mar.

$$ ✕ **Ristorante il Ritrovo.** Sitting in the tiny sky-high town square of Mon-
SOUTHERN tepertuso, 1,500 feet up the mountainside from Positano, the Ritrovo
ITALIAN has been noted for its cucina for more than 20 years. The friendly owners will organize a free shuttle service to and from Positano, making it easy to check out the terrace's dizzying view while sitting in the wood-paneled dining room. The menu features a combination of food from the sea and the hills—try the scialatielli ai frutti di mare accompanied by well-grilled vegetables or the speciality: zuppa saracena, a kind of paella brimming with assorted seafood. Leave space

The seaside walkway Via Positanesi d'America leads to Lo Guarracino, a restaurant-pizzeria with a view.

for the *sciuscella*, a homemade chocolate sweet with pine nuts paired with one of their 80 different kinds of a homemade liqueur (try the carob or even chamomile). Ask for advice on the excellent wine list from Teresa or Salvatore (if he's not too busy in the kitchen). Salvatore also runs a cooking school, so you can try to whip up his creations at home. ⊠ *Via Montepertuso 77, Montepertuso* ☎ *089/812005* ⊕ *www. ilritrovo.com* ⌁ *Reservations essential* ⊟ *AE, DC, MC, V* ⊗ *Closed mid-Jan.–mid-Feb.*

$ ✕ **Santa Croce.** Perched about 1,400 feet above sea level on the Path of the
SOUTHERN Gods, this is the only restaurant in the dreamy little hamlet of Nocelle
ITALIAN where the dress code is decidedly hiking gear. Try to get a window seat with its view fit for the gods—gazing over Positano, Li Galli islands, and the Fariglioni of Capri, you can sample their fresh pasta or grilled meat. On Saturday evenings, the olive wood-fired pizza oven produces godly delights. ⊠ *Via Nocelle 19, Nocelle* ☎ *089/811260* ⌁ *Reservations essential* ⊟ *AE, MC, V* ⊗ *Closed weekdays mid-Nov.–mid-Mar.*

$ ✕ **Saraceno D'Oro.** Although open also at lunchtime, this is most defi-
SOUTHERN nitely an evening venue (the outside tables are on the other side of the
ITALIAN busy Via Pasitea). Living up to its name, the restaurant's ambience inside is distinctly Moorish without being kitschy. This is one of the few restaurants patronized by the Positanesi. *Antipasti misti* is a favorite starter, while bass with leeks, veal with provolone, and local wines are all delicious. Pizza is also served. ⊠ *Via Pasitea 254* ☎ *089/812050* ⌁ *Reservations essential* ⊟ *MC, V* ⊗ *Closed Nov.–Dec. 26, Jan. 8–Feb.*

DID YOU KNOW?

The hotel Sirenuse is where John Steinbeck stayed while writing his famous essay "Positano" for *Harper's Bazaar* in 1953. He called the town "a dream place that isn't quite real when you are there and becomes beckoningly real after you have gone."

NEC LVMINE CLAVDIT

WHERE TO STAY

$$$–$$$$ ⊞ **Buca di Bacco.** Set in the very hub of Positano, this occupies stage-center on Positano's gorgeous Spiaggia Grande beach. First opened as a fisherman's tavern in 1916, it became a guesthouse in 1945 and is still run by the Rispoli family. It found fame as Positano's first nightclub (now La Pergola restaurant), and the photos of Steinbeck, Hemingway, and Jackie O that line the hotel walls prove the glitterati once flocked here. Today, some of the airy guest rooms look over the majolica dome of Santa Maria Assunta while all enjoy sea views. The dining terrace features such specialties as homemade *scialatielli ai frutti di mare* and *Gambaretti alla Clark* (named after the American general who docked here in 1943 and promptly requested a prawn cocktail). The hotel doesn't have a pool, but who needs one this close to the beach? **Pros:** right on the beach; uninterrupted views of the sea; a Jacuzzi with a view. **Cons:** a bit tricky to get to if not arriving by boat; poor service by some staff; located at the noisy "Times Square" crossroads of Positano. ⊠ *Via Rampa Teglia 4* ☎ *089/875699* ⊕ *www.bucadibacco.it* ↘ *47 rooms* △ *In-room: a/c, safe, refrigerator, Internet. In-hotel: restaurant, Wi-Fi hotspot* ▤ *AE, DC, MC, V* ⊗ *Closed Nov.–Mar.* ¶⊙| *MAP.*

$$$ ⊞ **Casa Albertina.** Clinging to the cliff, this little house was once one of just seven hotels in town before Positano became internationally famous. It continues to be well loved for its Italianate charm, its homey restaurant, and its owners, the Cinque family, with Mamma Annamaria ruling in the kitchen. Guest rooms have high ceilings, bright fabrics, tile flooring, and sunny terraces or balconies overlooking the sea and coastline (don't miss the view from the roof!). Car or motorboat excursions to surrounding towns and attractions can be arranged. You can't drive your car to the doorway, but porters will ferry your luggage. Note: It's 300 steps down to the main beach. Half board available on request. **Pros:** a home away from home; open all year. **Cons:** slightly removed from the action; have we mentioned the 300 steps? ⊠ *Via della Tavolozza 3* ☎ *089/875143* ⊕ *www.casalbertina.it/* ↘ *20 rooms* △ *In-room: a/c, refrigerator. In-hotel: restaurant, Wi-Fi hotspot, parking (paid)* ▤ *AE, MC, V.*

$$$$ ⊞ **Covo dei Saraceni.** In Positano, sea and town interact, and you see this best from the Covo dei Saraceni, spectacularly perched on the main beach at the foot of Monte Comune and just steps from the main pier (and the sometimes noisy ferries that moor here). Modern, charming, and increasingly luxe, this large hotel has a rooftop pool and bar set over the sea. Crisp and cool, the hand-painted tiled lobby is built around a curved staircase while the Savino restaurant's glass-walled dining area is overhung with bougainvillea vines. Guest rooms are simple but stylized, with wrought-iron balconies; suites are ultradeluxe and spacious, with whirlpools, larger terraces, and fanciful furnishings. The major plus here is the absolutely blissful location—you'd need to stay on a yacht to get any nearer the bay. **Pros:** top location; rooftop pool. **Cons:** a hike to get here, unless arriving by boat; hotel entrance is near dock where day-trippers arrive in Positano by ferry. ⊠ *Via Regina Giovanna 5* ☎ *089/875400* ⊕ *www.covodeisaraceni.it* ↘ *61 rooms* △ *In-room: a/c, safe, refrigerator. In-hotel: 2 restaurants, bar, pool, gym, Wi-Fi hotspot*

▤ AE, DC, MC, V ⊗ Closed Nov.–mid-Mar. ⦾ FAP.

$$
Fodor's Choice
★

⚄ **La Fenice.** Paradise found. This tiny and unpretentious hotel on the outskirts of Positano beckons with bougainvillea-laden vistas, castaway cottages, and a turquoise seawater pool, all perched over a private beach (250 steps away), just across a cove from Franco Zeffirelli's famous villa (now a superluxury hotel). Once past the gate, you climb a steep stairway to the main house—but tread slowly: the paths and stairways here enchantingly frame (sometimes literally with vines) vistas over land and sea. Thanks to the wonderful family of the owner, Constantino Mandara, you'll feel right at home in a few minutes—that's because this *is* his home. Guest rooms, accented with coved ceilings, whitewashed walls, and native folk art, are simple havens of tranquility. Several accommodations are in a house perched above the road (a bit noisy if trucks rumble by, but this rarely happens at night), although others are the adorable little cottages set close to the sea. All are linked by *very* steep walkways—covered with arbors and zigzagging across the hill, they tie together these little acres of heaven. **Pros:** paradise; private beach. **Cons:** some rooms overlook noisy road; a 10-minute walk to town. ⊠ *Via G. Marconi 4* ☎ *089/875513* ⊕ *www.lafenicepositano.com* ⇨ *14 rooms* ⚬ *In-room: no a/c, no TV. In-hotel: pool* ▤ *No credit cards* ⦾ *BP.*

$$$$
★

⚄ **Le Sirenuse.** As legendary as its namesake sirens, this exquisite, in-town 18th-century palazzo has long set the standard for superluxury in Italian hotels. Opened in 1951 with just eight rooms, when then-mayor Paolo Sersale converted the family home into a guesthouse (this is where John Steinbeck stayed while writing his famous essay, "Positano," for *Harper's Bazaar* in 1953), it now boasts 63 luxurious rooms sprawled over eight floors. Winner of countless awards, the hotel is still run by Baron Sersale and seduces all guests with Venetian and Neapolitan museum-quality antiques and artwork, stunning vine-entwined terraces that overlook town, and the coast's most beautiful pool terrace (*the* place to have lunch in Positano). Add in a private yacht for free boating excursions, an iPod for the duration of your stay, the in-house spa (designed by Gae Aulenti), and extravagantly stylish guest rooms—— each one special and many with whirlpool tubs, with all accented with elegant antiques (such as antique bedsteads or refectory tables) and the finest in hotel luxuries (such as the linen bedding)—and little wonder the price tags here are some of the highest in Italy. Enjoy some of the most luxurious cuisine in Campania either poolside or in the vine-draped La Sponda restaurant. Later, repair to the aristocratic reading room or the Champagne and Oyster bar, where contented patrons swap experiences and toast their good luck at being here—and *here*. **Pros:** unrivalled views; pure luxury; close to the bus stop. **Cons:** a bit of a climb from the town center; the restaurant is astoundingly expensive. ⊠ *Via Cristoforo*

Colombo 30 ☎ *089/875066* ⊕ *www.sirenuse.it* ➪ *63 rooms* ♿ *In-room: a/c, safe, Wi-Fi. In-hotel: 2 restaurants, bars, pool, spa, Internet terminal, Wi-Fi hotspot, parking (paid)* ▤ *AE, DC, MC, V* ⏍ *BP.*

$$$$ ⛫ **Palazzo Murat.** With a perfect location in the heart of town above the
★ beachside church of Santa Maria Assunta, and an even more perfect
entrance through a bougainvillea-draped patio and garden, the Murat
is one of Positano's winners. The courtyard—part orchard, part terrace—is one of the most drop-dead-gorgeous settings in all Campania,
the lower section of which offers a sublime area for dining alfresco (the
restaurant, Il Palazzo, has a superb and ambitious chef, who is proud
of using produce from the garden). The old wing is Positano's very
grandest palazzo, with massive limestone walls, carved Rococo delicacies, and wrought-iron balconies swimming in pink flowers; it was built
in the early 18th century and used as a summer residence by Joachim
Murat, King of Naples. The new wing, also overlooking the garden, is
a modern, Mediterranean-style building with arches and terraces—it's
cool, lovely, with scattered nautical motifs and tile accents, and very,
very pleasant in ambience. **Pros:** one-time home of a king; stunning
surroundings. **Cons:** only five rooms with seaside views; a constant
stream of curious day-trippers. ✉ *Via dei Mulini 23* ☎ *089/875177*
⊕ *www.palazzomurat.it* ➪ *31 rooms* ♿ *In-room: a/c, safe, refrigerator.
In-hotel: restaurant, bar, parking (paid)* ▤ *AE, DC, MC, V* ⊗ *Closed
Nov.–Mar.* ⏍ *BP.*

$ ⛫ **Pensione Maria Luisa.** The cheapest option in town, and it shows. But
just look past the downtrodden rooms to the stunning views over Torre
Clavel, and be welcomed by friendly proprietor Carlo Milo, and you
won't be disappointed. Very friendly, and wonderfully located in a quiet
winding street just above the Fornillo beach, this is as close to staying in
a friendly family home as you'll get in Positano. Not surprisingly, they
organize Italian language courses here. **Pros:** friendly staff; like residing
in a real Positano home. **Cons:** not very inviting decor; a bit far from
the main hub of the town. ✉ *Via Fornillo 42* ☎ *089/875023* ⊕ *www.
pensionemarialuisa.com* ➪ *10 rooms* ♿ *In-room: some a/c, refrigerator,
no TV* ▤ *No credit cards* ⏍ *BP.*

$$$–$$$$ ⛫ **Poseidon.** Set midway up the hillside amphitheater that is Positano
(and therefore a bit far from the beach and center of town), this hotel
offers ubiquitous breathtaking views. A family-run establishment, it has
recently been renovated (although we note the lobby still needs a new
paint job). The Poseidon, however, retains enough charms to make it
one of its most popular hotels thanks to an array of charms, beginning
with the pool and bar terrace dotted with orange and lemon trees. Guest
rooms are spacious, with hand-painted terra-cotta tile flooring and fresh
flowers provided daily. The oldest elevator in Positano takes you to
the Beauty Center's gym, sauna, and hydromassage. All rooms have a
private terrace, most overlooking the bay, and a range of events, from
boat rides to group excursions to weddings, can be organized. **Pros:**
very friendly staff. **Cons:** a steep climb from the town center. ✉ *Viale
Pasitea 148* ☎ *089/811111* ⊕ *www.hotelposeidonpositano.it* ➪ *48
rooms* ♿ *In-room: a/c, refrigerator, Wi-Fi (some). In-hotel: pool, gym,
parking (paid)* ▤ *AE, DC, MC, V* ⊗ *Closed Nov.–mid-Apr.* ⏍ *MAP.*

2

Set on its own clifftop promontory, the Grand Terrace of the San Pietro hotel is lined with beautiful majolica-tiled benches (inspired by those of the cloisters of Naples' Santa Chiara church).

$$$$ ★ **San Pietro.** Spectacular is the word for this luxurious oasis, favored by the likes of Julia Roberts, George Clooney, and Princess Caroline of Monaco, some of whom prefer this place because it's several leagues out of town (a shuttle bus whisks you back and forth), far from the crowds and the paparazzi. The place itself is more than camera-ready: set on a cliff high over the sea, with its own chapel for weddings, there are seven levels of gorgeous garden terraces. The San Pietro has a frilly, pretty decor that mixes modern (the hotel was built in the early 1970s) with magnificent (great antiques, elegant Vietri tilework). Who can resist idling away hours on the famous majolica benches of the grand terrace set on its own promontory over the Bay of Positano? All of the elegantly furnished guest rooms come with terraces (most look out to the sea, not toward Positano); room decors mix chic and charming in best country-style manner. The pool on an upper level is not large, so most guests opt to take an elevator fit for James Bond through the mountainside to the private beach with bar and Carlino, the new and exclusive (guest-only) restaurant, with its superambitious and stylish menu (don't dare leave without trying the hotel's incredibly delicious Elephant's Milk signature drink). **Pros:** enchanting gardens; million-dollar views of Positano; rubbing elbows with celebs. **Cons:** too far away from Positano to take a stroll but handy van shuttles you back and forth; not all rooms served by the elevator. ⊠ *Via Laurito 2* ☎ *089/875455* ⊕ *www.ilsanpietro.it* 🛏 *60 rooms* ⚬ *In-room: a/c, safe, refrigerator, Internet, Wi-Fi. In-hotel: restaurant, bars, tennis court, pool, gym, beachfront, Internet terminal, Wi-Fi hotspot* ➡ *AE, DC, MC, V* ✆ *Closed Nov.–Mar.* ❢◉❢ *BP.*

$$
★ **Villa Flavio Gioia.** For longer stays this is the ideal option, with a super location overlooking Piazza Flavio Gioia and the town's symbolic parish church, and a hop, skip, and a jump to the Spiaggia Grande. Each mini-apartment has its own terrace or large balcony, and a cooking area. For centuries a private home, it retains its old charm with bright rooms. Longer stays are preferred, and the minimum stay in high season is one week. The small garden hosts exhibitions by local painters, and is the ideal place to chill out, looking down at the tourists and Positanesi trekking down to the beach. **Pros:** prime location; ideal for longer stays. **Cons:** short stays are discouraged; no pool. ⊠ *Piazza Flavio Gioia 2* ☎ *089/875222* ⊕ *www.villaflaviogioia.it* ⤴ *13 rooms* ⚙ *In-room: a/c, safe, kitchen. In-hotel: parking (paid)* ▭ *AE, DC, MC, V* ⊗ *Closed Feb.*

NIGHTLIFE AND THE ARTS
Despite its past as a bohemian haven, nowadays Positano is remarkably quiet in the evenings. For entertainment, head down to the waterfront, where the restaurants lined up along the border of the Spiaggia Grande turn into an open-air party on summer nights.

CULINARY LESSONS On a centrally located roof garden with sweeping views of the coastline, **Diana Folonari** (of the famous wine family) holds four-day courses on Italian country cooking, offered in English from May through June and September through October, with wine tastings. Bring a notebook, pencils, and your own apron. ⊠ *Viale Pasitea 246* ☎ *089/875784* ⊕ *www. cookingschoolpositano.it.*

DANCE CLUBS **Music on the Rocks** (⊠ *Via Grotte dell'Incanto 56* ☎ *089/875874* ⊕ *www. musicontherocks.it* ⊗ *Closed Nov.–Mar.*) is a popular bar with live music on Wednesday and Saturday, run by the owners of the restaurants Chez Black and Le Terrazze. Set in a seaside cave off the Spaggia Grande beach, it is favored by the likes of Matt Dillon, Lenny Kravitz, Kate Moss, and Denzel Washington. Special events excepted, entrance is free as long as you buy a drink for around €10.

La Brezza (⊠ *Via del Brigantino 1* ☎ *089/875811* ⊗ *Closed Nov.–Mar.*) is a popular gathering place found just a few steps up from the Spaiggia Grande and is one of the prettiest places to enjoy a cocktail overlooking the beach.

FESTIVALS Yearlong, the Positano calendar is filled with festivities and religious *feste*. Sole, Mare e Cultura in July hosts national and international authors reading from their books in the shady gardens of Palazzo Murat. The first week in September sees the Premio Leonide Massine dance awards—officially known as the Positano Prize for the Art of Dancing, while the last Saturday brings the *Sagra del Pesce* (Fish Festival) on Fornillo beach. At Christmas, wreaths are fashioned from bougainvillea, and orchestra and choir concerts pop up all over town; the *Nuovo Anno* (New Year) is greeted with a big town dance and fireworks on the main beach, as well as other folklore and caffè-concerti musical events. In neighboring Montepertuso, a living crèche is enacted. The star event of the year and Positano's main religious festa is the **Feast of the Assumption**, held every August 15, with the painting of the Madonna with Child carried from the church to the sea, commemorated by evening fireworks and music on the main beach.

EATING WELL ON THE AMALFI COAST

Locals say they have "one foot in the fishing boat, one in the vineyard"—and a fortunate stance it is, as you can count on eating simple, fresh, seasonal food, and lots of it, with *tutti i sapori della campagna verace* (all the true flavors of the countryside). From the gulfs come *pesce alla griglia* (grilled fish), *calamari* (squid), *aragosta* (lobster), and *gamberone* (shrimp). Wood oven–baked thin-crust pizzas start with the classic *Margherita*—tomato sauce, basil, and cheese—and marinara—"marinated" with tomato, garlic, and oregano—and go from there to infinity.

La Cucina Costiera seems more sensuous amid all this beauty. Sun-dried tomatoes and chili peppers hang in bright red cascades on balconies and shopfronts. (*"Viagra naturale"* boasts a hand-lettered sign in Amalfi.) Ingredients grown in terraced plots include plump olives pressed into oil or eaten whole, tiny spring *carciofi* (artichokes), and sweet figs. *Sponzini,* or *pomodori del pendolo,* the tomatoes carried from Egypt long ago by fishermen, grow in the mountains and muddy fields of Furore and Conca dei Marini. Eggplant, asparagus, and mushrooms thrive in the Tramonte uplands, while tomatoes come from Campora. Soft *fior di latte* (cow's-milk cheeses) are from the high hill pastures of Agerola, while the world's best buffalo mozzarella comes from Paestum.

Pasta is often served with seafood, but regional dishes include *crespelle al formaggio*—layers of crepes with béchamel sauce—and fettuccine-like *scialatielli,* often a house specialty, served with varied sauces. Clams and pasta baked in a paper bag—"al *cartoccio"*—is popular in Amalfi. In Positano, try traditional squid with potatoes, stuffed peppers, and slow-simmering ragù (tomato sauce with meat, garlic, and parsley). Around Cetara, salted anchovies, eggplant, and peppers in oil are the base of the famed sauce called *"garum,"* handed down from the Romans. A lighter version is *colatura di alici,* an anchovy sauce developed by Cistercian monks near Amalfi, served on spaghetti as a traditional Christmas Eve treat. South of Salerno, you can visit working farms, and make friends with the buffalo, before sampling the best mozzarella known to mankind. Artichokes are also a specialty of the Paestum area. For the sweet tooth, don't miss Maiori's chocolate-covered eggplant.

Wine here is light, drinkable, and inexpensive, and often consumed mere months after crushing; don't be surprised if it's the color of beer, and served from a jug (*"sfuso"*–loose wine). Practically all of it comes from Campania, often from the town or village in which it's poured, perhaps even from the restaurant's own centuries-old vines. Little of it transports well. Furore, Gragnano, and Ravello produce good bottled wines, both rosso and bianco, with Furore's Cuomo perhaps the finest white.

Although a few restaurants are world renowned, most are family affairs, with *papà* out front, the kids serving, and mamma, aunts, and even old *nonna* in the kitchen. Smile a bit, compliment the cuisine, and you're apt to meet them all.

A festival devoted to chamber music, the **Corso Internazionale di Musica da Camera** (✉ *Via G. Marconi 45* ⊕ *www.icmcfestival.com*),twinned with a similar event in Shanghai, offers two-week master classes, lectures, and concerts open to the public for two weeks in July. The free summer concerts are staged in atmospheric settings throughout Positano.

The **Positano Myth Festival** (☎ *089/8122535* ⊕ *www.positanomythfestival. com*)is held at the end of August, with 10 days of cultural events—concerts, readings, dances—in colorful town settings.

SPORTS AND THE OUTDOORS

BEACHES

The Marina is the main boating area, with taupe, semisandy Spiaggia Grande the largest and widest beach of the six or so in the area. Fishermen—once the dominant workforce—now function as a cooperative group, supplying local kitchens; they can be seen cleaning their colorful, flipped-over boats and mending their torn nets throughout the day, seemingly oblivious to the surrounding throngs. To the west of town is the less-crowded Spiaggia di Fornillo, which you can get to by walking the gorgeous Via Positanesi d'America (leading from Spiaggia Grande). Fornillo is worth the walk, as it is vast and hemmed in by impressive cliffs. To the east of Positano is a string of small, pretty beaches, separated by coves—La Porta, Arienzo, San Pietro, and Laurito—most of which are accessible only by boat.

BOAT EXCURSIONS

From Spiaggia Grande you can board a scheduled day boat or hire a private one for as long as you'd like, to visit Capri, the Emerald Grotto in Conca dei Marini, or coves and inlets with small beaches. Close by, in the large caves of La Porta (650 feet east of the town center), Mezzogiorno and Erica, tools, utensils, and hunting weapons from the Paleolithic and Mesolithic ages have been discovered, the oldest known remains on the coast. The favorite boating destinations, however, are the rocky Li Galli islets (6 km [4 mi] southwest), seen from any point in Positano (as they are from the beaches of the peninsula), whose name derives from their importance in Greek mythology—resembling pecking birds, the islands were said to be the home of the sirens, part human, part feathered. Originally the site of an ancient Roman anchorage, the islands then became medieval fiefdoms of Emperor Frederick II and King Robert of Anjou. The isles remain tempting enough to lure purchasers in search of an exclusive paradise: Russian choreographer Leonide Massine in 1925, and, in 1988, dancer Rudolf Nureyev, who discovered the islands in 1984 when he came to accept the Positano Prize for the Art of Dancing, given each year in honor of Massine. The islands are still private, now belonging to a Sorrento hotelier, who also purchased the renowned Villa Zeffirelli in 2008—yours for a month for €500,000 or opt for a night at luxury hotel prices (grab a taste at ⊕ *www.villatreville.it*).**L'Uomo e il Mare** (✉ *Spiaggia Grande pier* ☎ *089/811613* ⊕ *www.gennaroesalvatore.it*) is an outfit run by brothers Gennaro and Salvatore Capraro (Gennaro's wife is English) offering boating excursions to Li Galli and many other coastal destinations, with lunch on board from €80 per person (less if you skip the lunch). Boating excursions can also be organized through **Cassiopea** (✉ *Spiaggia*

Grande ☎ *089/8123484* ⊕ *www.cassiopea-positano.com*), which also rents motorboats and rowboats by the hour.

HIKING

Hikers often pass through Positano on their way to the region's most famed mountainside trail, the **Sentiero degli Dei** (Pathway of the Gods), which can be picked up outside nearby Nocelle. For less professional hikers, Ponte dei Libri (a bridge several miles west) spans a pretty valley with soaring rock pinnacles and is a moderate walk. More serious climbers can hike up to Santa Maria del Castello (just more than 2,000 feet) from where paths radiate out eastward and westward along the Lattari Mountains. Plant lovers will find hillside walks particularly rewarding in May, when the mountains turn into a flowering rock garden with fine displays of orchids. As a general rule, allow plenty of time for what look like short distances on paper, take lots of water, and stick to the paths mapped out in red and white stripes by the CAI (Italian Alpine Club). Julian Tippet's hiking guide, *Landscapes of Sorrento and the Amalfi Coast* (available at stores on the coast), is a wonderful book—invest in it. You can also purchase the CAI's official map detailing all paths in the area.

SHOPPING

Although the traditional gaudily colored and lace-trimmed Positano-style clothes have started to look rather too frou-frou and dated, some contemporary designers are keeping the fashion alive with a more 21st-century spin. Goods still range from haute to kitsch, often tight tops and casual skirts in vibrant hues, with prices generally higher than in other coast towns. The fabric industry here began long ago with silk, canvas, and hand embroidery, then made headlines in 1959 when Positano introduced Italy to the bikini (following the reasoning that less is more, boutiques now sell even more highly abbreviated ones). The most concentrated shopping area, and the least difficult to maneuver, is the souklike area near the cathedral by the beach, where the crowded pedestrian pathway literally runs through boutiques. Lining steep alleyways covered with bougainvillea, small shops display items such as local foodstuffs, wood, lace, pottery, wines and limoncello, and ceramics; you'll even find artisans who can hand-stitch a pair of stylish sandals while you wait.

Pick up some great gifts from the tempting array of ceramics at **Ceramica Casola** (✉ *Via Laurito 49* ☎ *089/811382* ⊕ *www.ceramicacasola.com*). **Delikatessen Positano** (✉ *Via dei Mulini 5, 13, 15* ☎ *089/875489*) is the place to pick up your limoncello or biscuits and also offers candles and soaps made from lemons. At **I Sapori di Positano** (✉ *Via dei Mulini 6* ☎ *089/812055*) you can find anything that it's conceivably possible to make from citrus fruits. It's worth splurging at **Marilù** (✉ *Via del Saracino 20* ☎ *089/875631*) if you want to take home something unique in Positano wear.

MARINA DI PRAIA

★ *3½ km (2 mi) southeast of Positano, 2 km (1 mi) west of Vallone di Furore.*

"Whoever wants to live a healthy life spends the morning in Vettica and the evening in Praiano," according to a local adage. The larger township of Praiano may not fulfill that advice, but its scenic satellite, Marina di Praia, indeed does; it's home to a landmark eatery and famous disco. Nestled by the sea at the bottom of a dramatic chasm, this is the only anchorage along this rocky stretch where you can hire a boat and dock it and where ferries depart for points and islands along the coast.

GETTING HERE

By car, take the SS163 (Amalfitana) from outside Sorrento or Salerno. SITA bus from Sorrento–Positano–Amalfi, local bus from Praiano.

EXPLORING

The superpicturesque hamlet, with its year-round nativity scene perched on the cliff above, has a few parking spaces, a small sand beach tucked within cliffs, some excellent seafood restaurants, a hotel, and a tiny church. The legendary L'Africana disco, closed at the time of writing due to legal wranglings following the death of the owner, is tucked away on a pretty, winding path along the sea. All in all, Marina di Praia is like a little miniature and magical world nestled between two ageless cliffs.

WHERE TO EAT AND STAY

$$ ✕ **Alfonso a Mare.** Nestled in the Marina di Praia cove, this landmark
SOUTHERN restaurant and hotel is set in a rustic flagstone structure, once a dry
ITALIAN haul for boats, partly open to the sea breezes on one side with an open kitchen on the other. Inside are country-style wooden tables, netting, and ceiling baskets, while outside, colorful boats, peasant dwellings, and the chasm's sheer rock walls catch the eye. The hotel's small rooms have tile floors, windows opening to terraces overlooking the gulf, and a few antique touches. ⊠ *Via Marina di Praia* ☎ *089/874091* ⊕ *www. alfonsoamare.it* ⟿ *16 rooms* ⚭ *Restaurant, bar* ▭ *AE, DC, MC, V* ☾ *Closed mid-Nov.–Feb.* ⦿*MAP.*

$$$ ⬚ **Onda Verde.** Strikingly built on a rock dramatically jutting over the
★ tiny cove of Marina di Praia, this highly picturesque and popular hotel overlooks a Saracen tower and coastal ridges. Terraces overhang the sea, and common rooms and dining room feature panoramic glass walls and marble flooring. Later, you can climb down a winding path to the beach, where daily boat excursions leave for Positano, Capri, and Ischia. Several minutes away by footpath is the coast's most legendary disco, L'Africana, but you won't hear any music or disturbance from there—if you like to party, you can climb right into bed without having to drive. **Pros:** with these services there's no need to go into town at all; great views. **Cons:** a bit of a walk to get here; not great for mingling as you may never leave the hotel. ⊠ *Via Terra Mare 3* ☎ *089/874143* ⊕*www.ondaverde.it* ⟿ *26 rooms* ⚭ *In-room: a/c, safe, refrigerator, Internet. In-hotel: restaurant, bar* ▭ *MC, V* ☾ *Closed Nov.–mid-Mar.* ⦿*MAP.*

FURORE

18 km (12 mi) northeast of Positano; 14 km (9 mi) northeast of Praiano.

Furore, the *paese che non c'è,* the "town that doesn't exist," stretches for 8 km (5 mi) along the panoramic winding road climbing the Monti Latteri hills towards Agerola. Its nickname comes from the absense of any real focal point, or piazza, in the town, but, endearingly, it has billed itself as the *paese dipinto,* the "painted town," as the walls of the homes of local fishermen and wine cultivators are the "canvas" for an array of murals by local and international artists, who have mostly represented the traditions and culture of their town. This open air "gallery" was first initiated in 1980 with just three murals, and is regualary added to, with a different scene appearing around every bend. Other than artists, the most important residents of Furore are the local vintners. Townsfolk are said to live with one foot in a boat and one in a vineyard, and terraced vineyards cling to Furore's hillsides. Many vines uniquely grow horizontally from the stone walls, maximizing the use of the land here.

GETTING HERE

By car, take the Castellammare exit from the A3 motorway and follow the signs to Gragnano and Agerola, or take the SS163 (Amalfi Drive), and climb the hill 2 km (1 mi) west of Amalfi. There's a SITA bus service from Sorrento, and Positano. As for the Vallone di Furore, by car, take the SS163 (Amalfitana) from outside Sorrento or Salerno. There's SITA bus service from Positano and Amalfi.

EXPLORING

The most famous of Furore's vineyards is the Gran Furor Divina Costiera estate, which has produced top-quality "extreme" (so-called because of the conditions) wines here since 1942. Now named for owner Andrea Ferraioli's wife, the **Cantine di Marisa Cuomo** has won countless awards all over the world, including 2009's Gold Glass Award in San Francisco. The cream of its crop is undoubtedly Fior d'Uva (whose accolades include 2005's Best Limited Production Wines at L.A. County Fair) with an annual production around 16,000 bottles. Daughter Dorotea organizes wine tastings for a minimum of six people, while the cellar, hewn from the hillside Dolomitic limestone rock, can be visited outside the period of wine production (call for details). Andrea is also a talented photographer so don't miss the opportunity to see his stunning shots of the surrounding region. Ask them to show you the part of the stone wall (not far from the cellar) where you can see a magnificent 100-year-old horizontal vine. ⊠ *Via G.B.Lama, 16/18* ☏ *089/830348* ⊕ *www.marisacuomo.com.*

Fodor's Choice
★ From the lofty township of Furore, 944 steps (count 'em!) lead down to **Marina di Furore,** Italy's only fjord. Set on the coast, this enchanting hamlet—perhaps 10 houses?—beckons to most travelers as their SITA buses pass over it on a towering 90 feet (28 meters) high coastal viaduct (now the noted site of the Mediterranean Cup High-Diving Championship every July). The locale's name is from the "furor" of stormy water that once rushed down the Torrente Schiato here, now a mere trickle. Adorning the gorge is a tchotchke of a fishermen's village (once a favored

hideout of bandits and smugglers, with some houses renovated by Ingrid Bergman and Anna Magnani when they were involved with filming Roberto Rossellini's *L'Amore* in 1948); these *monazzeni* ("places to live in solitude") and the adjoining paper mill were abandoned when the tiny harbor closed. Today, the hamlet has been restored and the paper mill transformed into an "ecomuseum," with short botanical trails on which it's possible to see rare peregrine falcons as well as ancient species of plants found nowhere else in the region. From the beach, the *sentiero della Volpe Pescatrice* ("the fox-fish's path") and the *sentiero dei Pipistrelli Impazziti* ("the mad bats' path") climb up some 3,000 steps and were built to portage goods from the harbor to the town of Furore. The hard walk up takes a couple of hours, as you climb from sea to sky. To see any of this by car, you have to pay to park in the layby some 450 yards away on the Amalfi side of the gorge, just before the gas station. Unless you're in pretty good shape, it's better to boat to the beach and just rubberneck.

WHERE TO EAT AND STAY

$$
SOUTHERN
ITALIAN
★

✕ **Bacco.** One of the coast's oldest eateries, this has been a favorite for more than 80 years. The attractive interior is adorned unsurprisingly with images of the restaurant's synonymous Greek god of wine. The terrace is one of the best vantage points of the coast, with a cockerel weather vane lording it over a view of the Li Galli islands. The simple, but delicious, menu includes *ferrazzuoli alla Nannarella* (named after actress Anna Magnani, a notable diner here)—fresh pasta with tomatoes, tuna, swordfish, and pine nuts—and *vermicelli cu o' pesce fujuto*, a dish with no fish despite its moniker: the sea flavor of the local tomatoes gives the piscine *parfumo*. Try also the local dish, *totani alla volpe pescatrice* (flying squid with potatoes). Bacco also has 20 guest rooms, so feel free to indulge in that third glass of vino if you wish. ⊠ *Via G.B.Lama 9* ☎ *089/830360* ⊕ *www.baccofurore.it* ☱ *AE, DC, MC, V* ☉ *Closed 1 wk in Nov.*

$$$–$$$$
Fodor's Choice
★

🛏 **Furore Inn.** Suspended sky-high above the coast, commanding a stunning view stretching from Conca dei Marini to the Li Galli islands, this sleekly luxurious inn perches just below the pretty church of Sant'Elia (happily, a shuttle bus whisks guests to and from Amalfi). Surrounded by lush terraced gardens are the semi-Olympic pool, the infinity pool, and the heart-shaped pool—the triad making for the best swimming experience on the coast. A relaxing swim preps you for the sybaritic beauty spa (with Finnish sauna and Turkish bath) and your luxuriously comfortable guest room, each with its own private terrace and Jacuzzi (three are housed in the former residence of the Bishop of Amalfi, next to the church). Breakfast is served on a terrace while dinner is presented amid the Moorish arches of the Italian Touch restaurant, where you can enjoy the master chef's variations of ancient local recipes (cook them yourself in the hotel's cooking classes or get to know the famed local wines in tasting sessions). Far removed from the bustling Amalfi Drive, this is a restorative experience: a true spa for the soul. **Pros:** great pools; incredible views; shuttle bus. **Cons:** far from the main drag; you may never wish to leave the hotel grounds. ⊠ *Via dell'Amore, Piazza S. Elia* ☎ *089/8304711* ⊕ *www.furoreinn.it* ⇱ *22 rooms* ♨ *In-room: a/c,* *refrigerator, Internet, Wi-Fi. In-hotel: 2 restaurants, bar, tennis court, 3 pools, beauty center, gym, Wi-Fi hotspot, parking (paid)* ⊟*AE, D, MC, V* ☺ *Closed Nov.–mid-Mar.* ⦿*MAP.*

CONCA DEI MARINI

Fodor'sChoice ★ *2 km (1 mi) east of Vallone di Furore, 4 km (2½ mi) southwest of Amalfi.*

In her 2001 book of memories, *Happy Times,* Lee Radziwill declares that when she thinks of paradise, it is Conca dei Marini that first comes to mind. If you stay overnight here, we're sure you'll agree. Long a favorite of the off-duty famous and rich, the town hides many of its charms, as any sublime forgetaway should. On the most dramatic promontory of the coast, Conca dei Marini (the name means "seafarers' basin") was originally a province of ancient Rome called Cossa and later became an important naval base of the Amalfi Republic. Much later, it became a retreat for high-profile types, including John Steinbeck, Gianni Agnelli, and Carlo Ponti, who erected a white villa here by the sea (built for his first wife, not Sophia). You can see why: the green of terraced gardens competes with (and loses to) the blue sea, while the town's distinctive houses flanking the ridges have thick, white walls, with cupolas, balconies, and external staircases, testimony to former Arabic, Moorish, and Greek settlements. Below, on Capo di Conca, a promontory once used as a cemetery, a 16th-century coastal tower dramatically overlooks the sea. On a curve in the road sits the village's most famous attraction, the Emerald Grotto. Coral is still harvested in the waters off the coast here, while boats fish for sardines and squid through the night, their prow lanterns twinkling as if stars had slipped into the sea.

GETTING HERE

By car, take the SS163 (Amalfitana) from outside Sorrento or Salerno. There's SITA bus service from Positano and Amalfi.

EXPLORING

★ The main Conca dei Marini SITA bus stop is directly in front of the Hotel Belvedere. From here head west along the highway to the Sacred Tower and **Lido Capo di Conca** (☎*089/831512* ⦿ *www.capodiconca. it*) a privately run beach with bar and restaurant within the tower's shadow. Farther along you reach the Emerald Grotto. To the east, you can walk along the highway for views of Conca's harbor and lagoon. But the must-do is a jaunt down the staircase to the left of the Hotel Belvedere. This leads past some gorgeous houses to the dollhouse-size **harbor of Santa Maria della Neve,** one of the most idyllic sights along the entire coast. Closed for many years because of a major landside several years ago, its beach and marina have now reopened, and its darling little Chapel of Santa Maria della Neve should not be missed. From the Amalfi Drive high atop the hill, a view of this harbor is one of the coast's top photo-ops.

For Conca *in excelsis,* however, head up the mountainside to the northern reaches of the town (the road leads upward opposite the Hotel Belvedere, and then you can opt to take the gently climbing roads or

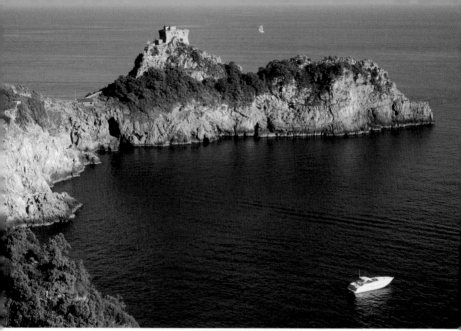

The coast's leading hideaway for off-duty celebrities, Conca dei Marini (*also see photo on this chapter's opening page*) is landmarked by its 16th-century Watch Tower.

the steeper staircase ever upward). Your reward as you climb up the hillside roads and steep scalinatelle is three stunningly sited churches. The first is neo-Byzantine **San Pancrazio,** set in a lovely palm-tree garden. Opposite this church, in the direction of Positano, is a road leading to a sky-high lookout over the coast. Back at San Pancrazio, head up the Scalinatella San Pancrazio to the tiny town piazza.

★   To the east along the cliff-side road is the sky-swimming church and **Convento di Santa Rosa,** which perches, "closer to heaven than to earth," on a bluff 1,000 feet over the sea, looking like some sort of Amalfitan Xanadu. Built as a theological university in the 15th century, and transformed into a Dominican monastery in the 16th century, the convent was abandoned in the 1920s and subsequently renovated into an *albergo* (inn). Alas, the owners closed up shop and for the past 40 years it has been one of the most coveted addresses in the world (rumor had it that Berlusconi himself was denied deed to the property). The big news in 2010, however, is that an American conglomerate has succeeded in snatching up the convent with plans to convert it to a luxury hotel in the distant future.

The convent found culinary fame in the 18th century when its nuns created one of the great local dishes, *sfogliata Santa Rosa* (a sweet cream-cheese-and-ricotta pastry shaped like a nun's hood). The mother superior distributed this delicacy free back then. Today, on Sunday and holy days, the pastries are baked, and savored, by locals and visiting revelers. You can head up to the Santa Rosa bluff by following the road leading up into Conca from the coastline, but if you want to take in the view of the convent from adjacent hills, use the mountaintop highway connecting Amalfi to Sorrento, which (unfortunately) runs right by the convent gates.

★ Heading back to the town piazza from the Convento di Santa Rosa, take Via Due Maggio and Via Roma to **Sant' Antonio di Padova**—an elegant Neoclassical white church spectacularly cantilevered hundreds of feet over the coastline on a stone parapet. The church is only open for Sunday-morning services, but you might ask locals if someone can open the church with a key for a quick visit (*"Dov'è la persona che ci può far visitare la chiesa?"*). For those who want to see churches in coastal villages, this may be the only way to gain entry.

On the outskirts of Conca dei Marini, the **Grotta dello Smeraldo** *(Emerald Grotto)* is a much-touted stop for day-trippers. The rather tacky sign on the road and the squadron of tour buses may put you off, but it's definitely worth a stop. Steps and an elevator bring you almost to sea level, but more delightful is to arrive by boat, which you can hire at just about any port up and down the coast; Coop. Sant'Andrea (☎ *089/873190 ⊕ www.coopsantandrea.com)* offers seven daily round-trips from Amalfi for €10. The karstic cave was originally part of the shore, but the lowest end sank into the sea when the peninsula subsided (the coast remains active, so it may eventually sink even lower—or rise). Intense greenish light filters into the water from an arch below sea level and is reflected off the walls of the cave, quite living up to emerald expectations. You wait to board a large rowboat with about 15 fellow passengers, and then you set off with a guide through the smallish cavern filled with huge stalactites and stalagmites. Don't let the boatman's constant spiel detract from the 20-minute experience—this is one of those tours that points out stalactites that look like Reagan (for Americans), Napoléon (for the French), and Dante (for the Italians) with an underwater nativity scene for the grand finale; just tune out and enjoy the sparkles, shapes, and Harry Winston–esque color. A tourist from Amalfi raved in a hotel log in 1858 that the cave ". . . can compete with Vesuvius," but it was forgotten about for years afterward until the grotto was rediscovered by a local fisherman in 1932. The light is best from noon to 3 pm, which is fortunately when hordes of potential visitors will be tucking into their pasta elsewhere. At Christmas there's a special celebration conducted around the underwater crèche. ✉ *Beyond Punta Acquafetente by boat, or off Amalfi Dr.* ☎ *089/871107 Amalfi tourist board* 🎫 *€5 ☉ Daily 9–4:30.*

WHERE TO STAY

$$$ 🏨 **Belvedere.** One of the coast's most beloved hotels, the Belvedere is
★ really not a hotel but a "home." This is the sort of place where guests ask for the room their great-grandparents favored. Happily, everyone, not just regulars, is treated like family here, and you'll find it difficult to say good-bye to the remarkably friendly and helpful staff. Set in one of the grande-dame villas of Conca dei Marini, featuring salons top-heavy with overstuffed sofas and a ravishing pool area, as well as a rocky beach, the Belvedere is handily located for exploring Conca dei Marini, as it's equidistant from the town's lagoon and Saracen tower. A shuttle service will take you to Amalfi. **Pros:** ideal location, with bus stop outside; a home away from home. **Cons:** be careful as you step

out the door—the entrance is on the busy Amalfi Drive; no elevator to the beach. ⊠ *Via Smeraldo 19* ☎ *089/831282* ⊕ *www.belvederehotel. it* ↪ *36 rooms* ⚹ *In-room: a/c. In-hotel: restaurant, bar, pool, Internet terminal, parking (free), some pets allowed* ▭ *AE, DC, MC, V* ⊘ *Closed mid-Oct.–mid-Apr.* ⓞ| *FAP.*

$$$–$$$$

Fodor's Choice

★

🖼 **Il Saraceno.** Gothic, Arabic, Oriental—and Las Vegas—influences combine to form this gorgeous extravaganza set on a chunk of cliff 3 km (2 mi) from Amalfi (note that this is its official address, but the hotel is really just a few steps away from Conca dei Marini). Bordering just a bit on kitsch, the evocatively exotic decor, which refers to Saracen pirates who roamed this coast centuries ago, begins in the lobby adorned with fantastic museum-quality 19th-century Orientalist oil paintings and antiques. Below, with more terraces than Babylon itself, the garden spills down the entire hillside to the enormous private beach, which features a saltwater pool. The Mushreq and El Qusayr restaurants are fine dining options in evocative Moorish surroundings. Mosaic floors, elaborate antique lighting fixtures, a medieval warrior in full armor, and gilded murals are accents, and guest rooms have crown-molded ceilings, rich colors, antiques, and terraces with floor-to-ceiling window panoramas. The hotel also maintains a private Romanesque stone chapel for weddings. Whew. **Pros:** if Xanadu was a hotel; ideal for living out your pirate fantasy; gorgeous garden terraces. **Cons:** too kitsch for some?; rather distant from the action (or is this a pro?). ⊠ *Via Augustariccio 33, Conca dei Marini/Amalfi* ☎ *089/831148* ⊕ *www.saraceno.it* ↪ *56 rooms* ⚹ *In-room: a/c, refrigerator. In-hotel: 2 restaurants, bars, pool, beachfront, Internet terminal, Wi-Fi hotspot, parking (free)* ▭ *AE, MC, V* ⊘ *Closed Nov.–Mar.* ⓞ| *FAP.*

AMALFI: FIRST OF THE SEA REPUBLICS

18 km (11 mi) southeast of Positano, 32 km (20 mi) west of Salerno.

At first glance, it's hard to imagine that this resort destination, set in a verdant valley of the Lattari Mountains, with its cream-colored and pastel-hued buildings tightly packing a gorge on the Bay of Salerno, was in the 11th and 12th centuries the seat of the Amalfi Maritime Republic, one of the world's great naval powers, and a sturdy rival of Genoa and Pisa for control of the Mediterranean. The harbor, which once launched the greatest fleet in Italy, now bobs with ferries and blue-and-white fishing boats. The main street, lined with leather shops and *pasticcerie,* has replaced a raging mountain torrent, and terraced hills where *banditti* (bandits) once roamed now flaunt the green and gold of lemon groves. Bearing testimony to its great trade with Tunis, Tripoli, and Algiers, Amalfi remains honeycombed with Arab-Sicilian cloisters and covered passages that suggest Asian caravansaries. In a way Amalfi has become great again, showing off its medieval glory days with sea pageants, convents-turned-hotels, ancient paper mills, covered streets, and its mosquelike cathedral.

A plaque under Amalfi's Porta Marina bears this inscription: "The judgment day, when Amalfitans go to Heaven, will be a day like any other." Visitors to this charming city, set in a verdant valley of the Lattari

Mountains, will soon understand what it means. For sheer picturesqueness, it can't be beat. Drinking in the vista of the town against the sea from the balcony of the town's historic landmark Convento di Amalfi is like getting an advance on paradise.

Amalfi's origin is clouded. One legend says that a general of Constantine's army, named Amalfo, settled here in 320; another tale has it that Roman noblemen from the village of Melphi (in Latin, "a Melphi"), fleeing after the fall of the empire, were first in these parts, shipwrecked in the 4th century on their way to Constantinople. Myth becomes fact by the 6th century, when Amalfi is inscribed in the archives as a Byzantine diocese, and the historical pageant really begins. Its geographic position was good defense, and the distance from Constantinople made its increasing autonomy possible. Continuously hammered by the Lombards and others, in 839 it rose against and finally sacked nearby Salerno, to which its inhabitants had been deported. In the 10th century, Amalfi constructed many churches and monasteries and was ruled by judges, later called doges—self-appointed dukes who amassed vast wealth and power.

From the 9th century until 1101, Amalfi remained linked to Byzantium but also was increasingly independent and prosperous, perhaps the major trading port in southern Italy. Its influence loomed large, thanks to its creation of the *Tavola Amalfitana*, a code of maritime laws taken up by most medieval-era kingdoms. Amalfi created its own gold and silver coins—or *tari*, engraved with the cross of Amalfi—and ruled a vast territory. With trade extending as far as Alexandria and Constantinople—where a large colony of Amalfitan merchants resided—it became Italy's first maritime republic, ahead of rivals Pisa, Venice, and Genoa; the population swelled to about 100,000, many of them seafarers and traders. As William of Apulia wrote in the 11th century, "No other city is richer in silver, cloth, and gold. A great many navigators live in this city . . . famous almost throughout the world as those who travel to where there is something worth buying."

But the days of wine and doges were about to end. In the 11th century Robert Guisgard of Normandy—in the duplicitous spirit of politicos to this day—first aided, then sacked the town, and the Normans from Sicily returned, after a short Amalfitan revolt, in the 12th century. Then, when the Republic of Pisa twice conquered it, Amalfi fell into decline, hastened by a horrific storm in 1343, then by an indirect blow from Christopher Columbus's discoveries, which opened the world beyond to competing trade routes. By the 18th century, the town had sunk into gloom, looking to its lemons and handmade paper for survival. After the state road was built by Ferdinand, the Bourbon king of Naples, in the 19th century, Amalfi evolved into a tourist destination, drawing Grand Tour–era travelers like Richard Wagner, Henry Wadsworth Longfellow, and Henrik Ibsen, all of whom helped spread Amalfi's fame.

GETTING HERE
By car, take the SS163 (Amalfitana) from outside Sorrento or Salerno, or take the Angri exit on the A3 motorway and cross the mountainous Valico di Chiunsi. SITA bus from Sorrento–Salerno, summer ferries

from Naples–Sorrento–Salerno. In Amalfi you can purchase tickets prior to boarding at the bar Il Giardino delle Palma bar, travel agency, or tobacco shop displaying a SITA sticker; all SITA buses leave Amalfi from Piazza Flavio Gioia. The special express bus to Naples departs from Monday to Saturday 5:30 to 11:40 am from the port;

WORD OF MOUTH

"I think the Amalfi coastal highway is very scary. Even riding the bus is scary. I can't imagine driving it myself. I took ferries whenever possible. Easy and fun to do."   —Cimbrone

catching this bus makes for an easy and scenic ride back to the city, allowing you to bypass a transfer from bus to the Circumvesuviana railway in Sorrento.

The Metro del Mare connects the town by boat to Naples and Sorrento in the summer months. Open-top **City Sightseeing buses** (☎ *081/8774707* ⊕ *www.sorrento.city-sightseeing.it*) make eight sightseeing daily trips from Amalfi and tour the main sites in the area, including Ravello for €3 (a daily four-trip ticket is €10).

VISITOR INFORMATION
Azienda Autonoma di Cura, Soggiorno e Turismo (✉ *Corso Reppubliche Marinare 27, Amalfi* ☎☎ *089/871107* ⊕ *www.amalfitouristoffice.it*) in Amalfi is open weekdays 8:30–1 and 2–6, Sunday 9–1.

EXPLORING AMALFI

Amalfi's compact tourist center is split between the bustling *lungomare* (waterfront), with its public and private transportation hubs, and the piazza in front of the Duomo. Parking is a big problem, as the tiny lot on the seafront (€3 per hour) fills up fast. There is a huge car park in the rock 400 yards east of the town, which has somewhat alleviated the situation. Traveling here via ferry and bus or staying in a hotel with a parking garage are good ideas. Once you explore the main sights near the waterfront, take off and explore the souklike center, then escape to the outskirts and the terraced hills of the Valle dei Mulini, site of Amalfi's ancient paper mills. At a little waterfall at the very north of the town, beyond the Museo della Carta, look to the left for a set of scalinatelle and climb the 100-plus steps; follow a footpath to the right, where you're in the middle of a lemon grove. If you buy a fresh lemon along the way—its leaves will be intact and its taste sweeter than you're accustomed to—and down its slices with a pinch of salt, you'll be passing time as the locals have since the age of its republic.

TOP ATTRACTIONS
Arsenale della Repubblica. From the middle of the 11th century, Amalfi's center of shipbuilding, customhouses, and warehouses was the Arsenale, today the only (partially) preserved medieval shipyard in southern Italy. Ships and galleys up to 80 feet long, equipped with up to 120 oars, were built at this largest arsenal of any medieval maritime republic. The boat now used for the historical regatta (held every four years, next in Amalfi in June 2012) and other ship models are kept in the arsenal's two large Gothic halls, which also hosts occasional exhibitions. Completely

Arsenale della
Repubblica **1**

Duomo di
Sant' Andrea **5**

Luna
Convento **3**

Museo Civico **4**

Piazza Flavio
Gioia **2**

Rua Nova
Mercatorum **6**

Valle dei
Mulini **7**

Amalfi

Maria Santissima ◆ ◆ Santa Maria
Aaddolorata   Maggiore

*Piazza
Duomo*

Porta della
Marina

Via M. Camera

Lungomare dei Cavalieri

◆ Bus stop

Golfo di Salerno

KEY
⫽ *Pedestrian Stairway*

0 ———— 1/4 mile

0 ———— 400 meters

renovated in 2008, 10 of the original 22 stone piers remain; the others were destroyed by storms and changes in the sea level on this ever-active coast. ✉ *South of Piazza dei Dogi, at Via Camera, by waterfront* ☎ *089/8736211 municipal office* ☉ *Mon.–Sat. 6–10, daily in Aug.*

Fodor'sChoice
★ **Duomo di Sant' Andrea.** Complicated, grand, delicate, and dominating, the 9th-century Amalfi cathedral has been remodeled over the years with Romanesque, Byzantine, Gothic, and baroque elements, but retains a predominantly Arab-Norman style. Cross and crescent seem to be wed here: the campanile, spliced with Saracen colors and the intricate tile work of High Barbery, looks like a minaret wearing a Scheherazadian turban, the facade conjures up a striped burnoose, and its Paradise Cloister is an Arab-Sicilian spectacular.

The power of Amalfi is evident in the approach to the cathedral, set atop 62 broad steps that lead to a mosaic facade, redone in the 19th century, and framed by bands, arches, and patterned squares. The imposing bronze doors, the first in Italy, were cast in Constantinople before 1066 and signed by Simeon of Syria; they were commissioned by the leader of the large Amalfitan colony there. Silver incrustations on the doors, now difficult to see, are images of Christ, Mary, and saints.

Visitors are now channeled first into the adjoining **Chiostro del Paradiso** (Cloister of Paradise): built around 1266 for Bishop Augustariccio as a burial ground for Amalfi's elite, it's one of the architectural treasures of southern Italy. Its flower-and-palm-filled quadrangle has a series of exceptionally delicate, intertwining arches on slender double columns in a combination of Byzantine and Arabian styles. Note the geometric patterns of colored mosaics in the walls, comprising parts of former pillars and pulpits of the earlier church. Of special note is a 14th-century crucifixion scene by Roberto d'Oderisio, a student of Giotto. The striking 12th-century bell tower in front of the complex has a Romanesque base and an elaborate yellow-and-green-tile top with arches in the local style, a round center surrounded by four smaller cupolas.

The chapel at the back of the cloister leads into the earlier (9th century) basilica. The structure, called the Basilica of the Crucifix, is in Romanesque style, with a nave, two aisles, and a high, deep apse. Note the 14th-century crucifixion scene by a student of Giotto. This section has now been transformed into a museum, housing sarcophagi, sculpture, Neapolitan goldsmiths' artwork, and other treasures from the cathedral complex.

Steps from the basilica lead down into the crypt of St. Andrew. The cathedral above was built in the 13th century to house the saint's bones, which came from Constantinople and supposedly exuded a miraculous liquid believers call the "manna of St. Andrew." Amalfi's cathedral had always lured pious devotees—from Francis of Assisi to Pope Urban IV—but after the 14th-century manna manifestation the pilgrim trade really picked up. The saint's remains (brought here in 1208) are kept under the 13th-century high altar in this exceptionally beautiful crypt adorned with marble statues sculpted by Pietro Bernini, father of the famed Gianlorenzo Bernini.

Following the one-way traffic up to the cathedral itself, you finally get to admire the elaborate polychrome marbles, and painted, coffered ceilings from its 18th-century restoration; art historians shake their head over this renovation, as the original decoration of the apse must have been one of the wonders of the Middle Ages. ⊠ *Piazza Duomo* ☎ *089/871324* 🖃 *€3* ◷ *Daily: Mar., Sept., 9:30–5:30; Apr.–June and Oct., 9–6:45; July and Aug., 9–7:45; Nov.–mid-Jan. 10–3:30, closed mid-Jan.–Feb. (daily services excepted).*

Museo Civico. The Municipal Museum of Amalfi, sharing space with the municipal offices (and therefore closed when council meetings take place), contains artifacts from Amalfi's medieval period, including paintings, ancient coins, banners, and jeweled costumes. The highlight is the original 66-chapter draft of the code of the *Tavole Amalfitana,* the sea laws and customs of the ancient republic, used throughout the Italian Mediterranean from the 13th to the 16th century. The Tavole established everything from prices for boat hires to procedures to be followed in case of shipwreck. Long one of the treasures of the Imperial Library of Vienna, the draft was returned to Amalfi after more than 500 years. Note the ceramic panel on the south outside wall of the museum, between Corso delle Repubbliche Marinare and Piazza del Municipio, created by Diodoro Cossa in the 1970s. The scenes provide an overview of local history: Roman refugees establishing themselves in nearby Scala

The piazza outside Amalfi's Duomo is a lively gathering place.

in the 4th century; the founding of Amalfi by these same Romans; Amalfi's commercial and diplomatic role in the Mediterranean; the arrival of St. Andrew's body; the invention of the maritime compass; and other historic events. ⊠ *Piazza Municipio 6* ☎ *089/8736211* 🖼 *Free* ⊘ *Weekdays 8:30–1:30, Tues. and Thurs. also 4:30–6:30 pm.*

Rua Nova Mercatorum. Also known as Via dei Mercanti, evocative Rua Nova was the main thoroughfare of medieval Amalfi, when the main road was a raging torrent, and it remains the most fascinating "street" in town. Claustrophobes, beware: it's completely covered, like a tunnel, but is especially wonderful when the light from alleys and windows plays on its white walls. Stretching almost the length of the main street, it ends at a medieval-era *contrada,* or neighborhood, with a fountain known as *Capo di Ciuccio* (Donkey's Head), where mules would refesh themselves after the climb down from the hills. ⊠ *Adjacent to Via Pietro Capuano.*

Valle dei Mulini. The Valley of the Mills, uphill from town, was for centuries Amalfi's center for papermaking, an ancient trade learned from the Arabs (who learned it from the Chinese). Beginning in the 12th century, former macaroni mills were converted to the production of paper made from cotton and linen, among the first in Europe to do so. In 1211 Frederick II of Sicily prohibited this lighter, more readable paper from being used in the preparation of official documents, favoring traditional sheepskin parchment; but by 1811 more than a dozen mills here, with more along the coast, were humming. Natural waterpower ensured that the handmade paper was cost-effective, but catastrophic flooding in 1954 closed most of the mills for good, and many of them have now been converted into private housing. The **Museo della Carta** (Museum of Paper) opened in 1971 in a 15th-century mill; paper samples, tools of the trade, old machinery, and the audiovisual presentation are all enlightening. The admission price gets you a guided tour in English, as well a demonstration of the papermaking process. A 20-minute stroll from the Piazza Duomo will take you to the valley via the main thoroughfare of Via Genoa, turning onto Via Capuano, at the edge of town. ⊠ *Via delle Cartiere 23* ☎ *089/8304561* ⚏ *€4* ⊕ *www.museodellacarta. it* ☉ *Mar.–Oct., daily 10–6:30; Nov.–Feb., Tues.–Sun. 10–3:30.*

WORTH NOTING

Luna Convento. Legendarily founded by none other than St. Francis of Assisi, the Luna Convento was built in the 13th century and retains its famous cloister, with distinctive Arab-Sicilian arcaded columns and a crypt with frescoes. Transformed into the earliest hotel on the Amalfi Coast in the early 19th century, the hotel was where Henrik Ibsen wrote a large chunk of *A Doll's House*. The hotel also owns the famous Torre Saracena (now home to a restaurant) that sits across the highway and stands guard over Amalfi's seaside promontory. ⊠ *Via Pantaleone Comite 19* ☎ *089/871002* ⊕ *www.lunahotel.it.*

Piazza Flavio Gioia. A statue, set in an ironically disorienting traffic roundabout in front of the harbor, honors the Amalfitan credited with inventing the maritime compass in 1302. Many say it was the Chinese who invented the compass, passing the idea along to the Arabs, who traded with Amalfi; Gioia may have adapted it for sea use (some even believe there was no such person as Gioia). ⊠ *On waterfront.*

WHERE TO EAT

$$
SOUTHERN
ITALIAN
✗ **Al Teatro.** Once a children's theater, this informal white-stucco restaurant in the medieval quarter is 50 steps above the main drag and most charming. A house specialty is grilled squid and calamari with mint sauce, reflecting the position of the place—suspended between sea and mountains. Try also the *Scialatielli al Teatro*, with tomatoes and eggplant. The pizzas, from their wood oven, are terrific. ⊠ *Via E. Marini 19* ☎ *089/872473* ▤ *AE, MC, V* ☉ *Closed Wed. and Jan.–mid-Feb.*

$$$
SOUTHERN
ITALIAN
✗ **Da Gemma.** Cognoscenti have sung the praises of this understated landmark since 1872. Tile floors, white tablecloths, and a terrace set above the main street are soothing elements. Admire the glistening kitchen in the entrance lobby before perusing the menu, printed on local handmade paper. Italian foodies appreciate dishes such as *tubettoni alla masaniello* (tiny pieces of pasta with capers, mussels, and prawns) and *pasta alla genovese*, a white ragù made with meat, onions, and black pepper. For dessert try the local specialty: eggplant with chocolate. ⊠ *Via Fra Gerardo Sasso 9* ☎ *089/871345* ⊕ *www.trattoriadagemma. com* ⚑ *Reservations essential* ▤ *AE, DC, MC, V* ☉ *Closed Wed. and mid-Jan.–Feb.*

$$$$
SOUTHERN
ITALIAN
★
✗ **Eolo.** One of the most sophisticated restaurants on the Amalfi Coast, Eolo is run by the owners of the Marina Riviera hotel. The decor is suavely tranquil—white-cove ceilings, Romanesque columns, mounted starfish—although the kitchen is anything but . . . it tosses out superb gastronomic delights, including raviolini stuffed with potatoes and

black truffles, branzino baked in a salt crust, and a souffle spin on the traditional Caprese salad of tomatoes and mozzarella. Many dishes are fetchingly adorned with blossoms and other visual allures, but nothing compares to the view of Amalfi's harbor from one of the tables in Eolo's picture-window alcove. If you don't land one of these three, don't fret—the entire room is pretty enough as it is. ⊠ *Via Pantaleone Comite 3* ☎ *089/871241* ⊕ *www.eoloamalfi.it* ⚘ *Reservations essential* ☐ *AE, MC, V* ☾ *Closed Nov.–Mar. and Tues.*

$$
SOUTHERN
ITALIAN
✕ **Il Tari.** Locals highly recommend this little *ristorante* named after the ancient coin of the Amalfi Republic and a few minutes' walk north of the Duomo. This used to be a former stable and the space has changed little since those equine days, but appealing local art, blue-and-white check tablecloths, old photos, and tile floors make this cozy enough, not to mention the vast menu, where winners include the wood-oven-baked thin-crust pizza with fresh sauces, and the *scialatielli alla Saracena*, long spaghetti-style pasta seemingly laden with everything you can imagine from the sea. ⊠ *Via P. Capuano 9–11* ☎ *089/871832* ⊕ *www. amalfiristorantetari.it* ☐ *AE, DC, MC, V* ☾ *Closed Tues.*

$$$$
SOUTHERN
ITALIAN
Fodor's Choice
★
✕ **La Caravella.** With tables adorned with lace tablecloths, *ciucciù* (donkey) ceramics, tall candles, and fresh floral bouquets, salons coved with frescoes and marble floors, it is little wonder this is considered the most romantic restaurant in Amalfi. Opened in 1959, it became the first restaurant in Southern Italy to earn a Michelin star (1966), and once drew the most gilded guest list in town, including such fans as Andy Warhol, Agnelli, and Federico Fellini. Now in its third generation, the menu maintains dishes favored fifty years ago, including slices of fish grilled in lemon leaves and marinated with an almond and wild fennel sauce. A tasting menu is available, but don't miss out on the antipasti—especially the *panzerottini neri* (ravioli stuffed with ricotta cheese and squid) or the fish *vellutata di limone* (dressed with lemon sauce). There is also an art gallery in the side alley displaying ceramics from Vietri sul Mare. ⊠ *Via Matteo Camera 12, near Arsenale* ☎ *089/871029* ⊕ *www. ristorantelacaravella.it* ⚘ *Reservations essential* ☐ *AE, MC, V* ☾ *Closed Nov. and Dec. and Tues.*

$$–$$$
SEAFOOD
✕ **Lo Smeraldino.** Open since 1949, this airy, popular fish restaurant presides over Amalfi's almost-emerald waterfront wharf, a setting that generates a festive holiday vibe that draws many diners. Another lure is the reasonably priced seafood, with a tourist menu showcasing the *cucina tipica Amalfitana,* such as the tasty penne with tomatoes, cream, eggplant, peppers, basil, and cheese, or excellent simply grilled fish (*grigliata di pesce*). You can see the boats bringing in the day's catch and at night there's pizza on the terrace amid the twinkling lights of hills, sea, and sky. ⊠ *Piazzale dei Protontini 1* ☎ *089/871070* ☐ *AE, DC, MC, V.*

$$
SOUTHERN
ITALIAN
✕ **Maccus.** In the heart of medieval Amalfi, with outside seating occupying the small *piazza* outside the churches of Santa Maria Maggiore and the Maria Santissima Addolorata, this gastronomical treat is a testimony to the *maschera* (mask) of Maccus, a lover of good food. Simple seasonal food is prepared by lovers of the craft, using grandma's recipes—try the grilled squid or the buffalo steak. The inside eating area is painted in vivid yellow and Pompeii red, reflecting the wheat

and wine used in this fine restaurant. ⊠ *Largo S. Maria Maggiore 1–3* ☎ *089/8736385* ⊕ *www.maccusamalfi.it* ⌂ *Reservations essential* ▤ *MC, V* ⊗ *Closed Jan. and Feb.*

$$
SOUTHERN
ITALIAN
✕ **Stella Maris.** Probably the first restaurant you see on arriving in Amalfi, with its distinctive blue-and-white awnings, this boasts a fine location on the beach. Dining directly on your sun lounger, on the terrace, or in front of the glass walls, you can gaze at the fishing boats bobbing in the bay. The *risotto al pescespada* (rice with swordfish) is a treat, or try a pizza. If you haven't yet worked up an appetite, you can choose an *aperitivo* or cocktail, joining the sun worshippers on the small strand of sand. ⊠ *Via della Regione 2* ☎ *089/872463* ⊕ *www.stella-maris.it* ▤ *AE, DC, MC, V* ⊗ *Closed Dec.–Mar.*

WHERE TO STAY

$
Fodor's Choice
★
🏨 **Albergo Sant'Andrea.** With everyone gazing at the magnificent steps leading to Amalfi's cathedral, few turn around to notice that this tiny, family-run pensione occupies one of the top spots in town. The cute "Room-with-a-View" lobby is as big as a Victorian closet, while guest rooms range from vast to cozy; most overlook the Duomo, with quieter ones on a side alley. Considering the location, the great air-conditioning, and the very friendly staff, this may be the *best* bargain in all Italy. **Pros:** on the main square; best views of Duomo; delightful staff. **Cons:** steep flight of steps to entrance; rooms very simple. ⊠ *Piazza Duomo* ☎ *089/871145* ⊕ *www.albergosantandrea.it* ⇥ *8 rooms* ⌂ *In-room: a/c* ▤ *AE, DC, MC, V* �🍽⊙ *EP.*

$$
🏨 **Aurora.** Regarded for its location near the beach of Spiaggia delle Sirene and the fishing harbor, this well-run little hotel is a good deal for sand potatoes who prefer absorbing rays to hiking the highlands. Amid a greenery-filled setting with three levels of arched windows, guest rooms are clean, 18 with water views and private terrace, and although just a flat and easy 10-minute walk from the Duomo, crowds rarely venture to this nook. Room prices follow a dynamic rate, making them cheaper the earlier you book. **Pros:** lovely terrace views of Amalfi harbor; away from the madding crowds; ideal for a beach-based trip. **Cons:** a bit of a walk to town; the smaller rooms are a bit cramped. ⊠ *Piazzale dei Protontini 7, between Scalo d'Oriente and Lungomare dei Cavalieri* ☎ *089/871209* ⊕ *www.aurora-hotel.it* ⇥ *29 rooms* ⌂ *In-hotel: a/c. In-hotel: bar, Internet terminal, parking (paid)* ▤ *MC, V* ⊗ *Closed Nov.–Mar.* 🍽⊙ *BP.*

$$$$
Fodor's Choice
★
🏨 **Grand Hotel Convento di Amalfi.** Under the moniker Hotel Cappuccini Convento this fabled medieval monastery was the most richly atmospheric hotel on the Amalfi Coast, if not in all of Italy. Immortalized in postcards and paintings, lauded by such guests as Longfellow and Wagner, the view of Amalfi's waterfront from the hotel terrace became one of the first travel icons of the Victorian age. The 13th-century monastery became a hotel in the mid-19th century and up to 2002 guests headed here to enjoy a magical retreat to the sepia-colored past. But that year NH Hotels began a seven-year restoration and reopened it in 2009. First impressions? The ugly outside elevator has been replaced by an indoor modern monstrosity; the new entrance area on Via Matteo Camera, now adorned with steel sculpted motifs, has been scorned by locals.

Ride up the cliffside and enter the hotel itself, however, and things look rosier. Still in place are some antiques of the past, such as Victorian lecterns and Savonarola chairs, along with the celebrated Arab-Sicilian cloister. But totally "corporatized" are the contemporary-styled guest rooms; once sublimely simple bare monk cells, they are now comfy cocoons with wicker settees and beds. Happily, the restaurant—long scorned as the worst on the coast—now takes dining seriously with a menu of local specialties served with "an international flair." The stunning ½-km-long (¼-mi-long) terrace promenade now holds the obligatory (small but glorious) infinity pool but, best of all, the time-burnished columns and clouds of bougainvillea still frame timeless views of Amalfi's harbor—among the most stunning vistas in Italy. Alas, nonguests are no longer welcome. **Pros:** a slice of paradise; iconic Amalfi. **Cons:** traditionalists will miss its old-world charm; a 10-minute walk to town. ✉ *Via Annunziatella 46* ☎ *089/8736711* ⊕ *www.ghconventodiamalfi. com* ↰ *53 rooms* ⚑ *In-room: a/c, refrigerator, Wi-Fi. In-hotel: restaurant, bar, pool, Internet terminal, Wi-Fi hotspot, parking (paid)* ▭ *AE, DC, MC, V* ☉ *Closed Nov.–Mar.* ⴲ *BP.*

$$ ⌂ **Hotel Amalfi.** Up a tiny side street not far from the Piazza Duomo, the Amalfi is unassumingly decorated with small, somewhat characterless modern-style rooms (get one with a geranium-filled balcony if you can) without a great view. However, the place's central location, the friendly welcome of the Lucibello family, the garden, and the roof terrace where you can breakfast in the warm morning sun not far from the cathedral's campanile, make this a fabulous deal if you want to be in the center of things and enjoy a rather gentle price tag. **Pros:** great central location; roof terrace. **Cons:** rooms are not very exciting; no access without negotiating steps. ✉ *Via dei Pastai 3* ☎ *089/872440* ⊕ *www.hamalfi.it* ↰ *40 rooms* ⚑ *In room: a/c, refrigerator (some), Wi-Fi. In-hotel: parking (paid), some pets allowed* ▭ *MC, V* ⴲ *FAP.*

$$ ⌂ **Hotel Floridiana.** With a great location right on Piazza Duomo, boast-
★ ing a fabulous ballroom as its breakfast room, and gently priced to boot, this is an option with many pluses. This was the residence of the famed Pisani family in the 12th century, and despite, or rather because of, restoration work in 2004, the surroundings bring you back to those times—look for the gloriously frescoed ceiling in the dining room, one of the grandest ballrooms in Campania that have come down to the present day. Guest rooms are simple, but comfortable, and the owner Agnese is extremely helpful and friendly, making you feel right at home in the heart of Amalfi. **Pros:** in the heart of the historic town; friendly owners; those frescoes! **Cons:** the rooms face inward, no sea view. ✉ *Via Brancia 1* ☎ *089/8736373* ⊕ *www.hotelfloridiana.it* ↰ *13 rooms* ⚑ *In room: a/c, refrigerator, Wi-Fi. In-hotel: parking (paid), some pets accepted* ▭ *AE, DC, MC, V* ⴲ *BP* ☉ *Closed Nov.–Mar.*

$$$$ ⌂ **Luna Convento.** Founded as a convent in 1222, allegedly by no less a personage than St. Francis of Assisi, the hotel has been owned by the Barbaro family since 1822 and visited by Otto van Bismarck, Wagner, Mussolini, Ingrid Bergman, and Tennessee Williams, among other noted figures. One of the restaurants is in the 15th-century Saracen tower, perched on a rock over the sea, providing a view that spans from Capo

dei Conca to Capo d'Orso. Coved ceilings, graceful arches, and marble columns mark the architecture, along with Flemish religious artwork, church and convent artifacts, antique furnishings, and mosaic flooring, all of which mix with modern comforts. That noted, some might say that this landmark is in dire need of a face-lift, both figuratively and literally. Traditionalists, however, would never carp about the "soul" of the Luna Convento: the beauty of its famed southern Romanesque cloisters and baroque chapel is timeless. Below the tower is a solarium and seawater pool. Ask for a room in the renovated wing, and try to get one with a grand balcony view over Amalfi's bay. **Pros:** the medieval convent vibe; a 270-degree view of Amalfi. **Cons:** you need to cross the busy road to get to the pool; not for all pockets; faded decor. ⊠ *Via P. Comite 33* ☎ *089/871002* ⊕ *www.lunahotel.it* ⤙ *43 rooms* ⌂ *In-room: a/c, safe, refrigerator, Wi-Fi. In-hotel: 2 restaurants, bar, pool, Wi-Fi hotspot* ▤ *AE, MC, V* ⭗*| BP.*

$$$–$$$$ ★ 🏨 **Marina Riviera.** Once the site of fishermen's cottages—these structures are that close to the sea—this hotel graces one of the coastal promontories in Amalfi town itself. At first look, however, guests could despair at the heavily trafficked seaside road just in front—but the good news is that the Marina Riviera is on a bend, traffic is never fast, and therefore not noisy. Thus, when you ascend to the hotel's second floor, you can easily escape into this cocoon decorated with antiques, 18th-century ceramics, and vintage photos. You'll feel right at home, thanks to the Gargano family, who greet you in the welcoming coved-ceiling reception area. Owner Antonio prides himself on his buffet-style breakfast (note also the sugar sachets, adorned with photos of Antonio carrying the 1960 Olympic torch!). Each guest room is different, with ceramic fittings in the bathrooms. The fourth floor solarium is decked out in Bali wood, and looks directly over the open sea (a small sea-water pool will be added in 2011). **Pros:** views to-die-for; friendly owers; great breakfasts. **Cons:** no internal elevator; entrance difficult to find; fronts busy road. ⊠ *Via Panteleone Comite* ☎ *089/871104* ⊕ *www.marinariviera.it* ⤙ *35 roors.* ⌂ *In-Room: a/c, safe, refrigerator. In-hotel: Wi-Fi hotspot, parking (paid)* ▤ *AE, DC, MC, V* ⊗ *Closed Nov.–Mar.* ⭗*| BP.*

$$$–$$$$ 🏨 **Miramalfi.** On the hill climbing the main coastal drive, this white-stucco hotel overlooks deep blue water and coastal ridges. The hotel's elevators, or a steep hike, deposit you at the seawater pool, with concrete platforms for sunbathing, and a lunch menu in the summer. Lobbies are sleekly decorated, and Le Onde dining room serves up wraparound panoramas; guests may also dine on the sea-air terrace. Rooms have vibrant tile flooring, brightly painted furnishings, floral fabrics, wicker, and lots of windows. All have private sea-view balconies, and some have whirlpools. **Pros:** an incredible view; all rooms have balconies. **Cons:** 1970s-style architecture; a bit far from town. ⊠ *Via Quasimodo 3* ☎ *089/871588* ⊕ *www.miramalfi.it* ⤙ *49 rooms* ⌂ *In-room: a/c, refrigerator, Internet, Wi-Fi. In-hotel: restaurant, bar, pool, beachfront, parking (paid), some pets allowed* ▤ *AE, DC, MC, V* ⭗*| BP.*

$$ 🏨 **Piccolo Paradiso.** A location in the Amalfi harbor area across from the Arsenale already makes this upscale bed-and-breakfast a special choice.

The atmosphere is more pleasing and elegant than that of a typical pensione. A common area has tile flooring, and rooms are smallish but comfortable, with wicker seating and wrought-iron headboards; three have private terraces. Run by two sisters, everything sparkles, and you'll get to know your fellow international guests in this little paradise. **Pros:** great location; friendly atmosphere. **Cons:** a little too close to the center for some; no credit cards. ⊠ *Via M. Camera 5* ☎ *089/873001* ⊕ *www. albergopiccoloparadisoamalfi.com* ⤳ *5 rooms* ☖ *In-room: a/c. In-hotel: Internet terminal* ⊟ *No credit cards* ⌾⎮ *BP.*

$$$$　☒ **Santa Caterina.** When Elizabeth Taylor and Richard Burton wanted to
Fodor's Choice　escape, they headed here and no wonder. Owned by the Gambardella
★　family for generations, this quietly elegant, supremely comfortable, and cherished hotel has long been one of the treasures of the coast. Indeed, many guests have been coming here since great-grandmother's day and, today, it remains as the last grand hotel of Amalfi. Just outside Amalfi proper (giving it a grand vista of the town), the Santa Caterina takes full advantage of its hillside location, with vast, terraced gardens and orchards overlooking the sea. Down by the water is a luscious heated seawater-pool area, complete with an idyllic thatched-roof, open-air seaside restaurant for fine dining. The main dining room may be the very best restaurant on the coast: white-linen stylish yet nouvelle, with an array of glamorously sophisticated delights coming out from the kitchen (this is the place to go if you want to enjoy one culinary blow-out on the coast). The lobby is charmingly coved, while decor is unobtrusively traditional, with Belle Epoque accents. Suites are in the main building, with various villas tucked in the vast gardens, such as the Follia Amalfitana (with its round bed and Jacuzzi-with-a-view; Hillary Clinton stayed in this one!) or the 19th-century hunting-box châlet, with its own pool, set at water's edge. Happily, the beauty center and restaurants are open to nonguests, so everyone can experience this treasure. **Pros:** the great traditions live on here; shuttle van to Amalfi. **Cons:** an uphill hike away from the town; entrance smack on Amalfi Drive. ⊠ *Strada Amalfitana 9* ☎ *089/871012* ⊕ *www.hotelsantacaterina.it* ⤳ *66 rooms* ☖ *In-room: a/c, safe, refrigerator, Wi-Fi. In-hotel: 2 restaurants, bar, pool, gym, spa, Internet terminal, Wi-Fi hotspot, parking (free)* ⊟ *AE, DC, MC, V* ⌾⎮ *BP.*

FESTIVALS

Amalfi's festivals best reflect the splendor of its past. The **St. Andrew Race** every June 27 and November 30, dedicated to Amalfi's protector of seamen, is a joyous religious celebration commemorating the defeat of Barbarossa and the Moslem fleet in 1544. A procession of white-robed men carry a silver-gilt replica of the saint to the harbor, and fishermen at the beach run it back to the cathedral and—in one dramatic dash— straight up its 62 steps. Later, the statue gleams silver in the sunshine of the piazza, as fishermen hang tiny wooden and gilt fish amulets from the saint's left wrist as tokens of gratitude. In the evening, guitar music drifts from many boats, and candlelight flickers.

Even more of a pageant is the **Regatta Storica delle Antiche Repubbliche Marinare** (*Historical Regatta* ☎ *089/871107*), the mock battles in which four boats, each with eight oarsmen, represent the medieval maritime

2

republics of Amalfi, Pisa, Genoa, and Venice. The prize, held by the winner for a year, is a scale-model gold-and-silver replica of an antique sailing ship. Each of the former republics is represented by 80 participants; Amalfi's musical contingent is adorned in jewel-encrusted costumes on loan from the town museum—doges, dogaressas, merchants, and commoners from the prosperous past come colorfully to life, with the day's festivities culminating in a show of fireworks. Held yearly on the first Sunday in June every four years, with the four cities alternating as the urban stage sets, the pageant is scheduled to be in Amalfi in 2012 (the 2009 edition was brought forward a year to coincide with the 800th anniversary of the arrival of St. Andrew's relics in Amalfi).

Amalfitans love to celebrate holidays. The Good Friday candlelight procession, Easter Sunday, and Christmas pageants with crèche competitions (with cribs mounted in the city fountains) are all excuses for lavish family occasions, with special foods and church ceremonies.

NIGHTLIFE
Amalfi doesn't have many clubs for music or dancing. However, flyers and posters often go up announcing concerts and theatricals during the peak summer months.

SHOPPING
Leading off from Piazza Duomo is the main street of Amafli, Via Genova, which is lined with some of the most adorable and interesting shops on the coast. Be sure to take a lovely passeggiata stroll along here at twilight! A true Aladdin's Cave of antique treasures, **La Scuderia del Duca** (⊠ *Largo Cesareo Console 8, near Arsenale* ☎ *089/872976* ⊕ *www.carta-amalfi.it*) is a publisher of fine books and postcards, but also selling antique accessories, objets d'art, and beautiful art tomes about Amalfi. They also now stock authentic paper from the Amatruda Mill, run by descendants of an Amalfi papermaking dynasty dating from at least 1400, and probably the oldest crafts papermaker in Italy. If you're pining for English-language newspapers, wanting a book on Amalfi's history, or just looking for a suitable poolside novel, try the **Libreria-Edicola Internazionale** (⊠ *Via Repubbliche Marinare 17* ☎ *089/871180*) near the tourist office.

Leather goods are popular items in small shops along the main streets; one good option is **Bazar Florio** (⊠ *Via P. Capuano 5/7* ☎ *089/871980*), with a fair and friendly owner. It features handbags, wallets, and backpacks.

Mostacciuolo (⊠ *Piazza Duomo 22* ☎ *089/871552*) has been run by a well-known and respected family of coral craftsmen since 1930.

ATRANI

Fodor's Choice   *1 km (½ mi) east of Amalfi, 5 km (3 mi) southwest of Ravello.*
★
In some respects this stage-set of a medieval town is a secret treasure: set atop a crag between cliffs overlooking the sea, and a 10-minute walk from the western outskirts of Amalfi—take the seaside stairs off the drive, just after the tunnel—this is the smallest municipality in Italy. Centered on a small and enchanting piazza, the town's special charms

The heart of Atrani is adorable Piazza Umberto I, a town square ringed in by buildings and corkscrew staircases, and looking for all the world just like an opera set.

are most evident from the sea, as it looks like an amphitheater ready for a royal pageant. Its closely packed, dollhouse-scaled backstreets are filled with pastel-and-white houses and shops, fragrant gardens, arcaded lanes, and spiraling scalinatelle. But the hamlet's stellar attractions are the baroque-style churches, which dominate the skyline, and around which parish houses cluster in true medieval style.

GETTING HERE

On foot from Amalfi; by car, take the SS163 (Amalfitana) from outside Sorrento or Salerno. There's SITA bus service from Sorrento, Positano, and Amalfi.

EXPLORING

Today, Atrani is often overlooked by tourists, who drive right by it over the riverbed of the Torrente Dragone. Tragically this river burst its banks in September 2010, burying the square in mud and destroying the beach (resulting in the death of a local girl). Don't worry, however, as the town now shows no traces of this devastation. In fact, it looks little changed from the days when it was closely linked to the Amalfitan republic, the residential choice of its aristocracy. It gained its independence from Amalfi in 1578, with which it maintains a friendly rivalry; locals say the town holds its processions on its narrow inner streets to discourage Amalfitans from participating.

Adorable Piazza Umberto I, entirely enclosed by four-story houses, is the setting for the basics of Italian life for Atrani's less than 1,000 residents: general store, stationery store, coffee shop, bar, fruit stand, restaurant, barber, and, of course, police station (the constable struts about as though in command of the pigeons strutting alongside him).

The uncrowded square is filled with simple scenes: children giggle at hide-and-seek, *duenas* gossip, and men debate and take sips from the venerable fountain as if the world had little changed from the days of the doges. An arcade to one side offers a glimpse of beach, fishing boats, a mule or two, and the sea beyond. At Christmas the whole town congregates here at dawn to drink cappuccino and share traditional cakes.

The bell of the 10th-century church of **San Salvatore de Bireto** tolled to announce the crowning of a new doge. The coronation ceremony was restricted to those wearing a *bireto,* the cloth cap that would be ceremoniously placed on the new doge's head, and someday worn attending his burial in the same church. The church was remodeled in 1810; the dome is beautifully tiled, and the paneled bronze doors cast in the 11th century came from Constantinople, as did the doors in the Amalfi Duomo. Within is a 12th-century marble plaque showing two peacocks, one standing over a human head between two sirens, the other on a hare being attacked by two birds; peacocks were considered immortal, but the symbolism of the two in this setting is open to interpretation.

The church of **Santa Maria Maddalena,** on a piazza, was built in 1274 and given a neo-baroque facade in 1852. The dome is covered in majolica tile, and the bell tower has an octagonal belfry similar to the campanile of the Carmine church in Naples. Among the treasures here are an altar in richly colored marbles and 16th-century paintings attributed to Amalfi Coast artists: *St. Magdalen between St. Sebastian and St. Andrew* by Giovannangelo D'Amato of Maiori, and *The Incredulity of St. Thomas* by Andrea da Salerno.

WHERE TO EAT AND STAY

$$

SOUTHERN
ITALIAN

✕ **A' Paranza.** Just up the hill behind the piazza is the best dining option in Atrani. White-cove ceilings reflect immaculate linen tablecloths in a place that is at once homely and quite formal. Entirely seafood-based, each day's menu depends on the catch, though a taster menu (antipasti ranging from marinated tuna to fried rice balls, with a helping of pasta and risotto, followed by a choice of dessert) is recommended. If that sounds like too much, go for the scialatielli ai frutti di mare, but be sure to leave room for the divine cakes. ✉ *Via Dragone 1/2* 🕾 *089/871840* 🖃 *AE, DC, MC, V* ⊙ *Closed Dec. 8–26 and Tues. Sept.–July.*

$$

SOUTHERN
ITALIAN

✕ **Le Arcate.** A cave is not where you'd normally expect to find good food, but this one changes the rules. The simple, dark, old restaurant tucked under the road also has a large terrace overlooking the beach. Folks dig its *scialatielli Masaniello*—fresh pasta named after the local boy who became a revolutionary in Naples—as well as its pizza and grilled fish. It's been here for 50 years, a drop in the gulf around these parts. Get a table out on the seafront where you can lean over and see exactly where your meal has come from. ✉ *Via G. Di Benedetto 4, under arcades of roadway connecting Amalfi and Atrani* 🕾 *089/871367* ⊕ *www.learcate.net* 🖃 *AE, DC, MC, V* ⊙ *Closed mid-Jan.–mid-Feb. and Mon. mid-Sept.–mid-June.*

$$–$$$
★

🖾 **Palazzo Ferraioli.** Occupying a 19th-century villa, this charming new entry on the coast is up the steps from Atrani's harbor, with an unrivalled view of the beach. Its pleasing modern design is evident from the moment you step into the lobby—guest rooms are colorful and individually designed with each dedicated to a famous movie actress (some with baths in the bedroom), and most with a sea view. The star attraction is the Nel Blue beauty center, with its mosaic walls and infused lighting—climb to the top-floor solarium for a 180-degree view over Atrani. **Pros:** the beauty center; the finest villa in town. **Cons:** all those steps; slightly removed from the action. ⊠ *Via Campo 16* ☎ *089/872652* ⊕ *www.palazzoferraioli.it* ⤸ *25 rooms* ⚭ *In-room: a/c, refrigerator. In-hotel: restaurant, bar, parking (paid)* ⊟ *AE, DC, MC, V* ⏐◎⏐ *BP.*

RAVELLO TO PAESTUM

A few minutes west of Amalfi, perched atop a ridge of Monte Cerreto, and "closer to the sky than the sea"—according to French writer André Gide—the achingly lovely town of Ravello gazes down on the Bay of Salerno and the humbler villages surrounding it. This cloud-riding perch is just one reason why some travelers give Ravello the laurel as the Amalfi Coast's—some say Italy's—most beautiful town. Languor becomes Ravello's mood, a bit out of sync with the world below, and it makes this town a lovely place to catch your breath. The slightly aloof star high above the coast, it remains there for the reaching and is worth the stretch. Hearty souls trek between Atrani and Ravello by a path that climbs through the Valle del Dragone, or Dragon's Valley, a name inspired by the morning mists here (the descent is easier than the ascent!). Most Ravello-bound travelers, however, take the SITA bus from Amalfi's Piazza Flavio Gioia, which corkscrews its way up 1,000 feet along a road in the southern Monti Lattari (although the road is infrequently closed due to landslides). Cars follow the same route and really come in handy when driving farther south along Statale 163 to the towns rimming the Bay of Salerno, which have their off-the-beaten-track appeal. If you're based in Naples and have singled out Ravello for a day's sampling of the Amalfi Coast, by far the quickest route is via the mountain pass called the Valico di Chiunzi, easily reached via the A3 Naples–Salerno Autostrada from the exit at Angri.

Many visitors end their southward journey along the Amalfi Coast in Ravello. They might have a point (what can top that mountaintop paradise?), but other savvy travelers keep heading southward, for ahead lie less crowded seaport villages, the bustling city of Salerno, and fabled Paestum, site of three of the greatest ancient Greek temples in the world.

After dropping down to sea level from Ravello or going eastward from Amalfi, the coast road, Statale 163, descends into Minori, known for its good beach and ancient Roman heritage. The road climbs up the cape by Torre Mezzacapo, then drops back down to sea level near the 15th-century church of San Francesco. Statale 163 then goes though the town of Maiori, with its much broader river valley producing another good beach, and passes Capo di Baia Verde, near the misleadingly named 17th-century Torre Normanna. The coast here becomes dramatic again, giving grand views of the sea as you climb past the promontory topped by Torre di Badia. Capo Tummolo and then Vallone di San Nicola, with the little village of Marina di Erchie, are ahead of you. The drive then

2

descends to the fishing village of Cetara, along a narrow inlet, continues along the coast, passing Torre de Fuenti and Vallone di Albori, and then faces the sea near Torre della Marina di Albori. At the junction of Raito, a lush little village, you cross the bridge over the Vallone Bonea to the town of Vietri, at which point traffic-light reality returns. Follow Statale 163 to the city of Salerno. Autostrada A3 south connects to E45, which leads to Battipaglia and the exit for the ancient temples of Paestum. Alternatively, hug the coast, driving along Salerno's *lungomare,* and continue along the fairly degraded coastline until you reach Paestum, 40 km (25 mi) from Salerno.

RAVELLO

Fodor'sChoice *6½ km (4 mi) northeast of Amalfi, 29 km (18 mi) west of Salerno.*
★

Positano may focus on pleasure, and Amalfi on history, but cool, serene Ravello revels in refinement. Thrust over Statale 163 and the Bay of Salerno on a mountain buttress, below forests of chestnut and ash, above terraced lemon groves and vineyards, it early on beckoned the affluent with its island-in-the-sky views and secluded defensive positioning. Gardens out of the *Arabian Nights,* pastel palazzos, tucked-away piazzas with medieval fountains, architecture ranging from Romano-Byzantine to Norman-Saracen, and those sweeping blue-water, blue-sky vistas have inspired a panoply of large personalities, including Wagner and Boccaccio, princes and popes, aesthetes and hedonists, and a stream of famous authors from Virginia Woolf to Tennessee Williams. Author and one time resident Gore Vidal, not an easy critic, has called the town's Villa Cimbrone panorama "the most beautiful view in the world." Today, many visitors flock here to discover this paradisical place, some to enjoy the town's celebrated music festival, others just to stroll through the hillside streets to gape at the bluer-than-blue panoramas of sea and sky.

GETTING HERE
By car, take the hill road climbing just east of Atrani, or take the Angri exit on the A3 motorway and cross the mountainous Valico di Chiunsi. SITA buses make the run up and down the mountain between Ravello and Piazza Flavio Gioia in Amalfi, where you can catch the main Amalfi Drive bus to Sorrento. In Ravello, you can purchase tickets prior to boarding at Punto e Virgola (Via Roma 5) and Bar Calce (Via Boccaccio 11). There are about two buses every hour. Open-top**City Sightseeing buses** ☎ *081/8774707* ⊕ *www.sorrento.city-sightseeing.it*) make eight sightseeing daily trips from Amalfi (and also connect with the more modern beach towns of Minori and Maiori) for €3 (a daily four-trip ticket is €10).

VISITOR INFORMATION
In Ravello, the **Azienda Autonoma Soggiorno e Turismo** is open daily 9 to 6, and 9 to 1, 2 to 6 November through March. ⊠ *Via Roma 18b, Ravello* ☎ *089/857096* 🖨 *089/877977* ⊕ *www.ravellotime.it.*

Auditorium
Niemayer **8**

Duomo **4**

Monastero
di Santa Chiara .. **2**

Museo del
Corallo **5**

Piazza
Fontana
Moresco **9**

San Giovanni
del Toro **7**

Santa Maria
a Gradillo **6**

Villa
Cimbrone **1**

Villa Rufolo **3**

EXPLORING

Though its origins are lost in obscurity, Ravello may have been settled by Romans fleeing the sack of their dying empire. The town itself was founded in the 9th century, under Amalfi's rule, until residents prosperous from cotton tussled with the superpower republic and elected their own doge in the 11th century; Amalfitans dubbed them *rebelli* (rebels). In the 12th century, with the aid of the Norman King Roger, Ravello even succeeded in resisting Pisa's army for a couple of years, though the powerful Pisans returned to wreak destruction along the coast. Even so, Ravello's skilled seafaring trade with merchants and Moors from Sicily and points east led to a burgeoning wealth, which peaked in the 13th century, when there were 13 churches, four cloisters, and dozens of sumptuous villas. Neapolitan princes built palaces; life was privileged.

But as is inevitable with all supernovas, Ravello's bright light diminished, first through Pisa's maritime rise in the 14th century, then through rivalry between its warring families in the 15th century. When the plague cast its shadow in the 17th century, the population plummeted from upward of 30,000 to perhaps a couple of thousand souls, where it remains today. When Ravello was incorporated into the diocese of Amalfi in 1804, a kind of stillness settled in. Despite the decline of its power and populace, Ravello's cultural heritage and special loveliness continued to blossom. Gardens flowered and music flowed in the ruined villas, and artists, sophisticates, and their lovers filled the crumbling palazzos. Grieg, Wagner, D.H. Lawrence, Chanel, Garbo and her companion, conductor Leopold Stokowski, and then, slowly, tourists, followed in their footsteps. Today, at the Villa Rufolo, the noted Ravello Festival is held in its shaded gardens. Here, special Wagnerian concerts are often held to pay homage to the great composer, who was inspired by these gardens to compose scenes of *Parsifal*.

With the exception of the Villa Rufolo concerts, however, the hush lingers, especially in off-season (at least until the Niemeyer Auditorium is opened), when there seem to be more cats than cars. Empty, narrow streets morph into whitewashed staircases rising into a haze of azure, which could be from the sea, the sky, or a union of both. About the only places that don't seem to be in pianissimo slow motion are Piazza Duomo, in front of the cathedral, during the evening passeggiata, or caffès at *pranzo* (luncheon) or *cena* (dinner). Note that the town likes to celebrate religious *feste* throughout the year—one of the nicest celebrations is the blossom-strewn celebration of Pentecost (usually the first week of June), when Piazza Duomo is ornamented with sidewalk pictures created with flower petals.

Although cars must park in the municipal lot, most arriving buses deposit their passengers near the hillside tunnel that leads to Piazza Duomo, which is lined with hoardings promoting the festival. On the square you'll find the Bric-a-Brac Shop, a great resource for books on Ravello.

TOP ATTRACTIONS

Fodor's Choice ★ **Auditorium Niemeyer.** Crowning Via della Repubblica and the hillside which overlooks the spectacular vista of the Bay of Salerno this startling new piece of modernist architecture has become the talk of all Ravello. Designed with a dramatically curved, all-white roof by Brazilian master architect Oscar Niemeyer (creator of Brasília), it was conceived as an alternative indoor venue for concerts (including those of the famed town music festival). The subject of much controversy since its first conception back in 2000, it has raised the wrath of some locals who have denounced such an ambitious modernist building in medieval Ravello. They need not have worried, as the result is a design masterpiece—a huge, overhanging canopied roof suspended over a 400-seat concert area, with a giant eye-shaped window allowing spectators to contemplate the extraordinary bay vista during performances. Although it was inaugurated in January 2010, the doors were immediately closed and, at the time of writing, the contoversy rages on, with authorities battling over who will run the structure. ⊠ *Via della Repubblica* ⊕ *www. auditoriumoscarniemeyer.it.*

Duomo. Pride of place on the town piazza is taken by the Duomo, the town cathedral, dedicated to patron San Pantaleone and founded in 1086 by Orso Papiro, the first bishop of Ravello. Rebuilt in the 12th and 17th centuries, and completely restored in 1973, the Duomo retains traces of medieval frescoes in the transept, an original mullioned window, a marble portal, and a three-story 13th-century bell tower playfully interwoven with mullioned windows and arches. The 12th-century bronze door features 54 embossed panels depicting Christ's life, and saints, prophets, plants, and animals, all narrating biblical lore. It was crafted by Barisano da Trani, who also fashioned the doors of the cathedrals of Trani and Monreale. (The door is currently under restoration—it was due in 2004, and made a cameo appearance in 2008 only to be whisked away again after it was found to be impossible to hang, due to incorrect measurements. It should be back by the end of 2010.) The nave's three aisles are divided by ancient columns, and treasures include sarcophagi from Roman times and paintings by southern Renaissance artist Andrea da Salerno. Most impressive are the two medieval *ambos,* or pulpits: The earlier one, used for reading the Epistles, is inset with a mosaic scene of Jonah and the Whale, symbolizing death and redemption. The more famous one, used for reading the Gospels, was commissioned by Nicola Rufolo in 1272 and created by Niccolò di Bartolomeo da Foggia. It seems almost Tuscan in style, with exquisite Cosmatesque mosaic work and bas-reliefs and six twisting columns sitting on lion pedestals. An eagle grandly tops the colonnette fronting the inlaid marble lectern.

A chapel left of the apse is dedicated to San Pantaleone, a physician, who was beheaded in the 3rd century in Nicomedia. Every July 27 devout believers gather in hope of witnessing a miracle (similar to that of San Gennaro in Naples), in which the saint's blood, collected in a vial and set out on an inlaid marble altar, appears to become clear and translucent. You can get closer look at the saint's blood by asking the caretaker nicely; after 4 pm, however, the small chapel where the vial is held behind the altar is unlocked. In the crypt is the **Museo del Duomo,** which displays treasures from around the 13th century, during the reign of Frederick II of Sicily, in an elegant setting. You'll find gold and silver work, sculpture, and a classic Campanian marble bust of a half-smiling woman from the Rufolo dynasty, whose name was Sigilgaita, adorning the cathedral's pulpit. Reliquaries of San Tommaso, Santa Barbara, and San Lorenzo are also displayed here. ⊠ *Museo del Duomo, Piazza del Duomo* ☎ *089/858311* ⊕ *www.chiesaravello.com* ⊠ *€2* ☉ *Sept.–May, daily 9–7; June–Aug., daily 9–9:30; between noon and 5:30 access to church is through museum, to right of steps.*

San Giovanni del Toro. Across the tiny piazza from the Hotel Caruso is the noted 11th-century church of San Giovanni del Toro. Its evocative interior has three high apses and a crypt with 14th-century frescoes of Christ and the apostles. A 12th-century ambo (pulpit) by Alfano da Termoli startles the eye with its blue Persian majolica and four columns topped with elaborate capitals. The chapel of the Coppola family in the left aisle has an exceptional 14th-century relief of St. Catherine of Alexandria. The small church's three porticos adorned with lunettes show an Arabian influence, and the tripartite back facade is exquisite. Restoration work on the church commenced in 2003, with the facade funded by the Hotel Caruso, but there is no sign of the interior being completed. ⊠ *Piazza San Giovanni del Toro.*

Fodor'sChoice
★ **Villa Cimbrone.** To the west of Ravello's main square, a somewhat hilly 15-minute walk along Via San Francesco brings you to Ravello's

CLOSE UP

Walking Versus Hiking?

Throughout this entire region, walking *is* hiking, so be prepared. Amalfi, where streets usually take the form of staircases, is a resort where you may leave more fit than you were when you arrived. These towns are picturesque for a reason, and you've probably never seen so many flights of steps—those bothersome *scalinatelle*: thousands of them, leading down to beaches, up to churches, across the hills.

Getting around will take a healthy set of lungs, strong calves, comfortable footwear, time-outs for rest, and a big bottle of Ferrarelle water—slow and steady is the way to go. As for intentional hiking, mule paths and footpaths were the only land-means to get around before the car, and most remain in place for hikers' delight.

Local tourist offices have maps of hikes, and can organize a guide. Check out Julian Tippett's excellent walking book, *Landscapes of Sorrento and the Amalfi Coast* (Sunflower Press), often found at bookstores and newsstands in the area. Even if you're not in shape, you can still participate: take transportation uphill, and let gravity guide you down.

2

showstopper, the Villa Cimbrone, whose dazzling gardens perch 1,500 feet above the sea. The ultimate aerie, this medieval-style fantasy was created in 1905 by England's Lord Grimthorpe and made world-famous when Greta Garbo found sanctuary from the press when she vacationed here with Leopold Stokowski in 1937. The Gothic *castello-palazzo* is in idyllic gardens, which are divided by the grand Allée of Immensity, leading in turn to the literal high point of any trip to the Amalfi Coast—the legendary **Belvedere of Infinity.** This grand stone parapet, adorned with amusing stone busts, overlooks the entire Bay of Salerno and is one of the most magical spots in all Europe. The name Cimbrone derives from the rocky ridge on which the villa stands, first colonized by the ancient Romans and hailed as Cimbronium back then. In the Middle Ages, the noble Accongiogioco clan built a house here. Centuries later, Ernest William Beckett, Lord Grimthorpe (whose main claim to fame is as designer of Big Ben's casement), fell in love with Cimbrone on a Grand Tour of Italy and, with the help of Nicolo Mansi, transformed the gardens into the extravaganza we see today. Since the lord hosted many of England's Bloomsbury set, it is now thought that Vita Sackville-West (just one of the many famous writers and artists who visited here) had some help in the garden design. Be sure to explore all the pathways to find the mock-Gothic crypt (now containing the restaurant Il Flauto di Pan), the Temple of Bacchus *tempietto* (under which Lord Grimthorpe is buried), the tea pavilion done in the style of Florence's Pazzi Chapel, and the Grotto of Venus. Many feel the Cimbrone is the most beautiful garden in Italy; be sure to visit here and decide for yourself. Better yet, overnight at this magical domain, as the villa itself is now a hotel. Begin by logging onto the villa Web site to see its wondrous photos. ⊠ *Via S. Chiara 26* ☎ *089/857459* ⊕ *www.villacimbrone.it* 🖃 *€6* ☉ *Daily 9–half hr before sunset.*

The view from Villa Cimbrone's Belvedere of Infinity may be the finest on the coast.

Fodor's Choice   **Villa Rufolo.** To the right of the Duomo is the Villa Rufolo, home to some
★   of the most spectacular gardens in Italy, many of which stunningly frame
a Cinerama vista of the Bay of Salerno, often called the "bluest view
in the world." If the master storyteller Boccaccio is to be believed, the
villa was built in the 13th century by Landolfo Rufolo, whose immense
fortune stemmed from trade with the Moors and the Saracens. Now
the setting for the Ravello Music Festival, its Romanesque walls contain a scene that seems from the earliest days of the Crusades. Norman
and Arab architecture mingle in a welter of color-filled gardens so lush
that composer Richard Wagner used them as inspiration for Klingsor's
Garden, the home of the Flower Maidens, in his opera *Parsifal*. Beyond
the Arab-Sicilian cloister and the Norman tower are two flower-bedded
terraces that offer the prime vista of the Bay of Salerno, set off by the
twin cupolas of the 13th-century church of Santissima Annunziata and
a dramatic umbrella pine tree (all three adorn the favorite poster image
of Ravello). In 1851 the villa was acquired by Sir Francis Nevile Reid,
a Scotsman, who hired Michele Ruggiero, head of the excavations at
Pompeii, to restore the villa to its full splendor and replant the gardens
with rare cycads, cordylines, and palms. Highlights of the villa are its
Moorish cloister—an Arabic-Sicilian delight with interlacing lancet arcs
and polychromatic palmette decoration—and the 14th-century Torre
Maggiore, the so-called Klingsor's Tower, renamed in honor of Richard
Wagner's landmark 1880 visit and today a dramatic spot for chamber
music recitals (note that when weather is rainy, concerts are moved into
a charmless auditorium; in the future, these may be moved to the town's
new Auditorium Niemeyer). Beyond lie the two spectacular terrace
gardens, with the lower one, the "Wagner Terrace," often the site for

concerts, with the orchestra perched on a precarious-looking platform constructed over the precipice. Villa Rufolo also houses a library of rare documents and manuscripts. ⊠ *Piazza Duomo* ☎ *089/857866* ⊕ *www. villarufolo.it* ▢ *€5, concerts extra charge* ☉ *Daily 9–8; closes earlier when concert rehearsals are taking place; winter 9–6.*

Continue down Via della Repubblica and take a sharp right up the Via dell'Annunziata stair path for a closer look at the **Santissima Annunziata** (now a conference center closed to the public).

Head back to the town square and climb the steps of Via Richard Wagner, to the left of the Duomo, to Via San Giovanni a Toro, the address of Ravello's grandest palazzi (now hotels). **Villa Episcopio,** a 12th-century bishop's residence, was formerly called Villa di Sangro. It is currently being renovated, though there's a chance it will be open to the public in 2011. Amid the gardens and ruins, Italy's King Vittorio Emanuele III abdicated in favor of his son, and Jackie Kennedy enjoyed breaks from her public obligations. Wine merchants here have been cultivating grapes since 1860, and varieties of Ravello rosso and bianco, as refined as their namesake, can be purchased in town.

WORTH NOTING

Monastero di Santa Chiara. Majolica flooring in the 13th-century Monastery of Santa Chiara, now a closed order, is one special element; another is the *matronaeum,* or women's gallery, the only one left on the Amalfi Coast (not known for segregating the sexes, or anything else). You can visit this church for the early-morning Sunday service, but the wheel used to deliver food (and at one time unwanted children) to the nuns can be seen anytime. Closer to town, along Via S. Francesco, is the church and convent of **San Francesco,** founded in 1222 by St. Francis of Assisi, with a small Gothic cloister; the church was rebuilt in the 18th century. ⊠ *Via S. Chiara.*

Museo del Corallo *(Coral Museum).* To the left of the Duomo is the private Coral Museum, which shows the venerable tradition of Italian workmanship in coral, harvested in bygone centuries from the gulfs of Salerno and Naples and crafted into jewelry, cameos, and figurines. This is a fascinating collection, not confined solely to coral work, with a painting of Sisto IV from the 14th century and what may be an original Caravaggio. Look also in particular for a carved Christ from the 17th century, for which the J. Paul Getty Museum offered $525,000 in 1987 (he was refused) and a tobacco box covered in cameos, one of only two in the world. There is also a statue of the Madonna dating from 1532. Master craftsman in residence Giorgio Filocamo has crafted coral for Pope John Paul II, the Clintons, and Princess Caroline, as well as numerous Hollywood stars. ⊠ *Piazza Duomo 9* ☎ *089/857461* ▢ *Free* ☉ *Mon.–Sat. 10–noon and 3–5, shop open longer.*

Piazza Fontana Moresco. Buy some gelati on the piazza by the Duomo and walk east to the Piazza Fontana Moresco, below the Hotel Parsifal and above the gates of the walled perimeter, to check out the stone lion and cow on the fanciful 1,000-year-old fountain, still spewing water. Unfortunately the statues are imitations; the originals were stolen some 40 years ago.

Santa Maria a Gradillo. Three hundred and fifty yards along Via Roma, to the left of the Duomo, is the three-aisle 13th-century **Santa Maria a Gradillo** with its lovely dome. This was the place where the town noblemen gathered to discuss civic issues; its atrium collapsed in the 18th century. The small Sicilian-Saracenic bell tower has two light mullion windows.

WHERE TO EAT

$$$
SOUTHERN
ITALIAN
★

✕ Cumpa' Cosimo. Lustier-looking than most Ravello spots, Cumpa' Cosimo is run devotedly by Netta Bottone, who tours the tables to ensure her clients are content. Her family has owned this *cantina* for 75 of its 300-plus years, and she has been cooking under the arched ceiling for around 60 of them. You can't miss here with any of the dishes featuring classic Ravellian cuisine. A favorite (share it—it's huge) is a *misto* of fettuccine, fusilli, tortellini, and whatever other homemade pasta inspires her, served with a fresh, fragrant pesto. Meats are generally excellent—after all, they are supplied by the butcher shop next door, also run by Netta. The *funghi porcini* mushroom starter and the house cheesecake are so delicious you'll drop your fork. Local wines ease it all down gently, and homemade gelato is a luscious ending. ⊠ *Via Roma 46* 🕾 *089/857156* 🔥 *Reservations essential* 🗖 *AE, MC, V* ⊗ *Sometimes closed Mon. in winter.*

$$
SOUTHERN
ITALIAN

✕ Da Salvatore. Adjacent to the Hotel Graal and sharing the same glorious view of the Bay of Salerno, this has a large terrace and room for dining just beyond its small garden. Classic Campanian cuisine—try the *crespolini alla Ravellese* (cheese-filled crêpes) or the day's specialty, changing by the season—is on tap here, along with friendly service and That View, which is a real bargain at these prices (the same can be said for the six surprisingly upscale guest rooms found upstairs). ⊠ *Via della Repubblica 2* 🕾 *089/857227* ⊕ *www.salvatoreravello.com* 🗖 *AE, DC, MC, V* ⊗ *Sometimes closed Mon. in winter.*

$
SOUTHERN
ITALIAN

✕ Figli di Papà. The young chef-owners of this restaurant attempt to turn Campania classics into something more—and they usually succeed. Past a fireplace that flickers in season and watercolors by Irish artist Leo Kennedy, resident in Ravello, you descend into a white, modernized 13th-century setting. The daily menu *turistica* may offer such dishes as *crespolini di pesce* (fish-stuffed crepes), and *lombo di agnello al rosmarino con spinaci all'uvetta* (lamb cutlets with spinach and raisins). Tasting menus—to suit various appetites and wallet sizes—are even more creative, with unexpected combinations. To match the food, the owners provide a wine list featuring the best of the region, which can also be enjoyed on the outside terrace. ⊠ *Via della Marra 7* 🕾 *089/858302* ⊕ *www.ristorantefiglidipapa.it* 🗖 *AE, DC, MC, V* ⊗ *Closed 3 wks in Nov., 6 wks in Jan. and Feb., Tues. in winter.*

¢
SOUTHERN
ITALIAN

✕ Giardini Caffè Calice. Located on a corner of Piazza Duomo, this popular café showcases Irish painter Leo Kennedy's watercolors of Ravello. With an alfresco area in the one-time gardens of the Hotel Toro and three guestrooms, this is a favorite of locals and visitors alike. ⊠ *Via Wagner 3* 🕾 *089/857152* 🗖 *MC, V.*

$$
PIZZA
★

✕ Vittoria. Between the Duomo and the church of San Francesco, this is a good place for a return to reality and an informal bite. Vittoria's thin-crust pizza with loads of fresh toppings is the star attraction, and locals praise it *molto*—it was a favorite of Gore Vidal. But also try the pasta, maybe fusilli with tomatoes, zucchini, and mozzarella. Vittoria is pretty, too, with arches and tile floors. All this adds up to crowds, so try to get here on the early side. ⊠ *Via dei Rufolo 3* ☎ *089/857947* ⊕ *www.ristorantepizzeriavittoria.it* ☰ *AE, MC, V* ☺ *Closed Nov.–Mar.*

WHERE TO STAY

$$$$
Fodor's Choice
★

Caruso. One of the new benchmarks for 21st-century luxury on the Amalfi Coast, the Caruso has created a whole new fan base since it reopened its doors after a 10-year renovation in 2005. Old-timers (who once included Virginia Woolf, Tennessee Williams, the Khedive of Egypt, and Margot Fonteyn) continue to mourn the sad loss, however, of the medieval palazzo's priceless patina (the legendary belvedere window was given a hideous Lucite plastic makeover). But since guest rooms had become threadbare, Orient-Express Hotels ordered a restoration. Forsaking the yesteryear charm of the spectacular *gran salone*, they banished the dazzling 19th-century Italian paintings, the romantic *giardino*, and the terraced restaurant. In place arrived high-roller luxury: the strawberries-and-Champagne welcome, the best Bellinis on the coast; a grand, rooftop heated infinity pool; newly restored baroque frescoes; and the ambitious Belvedere Restaurant. While fans rave about the sumptuous guest rooms (most with sea view) and boat trips on the coast (with a shuttle to Amalfi), others find the renovation a complete desecration of old-world Ravello. **Pros:** experience Ravello like a VIP; pure luxury. **Cons:** antique furniture traded in for beige rattan sofas; out of the price range of most; heavy-handed restoration. ⊠ *Piazza San Giovanni del Toro 2* ☎ *089/858801* ⊕ *www.hotelcaruso. com* ⤴ *48 rooms* ♿ *In-room: a/c, safe, refrigerator, Internet, Wi-Fi. In-hotel: 3 restaurants, bar, pool, gym, spa, Internet terminal, Wi-Fi hotspot, parking (paid), some pets allowed* ☰ *AE, DC, MC, V* ☺ *Closed Jan. and Feb.* ❢⊙❢*FAP.*

$$
Graal. The name comes from the Holy Grail, as in Wagner's opera *Parsifal*, but this inn is more an operetta. The walls are adorned with the work of Roman artist Bruno Canova, colorful tiled murals outside, and paintings inside. It's much less grand than Ravello's famous hotels, with a modern decor that's a bit of a downer. Nevertheless, it reaches high-Cs for comfort, cleanliness, and contentment. Hovering over the water on the Via della Repubblica, overlooking the new Niemeyer auditorium, with a nearly unobstructed view of the breathtaking bay, this hotel possesses one of the friendliest staffs around, a pretty pool area, and whirlpools and fancy baths. In the dining room, meals from a family kitchen are delivered to tables dressed in linen and set near large, arched windows. Most rooms are smallish, some are deluxe (especially No. 342, with a double whirlpool and a bed from which you can see the great view), but all have tiled floors and balconies. **Pros:** friendly staff; great views. **Cons:** rooms on the lower level are disappointing; the modern decor doesn't fit with the surroundings. ⊠ *Via della Repubblica 8* ☎ *089/857222* ⊕ *www.hotelgraal.eu* ⤴ *43 rooms* ♿ *In-room: a/c, safe, refrigerator, Internet, Wi-Fi. In-hotel: 2 restaurants, bar, pool* ☰ *AE, DC, MC, V* ☺ *Restaurant closed Mon. Oct.–Mar.* ❢⊙❢*BP.*

$$$$ ⚅ **Palazzo Sasso.** In this 12th-century home of the aristocratic Sasso family, Wagner penned part of his opera *Parsifal* in the 1880s, and in the fashionable 1950s, the palazzo hosted Ingrid Bergman and Roberto Rossellini. Once part of the adjacent Hotel Palumbo, it was opened in its own right by Sir Richard Branson in 1997, after a 19-year hiatus, luring the glitterati—its first guests were Placido Domingo and his entourage. Ordinary mortals, too, can come to sightsee and peek at the gleaming marble lobby (once a chapel), glass elevators, two rooftop hot tubs, and roaring waterfall replete with *Playboy* Mansion statuary. Traditionalists might look askance (if not be totally horrified) at all this glitz in quaint old Ravello, but no one will complain about immaculately furnished guest rooms, with the latest computer-operated lighting and air-cooling systems. Even better, the gilded, Empire-style Rossellini restaurant, with two Michelin stars, is now among the finest in Campania and offers the latest in regal, nouvelle fare. If you can tear yourself away from the hotel, you can be whisked down to their intimate (no more than 26 guests) beach club on the coast. **Pros:** one of the finest restaurants in the region; pure luxury. **Cons:** out of the price-range of most; traditionalists beware! ⊠ *Via San Giovanni del Toro 28* ☎ *089/818181* ⊕ *www.palazzosasso.com* ⇥ *38 rooms, 5 suites* ⚿ *In-room: a/c, safe, refrigerator, Internet, Wi-Fi. In-hotel: 2 restaurants, bar, pool, gym, spa, parking (paid), some pets allowed* ⊟ *AE, DC, MC, V* ⊗ *Closed Nov.–Feb.*

$$$$ ⚅ **Palumbo.** This is the real deal—the only great hotel left in Ravello that

Fodor's Choice   is still a monument to the Grand Tour sensibility that first put the town
★   on the map. Legendarily old-fashioned, built in the 12th century as a palazzo, this famous hotel has long been a stop for visiting somebodies: Wagner, who composed on the piano in the lobby; Bogart, filming *Beat the Devil*; a young Jack and Jackie. Hollywood's golden couple Brad Pitt and Angelina Jolie filmed a (deleted) scene from *Mr. & Mrs. Smith* here, so it's unsurprising their relationship also blossomed in real life. Ancient marble columns, mosaic-tile floors, and museum-quality antiques combine to provide an elegant ambience throughout the hotel, while incredible views of the Bay of Salerno can be enjoyed from your terrace or the lush gardens that sit below the hotel on the hillside. The innovative Continental cuisine is served in the exclusive Confalone restaurant, a magnificently gilded ballroom with its original frescoed ceiling and old-master paintings. Or you can enjoy a view as delicious as the food atop the restaurant terrace—finish off your feast with lemon soufflé and Episcopio estate wine (note the restaurant is closed from November to March). Most guest rooms have antiques, vintage fabrics, and modern marble baths, except for those in the annex, where at just over half the cost you still have access to all the facilities of the main palazzo. Lodging prices can include both a sumptuous breakfast and a choice of either a gourmet lunch or dinner. **Pros:** impossibly romantic; wonderful coastal retreat. **Cons:** with all this finery it can be difficult to relax; great restaurant closed in winter. ⊠ *Via S. Giovanni del Toro 16* ☎ *089/857244* ⊕ *www.hotelpalumbo.it* ⇥ *17 rooms* ⚿ *In-room: a/c, safe, refrigerator, Internet, Wi-Fi. In-hotel: restaurant, bar, parking (paid)* ⊟ *AE, DC, MC, V* ⊧◎ *MAP.*

$$ ⌂ **Parsifal.** In 1288 this diminutive property was a convent housing an order of Augustinian friars. Today the intact cloister hosts travelers simply intent on enjoying themselves mightily. Ancient, ivy-covered stone arches and a tiled walkway looking out over the coastline lead to a cozy interior that still feels a bit like a retreat. Sun lounges, a garden, a fishpond, a Ping-Pong table, and alfresco dining all overlook the sea. Restoration work is ongoing in the low season, and the swimming pool should be ready for 2012. Guest rooms are small with coved ceilings (monk's cells, after all), and some have Ravello's breathtaking view. The charming young manager dotes on Americans, and gladly accommodates guests all year round. Half board is often required at peak season. **Pros:** staying in a convent in Ravello; friendly staff. **Cons:** slightly removed from the main town; tiny rooms. ⌂ *Viale Gioacchino d'Anna 5* ☎ *089/857144* ⊕ *www.hotelparsifal.com* ⤴ *17 rooms* ⚐ *In-room: a/c, safe, refrigerator, Internet, Wi-Fi. In-hotel: restaurant, bar, parking (paid), some pets allowed* ⊟ *AE, DC, MC, V* ⍟ *FAP.*

$$$–$$$$ ⌂ **Rufolo.** D. H. Lawrence worked on *Lady Chatterley's Lover* during his 1926 visit, so it might be fun to revisit the novel's groundbreaking love scenes while you're here. Some rooms have balconies to liven up the snug quarters with gorgeous sea and sky vistas framed by the palm trees of the Villa Rufolo, just below the hotel. Author Gore Vidal could often be seen strolling along the path beside the hotel—he owned La Rondinaia, the villa at the end of the path, but sold it to a private investor in 2006. **Pros:** as close to La Rondinaia as mere mortals can get; beautiful views over Villa Rufolo. **Cons:** car park clutters the entrance; the staff have been known to be unhelpful. ⌂ *Via San Francesco 1* ☎ *089/857133* ⊕ *www.hotelrufolo.it* ⤴ *34 rooms* ⚐ *In-room: a/c, safe, refrigerator, Internet, Wi-Fi. In-hotel: restaurant, bar, pool, parking (free), some pets allowed* ⊟ *AE, DC, MC, V* ⍟ *Closed mid-Nov.–mid-Mar.* ⍟ *FAP.*

$ ⌂ **Toro.** Two minutes from the Duomo, this little hotel with a garden and lots of antiques has been in the Schiavo family for three generations. Even this modest inn once boasted visiting VIPs: composer Edvard Grieg wrote in the guest book that he was *"molto contento"* and artist M. C. Escher also stayed here (his celebrated prints of spiraling staircases were inspired by those he discovered in Ravello and Atrani). **Pros:** a small piece of Ravello's artistic history; very central. **Cons:** long flight of steps to climb; space rather cramped. ⌂ *Via Roma 16* ☎ *089/857211* ⊕ *www.hoteltoro.it* ⤴ *10 rooms* ⚐ *In-room: a/c, safe, refrigerator, Internet, Wi-Fi. In-hotel: some pets allowed* ⊟ *AE, MC, V* ⍟ *Closed Nov.–mid-Apr.* ⍟ *BP.*

$ ⌂ **Villa Amore.** A 10-minute walk from the Piazza Duomo, this charmingly secluded hotel with a garden is family-run and shares the same exhilarating view of the Bay of Salerno as Ravello's most expensive hotels. Rooms are small, with modest and modern furnishings. Reserve ahead, and specify time of arrival if you need help with luggage from the parking lot or bus stop (you pay about €5 per bag). **Pros:** charmingly secluded; wonderful views. **Cons:** rather far from the main drag; modest rooms. ⌂ *Via del Fusco 5* ☎ *089/857135* ⊕ *www.villaamore.it* ⤴ *10 rooms* ⚐ *In-room: a/c, safe, refrigerator, Internet, Wi-Fi. In-hotel: restaurant, bar, some pets allowed* ⊟ *DC, MC, V* ⍟ *FAP.*

$$$$ 🏨 **Villa Cimbrone.** Suspended over the azure sea and set amid rose-laden
Fodor'sChoice gardens, this magical place was once the home of Lord Grimthorpe and
★ the holiday hideaway of Greta Garbo. In the mid-1990s it was exquisitely transformed into a hotel by the Vuillemeier family. The hotel is
in an intact Gothic-style castle, replete with guest rooms ranging from
palatial to cozy. Two rooms are covered with frescoes, and all follow
a basic floral theme—we love the small Peony Room because it's the
only one in the main castello with its own terrace overlooking the
bay (Garbo's former room only has an enclosed balcony). Happily, a
newer wing—antiques and a parchment-hue color scheme make it look
as time-burnished as the main house—has a bevy of rooms overlooking the sea bluff and the gorgeous pool. Tapestried armchairs, framed
prints, and vintage art books, which belonged to Viscountess Frost, the
lord's daughter, still grace the enchantingly elegant sitting room and the
19th-century Music Room. On special occasions food is served near
the Cripta, or porticoed crypt, which was built by Lord Grimthorpe
to resemble the one at Fountains Abbey, England. Best of all, guests
have the villa's legendary gardens—famed for the spectacular Terrace
of Infinity—all to themselves once their gates are closed at sunset. The
villa is a bit of a hike along lanes and alleys from the town center, but
porters will carry your luggage and the distance helps keep this the
most peaceful place on the Amalfi Coast. Get an advance view at the
hotel's splendid Web site. **Pros:** the gardens are all yours after closing
time; stay where Garbo chose to "be alone." **Cons:** a longish hike from
town center; daily arrival of respectful day-trippers. ⊠ *Via Santa Chiara
26* ☎ *089/857459* ⊕ *www.villacimbrone.com* ⇆ *19 rooms* ♿ *In-room:
a/c, safe, refrigerator, Internet, Wi-Fi. In-hotel: restaurant, bar, pool,
gym, spa, Internet terminal, Wi-Fi hotspot, some pets allowed, parking
(paid)* ▭ *AE, DC, MC, V* ⊘ *Closed Nov.–Mar.* �𝖎⃝⃒ *BP.*

$$$ 🏨 **Villa Maria.** This pretty-as-a-picture option is fronted by a vast gar-
★ den terrace and has more sunny warmth than most formal hotels in
Ravello. Hued in glowing terra-cotta, adorned with gorgeous flowers,
and offering a sweet welcome thanks to entry salons replete with tiled
floors, high ceilings, lace, and antiques, the Villa Maria has long been
a popular option in Ravello. The award-winning terrace restaurant (a
lovely place for breakfast and cooking courses) uses produce from the
organic vegetable garden just up the road. Another plus is the hands-on
management of Professor Vincenzo Palumbo (who bagged Gore Vidal's
La Rondinaia villa in 2006). All but two rooms are standard, and there's
an airy suite that has a large balcony overlooking the coast. The view
here is unique, looking out over the Vallone del Dragone, not the bay.
Also check out Maria's sibling, the recently renovated 18th-century
manor house Hotel Giordano, a few minutes away, where guests can
use the pool. **Pros:** delightfully friendly staff; convenient restaurant.
Cons: few coastal views; pool at nearby hotel. ⊠ *Via Santa Chiara 2*
☎ *089/857255* ⊕ *www.villamaria.it* ⇆ *23 rooms* ♿ *In-room: a/c, safe,
refrigerator, Internet, Wi-Fi. In-hotel: restaurant, bar, pool, parking
(free)* ▭ *AE, DC, MC, V* �𝖎⃝⃒ *FAP.*

NIGHTLIFE AND THE ARTS

Until the Auditorium Niemeyer opens, there's little nightlife activity other than the concerts offered by the Ravello Concert Society and the Ravello Music Festival, unless you count moongazing. A few caffè and bars are scattered about, but the general peacefulness extends to evening hours. Hotels and restaurants may offer live music and can advise you about the few nightclubs, but around these parts the sound is soft and classical—or silence.

CONCERTS AND FESTIVALS Starting in the 1950s, Ravello became famed as the "City of Music," when concerts began to be performed in the spectacular gardens of the Villa Rufolo.

Fodor's Choice ★ The celebrated **Ravello Music Festival** (⌧ *Viale Wagner 5* ☎ *089/858360* ⎙ *089/8586278* ⊕ *www.ravellofestival.com*), which evolved from the Festivalè Musicale di Ravello, runs from June to October, with full orchestras performing Wagner, Bach, Mozart, Beethoven, Brahms, Chopin, and slightly less well-known Italian composers such as Scarlatti and Cimarosa. Each year's festival is based on a theme—in 2010 it was Madness—and this has allowed them to also expand into other genres. The most popular event is the *Concerto all'Alba* (dawn concert), when the entire town wakes up at 4:30 to watch the sunrise over the bay to the accompaniment of music from a full symphony orchestra; this event takes place on the night of August 10 to coincide with the shooting stars on the night of San Lorenzo. The older **Ravello Concert Society** (☎ *089/858149* ⎙ *089/858249* ⊕ *www.ravelloarts.org*) runs a yearlong program, with a few concerts also held in coastal churches and, ostensibly, the new Auditorium Niemeyer. Most evening concerts are held at 9:30, with occasional performances starting at 6:30. Note that the 9:30 concerts begin well after sunset, so come earlier if you want to catch the evening glow. Annual concert schedules—listed on the Ravello Concert Society Web site—are posted outside Villa Rufolo and may also be picked up at tourist information offices on the Amalfi Coast

Fodor's Choice ★ At the foot of Ravello's mountain sits the satellite seaside borgo of **Torello.** On the second Sunday of September, this time-stained medieval hamlet reenacts its Saracen invasion with an unforgettable firework display. Replete with exploding stars that whiz through the streets on cables, this has to be seen to be believed. In addition, the town is illuminated for the preceding week, a magical sight even when viewed from Ravello, set 1,000 lofty feet up the hill.

CULINARY LESSONS If you fancy learning how to make some of the things you've been eating, **Mamma Agata** (⌧ *Piazza San Cosma 9* ☎ *089/857019* ⎙ *089/858432* ⊕ *www.mammaagata.com*), who has cooked for Elizabeth Taylor, Federico Fellini, Jackie Kennedy, and Marcello Mastroianni, will take you into her kitchen—with the almost obligatory stunning view—and take you through the preparation of the area's pasta dishes and sweets. A three-hour morning session is followed by lunch—that you yourself will have made. She published a cookbook in 2009, so you can cook like Mamma at home.

SHOPPING

Bric-a-Brac (⌧ *Piazza Duomo 4* ☎ *089/857153*) has some 19th-century antiques, including historic crèche scenes; in the front of the store is a must for history and art lovers—a great selection of books and antique prints about Ravello.

Ceramiche d'Arte Carmella (✉ *Via dei Rufolo 16* ☎ *089/857303*) ships its good stock of Vietri-made and other hand-painted ceramics all over the world. Bargaining may reward you with a 10% discount, maybe more if you have a talent for it.

Run by the Hotel Palumbo across the vicolo, **Episcopio Winery** (✉ *Via Giovanni a Toro* ☎ *089/857244* ⊕ *www.hotelpalumbo.it*), offers selections of fine Ravello vintages.

Gerardo Sacco (✉ *Piazza Duomo 8* ☎ *089/858125*) is jeweler to several divas; a brochure in the shop shows Glenn Close, Elizabeth Taylor, Mel Gibson, and Caroline of Monaco (among others) flashing his creations. Theatrical to say the least, his earrings, necklaces, and bracelets are large and showy and not to everyone's taste, but certainly worth a look.

Gruppo Petit Prince (✉ *Via San Francesco 9* ☎ *089/858033*) has a nice selection of stationery, prints, and artworks.

Ravello Gusti & Delizie (✉ *Via Roma 28* ☎ *089/857716*) is stocked to the ceiling with *prodotti tipici e naturali della costiera Amalfitana*; this is the place for foodstuffs, as well as delicacies and wines from all over Italy. Sun-dried-tomato pasta, olive oil, and other treats are available, but most intriguing are the lemon products—candles and soaps, and even lemon honey.

CETARA

3 km (2 mi) northeast of Erchie, 4 km (2½ mi) southwest of Vietri.

Back in the days of the Caesars, this little town ranked high on their menus, as it was said the most delectable tunas hailed from Cetara, thanks to the town's special *garum* recipe. Today, gourmands still flock here to eat like emperors, while others head here because the waterfront is so delightfully laid-back and "real."

GETTING HERE

By car, take the SS163 (Amalfitana) from outside Sorrento or Salerno, or take the Angri exit on the A3 motorway and cross the mountainous Valico di Chiunsi. The SITA bus line runs here from Amalfi and Salerno.

EXPLORING

Tourists tend to take a pass on the village of Cetara. A quaint and quiet fishing village below orange groves on Monte Falerzo, it was held in subjugation to greater powers, like most of these coastal sites, throughout much of its history. From being a Saracen stronghold in the 9th century, it became the final holding of Amalfi at the eastern edge of the republic, which all through the 11th and 12th centuries tithed part of Cetara's fishing catch, *ius piscariae*—the town's claim to fame. It's rumored that the village's Latin name comes from this big catch—*cetaria* (tuna net), but the town haul is most famous for its anchovies—thousands of years ago, salted and strained, they became a spicy liquid called *garum*, a delicacy to the rich of ancient Rome (this, as well as the lighter *colatura di alici*, can be purchased at local grocery stores or at Cetarii [⊕ *www.cetarii.it*] on the beachfront). After the Middle Ages, the village came under the dominion of the Benedictine abbey of neighboring Santa Maria di Erchie and then became the port of the abbey of Cava, above the coast, which traded with Africa and

Paestum is the site of remarkably well-preserved Greek temples, including the Tempio di Cerere.

extracted anchorage dues. In 1534 the Turks, led by the tyrant Sinan Pasha—on the invitation, no less, of Prince Ferdinando Sanseverino of Salerno—enslaved 300 Cetaran villagers, spiriting them away in 22 galleys and executing those who would not cooperate. A few survivors fled to Naples, which immediately ordered a watchtower to be raised in Cetara to ward off future raids. This is one of the many landmarks that remind tourists that there were coastal perils previous to the one of driving on Statale 163. Beneath the tower is a rocky little beach, and a small park overlooks the harbor, where fishermen mend their nets and paint their boats. They often are away from home for months, fishing in deep waters. Other than the scenic charm of the waterfront, there are no main sights here, other than the church of San Pietro, near the harbor.

WHERE TO EAT AND STAY

$$–$$$
SEAFOOD
✕ **Acqua Pazza.** Locals along this part of the coast rave about this tiny restaurant. On the main street, a stone's throw from the harbor, it has a colorful decor occupying two small rooms with an outside wooden terrace. The raison d'être is remarkably fresh seafood, with the spaghetti with *colatura di alici* also a specialty here. ⊠ *Via Garibaldi 38* ☎ *089/261606* ⊕ *www.acquapazza.it* ▭ *AE, DC, MC, V* ☯ *Closed on Mon. mid-Oct.–mid-Mar.*

$
SOUTHERN
ITALIAN
✕ **Al Convento.** In a covered cloister of a former convent, this restaurant receives glowing reviews for its different permutations of the anchovy. The less adventurous might order the excellent pizza from their wood oven. The decor is whitewashed with soaring arches and a ceiling adorned with beautiful old frescoes. Cooking classes are also organized

2

here. ⊠ *Piazza San Francesco 16* ☏ *089/261039* ⊕ *www.alconvento.net* ▤ *AE, DC, MC, V* ⊙ *Closed on Wed. mid-Oct.–mid-Mar.*

$$
SEAFOOD
✕ **San Pietro.** Just down from the bus stop, this is a pioneering restaurant in Cetara. You can enjoy romantic outdoor seating overlooking the town square (and even savor dinner by candlelight). Owner Franco has been here for almost 30 years, and also doubles as the chef. Every now and then he'll pop out of the kitchen to explain his original anchovy recipes—fried, marinated, *colatura*, and even in the bread (he has any number of combinations to choose from). Book early enough (at least two days in advance) and he can prepare a typical menu from ancient Roman times. ⊠ *Via della Marra 7* ☏ *089/858302* ⊕ *www.ristorantefiglidipapa.it* ▤ *AE, DC, MC, V* ⊙ *Closed 3 wks in Nov., 6 wks in Jan. and Feb., Tues. in winter.*

$$–$$$
▦ **Cetus.** Cetara's leading hotel is set in a white-stucco building that seems to have grown right out of the living rock. The natural theme is continued within. A summer-light restaurant has floors of marble tile, a window-wall, and terraces. The beauty center and gym are in sleek, relaxing surroundings. A steep walk leads to the hotel's private beach and summertime "American" bar. Shutter doors open onto broad, stone-flagged spaces, with umbrella tables, casual seating, overflowing flower boxes, and close-up sea views with the city of Salerno shimmering from afar. **Pros:** amazing view floating above the sea; no better place in Cetara. **Cons:** 350 yards from town along Amalfi Drive, not ideal for walking; steep descent to beach. ⊠ *Corso Umberto I 1* ☏☏ *089/261388* ⊕ *www.hotelcetus.com* ↩ *37 rooms* ᕫ *In-room: a/c, safe, refrigerator, Internet, Wi-Fi. In-hotel: restaurant, bar, beachfront, parking (free)* ▤ *AE, DC, MC, V* ⦿ *BP.*

SHOPPING

Cetarii (⊠ *Via Largo Marina 48/50* ⊕ *www.cetarii.it*) is the place to buy a bottle of the special anchovy delicacy called *colatura di alici* and other local products such as lemon honey.

PAESTUM

★ *45 km (27 mi) southeast of Cetara, 42 km (25 mi) southeast of Salerno, 99 km (62 mi) southeast of Naples.*

One of Italy's most majestic sights lies on the edge of a flat coastal plain: the remarkably well-preserved **ancient Greek temples** of Paestum. The S18 from the north has now been rerouted via the train station (Stazione di Paestum), which is about 800 yards from the ruins. Access can be gained through the perfectly preserved archway **Porta Sirena,** or—if motorized—through the northern gate of **Porta Aurea.** The ruins are part of the ancient city of Poseidonia, founded by Greek colonists in the 7th century BC. When the Romans took over the colony in 273 BC and its name was latinized to Paestum, they changed the layout of the settlement, adding an amphitheater and a forum.

GETTING HERE

By car, take the A3 motorway south from Salerno, take the Battipaglia exit to SS 18. Exit at Capaccio Scala. By CSTP or SCAT bus hourly from Salerno, by State railway from Salerno.

EXPLORING

Much of the archaeological material found on Paestum's site is displayed in the helpfully labeled **Museo Nazionale.** Several rooms are devoted to the unique tomb paintings discovered in the area, rare examples of Greek and pre-Roman pictorial art. About 600 feet from the museum (in front of the main site offices), framed by banks of roses and oleanders, is the **Tempio di Nettuno** (Temple of Poseidon), a magnificent Doric edifice with 36 fluted columns and an extraordinarily well-preserved entablature (area above the capitals), which rivals the finest temples in Greece. On the left of the temple is the so-called **Basilica,** the earliest of Paestum's standing edifices; it dates from early in the 6th century BC. The name is an 18th-century misnomer, for the structure was in fact a temple sacred to Hera, the wife of Zeus. Behind it an ancient road leads to the **Foro Romano** (Roman Forum) and the single column of the **Tempio della Pace** (Temple of Peace). Beyond—on the north side of the site—is the **Tempio di Cerere** (Temple of Ceres), thought to have originally been dedicated to the goddess Athena. From the thankfully pedestrianized road that runs past the site—actually it cuts the site in half—you can view the temples in the late afternoon or early evening, when the light enhances the deep gold of the limestone. Many people touring the Amalfi Coast take a day trip down to Paestum. ⊠ *Via Magna Grecia* ☎ *0828/722654* ⊠ *Site €4, museum €4, combination ticket €6.50* ⊗ *Excavations daily 8:45–2 hrs before sunset, 8:45–4 in winter; museum daily 8:30–6:45; museum closed 1st and 3rd Mon. of month.*

WHERE TO STAY

$ ⚇ **Azienda Agrituristica Seliano.** This working-farm-with-a-difference is about 3 km (2 mi) from the temples and consists of a cluster of 19th-century baronial buildings. The Baronessa Cecilia herself presides over all, with sons Ettore and Massimino handling visitor logistics. Top priority once you have settled in to your refurbished rooms is to make friends with all the farm dogs, who will then be your faithful companions on country walks past apricot orchards and fields of artichokes. Opt for half-board terms as most of the food is home-produced, including the rich buffalo stew, fresher-than-ever mozzarella, and more elaborate dishes brought with relentless regularity from the kitchens; you'll be seated, as is the tradition, with other guests around a banquet table. For those without transport, transfers can be arranged from Paestum main-line station; bicycles may be borrowed on a first-come, first-served basis. **Pros:** a great taste of a working farm; a banquet every evening. **Cons:** confusing to find; not for non–dog fans. ⊠ *Via Seliano, about 1 km (½ mi) down dirt track west off main road from Capaccio Scalo to Paestum, Paestum* ☎ *0828/723634* ⊕ *www.agriturismoseliano.it* ⟲ *14 rooms* ♿ *In-hotel: restaurant, pool, bicycles, some pets allowed* ⊟ *AE, DC, MC, V* ⊗ *Closed Nov.–Mar., will open for bookings* ⟦⊘⟧ *FAP.*

SHOPPING

If you want to visit a working farm, **Tenuta Vannulo** (⊠ *Via G. Galilei* ☎ *0828/724765* ⊕ *www.vannulo.it*) produces a wide range of award-winning cheeses and yogurts. Say hello to the pen of buffaloes before sampling their sublime mozzarella.

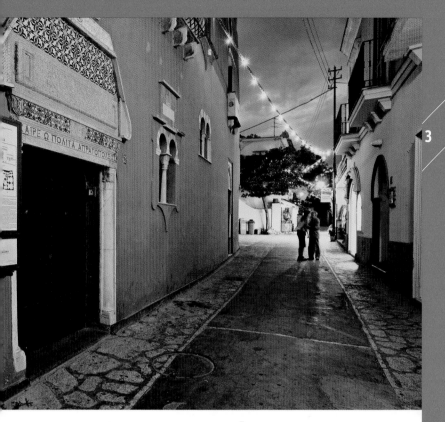

Capri, Ischia, and Procida

WORD OF MOUTH

"We spent three nights on Capri in May, and had a wonderful time. We did a lot of hiking, and I mean a lot. One must really walk to see this beautiful island."

—Tuscanlifeedit

WELCOME TO CAPRI, ISCHIA, AND PROCIDA

TOP REASONS TO GO

★ **The living room of the world:** Pose oh-so-casually with the beautiful people sipping their Camparis on La Piazzetta, the central crossroads of Capri Town: a stage-set square that always seems ready for a gala performance.

★ **Spa-lendid Ischia:** Rebellious daughter of a distant volcanic eruption, Ischia was compensated for her rocky complexion with gorgeous spas famed for their seaweed soaks and fango mud cures.

★ **Marina di Corricella, Procida:** Lilliputian-size Procida has numerous harbors, but none will have you reaching for your paintbrush as quickly as this rainbow-hued, horizontal version of Positano.

★ **Anacapri's Siren Heights:** Be sure to be nice to the bus driver when you take the precipitously steep road up to Capri's bluff-top village—you're nearly a thousand feet above the Bay of Naples here.

1 Capri. A tiny energy point in the universe with a magnetic pull far exceeding its size, Capri is a balmy and palmy never-never land that has been the darling of tourism for 2,500 years. Although its hotels rank among the priciest (and perchiest) around, its incomparable views and natural wonders—I Faraglioni and the Arco Naturale, to name but two—come with no price tags. Capri Town is the place to head for jet-setter glamour, while Anacapri—sitting high up on Monte Solaro—is noted for its understated charm, a fact that accounts for a disproportionate number of easel-toting visitors at the Villa San Michele, with its nonpareil bay view.

Panorama of Capri's harbor

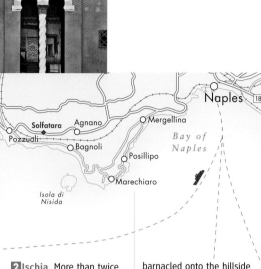

GETTING ORIENTED

Geological stepping-stones anchored in the Bay of Naples, the islands of Capri, Ischia, and Procida tip the two points of the bay's watery crescent. A mere drop in the blue Mediterranean with a popularity way out of proportion to its size, Capri is a *piccolo paradiso* often swamped by tidal waves of day-trippers. Happily, its more rustic sister islands in the archipelago offer something for escapists of every ilk.

2 **Ischia.** More than twice the size of Capri, lesser-known Ischia may have lost the beauty contest to its sister, but it has something Capri doesn't: paradisial white-sand beaches, thermal hot-spring spas, and many fewer day-trippers. Trekkers climbing Monte Epomeo can enjoy a 360-degree view of the gulf.

3 **Procida.** Although it's a short trip, 3 km (2 mi) from the mainland, this little volcanic outcropping remains a secret to many. Sun, cliffs, and sea combine to create the distinctive atmosphere so memorably immortalized in the film *Il Postino.* The town of Terra Murata is barnacled onto the hillside with its ancient baroque abbey of San Michele glittering amid the rocky terrain. The Vivara nature preserve is a paradise for bird lovers.

CAPRI, ISCHIA, AND PROCIDA PLANNER

Making the Most of Your Time

Each of the three islands has its own individual charm—the chic resort of Capri, the volcanic spas of Ischia, and the rustic Procida. If you are unable to overnight, it is worth getting to Capri as early in the morning as possible, to see the main sites before the human tsunami hits the island. Take a round-the-island boat trip and gaze at the natural beauty of the Fariglioni and the Blue Grotto, two of the unmissable sights on this fabled isle.

If archaeology and history are at the top of your list of priorities, choosing between Ischia and Capri can be difficult. Ischia has the added bonus of its natural thermal baths—if you want the gamut of natural saunas and access to a dreamy beach, head to Poseidon in Forio or landscaped Negombo in Lacco Ameno.

Moving around Capri to the main sites is generally easier—and can be done in a day if pushed—while Ischia calls for more chilling out at your destination. If time is limited, Procida and its magical waterfront, as immortalized in the Oscar-winning film *Il Postino*, can be tacked on to your stay as a day trip from Ischia or from the mainland.

Getting Around

Lying equidistant from Naples (about 25 km [16 mi]), Ischia and Capri stand like guards at the main entrance to the Bay of Naples, with Ischia to the west and Capri to the south, while Procida is like a small stepping-stone halfway between Ischia and Capo Miseno (Cape Misenum), on the mainland. The islands can be reached easily from various points in and near Naples, such as the port of Pozzuoli. However, most people head first to Capri using ferries and hydrofoils from two main port terminals in Naples—the Molo Beverello (in the downtown city center) and Mergellina (on the far western border of the city)—along with the thousands who travel via the popular ferries connecting with Sorrento. There are also boat connections between the islands. *For details, see the "Getting Here" and" Getting Around" sections for each island in this chapter.*

Schedules for many routes are listed every day in the local newspaper *Il Mattino*—buy a single ticket rather than a round-trip, which would tie you to the same line on your return journey. Day-trippers need to remember that the high-season crowds on the last ferries leaving the islands make this crossing riotously reminiscent of packed subways and buses back home; in addition, rough bay waters can also delay (and even cancel) these boat rides.

Once on the islands you can do without a car, as the bus service is good—the trip from Capri to Anacapri is breathtaking both for its views and the sheer drops just inches away. Tickets should be bought before boarding, and then stamped on the bus.

For those with (much) deeper pockets, microtaxis are readily available to whiz you to your destination.

Capri's funicular from Marina Grande to Capri town is an attraction in itself, as is the spectacular chairlift to Monte Solaro.

Be prepared, especially on Capri and Procida, to do a lot of walking—many of Capri's narrow alleys allow no alternative, and it is the only real way to find the hidden wonders of Procida.

Renting a scooter on Ischia gives you the freedom to explore at will, as well as giving you that real Italian experience.

Finding a Place to Stay

On Capri, hotels fill up quickly, so book well in advance to be assured of getting first-pick accommodations. Although island prices are generally higher than those on the mainland, it's worth paying the difference for an overnight stay. Once the day-trippers have left center stage and headed down to the Marina Grande for the ferry home, the streets regain some of their charm and tranquillity.

Although Ischia can be sampled piecemeal on day excursions from Naples, given the size of the island, you'd be well advised to arrange a stopover. Ischia is known for its natural hot-water spas, and many hotels have a wellness or beauty center, meaning you may be tempted not to venture any farther than the lobby for the duration of your stay. Hotels in Procida tend to be family run and more down-to-earth. Note that booking is essential for the summer months, when half board may be required. Most hotels close from November to Easter, when the season is at its lowest.

Word of Mouth

"Buses on Capri are very small. There are just six or eight rows of seats and the seat configuration is two seats on one side and 1 seat on the other. As you can imagine, the seats fill up very fast, leaving standing room only for many people." —dcd

"When we arrived in the center of Anacapri we decided the first thing we wanted to do was ride the chairlift up to the top of Mt. Solaro. This was one of the things that was on my 'really want to do this' list, and I'm very happy that we did. It was such a beautiful day . . . clear blue sky, sun shining, sharing the experience with great friends, I couldn't have asked for a more perfect setting." —LowCountryIslander

Taking to the Water

Unsurprisingly the islands are a haven for fans of water sports. Apart from the ample opportunities for swimming in crystal-clear water (but if it's sandy beaches you want, avoid Capri), all three islands have long-established scuba-diving centers (although the prices on Capri are exorbitant). Windsurfers should head to Ischia, while Procida is the ideal place to rent a yacht for short or long trips. Boat and canoe rental is available on all three islands. You might prefer, however, to just avail yourself of the thermal baths for which Ischia is renowned.

Walking and Hiking

With their high peaks, both Capri and Ischia offer spectacular trekking opportunities. Ischia's Monte Epomeo, at 2,582 feet, is somewhat more challenging than the 1,932 feet of Monte Solaro in Capri, especially as on the latter you can choose to use the chairlift for one leg (if not both) of the trip.

The path from Capri Town to the Faraglioni is one of the most beautiful seaside walks in the world, although a strong competitor is the four-hour trek past five Napoleonic towers on the island's west coast.

WHAT IT COSTS (IN EUROS)	¢	$	$$	$$$	$$$$
Restaurants	under €20	€20–€30	€30–€45	€45–€65	over €65
Hotels	under €75	€75–€125	€125–€200	€200–€300	over €300

Restaurant prices are for a first course (*primo*), second course (*secondo*), and dessert (*dolce*). Hotel prices are for two people in a standard double room in high season, including tax and service.

CAPRI IS FOR WALKERS

While Capri may first conjure up chichi cafés and Gucci stores, it's also hiking heaven. Get ready for idyllic pathways running beside cactus-covered cliffs and whitewashed Arabian houses overlooking some of the bluest water on Earth.

Above: Atop Monte Solara leading to the lovely Santa Maria a Cetrella look-out point. Opposite top: The Lighthouse at Punta Carena from the Belvedere di Migliara. Opposite bottom: Via Krupp

When Capri Town swarms with summer crowds and begins to feel like an ant farm, take to the hills—in a few minutes, you can find yourself atop a cliff without a trace of humanity in sight. Many trails here run past famous sights and they offer something for everyone. Novices will love the unique-in-all-the-world zigzag of Via Krupp—a work of art in itself—while pros will dare themselves with Il Passetiello, the ancient mule track that connected the island's two towns, from Via Capodimonte in Anacapri past 14th-century Carthusian pathways to stunning Santa Maria a Cetrella, plus some *very* steep cliff paths. On this trail, don't get too distracted by the amazing view of I Faraglioni as you descend into Capri Town or you may get there quicker than planned!

A SHORTCUT

The Monte Solaro chairlift, built in 1952 (and overhauled in 1998), hoists you to the peak in just over ten minutes, your feet dangling, at times, less than one hundred feet above the houses and treetops. From here you can access some great hikes—namely one down to the famously scenic vista from Santa Maria a Cetrella. To save yourself a climb, remember to use the chairlift!

IL SENTIERO DEI FORTINI

Vying with the Amalfi Coast's Sentiero degli Dei for the title of most beautiful coastal walk in the world, this "Path of the Forts" stretches along the western side of the island for 5.2 km (3.2 mi). Jaw-dropping views are accented by four Saracen fortresses (used mainly during the Napoleonic wars). Starting from the Grotta Azzurra (Blue Grotto), you soon meet the first fort, Fortino di Orrico, set just 30 meters (100 feet) above the water. The path continues through rich Mediterranean maquis to Fortino di Mesola, with great views around this strategically placed fort. The path then rises past Fortino del Pino to the tiny Fortino del Tombosiello and then ends at the famous Faro lighthouse. Along the path ceramic panels—inscribed with reflective haikus—describe your surroundings, the final touch to this unmissable open-air ecomuseum. This walk is not difficult, but lasts up to 5 hours, with no watering spots along the way, so bring lots of water!

BELVEDERE MIGLIARA TO PUNTA CARENA

The 40-minute walk along the paved Via Migliara from Anacapri to the Belvedere Migliara—with one of the most beautiful views on the island—and the Philosophy Park may be some folks' idea of a hike, but the blisters are truly worth it when you head on down the mountainside via the tiny path for 20

minutes to the Torre della Guardia, a Saracen tower once belonging to Axel Munthe. Stone steps take you down to Punta Carena, with its shell-shaped rocky bay: perfect for a well-deserved swim!

SCALA FENICIA

Workout fans will have no hesitation in climbing (of course!) the 921 steps of the—probably—Greek (Phoenician)-built steps, once the main "road" from Capri to Anacapri. From Marina Grande follow the street (not the funicular) to Capri Town for five minutes until you see the signpost on your right. A paved residential path then takes you to the base of the stairway, with the next stop (apart from some time to catch your breath!) just under Villa San Michele, 290 meters (950 feet) above the sea. Take a break along the way, just before passing under the main car road, to admire the 17th-century chapel of Sant'Antonio da Padova, dedicated to the patron saint of Anacapri.

GIRO DELL'ARCO NATURALE

Where else can you see the Arco Naturale, the Grotta di Matermaia, Villa Malaparte, and I Faraglioni in under two hours? This walk, which is truly spectacular, along beauteous Via Pizzo Longo, is detailed in our box: "Classic Capri: A Good Walk."

Updated
by Fergal
Kavanagh

The islands off Naples are so different from each other that you wonder how they can possibly be in the same bay—indeed, some would say that Capri, Ischia, and Procida are not true water mates, as they lie just beyond the bay's outer fringes. More tellingly, their contrasts go beyond mere geology and vegetation. They all occupy different niches in the traveler's mind.

Capri panders to the whims of the international great-and-good. Ischia serves the needs of a predominantly German and Italian clientele. Procida—the closest to the mainland—is more dependent on the weekend and summer influx of Neapolitans. But together, the islands of Capri, Ischia, and Procida—chosen by the Greeks, the supreme connoisseurs and aesthetes of antiquity, as their first base in Italy—combine a broad and delightful gamut of experiences.

Islandophiles, of course, have always had a special love for Capri (the first syllable is accented—"*Ca*-pri"). Pleasure dome to Roman emperors and still Italy's most glamorous seaside getaway, this craggy, whale-shaped island has an epic beauty: cliffs that are the very embodiment of time, bougainvillea-shaded pathways overlooking the sea, trees seemingly hewn out of rock by the Greeks. It's little wonder that tales tell of tourists snapping up villas while their unsuspecting wives were, so they thought, doing last-minute souvenir shopping, or of American industrialists who, determined to stay on, sent a wire home with a brisk "sell everything" order. Capri has always been a stage that lesser mortals could share with the Beautiful People, often an eclectic potpourri of duchesses who have left their dukes home, fading French film actresses, pretenders to obscure thrones, waspish couturiers, and sleek supermodels.

Today Capri's siren song continues to seduce thousands of visitors. On summer days the port and *piazzetta* are often crammed, so if you can visit in spring or fall, do so. Yet even the crowds are not enough to destroy Capri's very special charm. The town itself is a Moorish stage set of sparkling white houses, tiny squares, and narrow medieval alleyways hung with flowers, while its hillsides are spectacular settings for luxurious seaside villas. The mood is modish but somehow unspoiled. The upper crust does its sun-baking in private villas, hinting that you, also, should retreat when the day-trippers take over—offering yourself to the sun at your hotel pool or exploring the hidden corners of the island. Even in the height of summer, you can enjoy a degree of privacy on one of the many paved paths that have been mapped out through species-rich Mediterranean maquis, winding around the island hundreds of feet above the sea.

Recent years have seen a diversification of the experiences offered on the three islands. Once entirely dependent on its thermal springs, Ischia is now the archaeological front-runner in the bay, thanks to its noted museum in Lacco Ameno. Procida has opened up to tourism, with some newer, smaller hotels remaining open throughout the year. All the islands are well served by road networks, with buses plying the main roads and a funicular on Capri reaching the main town from the Marina Grande, as well as a chairlift ascending to the top of Monte Solaro (1,932 feet) from Anacapri. Life on Capri gravitates around the two centers of Capri Town (on the saddle between Monte Tiberio and Monte Solaro) and Anacapri, higher up (902 feet).

CAPRI: A SIREN LANDSCAPE

D.H. Lawrence once called Capri "a gossipy, villa-stricken, two-humped chunk of limestone, a microcosm that does heaven much credit, but mankind none at all." He was referring to its once rather farouche reputation as well as its unique natural beauty. Fantastic grottoes, soaring conical peaks, caverns great and small, plus villas of the emperors and thousands of legends combine with Suetonius's ancient Roman tales of "exquisite tortures" to brush the isle with an air of whispered mystery and an intoxicating quality as heady as its rare and delicious wines. Emperor Augustus was the first to tout the island's pleasures by nicknaming it *Apragopolis*—the City of Sweet Idleness—and Capri has drawn escapists of every ilk since. Ancient Greek and Roman goddesses were moved aside by the likes of Jacqueline Onassis, Elizabeth Taylor, and Brigitte Bardot, who made the island into a paparazzo's paradise in the 1960s. Today, new generations of glitterati continue to answer the island's call.

Of all the peoples who have left their mark on the island during its millennia of history, the Romans with their sybaritic wealth had the greatest effect in forming the island's psyche. Capri became the center of power in the Roman Empire when Tiberius scattered 12 villas around the island and decided to spend the rest of his life here, refusing to return to Rome even when, 10 years on, he was near death. Far from being a dirty old man only interested in orgies, this misunderstood gentleman used Capri as a base to run the ancient Roman Empire. All Tiberius's hard work and happy play—he indulged in his secret passion for astronomy here—were overlooked by ancient scandalmongers, prime among them Suetonius, who wrote: "In Capri they still show the place

Capri is laced with spectacular walking paths.

at the cliff top where Tiberius used to watch his victims being thrown into the sea after prolonged and exquisite tortures. A party of mariners were stationed below, and when the bodies came hurtling down, they whacked at them with oars and boat-hooks, to make sure they were completely dead." Thankfully, present-day Capri is less fraught with danger for travelers, or even to dignitaries from afar. The main risks now are overexposure to the Mediterranean sun, overindulgence in pleasures of the palate, and a very sore wallet.

Life on Capri gravitates around the two centers of Capri Town (on the saddle between Monte Tiberio and Monte Solaro) and Anacapri, higher up (902 feet). The main road connecting Capri Town with the upper town of Anacapri is well plied by buses. On arriving at the main harbor, the Marina Grande, everyone heads for the famous funicular, which ascends (and descends) several times an hour. Once you're lofted up to Anacapri by bus, you can reach the island heights by taking the spectacular chairlift that ascends to the top of Monte Solaro (1,932 feet) from Anacapri's town center. Life on Capri gravitates around the two centers of Capri Town (on the saddle between Monte Tiberio and Monte Solaro) and Anacapri, higher up (902 feet). Within Capri Town and Anacapri foot power is the preferred mode of transportation, as much for convenience as for the sheer delight of walking along these gorgeous street and roads.

VISITOR INFORMATION

Azienda Autonoma di Cura, Soggiorno e Turismo (⊠ *Banchina del Porto, Marina Grande* ☎ *081/8370634* ⊠ *Piazza Umberto I, Capri Town* ☎ *081/8370686* ⊠ *Via G. Orlandi 59, Anacapri* ☎ *081/8371524*

CAPRI: GETTING HERE AND AROUND

GETTING HERE BY BOAT

Capri is well connected with the mainland in all seasons, though there are more sailings between April and October. However, you can't return to Naples after about 10:20 pm in high season (in low season often 8 pm or even earlier). Hydrofoils, Seacats, and similar vessels leave from Molo Beverello (below Piazza Municipio) in Naples, while ferries leave from Calata Porta di Massa, 1,000 yards to the east, and *aliscafi* (hydrofoils) also sail from the small marina of Mergellina, a short distance west of the Villa Comunale in Naples. There's also service to and from Sorrento's Marina Piccola. Much of Capri is pedestrianized, and a car is a great hindrance not a help.

Several ferry and hydrofoil companies ply the waters of the Bay of Naples, making frequent trips to Capri. Schedules change from season to season; the most reliable source for departure times is *Il Mattino*, Naples' daily newspaper. There's little to be gained—sometimes nothing—from buying a round-trip ticket, which will just tie you down to the return schedule of one line. Book in advance in spring and summer for a Sunday return to the mainland.

Caremar (☎ 892/123 or 081/8370700 ⊕ www.caremar.it) has up to seven ferry departures per day from Calata Porta di Massa (€9.60, with a travel time of 1 hour, 20 minutes). Three ferries leave daily from Sorrento (€9.80, travel time 25 minutes).

Linee Marittime Partenopee (☎ 081/8781430 or 081/8071812 ⊕ www.consorziolmp.it) has one to three hydrofoil departures every hour from Sorrento (€14, travel time 20 minutes) and one hydrofoil per day from Ischia (in the morning, €13, one hour).

From Naples, **Navigazione Libera Del Golfo** (☎ 081/5520763 ⊕ www.navlib.it) has roughly one hydrofoil departure per hour from Molo Beverello (€16, travel time 40 minutes).

SNAV (☎ 081/4285555 ⊕ www.snav.it) offers one hydrofoil every hour from Mergellina or Molo Beverello (€16, travel time 40 minutes).

From Easter to October, Volaviamare (☎ 081/4972222 ⊕ www.volaviamare.it) offers three jet foils from Positano and Amalfi (approximately €17, travel time 50 minutes), and two ferries from Positano and Amalfi (€15, travel time 1 hour, 20 minutes).

GETTING AROUND

Most of Capri's sights are reasonably accessible by either boat or bus, except for Villa Jovis and Cetrella, which require some walking (about 40 minutes). The bus service is relatively cheap (€1.40) and frequent, while taxis are likely to cost 10 to 20 times as much as public transport. Don't buy a *biglietto giornaliero* (day pass) for the bus and funicular unless you're thinking of covering almost every corner of the island—it costs €6.90, so you would need to make five separate trips to make it pay, and locals deem it a bit of a rip-off. Conveniently located at the traffic hub of the island, **Rent a Scooter** (✉ Via Roma 70, Capri Town ☎ 081/8375863 ⊕ www.caprirentalagency.com) offers scooters from €25 for two hours (add €5 in August).

⊕ *www.capritourism.com*) offices in Capri, Capri Town, and Anacapri are open daily 8:30–8:30 in high season (9–3 on Sunday), and 8:30–2:30 in winter. Their excellent Web site has an English-language version.

CAPRI TOWN AND ENVIRONS

This fantasy of white-on-white Capriote architecture, flower-filled window boxes, and stylish boutiques rests on a saddle between rugged limestone cliffs to the east and west, where huge herds of *capre* (goats) once roamed, hence the name of the island. Beyond Capri Town lies some of the island's most spectacular sights, including I Faraglioni and the Villa Jovis. As you disembark at the marina quay, note that unlike the other islands in the Bay of Naples, Capri is not of volcanic origin but was formed by marine deposits laid more than 100 million years ago and then uplifted during plate tectonic activity in the Pleistocene era (as recently as 1 to 2 million years ago); Monte Tiberio, to the south of the Marina Grande, and Monte Solaro, to the west, powerfully attest to these upheavals.

GETTING HERE

From the main harbor, Marina Grande, follow the crowds to the main ticket office for the famous funicular, located near where the pier juts out into the harbor. Look for the rounded arcadelike entrance set in the wall of stores and houses. The funicular heads up from the Marina Grande, fun in itself, to the main attraction, Capri Town, the island's hub, which lies above in the saddle of the island. Across the way from the funicular office are ticket offices for many boat lines, near the small police station, plus for tickets to take buses up the hill to Capri Town.

TOP ATTRACTIONS

Arco Naturale *(Natural Arch)*. One of Capri's most famous natural wonders, this geologic arch is all that remains of a large limestone cave that has suffered the erosive effects of wind and rain over the millennia. Once a cave that was likely hollowed out by wave action, it broke apart when lifted up to its present position, hundreds of feet above sea level, in relatively recent geological times (about 1 to 2 million years ago). Engraved by 19th-century artists, it became a favorite landmark for travelers in the Romantic era. ⊠ *Via Arco Naturale, at end of Via Matermania.*

Fodor'sChoice ★ **Certosa di San Giacomo** *(Charterhouse of St. James)*. Nestled between the Castiglione and Tuoro hills, this grand, palatial complex was for centuries a Carthusian monastery dedicated to St. James. It was founded between 1371 and 1374, when Queen Giovanna I of Naples gave Count Giacomo Arcucci, her secretary, the land and the means to create it. The count himself then became devoutly religious and retired here until his death. After the monastery was sacked by the pirates Dragut and Barbarossa in the 16th century, it was heavily restored and rebuilt—thanks in part to heavy taxes exacted from the populace. The friars within were detested by many Capresi for refusing to open the gates to minister to the people when plague broke out.

Capri

TO
NAPLES-SORRENTO

P. del Capo
P. della Chiavica

Villa Jovis
Monte Tiberio
Villa Lysis
Via Tiberio
Moneta

Arco Naturale
Grotta di Matermania
Villa Malaparte
P. Massullo

Matermania
Capri Town
Via Mater Mania
Monte Tuoro
Via Pizzolungo
Porto de Tragara
Monacone

La Piazzetta
Santo Stefano
Certosa di San Giacomo
Punta Tragara
P. di Tragara
I Faraglioni

Strada S Francesco Stairway
Via Tragara
Faraglioni de Fuori

Marina Grande
Funicolare
Museo Caprense Ignazio Cerio
Giardini di Augusto

S. Constanzo
Phoenician Stairway
Via Krupp
Santa Maria a Cetrella
Marina Piccola
P. Mulo

Bagni di Tiberio
Villa San Michele
Castello Barbarossa
Monte S. Maria
Monte Cappello
P. di Terita

P. Trasele
Monte Solaro
Segovia cable car
P. Ventroso

Piazza Vittoria
Anacapri
Caprile

Casa Rossa
San Michele
Pagliaro
Philosophical Park
Belvedere del Migliara
P. del Tuono

Grotta Azzurra
Materita
Faro

P. dell' Arcera
P. Capocchia
Cala del Rio
Compatiello
P. del Pino
P. Carena

1000 yards
1000 meters

KEY
Ferry Lines

CLASSIC CAPRI: A GOOD WALK

Capri is a walker's paradise, with the added bonus of a detailed history of the main streets displayed on painted tiles at many points, erected by the Lions Club. Once you get off the ferry and have picked up a decent map of Capri (€1 at the information office on the main jetty), take a funicular ride up from the harbor area of **Marina Grande** to Capri Town (only one stop, €1.40 one way; if for any reason it's not working, there's a bus and taxi service). For energetic foot soldiers, there's a former mule track starting from a small square on the quayside called Largo Fontana that will place you at the top in about 15 minutes, emerging just below the clock tower in Capri Town. The top funicular station brings you out onto Piazza Umberto I, better known locally as **La Piazzetta**.

On peak days in summer this area gets extremely crowded, so don't expect to be allowed to sip your Campari for more than 20 minutes without being encouraged to move on. Admire the majolica decoration of the clock tower dial and inspect the 17th-century church of **Santo Stefano**, just off the upper side of the square in Piazzetta Cerio. On the same tiny square is the **Museo Caprense Ignazio Cerio**, a small four-room exhibition of archaeological and fossil finds, and useful as a backup site on a rainy day. Then forge your way across the main Piazzetta to Via Le Botteghe; if you're thinking about a picnic lunch, you can stock up on provisions here (try Sfizi di Capri, a baker at Via Parocco Canale 7, just off Via Le Botteghe, for a slice of frittata *di spaghetti* or a more orthodox *panino*, or roll, and fixings). Just opposite the alleyway

is a small supermarket to complete the meal or just to stock up on liquid refreshments at reasonable prices. Take the small Via Madonna delle Grazie behind the fruit stall to see the Chiesa di Sant'Anna, with its restored 14th-century frescoes.

The farther away you get from La Piazzetta, the quieter this pedestrianized road becomes. Via Le Botteghe becomes Via Fuorlovado and then Via Croce, developing gradually into an avenue fringed by bougainvillea and spreading oleander trees. This is an area where real estate now changes hands for upward of €14,000 a square meter (more than $1,300 per square foot).

After about 10 minutes, at the Bar Lindos, the road to the Arco Naturale branches off to the right. Art and archaeology buffs will instead want to continue straight on, past the Chiesa di San Michele (a powder store in the 19th-century French occupation), and up Monte Tiberio.

A turnoff along the way takes you to the **Villa Lysis**, one of Capri's most legendary private homes, built by the poet Baron Fersen and now open to the public (look for the signpost off Via Tiberio). Return to Via Tiberio and continue onward—the full hike may take 45 minutes up the hill—to reach Tiberius's famous mountaintop **Villa Jovis**. Heading back down Via Tiberio, the caffè at the crossroads is one of the last watering holes before heading out to the Arco Naturale. Follow the ceramic signs for Arco Naturale along Via Matermania for about 15 minutes until the path forks (Arco Naturale, to the left; Grotta di Matermania, to the right).

Peer at the **Arco Naturale**, keeping in mind that the path is a cul-de-sac, so every step you go down has to be retraced. Then, knee joints permitting, take the hundreds of steps—and we mean hundreds (don't worry, you won't have to backtrack)—down to the **Grotta di Matermania,** an impressive natural cave where ancient Romans worshipped the goddess Cybele every dawn.

Where the path levels out begins one of the most beautiful seaside walks in the world—the Via Pizzo Lungo. This path continues south through fine Mediterranean maquis vegetation (most of the evergreen trees are holm oak) high above the shoreline, affording fine views of Punta Massullo where **Villa Malaparte**—possibly the most important creation of 20th-century Italian architecture—perches over the sea. Two hundred yards farther is a panoramic point from which you can gaze at **I Faraglioni,** Capri's famous cluster of offshore rocks.

As you continue west, look first for the most romantic house on Capri, the Villa Solitaria—once home to novelist Compton MacKenzie, it's set on a bluff over the sapphire sea and was built in the early 1900s by famed Capriote architect Edwin Cerio—then look for the towering rock pinnacle Pizzo Lungo (High Point), which the ancients thought was the petrified form of Polyphemus, the giant blinded by Odysseus's men.

At the end of the Giro dell'Arco Naturale (Natural Arch Circuit) is another panoramic point, the **Punta Tragara,** which marks your arrival back in Capri Town. From here take Via Tragara, lined with elegant hotels and villas, until it joins with Via Camerelle. Look for a left turn down Via Cerio to the **Certosa di San Giacomo** (Charterhouse of St. James), a former monastery that is Capri's grandest architectural set piece.

About five minutes' walk away up Via Matteotti are the **Giardini di Augusto** (Gardens of Augustus), which give an excellent view over the southern side of the island toward the Faraglioni.

The impressive **Via Krupp** was reopened in 2008 after 32 years, and it's well worth taking this hairpin-turned walkway to Marina Piccola. Alternatively retrace your steps until you get to Via Serena, a mere five-minute walk from the Piazzetta. Once back at base, you might splurge on a *granita* or a cocktail at the Piccolo Bar, the very first bar to grace the square and the only one with an upstairs terrace.

TIMING

Allowing time for a refreshment stop, a little shopping, and a fair amount of photo snapping, the walk will take between three and five hours, plus an extra half hour if you visit the Certosa museum. Those who aren't up for much hiking should choose either the trek to the Villa Jovis or the Giro dell'Arco Naturale; the latter is a cliffside path that includes hundreds of steps (going downhill mostly), so be prepared. Most of the sites and shops are open throughout the day, but as there's more than a fair amount of up and down, you'd be well advised to avoid the stickiest hours—weatherwise—from noon to 3 in summer.

3

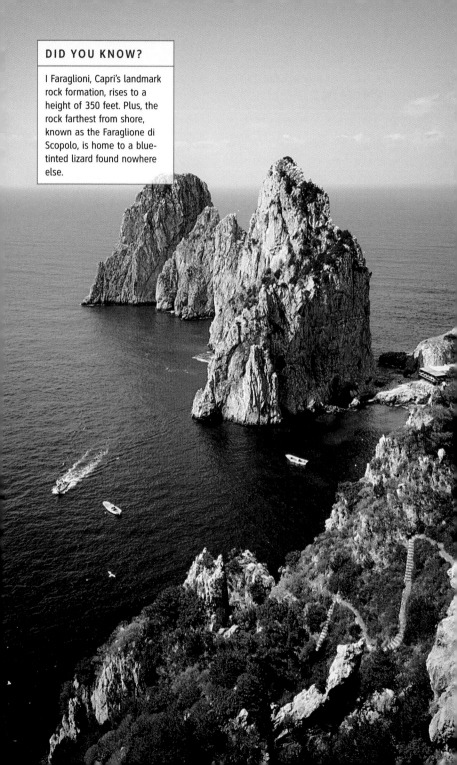

3

The complex was reopened to the public in 2008 after major renovations lasting four years. You enter via a grandly imposing entryway, which leads to the **Biblioteca Comunale Popolare Luigi Bladier** (public library—Capri's only free Internet point) and the spacious church of **San Giacomo** (built in 1690, reopened after renovations in 2010). After admiring the church's baroque frescoes, follow the signpost down toward the *Parco,* which leads down an avenue flanked by pittosporum and magnolia toward the magnificent monastery gardens and some welcome benches with stunning views. Take heed of the signs reminding you to watch your step, as the ground is uneven in places. Beyond a covered road lies the **Chiostro Grande** (Large Cloister)—originally the site of the monks' cells and now the home of a high school; nearby is the 15th-century **Chiostro Piccolo** (Small Cloister), both often the venues for summertime open-air concerts. The newly reopened (2010) Quarto del Priore hosts art exhibitions from international artists, but the showstopper here is the **Museo Diefenbach,** comprising a collection of recently restored large canvases by the German painter K. W. Diefenbach, who visited Capri in 1900 and stayed until his death in 1913. Although his protracted stay may have cured Diefenbach of his chronic depression, his tormented soul emerges clearly in his powerful paintings, filled with apocalyptic storms and saintly apparitions. For years, Diefenbach rivaled the Blue Grotto for sheer picturesqueness—he was given to greeting visitors replete with flowing white beard, monk's cowl, and primitive sandals. From La Piazzetta take Via Vittorio Emanuele and then Via F. Serena to reach this beautiful monastic complex, one of the true highlights of historic Capri. ✉ *Viale Certosa 40, Capri Town* ☎ *081/8376218* ⊕ *www.capricertosa.com* ✉ *Free* ☉ *Tues.–Sun. 9–2 (also 6–8 during exhibitions), park 9–1 hr before sunset.*

Fodor'sChoice ★ **I Faraglioni.** Few landscapes set more artists dreaming than that of the famous Faraglioni—three enigmatic, pale ocher limestone colossi that loom out of the sea just off the Punta Tragara on the southern coast of Capri. Soaring almost 350 feet above the water, the Faraglioni have become for most Italians a beloved symbol of Capri and have been poetically compared to Gothic cathedrals or modern skyscrapers. The first rock is called Faraglione di Terra, since it's attached to the land; at its base is the famous restaurant and bathing lido Da Luigi, where a beach mattress may accompany the luncheon menu. The second is called di Mezzo or Stella, and little boats can often be seen going through its picturesque tunnel, which was caused by sea erosion. The rock farthest out to sea is Scopolo and is inhabited by a wall lizard species with a striking blue belly, considered a local variant by biologists although legend has it that they were originally brought as pets from Greece to delight ancient Roman courtiers—you can see an embalmed specimen at the Museo Caprense Ignazio Cerio. ✉ *End of Via Tragara, Capri Town.*

La Piazzetta. The English writer and Capriophile Norman Douglas called this square, officially known as Piazza Umberto I, "the small theater of the world." The rendezvous point for international crowds, this "*salone*" became famous as the late-night place to spot heavenly bodies—of the Hollywood variety, that is. Frank Sinatra, Rita Hayworth, Julie Christie, Julia Roberts, and Mariah Carey are just a few of the

THE ISLANDS THROUGH THE AGES

In terms of settlements, conquests, and dominion, the history of the islands echoes that of Campania's mainland. For eastern Mediterranean traders in the second and first millennia BC, Capri and Ischia were both close enough to the mainland to provide easy access to trade routes and impervious enough to afford natural protection against invaders.

Ischia, or Pithekoussai, as it used to be called—a word probably derived from the Greek term for a large earthenware jar (*pithos*) rather than the less plausible word, *pithekos*, meaning monkey—is renowned in classical circles as the first colony founded by the Greeks on Italian soil, as early as the 8th century BC.

Capri, probably colonized in the 7th century BC, a century or so later than Ischia, is amply described in the early years of the Roman Empire by authors such as Suetonius and Tacitus, as this was the island where Tiberius spent the last 10 years of his life.

After the breakup of the Roman Empire, the islands, like many other parts of the Mediterranean, suffered a succession of incursions. Saracens, Normans, and Turks all laid siege to the islands at some stage, between periods of relative stability under the Swabians, the Angevins, the Aragonese, and the Spanish.

After a short interregnum under the French at the beginning of the 19th century, a period of relative peace and prosperity ensued. Over the next century, from the opening of its first hotel in 1826, Capri saw an influx of visitors that reads like a who's who of literature and politics, especially in the first decades of the 20th century. Ischia and Procida established themselves as holiday resorts much later, with development taking place from the 1950s onward.

celebs who have made La Piazzetta the place where the rich and famous come to watch other rich and famous folk. These days, if the high fly-ers bother to make an appearance, they're likely to show up at 8 in the evening for an aperitif and some peppery *tarallucchi* bread sticks, with a possible return visit for a late-night limoncello.

In any event, the square is never less than picturesque and has been a natural crossroads and meeting point since Roman times. The religious complex of Santo Stefano was built around the square in the 17th century, but the clock tower and Municipio, or town hall (once the archbishop's palace) are the only remnants of its cathedral. Capri's version of Big Ben—the charming bell tower, or Torre dell'Orologio—is perched over the ancient gateway. ⊠ *At intersection of vias Botteghe, Longano, and Vittorio Emanuele, Capri Town.*

Fodor'sChoice ★ **Marina Piccola.** A 10-minute ride from the main bus terminus in Capri (Piazzetta d'Ungheria), Marina Piccola is a delightfully picturesque inlet that provides the Capresi and other sun worshippers with their best access to reasonable beaches and safe swimming. The entire cove is romantically lined with *stabilimenti*—elegant bathing lidos where the striped cabanas are often air-conditioned and the bodies can be Modigliani-sleek. The most famous of these lidos (there's a fee to use

Villa Jovis was the home of Emperor Tiberius during the final years of his rule over ancient Rome.

the facilities), found closest to I Faraglioni, is **La Canzone del Mare**, once presided over by the noted British music-hall singer Gracie Fields and for decades favored by the smart set, including Noël Coward and Emilio Pucci (who set up his first boutique here). La Canzone del Mare's seaside restaurant offers a dreamy view of I Faraglioni and a luncheon here, although pricey, can serve as an iconic Capri moment. Jutting out into the bay at the center of the marina is the **Scoglio delle Sirene**, or Sirens' Rock—a small natural promontory—which the ancients believed to be the haunt of the Sirens, the mythical temptresses whose song seduced Odysseus in Homer's *Odyssey*. This rock separates the two small beaches: Pennaulo, to the east, and Marina di Mulo, site of the original Roman harbor, to the west. The small church, **Chiesa di Sant'Andrea**, was built in 1900 to give the local fishermen a place of worship. ⊠ *Via Marina Piccola.*

Punta Tragara. The "three sons of Capri"—to use one of the many poetic nicknames for the three giant rocks of I Faraglioni—can be best seen from the famous lookout point at Punta Tragara at the end of gorgeous Via Tragara. At this point, a path—marked by a plaque honoring the poet Pablo Neruda, who loved this particular walk—leads down hundreds of steps to the water and the feet of I Faraglioni, and perhaps to a delightful lunch at one of the two lidos at the rock base: Da Luigi, a household name in the Bay of Naples, or La Fontelina, an exclusive sun-drenched retreat nearby. After lunch, habitués then use the little boat (fee charged) that ferries back and forth to nearby Marina Piccola and then take the bus back to town. Near the start of the Neruda path turn left to find the most gorgeous seaside walk in Capri—the **Via**

Pizzo Lungo. Another place to drink in the view of I Faraglioni, which is most romantic at sunset, is the **Punta Del Cannone,** a hilltop belvedere reached beyond the Certosa di San Giacomo and the Giardini di Augusto. ✉ *End of Via Tragara, Capri Town.*

Fodor'sChoice **Villa Jovis.** Named in honor of the ancient Roman god Jupiter, or Jove,
★ the villa of the emperor Tiberius is riveted to the towering Rocca di Capri like an eagle's nest overlooking the strait separating Capri from Punta Campanella, the tip of the Sorrentine peninsula. Lying near the easternmost point of the island, the villa is reached by a well-signposted 50-minute walk that climbs gradually from the Piazzetta in Capri Town and offers several opportunities along the way to slake your thirst and catch your breath (if possible, resist temptation until you get to the welcoming Bar Jovis, on Via Tiberio, about five minutes' walk from the site). Although criticized by locals for the visible conditions of neglect, Villa Jovis is nonetheless a powerful reminder of the importance of the island in Roman times. What makes the site even more compelling are the accounts of the latter years of Tiberius's reign from Capri, between AD 27 and 37, written by authors and near-contemporaries Suetonius and Tacitus. They had it that this villa was famous for its sybaritic living, thus sounding a leitmotif whose echo can be heard at the luxurious hotels of today.

There are remarkably few discrepancies between the accounts of the two historiographers. Both point to Tiberius's mounting paranoia in Rome, while Tacitus outlines his reason for choosing Capreae (*Annals,* Book IV). "Presumably what attracted him was the isolation of Capreae. Harborless, it has few roadsteads even for small vessels; sentries can control all landings. In winter the climate is mild, since hills on the mainland keep off gales. In summer the island is delightful, since it faces west and has open sea all round. The bay it overlooks was exceptionally lovely, until Vesuvius's eruption transformed the landscape." Capri in Roman times was the site of 12 spacious villas, but Villa Jovis is both the best preserved and must have been the largest, occupying nearly 23,000 square feet.

The entrance to the site lies just beyond the *pharos* (lighthouse) built under Tiberius and used until the 17th century to warn ships away from the narrows between Capri and the mainland. Pick up a site map at the ticket office, which gives a useful breakdown of the various areas of the villa to be visited. Nearby, you can find the **Salto di Tiberio** (Tiberius's Leap), the place where ancient gossips believed Tiberius had enemies, among them his discarded lovers and even unfortunate cooks, hurled over the precipice into the sea some 1,000 feet below. After taking stock of this now-harmless viewing platform and its information panels, take the upper path past the baths complex around the palace residential quarters to view the heavily restored Chapel of Santa Maria del Soccorso and its large bronze statue of the Madonna, a gift to the island from the Caprese painter Guido Odierna in 1979. The walk around the perimeter of the site gives an idea of the overall layout of the palatial residence, which in places rose to five stories in height. From here descend some steps and then a ramp to the *ambulatio* (walkway), which offers additional spectacular views and plenty of shade, as well

DID YOU KNOW?

After being off limits for 32 years, winding Via Krupp was reopened in 2008, complete with a plaque unveiled by Italian president Giorgio Napolitano proclaiming the road a symbol of liberty and an homage to beauty.

as a *triclinium* (dining room) halfway along. The center of the site is a complex devoted to cisterns. Unlike in Pompeii, there was no aqueduct up here to provide fresh running water, so the cisterns next to the bath complex were of prime importance. ⊠ *Via A. Maiuri* ☎ *081/8374549* ⊡ *€2* ⊙ *Feb.–Oct., daily 9–1 hr before sunset; Nov.–Jan., daily 9–3:15.*

Fodor's Choice **Villa Lysis.** Opened to the public in 2003, this legendary domain looms
★ large in Capri's consciousness. The island's Xanadu, Manderlay, and San Simeon, it was originally known as the Villa Fersen, after Baron Jacques d'Adelsward-Fersen, the builder. Fleeing to the island from a scandal involving Parisian schoolboys, the French aristocrat had this white-stucco pile designed by Edouard Chimot in 1903 in shimmering Belle Epoque style, replete with gilded-mosaic columns and floors looted from the island's ancient Roman sites. Past the impressive columned entrance, inscribed in stone with "Amori et Dolori Sacrum" (A Shrine to Love and Sorrow), the baron would retire to write poems and paint pictures in his *Stile Liberty* (Art Nouveau) salons. Sadly all the furnishings are gone, but you can still gasp at the ballroom open to the sea and the large smoking room in the basement, where, in a tiled pool, Fersen committed suicide by ingesting a lethal mix of opium and champagne in 1923. Outside are magical terraces with views to rival the adjacent Villa Jovis. Unfortunately, the gardens still needed a good deal of restoration at this writing (fall 2010). ⊠ *Via Lo Capo* ☎ *081/8386214 Capri municipal office* ⊡ *Free* ⊙ *Apr.–mid-Oct., Mon.–Sat 9:30–12:30 and 2:30–5:30.*

WORTH NOTING

Giardini di Augusto *(Gardens of Augustus)* and **Via Krupp.** You'll see some spectacular views of the southern side of Capri from the southernmost terrace of this well-kept park lying on both sides of Via Matteotti. In one corner of the gardens is a monument to Lenin, who visited Gorky and his Capri-based school for revolutionaries between 1907 and 1913. This school, above the gardens, is now the hotel Villa Krupp, named after the German industrialist Friedrich Alfred Krupp. An amateur marine biologist, Krupp fell in love with Capri after coming to Naples to visit its aquarium. In 1900 he decided to fund a paved walkway to connect the Hotel Quisisana, where he then lived, to the Marina Piccola. A bust of the benefactor stands at the start of the zigzagging Via Krupp, considered a masterpiece, demonstrating that roads can be works of art in themselves. Designed by Emilio Mayer, it features no less than eight whiplash switchbacks, hugging the cliff face and engaging the stroller in an ever-changing panorama that stretches from the Giardini di Augusto and the Punta del Cannone to the waterfront. After a hiatus of 32 years the road was reopened in 2008 by Italian president Giorgio Napolitano, who unveiled a plaque exulting the sinuous curves as an eternal symbol of liberty and homage to the beauty of nature. Although heir to the great munitions fortune, Krupp was the most peaceful of men and bestowed monies on many island charities. Despite his good works, he was hounded by malicious gossip that he held orgies at his villa and in the island grottoes, and he committed suicide in 1902 (such stories support the long-held tradition that the native Caprese continue

Continued on page 125

CAPRI BY BOAT

To savor Capri to the fullest you must sail its blue waters as well as wander through its squares and gardens. Happily, the famous "giro" cruises around the island allow you to enjoy the perfect sailing safari.

Sooner or later, the beautiful coastline of Capri will lure you to its shores, where you'll be in good company: ancient heroes, emperors, Hollywood divas, and legions of mere mortals have been answering the same siren call from time immemorial. Fact is, you haven't fully experienced Capri until you've explored its rocky shoreline, a veritable Swiss cheese of mysterious grottoes tucked into its myriad inlets and bays. As you'll learn, the Blue Grotto may be world famous, but there's also a Green Grotto, a Yellow Grotto, a Pink, and a White. And unless you possess fins, the only way to penetrate many of these secret recesses is to book yourself on one of the island's giro (tour) cruises—they have been an iconic Caprese experience since the 19th century. Offered by a flotilla of companies ranging from bare-bones to high luxe, these round-about tours—many last only two hours but you can also sign on for daylong cruises—give you the chance to travel the island's "highway," marvel at sights immortalized in 1,001 travel posters, and, for one magical afternoon, take possession of one of the horseshoe-shape inlets where movie stars are as much at home as dolphins.

above, Capri's iconic Faraglioni rock formation

A "GIRO" TOUR AROUND CAPRI

An aquatic version of the famous Italian *passeggiata* (stroll), the Capri giro cruise is offered on two main types of boat. The classic craft is a *gozzo*—once the traditional fishing boat of the Bay of Naples, it now varies in comfort from luxe (shower, lunch, aperitif) to basic (BYO *panino*). Or opt for a *gommone*, a speedboat: this gives you a chance to create your own itinerary—but watch out for gas prices. Coastal highlights are outlined below, but you can always opt to follow your instincts, take an inviting side lagoon, and Robinson Crusoe the day away in one of the innumerable small inlets.

*Map labels:*
Punta Capo/ Rocca di Capri
Villa Lysis
Villa Jovis
Marina Grande
Grotta del Bove Marino
S. Constanzo
Moneta
Via Tiberio
Grotta dei Polpi
Grotta Meravigliosa
Capri Town
Grotta Bianca
Matermania
Cala di Matermania
Via Mater Mania
Giardini di Augusto
Via Tragara
Villa Malaparte
Punta Massullo
Marina Piccola
Via Krupp
Grotta Oscura
Via Pizzolungo
Grotta Albergo Marinari
Tragara
Mar Tirreno
I Faraglioni

Grotta Bianca

a 19th-century Xanadu that clings like a wasps' nest to the cliff and, perched atop the looming peak, the ruins of Emperor Tiberius's fabled **Villa Jovis**.

SEA FOR YOURSELF

Rounding Capri's eastern coast you arrive at the **Grotta dei Polpi**, originally named for its abundance of octopus and cuttlefish; recently fished dry; it is now called the Coral Cave. Past a gorge, you'll arrive at **Grotta Meravigliosa**—the "cave of marvels," as its innumerable stalagmites and stalactites prove (look, as most people do, for one that is said to resemble the Madonna). You'll need a sweater and even a scarf in here—it's glacial even in peak summer.

Farther along is the **Grotta Bianca** (White Grotto), whose opal waters—their

STARTING YOUR ROUNDS

Capri's gateway harbor, the **Marina Grande**, is where most giro cruises start. Time, budget, weather, and confidence will determine your choice of tour—long or short, cheap or ritzy, guided

Villa Jovis

or independent—but the more extensive ones should cover the following sites. East of the marina lies the **Grotta del Bove Marino** (Sea Lion's Cave). Listen for the distinctly mammalian howl, amplified naturally by the cave walls: local fishermen may tell you the creature is still in residence, but what you're hearing is the wail of the wind and sea. You soon reach **Punta Capo**, marked by its welcoming statue of the Madonna del Soccorso. Here, atop the **Rocca di Capri**—Capri's own Gibraltar—catch a glimpse of the **Villa Lysis**,

Marina Grande

color is due to the mix of seawater and deep-spring water—shimmer against a spectacularly jagged white backdrop; past the entrance a large crevice has produced a natural swimming pool, known as the Piscina di Venere (Pool of Venus). Entering the **Cala di Matermania**, spot the distant square-shaped sea rock known as Il Monacone, once home to a hermit-monk who kept a net hanging off its side (woe betide any fisherman who did not throw in some fish!). Astride the promontory of **Punta Massullo** is that modernist eyeknocker, the red-hued **Villa Malaparte**.

Past the ancient Roman port of **Tragara** lies the famed **Faraglioni**, the earthen powerhouse of three massive rocks rising from the sea that remain the scenic masterpiece of Capri. The "Faraglione di Terra" is linked to land and nestles two famous lido restaurants, Da Luigi and La Fontelina. The next rock monolith out is the "Faraglione di Mezzo"

(Middle)—this one has the tunnel that is so much fun to sail through—while the farthest one out is the Scopolo, or "Faraglione di Fuori" (External). If you have an expert guide ask him to take you into the little blue grotto—a small cave illuminated by an underwater window of aquamarine light—tucked behind the Faraglioni.

Faraglioni

Villa Malaparte

Cala di Matermania

WATER COLORS

Farther on sits the **Grotta Albergo Marinari**. Despite its name, there is no hotel here; the cave was used by sailors as shelter from sudden sea storms. Next lies the **Grotta Oscura**, whose deceptively narrow entrance opens up to reveal the largest cave on the island, its two large oval caverns a showplace of stunning light reflections. Drifting up the southern coast of Capri, the

Faro

zigzagging drama of **Via Krupp** threads its way over the hillside to chic **Marina Piccola**. It was here on the Scoglie delle Sirene (Siren's Rock), immortalized in Canto XII of the *Odyssey*, that mermaids tried to lure Odysseus, the world's first tourist, onto its hazardous shoals.

Just after **Punta Ventroso** look for the Cala di San Costanzo, where a "face" in the rock presumably resembles St. Costanzo, the patron saint of Capri. A few hundred meters farther on is the **Grotta Verde** (Green Grotto), whose waters resemble an enormous deep-sea daiquiri, and which in turn is followed by the **Grotta Rossa**, whose red hue is caused by algae buildup. A little way beyond

Marina Piccola

is the **Grotta dei Santi** (Saints' Cave), whose rocky outcrop resembles human figures at prayer. Take some time to enjoy the truly stunning waters of **Cala Marmolata**, which you'll sail through before coming to the lighthouse, or **Faro**. Sail the length of the west coast to the cape landmarked by the Torre Damecuta. From the Gradola shore you will find your spectacular finale, the **Grotta Azzurra** (Blue Grotto).

MAKING THE MOST OF THE GROTTA AZZURA

native Capresi insist that the optimum time to see the unearthly blue is between 10 AM and 1 PM. However, more objective observers advise that the best time is around 4 PM or 5 PM, when the raking light of the sun is most brilliant. At this hour, many—though not all—of the boatmen have departed along with the tour buses, so you may have the Blue Grotto pretty much to yourself.

Today, many travelers visit Capri's fabled Grotta Azzura (Blue Grotto) using tour boats departing either from Capri's Marina Grande or from the small embarkation point below Anacapri (reached by bus from Anacapri Town). This approach can prove frustrating: you have to board one boat to get to the grotto, then transfer to a smaller one to pass through the 3-foot-high cave opening, and then are allowed—due to the midday traffic jam of boats—disappointingly little time once inside the cave. Instead, in late afternoon—not midday—take the bus from Anacapri's Piazza Vittoria to the Strada della Grotta Azzurra. Interested in protecting the early-afternoon hours for their traditional siesta, many

🚤 € 15 from Marina Grande, €10 by rowboat from Grotta Azzurra

🕐 8:30–1 hr before sunset, closed if sea is even minimally rough

Grotta Azzurra

THE BEST CRUISE OUTFITTERS

INDEPENDENCE

If you're keen on exploring the island on your own, you can hire a speedboat (gom-mone)—with a skipper provided on request—from the following:

LEOMAR (follow the stairs to the passage-way; Spiaggia Marina Grande, 081/8377181). Based on the beach at Marina Grande next to the bus stop, Leomar offers hourly and full-day rentals starting at €35–€45 per hour, six people maximum.

BANANA SPORT (Spiaggia Pontile Privato, 081/8375188, www.capri.com/en/c/capri-boat-banana-sport). Rent boats starting at €70 for a minimum two-hour trip.

QUICK OVERVIEW TOURS

If time is short, catch a tour on a larger, quicker, and sometimes more fun-packed boat.

MOTOSCAFISTI CAPRI (Via Provinciale 282, 081/8377714, www.motoscafisticapri.com). With offices right on the dock at Marina Grande, this cooperative of gozzo boat owners offers three set tours that leave on the hour. Admission is depending on choice of tour, €12–€14. Their "Blue" and "Yellow" tours include the Blue Grotto.

LASER CAPRI (Via Don Giobbe Ruocco 45, 081/8375208, www.capri.net/en/c/laser-capri). For those who want to make a tour on a larger, sturdier sightseeing boat, Lazer has a fleet of larger ships which can take up to 100 people. Tickets run €21.50 to the Blue Grotto, €14 for full-island tour. Their ticket booth is just past the main funicular station landing.

Grotta Verde

A PERSONAL TOUCH

On some of these guided tours, a lively combination of anecdotes (and folk songs!) accompany you throughout: Proffer a gratu-ity if you are happy with the trip.

CAPRI RELAX BOATS (Via Cristoforo Colombo 34, 081/8374559, www.caprirelax boats.com). One of the best and most stylish of the outfitters, Capri Relax has a compre-hensive range of tours. The island tour will take you into caves that larger boats can't reach, and their flexibility allows you to decide the itinerary.

GENNARINO ALBERINO (Capri Whales, Via Cristoforo Colombo 17, 081/8378894, www.capriwhales.it). These tours are virtually living island history, as he was one of the divers who unearthed the ancient marble statues found in the Blue Grotto. Each of his boats is furnished with freshwater showers and iceboxes. Gennarino's knowledge of the island is encyclopedic, and few others can match it.

CAPRI TIME BOATS (Truglio 19, 081/3509173, www.capritimeboats.com). This very suave option not only offers island tours but goes beyond to the Amalfi Coast and islands in the bay.

CAPRI SEA SERVICE (Via Cristo-foro Colombo 64, 081/8378781, www. capriseaservice.com). A wide panoply of options are offered, from gozzo tours to spe-cialized diving trips.

CAPRI BOATS (Via Largo Fontana 53, 081/19726872, www.capriboats.com). Those wanting to experience the "Capri moon" over the Faraglioni, nighttime fishing expedi-tions, and an array of gozzo tours should contact this outfitter.

■ TIP→ Giro passengers often have to purchase separate tickets (€12) to use the rowboats that tour the Blue Grotto. Check when signing up for your giro cruise.

to detest, somewhat ironically in this fabled vacationland, all outsiders). ⊠ *Via Matteotti and Via Krupp, Capri Town.*

Grotta di Matermania. Set in the bowels of Monte Tuoro, this legend-haunted cave was dedicated to Cybele, the Magna Mater, or Great Mother of the gods—hence the somewhat corrupted name of the cave. A goddess with definite Eastern origins, Cybele did not form part of the Greek or Roman pantheon: worship of her was introduced to Italy in 204 BC at the command of the Sibylline oracle, supposedly for the purpose of driving Hannibal out of Italy. At dawn the cave is touched by the rays of the sun, leading scholars to believe it may also have been a shrine where the Mithraic mysteries were celebrated. Hypnotic rituals, ritual sacrifice of bulls, and other orgiastic practices made this cave a place of myth, so it's not surprising that later authors reported (erroneously) that Emperor Tiberius used it for orgies. Nevertheless, the cave was adapted by the Romans into a luxurious nymphaeum (small shrine), but little remains of the original structure, which would have been covered by tesserae, polychrome stucco, and marine shells. If you want to see the few ancient remains, you have to step inside the now-unprepossessing cavern. ⊠ *Giro del'Arco Naturale.*

Marina Grande. Besides being the main harbor gateway to Capri and the main disembarkation point for the mainland, Marina Grande is usually the starting point for round-island tours and trips to the Blue Grotto. The marina has faded in the glare of neon since the days when it was Sophia Loren's home in the 1958 film *It Started in Naples*. Originally a conglomeration of fishermen's houses built on ancient Roman foundations, it's now an extended hodgepodge of various architectural styles, with buildings that almost exclusively service the tourist industry. Warehouses and storerooms in which fishermen once kept their boats and tackle are now shops, restaurants, and bars, most either tacky or overpriced. To the west, however, lie three sights worth exploring: the historic church of **San Costanzo,** dating from the 5th century, the ruins of the **Palazzo a Mare** (a villa built for Emperor Augustus), and the chic **Bagni di Tiberio beach.** Sun-worshippers bathe here, oblivious to the partly submerged remains of the harbor section of Augustus' palace (subsequently added to by Tiberius), with its nympheum, baths, and tanks used for fish breeding. This is a 30-minute walk from the Marina Grande, alternatively use the boat service (€5). ⊠ *Marina Grande, Capri Town.*

Santo Stefano. Towering over La Piazzetta, with a dome that is more sculpted than constructed and with *cupolettas* that seem molded from frozen zabaglione, Capri's mother church is a prime example of *l'architettura baroccheggiante*—the term historians use to describe Capri's fanciful form of baroque architecture. Often using vaulting and molded buttresses (since there was little wood to be found on such a scrubby island to support the ceilings), Capri's architects became sculptors when they adapted Moorish and Grecian styles into their own "homemade" architecture. Sometimes known unglamorously as the ex-cathedral, the church was built in 1685 by Marziale Desiderio of Amalfi on the site of a Benedictine convent (founded in the 6th century), whose sole relic is the clock tower campanile across the Piazzetta. As in so many churches in southern Italy, there has been a good deal of recycling of ancient building materials: the flooring of the chapel to the left of the high altar was laid with polychrome marble from Villa Jovis, while the marble in the Cappella del Sacramento was removed from the Roman villa of Tragara. Inside the sacristy are some of the church treasures, including an 18th-century silver statue of San Costanzo, the patron saint of Capri, whose holy day is celebrated every May 14. Opposite the church on the tiny Piazzetta I. Cerio are the Palazzo Cerio Arcucci, with its Museo Caprense Ignazio Cerio; the Palazzo Farace, which houses the Biblioteca Caprense I. Cerio (I. Cerio Library); and the Palazzo Vanalesti, the executive offices of the Capri tourist board. ⊠ *Piazza Umberto I, Capri Town* ☎ *081/8370072* ☉ *Daily 7–1, 4 after evening service.*

Villa Malaparte. Nicknamed the *Casa Come Me* (House Like Myself) and perched out on the rocky Punta Massullo, this villa is considered by some historians to be a great monument of 20th-century architecture. Built low to be part of the ageless landscape, the red-hued villa was designed in Rationalist style by the Roman architect Adalberto Libera in the late 1930s for its owner Curzio Malaparte (author of the novel *La Pelle,* which recounts various World War II experiences in Naples). Unfortunately, the aesthetic concerns of the villa are inextricably entailed with political ones: Curzio Malaparte was a full-blown Fascist, and the only reason why this house was allowed to be built along this otherwise unsullied stretch of coast was by special fiat from none other than Mussolini. Malaparte was unhappy with the design and made a number of alterations during the construction phase, including the famous trapezoidal staircase that seems to grow out of the roof. The villa is private, but if you want to see it up close, it was featured as a suitably striking backdrop for Brigitte Bardot in Jean-Luc Godard's underrated film *Contempt* (1963). ⊠ *Giro dell'Arco Naturale.*

ANACAPRI AND ENVIRONS

One of the most breathtaking bus rides anywhere follows the tortuous road from Capri Town 3 km (2 mi) up a dramatic escarpment to Anacapri. At 902 feet over the bay, Anacapri is the island's only other town and leading settlement on the island's peaks, poetically referred to as the Monte Sirene (Siren Heights). Crowds are thickest around the square, which is the starting point of the chairlift to the top of Monte Solaro and close to Villa San Michele, the main magnet up here for tour groups. Allow plenty of time when traveling to or from Anacapri, as space on the local buses is usually at a premium. Alternatively, the athletically inclined can hike from Capri up to Anacapri by taking the 921 steps of the Scala Fenicia (the Phoenician Stairway, more likely to have been built by the Greeks than the Phoenicians), leading almost down to Marina Grande, to a point on the main road about 15 minutes' walk from Capri Town. For access, continue walking past Villa San Michele away from Piazza Vittoria. Needless to say, most people will want to tackle the Scala Fenica going down, not up. As a fitting finale to a visit

AROUND ANACAPRI: A GOOD WALK

From Anacapri's main square of Piazza Vittoria, take Via Capodimonte opposite the *Seggiovia* (chairlift) to **Villa San Michele,** about a five-minute walk, past a formidable array of garish boutiques, bars, and liqueur factories, all vying to ensnare passersby.

As with many sites on the island, it's best to get to the villa shortly after it opens, or in the early evening when the day-trippers have moved through.

After browsing through its rooms and strolling through the gardens and the ecomuseum, retrace your steps to Piazza Vittoria and make for the lower station of the Seggiovia to **Monte Solaro.** You'll soon be whisked out of town over whitewashed houses and carpets of spring-flowering broom and rockrose to the viewing platform at the top of Solaro.

From here a path leads north downhill toward the sublimely picturesque church of **Santa Maria a Cetrella** through some of the most beautiful wooded countryside on Capri.

In spring and autumn watch for migrating birds. A splash of yellow combined with an undulating flight could be the golden oriole; the multicolor bee-eater also migrates via Capri in May and September.

On the way back down from Cetrella, follow the signs to Anacapri along Via Monte Solaro (downhill), passing close to the ruins of the **Castello Barbarossa** and then emerging close to the Villa San Michele.

If you have time and energy left over, make for Via Orlandi, a useful street for stocking up on provisions.

Pass the impressive **Casa Rossa** (Red House), on your right, and then take the next right turn (Via San Nicola) to Piazza San Nicola and the church of **San Michele.** Climb to the organ loft to savor its magnificent majolica-tile floor depicting the Garden of Eden, then head back to the Piazza Vittoria.

At this point choose between the Belvedere di Migliara and the Grotta Azzurra. A 40-minute walk to Belvedere di Migliara is rewarded with an iconic view as well as the world's first Philosophical Park. By mid- to late afternoon, the crowds will have vanished from the **Grotta Azzurra** (Blue Grotto), at the sea below Anacapri.

Catch the convenient bus that links the town with the grotto and enjoy this fabled sight around 4 pm or 5 pm, when connoisseurs swear that the light is best.

TIMING
The walk takes approximately four hours, allowing at least one hour for the visit to Villa San Michele and its gardens, and a further two hours' leisurely amble on the roundtrip. Add a half hour if visiting the Belvedere di Migliara as it is off the beaten track.

If armed with a packed lunch, you're most likely to find a picnic site near Cetrella—in attempts to discourage low-spending day-trippers from the mainland, consumption of picnics is made fairly difficult on Capri.

3

A chairlift makes ascending Monte Solaro a breeze.

to Anacapri, take the convenient bus down the hill to the water's edge and the fabled Blue Grotto.

GETTING HERE

There's regular bus service to Anacapri from Marina Grande or Capri Town (Piazzetta d'Ungheria).

TOP ATTRACTIONS

★ **Casa Rossa** *(Red House)*. Capri is famous for its villas built by artists, millionaires, and poets who became willing prisoners of Capri during the Gilded Age. Elihu Vedder, Charles Coleman, Lord Algernon, and the Misses Wolcott-Perry were some of the people who constructed lavish Aesthetic Movement houses. Built by the American colonel J. C. MacK-owen, this particular villa, near the center of Anacapri, was erected between 1876 and 1899. With wall hues in distinctive Pompeian red, the villa incorporates a noted 15th-century Aragonese tower. The villa now houses a wonderful don't-miss permanent exhibition called "The Painted Island," featuring 33 canvases from masters such as Giordano and Brancaccio, depicting images of Capri in the 19th and 20th centuries. ⊠ *Via G. Orlandi, Anacapri* ☎ *081/8382193* ✉ *€3* ⊘ *Apr.–Sept., Tues.–Sun. 9:30–1 and 5:30–8:30.*

Fodor's Choice **Grotta Azzurra** *(Blue Grotto)*. Contrary to the legend claiming that the ★ Blue Grotto was discovered by two travelers as recently as the 19th century, the truth is it has been an island landmark since time immemorial. Extensive sub-sea-level remains as well as several large statues (some now on view at Anacapri's Casa Rossa, others in Naples) reveal it had been in use as the elegant, mosaic-decorated nymphaeum of the adjoining Roman villa of Gradola. Historians can't quite agree if it was simply a lovely little pavilion where rich patricians would cool themselves in preparation for midday picnics, or if it was a site where sacred rituals were practiced. It is thought that Tiberius may have accessed the grotto through Anacapri's *cloaca maxima* (sewer) from his adjacent Villa Damecuta.

The Blue Grotto famously burst upon the modern consciousness with its rediscovery on August 18, 1826, by the Polish poet August Kopisch and his Swiss friend, the artist Ernest Fries. Two years later, the poet Wilhelm Waiblinger wrote an ode to it as a tribute to the era of Romanticism and man's "return to nature." It subsequently inspired Hans Christian Andersen's 1835 novel, *The Improvisor,* a 19th-century bestseller that triggered an unending flow of Grand Tour visitors to Capri.

Hues in such vivid blue as to demote cerulean to green, the Grotta Azzura remains Capri's greatest natural wonder. Don't be surprised to see visitors dunk glasses into its opaline liquid, half-expecting to see the glasses filled with neon blue water. In fact, the intense color is caused by sunlight refracting through the entrance's enormous underwater arch. Back when Emperor Tiberius used to haunt this cave, the water level was considerably lower than now, so today's visitors are enjoying a light spectacle the ancient Romans missed out on.

The Grotta Azzurra can be reached from Marina Grande or from the small embarkation point below Anacapri on the northwest side of the island, served by bus from Anacapri. It must be said that while the grotto is spectacular, the experience of viewing it can be frustrating. You board one boat to get to the grotto and transfer to another smaller one in order to get inside (the opening is only just over 3 feet high). If there's a backup of boats waiting to get in, you'll be given precious little time to enjoy the gorgeous color of the water and its silvery reflections. Instead of taking a boat from Marina Grande, from Anacapri you can head to the Piazza Vittoria for the bus that connects the town with the seaside grotto. Either way you go, though, is going to be time-consuming. Be prepared to dicker with the boatmen at the grotto entrance. Some foolhardy swimmers brave the heavy fines applicable when the boats have left. ⊠ *Grotta Azzurra* 🖷*€21 from Marina Grande, €7 by rowboat from Grotta Azzurra near Anacapri* ⊘ *9–1 hr before sunset, closed if sea is even minimally rough.*

Monte Solaro. An impressive limestone formation and the highest point on Capri (1,932 feet), Monte Solaro affords gasp-inducing views toward the bays of Naples and Salerno. A 12-minute chairlift ride will take you right to the top (refreshments available at bar), which is a starting point for a number of scenic trails on the western side of the island, most particularly down the slope to the lovely area around Santa Maria a Cetrella. Picnickers should note that even in summer it can get windy at this height, and there are few trees to provide shade or refuge. ⊠ *Piazza Vittoria, Anacapri* 🕿 *081/8371428* 🖷*€7 one-way, €9 round-trip* ⊘ *Daily 9:30–5. Closed in adverse weather conditions.*

Fodor's Choice ★ **Santa Maria a Cetrella.** Scenically perched on the slopes of Monte Solaro, this small sanctuary in late-Gothic style—with its older parts dating to the late 14th century—offers a truly picturesque frame for a panorama that takes in much of the island. It also marks the top of the second access route (Il Passetiello) used in ancient times, which linked Capri Town with Anacapri. Steep, slippery, and in spots still dangerous, this is the pathway that the Carthusian monks of San Giacomo would have used to reach their properties in the upper part of the island. Congregants were mainly fisherfolk whose boats were moored in the Marina Piccola directly below; they also used this cliff-top aerie as a lookout against Saracen pirates. The church was substantially rebuilt by Franciscan monks in the early 17th century, when a sacristy was added. To reach Santa Maria, you can climb a path leading off Viale Axel Munthe (an hour-long walk); an alternative is to descend a path leading from the Monte Solaro chairlift. The church has erratic opening times; ask at the chairlift for further information. Mass is celebrated at dawn every Sunday in September, but the site remains unforgettable year-round. ⊠ *Monte Solaro.*

Fodor's Choice   **Villa San Michele.** Henry James called this villa and garden "the most
★   fantastic beauty, poetry, and inutility that one had ever seen clustered together." At the ancient entranceway to Anacapri just at the top of the Scala Fenicia and occupying the site of an ancient Roman villa, Villa San Michele was built (beginning in 1895) in accordance with the instructions of its owner, Axel Munthe (1857 to 1949). Physician to the Swedish royal family, Munthe practiced both in Paris and in Rome, thereby building up a substantial fortune, much of which he plowed into real estate in Anacapri. He was a philanthropist with a lifelong dedication to the sick and destitute. Munthe's *The Story of San Michele* is an evocative—if not entirely reliable—autobiography.

The 19th-century artists Alma-Tadema and Lord Leighton—specialists in painting scenes *all'antica* ("of antiquity")—would have set up their easels in a minute at the villa, thanks to its Roman-style courtyards, marble walkways, and atriums. Rooms display the doctor's varied collections, which range from bric-a-brac to classical antiquities (once thought so important J. Pierpont Morgan offered millions for them, but the good doctor knew that most were fakes so refused all offers). Medieval choir stalls, Renaissance lecterns, and gilded statues of saints adorn various rooms, while the doctor's personal memorabilia enables the visiting public to learn more about this enigmatic patron of the arts and humanist.

The villa is connected by a spectacular pergola path overlooking the entire Bay of Naples. This leads to the famous **Sphinx Parapet,** where an ancient Egyptian sphinx from 1200 BC looks out over to Sorrento (you cannot see its face—on purpose). It's said that if you touch the sphinx's hindquarters with your left hand while making a wish, it will come true. The parapet is connected to the adorable little Chapel of San Michele. Dr. Munthe was initially drawn to San Michele because of this chapel, abandoned at the time, which stands on the grounds of one of Tiberius's villas. Rumor has it that its missing bells were said to ring as a sign that the emperor was seeking forgiveness for having sentenced a certain carpenter from Galilee to death. Munthe proceeded to banish all shadows, converting the chapel into a library and concert hall, and making his new home Capri's most welcoming showplace.

Besides hosting summer concerts on Friday evenings, the Axel Munthe Foundation has an ecomuseum that fittingly reflects Munthe's fondness for animals, where you can learn about various bird species—accompanied by their songs—found on Capri. Not only did Munthe aid people, he bought up the hillside as a sanctuary for birds, which prevented the Caprese from capturing quail by terrible means (lured by songbirds that had been blinded to make them sing better). Munthe left this Italian jewel to the Swedish state, on condition it was used to further cultural relations between the two countries. Today, thanks to Dr. Munthe, this little realm is still an Eden. ⊠ *Viale Axel Munthe 34, Anacapri* ☎ *081/8371401* ⊕ *www.villasanmichele.eu* ▣ *€6* ☉ *Nov.– Feb., daily 9–3:30; Mar., daily 9–4:30; Apr. and Oct., daily 9–5; May– Sept., daily 9–6.*

WORTH NOTING

Castello Barbarossa. The foundation of this ruined castle, almost clinging to the side of the cliff above Villa San Michele, dates to the late 10th century, when Capri was ruled by the ancient maritime republic of Amalfi. Named after the admiral of the Turkish fleet, Kheir-ed-Din, or Barbarossa (Redbeard), who stormed and took the castle in 1535, much of the original layout has been changed over the centuries. Axel Munthe bought the property in order to make it a sanctuary for migrating birds—following his initiative, bird hunting was forbidden on the island in 1932. The Villa San Michele organizes free weekly guided visits of the surrounding grounds on Thursday afternoons from May to October (call to reserve a place) besides carrying out ornithological research in the area. ⊠ *Axel Munthe Foundation, Anacapri* ☎ *081/8371401* ⊕ *www.villasanmichele.eu* ▣ *Free.*

Philosophical Park. Frustrated by Capri's ongoing commercial overdevelopment, Swedish professor Gunnar Adler-Karlsson acquired the land around the Belvedere Migliara with the intention of maintaining an ecologically pure area. Covering 11,000 square meters (36,000 square feet), paths lead through rich Mediterranean maquis with over sixty ceramic panels lining the way with quotes from great thinkers from Aristotle to Einstein. Allegedly the first of its kind in the world, just feet away from one of the most gorgeous views in the world, this park is devoted to peace and reflection. A complete guide, called "Meditation Upon Western Wisdom," hangs from the trees (and is also available free from the adjacent Da Gelsomino restaurant). ⊠ *Via Migliara, Anacapri* ⊕ *www.philosophicalpark.org* ▣ *Free.*

San Michele. The octagonal baroque church of San Michele on Piazza San Nicola, finished in 1719, is best known for its exquisite majolica pavement (1761), designed by Solimena and executed by the Abruzzese *mastro-riggiolaro* (master tiler) Leonardo Chiaiese. A walkway skirts the rich ceramic carpet depicting Adam and a duly contrite Eve being expelled from the Garden of Eden, but you can get a breathtaking overview from the organ loft, reached by a winding staircase near the ticket booth. Outside the church is the Via Finestrale, which leads to Anacapri's noted **Le Boffe quarter.** This section of town, slightly lower on the hillside, is centered on the Piazza Diaz and the church of Santa Sofia and owes its name (from the Neapolitan dialect for "swollen") to

the distinctive domestic architecture prevalent here, which uses vaults and sculpted groins instead of crossbeams. ✉ *Piazza S. Nicola, Anacapri* ☎ *081/8372396* ⊕ *www.chiesa-san-michele.com* 🎫 *€2* 🕐 *Apr.–Oct., daily 9–7; Nov and Mar., daily 10–2.*

WHERE TO EAT

IN AND AROUND CAPRI TOWN

$$
SOUTHERN
ITALIAN

✕ **Al Grottino.** This small and friendly family-run restaurant, which is handy to the Piazzetta, in a 14th-century building, has arched ceilings and lots of atmosphere; autographed photos of celebrity customers cover the walls. House specialties are *scialatielli ai fiori di zucchine e gambaretti* (homemade pasta with zucchini flowers and shrimps) and linguine *ai scampi*, but the owner delights in taking his guests through the menu. ✉ *Via Longano 27, Capri Town* ☎ *081/8370584* 🍴 *Reservations advised* 🟰 *AE, DC, MC, V* 🕐 *Closed Nov.–mid-Mar.*

$$$$
SOUTHERN
ITALIAN

✕ **Aurora.** Though often frequented by celebrities—photographs of famous guests adorn the walls inside and out—this restaurant offers courtesy and *simpatia* irrespective of your persona. Although the oldest restaurant on the island (it used to be set high on the hill), now in its third generation, its decor is sleekly minimalist. If you want to see and be seen, reserve a table outside on one of Capri's chicest thoroughfares; otherwise go for extra privacy and ambience within. The cognoscenti start by sharing a pizza all'Acqua, a thin pizza with mozzarella and a sprinkling of *peperoncino* (chili). If tiring of pasta, try the *sformatino alla Franco* (rice pie in prawn sauce) but leave room for the homemade sweets. The place fills up quickly, so be sure to reserve. ✉ *Via Fuorlovado 18/22, Capri Town* ☎ *081/8370181* ⊕ *www.auroracapri.com* 🍴 *Reservations essential* 🟰 *AE, DC, MC, V* 🕐 *Closed Jan.–mid-Mar.*

$$$
SOUTHERN
ITALIAN

✕ **Capri's.** With an unrivaled view over the bay, this sleek restaurant is just feet away from the Piazzetta. In fact, since it is on one of the island's most congested streets, you'll find passersby often gathering to watch the sushi chef preparing "Capri Crudo" (raw Capri) in one window or to study the gallery of celebrity diners in another—Kanye West got engaged here. Result: Groups of "street traffic" do come in for a quick bite. You can't blame them: Across the threshold two all-window, no-wall dining terraces (one uncovered in good weather) afford spectacular vistas across to Procida and Ischia—the only restaurant on the island that can boast this. But the food here deserves hours to savor such treats as the Mediterranean sushi or *scialatielli con aragosta (homemade pasta with lobster)* or *paccheri al coccio* (pasta with shellfish). Open all year, the owner also runs the whitewashed Capricorno restaurant on Via Longano. ✉ *Via Roma 38, Capri Town* ☎ *081/8377108* ⊕ *www.capris. it* 🟰 *AE, DC, MC, V* 🕐 *Open all year.*

$$$
SOUTHERN
ITALIAN

✕ **Edode.** When you've had enough of florid, flowery Caprese decor, head here to this sleek entry among the island's restaurants. The name may come from the ancient Greek for food, the seats may have been imported from Austria, the gray-on-white columns hail from Paris, but the ambience conjures up New York's hot cool Meatpacking district. From the menu, you can't go wrong with the fresh fish, the specialty being *paccheri con gamberi e crema di zucchini* (large pasta with shrimp and cream of zucchini). The wine list has more than 900 choices from all over the world. Enjoy a fine bottle and settle in for some nice people-watching—they serve until after 1 am. ⊠ *Via Camerelle 81/83, Capri Town* ☎ *081/8388252* ⊕ *www.edodecapri.com* ⊟ *AE, DC, MC, V* ⊘ *Closed mid-Oct.–Mar.*

$$$ ✕ **La Canzone del Mare.** Although not primarily a restaurant, luncheon
SOUTHERN in the covered pavilion of this legendary bathing lido of the Marina
ITALIAN Piccola is Capri at its most picture-perfect. With two seawater pools
★ as well as rocky beach, and I Faraglioni in the distance, this was the erstwhile haunt of Gracie Fields, Emilio Pucci, Noël Coward, and any number of 1950s and '60s glitterati. The VIPs may have departed for more private beaches, but this setting is as magical as ever. You need to pay a fee (€20) to actually use this bathing *stabilimento* (club) but why not make a day of it? There are also five suites available if a day is not enough. Boats also depart from here for Da Luigi, the lido/restaurant at the base of I Fariglioni. ⊠ *Via Marina Piccola 93, Capri Town* ☎ *081/8370104* ⊕ *www.lacanzonedelmare.com* ⊟ *AE, DC, MC, V* ⊘ *Closed Oct.–Mar. No dinner.*

$$$ ✕ **La Capannina.** For decades one of Capri's most celebrity-haunted res-
SOUTHERN taurants, La Capannina is a few steps from the busy social hub of the
ITALIAN Piazzetta. The walls are covered with photos of celebrities enjoying
★ their meal here, and the discreet covered veranda, with its hanging baskets, is ideal for dining by candlelight in a florid garden setting, all pink, green, and white. Another alternative to avoid the stuffy indoor rooms is to join the regulars in the outdoor courtyard. The specialties, aside from an authentic Capri wine with the house label, are home-made *ravioli capresi* and *linguine con lo scorfano* (flat spaghetti with scorpion fish), the squid stuffed with caciotta cheese and marjoram, and the "Pezzogna," an exquisite sea bream cooked whole in a copper casserole and garnished with a layer of baked potatoes. The small bar across the side alleyway is run by the same owners. ⊠ *Via Le Botteghe 12b, Capri Town* ☎ *081/8370732* ⊕ *www.capannina-capri.com* ⌂ *Reservations essential* ⊟ *AE, DC, MC, V* ⊘ *Closed Nov.–mid-Mar. and Wed. in Mar. and Oct.*

$$ ✕ **La Fontelina.** Lying just below Punta Tragara at the base of Capri's
SOUTHERN impressive offshore rocks (the Faraglioni), this is the place to enjoy a
ITALIAN delightfully comatose day on the island. Given its position right on
★ the water's edge, seafood is almost de rigueur. For a slightly different starter, try the *polpette di melanzane* (eggplant fritters), and then dip into the vegetable buffet. Highly recommendable is the house sangria, a blissful mix of white wine and fresh fruit. La Fontelina also functions as a lido, with steps and ladders affording access to fathoms-deep blue water. Access is by boat from Marina Piccola or on foot from Punta Tragara (10 minutes). Only lunch is served. Across the way is the archrival lido-restaurant, Da Luigi, with a more evocative setting but now a bit too famous for its own good. ⊠ *I Faraglioni, at end of Via Tragara, Capri Town* ☎ *081/8370845* ⊟ *AE, MC, V* ⊘ *Closed mid-Oct.–Easter. No dinner.*

$$$ ✕ **Le Grottelle.** Enjoying one of Capri's most distinctive settings, this
SOUTHERN extremely informal trattoria is built up against the limestone rocks not
ITALIAN
★

far from the Arco Naturale—a cave at the back doubles as the kitchen and wine cellar. Whether you stumble over this place, or make it your destination after an island hike, Le Grottelle will prove memorable, thanks to that ambience and sea view taking in the Amalfi Coast's Li Galli islands. The food? Oh, that . . . the menu includes ravioli and local rabbit, but go for the seafood, with *linguine con gamberetti e rucola* (pasta with shrimp and arugula) one of the more interesting specialties. ⊠ *Via Arco Naturale 13* 🕾 *081/8375719* 🖄 *Reservations essential* ▭ *DC, MC, V* ⊙ *Closed Nov.–mid-Mar.*

IN AND AROUND ANACAPRI

$ × **Barbarossa.** This ristorante-pizzeria is the first you'll see if you arrive
PIZZA in Anacapri by bus. Its panoramic covered terrace takes in views of the Barbarossa castle on the hill as well as the sea. The no-frills ambience belies the quality of the *cucina*: besides *pizze* they specialize in local dishes—be sure to try the *risotto con gamberi a limone* (shrimp with lemon). Barbarossa is open all year. ⊠ *Piazza Vittoria 1, Anacapri* 🕾 *081/8371483* ▭ *AE, DC, MC, V.*

$$ × **Da Gelsomina.** Set amid its own terraced vineyards with inspiring
SOUTHERN views to the island of Ischia and beyond, this is much more than just
ITALIAN a well-reputed restaurant. The owner's mother was a friend of Axel
★ Munthe and encouraged her to open a kiosk serving hot food, which evolved into Da Gelsomina. It has an immaculately kept swimming pool, which is open to the public for a small fee—a buffet is served as you lounge here. Located close to one of the island's finer walks as well as the Philosophy Park, it's an excellent base for a whole day or longer. There's also a five-room pensione, with free transfer service by request from Anacapri center. ⊠ *Via Migliara 72, Anacapri* 🕾 *081/8371499* ⊕ *www.dagelsomina.com* ▭ *AE, DC, MC, V* ⊙ *Closed Jan.–mid-Feb. and Tues. in winter. No dinner in winter.*

$$ × **Il Cucciolo.** Nestling in thick maquis high above the Blue Grotto and a
SOUTHERN five-minute walk from the Roman site of Villa di Damecuta, this must be
ITALIAN one of the most romantic locations on Capri, perfectly placed to catch the setting sun. The cucina is refreshingly inventive with fish being a specialty: ask for *pasta fresca con zucchini e gamberi* (fresh pasta with zucchini and shrimp). There's a free evening chauffeur service to and from Anacapri. Reservations are essential in the evening. ⊠ *Via La Fabbrica 52, Anacapri* 🕾 *081/8371917* ▭ *AE, DC, MC, V* ⊙ *Closed Nov.–mid-Jan. and Tues. in Oct. and Feb.–May.*

$$$ × **La Rondinella.** This is an airy ristorante-pizzeria looking onto the main
SOUTHERN pedestrianized street of Anacapri. In summer make sure you reserve a
ITALIAN table out on the popular terrace. If you have difficulty choosing from the extensive menu, ask for advice or opt for one of their best pasta dishes, linguine *macchiavelle* (with capers, olives, and cherry tomatoes). ⊠ *Via Orlandi 295, Anacapri* 🕾 *081/8371223* ▭ *DC, MC, V* ⊙ *Closed Nov.–Feb. and Thurs. Oct.–May.*

WHERE TO STAY

IN AND AROUND CAPRI TOWN

$$$–$$$$ 🖼 **Il Gatto Bianco.** The spot where Jacqueline Kennedy famously sought refuge when hounded by paparazzi, this is still a favorite destination to channel Capri's Sunset Boulevard-y ghosts. With greater crowds packing Capri, the hotel does suffer a bit from its location—just around the corner from the Piazzetta and right in the thick of crowds, caffè, and discos. That noted, the lovely atmosphere inside the public salons is quintessential Caprese—it was recently refurbished, with a new blue-on-white bar area, majolica-lined stairs, and antique-y accents. It used to be a bargain option but has grown pricier over the years. Matisse, the resident *gatto bianco* (white cat), adds an authentic touch to this taste of Capri. **Pros:** central location; wonderful atmosphere. **Cons:** perhaps too close to the action; no sea view; lack of hotel facilities for this price range. ✉ *Via Vittorio Emanuele 32, Capri Town* ☎ *081/8370203* ⊕ *www.gattobianco-capri.com* ⤸ *40 rooms* ⚏ *In-room: a/c, refrigerator. In-hotel: Wi-Fi hotspot* ☰ *AE, DC, MC, V* ⊘ *Closed Nov.–Apr.* ❖❘ *BP.*

$$$$ 🖼 **J. K. Place.** The most supremely stylish hotel in southern Italy, this
Fodor's Choice   luxurious Xanadu has almost made every other accommodation on
★   Capri seem dowdy and dull since it opened in 2007. Set in an 1876 villa perched over the island's Marina Grande harbor (yet removed from its hurly-burly), the hotel welcomes you into salons so glamorous they graced the cover of Europe's *Architectural Digest*. Nautical blue walls and white Corinthian columns set off a symphony of vintage photographs, 19th-century bronzes, starched white-linen wing armchairs, and enough coffee-table books to keep even the pickiest fashionista happy. Outside, regal stone sphinxes patrol teak-lined bay-side terraces; across a vast lawn, flowering fruit trees shade the gargantuan pool. The guest rooms have a Hamptons-meets-Mediterranean Modern vibe, thanks to billowing white drapes, four-poster beds, 1940s French commodes, and big plasma TVs. More like a superrich aunt's villa on Capri than a regular hotel, this is the place that all high lifers (sorry, rooms start at €700) must check out. **Pros:** gorgeous decor; exquisite pool; very close to chic Tiberio beach; free shuttle to town. **Cons:** only for high rollers; many guests clear out for Capri nightspots. ✉ *Via Provinciale Marina Grande 225, Marina Grande* ☎ *081/8384001* ⊕ *www.jkcapri.com* ⤸ *22 rooms* ⚏ *In-room: a/c, safe, refrigerator, Wi-Fi. In-hotel: pool, gym, spa, Wi-Fi hotspot* ☰ *AE, DC, MC, V* ⊘ *Closed mid-Oct.–mid-Apr.*

$$$$ 🖼 **La Palma.** Though the oldest on Capri (1822), this attentively run hotel has not rested on its laurels. At the front door you're immediately given a blast of island glamour, with gleaming lobby, and majolica-tile rooms providing a delightful contrast to the hustle at street level outside (this is just down the street from La Piazzetta) and the sorry looking sculpture deposited here from the 2008 Cow Parade. Through the lobby, make for the hotel's magical courtyard, lined with coves and columns sculpted in archetypal Caprese "zabaglione" stucco. Beginning life as the Locando Pagano, this hostelry first hosted August Kopisch, who then went on to "discover" the Blue Grotto. What he would think of the highly lush guest rooms, now dripping with "frescoes" and *dolce*

vita accents remains to be seen. The outdoor restaurant is on the much-frequented Via Vittorio Emanuele—*the* place to see and be seen. **Pros:** the most central of Capri's luxury hotels; real island glamour. **Cons:** perhaps too central; rather far from the sea. ⊠ *Via V. Emanuele 39, Capri Town* ☎ *081/8370133* ⊕ *www.lapalma-capri.com* ➟ *72 rooms* ♿ *In-room: a/c, safe, refrigerator, Wi-Fi. In-hotel: restaurant, bar* ⊟ *AE, DC, MC, V* ⊗ *Closed Nov.–Easter* ⦿ *MAP.*

$$$$ ⛨ **La Scalinatella.** If you're bronzed and beautiful, or just bronzed, or even just beautiful, this is your kind of hotel. A white Moorish mansion out of the *Arabian Nights*, it conjures up Capri in finest Hollywood fashion. The name means "little stairway," and that's how this charmingly small hotel is built, on terraces following the slope of the hills, with winding paths and bougainvillea arbors. Inside, the decor is *Architectural Digest*–opulent, with Venetian blackamoor statues, Empire-era consoles, and Valentino fabrics. Guest rooms have overstuffed sofas, bright colors, large terraces, and some even have his-and-her bathrooms (most have whirlpool baths). Outside, one of Capri's bluest pools is the fetching setting for delicious luncheons. **Pros:** all rooms have a sea view; his-and-her bathrooms. **Cons:** a bit removed from the center; main pool visible from main road. ⊠ *Via Tragara 10, Capri Town* ☎ *081/8370633* ⊕ *www.scalinatella.com* ➟ *30 rooms* ♿ *In-room: a/c, safe, refrigerator, Wi-Fi. In-hotel: restaurant, bar, tennis court, pools, Wi-Fi hotspot* ⊟ *AE, DC, MC, V* ⊗ *Closed Nov.–Mar.* ⦿ *BP.*

$$$$
Fodor's Choice
★
⛨ **Punta Tragara.** The most beautiful hotel on Capri, this has a hold-your-breath perch directly over the famed rocks of I Faraglioni. Clinging to the Punta Tragara lookout point and originally a villa designed by Le Corbusier, it once hosted a secret wartime meeting between Churchill and Eisenhower. Opened as a hotel in the 1970s by Count Manfredi, baronial fireplaces, gilded antiques, and travertine marble set the style in the main salons, while guest rooms—no two are alike—are sumptuously cozy-casual. The dreamy garden area is the showstopper here and it comes studded with two pools. One is a heated, jet-powered, aquamarine jewel set a foot away from Monzù, an idyllic, arbor-covered restaurant that just might be the prettiest spot on the island. To top it off, the entire staff seems to have been sent to the finest finishing schools. **Pros:** a taste of the good life; the view of I Faraglioni. **Cons:** a 10-minute walk from the center; some find the decor dated but others find that a plus. ⊠ *Via Tragara 57, Capri Town* ☎ *081/8370844* ⊕ *www.hoteltragara.com* ➟ *44 rooms* ♿ *In-room: a/c, safe, refrigerator. In-hotel: restaurant, bar, pools, Internet terminal, Wi-Fi hotspot* ⊟ *AE, DC, MC, V* ⊗ *Closed mid-Oct.–mid-Apr.* ⦿ *BP.*

$$$$
★
⛨ **Quisisana.** Some people say there are really three villages on Capri: Capri Town, Anacapri, and this celebrated landmark, which looms large in the island's mythology. Superstar of Capri hotels, the "Quisi" draws "didn't-I-meet-you-in-Saint-Tropez?" guests who wouldn't *dream* of staying anywhere else. The Quisi's popularity has led to its expansion over the years: the lobby is enormous, the pool seems ready for an Esther Williams MGM production number, and the theater-cum-convention center is a jewel designed by noted modernist Gio Ponti back in the 1930s. But the hotel can't be beat for its shiny and luxe restaurants,

see-and-be-seen bars, QuisiBeauty parlor, professional service, and location (just down the street from the crowded Piazzetta, this may be *too* convenient). These days, the Quisisana legend remains strong: if you want to plug into Capri's network of the rich and famous, one of the best places to start is the hotel's Bar Quisi with its Krug Room. The fact remains that even though this is Capri's biggest hotel, it is also its hardest-to-get reservation in high season. **Pros:** luxe atmosphere on a large scale. **Cons:** the food isn't all star quality (steer clear of the pizza); convention-size and far from cozy. ⊠ *Via Camerelle 2, Capri Town* ☎ *081/8370788* ⊕ *www.quisisana.com* ↴ *148 rooms* ⚘ *In-room: a/c, safe, refrigerator, Wi-Fi. In-hotel: restaurant, bar, tennis court, pools, gym, Internet terminal, Wi-Fi hotspot* ☐ *AE, DC, MC, V* ☺ *Closed Nov.–mid-Mar.* ¶⊙¶ *BP.*

$$ ᵀᵛ **Villa Krupp.** Occupying a beautiful house overlooking the idyllic Gardens of Augustus, this historic hostelry was once the home of Maxim Gorky, whose guests included Lenin. Rooms are plain but spacious, with comfy beds, and some have south-facing terraces with awesome views. Breakfast is served on the glorious terrace and Certosa di San Giacomo and I Faraglioni are just a few minutes away. **Pros:** direct access to the Gardens of Augustus. **Cons:** a lot of steps to be negotiated; rooms are simple. ⊠ *Viale Matteotti 12, Capri Town* ☎ *081/8370362* ⊕ *www.villakrupp.it* ↴ *12 rooms* ⚘ *In-room: no TV. In-hotel: restaurant, bar, tennis court, pools, gym, Wi-Fi hotspot* ☐ *MC, V* ☺ *Closed Nov.–Mar.* ¶⊙¶ *BP.*

$$$
Fodor'sChoice
★

ᵀᵛ **Villa Sarah.** Few hotels offer such a quintessentially Caprese spirit as this villa jewel. Set in one of Capri's nicest residential quarters and lovingly run by the De Martino family, their Capri-yellow Mediterranean building has a sweet island style and comes wonderfully surrounded by lush gardens, abloom with flowers, fruit, and peace. Only after threading leafy paths and climbing some gentle steps do you spot the two-story villa, which is done up in white and golds with some of those iconic round Capri windows as accents. You immediately feel as if you are a guest in one of those multimillion-dollar private Capri villas. Inside, guest rooms are homey and furnished with bright, simple accents. The quiet and restful nights do come at a price: a long 15-minute walk downhill is needed to get to the action of Capri town's Piazzetta. Particularly lovely and gently priced (for Capri), this is truly a wonderful option. **Pros:** gorgeous pool; wonderful gardens. **Cons:** a steep and long climb back from the Piazzetta; no elevator. ⊠ *Via Tiberio 3/a, Capri Town* ☎ *081/8377817* ⊕ *www.villasarah.it* ↴ *19 rooms* ⚘ *In-room: a/c, refrigerator. In-hotel: hotel: bar, pool* ☐ *AE, DC, MC, V* ☺ *Closed Nov.–Mar.* ¶⊙¶ *BP.*

IN AND AROUND ANACAPRI

$$ ᵀᵛ **Biancamaria.** This tastefully refurbished hotel with its pleasing facade and whitewashed spreading arches lies in a traffic-free zone close to the heart of Anacapri. The front rooms have large terraces looking toward Monte Solaro; those at the back are quieter and more private. **Pros:** friendly staff; Anacapri literally at your doorstep. **Cons:** on the main pedestrian road; no gardens. ⊠ *Via G. Orlandi 54, Anacapri* ☎ *081/8371000* ⊕ *www.hotelbiancamaria.com* ↴ *25 rooms*

⚲ *In-room: a/c, refrigerator. In-hotel: bar, pool* ▭ *MC, V* ⊘ *Closed mid-Oct.–Mar.* ❐ *BP.*

$$$$
Fodor's Choice
★

🏨 **Caesar Augustus.** A continuing favorite of the Hollywood set, this landmark has long been considered a Caprese paradise thanks to its breathtaking perch atop an Anacapri cliff. Of course, let's not forget the grandeur of its villa, gardens, terraces, and pool. As for accommodations, think chic, charming, and casual: the chairs are plump, the beds enormous, the bouquets fragrant, and most rooms have a Jacuzzi. You won't give a second's thought to decor, however, once you catch sight of the fabled stone terrace and its Cinerama view of the Bay of Naples or the infinity pool—a jaw-dropping extravaganza nearly levitating 1,000 feet over the sea and easily one of the most glamorous spots on Earth. But beware: the rooms on the back of this hotel are very close to the main Anacapri road—be sure to get a bay-side room (or better still, one of the new suites set in the cliff side far from the main building). Blissfully distant from Capri Town's crowds, the hotel has a private van to shuttle pampered guests back and forth. The poolside restaurant is open to nonguests, as are the hotel's lovely summer weekly classical concerts. **Pros:** pool area possibly the most glamorous place in Campania; staggering bay views if you get the right rooms. **Cons:** a bit far from the action; near noisy main road. ✉ *Via G. Orlandi 4, Anacapri* ☎ *081/8373395, 081/8371421 reservations* ⊕ *www.caesar-augustus. com* ✆ *55 rooms* ⚲ *In-room: a/c, safe, refrigerator, Wi-Fi. In-hotel: restaurant, bar, pool, Wi-Fi hotspot* ▭ *AE, DC, MC, V* ⊘ *Closed Nov.–mid-Apr.* ❐ *BP.*

$$$$
Fodor's Choice
★

🏨 **Capri Palace.** It is no surprise that this is a favorite of the *cogniscenti*, famous or otherwise. The hotel is vast, perhaps part of the problem on tiny, chic Capri for, like the Quisisana, this place borders on convention-group size. Big size, however, can also deliver bonuses, such as the top-rated L'Olivo restaurant, whose sleek decor of vintage photography, spotlights, and antique-style columns make a fitting showcase for Michelin-starred chef Oliver Glowig (best bet: Mediterranean blue lobster with saffron, black lentils, and cacao beans). Many rooms are also enormous and are adorned with lantern lights, billowing linens, and teakwood cabinetry. Some opt for the art- and film-theme Monroe, Callas, or Warhol suites—while others can afford the rooms with private pools. A shuttle bus will whisk you to their beach club and its Il Riccio restaurant. **Pros:** superb cuisine; the finest quality service. **Cons:** too close to the center of Anacapri; as for prices, if you don't go first class, your heirs will. ✉ *Via Capodimonte 2b, Anacapri* ☎ *081/9780111* ⊕ *www.capripalace.com* ✆ *77 rooms* ⚲ *In-room: a/c, safe, refrigerator, Wi-Fi. In-hotel: restaurant, pool, gym, spa, Wi-Fi hotspot* ▭ *AE, DC, MC, V* ⊘ *Closed Nov.-mid-Mar.*

NIGHTLIFE AND THE ARTS

As would be expected, Capri offers a fair spread of evening entertainment, especially on weekends and during the busier months of July and August, when many upper-crust Italians from the mainland occupy their holiday homes on the island. For music that's fairly gentle on the ears, try one of the traditional *taverne*, which are peculiar to Capri Town.

There are also a number of discos and piano bars from which to choose, but the nightlife is more laid-back than Naples or even Ischia. On summer nights the place to be seen showing off your tan and sipping your extra-dry martini is the Piazzetta.

BARS

Panta Rei. Billing itself as a sophisticated bar, this is where to find the cognoscenti sipping their *aperitivi* on the terrace overlooking Marina Grande. In a converted cinema down a short flight of stairs off Via Roma, this doubles as a Beauty Spa by day, with sauna and heated pool, but by night the minimalist lounge bar area comes alive with the coolest sounds from the "guru DJ," live music, or piano bar. ⊠ *Via Lo Palazzo 1, Capri* ☎ *081/8378898* ⊕ *www.pantareicapri.it* ☎ *€20 including drink at bar* ⊗ *Beauty spa daily 10 am–8 pm, lounge bar daily 7 pm–1:30 am. Closed mid-Nov.–mid-Dec., Jan.–Mar.*

Under the shadow of the Piazzetta's clock tower is **Pulalli** (⊠ *Piazza Umberto I 4* ☎ *081/8374108*), where you can enjoy tapas-style snacks while sipping wine on the open terrace.

DISCOS

Capri Town's Via Camerelle has the island's most popular late-night spots, often found in underground cellars. If you are looking for the nightlife edge, try **Number Two** (⊠ *Via Camerelle 1, Capri Town* ☎ *081/8377078*), as admission (€20) also includes access to sister club Number One, where live music is performed until the small hours. Another Camerelle hot spot is **Le Clochard** (⊠ *Via Camerelle 63, Capri Town* ☎ *081/8377308*), the chicest club to open in 2010 and frequented by the same crowd who flock to Anema e Core; house music and hip-hop is the order of the night.

For 360-degree music almost any night of the year, **Red** (⊠ *Via Orlandi 259, Anacapri* ☎ *081/8372523*) is the clubbing spot for cognoscenti of various ages. Unlike most other clubs in Italy, no admission fee is charged, though you're expected to knock back the odd drink (about €15 each). A new "wine corner" is pulling in the thirtysomethings. This is the only club open all year. On Thursday in July and August, make a point of going down to Antonio Beach near the Faro, where Red arranges open-air discos by the water's edge beginning at 10:30 pm.

TAVERNE

Anema e Core (⊠ *Via Sella Orta 39/e, Capri Town* ☎ *081/8376461* ⊕ *www.anemaecore.com*) means "soul and heart" in Caprese dialect. This popular place is tucked down a quiet side street, a two-minute walk from the Piazzetta. Admission (€40) includes an eclectic range of lightish live music (after 11 pm) and a drink from the bar. No food is served, so come well sated. Frequented by celebrities, dancing here occasionally takes to the tables. The spot is closed Wednesday and is usually open from 9 pm in summer months. Reservations are essential on weekends. Tucked well away from the hub of the Piazzetta is **Guarracino** (⊠ *Via Castello 7, Capri Town* ☎ *081/8370514*), the place for traditional Neapolitan guitar music with a hint of Latin-American rhythm.

THE ARTS

Culturally speaking, Capri has a fairly long hibernation, awakening briefly for the New Year celebrations. Recitals and other low-key cultural events are held in October and January in the Centro Caprense Ignazio Cerio, though from June through September the island comes alive with various events, including an outdoor concert season. It's a magical experience to see works performed at Anacapri's Villa San Michele (on Friday evenings) or on the spectacular terrace of the Hotel Caesar Augustus. In general, for information about cultural events and art exhibitions, ask at the local tourist information office or scan the posters in shop windows.

The Certosa di San Giacomo is the cultural heart of the island, hosting events throughout the year. Concerts are held in the two attractive cloisters from June through September. The beginning of September sees the Certosa International Arts Festival, hosting film screenings, recitals, and readings (⊕ *www.capricertosa.com*), while the New Year's Eve festivities are eclipsed by the film festival Capri Hollywood (⊕ *www. caprihollywood.com*).

Capri also caters for the literati, with Le Conversazioni (⊕ *www. leconversazioni.it*) presenting well-known authors reading from their works in Piazzetta di Tragara. Held at the beginning of July, previous editions have featured David Byrne, Martin Amis, and Ethan Coen.

SPORTS AND THE OUTDOORS

Although there are several tennis courts on the island, most are restricted access, so the vast majority of people looking to burn excess energy do so at sea level or below. For naturalists, bird-watching is particularly good in spring and autumn as Capri lies on a migration pathway, and botany lovers will be thrilled by the island's various nature trails, especially from April to June. For a simple workout, the **Capri Gym Fitness Center** (⊠ *Via Roma 10, Capri* ☎ *081/8375430*) allows one-off visits.

SWIMMING AND STABILIMENTI

Sorry—Capri is not noted for fine beaches. "Strand-ed" habitués cram onto **Marina Piccola**, generally considered to have the best beach on the island. It's certainly the most historic: Homer believed this to be the legendary spot where the Sirens nearly snared Odysseus. Social go-getters seem to prefer the less picturesque Bagni di Tiberio beach near Marina Grande. At Marina Piccola, expect to pay about €15 per person for the use of showers, lockers, and a sun chair/sun bed. It's definitely worth investing in snorkeling gear, as the sea is rich in marine life, and visibility is often excellent.

Rather than visiting public beaches, many sun worshippers opt to enjoy the fabled *stabilimenti balneari* (private bathing lidos) scattered around the island, some of which offer real relaxation and unbelievable views. One of the most famous is **La Fontelina** (⊠ *Località Faraglioni, Capri Town* ☎ *081/8370845* 🎫 *€18 admission includes locker and sun chair, €9 for beach umbrella*), open from April to October. At the foot of the Faraglioni rocks, the lido has a magical setting. There's no beach here, so the lido isn't suitable for children. You can get to La Fontelina by using a rocky path that begins at the end of Via Tragara; others prefer to take a ferry (€4) from the more accessible Marina Piccola during the afternoon. The excellent but pricey restaurant is only open for lunch. The **Lido del Faro** (✉ *Località Punta Carena, Anacapri* ☎ *081/8371798* ⊕ *www.lidofaro.com* ✎ *€20 admission includes locker and sun bed, €6 beach umbrella*), on the Anacapri side of the island, is set amid rocks with a natural basin as a seawater swimming pool and is open from April to October during daylight hours. The sun usually beats down on this westerly headland all day while on summer nights the restaurant provides a unique setting for enjoying the freshest fish. The lido is easily accessible by bus from Anacapri. Note that many other stabilimenti are set on the enchanting Marina Piccola, particularly the famous Canzone del Mare.

SHOPPING

Although Capri is unlikely to be a bargain-hunter's paradise, shopping here is almost an experience in its own right. Frustratingly though, goods are often displayed without price tags, which means you have to shop Italian-style: decide whether you like an article first and then inquire about its price, rather than vice versa.

BOOKSTORES

An antiquarian's delight and one of the most elegant bookstores in Italy, **La Conchiglia** (✉ *Via Camerelle 18, Capri Town* ☎ *081/8378199* ⊕ *www.laconchigliacapri.com* ✉ *Via Le Botteghe 12, Capri Town* ☎ *081/8376577* ✉ *Via Orlandi 205, Anacapri* ☎ *081/8372646*) not only offers the largest selection of books on Capri and the Bay of Naples islands but publishes many sumptuous tomes through its own imprint. In addition to their own books, an attractive array of 19th-century prints, gouaches, and vintage editions of English books on Capri and the south of Italy is offered at their art gallery–cum–store on Via Camerelle, although a greater variety of titles is offered at their Via Le Botteghe location. There's also a branch in Anacapri.

JEWELRY

The extra security of being on a virtually crime-free island means that you can actually wear the expensive items you might want to buy. Some tax-free "bargains" might be possible from that Capri institution, **Chantecler** (✉ *Via Vittorio Emanuele 51, Capri Town* ☎ *081/8370544* ⊕ *www.chantecler.it*), where you can find those distinctive locally crafted brooch or some cuff links made from ancient Roman coins. **La Campanina** (✉ *Via Vittorio Emanuele 18/20, Capri Town* ☎ *081/8370643* ⊕ *www.lacampaninacapri.com*) is the place to head to snag a miniature replica of the "Bell of Good Fortune" from Anacapri's church of San Michele, first produced for President Roosevelt in 1944.

PERFUME

If you're looking for something that's easily portable to take back from Capri, then eau de toilette, a potpourri, or perfumed soap might be just the thing. **Carthusia** has been making perfumes since 1948, but—as they will proudly tell you—the tradition of perfumery on the island stretches back hundreds of years to the days of Queen Giovanna of Anjou. The factory, close to the Certosa di San Giacomo, is open for visits and a limited range of purchases, although there are no official guided tours of the premises. ⊠ *Factory: Via Matteotti 2d, Capri Town* ☎ *081/8370368; Showroom:*⊠ *Via Camerelle 10, Capri Town* ☎ *081/8370529; Showroom:*⊠ *Via Capodimonte 26, Anacapri* ☎ *081/8373668* ⊕ *www.carthusia.com.*

RESORTWEAR
Capri's main shopping streets—the Via Vittorio Emanuele and Via Camerelle, down the road from the island's main square, La Piazzetta—are crammed with world-famous names (Fendi, Gucci, Prada, Dolce & Gabbana, Benetton, Ferragamo, Hermès). But if you're overwhelmed by the choice and are looking for something stylish but Capri-distinctive—in an astonishing range of colors—then check out the bright hand-block prints on clothes, bags, and shoes by Capri-local Livio De Simone at **La Parisienne** (⊠ *Piazza Umberto I 7, Capri Town* ☎ *081/8370283* ⊕ *www.laparisiennecapri.it*)occupying this spot for over a century; here, too, you can purchase copies of the original capri pants worn by such gilded folk as Audrey Hepburn. The boutiques of Roberto Russo are favored by fashion folk. **Russo Uomo** (⊠ *Piazzetta Quisisana, Capri Town* ☎ *081/8388200*) has one of the largest selections of chic togs in town. Sandals are a Capri specialty. With a family business stretching back to 1917, **Vincenzo Faiella** (⊠ *Via Le Botteghe 21, Capri Town* ☎ *347/6780079*) is justifiably proud of his made-to-measure footwear. Expect to pay €60 to €110 for a carefully handcrafted pair.

Da Costanzo (⊠ *Via Roma 49, Capri Town* ☎ *081/8378077*) is the "king" of Caprese sandalmakers since Jackie O, Sophia Loren, and Grace Kelly all purchased pairs here in the good old days.

ISCHIA: THE SEASIDE CURE

While Capri leaves you breathless with its charm and beauty, Ischia (pronounced EES-kee-ah, with the stress on the first syllable) takes time to cast its spell. In fact, an overnight stay is definitely not long enough for the island to get into your blood. Here you have to look harder for the signs of antiquity, the traffic can be reminiscent of Naples—albeit on a good day—and the island displays all the hallmarks of rapid, uncontrolled urbanization. Ischia does have its jewels, though. There are the wine-growing villages beneath the lush volcanic slopes of Monte Epomeo, and unlike Capri, the island enjoys a life of its own that survives when the tourists head home. Ischia has some lovely hotel-resorts high in the hills, offering therapeutic programs and rooms with dramatic views. If you want to plunk down in the sun for a few days and tune out the world, go down to sea level: against the towering backdrop of Monte Epomeo and with one of the island's inviting beaches—or natural hot baths—close at hand, you might wonder what Emperor Augustus could have been thinking when he surrendered Ischia to the Neapolitans in return for Capri.

Ischia

Unlike Capri, Ischia is volcanic in origin. From its hidden reservoir of seething molten matter come the thermal springs said to cure whatever ails you. Today the island's main industry, tourism, revolves around the over 100 thermal baths; most of them are attached to hotels. In the height of summer, the island's population of 60,000 swells more than sixfold, with considerable strain placed on local water resources and with public transport facilities and with decibel counts rising notably. However, most of the *confusione* is concentrated within the island's six towns and along its main roads, and it's relatively easy to find quiet spots even close to the beaten path.

Much of the 23 mi (37 km) of coastline are punctuated with a continuum of *stabilimenti balneari* (private bathing establishments) in summer (there are also lots of public beaches), set against the scenic backdrop of Monte Epomeo and its verdant slopes. Most port traffic to the island—mainly ferries and hydrofoils from the mainland—is channeled into Ischia Porto with some arrivals at Casamicciola and Forio, burgeoning resorts and busy spa centers. The Castello Aragonese in Ischia Ponte, which is a vast medieval complex rather than just a castle, is one of the island's main historic sights; Lacco Ameno, with its immense archaeological heritage and more upscale ambience, is a good base for exploring the north of the island; Forio is famous for the grand gardens of La

Ischia's Castello Aragonese sits on its own island, just offshore from Ischia Ponte.

Mortella and the Poseiden thermal baths. Buses between the main towns are frequent and cheap, though somewhat overcrowded.

VISITOR INFORMATION

Housed in the historic municipal bath building, **Azienda Autonoma di Cura, Soggiorno e Turismo** (✉ *Ufficio Informazioni, Banchina Porto Salvo, Ischia Porto* ☎ *081/5074231* 📠 *081/5074230* ⊕ *www.infoischiaprocida. it*) in Ischia Porto is open Monday–Saturday 9 am–2 pm and 3–8.

ISCHIA PORTO

4 km (3 mi) east of Casamicciola.

Ischia Porto is the largest town on the island and the usual point of debarkation. It's no workaday port, however, but a pretty resort with plenty of hotels and low, flat-roofed houses on terraced hillsides above the water. Known by the Romans as Villa dei Bagni, its villas and gardens are framed by umbrella pines and locals mingle with German tourists in the narrow streets.

GETTING HERE

Ferries and hydrofoils bring you here from Naples and Pozzuoli.

EXPLORING

Ischia Porto's harbor area was originally a landlocked lake in a volcanic crater: the Bourbon king Ferdinand II had a channel cut to create an opening seaward, and then created a sheltered port (1854). As you walk into the town along the waterfront, note the grandiose facade of the municipal baths (where Ferdinand II used to take the waters), now used for town council offices and occasional art exhibitions. While exploring

ISCHIA: GETTING HERE AND AROUND

GETTING HERE

Ischia is well connected with the mainland in all seasons. The last boats leave for Naples and Pozzuoli at about 8 pm (though in the very high season there is a midnight sailing), and you should allow plenty of time for getting to the port and buying a ticket. Ischia has three ports—Ischia Porto, Casamicciola, and Forio (hydrofoils only)—so you should choose your ferry or hydrofoil according to your destination. Non-Italians can bring cars to the island relatively freely.

Alilauro (☎ 081/4972222 ⊕ www. alilauro.it) has roughly one hydrofoil per hour traveling from Beverello and Mergellina, Naples, to Ischia Porto (€16, travel time 40 minutes). From May through September, seven hydrofoils per day, at weekends, depart for Forio (€17, travel time 50 minutes).

Caremar (☎ 892/123 ⊕ www. caremar.it) has six hydrofoil departures from Molo Beverello, Naples, to Ischia Porto (€16, travel time between 45 minutes and 1 hour) and six ferry departures per day, from Calata Porta di Massa, Naples (€9.60, travel time 1 hour, 30 minutes). Ferry departures are also available from Pozzuoli (€8.60, travel time 1 hour).

MedMar (☎ 081/3334411 ⊕ www. medmargroupi.it) has seven daily departures from Calata Porta di Massa, Naples (€10.65, travel time 1 hour, 30 minutes), and twelve ferries daily departing from Pozzuoli, sometimes docking at Casamicciola (€9.65, travel time 1 hour).

SNAV (☎ 081/4285555 ⊕ www.snav. it) offers four hydrofoils every hour from Mergellina or Molo Beverello,

Naples, to the marina of Casamicciola (€19, travel time 50 minutes).

In 2010 **TrenItalia** (☎ 892021 ⊕ www.trenitalia.com) introduced the integrated "Treno + Nave" ticket, which transports travelers from Naples's train station to the ferry port and the next island departure.

GETTING AROUND

Ischia's bus network reaches all the major sites and beaches on one of its 15 lines. The principal lines are CD and CS, circling the island in clockwise and counterclockwise directions—in the summer months runs continue until after midnight. The main bus terminus is in Ischia Porto at the start of Via Cosca, where buses run by the company SEPSA (☎ 081/991808 ⊕ www. eavbus.it) radiate out around the island. There are also convenient *fermate* (stops) at the two main beaches—Citara and Maronti—with timetables displayed at the terminus. Tickets cost €1.30 for 90 minutes, €4.20 for 24 hours; note that conditions can get hot and crowded at peak beach-visiting times.

A number of car and scooter rental facilities are available. Note that police are vigilant about seat-belt violations. About 200 yards from Ischia Porto's ferry terminal, **Del Franco** (✉ Via Alfredo De Luca 127, Ischia Porto ☎ 081/991334), opposite Hotel Jolly, has a fair range of sturdy bicycles costing €12 per day. Closer to the port, facing the marina, **EuroScooterCar** (✉ Via Iasolino 45, Ischia Porto ☎ 081/982722) offers cars from €35 daily and scooters from €30 (add €5 in August).

Ischia Porto, be sure to stop by **Ciccio** (✉ *Via Jasolino, 1*), near the ferry piers, for the best gelato on Ischia. As for serious dining, note that most restaurants are concentrated around what the locals call the *Riva Destra* (Left Bank) or the eastern side of the port harbor.

WHERE TO EAT AND STAY

$$
SOUTHERN
ITALIAN
✕ **Da Gennaro.** The oldest restaurant on the island, this has been a favorite of the stars, including Tom Cruise and Sophia Loren. Family-run, it opened on the seafront overlooking the boats in 1965 and continues to serve excellent fish in a convivial atmosphere. Specialties include *risotto alla pescatore* (rice with shellfish) and linguine *all'aragosta* (with lobster). In perfect English, friendly owner Gennaro will happily take you through the celebrity-laden wall of photos. ✉ *Via Porto 59* 🕾 *081/992917* ▤ *AE, DC, MC, V* ⊘ *Closed Nov.–mid-Mar.*

$$$
🏨 **Hotel La Villarosa Terme.** Part of a family-run chain of four hotels in the town of Ischia, this is set in a villa and garden, with a thermally heated pool. Guest rooms are bright and airy, with varied decor—some rooms have charming antiques, others are more modern. Meals are served in the roof garden, overlooking the town of Ischia and the Bay of Naples— and you must reserve well in advance. It's in the heart of Ischia Porto, just off the busy shopping street Via Roma, and a short walk from the beach. **Pros:** view from roof garden; wonderful pool. **Cons:** maybe too close to the town; some rooms are more attractive than others. ✉ *Via Giacinto Gigante 5,* 🕾 *081/991316* ⊕ *www.dicohotels.it* ⟿ *37 rooms* △ *In-room: a/c, safe, refrigerator. In-hotel: restaurant, pool* ▤ *DC, MC, V* ⊘ *Closed Nov.–Mar.* ⅰⓄⅰ *MAP.*

NIGHTLIFE AND THE ARTS

Nightlife on Ischia starts late in the evening and you should be prepared to stay the course until the early hours. In some private gardens, occasional concerts and cultural events are offered during the summer months, with the highlight being the **Ischia Jazz Festival** (⊕ *www. ischiajazz.eu)* at the beginning of September.

Valentino Club (✉ *Corso Vittorio Colonna 97, Ischia Porto* 🕾 *081/982569* ⊕ *www.valentinoischia.eu)*, in the center of Ischia Porto, is the focal point for all but the gel-and-scooter set, with clientele in its early twenties and above. Admission varies between €16 and €25, depending on what's on offer.

Offering live music and DJ sets, **Blue Jane** (✉ *Pagoda Beach, Ischia Porto* 🕾 *081/993296* ⊕ *www.janeischia.it)*, shaped like a boat, has a spectacular setting on the port's entry overlooking the bay. The club is a landmark, and visitors have included Mick Jagger and Gianni Agnelli.

ISCHIA PONTE

2 km (1 mi) southeast of Ischia Porto.

The spectacular Castello Aragonese, towering atop an islet just off the main shore, landmarks Ischia Ponte. The town's name (Ischia Bridge) refers to the striking causeway built in the mid-15th century to connect it with the rest of Ischia. While it has an amazing history, the castle also looms large in today's Ischia, as it becomes the appropriately cinematic setting for the Ischia Film Festival every July, with occasional exhibitions held in the Chiesa dell'Immacolata.

GETTING HERE

Take Bus No. 7 from Ischia Porto. If arriving by car or scooter, bear in mind that the access to the town is pedestrianised during peak hours (there is, however, a large car park).

EXPLORING

★ Access to the spectacular citadel of the **Castello Aragonese** is via an elevator from its base, and the various walks at the top are clearly signposted. While taking in the whole site, pause at one of the two bars and enjoy the stunning views from the various vantage points. The little island was settled as early as the 5th century BC, when the tyrant Hiero of Syracuse came to the aid of Cumae in its power struggle against the Etruscans. This was his reward: an almost unassailable natural islet more than 300 feet high, on which he erected high watchtowers to monitor movements across the Bay of Naples. The island changed hands in the succession of centuries, with Greeks from Neapolis, Romans, Visigoths, Vandals, Ostrogoths, Saracens, Normans, Swabians, and Angevins successively modifying the fortifications and settlements. Ischia Ponte was where the population of Ischia sought refuge in 1301, when Epomeo's last eruption buried the town of Geronda on the other side of the causeway. The new influx of inhabitants led to a flurry of building activity, most notably the **Cattedrale dell'Assunta,** built above a preexisting chapel that then became its crypt. In the following century the Angevin castle was rebuilt by Alfonso of Aragon (1438), who gave it much of its present form. However, its turbulent history continued well into the 19th century, when it was seriously damaged by the English in their attempts to dislodge the French during the Napoleonic Wars (1809).

Two hours should be enough to give you a feel of the citadel, stroll along its ramparts, and visit its key religious sites. Don't miss the frescoed 14th-century crypt beneath the cathedral (Giotto school), although the ruined cathedral itself, with its noticeable 18th-century additions—such as the baroque stucco work—is quite atmospheric. ✉ *Castello Aragonese, Ischia Ponte* ☎ *081/992834* ⊕ *www.castelloaragonese.it* ✉ *€10* ⊙ *June–Sept., daily 9–8; Mar.–May, Oct.–Jan. 8, daily 9–5.*

Housed in the Palazzo dell' Orologio, the town's **Museo del Mare Ischia** is dedicated to the daily life of fishermen. Ship models, archaeological finds, nautical instruments, and the stray modern art show make up the small holdings. ✉ *Via Giovanni Da Procida 3* ☎ *081/981124* ⊕ *www.museodelmareischia.it* ✉ *€2.60* ⊙ *July and Aug., daily 10:30–12:30 and 6:30–10; Sept. and Oct., Apr.–June, daily 10:30–12:30 and 3–7; Nov.–Jan. and Mar., daily 10:30–12:30. Closed Feb.*

WHERE TO EAT AND STAY

$$
SOUTHERN
ITALIAN

✗**Ristorante Cocò Gelo.** This inviting restaurant sits on the causeway linking the Aragonese castle to the rest of Ischia and is renowned for its fresh fish, which is highly prized by the Ischitani. Try the linguine *ai calamaretti* (with squid); a good starter in winter months is the vegetable-based *zuppa di fagioli e scarola* (bean and escarole soup). ✉ *Via*

Aragonese 1 ☎ *081/981823* ⊟ *AE, DC, MC, V* ⊗ *Closed Jan. and Feb. and Wed. Oct.–Mar.*

$–$$
Fodor'sChoice
★

🏨 **Albergo Il Monastero.** Within the Castello Aragonese at Ischia Ponte, with rustic rooms that peer down into the Mediterranean hundreds of feet below, this is the ultimate in ambience combined with the peace and quiet of a traffic-free area. Guest rooms are on the simple side, but the management is friendly and tries to warm things up. You can also choose to dine here (guests only) on the spectacular terrace, if you can't face the climb down to the town; there is no printed menu but the resident chef specializes in the island cuisine and, if you're lucky, you might be in for real treats like Ischian rabbit. This is a highly popular hotel, so book way in advance. **Pros:** stunning views; how often do you get to stay in a real castle? **Cons:** rather difficult to negotiate the steps before reaching the elevator; some consider this too far away from the town's action. ⊠ *Castello Aragonese 3* ☎ *081/992435* ⊕ *www. albergoilmonastero.it* ⟿ *21 rooms* ⌂ *In-room: no a/c, no TV, Internet. In-hotel: restaurant* ⊟ *AE, DC, MC, V* ⊗ *Closed Nov.– Mar.* ﴾⦿﴿ *BP.*

$
★

🏨 **Villa Antonio.** Blessed with a stunning perch over the Bay of Cartaromana, with the Castello Aragonese posing front and center in a panoramic vista, the Antonio offers a quiet haven five minutes from the crowds. Direct access to the sea is a few private steps away from the lovely whitewashed and casual villa, but sun beds abound at several garden levels so most guests tend not to stray too far. Owner Antonio's brother Giovanni is a sculptor—his granite and marble works are scattered around the flower-decked terraces. Rooms are basic, but most have air-conditioning and all have sea views. **Pros:** no better view of the castle; seaside location. **Cons:** many steps to negotiate before elevator; guest rooms' small windows don't do justice to the view. ⊠ *Via S. Giuseppe della Croce* ☎ *081/982660* ⊕ *www.villantonio.it* ⟿ *18 rooms* ⌂ *In-room: a/c, safe, refrigerator. In-hotel: bar* ⊟ *No credit cards* ⊗ *Closed Nov.–mid-Mar.* ﴾⦿﴿ *BP.*

NIGHTLIFE AND THE ARTS

There's a rich tradition in Ischian local festivals, with the **Feast of Sant'Anna** (July 26) holding pride of place with its skillful choreography and floating procession in the marina at Ischia Ponte below the Aragonese Castle.

THE ARTS

The free **Ischia Film Festival** (⊕ *www.ischiafilmfestival.it*) takes over the Castello Aragonese for a week each July, focusing—appropriately, given its unbeatable location—on films with stunning landscapes.

Midway between Ischia Porto and Ischia Ponte, **Bar Calise** is allegedly "the biggest bar in Europe." Here is all you need for a good night out in one garden—you can choose between live music, a nightclub ('O Spasso), a piano bar, a restaurant-pizzeria, or a more traditional caffè. And if you have a hankering for a *cornetto* late at night, this is the only place on the island to find such pastry delicacies after midnight. Vetern Emiddio Calise runs this complex as well as four other bars and *pasticcerie* (try their specialty Monte Epomeo on Sunday) around the island. ✉ *Piazza degli Eroi, Ischia* ☎ *081/991270* ⊕ *www.barcalise.com* ⊘ *Nov.–Easter, Thurs.–Tues. 7–1.*

CASAMICCIOLA

2 km (1 mi) east of Lacco Ameno.

Known properly as the spa town of Casamicciola Terme, with the largest concentration of thermal baths on the island, the lower town revolves around the busy Piazza Marina with its large bust of the Italian king Vittorio Emanuele II and its marble plaque honoring Henrik Ibsen, who was inspired by the beauty of the area to write *Peer Gynt* here. Although much of the town was destroyed in an 1883 earthquake, it has retained some charming examples of 19th-century architecture.

GETTING HERE

Take Bus No. 1/CD/CS from Ischia Porto. Bus No. 3 climbs to the upper part of the town.

EXPLORING

Other than a small 19th-century geophysical observatory there are few sights in town but that doesn't bother most visitors, who have headed here to enjoy the famous spa hotels. Note the stunning, although now derelict, building on the left as you approach the town from Ischia: it is Pio Monte della Misericordia, opened in 1604 as a hospital that is in the history books because it housed Europe's first spa.

WHERE TO EAT AND STAY

$ ✕ **Ristorante Calise Capriccio.** The town's most centrally located restaurant
SOUTHERN is run by Caffè Calise, which has been in the business since 1925. Bang
ITALIAN in the middle of the square, this one-time nightclub has a terrace overlooking the busy road and the boats of the tourist marina. Presided over by Giuseppe Marra (with an impressive international CV), the menu is based on the day's catch with an experimental twist. Starters include fried *calamaretti* (squid) with onion and swordfish with capers. Local wine accompanies *paccheri con cozze e pecorino*, a bold combination of pasta with mussels sprinkled with cheese. Leave space for the glorious deserts, all from the renowned Calise *pasticceria*—try the yummy Valentina cake (strawberries and cream on a sponge base). ✉ *Piazza Marina* ☎ *081/994724* ▭ *AE, DC, MC, V* ⊘ *Closed Nov.–Mar.*

$$ 🏨 **Albergo l'Approdo.** Near Casamicciola's port, spas, and town center, this is a small hotel with a fine array of facilities. The spa has an indoor pool, and pampers guests with the beauty treatments on offer, including ayurveda massage and reflexology. An elevator whisks those who prefer the beach down to sea level, but most stick by the outdoor pool. **Pros:** wonderful elevated views; pool perched above bay. **Cons:** the beach is across a busy road; showers are tiny. ✉ *Via Eddomade 29* ☎ *081/994077* ⊕ *www.lapprodohotel.com* ⤵ *39 rooms* 🛏 *In-room: a/c, safe, refrigerator. In-hotel: restaurant, bar, pools, spa* ▭ *AE, DC, MC, V* ⑩ *MAP.*

$$$$ 🏨 **Terme Manzi.** One of Ischia's newest luxury hotels (yet also the oldest),
★ Terme Manzi originally opened in the mid-19th century and reopened in 2006 after four years of restoration. It was here that so-called "thermal

tourism" began, in the Gurgitello springs, one of the largest spas in the south of Italy—the bath where Giuseppe Garibaldi bathed is conserved in a corner. Sybaritic is the word to describe the decor: hypercolorful mosaic columns, gilded Stil Empire furniture, and lots of Las Vegasian glitz. The exterior is glamorously white-on-white, lined with balconies, and with a roofline topped with Moroccan-style onion domes. The staff is ready to pamper you with every kind of beauty treatment imaginable, and you can top it all off in the open-air roof pool, surrounded by Ischia's rich vegetation. The Mosaic restaurant, the only establishment on the island with two Michelin stars, is successfully ambitious. **Pros:** some say five stars is not enough; wonderful indoor pool. **Cons:** located in a nondescript square; very far from beach. ⊠ *Piazza Bagni 4* ☎ *081/994722* ⊕ *www.termemanzihotel.it* ⤵ *61 rooms* ⌂ *In-room: a/c, safe, refrigerator, Internet. In-hotel: restaurant, bar, pool, spa, Wi-Fi hotspot, parking* ⊟ *AE, DC, MC, V* ⦿*BP.*

LACCO AMENO

6 km (4 mi) west of Ischia Porto, 3 km (2 mi) north of Forio.

Lacco Ameno was colonized by the Greeks as early as the 8th century BC, and the landscape here has remained epic: it was used as the backdrop for the barge scene in Elizabeth Taylor's *Cleopatra*. For all its famous visitors, the town does not have a jet-setty vibe and looks lackluster on first impression. But take a walk down the main road, which turns into the Corso Rizzoli along the seafront and you will find a pedestrianized heaven: flanked by low-key shops, caffès, and restaurants and lined with cobblestones, the promenade runs for several idyllic blocks with the bay rarely out of sight.

GETTING HERE
Take Bus No. 1/CD/CS from Ischia Porto.

EXPLORING
The smallest of the six *comuni* (municipalities) on the island, Lacco Ameno is a mecca for some of Italy's rich and famous. Magnate Gianni Agnelli used to anchor his yacht every summer close to the Fungo, a most distinctive mushroom-shaped rock in volcanic tufa sculpted by wave action in the small marina, now one of the most notable natural landmarks on Ischia. Luchino Visconti, the noted realist film director and opera designer, had his Villa La Colombaia nearby in Baia San Montano, now used by the local council to promote the film industry on the island. The Bay of San Montano, a brilliant blue-sapphire buckle along the coast, is now the setting for the Giardini Negombo, the most stylish of the thermal complexes on the island. At sunset, Corso Rizzoli becomes a romantic's heaven.

★ Lacco Ameno's archaeological importance—it rests below the first Greek settlement on Italian soil on the island, at Monte Vico to the west—is amply reflected by the finds displayed in Ischia's top museum, the **Museo Archeologico di Pithecusae,** and the ancient site beneath the church of Santa Restituta. The museum occupies much of the Villa Arbusto, built by Carlo d'Aquaviva in 1785 on top of a Bronze Age settlement. Inaugurated in 1999, with the directors of both the British

The Santuario del Soccorso in Forio is Ischia's most picturesque church.

Museum and the Louvre in attendance, its eight rooms house a wide range of Greek pottery unearthed at the ancient necropolis site near the Baia di San Montano, much of it dating to the earliest years of the Greek colony (late 8th century BC), including Nestor's Cup, the oldest known kotyle vase in existence. Villa Arbusto hosts occasional musical *serate,* or evening soirées, in summer months. ⊠ *Villa Arbusto* ☎ *081/900356* ⊕ *museopithecusae.campaniabeniculturali.it* ✉ *€5* ⊗ *June–Sept., Tues.– Sun., 9:30–1 and 4–8; Apr., daily 9:30–1 and 3–5.*

Beside the nearby church of Santa Restituta, almost completely rebuilt following a catastrophic earthquake in 1883, you can gain access to the underground excavations at the **Museo e Scavi Santa Restituta,** which are a memorable lesson in stratigraphy. Discovered in 1950 when the old majolica pavement above was removed, the underground site shows the building activities of several different periods (archaic Greek, Hellenistic, Roman, and Early Christian), faithful reconstructions of an ancient loom and a miller's workshop, and the various finds discovered in situ. Although the structures are poorly labeled and it takes an expert eye to discern which buildings belong to which periods, this gives you a good idea of historical continuity on the island. ⊠ *Piazza Santa Restituta* ☎ *081/992442* ✉ *€3* ⊗ *Apr.–Oct., Mon.–Sat. 9:30–1 and 4:30–8, Sun. 9:30–1.*

WHERE TO STAY

$$$$ 🏨 **Albergo della Regina Isabella.** Built in 1956 and tucked away in an exclusive corner of the beach in Lacco Ameno, Ischia's largest luxury hotel is synonymous with the island's celluloid history—when filming *Cleopatra* on Ischia, Elizabeth Taylor and Richard Burton camped

out here. With full resort facilities and its own private pier (transfers from Naples and Ischia can be arranged), it pampers VIPs and normal mortals with spa treatments. Guest rooms are ample and decorated in warm Mediterranean colors, and most have terraces or balconies, many overlooking the sea. Don't miss the fun of socializing with chic vacationers in the elegant Indaco restaurant—a meal here is worth it just for the fabulous views over the harbor. The Ischia Global Film & Music Festival is held here in July, giving guests a chance to mingle with the stars. **Pros:** central location; considered by locals the best hotel on Ischia. **Cons:** built in the 1950s, not the most elegant of times; rooms are fairly spartan for a hotel in this price category. ⊠ *Piazza Santa Restituta* ☎ *081/994322* ⊕ *www.reginaisabella.it* ⇥ *128 rooms, 8 suites* ⚑ *In-room: a/c, safe, refrigerator. In-hotel: restaurant, bar, tennis court, pools, spa, beachfront, Wi-Fi hotspot, parking* ☰ *AE, DC, MC, V* ⊘ *Closed Nov.–27 Dec. 7; Jan.–mid-Apr.* ¶ *BP.*

$$$$
Fodor's Choice
★

⛺ **Mezzatorre Resort & Spa.** Far from the madding, sunburned crowds that swamp Ischia, this luxurious getaway perches in splendid isolation on the extreme promontory of Punta Cornacchia. The complex is reached through an imposing gate, and a mile or so along a country lane. Standing on the terraces of this renovated fortress, set over the blue Bay of San Montano, with yachts parading below you, it's not hard to understand why film director Luchino Visconti chose to live just up the hill. This hotel has nearly everything to tempt its privileged guests to stay put and *relax*: a glamorous heated pool overlooking a storybook cove, two cosseting restaurants, full health and beauty treatments and hundreds of pine and pomegranate trees for true peace and quiet. The ancient fortress has been sleekly renovated, perhaps too much so from the look of its umber-red exterior. Inside, all is white-on-white glamour with antiques and ancestral portraits as accents. Most guest rooms are in the 16th-century Saracen tower (where Jennifer Lopez shacked up in 2009). The restaurants, Chandelier (haute cucina, evenings only) and the informal Sciué Sciué, are open to nonguests but book in advance. The official address is Forio but this is much closer to Lacco Ameno, where a shuttle bus is available to pick you up. **Pros:** the ideal getaway location; wonderful views. **Cons:** very isolated. ⊠ *Via Mezzatorre 13, Forio d'Ischia* ☎ *081/986111* ⊕ *www.mezzatorre.it* ⇥ *57 rooms* ⚑ *In-room: a/c, safe, refrigerator. In-hotel: restaurant, tennis court, pools, spa, Wi-Fi hotspot, parking* ☰ *AE, DC, MC, V* ⊘ *Closed Nov.–Apr.* ¶ *BP.*

THE ARTS

Though it's only been in existence since 2002, the weeklong **Ischia Global Film & Music Festival** (⊕ *www.ischiaglobal.com*) has become an important festival, attracting such stars as Burt Bacharach, Val Kilmer, Harry Belafonte, Naomi Watts, and Jean-Claude Van Damme. Hosted in July by the luxurious Albergo della Regina Isabella in Lacco Ameno, the event is pleasingly informal.

THE OUTDOORS

If you visit one of Ischia's many *terme,* or spa baths, you will not only be following a well-established tradition stretching back more than 2,000 years but also sampling one of the major contemporary delights of the island. You should allow at least half a day for this experience, but better value is to get there early and indulge until sunset. If you do decide to restrict yourself to half a day, then go in the afternoon, when the hefty entrance fees are slightly lowered. The larger establishments have a plethora of pools offering natural hydromassage at different temperatures and in different settings, with a complement of bars and restaurants to enable customers to stay on the premises right through the day. Most terme are equipped with beauty centers, offering an unbelievably broad range of services, from mud-pack treatments and manicures to tattoo removal and bioenergetic massage.

For the ultimate Ischian spa escape, try the stylishly landscaped park of **Giardini Negombo.** Designed around a beach of the finest sand, by the scenic bay of San Montano, it was created decades ago by Duke Luigi Camerini, a passionate botanist (who named his resort in honor of its resemblance to a bay in Sri Lanka). There are 13 saltwater or thermal pools here, plus facilities for hydromassage, a beauty center with sauna and Turkish bath, five bars, two restaurants, canoe and pedal-boat rental, and, according to the brochure, "a boutique for irresponsible purchases." All this is set in gardens with 500 species of Mediterranean plants and several panoramic views. Everything here—modern stone waterfalls, elegant poolside tables with thatched-leaf umbrellas, sensitive landscaping—is in the finest taste. At night the outdoor arena hosts big-name concerts. ⊠ *Baia di San Montano, Lacco Ameno* ☎ *081/986152* ⊕ *www.negombo.it* 🎫 *€29 all day, €24 after 1 pm; €17 after 4 pm; prices rise by €2–€4 in July and Aug.* ☉ *Mid-Oct.–mid-Apr., daily 8:30–7.*

FORIO

9 km (6 mi) west of Ischia Porto.

Lying close to the main wine-producing area of the island, Forio is a busy seaside resort with beaches barely a minute's walk from its town center. Further along are the small San Francesco and the larger Citara, two of the island's better-known beaches. At first glance, the town seems to provide sad evidence of suburban sprawl (there are more houses without planning permits here than with), and its natural setting of flat coastline is not the most alluring.

GETTING HERE

Take Bus No. 1/CS/CD from Ischia Porto. Bus No. 2 continues to Citara beach and the popular Poseidon Gardens.

EXPLORING

★ However, the island's most picturesque church sits here overlooking the water: the 14th-century whitewashed church of Santa Maria della Neve, down at the harbor, better known as the **Santuario del Soccorso.** This is a good spot for a sunset stroll. You can also get an overview of the town from the Torrione, one of 12 towers built under Aragonese rule in the 15th century to protect Forio's inhabitants from the ever-present threat of pirate raids.

Fodor's Choice
★

Two kilometers (1 mi) north of Forio is one of the most famous gardens in Mediterranean Italy, **La Mortella.** The garden was a labor of love designed in 1956 by the landscape architect Russell Page for Sir William Walton and his Argentine-born wife, Susana. The garden was created within a wide, bowl-shaped, rocky valley, originally not much more than a quarry, overlooking the Bay of San Francesco and with spreading views toward Monte Epomeo and Forio. Lady Walton, who passed away in 2010, was a talented gardener in her own right. She first planted the trees of her childhood here: jacaranda and the rare bromeliad. Native wild plants were encouraged in the upper reaches of the gardens, with dainty vetches and orchids as well as myrtle, from which the garden got its name, La Mortella. Considering the volcanic valley out of which the gardens were sculpted, they are appropriately threaded with pathways of rocks hewn from Vesuvius. In homage to the hot springs of the island, the centerpiece is an elliptical pond with three small islands adorned with the immense boulders that once littered the grounds.

Besides some soothing strolls among the well-labeled flower beds and landscaped rock gardens, try to spend some time in the museum dedicated to the life and works of the late English composer, William Walton. The gardens have excellent facilities, including a shop selling Sir William's music and Lady Walton's lively biography of her husband, *Behind the Facade,* along with two books by her on the Mortella gardens, as well as light, homemade refreshments. A theater was opened in 2006, and hosts a concert series on most weekends. Book well in advance for these tickets. ✉ *Via Francesco Calise 39* ☎ *081/986220* ⊕ *www.lamortella.org* 🎫 *€12, €20 for concert, including visit to garden* ☉ *Apr.–Oct., Tues., Thurs., and weekends 9–7.*

A crenellated white fortress, **La Colombaia** was once the summer residence of noted film director Luchino Visconti, and now houses a permanent exhibition of photographs outlining the history of cinema and theater, as well as promoting art and cultural activities on the island. Built in the early 1900s, it was acquired by Visconti in the 1960s. The Visconti Foundation here has regular film screenings and a literary caffè, as well as occasional contemporary art exhibitions. The villa itself, reopened in 2010 after years of restoration work, boasts stunning views over the Baia San Montano, with the director's ashes housed in the gardens. The official address is the town of Forio but the site is actually closer to Lacco Ameno. ✉ *Via Salvatore Calise 130* ☎ *345/9608296* 🎫 *€5* ☉ *Apr.–Oct., Tues.–Sun. 10–1, 4–7.*

WHERE TO EAT

$

SOUTHERN
ITALIAN

✗**Bar-Ristorante Bagno Teresa.** This is an unpretentious restaurant on Citara Beach (no dress code) that offers a range of fresh seafood at reasonable prices served with lively local wine. If you want to stay light for the afternoon swim, and rent a bed and brolly, this is the place to come—there's no need to order a full Mediterranean splurge. ✉ *Baia di Citara* ☎ *081/908517* 🍽 *AE, MC, V* ☉ *Closed mid-Nov.–Mar.*

$$$

MODERN ITALIAN

✗**Il Melograno.** One of the island's finest restaurants, one of only two with a Michelin star, is tucked away on the road leading to Citara Beach. Try the *crudo italiana* (an Italian take on sushi) to start and then just indulge in food that tastes as good as it looks. New dishes with a twist are regularly introduced—the fried anchovies stuffed with provola cheese and homemade tomato bread was one year's winner. Another specialty is the *beccaccia,* a rabbit dish. Those on a higher budget and with a healthy appetite should treat themselves to the featured special menu, particulary the *Mano Libera,* the chef's choice, replete with local fish and vegetables given a nouvelle twist. Popular as this place is, be sure to reserve for summer dinners. ⊠ *Via G. Mazzella 110* ☎ *081/998450* ⊕ *www.ilmelogranoischia.it* ⊟ *AE, DC, MC, V* ☺ *Closed Jan.–mid-Mar., Mon. and Wed. Nov.–Dec.*

3

WHERE TO STAY

$$ ⛺ **Hotel Semiramis.** A quiet family-run hotel, this is within a minute's walk of Citara Beach and the crowded Giardini Poseidon spa. The rooms are decorated tastefully in thematic styles, with the best and most expensive in the panoramic wing on the upper terrace. Breakfast is served overlooking the beach, and to cap it all, there's a child-friendly, secluded swimming pool tapping water from geothermal aquifers 30 feet down. **Pros:** great views; friendly staff. **Cons:** a lot of steps to negotiate; not much action in the evening. ⊠ *Via G. Macella 236* ☎ *081/907511* ⊕ *www.hotelsemiramisischia.it* ↩ *33 rooms* ⚭ *In-room: a/c, safe, refrigerator. In-hotel: bar, pool* ⊟ *AE, DC, MC, V* ☺ *Closed Nov.–Mar.* ⏹ *BP.*

$$ ⛺ **Il Gattopardo.** Surrounded by verdant Ischian maquis and a vineyard,
★ this modern-style hotel is in the most striking and quiet area of Forio. The two solariums are the ideal place to enjoy the splendid view of the Citara bay and the Epomeo mountain. Thermally heated swimming pools, both indoor and outdoor, are part of the facilities offered in the beauty farm, along with mud therapy, Finnish sauna, and massages. Guest rooms are airy and comfortable, with either terrace or balcony, and the restaurant boasts a wine cellar where you can sample the fruits of the surrounding vineyard. **Pros:** the outdoor pool under the olive trees; friendly staff. **Cons:** the entrance is more akin to a sports club than hotel; some rooms are too close to the action. ⊠ *Via G. Mazzella 146* ☎ *081/997714* ⊕ *www.ilgattopardo.com* ↩ *72 rooms* ⚭ *In-room: a/c, safe, refrigerator. In-hotel: restaurant, bar, tennis court, pools, Wi-Fi hotspot, parking* ⊟ *AE, DC, MC, V* ☺ *Closed Nov.–Mar.* ⏹ *MAP.*

SPORTS AND THE OUTDOORS

The largest spa on the island, with the added boon of a natural sauna hollowed out of the rocks, is the **Giardini Poseidon Terme.** Here you can sit like a Roman senator on two stone chairs recessed in the rock and let the hot water cascade over you. With countless thermally regulated pools, promenades, and steam pools, plus lots of toga-clad kitschy statues of the Caesars, Poseidon exerts a special pull on Germans, many of them grandparents shepherding grandchildren. On certain days, the place is overrun with people, so be prepared for crowds and wailing babies. ⊠ *Citara Beach, Forio* ☎ *081/9087111* ⊕ *www.giardiniposeidonterme. com* ▤ *€30 all day, €25 after 1 pm; add €3 to prices in Aug., €5 for visitors (no bathing) between 6 pm and 7 pm* ☺ *Apr.–Oct., daily 9–7.*

The Giardini La Mortella was built by British composer Sir William Walton and his wife, Lady Susana.

SHOPPING

With all the beauty farms on Ischia, ladies might enjoy visiting the main cosmetics factory on the island, **Ischia Thermae** (⌧ *Via Schioppa 17, Forio* ☎ *081/997745* ⊕ *www.ischiathermae.com*), which occupies an 18th-century palazzo in the town center of Forio. Besides poring over some of the formidably named articles in their retail outlet (such as Thermal Mud Purifying Mask Exfoliator), you might enjoy guided tours of the factory, offered three days a week (Monday, Wednesday, and Friday at 4:30 and 7:30) with the bonus of a free sample of their products.

PROCIDA: ISLAND OF CONTRASTS

Lying barely 3 km (2 mi) from the mainland and 10 km (6 mi) from the nearest port (Pozzuoli), Procida is an island of enormous contrasts. It's the most densely populated island in Europe—just over 10,000 people crammed into less than 3½ square km (2 square mi)—and yet there are oases like Marina Corricella and Vivara, which seem to have been bypassed by modern civilization. The inhabitants of the island—the *Procidani*—have an almost symbiotic relationship with the Mediterranean: many join the merchant navy, others either fish or ferry vacationers around local waters. And yet land traffic here is more intense than on any other island in the Bay of Naples.

In scenic terms this is the place to admire what the Italians call "Spontaneous," or folkloric Mediterranean, architecture: look for the tall archways on the ground floor, which signal places where boats could be stowed in winter, the outside staircases providing access to upper

PROCIDA: GETTING HERE AND AROUND

GETTING HERE

Procida's ferry timetable caters to the many daily commuters who live on the island and work in Naples or Pozzuoli. The most frequent—and cheapest—connections are from the Port of Pozzuoli. After stopping at Procida's main port, Marina Grande (also called Sancio Cattolico), many ferries and hydrofoils continue on to Ischia, for which Procida is considered a halfway house.

Caremar (☎ 892/123 ⊕ www. caremar.it) has five hydrofoils departing from Molo Beverello, Naples (€13.35, travel time 35 minutes), and up to seven ferry departures per day from Calata Porta di Massa, Naples (€8.50, travel time 1 hour). There are three ferries per day from Pozzuoli (€6.60, travel time 40 minutes).

Ferries of **Procida Lines** (☎ 081/8960328) leave seven times a day from Pozzuoli (€5.50 travel time 40 minutes).

SNAV (☎ 081/4285555) four daily hydrofoils leave from Mergellina or Molo Beverello, Naples (€13, travel time 35 minutes).

As with the other islands, buy a single ticket rather than a round-trip (there's virtually no saving on a round-trip ticket, which is usually twice the single fare, and it ties you down to one operator on your return).

GETTING AROUND

There are four main bus routes that will take you to practically every corner of the island as well as a fleet of microtaxis operating round island tours and plying the route between the port and the Marina di Chiaiolella, on the southwest of the island. To get to Vivara, a road climbs westward out of Chiaiolella, and motorized access is barred shortly before reaching the bridge linking the two islands.

The bus terminus in Procida is at the disembarkation point in Via Roma. Provided there's no traffic gridlock along the island's narrow streets, the buses run by the company SEPSA (☎ 081/991808 ⊕ www.eavbus.it) will get you to most destinations within about 10 minutes for €1.

Chiaiolella is the most frequently served destination (about every 15 minutes) and timetables are displayed—and tickets bought—at a newsstand next to the hydrofoil ticket office.

In summer the bus service runs until about 1 in the morning. Tickets can be bought for €1.30 from the bus driver. Keep in mind that on-the-spot checks and hefty fines are frequently imposed on riders without a ticket.

Although Procida has fewer hills than either Ischia or Capri, cycling is really only feasible when the roads are closed to motorized traffic (evenings in summer).

Most islanders get around on mopeds and scooters, which means the streets between the port and the center of the island are both noisy and loaded with pollutants, making casual strolling and window-shopping stressful.

Beaches can be reached by sea or land, with fishermen improvising as water-taxi drivers.

Procida is famed for its Good Friday procession.

floors without cramping interior living space, and the delicate pastel colors of the facades contrasting with the deeper, bolder blues of the sea. Picturesquely scenic, it's no surprise that Procida has strong artistic traditions and is widely considered the painters' island par excellence.

VISITOR INFORMATION

Procida Tour (⊠ *Via Roma 109, Procida* ☎ *081/8968089* ⊕ *www. procidatour.it*) can give you a map of the island and accepts left luggage. It's open daily 10–1 and 4–8.

TERRA MURATA AND ABBAZIA DI SAN MICHELE

Boats pull into the main port, **Marina Grande** (or **Sancio Cattolico** the local dialect for "safe place"), which is fetchingly adorned with pastel-hued houses and the church of Santa Maria della Pietà (1760). For your introductory look, hike up to the Piazza di Martiri on your way up to the **Castello.** Magnificent views can be seen from the piazza in front of the castle, including the enchanting fishing village of the Marina della Corricella. For a fascinating glimpse of the traditional architecture, once you reach the piazza turn left and walk about 600 feet until you come to a tiny passageway that leads to the Casale **Vascello,** originally a gated area of tumbling-down cottages.

GETTING HERE

Take Bus C2 to get to this popular town.

EXPLORING

After exploring on your way to the Cascale Vascello district, continue along Via San Michele to the highest point on the island, the old town of **Terra Murata**—a fascinating cluster of ancient buildings, including a church, palazzi, fortifications, ancient walls, and gateways, mostly in yellow-gray tufa stone. A Benedictine abbey was founded here in the 11th century, safely tucked away from mainland marauders, and the area became the focal point for the inhabitants of the island.

3

Perched precariously at the top of a cliff facing the small bay of Corricella is the 16th-century **ex-convent of Santa Margherita Nuova.**

The easily distinguishable and now abandoned **Palazzo d'Avalos,** built at the same time—confusingly, sometimes called Palazzo Reale or Il Castello—was the 17th-century residence of Innico d'Avalos, cardinal and mayor of Procida, and used as a prison from 1832 until 1987. Rumor has it that its inmates were a little miffed at having to abandon the sun-drenched island of Procida. Now it is for sale for a cool €28 million.

Within Terra Murata is the **Abbazia di San Michele.** San Michele (St. Michael) is the island's patron saint and a key figure in its history and traditions. Legend has it that in 1535, when the sultan of Algeria's admiral laid siege to the island, San Michele appeared above the pirate force and put them to flight (the 17th-century painting depicting the scene is in the choir of the abbey's 17th-century church; one of the invaders' anchors can also be viewed). On the wall close to the richly coffered ceiling of the church is another depiction of San Michele, this time by the grand master Luca Giordano (1699). As you walk around the church, note the holes in marble flagstones on the floor, which were in effect trapdoors through which bodies could be lowered to the underground crypt below. Children will be fascinated by the skulls still lurking in the catacombs. The cultural association Milennium offers guided tours for a small fee. ⊠ *Terra Murata* ☎ *081/8967612* ⊕ *www.abbaziasanmichele. it* ☜ *Free* ☉ *Apr.–Oct., Tues.–Sat. 10–1 and 3–5:30, Sun., Mon. 10–1; Nov.–Mar., call for times.*

CORRICELLA

Fodor's Choice
★

Perched under the citadel of the Terra Murata, the **Marina di Corricella** is Procida's most iconic sight. Singled out for the waterfront scenes in *Il Postino* (*The Postman,* the 1995 Oscar winner for Best Foreign Film—the bar in the film is now a restaurant), this fishermen's cove is one of the most eye-popping villages in Campania—a rainbow-hued, horizontal version of Positano, comprising hundreds of traditional Mediterranean-style stone houses threaded by numerous *scalatinelle* (staircase streets).

GETTING HERE

Take Bus C2 from Marina Grande Sancio Cattolico to Terra Murata, then on foot.

EXPLORING

The inhabitants of Corricella have been relatively immune to life in the limelight—cinematic and otherwise—and apart from the opening of an occasional restaurant and bar, there have been few changes in this sleepy but magical village. This is the type of place where even those of us with failing grades in art classes feel like reaching for a paintbrush to record the delicate pinks and yellows of the waterfront buildings. Others will use up their camera's flash cards in a jiffy.

WHERE TO EAT

$

SOUTHERN
ITALIAN

✕ **Graziella.** This atmospheric restaurant sits right on the waterfront down at Corricella. It's family run and as rustic as they come, with food served on plastic tables outside. For starters try the *bruschette* and the seafood specialty, a selection of shellfish, octopus, and anchovies big enough for two. The *impepata di cozze* (mussels in pepper) is a must, and top it all off with a homemade *granita di limone* (lemon crushed ice), made freshly everyday here, and undoubtedly the best on the island. ⊠ *Via Marina Corricella 14* ☎ *081/8967479* 🗖 *No credit cards* ⊘ *Closed Dec.–Feb.*

$$

SOUTHERN
ITALIAN

★

✕ **La Conchiglia.** A dinner at this beachfront spot really lets you appreciate the magic of Procida. Beyond the lapping of the waves, Capri twinkles in the distance. The seafood is divinely fresh, the pasta dishes usually soul-warming. Access here is either by foot down the steps from Via Pizzaco or by boat from the Corricella harborfront—phone owner Gianni if you want the boat to pick you up (free for diners). ⊠ *Via Pizzaco 10* ☎ *081/8967602* ⊕ *www.laconchigliaristorante.com* 🗖 *AE, MC, V* ⊘ *Closed mid-Nov.–Mar.*

WHERE TO STAY

$$

La Casa sul Mare. One of Procida's nicest boutique hotels, this charmer overlooks the fishing village of Corricella and the bay. The south-facing private terraces of the jewel-like bedrooms have stunning views and are the perfect place to lap up winter sunshine. Antiques and traditional ceramic flooring complete the decor. Breakfast is served in the garden, and in the summer months a shuttle bus or boat will take you to any beach on the island. **Pros:** stunning views; wonderful atmosphere. **Cons:** tiny bathrooms; not-great service. ⊠ *Salita Castello 13* ☎ *081/8968799* ⊕ *www.lacasasulmare.it* ⤶ *10 rooms* ⚬ *In-room: a/c, safe, refrigerator. In-hotel: bar* 🗖 *AE, DC, MC, V* ⎢○⎢ *BP.*

$$

Fodor's Choice

★

La Tonnara. In one of Procida's cutest corners, this inviting new hotel option (take the Bus L1/L2 from Marina Grande Sancio Cattolico to the Marina di Chiaiolella) has been renovated from a former warehouse for tuna fishers. Set in a small but immaculate garden it maintains the characteristics of its marine history while now flaunting a sleek and modern décor. Guest rooms are bright and airy, each individually decorated—all but two (on the ground floor) have a view of the beach. The marina, beach, and Vivara island park are just steps away. **Pros:** lovely setting; on the beach. **Cons:** constant stream of beachgoers outside the gate. ⊠ *Via Marina Chiaiolella 33* ☎ *081/8101052* ⊕ *www.latonnarahotel. it* ⤶ *14 rooms* ⚬ *In-room: a/c, safe. In-hotel: bar, parking (free)* 🗖 *DC, MC, V* ⎢○⎢ *BP.*

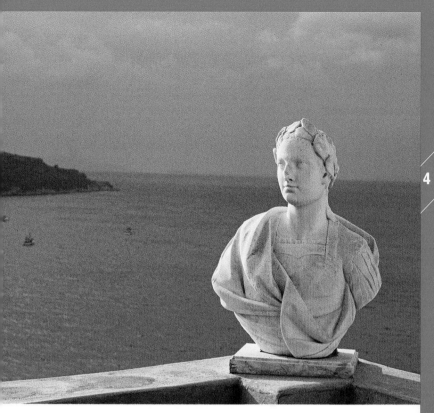

Sorrento and the Sorrentine Peninsula

WORD OF MOUTH

"Sorrento is a fine place to spend a few days. Easy to catch ferries to islands. Convenient to Naples, Pompeii, etc."

—Julia 1

WELCOME TO SORRENTO AND THE SORRENTINE PENINSULA

TOP REASONS TO GO

★ **"Torna a Surriento":**
Sorrento's old town quarter is one of the most romantic places in Italy—be sure to dine in front of the Sedile Dominova, a 16th-century frescoed loggia that is a colorful backdrop for caffè and serenading waiters warbling "Come Back to Sorrento."

★ **A View with a Room:**
Give in to suite temptation and splurge on Sorrento's grand hotels perched by the Bay of Naples—the best are Belle Epoque extravaganzas with enough gilded salons to make even a Proust heroine swoon.

★ **Shopping along Via San Cesareo:** Sorrento's regional trifles are world famous, and this charming street is just the place to find embroideries, inlaid wooden intarsia, music boxes, leather items, and dolls in tarantella costumes.

★ **Passeggiare:** Join the *passeggiata* (evening strolling ritual) at Piazza Tasso and follow the locals as they make the rounds of Sorrento's historical center to gossip, strut, and see and be seen.

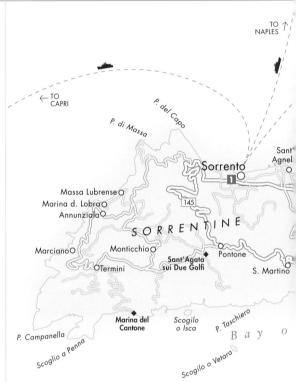

1 Sorrento. When literati sang Sorrento's praises in the Grand Tour era, palatial hotels went up to accommodate the titled lords who rushed to visit. The English, especially, left their stamp on the city, which is still notably civil and genteel. Perched on a cliff across the bay from Naples—with Vesuvius front and center—it has no major tourist attractions; the Belle Epoque city itself, with its enchanting sherbet-hued *palazzi* and bouquets of villas, is the draw. The charming historic quarter is centered on Piazza Tasso. Follow Via San Cesareo through a labyrinth of alleys to the Chiesa di San Francesco (with a

P. Orlando

Castellammare

Circumvesuviana
Rail Line 163

Gradelle

Marina
de Equa

Vico
Equense

Monte
Faito

Alimuri

Massaquano

Meta 2

P E N I N S U L A

Moiano

Monte
Creasuolo

Piano
di Sorrento

163

163

Positano

P. Germano

S a l e r n o

La Rotonda

TO
CAPRI

0   1 mi

0   1 km

4

GETTING ORIENTED

Connected to Naples via the famous Circumvesuviana train and the Metro del Mare, to Capri and Amalfi via the ferries and hydrofoils that depart its Marina Piccola, and set equidistant from Pompeii and the Amalfi Coast, Sorrento is a convenient home base for visiting the region. Set high atop a bluff on the peninsula created by the Lattari Mountains, it has a stunning view of the Bay of Naples. Beyond the town lies a scenery-rich peninsula famous for fabulous restaurants, Edenic parks, and a famously popular beach at Marina del Cantone.

gorgeous, bougainvillea-draped cloister) and the Villa Communale, where you get a Cinerama view of the bay.

2 The Sorrentine Peninsula. When the crowds of Sorrento get too much, you can always get out of town. Northeast of the city, the route leads to Sant'Agnello, an aristocratic beauty spot hallowed by two historic

hotels, the Cocumella and the Parco dei Principi (the latter with a famous botanical park). South of Sorrento, Sant'Agata sui Due Golfi crowns a peak that overlooks both the Bay of Naples and the Bay of Salerno. Travel south down the peninsula to reach the delightfully festive beach at Marina del Cantone.

SORRENTO PLANNER

Making the Most of Your Time

Sorrento has plenty of appeal in its own right, but its greatest virtue is its central location—it makes a fine base, putting you within day-trip distance of Pompeii, the Amalfi Coast, and the islands of the bay.

You should spend a day taking in Sorrento itself and the surrounding area, plus another leisurely day exploring the Sorrento Peninsula, enjoying the best beaches and restaurants in the area or taking a rural hike. For day trips, an excursion along the Amalfi Drive is a rise-early, full-day excursion. You can easily get from Sorrento to the Amalfi Coast by bus, or ferry around the peninsula in the summertime. Other day-trip alternatives include an excursion to the archaeological sites around the Bay of Naples—the train from Sorrento will deposit you right in front of Pompeii or a short distance from Herculaneum. Boat, ferry, and hydrofoil services also connect you with Naples and environs, plus the islands of Capri and Ischia, all valid day-trip alternatives.

Keep in mind that if you're driving, and you wind up not heading back to Sorrento until after dark, you should stick to the main roads. It's easy to get lost on back roads at night.

Sorrento Was Made for Strollers

Divinely picturesque, the old town of Sorrento is like a Belle Epoque stage set—festooned with palazzi, charming streets, and gorgeous landmarks, it is custom-tailored for one of the most enjoyable promenades you will ever take.

Begin at Sorrento's historic center, **Piazza Tasso,** watched over by statues of the namesake poet. Avoid busy Corso Italia to head instead to the southwest corner of the piazza to Via Santa Maria della Pietà to take a look at the noted **Palazzo Correale** (No. 24), whose 18th-century majolica courtyard, now a flower shop, overflows with charm. Follow this street until you reach the Largo Arcivescovado, site of the **Duomo dei SS Filippo e Giacomo.**

After viewing this grand cathedral, head for its wedding-cake campanile, then make a right off Corso Italia down Via Giuliani to enter Sorrento's most picturesque quarter.

Here, on Via San Cesareo, is the beautifully frescoed **Sedile Dominova,** the ancient, open-air site of civic discourse (at night illuminated for caffè sitters—one of your best "big exhale" hours will be spent here). Return to Piazza Tasso along Via San Cesareo, lit with 19th-century lanterns and the main shopping drag. When you arrive at the edge of Piazza Tasso, go left toward the bay, a block or so along Via De Maio, to pretty Piazza Sant'Antonino, the site of the 11th-century **Basilica di Sant'Antonino.** Past this piazza take Via Santa Maria delle Grazie and Via Donnorso to the church of **San Francesco** to feast your eyes on its legendary 14th-century "Paradise" cloister.

Relax in the adjoining **Villa Communale** gardens and enjoy the Cinemascope-wide view of the Bay of Naples. Continue on Via Veneto to the **Piazza della Vittoria** to see the faded "Casa di Tasso" sign that marks the birthplace of the town's revered poet. Cross the piazza to the aristocratic Hotel Bellevue Syrene, whose fabulous garden belvedere is the most beautiful place to have drinks. Pass the hotel to exit the walls near the Porta Greca (Greek Gate) and take the stairway down to **Marina Grande** for dinner at a festive seafood restaurant. Catch a bus on the Via del Mare to return.

Guided Tours

A much better sightseeing alternative to driving yourself around Sorrento (and driving yourself crazy in the process) is the double-decker tour bus operated by **City Sightseeing Sorrento** (✉ *Via degli Aranci 172* ☎ *081/8774707* ⊕ *www.sorrento.city-sightseeing.it*).

For a daily fare of €12, this outfit takes you from its terminus at Piazza De Curtis (by the Circumvesuviana station) out of Sorrento to Massa Lubrense, Termini, and Sant'Agata.

You can get off along the way, hike perhaps for a few hours (especially from Termini Punta Campanella) and then board once again.

For guided tours of the Sorrento Peninsula—but also departing from Sorrento to Capri, Pompeii, and the Naples area—check out the knowledgeable and passionate team of **Vesuvius vs. Pompeii** (☎ *333/6409000* ⊕ *www.vesuviusvspompeii.com*). They can also arrange private transfers and vehicles for people with disabilities.

Finding a Place to Stay

The ghosts of a vacationing Empress Eugénie and an ailing Caruso haunt Sorrento's hotel corridors. Sorrento has a plethora of upper-range hotels with fin de siècle charm, perched on top of impressive tuff cliffs, with balconies and terraces giving an immediate this-is-it sensation.

If traveling on a tighter budget, you can choose between a three-star accommodation or a B&B in the town center or a quieter hotel farther from Sorrento's hub and from the sea.

If staying on the peninsula, don't assume you'll be a stone's throw from the shoreline: at times access to the sea is lengthy and arduous, and most of the coastline is rocky.

WHAT IT COSTS (IN EUROS)

	¢	$	$$	$$$	$$$$
Restaurants	under €20	€20–€30	€30–€45	€45–€65	over €65
Hotels	under €75	€75–€125	€125–€200	€200–€300	over €300

Restaurant prices are for a first course (*primo*), second course (*secondo*), and dessert (*dolce*). Hotel prices are for two people in a standard double room in high season, including tax and service.

When to Go

Guess what? Summer months may, in fact, be the new "off-season"—horror stories of torrid days and humungous crowds have driven ever more people to travel here during May/June and September/October and the region is packed to the gills with travelers during those months. That doesn't mean that this region isn't crowded during July and August.

Let's not forget that summer is filled with festivities and offers the best weather for sunning and swimming, bringing dense crowds and higher prices, especially during the middle two weeks of August, when Italians vacation en masse. But no time is perfect: although April and May are sublime, Italian students are then on break and can overrun major sites.

The news is usually wonderful for the weather. Sheltered by the Lattari Mountains arcing east to west across the peninsula and inland from the Amalfi Coast, and exposed to cool breezes from two bays, the Sorrentine Peninsula enjoys a climate that is among the mildest in Italy; the temperature rarely falls below 10°C (50°F) in winter, or climbs above 31°C (90°F) in summer. In winter many hotels close, from November to March. As for rain, or what the locals call *passione de Pasqua* ("tears of passion" at Easter), it's rare although weeklong storms can strike.

GETTING AROUND

Ottima Cucina

So your Grail is fine gastronomy, calorie-laden ice cream or just a humble glass of limoncello liqueur? You need look no further. The Sorrento peninsula has an excellent range of eateries. With southern Italy's best restaurant in Sant'Agata, a cluster of gastronomic destinations in Marina del Cantone, and excellent *trattorie* in Sorrento itself, the choice turns into a dilemma of delights. And then, you may well "discover" an out-of-the-way *osteria* up in the hills, with no written menu but plenty of character, *vino locale* and, more often than not, *ottima cucina*—the best food. Having much higher levels of tourism than Naples, the area around Sorrento has fewer cheap and cheerful restaurants for locals, but you are more likely to find waiters who speak some English, *trattorie* which stay open right through August, and generally higher levels of cuisine. As a rule of thumb, avoid set menus (often called *menu turistico)* and go for whatever looks freshest to you. Remember that fish and steak prices on menus are often indicated by a price per 100 grams—look carefully if it seems suspiciously cheap!

Car Travel

All traffic from Naples to Sorrento is ultimately channeled onto the SS 145, which must be one of the slowest state highways in southern Italy.

The road is single lane all the way from the A3 Autostrada turnoff at Castellammare di Stabia.

Though you'll get some scenic vistas as you inch along the peninsula, it's only when you get beyond Sorrento, on the road to Massa Lubrense or Sant'Agata, that a car becomes more of a benefit than a liability.

Don't expect excellent driving standards in the Sorrento area, and be especially careful of scooters, which tend to take considerable liberties.

Avoid traveling from Naples to Sorrento on Saturday evenings and on fine Sunday mornings even in winter.

The same applies to the SS 145 late on a Sunday afternoon, when immense numbers of day-trippers and weekenders return home to the Naples area.

Parking in Sorrento

If you make a stop in Sorrento by car, head for the large parking lot called Ulisse (after the hotel of which it is a part): take a left turn into Via degli Aranci when you meet the "no entry" signs as you enter Sorrento, pass under the railway bridge, and turn right at the roundabout.

This road skirts the town center (to the right). At the stop sign on Corso Italia take a right turn, and turn right immediately down toward the Marina Grande. **Ulisse Parking** (✉ *Via Del Mare 22* ✉ *€2 per hr*) is on your left after the road bridge, and within easy walking distance of the town center and Marina Grande.

Train Travel

The train stations on the **Circumvesuviana** (☎ 081/7722444 ⊕ www.vesuviana.it) line serving the Sorrento Peninsula are Meta, Piano di Sorrento, Sant'Agnello, and Sorrento, in order of increasing distance from Naples. The main transport hub for cheap, efficient bus services radiating to destinations along the coast and inland is the Circumvesuviana station in Sorrento.

If heading to Sorrento from Naples, use the Stazione Centrale (Piazza Garibaldi), which is the second stop on the Circumvesuviana line as it departs from Naples. Follow the *Circumvesuviana* signs, which will take you through the ticket barriers down into the train stations.

Trains to Sorrento run every half hour from Naples; some trains are *direttissimo* (express), only stopping at major stations; they take half the time of local trains. Round-trip fares are €6.60 for Naples to Sorrento (if traveling round-trip on the weekend, purchase a day pass good for unlimited stops on the line for €6.50) and €3.60 for Pompei Scavi–Sorrento. In Sorrento the train station is opposite Piazza Lauro and a five-minute walk from Piazza Tasso.

Bus Travel

At €1.10 for a one-way *extraurbano* bus ticket from Sorrento to other locations on the peninsula—and some lines with departures every 20 minutes—the bus is a good way to get around quickly and cheaply. Municipal **Circumvesuviana** (☎ 081/7722444 ⊕ www.vesuviana.it) buses radiate out from the Circumvesuviana station to most major destinations on the peninsula, while **SITA** (☎ 089/405145 ⊕ www.sitabus.it) buses go farther afield to Positano, Amalfi, and Naples.

Inform the driver of your destination when boarding to avoid missing your stop. If traveling up from the port of Sorrento at Marina Piccola, or the waterfront at Marina Grande, you'll need to get a Circumvesuviana orange bus. The main orange bus stop in Sorrento is on Piazza Tasso.

Tickets must be purchased in advance (though for a surcharge of €0.50 you can buy a ticket on the orange bus). Time-stamp your ticket in the machine at the front of the bus as you board. You can buy tickets at caffè, bars, tobacco shops, and newsstands area-wide.

Boat Travel

Headquartered in Naples, the **Metro del Mare** (☎ 199600700 ⊕ www.metrodelmare.net) is a scenic, seasonal alternative to ground transport around the bay. Commuter ferries service all the main ports throughout the gulf and, although more expensive and slower than ground travel, offer spectacular views of the coastline and Vesuvius. Lines 1, 2, 3, and 6 all connect Sorrento with Naples and numerous other locations.

Fares are roughly €7 to €10, depending on the trip. Check the local paper (*Il Mattino*) for timetables or go to ⊕ www.metrodelmare.net for departure times.

In addition, many commercial ferries and hydrofoils run year-round (with more trips in high season). To get to smaller towns or to take private boats, you can make arrangements with private boat companies or independent fishermen. Seek out people who are recommended by the tourist office or your hotel.

Ferries and hydrofoils to and from Sorrento, with connections to Naples, Capri, Positano, and Amalfi, are operated by **Alilauro** (☎ 081/8781430 or 081/4972222 ⊕ www.alilauro.it), **SNAV** (☎ 081/4285555 ⊕ www.snav.it), **Caremar** (☎ 892/123 ⊕ www.caremar.it), and **Linee Maritime Partenopee** (☎ 081/8781430 ⊕ www.consorziolmp.it).

CAMPANIA'S WINE RENAISSANCE

Two thousand years ago, wine from Campania was considered some of the best in the Roman Empire. But in recent centuries, the region's wine production—and quality—declined precipitously, only to be raised from mediocrity in the past 20 years. Now Campanian wine is once again arousing the passions and palates of wine connoisseurs.

A vinous renaissance is underway: traditional grape varieties like Aglianico and Piedirosso (reds), and Fiano and Falanghina (whites) have halted the southward expansion of "foreign" (i.e., Northern Italian) intruders like Sangiovese and Trebbiano. There is a new spirit of pride and achievement in the region, evidenced by the rapid increase in production of DOC—Controlled Denomination of Origin—wines, meaning they are recognized by Italy's system for ensuring quality wines. Like those in Tuscany to the north, wineries are increasingly opening their doors to the public.

LABEL TERMS

Italian wine laws are complex. Fortunately wine labels feature some indications of quality and style. The most rigorous classification—with restrictions on geographic zone, grape variety, and production methods—is DOCG (*Denominazione di Origine Controllata e Garantita*), followed by DOC (*Denominazione di Origine Controllata*); and IGT (*Indicazione Geografica Tipica*), which has the fewest restrictions. Other wine label terms to look out for: *vino di tavola* means basic table wine; *riserva* indicates the wine was aged longer than usual; *classico* signifies a well-respected, traditional style; *secco* means dry; and *dolce* indicates sweet.

AGLIANICO (TAURASI)

The most renowned regional red variety is Aglianico, which makes Taurasi near Avellino, the first-ever southern Italian wine to receive a DOCG label in 1993. The varietal has been called "the Barolo of the south" for its structure and ability to age. Aglianico produces full-bodied red wines with crisp acidity, robust tannins, and complex flavors of plum and spice. These wines are excellent with grilled steak, pizza, and pasta with meat ragù.

FIANO (FIANO DI AVELLINO)

This classical white grape shows best in the volcanic soils of Avellino, where it has garnered DOCG status. The wine expresses strong flavors of honey, spices, and nuts. It is excellent as an aperitivo, and pairs well with tough-to-match artichokes, as well as seafood fettucine and most fish dishes.

CODA DI VOLPE

An ancient full-bodied white grape grown near Naples. Until recently, it was used as a blending grape with Falanghina and Greco (in the white Vesuvio DOC) or Fiano. Now it is possible to find the crisp, medium-bodied Coda di Volpe bottled by itself. The varietal is excellent with gently prepared (not grilled) shellfish dishes or panfried fish, as it is fairly neutral and can be overwhelmed by strongly flavored foods.

FALANGHINA

An ancient white grape that may have been a base for the fabled Falernum, the most highly prized wine of the Roman period. This varietal has experienced a revival in recent years. It is a full-bodied, fresh tasting white wine with fruity notes. Falanghina can be found in many DOC wines by itself, and famously is blended with Greco and Biancolella to make Capri Bianco, the DOC white wine from the island of Capri. Falanghina is acidic enough to pair well with grilled and fried seafood dishes.

GRECO (GRECO DI TUFO)

Greco is a Campanian variety that does best around the village of Tufo, where it has DOCG status. The soil there is a sulphurous soft rock called *tufo* (*tuffeau* in French). Greco is a light white wine that expresses ripe stone fruits, like peaches, with notes of almond and citrus. It is great served as an aperitivo and matched with cold antipasto.

PIEDIROSSO (AKA PER'E PALUMMO)

This late-ripening red grape variety produces a fruity wine with notes of cherries and herbs. It is the main grape in the red wines of Vesuvio DOC and Capri DOC. Piedirosso pairs well with pizza, cured meats, and grilled vegetables.

Opposite page: A wine cellar in Campania.
top right: A Campania vineyard.
bottom left: Black grapes grow in Naples.

Updated
by Fiorella
Squillante

Like the familiar song "Come Back to Sorrento," with its long, mournful closing notes (listen to the Pavarotti version and you may shed a few tears), the beautiful, Belle Epoque resort town of Sorrento is tinged with melancholy.

Its streets seem like 19th-century sepia photographs, vestiges of the Roman Empire's ruins are strewn about, and tiers of votive offerings of hopeful Sorrentines flicker in the crypt of the basilica of Sant'Antonino. Vesuvius, as always, looms in the distance. And with the sun's heart-stopping descent into the Bay of Naples, the isle of Capri fades into the purple twilight, as if to disappear forever.

Gently faded, in the manner of a stereopticon image, Sorrento still exudes a robust appeal. For anyone suffering "nostalgia di Napoli"—a longing for tarantellas, strumming mandolines, and *dolce far niente*—this is the ideal place, since it's relatively free of the urban grit found in the real Naples. Sorrento's tourist industry that began centuries ago is still dominant, although the lords and ladies of bygone days have been replaced with (mainly English, German, and Japanese) tour groups.

The Sorrento Peninsula was first put on the map by the ancient Romans. Emperors and senators—who knew a good thing when they saw it—claimed the region for their own, crowning the golden, waterside cliffs of what was then called "Surrentum" (in reference to the Sirens that reputedly haunted the nearby Li Galli islets) with palatial villas. Modern resorts now stand where emperors once staked out vacation spots. Reminders of the Caesars' reigns—broken columns, capitals, marble busts—lie scattered among the area's orange trees and terraces. Sorrento goes as far back as the Samnites and the Etruscans, the *bons viveurs* of the early ancient world, and for much of Sorrento's existence it has remained focused, in fact, on pleasure. The Sorrento Peninsula became a major stop on the elite's Grand Tour itineraries beginning in the late 18th century, thanks to glowing reports from Goethe, Lord Byron, Shelley, and Richard Wagner, Keats, Scott, Dickens, and Ibsen. By the mid-19th century, grand hotels and wedding-cake villas had sprung up to welcome the flow of princes, khans, and tycoons.

As a hub for a banquet of must-see sites—Pompeii and Naples to the north, Capri to the west, and the Amalfi Coast to the south—Sorrento remains unequaled. Because of its convenient location, the city can become overrun with visitors in summer, so it's fortunate that the rest of the Sorrento Peninsula, with plains and limestone outcroppings, watchtowers and Roman ruins, groves and beaches, monasteries and villages, winding paths leading to isolated coves and panoramic views of the bays of both Naples and Salerno, remains relatively undiscovered. Eons ago, when sea levels dropped during the glaciations, the peninsula's tip and Capri were joined by an overland connection, and today it still seems you can almost make it in a single jump. Separating grande dame Sorrento from the relatively arriviste Amalfi Coast, this hilly, forested peninsula provides the famed rivals breathing space, along with inviting restaurants and an uncrowded charm all its own.

4

SORRENTO

Sorrento may have become a jumping-off point for visitors to Pompeii, Capri, and Amalfi, but you can find countless reasons to love it for itself. The Sorrentine people are fair-minded and hardworking, bubbling with life and warmth. The tufa cliff on which the town rests is like a great golden pedestal spread over the bay, absorbing the sunlight in deepening shades through the mild days, and orange and lemon trees waft a luscious perfume in spring. In the evening, people fill caffè to nibble, sip, and talk nonstop; then, arms linked, they stroll and browse through the maze of shop-lined lanes.

It has been this way for centuries, ever since Sorrento became a prescribed stop for Grand Tour travelers, who savored its mild winters while sopping up its culture and history. According to a letter from his traveling companion in 1876, the philosopher Nietzsche, not generally known for effervescence, "laughed with joy" at the thought of going to Sorrento, and French novelist Stendhal called it "the most beautiful place on earth." Many visitors still share his opinion.

GETTING HERE
From downtown Naples, take a Circumvesuviana train from Stazione Centrale (Piazza Garibaldi), SITA bus from in front of the station, or hydrofoil from Molo Beverello. If you're coming directly from the airport in Naples, pick up a direct bus to Sorrento. By car, take the A3 Naples–Salerno highway, exiting at Castellammare, and then following signs for Penisola Sorrentina, then for Sorrento.

Tourist Information In Sorrento the office of the **Azienda Autonoma di Soggiorno Sorrento-Sant'Agnello** (✉ Via L. De Maio 35, Sorrento ☎ 081/8074033 ⊕ www.sorrentotourism.com) is open weekdays 8:30–4:15. Besides dispensing a wealth of information, they also have a useful booking service for hotels, B&Bs, and holiday flats throughout the peninsula.

EXPLORING SORRENTO

Winding along a cliff above a small beach and two harbors, the town is split in two by a narrow ravine formed by a former mountain stream. To the east, dozens of hotels line busy Via Correale along the cliff—many have "grand" included in their names, and some indeed still are. To the west, however, is the historic sector, which still enchants—it's a relatively flat area, with winding, stone-paved lanes bordered by balconied buildings, some joined by medieval stone arches. The central piazza is named after the poet Torquato Tasso, born here in 1544. This part of town is a delightful place to walk through, especially in the mild evenings, when people are out and about, and everything is open. Craftspeople are often at work in their stalls and shops and are happy to let you watch; in fact, that's the point.

TOP ATTRACTIONS

Basilica di Sant'Antonino. Gracing Piazza Sant'Antonino and one of the largest churches in Sorrento, the Basilica di Sant'Antonino honors the city's patron saint, St. Anthony the Abbot. The church and the portal on the right side date from the 11th century. Its nave and side aisles are divided by recycled ancient columns. Among the paintings, is the one on the nave ceiling signed and dated by Giovan Battista Lama in 1734. The crypt, housing the saint's bones, is enriched by polychrome marble and votive offerings. In addition, a relic case contains two whale ribs, which commemorates one of the saint's miracles, when he saved a child from the cetacean. Directly opposite across the piazza is the turn-of-the-20th-century *Municipio* (town hall). ⊠ *Piazza Sant'Antonino* ☎ *081/8781437* ⊠ *Free* ☾ *Daily 7–noon and 5–7.*

Fodor's Choice
★
Convento di San Francesco. Near the Villa Comunale gardens and sharing its vista over the Bay of Naples, this church is celebrated for its 14th-century cloister. Filled with greenery and flowers, the Moorish-style cloister has interlaced pointed arches of tufa rock, alternating with octagonal columns topped by elegant capitals, supporting smaller arches, and makes a suitably evocative setting for summer concerts and theatrical presentations—make this a must if you can catch an event. The church portal is particularly impressive, with the original 16th-century door featuring intarsia (inlaid) work. The interior's 17th-century decoration includes an altarpiece depicting St. Francis receiving the stigmata, by a student of Francesco Solimena. The convent is now an art school, where students' works are often exhibited. ⊠ *Piazza S. Francesco* ☎ *081/8781269* ⊠ *Free* ☾ *Daily 8–8.*

Duomo dei SS Filippo e Giacomo. Ancient, but rebuilt from the 15th-century right up to 1924, the town's cathedral follows a Latin-cross design; its nave and two side aisles are divided by thick piers with round arches. A Renaissance-style door and artworks, including the archbishop's 16th-century marble throne and ceiling paintings attributed to the 18th-century Neapolitan school, are easily viewable. Twentieth-century local marquetry magnificently ornaments the choir stalls, with pictures of the Stations of the Cross. In this church Torquato Tasso—Sorrento's most famous native son, his books such as *Jerusalem Liberated* were among the top "bestsellers" of the 16th century—was baptized (probably at the

Sorrento

Basilica di
Sant'Antonino **5**
Convento di
San Francesco **6**
Duomo dei SS Filippo
e Giacomo **3**
Marina Grande **10**

Museo Bottega della
Tarsia Lignea **9**
Museo Correale
di Terranova **11**
Palazzo Correale **2**
Piazza Tasso **1**
Piazza della
Vittoria **8**

Sedile Dominova **4**
Villa Comunale **7**

Golfo di Napoli

Marina Piccola

Porto

Marina Grande

Via Capo

Via Nastro Verde

TO
SANT'AGNELLO →

Via Califano

Via Rota

Viale Nizza

Via Capasso

Corso Italia

Piazza A.
Lauro

Corso Italia

Stazione
Circumvesuviana

Bus stop

Via S. Renato

Via degli Aranci

SS145

SS145

Via Correale

Viale de Maio

Via S. M. Grazie

Via Cesareo

Via Pietà

Via S. Antonino

Via S. Sersale

Corso Italia

Via degli Aranci

Via L. Veneto

Via Accademia

Via Tasso

Vico I Fuoro

Vico II Fuoro

Vico III Fuoro

Via S. Nicola

Via S. Vincenzo

Via Marina Grande

SS145

0   1/4 miles
0   1/4 km

font in the first chapel on the right). The delightfully florid three-story campanile, topped by a clock and a belfry, has an open arcaded base and recycled Roman columns. ⊠ *Largo Arcivescovado at Corso Italia* ☏ *081/8782248* ✆ *Free* ⊙ *Daily 8–noon and 5–8.*

Museo Correale di Terranova. In an 18th-century villa and lovely garden on land given to the patrician Correale family by Queen Joan II of Anjou in 1428, this museum has an excellent private collection amassed by Pompeo and Alfredo Correale, Counts of Terranova. The garden offers an allée of flowers, palms, pine trees, citrus groves, and an esplanade with a panoramic view of the Sorrento coast. Head instead the somewhat charmless buildings to find one of Europe's most charming collections of the decorative arts, with specialties that will especially delight connoisseurs of the *Seicento* (Italian 17th century), along with treasures of Neapolitan paintings from the 16th to the 19th centuries. On the ground floor there are magnificent 18th- and 19th-century inlaid tables by Giuseppe Gargiulo, along with Rococo portrait miniatures. The first and second floors house a notable collection of paintings, including Caravaggesque, baroque, and delightful 19th-century Campanian landscapes of the Posillipo School. Glassware, fans, intriguing clocks, and a *biribì* (a game of chance) remind us of the age when pleasure and delight was all. A series of majolica introduce an exhaustive collection of porcelain from all the 18th-century European factories, with Royal Capodimonte taking pride of place. ⊠ *Via Correale 50* ☏ *081/8781846* ⊕ *www.museocorreale.it* ✆ *€6* ⊙ *Tues.–Mon. 9:30–1:30.*

Fodor'sChoice ★ **Sedile Dominova.** Enchanting showpiece of the Largo Dominova—the little square that is the heart of Sorrento's historic quarter—this is a picturesque open loggia with expansive arches, balustrades, and a green-and-yellow-tile cupola, originally constructed in the 16th century. The open-air structure is frescoed with 18th-century trompe l'oeil columns and the family coats of arms, which once belonged to the *sedile* (seat), the town council where nobles met to discuss civic problems as early as the Angevin period. The sediles resolved regional differences and members were granted privileges by powerful Naples during the days of the Spanish occupation. Today, Sorrentines still like to congregate around the umbrella-topped tables near the tiny square; in the evening, under the still vibrant and now softly illuminated frescoes, men sitting in the forecourt may still be discussing civic problems while playing cards. ⊠ *Largo Dominova, at Via S. Cesareo and Via P.R. Giuliani.*

Fodor'sChoice ★ **Villa Comunale.** The largest public park in Sorrento, the Villa Comunale sits on a cliff top overlooking the entire Bay of Naples and offers benches, flowers, palms, and people-watching, plus a seamless vista that stretches from Capri to Vesuvius. From here steps lead down to Sorrento's main harbor, the Marina Piccola. ⊠ *Adjoining church of San Francesco.*

NEED A BREAK?

The unassuming **Bar Villa Comunale** (⊠ *Villa Comunale* ☏ *081/8074090*), closed mid-November to March, is the perfect spot to sit with Sorrento's card players or just gaze across the Bay of Naples at the perfect scenery. For an afternoon delight, why not head across the road to **Davide** (⊠ *Via*

Giuliani 39 ☎ *081/8781337*) to indulge in a gelato? For something with a local twist, try *profumi di Sorrento,* the in-house citrus fruit sorbet, or a cream-laden *semifreddo delizia al limone.* Davide is closed November through March.

WORTH NOTING

Marina Grande. Close to the historic quarter (but not that close—many locals prefer to use the town bus to shuttle up and down the steep hill), the port, or *borgo,* of the Marina Grande is Sorrento's fishing harbor. In recent years it has become unashamedly touristy, with outdoor restaurants and caffè encroaching on what little remains of the original harbor. Most establishments down here are geared to the English-speaking market—expect a *Good evening* rather than a *Buona sera* as you enter, and menu listings that may make you think you've been teleported into a British fish-and-chip shop. The marina still remains a magical location for an evening out on the waterfront, but if you're interested in a dip—given the dubious seawater quality here and the cramped conditions—head out instead toward Massa Lubrense and Nerano. Don't confuse this harbor with Marina Piccola, at the base of the cliff, below Piazza Tasso and the Hotel Excelsior Vittoria; that's the area where ferries and hydrofoils dock. ⊠ *Via del Mare.*

Museo Bottega della Tarsia Lignea (Museum of Intarsia Work). The 18th-century Palazzo Pomaranci Santomasi houses an assorted collection of the celebrated Sorrentine decorative art of intarsia, or *intarsi* (inlays), comprising mainly 19th-century furniture and some modern artistic creations. Also on view are 19th-century paintings, prints, and photographs of the Sorrento Peninsula. ⊠ *Via San Nicola 28* ☎ *081/8771942* ⌑€8 ⊙ *June–Sept., Mon.–Sat. 10–1 and 4–7:30; Oct.–May, Mon.–Sat. 10–1 and 3–6:30.*

★ **Palazzo Correale.** Just off the southeast corner of Piazza Tasso, this palazzo was built in the 14th century in Catalan style but transformed into a Rococo-era showstopper, thanks to its exquisite **Esedra Maiolicata** (Majolica Courtyard, 1772). This was one of the many examples of majolica and faienceware created in this region, a highlight of Campanian craftsmen. (Other notable examples are the Chiostro delle Clarisse at Naples' Santa Chiara and the grand terrace of Positano's Hotel San Pietro.) In 1610 the palazzo became the Ritiro di Santa Maria della Pietà and today remains private, but you can view the courtyard beyond the vestryway. Its back wall—a trompe l'oeil architectural fantasia, entirely rendered in majolica tile—is now a suitably romantic setting for the Ruoppo florist shop. Buy a rose here and bear it through the streets of old Sorrento, an emblem of your pleasure in the moment. As you leave the palazzo, note the unusual arched windows on the palace facade, a grace note also seen a few doors away at **Palazzo Veniero** (No. 14), a 13th-century structure with a Byzantine-Arab influence. ⊠ *Via Pietà 24.*

★ **Piazza della Vittoria.** Tree-shaded Piazza della Vittoria is book-ended by two fabled hotels, the Bellevue Syrene and the Imperial Hotel Tramontano, one wing of which was home to famed 16th-century writer Torquato Tasso. Set by the bay-side balcony, the facade of the **Casa di**

Marina Grande is Sorrento's main fishing harbor, as well as a popular tourist hangout.

Tasso is all the more exquisite for its simplicity and seems little changed since his day. The poet's house originally belonged to the Rossi family, into which Tasso's mother married, and was adorned with beautiful gardens (Tasso wove gardens into many of his poems). The piazza itself is supposedly the site where a temple to Venus once stood, and the scattered Roman ruins make it a real possibility. ⊠ *Via Veneto and Via Marina Grande.*

Piazza Tasso. This was the site of Porta Catello, the summit of the old walls that once surrounded the city. Today it remains a symbolic portal to the old town, overflowing with apricot-awning caffè, *Stile Liberty* (Italian Art Nouveau) buildings, people who congregate here day and night, and horse-drawn carriages clip-clopping by. In the center of it all is Torquato Tasso himself, standing atop a high base and rendered in marble by sculptor Giovanni Carli in 1870. The great poet was born in Sorrento in 1544 and died in Rome in 1595, just before he was to be crowned poet laureate. Tasso wrote during a period when Italy was still recovering from devastating Ottoman incursions along its coasts—Sorrento itself was sacked and pillaged in 1558. He is best known for his epic poem *Jerusalem Delivered,* which deals with the conquest of Jerusalem during the First Crusade. At the northern edge of the piazza, where it merges into Corso Italia, is the church of Maria del Carmine, with a Rococo wedding-cake facade of gleaming white-and-yellow stucco. Step inside to note its wall of 18th-century tabernacles, all set, like a jeweler's display, in gilded cases, and the fine ceiling painting of the Virgin Mary. ⊠ *Western end of Corso Italia and above Marina Piccola, at eastern edge of historic district.*

The Majolica Courtyard is a highlight of the Palazzo Correale.

WHERE TO EAT

$$
SOUTHERN
ITALIAN

✕ **Da Emilia.** Right at the Marina Grande, and not the most visually prepossessing place in Sorrento, this spot has a happy plus with Irene in the kitchen. The rickety wooden tables and blue-check tablecloths are a refreshing change from the town's (occasionally pretentious) elegance. Go for a plate of honest spaghetti with clams, wash it down with a carafe of white wine, and watch the fishermen mending their nets. Fresh fried *paranza* (small local fish) or anchovies are also top-notch. *Gnocchi* (dumplings in tomato and basil sauce) and eggplant Parmesan are also highly recommended. ⊠ *Via Marina Grande 62* ☎ *081/8072720* ▭ *No credit cards* ⊘ *Closed Tues. during Nov.–Feb.*

$$
MODERN ITALIAN

✕ **Il Buco.** In the spirit of "Slow Food," this restaurant just off Piazza Sant'Antonino uses only local and seasonal ingredients of the highest quality in its nouvelle creations. Dine on inventive sea and land dishes like risotto with buffalo cheese topped with prawns and fresh mint. Round out the meal with a sponge apple cake with Calvados sauce. Reservations are recommended for dinner. ⊠ *Seconda Rampa di Marina Piccola, 5* ☎ *081/8782354* ⊕ *www.ilbucoristorante.it* ▭ *AE, DC, MC, V* ⊘ *Closed Wed. and Jan.*

$
SOUTHERN
ITALIAN

✕ **La Basilica.** Opened by the same owner as the **Ristorante Museo Caruso**, this is a budget alternative to its famous brother. No cover, no service charge, but the same extensive wine list (about 1,700 different labels) plus a bountiful choice of hearty Italian dishes. In a tiny alley between piazzas Tasso and St. Antonino, its main salon is decorated with modern paintings of an erupting Vesuvius. You can watch the *pizzaiolo* baking pizza or bread for you in the wood oven, but if you want a romantic dinner, choose the smaller room on the opposite side of the road. Here—vertigo permitting!—you can dine on a tiny balcony overlooking the tortuous road leading to the harbor. There is also outside seating for the less adventurous. Choose the *strozzapreti* (priest-chokers) pasta with scampi and cherry tomatoes or go for the fabulous rice cake on zucchini sauce. ✉ *Via S. Antonino 28* ☎ *081/8774790* ⊕ *www. ristorantelabasilica.com* ▤ *AE, DC, MC, V.*

$$
SOUTHERN
ITALIAN
Fodor's Choice
★
✕ **La Favorita—'O Parrucchiano.** This restaurant is in a sprawling, multi-level, high-ceiling greenhouse and orchard, with tables and chairs amid enough tropical greenery to fill a Victorian conservatory—the effect is enchantingly 19th century. Opened in 1868 by an ex-priest ('o Parrucchiano means "the priest's place" in the local dialect), La Favorita continues to serve classic Sorrentine cuisine. The shrimp baked in lemon leaves, cannelloni, homemade Sorrentine pasta, chocolate and hazelnut cake, and lemon profiteroles are all excellent, but they can't compete with the unique decor. ✉ *Corso Italia 71* ☎ *081/8781321* ⊕ *www. parrucchiano.it* ▤ *MC, V* ☽ *Closed Wed. only mid-Nov.–mid-Mar.*

$$
ITALIAN
✕ **La Lanterna.** On the site of ancient Roman thermal baths (you can still see ruins under a glass section in the floor), this is a historic venue as well as a beloved eatery. Whether dining outdoors under the lanterns, or indoors under the beamed ceiling and stucco arcades, you'll enjoy *cucina tipica, locale e nazionale*, traditional local and national dishes, including old favorites such as *calamaro ripieno* (stuffed calamari). ✉ *Via S. Cesareo 25* ☎ *081/8781355* ⊕ *www.lalanternarestaurantsorrento.com* ▤ *AE, DC, MC, V* ☽ *Nov. and Jan.–Mar., closed Wed.*

$$
SOUTHERN
ITALIAN
✕ **Osteria del Buonconvento.** If you are looking for a trattoria with outside seating and a good assortment of local dishes and *real* pizza, go for this little osteria in the heart of Sorrento. The owner speaks only Neapolitan but has a special talent of suggesting the dish of the day (don't worry, the waiters do speak English). First-class *gnocchi alla sorrentina*—dumplings with tomato sauce, basil, and mozzarella—baked and served in the *pignatiello* (terracotta pot), or the pasta with clams and pumpkin cream, or the delicious vegetable side dishes to be eaten with *focaccia* (baked pizza dough) instead of bread, are some of the delights that announce this is truly authentic *cucina sorrentina*. ✉ *Via B. Donnoroso 5* ☎ *081/8773637* ⊕ *www.osteriadelbuonconvento.it* ▤ *DC, MC, V* ☽ *Closed Mon. and Feb.*

$$$
SOUTHERN
ITALIAN
Fodor's Choice
★
✕ **Ristorante Museo Caruso.** A classic international and operatic theme is carried out from *preludio* appetizers, such as shrimp in a limoncello dressing, to the *rapsodia delicatesse* desserts, including crêpes suzette. Sorrentine favorites are tweaked creatively as well, including ravioli with broccoli sauce and squid with almonds. The staff is warm and helpful, the singer on the sound system is the long-departed "fourth tenor" himself, and the operatic memorabilia with posters and old photos of Caruso is viewed in a flattering blush-pink light. This elegant restaurant deserves its longtime popularity. It is open from noon to midnight to cater for hunger pangs at any time of day. There are five-course tasting menus from €50. ✉ *Via S. Antonino 12* ☎ *081/8073156* ⊕ *www.ristorantemuseocaruso.com* ▤ *AE, DC, MC, V.*

WHERE TO STAY

$$$$ ☷ **Bellevue Syrene.** In the late 19th century, Empress Eugénie of France
Fodor's Choice   came here for a week and wound up staying three months. You'll under-
★   stand why if you stay at this retreat magisterially placed on a bluff high
over the Bay of Naples—just wait until you see the view from the glass-
enclosed lobby. One of Italy's most legendary hotels, this connoisseur's
favorite is a gentle fantasia of Venetian chandeliers, Louis-Phillipe rugs,
and Belle Epoque murals (painted to make the King of Bavaria feel
more at home back in the 1860s). Or was, until a recent renovation
transformed a block of the guest rooms into visions right out of today's
sizzling South Beach. The gilded chandeliers have been replaced by
hip and modern ones, avant-garde artworks rub shoulder with trompe
l'oeil frescoes, and plate-glass coffee tables now adorn the ducal salons.
Don Giovanni, the main restaurant, has plate-glass panoramic vistas
over the bay and a truly tempting menu (Li Galli Lobster with Melon
Pearls, anyone?). Many, however, will want to head outdoors to enjoy
elegant meals under the cliff-top wisteria pergola. **Pros:** spectacular
views; impeccable design elements; elegantly furnished common areas;
half board available. **Cons:** very expensive (parking alone costs €25 a
day). ⊠ *Piazza della Vittoria 5* ☎ *081/8781024* ⊕ *www.bellevue.it* ⇗ *49
rooms* ♨ *In-room: a/c, safe, refrigerator, Internet, Wi-Fi. In-hotel: 4 restaurants, bar, gym, beachfront, Internet terminal, Wi-Fi hotspot, some
pets allowed* ⊟ *AE, DC, MC, V* ⊘ *Closed Jan.–Mar.* ⍓ *BP.*

$$ ☷ **Del Corso.** This centrally located, family-run hotel close to Sorrento's
major hub, Piazza Tasso, is homey and comfortable, with pleasant com-
mon areas and basic, clean rooms. A solarium, courtyard entrances
for some rooms, and a breakfast terrace nudge up the comfort level.
Reception is on the second floor (via the elevator). For a quieter stay,
opt for a room away from the front overlooking the busy Corso Italia.
Pros: pleasant, accommodating staff; centrally located. **Cons:** no pool;
some rooms are small; no parking. ⊠ *Corso Italia 134* ☎ *081/8071016*
⊕ *www.hoteldelcorso.com* ⇗ *26 rooms* ♨ *In-room: a/c, safe. In-hotel:
bar, Wi-Fi* ⊟ *AE, MC, V* ⊘ *Closed Jan. and Feb.* ⍓ *BP.*

$$$$ ☷ **Excelsior Vittoria.** Overlooking the Bay of Naples, this Belle Epoque
Fodor's Choice   dream offers gilded salons worthy of a Proust heroine; gardens and
★   orange groves; and an impossibly romantic terrace where musicians
sometimes lull guests with equal doses of Cole Porter and Puccini. This
complex of two mansions and two 19th-century chalets has been run by
the same family for 175 years; they have traded witticisms with Alexan-
dre Dumas and Oscar Wilde, welcomed crowned heads, and comforted
Caruso in his final days. The public salons are virtual museums, with
potted palms, Victorian love seats, and Stile Liberty ornamentation;
like the Bellevue Syrene hotel, this hotel offers the truly magical experi-
ence of staying in a veritable "palace" in a casual resort. Guest rooms
are usually spacious and airy, with tile floors, soigné furnishings, and
balconies and terraces overlooking bay or gardens. Dine in the open-
air seaside restaurant Bosquet or in the magnificently grand dining hall
of Vittoria, where waiters in starched white jackets don't look a bit
foolish. Outside is a gorgeous park, lined with arbored promenades,
shaded by orange trees, studded with statues, and home to a giant pool.

Once part of a villa constructed by Lord William Waldorf Astor, the Villa Pompeiana is now a place reserved for special parties at the Hotel Bellevue Syrene.

Step outside the protected gates and you're right in the heart of Sorrento. **Pros:** unbeatable location in the center of town; gardens buffer city noise. **Cons:** not all rooms have sea views; some rooms are on the small side; front desk can be cold. ⊠ *Piazza Tasso 34* ☎ *081/8071044, 800/980053 in Italy only* ⊕ *www.exvitt.it* ⤵ *98 rooms* ⌂ *In-room: a/c, safe, refrigerator, Wi-Fi. In-hotel: 2 restaurants, bars, pool, gym, spa, Internet terminal, Wi-Fi hotspot, parking (free), some pets allowed* ⊟ *AE, DC, MC, V* ⦿⏐ *BP.*

$$ ⛨ **Hotel Astoria.** In the heart of Sorrento's historical center, down a quiet pedestrian-only narrow street, this charming hotel has been completely renovated in a light and gracious Mediterranean style. There is no view but you are in an old building (replete with majolica-tile floors) with comfortable modern facilities. You can enjoy your breakfast in the lunchroom or alfresco in the courtyard. There's also a little pool (not for swimming, unfortunately) for kids and a terrace with sun beds. A nice touch is the bowl with fresh apples for the guests at reception . . . everybody knows that an apple a day keeps the doctor away! **Pros:** central location; friendly staff. **Cons:** no views. ⊠ *Via Santa Maria delle Grazie 24* ☎ *081/8074030* ⊕ *www.hotelastoriasorrento.com* ⤵ *32 rooms* ⌂ *In-room: a/c, refrigerator, safe. In-hotel: bar, Wi-Fi hotspot* ⊟ *AE, MC, V* ⊗ *Closed Jan. and Feb.* ⦿⏐ *BP.*

$$$–$$$$ ⛨ **La Favorita.** Sorrento is home to some of the most gorgeous and
★ sumptuous hotels in Italy, but they all now have to make room for this newborn, a striking beauty that can hold its own against some great hotel names. The official name is Grand Hotel La Favorita and it earns the encomium with its exceedingly glamorous lobby: a white-on-white extravaganza of Caprese columns, tufted sofas, shimmering

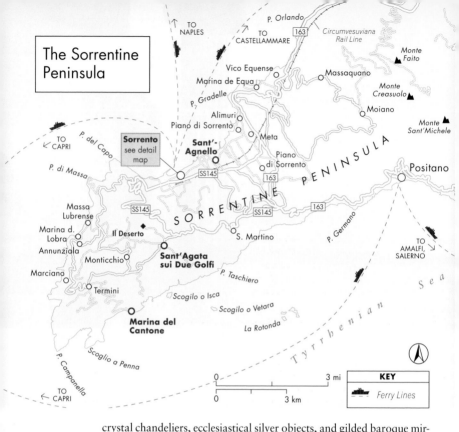

crystal chandeliers, ecclesiastical silver objects, and gilded baroque mirrors. Happily, the vibe is also elegantly casual, the staff is charming and helpful, and the guest rooms well equipped and spacious (they need to be as they don't offer any views to speak of). The garden is a delight but that's no surprise, as owner Enzo Manniello also runs Sorrento's famous garden-restaurant Parrucchiano. If you want a view, just head up to the rooftop pool area, where you can savor a magnificently scenic vista of the bay and Vesuvius. **Pros:** central location; beautiful terrace; idyllic garden. **Cons:** no views from the guest rooms. ⊠ *Via T. Tasso 61* ☎ *081/8782031* ⊕ *www.hotellafavorita.com* ⇆ *85 rooms* ⌂ *In-room: safe, Wi-Fi. In-hotel: restaurant, 2 bars, pool, parking, some pets allowed* ≡ *AE, DC, MC, V* ☾ *Closed Nov. and Jan.–Mar.* ⊚|*BP.*

¢–$ 🏠 **Relais Palazzo Starace.** There may be no elevator, no lobby, and no view but this place does boast a gentle price tag in a central part of town, and that's a winning combo for sizzling, summertime Sorrento. The entrance hall might be discouraging at this B&B but once you get to the third floor (your luggage goes up in a freight elevator), you'll be happy to find guest rooms that are tastefully furnished and equipped with TV, air-conditioning, and a supermarket-priced minibar. Breakfast is served in a bar a few minutes' walk away. The two-bedroom apartment with kitchenette is ideal if you have children. The owner, Signora Giovanna, is happy to give you tips about Sorrento. Note that the rooms with a balcony are prettier but do face onto Corso Italia, one of Italy's busiest streets but one that is closed to traffic at night. **Pros:** great location; competitive prices; discounted parking at nearby garage. **Cons:** no elevator; no views; room with the air conditioner on balcony is noisy. ⊠ *Via Santa Maria della Pietà 9* ☎ *081/8784031* ⊕ *www.palazzostarace.com* ⤏ *5 rooms* ⌂ *In-room: a/c, safe, refrigerator* ⊟ *MC, V* ⊗ *Closed Jan. and Feb.*

NIGHTLIFE AND THE ARTS

Music spots and bars cluster in the side streets near Piazza Tasso, among them Fauno Notte Club, Artis Domus, and Chantecler's. Ask at your hotel about clubs that might interest you and to get the latest news. The main watering hole for Sorrento visitors is the **Circolo dei Forestieri** (⊠ *Via L De Maio 35* ☎ *081/8773012* ⊕ *www.circolodeiforestieri. com* ⊗ *Closed Dec.–Feb.*), traditionally packed with Americans, Brits, and Australians. Crowds begin to descend (also home to the Sorrento tourist office) for an aperitif at sunset; others arrive for dinner, while merrymakers hold out for the late-night karaoke.

Incontri Musicali Sorrentini (⊠ *Cloister of Chiesa di San Francesco* ⊠ *Piazzetta Angri and Largo Annunziata in Sant'Agnello*) is the main cultural event of the year, offering a bevy of concerts and theatrical entertainments from the last week of August to the end of September, many held in the famous Moorish-style cloister of the church of San Francesco. There are several outdoor venues in Sant'Agnello nearby. Tickets cost €15–€30; check with your hotel or the Sorrento tourist office (⊕ *www.sorrentotourism.com*) for schedules and information. Throughout the year, free municipal concerts—usually jazz or classical music—are held in several other venues.

The **Tarantella Show** (⊠ *Fauno Notte Club, Piazza Tasso 1* ☎ *081/8781021* ⊕ *www.faunonotte.it*) presents tarantella dances with masks, costumes, and tambourines, as well as classic Neapolitan folklore performances complete with *pulcinella* (comedic prankster figures in Neapolitan theater) and *pazzarielli* (jesters).

SHOPPING

The main shopping street is Via San Cesareo—along this pedestrian thoroughfare, lined with dozens of shops selling local and Italian crafts, the air is pungent with the perfume of fruit and vegetable stands. Corso Italia has more modern boutique offerings. Wood inlay (*intarsia*) is the most-sought-after item, but you'll be surprised by the high quality of embroidery and metalwork. Keep your eye out for stalls selling tiny crèche figures that go beyond the traditional Nativity participants—miniature *Pulcinella*, hunchback dwarfs, and elaborate market scenes. Local crafts, but in line with a contemporary art spirit, can be found in Via Fuoro, while some classic antique dealers are in Via P.R.Giuliani.

Far from the tourist streets, hunt down Aromi di Sorrento-Mezzo Kilo (⊠ *Via Fuoro 62/A* ☎ *333/3718544*for a little shop crammed with Sorrento's best soaps and essences. Or delight in ingenious Giuseppina

Gambardella's unique creations of lovely Christmas decorations made with peppers.

Right in the *centro storico*, but not easy to find, the tiny store of Arte e Dimora (⊠ *Vico 1, Fuoro 9 bis* might be just the place to fall in love with a unique *souvenir de voyage*. With no e-mail or telephone, the extravagant Michele tends his tiny space full of hundreds of different kinds of bric-à-brac, including watercolors, frames, old tin boxes, and one-of-a-kind vintage items.

Sorrento for sandals? Forget Positano and Capri and head to **La Conchiglia** (⊠ *Via Fuoro 29* ☎ *081/8774605*). You choose one of the hundreds of designs and one of the resident maestri creates your own made-to-measure sandals on the spot.

Vincenzo and his son Nicholas make distinguished jewels with both coral and lava at their **Leonard Jewels** (⊠ *Via S. Cesareo 24* ☎ *081/8772923*) ; for those famous carved Sorrentine cameos head to the mezzanine floor.

Libreria Tasso (⊠ *Via S. Cesareo 96* ☎ *081/8071639* ⊕ *www.libreriatasso. com*) has a browse-worthy stock of English books and maps.

Limonoro (⊠ *Via S. Cesareo 49/53* ☎ *081/8785348* ⊕ *www.limonoro.it*) produces the lovely local lemon liqueur, limoncello. You can observe the production process in the back of this tiny white shop, and watch the owners paint designs on the pretty bottles.

At **Sepe–Vetri d'Arte** (⊠ *Via P. R. Giuliani 19* ☎ *081/8072848*) Yvonne Adriaens and Massimo Sepe make impressive examples of artistic glass, ranging from stained glass for houses or churches to smaller items made of fused glass, including clocks, lamps, frames, mirrors, and plates. Exquisite, unusual jewelery is also for sale.

Stinga Tarsia (⊠ *Via L. De Maio 16* ☎ *081/8781165*) has been crafting fine-quality marquetry, coral, and cameos since 1890.

SANT'AGNELLO TO MARINA DEL CANTONE

Grand monasteries, the finest beach along the Gulf of Positano, an Edenic botanical park, and southern Italy's finest restaurant are just a few of the discoveries that await the traveler willing to leave Sorrento's Belle Epoque splendor behind and take to the scenic hills and coasts of the Sorrento Peninsula. As it turns out, many people do just that—the towns here get crowded with weekenders from Naples and Rome, and the two-lane state roads 145 and 163 are often congested. The sights here, however, are worth the bother. For those without a car, blue-colored SITA lines and Circumvesuviana orange-colored buses run regularly throughout the peninsula, with most routes stopping in Sorrento. Bus stops are frequent along the peninsula roads, but it's always best to be armed with a local timetable to avoid long waits at stops. Buses stop by request and only at official stops, so flag them down when you would like to get picked up and on boarding request the desired stop.

The gardens of the Cocumella hotel overlook the villas of Sant'Agnello, the Bay of Naples, and Vesuvius.

SANT'AGNELLO

2 km (1 mi) east of Sorrento.

Back in the 18th and 19th centuries, the tiny hamlet of Sant'Agnello was an address of choice. To escape Sorrento's crowds, Bourbon princes and exiled Russian millionaires vacationed here, some building sumptuous villas, others staying at the Hotel Cocumella, the oldest hotel on the Sorrento Peninsula. On the quieter coastal side of town, Sant'Agnello still possesses a faintly ducal air. The 15th- to 16th-century parish church, Chiesa Parrocchiale di Sant'Agnello, is as lyrical as its name: swirls of lemon yellow and white, decorated with marble-gloss plasterwork. Nearby is a spectacular belvedere, the Terrazza Punta San Francesco, complete with café, which offers a hold-your-breath view of the Bay of Naples.

GETTING HERE

Take the A3 Napoli–Salerno highway to the Castellammare di Stabia exit. Take SS145 south and follow signs for "Penisola Sorrentina" and Sant'Agnello. By train, take the Circumvesuviana to the Sant'Agnello stop. There is regular municipal bus service from downtown Sorrento.

EXPLORING

Sant'Agnello's two most famous estates sit side by side nearby. In the early 19th century, the Jesuit **Cocumella monastery** was transformed into a hotel, welcoming the rich and famous. Today, only lucky guests can enjoy its gardens. Next door is the **Parco dei Principi, a hotel built by Gio Ponti in 1962 surrounded by** a botanical park laid out in 1792 by the Count of Siracusa, a cousin to the Bourbons. Traversed by a diminutive Bridge of Love, this was a favorite spot for Désireé, Napoléon's first amour, who came here often. Shaded by horticultural rarities, this park leads to the count's Villa di Poggio Siracusa, a Rococo-style iced birthday cake of a house perched over the bay. Green thumbs and other circumspect visitors can stroll through the romantic park, now part of the Hotel Parco dei Principi.

WHERE TO STAY

$$$$ ☒ **Cocumella.** Many cognoscenti adore this hotel, once one of the most
★   aristocratic in Italy. Set in a cliff-top garden overlooking the Bay of Naples, the Cocumella occupies a baroque monastery, complete with frescoed ceilings, antique reliquaries, a marble cloister, just next to the 17th-century church of Santa Maria. The lobby is Italian-Victorian (note the ceiling frescoes of the four seasons) and 19th-century grace notes continue in grand suites, which have stone fireplaces, Empire-style bureaus, and marble-clad bathrooms; even smaller rooms have their charm. Added amenities include a semi-Olympic pool set among orange trees, tennis courts, a beauty-spa and exercise room, and a 90-foot-long 19th-century tall ship for daily excursions on the bay. Opened in 2009, the Coku Restaurant serves Mediterranean-style sushi on one of the most enchanting terraces in Campania. A bus frequently runs between Sant'Agnello and central Sorrento. **Pros:** quiet location; amazing gardens. **Cons:** far from off-site restaurants; car could be seen as necessity. ☒ *Via Cocumella 7* ☎ *081/8782933* ⊕ *www.cocumella.com* ↘ *53 rooms* ☌ *In-room: a/c (some), safe (some), refrigerator, Wi-Fi. In-hotel: 2 restaurants, tennis court, pool, gym, beachfront, Wi-Fi hotspot, some pets allowed* ▭ *AE, MC, V* ⊙ *Closed Nov.–Mar.* ❢⊙❢ *BP.*

$$$–$$$$ ☒ **Grand Hotel Parco dei Principi.** This hotel offers the best of both
Fodor'sChoice   worlds—a stunningly romantic park, complete with gilded 19th-century villa, plus a hotel that's 1960s modern. Up to a decade ago, the latter might have been considered a debit, but now that Sixties Moderne has entered the history books, this building is newly chic. In fact, when opened, this striking white-on-white structure raised the bar for '60s design, thanks to Gio Ponti, Italy's coolest designer of the era. Inside, all is white walls and blue-glass accents; outside blooms the fabled Parco dei Principi, the lush giardino laid out by the Duke of Siracusa, cousin to the Neapolitan Bourbons, in the early 19th century. Paths lead to a romantic Rococo villa set on the bay—today, a splendiferous setting for the hotel's pool area. A shuttle bus connects with downtown Sorrento. **Pros:** stunning garden; grand bay views; fun '60s décor; exquisite pool area. **Cons:** rooms in road-side wing fall short of those in main bay-side building. ☒ *Via Rota 1* ☎ *081/8784644* ⊕ *www. grandhotelparcodeiprincipi.net* ↘ *96 rooms* ☌ *In-room: a/c, refrigerator, Internet, Wi-Fi. In-hotel: restaurant, bar, pool, beachfront, Wi-Fi hotspot, parking (paid)* ▭ *AE, DC, MC, V* ⊙ *Closed Nov.–Mar.* ❢⊙❢ *BP.*

SANT'AGATA SUI DUE GOLFI

7 km (4½ mi) south of Sorrento, 10 km (6 mi) east of Positano.

Because of its panoramic vistas, Sant'Agata was an end-of-the-line pilgrimage site for beauty lovers through the centuries, especially before the Amalfi Drive opened up the coast to the southeast. As its name suggests, this village 1,300 feet above sea level looks out over the bays of Naples and Salerno (Sant'Agata refers to a Sicilian saint, honored here with a 16th-century chapel), and it found its first fame during the Roman Empire as the nexus of merchant routes uniting the two gulfs. Now that the town has become slightly built up, you have to head to its outskirts to take in the vistas.

GETTING HERE

By car, take the A3 Napoli–Salerno highway to the Castellammare di Stabia exit. Take SS145 south and follow signs for "Penisola Sorrentina." Once you reach Piano di Sorrento, take SS163 (direction Positano) and after about 3 km (2 mi), turn back onto SS145, following signs for Sant'Agata sui Due Golfi. By public transport, take the Circumvesuviana to Sorrento, then a SITA bus to Sant'Agata sui Due Golfi.

EXPLORING

Sant'Agata's most famous vantage point is on the far north side of the hill, where an ancient Greek sanctuary is said to have been dedicated to the Sirens of legend. That choice location became **Il Convento di San Paolo al Deserto**, a monastery built by the Carmelite fathers in the 17th century and now occupied by an order of nuns. Partly restored, the monastery's famed belvedere—with panoramic views of the blue waters all around, and of Vesuvius, Capri, and the peninsula—was a top sight for Grand Tour–era travelers. To access the belvedere's tower, ring the bell at the monastery and ask for the key to open the gate. To get to the Deserto from the center of Sant'Agata, take the main road (Corso Sant'Agata) past the church of Santa Maria delle Grazie on your right, and keep walking uphill on Via Deserto for a little more than half a mile. If traveling by car, park in the raised lot opposite the hotel O Sole Mio. ⊠ *Via Deserto* ☎ *081/8780199* 🖃 *Donations welcome* ☉ *Oct.–Mar., daily 3–4; Apr.–Sept., daily 5–8.*

Today's travelers head to Sant'Agata less for the sublime beauties of Il Deserto than for its lodging options and to dine at Don Alfonso 1890, the finest restaurant in Campania. Across the way from Don Alfonso on the town square is the beautiful 16th-century Renaissance church of **Santa Maria delle Grazie**. The shadowy, evocative interior features an exceptional 17th-century altar brought from the Girolamini church in Naples in the 19th century. Attributed to Florentine artists, it's inlaid with lapis, malachite, mother-of-pearl, and polychrome marble.

WHERE TO EAT AND STAY

$

SOUTHERN
ITALIAN

Fodor's Choice

★

✕ **Antico Francischiello da Peppino.** Halfway between Sant'Agata and Massa Lubrense and overlooking olive groves that seem to run into the sea, this fourth-generation establishment has been welcoming hungry travelers for more than 100 years. Two huge, beamed rooms with sprays of fernery, antique mirrored sideboards, hundreds of mounted plates, brick archways, old chandeliers, fresh flowers, and tangerine-hue tablecloths are quite a sight—a virtual living museum to traditional Sorrentine arts and crafts. *Tagliolini con zafferano, zucchine e gamberi* (pasta with saffron, zucchini, and prawns), ravioli with clams and arugula, and other bountiful country cuisine is *tutto buono*. Reservations

While enjoying a spectacular feast at Don Alfonso 1890, why not treat yourself to a "Vesuvio" flambé cocktail?

are essential for weekend dinners and Sunday lunch. Perched above the restaurant, with sweeping views over to Capri and across the Bay of Naples, are eight well-appointed rooms ($). ✉ *Via Partenope 27, halfway between Sant'Agata and Massa Lubrense* ☎ *081/5339780* ⊕ *www.francischiello.com* 🍴 *AE, DC, MC, V* ⊗ *Closed Wed. in Nov.–Mar.*

$$$$

MODERN ITALIAN

Fodor's Choice

★

✕ **Don Alfonso 1890.** The greatest restaurant in Campania, this is the domain of Alfonso Iaccarino. Haute-hungry pilgrims head here to feast on culinary rarities, often centuries-old recipes given a unique Iaccarin-ian spin. Lobster, for instance, is breaded with traditional Sorrentine "porri" flour, then drizzled with sweet-and-sour sauce influenced by the Arabian traders who came to Naples. The braciola of lamb with pine nuts and raisins is a recipe that also shows an Arab influence, while the cannoli stuffed with foie gras pays homage to the age of Napoleon. Nearly everything is homegrown, with olive oils *di produzione propria* (created on the family farm), vegetables so lovingly grown they have bodyguards, not gardeners (so jokes the staff). Hand-churned butter finds its way into sublime desserts such as the *pizza di cioccolato* (white sugar "mozzarella" on a chocolate "pizza") or the *soufflé di liquore di limone*. The restaurant decor is pastel and staidly traditional—the fireworks are reserved for the food (and the occasional Vesuvio flambéed cocktail). Don Alfonso has one of the finest wine cellars in Europe, set deep in an Oscan cave—don't be surprised if the sommelier tells you his earliest bottle is a Roman amphora dating from 30 BC. If you want to make a night of it, Alfonso and his enchanting wife, Livia, also run an inn ($$$) above the restaurant, with eight suites and an apartment furnished in traditional style. Light sleepers should note that the nearby church bells ring on the half hour throughout the entire night. ✉ *Corso*

Sant'Agata 13 ☎ *081/8780026* ⊕ *www.donalfonso.com* ▤ *AE, DC, MC, V* ☺ *June–Sept., no lunch and closed Mon.; Apr., May, and Oct. closed Mon. and Tues.; closed Nov.–Mar.*

$$–$$$ 🏨 **Sant'Agata.** Like a mirage in off-the-beaten-path Sant'Agata sui Due Golfi, this vast and grand hotel rises not far from cow paths and the monks found at the Il Deserto monastery. One can only imagine what the fathers at the latter would make of this place's gigantic pool, its even larger restaurant, or the generic luxe look of it all, but in the wilds of the Sorrentine peninsula this is a shot of big-city pizzazz. The second floor on the road side has a glimpse of a sea view, but for mere stylish furnishings you should opt for the giant new annex. And if you don't want to trek down for a dip at sea level, boy, does that swimming pool come in handy. **Pros:** recently renovated; easily accessible by SITA bus; free Wi-Fi; quiet location. **Cons:** far from the beach. ⊠ *Via dei Campi 8/A* ☎ *081/8080800* ⊕ *www.hotelsantagata.com* 🛏 *48 rooms* 🔑 *In-room: a/c, safe, refrigerator, Wi-Fi. In-hotel: restaurant, bars, pool, parking (paid), Wi-Fi hotspot* ▤ *AE, DC, MC, V* ☺ *Closed Dec.–Feb.* 🍴 *BP.*

MARINA DEL CANTONE

★ *5 km (3 mi) southwest of Sant'Agata sui Due Golfi.*

As the largest (pebble) beach on the Sorrento Peninsula, Marina del Cantone attracts weekend sun worshippers and foodies drawn by the seaside restaurants here. To get to the beach, usually dotted with dozens of festive umbrellas, a slender road winds down to the sea through rolling vineyards and the small town of Nerano, ending at the Gulf of Positano near the Montalto watchtower.

GETTING HERE

By car, take the A3 Napoli–Salerno highway to the Castellammare di Stabia exit. Take SS145 south and follow signs for "Penisola Sorrentina." Once you reach Piano di Sorrento, take SS163 (direction Positano) and after about 3 km, turn back onto SS145, following signs for Sant'Agata sui Due Golfi, then Metrano, then Nerano-Marina del Cantone. By public transport, take the Circumvesuviana to Sorrento, then a SITA bus to Nerano-Marina del Cantone.

EXPLORING

While enjoying Marina del Cantone's wonderful beach and kick-back village vibe, it also offers a front-row seat to the haunting geological spectacle that is the islets of **Li Galli,** which seems to follow you around as you drive up and down the Amalfi Coast. Other than Positano, Del Cantone is the best place to hire a boat to visit these tiny islands—Gallo Lungo, Castelluccia, and La Rotonda—which sit on the horizon to the east of the beach. They're also called Isole Sirenuse (Isles of the Sirens), after the mythical girl group that lured unwitting sailors onto the rocks. What goes around comes around: legend says the Sirens' feet became flippers, because the Three Graces were envious of how they danced the tarantella; and, as the folkloric tale concludes, the mermaids' dancing days were really *finito* when they petrified into the isles themselves. With all this dancing going on, it's not surprising that the great Russian ballet choreographer Leonide Massine purchased the Li Galli islands as his home in the 1950s; in the 1980s, they were sold to Rudolf Nureyev, who made them his last residence. The beach at Marina del Cantone was reputedly the superstar dancer's favorite coastal hangout.

Nautica 'O Masticiello (✉ *Waterfront, Marina Del Cantone* 🕾 *081/8081443* ⊕ *www.masticiello.com*) runs daily trips to Capri from June to September, and regular tours along the Amalfi Coast including Li Galli, Amalfi, and Positano, weather permitting. They also offer a wide selection of boat rentals, with or without a captain.

WHERE TO EAT AND STAY

$$

SOUTHERN
ITALIAN

✕ **Maria Grazia.** A great story lies behind this area favorite. Signora Maria was running this little waterfront trattoria between the world wars when an aristocrat came round unexpectedly to eat; Maria cooked up the best she had on hand—spaghetti with stuffed zucchini blossoms. Through the well-satisfied aristocrat, the restaurant soon became famous. You can still enjoy it, even without a noble title, in season. ✉ *Spiaggia di Marina del Cantone* 🕾 *081/8081011* ▤ *AE, DC, MC, V* ☺ *Closed mid-Nov.–Feb. except on weekends.*

$$$

SOUTHERN
ITALIAN

✕ **Taverna del Capitano.** The fascinating cuisine here is based on old recipes from the various cultures—Norman and Moorish among them—that loom large in the history of the region. The captain's son, chef Alfonso Caputo, is a wizard at conjuring up not-available-anywhere-else combinations: for example, chicory-and-prawn soup, and tagliatelle with anchovies, sardines, and fennel. You can rely on the knowledgeable maître d' for an absorbing commentary on the various dishes and advice on the right wine from a siege-ready cellar. For dessert, opt for candied eggplant filled with ricotta and topped with chocolate sauce. Above the restaurant area is a select 10-room hotel—called La Locanda del Capitano—run by the same family, with the best rooms overlooking the waterfront. Lodging prices ($$–$$$) include full beach facilities. ✉ *Piazza delle Sirene 10/11, Massa Lubrense, loc. Marina del Cantone* 🕾 *081/8081028* ⊕ *www.tavernadelcapitano.com* ▤ *AE, DC, MC, V* ☺ *Closed Jan. and Feb. and Mon. and Tues., except in summer.*

5

The Bay of Naples

POMPEII TO THE PHLEGREAN FIELDS

WORD OF MOUTH

"I love both Herculaneum and Pompeii, but if I had to choose I would say Herculaneum—it seems to be more personal somehow. It is more compact and easier to do justice to it if time is limited."

—travel2live2

0

WELCOME TO THE BAY OF NAPLES

TOP REASONS TO GO

★ **Archaeological Treats:** Thanks to the destructive yet preserving powers of Vesuvius, you can see what ancient Roman life was like when visiting Pompeii and Herculaneum.

★ **Sweeping Views:** Look seaward from the Acropolis at ancient Cumae and imagine you're a Greek colonist just arrived on the Italian mainland in the 8th century BC.

★ **A Gastronomic Splurge:** See how the Romans have revived their reputation as *bons viveurs* in restaurants at modern Pompeii, or enjoy the day's catch on the waterfront at Pozzuoli.

★ **Home to Mr. and Mrs. Nero:** As an alternative to the tourist bustle at other sites, head for Oplontis, a Roman villa oozing charm and tranquility with astoundingly well-preserved frescoes.

★ **The Dream Volcano:** Geothermal energy has been trapped since time immemorial under the cone of Vesuvius—as you'll see on a hike around the peak.

1 **Vesuvius and environs.** If you head southeast from Naples you immediately run into the *Comuni Vesuviani*, towns with wondrous archaeological sites often sandwiched between once-opulent Bourbon-era villas and ugly 20th-century housing developments, all set against the fertile but threatening backdrop of Vesuvius. This is the place to immerse yourself in Roman society, art, and architecture.

2 Campi Flegrei. Starting from the western suburbs of Naples, the Phlegrean Fields stretch in a coastal belt all the way to the coast at Cumae. Pockmarked with volcanic craters, this was where Rome's senators and emperors came to spend the summer months, tapping the geothermal energy to enhance their downtime with steam baths and swims. It is no coincidence that this remains a favorite excursion for Neapolitans in the 21st century.

GETTING ORIENTED

The Bay of Naples chapter includes two main areas: southeast of Naples, the famous region dominated by Vesuvius and home to the spectacular ancient sites of Pompeii and Herculaneum and, along the coast west of Naples, the Campi Flegrei region, also home to a myriad of ancient wonders. The Vesuvian area is served by the Circumvesuviana railway from both Naples and Sorrento, which are the major bases for day trips. Although Naples is the obvious base for the Campi Flegrei, public transportation from Naples to the main sites beyond Pozzuoli becomes more sporadic, so if you have a few days to spare, opt to stay in one of the fetching country-style hotels in situ.

5

THE BAY OF NAPLES PLANNER

When to Go

This part of the Mediterranean is at its best in spring and fall.

Winter months occasionally reserve chilly surprises for visitors. For instance, roads on the upper slopes of Vesuvius become dangerously icy at times.

In April, May, September, and October watch out for the hordes of (nonpaying) school-children at archaeological sites.

Check out sites such as the ancient Roman baths at Baia and the ancient Roman theaters at Pompeii for spectacular summertime events.

Nature lovers will be pleased to know that this part of the Mediterranean, especially the verdant Campi Flegrei, becomes a floral feast at springtime.

As late as June and July, the north-facing slopes of Vesuvius are still awash with color.

Word of Mouth

"You can't beat the views from the top of Vesuvius, and it is pretty cool to watch the volcano smolder and smoke. You get a good overview of the region and can see the entire gulf all the way from Naples to Sorrento and out to Capri."
—nnolen

Making the Most of Your Time

Allow two full days for visiting the major sites of Herculaneum, best combined with Vesuvius, and Pompeii, which can be neatly bracketed with more rarefied Oplontis.
All these sites will need to be backed up by a visit to the Museo Archeologico Nazionale in Naples, which houses all the major finds from the various sites and also one to Herculaneum's new MAV museum where, thanks to cutting-edge computer technology, ruins are virtually restored to their original glory. For several buildings in Pompeii you need to make Internet reservations at least 24 hours ahead of time (⊕ www.arethusa.net), so a little advance planning is necessary. In the Campi Flegrei, prioritize the sites in Pozzuoli (especially the amphitheater), the outlying site of Cumae, or the monumental archaeological park in Baia.

Finding a Place to Stay

Though much of the Vesuvian area is embraced by the Vesuvius National Park, don't expect well-appointed *agriturismi* or rustic lodgings—or, for that matter, hotels that have you sighing with pleasure when you throw open the shutters. But don't fear. East of Naples there are some great bets for hotels, with two of them found along Herculaneum's Miglio D'Oro. One is the impressive Miglio d'Oro Park Hotel, which provides a chance not just to visit one of the classic and famed Vesuvian villas but to actually stay in one. As well as being convenient for the two days more or less needed to combine visits to Herculaneum's archaeological site and its nearby MAV museum, this hotel and also the convenient Hotel Ercolano are also well placed for Pompeii and Oplontis.

WHAT IT COSTS (IN EUROS)

	¢	$	$$	$$$	$$$$
Restaurants	under €20	€20–€30	€30–€45	€45–€65	over €65
Hotels	under €75	€75–€125	€125–€200	€200–€300	over €300

Restaurant prices are for a first course (*primo*), second course (*secondo*), and dessert (*dolce*). Hotel prices are for two people in a standard double room in high season, including tax and service.

Train Travel

The main station in Naples (Stazione Centrale, at Piazza Garibaldi) is the main hub for public transport both east and west of Naples. A branch of the aptly named **Circumvesuviana railway** (☎ 800/053939 ⊕ www.vesuviana.it) serves the main archaeological sites at the foot of Vesuvius. Trains leave from the Porta Nolana–Corso Garibaldi station in Naples, stop at the main terminal at Piazza Garibaldi 10 blocks away, and then head southeast for Sorrento (about two trains per hour; €1.80 to Ercolano and Torre Annunziata, €2.40 to Pompei Scavi–Villa dei Misteri).

For the Phlegrean Fields to the west of Naples, take the Cumana line run by **SEPSA** (☎ 800/001616 ⊕ www.sepsa.it), with trains every 15–20 minutes, from the terminus at Piazza Montesanto near Montesanto Metropolitana station. Alternatively, take the **FS Metropolitana Linea 2** (☎ 800/568866 ⊕ www.trenitalia.com) to Pozzuoli from either the main Piazza Garibaldi station or the more welcoming station of Mergellina, with departures every 10–15 minutes. This will drop you near the amphitheater and the Solfatara crater.

Bus Travel

Train travel is generally preferable to bus; local roads can be frustratingly slow. The cultural association **Retour** (⊕ www.retourcampiflegrei.com) organizes seasonal departures of the Campi Flegrei on a hop-on-hop-off sightseeing bus from Piazza Municipio–Largo Castello in Naples. Tickets cost €10 a day or €15 for two consecutive days. The bus makes various stops in Naples before heading on to Pozzuoli, Cumae, Baia, Lucrino, and Monte Nuovo.

Boat Travel

The **Metro del Mare** (☎ 199/600700 ⊕ www.metrodelmare.it) is a scenic seasonal option for getting around the bay. Commuter ferries serve all the main ports; they're more expensive and slower than ground transport, but provide spectacular views. Line 1 is particularly useful, with stops in Bacoli (Baia), Pozzuoli, Naples, Portici, Ercolano, Torre del Greco, Torre Annunziata, Castellmmare di Stabia, and Sorrento. Line 2 connects Pozzuoli and Sorrento (€9). Consult the Web site for departure times, which vary with the season.

Car Travel

Pompeii is a short distance off the A3 Naples–Salerno Autostrada (toll from Naples or Nocera: €1.60), but this major highway with only two lanes in each direction can get congested with ill-disciplined drivers and seemingly never-ending roadwork. A car could be useful for exploring the Campi Flegrei region on the west side of Naples, especially for sites like Cumae and Lake Avernus where public transport is either infrequent or nonexistent. From Naples, travel toward Pozzuoli on the Tangenziale—the Naples bypass (toll: €0.65)—exiting at the appropriate junction.

Most archaeological sites are fairly accessible by car. Use a *parcheggio custodito* (attended parking lot), particularly at Pompeii and Herculaneum, and avoid on-street unattended parking. Metered parking (look for the blue lines on the street) is scarce in most places.

Off the main highways, signposting is sometimes poor, with road signs suffering intense competition from advertising placards, so navigating becomes an invaluable skill. The westbound Tangenziale (Napoli–Pozzuoli) should be avoided Saturday evenings and Sunday in summer (crowds heading out of Naples for nightlife or beaches). Road conditions are usually good, though surfaces near the top of Vesuvius can become icy in winter.

5

CAMPANIA'S ANCIENT TREASURES
AN ARCHAEOLOGICAL "DISNEYLAND"

As so often happens in history, other people's catastrophes are an archaeologist's dream: Pompeii, Herculaneum, and nearby ancient sites were remarkably preserved for posterity thanks to Vesuvius's biggest eruption.

Above: The Castle at Baia is home to the Museo Archeologica dei Campi Flegri. Opposite top: Roman temple at Pozzuoli. Opposite bottom: Temple of Venus, Baia.

Pompeii, Herculaneum, Baia, Cumae, Oplontis . . . no wonder the regions to the west and east of Naples are considered two of the world's greatest treasure troves of Greek and Roman antiquity. Why are these regions the "Disneylands" of classical antiquity? The area surrounding the big city has a Greco-Roman history that makes Naples itself look like the new kid on the block. The Greeks first Hellenized Italy's boot in the 6th century BC at Cumae. From the 1st century AD, the Romans made the region a vast playground. Favored by upper-middle-class Romans, Pompeii and Herculaneum were like French Riviera towns of today. And when emperors wanted to indulge in sybaritic living they headed west instead, from Puteoli to Baia, to build palatial residences for indulging in vices that would have been unseemly in Pompeii or (just read Petronius' *Satyricon*) Rome.

THE EMPRESS'S DUGOUT

Its ownership attributed to Mrs. Nero, the Empress Poppaea, the spectacular villa at Oplontis, when Vesuvius erupted, was probably empty, suggesting that it was undergoing restructuring. The villa does, though, have ravishing Roman murals done in the ultimate in the 2nd and 3rd Pompeiian Styles, and with often whole rooms to yourself to view them in.

POMPEII

When it comes to Campania's overflowing basket of treasures of the ancient world, everyone starts with Pompeii, and rightly so. Rome's Forum might be more majestic, but for a cross-section of Roman everyday life Pompeii is UNESCO World Heritage site "numero I."

Not only are everyday people commemorated but in the Orchard of the Fugitives they are preserved as death left them. In the newly restored Thermopolium, the day's takings were found in the till. Graffiti abound (one, the Latin version of "House done," advice from one thief to another).

Or head to the Villa dei Casti Amanti, where recent excavations uncovered the skeleton of a mule used to work the flour mill. In the Domus of Julius Polybus the past reemerges via virtual technology, missing pieces put back to recreate the house while the original owner is given an eerie voice-over. To carry historical continuity further, inspired by Pompeii's Cave Canem mosaic, you can even adopt a local dog. (⊕ *www. icanidipompeii.it*).

HERCULANEUM

More compact than Pompeii, Herculaneum was discovered by chance after sinking a well in 1711. An archaeological dream come true, the mix of mud and pyroclastic matter meant that much

organic material remains eerily intact, down to a carbonized Roman boat recently given its own pavilion, along with spectacular frescoes and mosaics. To see it all come alive, visit the new and spectacular MAV museum, including a computer recreation of that fateful day when Vesuvius blew in 79 AD.

BAIA

With its thermal springs, this bay of bays boasted antiquity's most extensive bath complex as Rome's Great and the Good (and not-so-good) undertook some private colonization for leisure purposes.

Much of the complex is still there on the slopes while part of one pleasure palace—Emperor Claudius' Nymphaeum—now lies submerged, the highlight of a submarine area visitable from a glass-bottomed boat. Replica statues rear from the depths, the originals being in Baia's grand castle-turned-museum.

CUMAE

Here Greeks established their first foothold on Italy's mainland, introducing the cult of Apollo whose priestess, the Cumaean Sibyl, prophesied for Aeneas the founding of Rome.

Eight centuries later she was still in business, predicting to a young Claudius his future emperorship, albeit her "cave"—one of the ancient wonders of the world—is actually part of a Roman military tunnel.

5

Updated by
Martin Wilmott
Bennett

You can get to Naples by train, bus, or car, or you can "arrive" aboard a boat. If you're lucky enough to travel by water, a peacock's tail of splendor unfolds before you as you enter the vast Golfo di Napoli, the Bay of Naples. Enshrined in 1,001 travel posters, this pulse-tingling vista offers a turquoise-rimmed crescent of isles, hills, azure sea, ancient cities, and modern villas, all arrayed around the bay to the east and west of Naples.

But on each side of the city the earth fumes and grumbles, reminding us that all this beauty was born of cataclysm. Along the coast to the west are the Campi Flegrei, the Phlegrean Fields of the ancients, where the crater of the Solfatara spews satisfyingly Dante-esque gases and where hills like Monte Nuovo have a habit of emerging overnight. Nearby are the dark, deep waters of Lago d'Averno, the lake that was allegedly the ancient doorway to the Underworld, realm of the pagan afterlife ruled over by the god Hades. To the southeast of Naples slumbers Vesuvius, the mother of all mounts, looking down from its 4,000-foot height at the coastal strip stretching from modern and ancient Pompeii all the way to Naples. With potential destruction ever at hand, it is small wonder that southern Italians—and in particular Neapolitans—obey to the letter Horace's precept, *carpe diem,* "seize the day."

Even with the world's most famous volcano looming over the scene like a perpetual standby tombstone, visitors should feel relatively safe. The observatory on Vesuvius's slopes keeps its scientific finger on the subterranean pulse and will warn when signs of misbehavior become evident, so you need not worry about becoming an unwilling exhibit in some encore of Pompeii. You can simply concentrate on the memorable sights that fringe the spectacularly blue bay. The entire region is rife with legend and immortal names. Sixteen kilometers (10 mi) to the west of Naples lies an area where the emperors Claudius and Nero schemed and plotted in their villas, Virgil composed his poetry, and the Apostle Paul landed to spread the Gospel. Here, in and around what was called the Phlegrean (burning) Fields, are ancient sites, such as the Greeks' first colony in mainland Italy, the city of Cumae, home of the famed Cumaean Sibyl; the luxury-loving Baia, whose hot springs and dissolute living made it ancient Rome's most fashionable pleasure dome; and the Amphitheater of Pozzuoli, whose subterranean galleries are better preserved than even those at Rome's Colosseum. Here are the Campi Flegrei—inspiration for Dante's *Inferno*—and the sulfur-bound Solfatara, the "Little Vesuvius." Leapfrogging over Naples and spread out east along the bay are the ancient noble villa at Oplontis and, in the shadow of Vesuvius, Herculaneum and Pompeii—among the largest archaeological sites in Europe. Nowhere else in Italy is there a comparable mingling of natural vigor with the remains of antiquity.

VESUVIUS AND ENVIRONS

Though barely more than a third as tall as the perennially active Mt. Etna, its Sicilian counterpart, Vesuvius, with its relatively modest 4,189-foot height, has achieved unparalleled status in the collective consciousness of the Italians and the world. For centuries this intermittently active volcano had offered a spectacle to visitors who flocked to the Bay of Naples to marvel at its small-scale eruptions, ever-present plumes of smoke, and thundering fumaroles. In the mid-18th century, in fact, the entire court of Naples set up shop in Portici, at the foot of the mountain, building summer villas that served as ringside seats to the volcano's hypnotic pyrotechnics.

Artists painted the mountain in eruption, streams of lava rendered in lurid hues of blood. Romantic poets climbed the peak under the full moon to create odes extolling its sublime and terrible power. Duchesses (fashionably attired with earrings and cameos exquisitely carved of seashells) would hire chair porters to bear them up to the rim, where, down below, rainbow mounds of sulfurous ash, vents of hissing steam, lunarlike boulders—everything, it seems, but little imps dashing about with long Luciferian pitchforks—presented a hellish sight.

Vesuvius's eruptions—from the ancient era through the 18th century—had long been legendary, but the volcano's lethal handiwork only became apparent to modern minds when the Roman towns of Pompeii and Herculaneum were discovered by accident and then excavated in the late 18th century. As it turned out, having been buried since the famous AD 79 eruption, these towns promptly became the most celebrated archaeological sites in Europe, offering up untold artistic treasures (the finest of which are on display at Naples's incredible Museo Archeologico Nazionale).

Today, thousands of visitors arrive every day to sites around the bay, most with one eye monitoring 'O Vesuvio, just a few miles away. There have been around 30 eruptions of various magnitudes in the past 2,000 years, the most recent of which took place in 1944. This might be construed as good news, but many volcanologists think it's ominous when a living volcano is so silent—only two eruptions have occurred in the 20th century—and they now maintain a constant watch.

5

HERCULANEUM (ERCOLANO)

Fodor's Choice   *12 km (8 mi) southeast of Naples, 40 km (25 mi) northwest of Salerno.*

★   A visit to the archaeological site of Herculaneum neatly counterbalances the hustle of its larger neighbor, Pompeii. And although close to the heart of the busy town of Ercolano—indeed, in places right under it—the ancient site seems worlds apart, and you have the sensation of being catapulted back into the past, for here there is ample supply of ancient allure and splendor (unlike Pompeii, whose site is much more ruined). Like Pompeii, Herculaneum was buried by Vesuvius's eruption in AD 79. Unlike Pompeii, it was submerged in a mass of volcanic mud that sealed and preserved wood and other materials including food (whereas at Pompeii, most organic matter rotted away over time). Much smaller than its famous neighbor, the settlement of Herculaneum was a wealthy resort town, and a greater portion of what was found has been left in place. Several villas have inlaid marble floors that evoke the same admiration as the mosaics in Naples' Museo Archeologico. Elsewhere it's possible to gauge how the less privileged lived: more remains of the upper stories than in Pompeii, so you can view the original stairs to the cramped, poorly lighted rooms that gave onto the central courtyard. Here there's more of a sense of a living community than Pompeii is able to convey.

GETTING HERE

To get to Herculaneum by car, take the A3 Naples–Salerno highway and exit at "Ercolano." Follow signs for the "*Scavi*" (excavations). The Circumvesuviana connects Herculaneum to Naples, Portici, Torre del Greco, Torre Annunziata, Pompeii, and Sorrento with frequent departures and arrivals. City buses No. 157 and 255 depart Naples' Piazza Municipio for Herculaneum, via Portici, regularly. No. 255 continues on to Torre del Greco as well.

VISITOR INFORMATION

The **Ufficio Turistico** (⊠ *Via IV Novembre 82, Ercolano* ☎ *081/7881243*) is open 9–2, closed Sunday.

EXPLORING

Like all the other sites in the Vesuvian area, **Herculaneum, or the ancient site of Ercolano** is served efficiently by the Circumvesuviana railway, which provides fast, frequent, and economical connections; from Naples' Stazione Centrale in Piazza Garibaldi, take the Circumvesuviana train to the Ercolano stop (five per hour, 20 minutes east, €1.80). The ruins are a five-minute walk downhill along Via IV Novembre toward the Bay of Naples. ■TIP➔ Archaeology buffs will want to bring a flashlight to better see into the dark corners of the excavated houses and bottled water to pour on in situ mosaics to brighten them up.

Herculaneum was named, like several other Greek colonies around the Mediterranean, after its legendary founder Heracles (Hercules), but details surrounding the date of its foundation by its Greek settlers have yet to be revealed. Certainly the grid plan of the town's layout suggests affinities with nearby Neapolis (now Naples), so it could have been an offshoot of its neighbor on the Bay of Naples. Like many Greek sites

East of Naples: Vesuvius and Environs

KEY

⊢+⊢ Rail Lines
········· Foot Trails

Golfo di Napoli

Naples

Stazione Centrale Napoli

S. Giorgio Cremano

Portici

Herculaneum (Ercolano)

Torre del Greco

S. Sebastiano

Pollena Trocchia

S. Anastasia

Somma

S. Gennaro

S. Guiseppe

Ottaviano

Vesuvius

Parco Nazionale del Vesuvio

Terzigno

Boscotrecase

Boscoreale

Oplontis (Torre Annunziata)

Villa dei Misteri

Pompeii

Scafati

Poggiomarino

Striano

S. Valentino

S. Marzano

Palma

Carbonara

A1

A3

A30

268

162

18

var. 268

0 2 mi
0 2 km

in southern Italy, in about the 4th century BC it fell under Samnite influence. It finally became a *municipium* (municipality) under Roman dominion in 89 BC. At the time of its destruction in AD 79, it had fewer than 5,000 inhabitants (as compared to Pompeii's 10,000–20,000), many of whom were fishermen, craftsmen, and artists, while a lucky few patricians owned summer villas overlooking the sea. In contrast to Pompeii, most of the damage here was done by volcanic mud. This semiliquid mass seeped into the crevices and niches of every building, covering household objects and enveloping textiles and wood—sealing all in a compact, airtight tomb.

Casual excavation—and haphazard looting—began at the beginning of the 18th century under the prince of Elboeuf, who purchased the land after a farmer had made several chance finds of marble relics while digging for a well. The excavation technique at the time consisted of digging vertical shafts and horizontal galleries, and whenever possible, gunpowder was used to speed up the work—techniques that make those of the much-maligned Heinrich Schliemann, discoverer of Troy, sound positively scrupulous. It was precisely through this network of underground tunnels that 18th-century visitors from northern Europe on their Grand Tour—such as Horace Walpole and Thomas Gray—were to experience the buried city.

Open-air digs were not initiated until 1828 and, using much more scientific techniques, continue to this day. One recent is a carbonized Roman ship, another example how the relics unearthed here are generally better preserved than Pompeii's. In some cases you can even see the original wooden beams, staircases, and furniture. Lending a touch of verdant life, some of the peristyle gardens have been replanted. Today much excitement is focused on one excavation adjacent to the main site, the **Villa dei Papiri,** built by Julius Caesar's father-in-law. The building takes its name from the 1,800 carbonized papyrus scrolls dug up here in the 18th century, and is believed to have been a center for Epicurean philosophy. ■ TIP➡ The villa is closed to the public for restoration, but you can see more than 100 bronze statues recovered from the villa at the Museo Archeologico Nazionale in Naples while an impressive virtual version of the building inside and out is to be seen just up the road in the newly opened Museo Archeologico Virtuale museum.

Enter the real archaeological site through the entrance on Corso Resina. Make your way down a Nature section planted with local flora with a Roman connection—myrtle, lavender, holm oaks—offset by the most modern hydrography. Pick up a splendid map at the ticket office and proceed alongside the excavated town. Its grid pattern, with three *cardines* (avenues running north–south) intersected by two *decumani* (east–west axes), is reminiscent of that found in Spaccanapoli. The sloping path leads you to a bookshop and a kiosk where you can hire an audio guide (€6.50).

The main *"percorso"* (guided path) starts, fittingly enough, with a recently built tunnel taking you down to what would have been, pre-AD 79, the now slimy green seafront. First stop is the **Terrace of M. Nonius Balbus,** proconsul of Crete and Cyrene, supporter of the emperor

Much better preserved than Pompeii, Herculaneum boasts houses with frescoes whose colors remain much more vivid.

Augustus, and a great benefactor to the town. His statue gazes down at a sea that is no longer there, having been pushed back some 400 meters by debris from the 79 eruption. Directly below, on the one-time harbor front, 300 skeletons were famously found together with sundry jewelry: Archaeologists have identified them as would-be refugees from the volcano who became asphyxiated by the fumes. Two years later, in 2008, a 9-meter-long Roman ship was found, its wood preserved through the process of carbonization (now on view in a pavilion open Saturday).

Beyond the terrace you can descend into the **Terme Suburbane** (*Suburban Baths*) communal baths, the benches and marble floors giving the appearance of having been laid down only decades ago. Further evidence of the volcanic mud's sealing effect is the two-millennia-old firewood stacked in the furnace area, with gods and putti emerging from the stucco wall in pristine detail. Next on the percorso is the Area Sacra, notable for the recently unearthed "Sacellum of the Four Gods" friezes.

A few doors down the Cardo V Inferiore, the star attraction of the **House of Telephus** is another wonderful relief showing this Greek hero being cured by Achilles. With 60 rooms built on three levels, the building (Herculaneum's second largest) is thought to have belonged to M. Nonius Balbus, he of the statue down the street. By contrast at No. 8 Cardo V Superiore is the small shop of one Sextus Palulculus Felix, with twin phalli to ward off accidents and at the back 25 bronze hotplates for baking cakes. ⊠ *Il Quartiere Suburbano*.

★ Also in Cardo V Inferiore is the **Casa dei Cervi**. This would have been one of the first houses that visitors to the town would have passed as they entered the city from the seaward side. As in most top-notch

THE BAY OF NAPLES THROUGH THE AGES

Rich archaeological and literary evidence reveals a continuous human presence in Campania for millennia. Used as an outpost probably by the Minoans and Mycenaeans in the second millennium BC, the area was first colonized by Greeks from Euboea in the 8th century BC; they settled on the island of Pithekoussai (modern-day Ischia) and later on the mainland at Cumae. The Greek geographer Strabo (64 BC–after AD 21), who appears to have traveled extensively in the area, provides further documentation to the area's history. The early Greeks traded widely with the Etruscans and local Italic peoples, eventually extending their sphere of influence to Neapolis and southward and northward along the shores of the Tyrrhenian Sea.

Greek civilization flourished for hundreds of years along this seaboard, but there was nothing in the way of centralized government until centuries later, when the Romans extended their domain southward and began to set up colonies of their own for added protection, especially after incursions led by such flamboyant figures as Pyrrhus and Hannibal in the 3rd century BC.

The Romans transformed Pompeii and Herculaneum into the Hamptons of their day, but all their merry-making was stilled in AD 79 by a jolt from Vesuvius, believed by few at the time to harbor any danger for those living at its base. We are fortunate to have Pliny the Younger's memorable description of his uncle being overwhelmed by fumes and dying of asphyxiation in Stabiae, now Castellammare di Stabia. Although written some years after the event, Pliny's letter to Tacitus is a unique and moving account of the disaster.

town residences, however, the entranceway is plain and leads into a *vestibulum*, a small vestibule that opens onto an open courtyard called a *peristylium*. The showpiece in this particular house is the garden area, surrounded by a so-called *cryptoporticus* embellished with fine still life frescoes and terminating in a partially reconstructed gazebo. Of course, prior to the eruption, the house would have had a fine view over the Bay of Naples. ⊠ *Insula IV.*

As you walk around Herculaneum, you'll notice the narrow entrances of the houses and the wider entrances for shops, inns, and other buildings where large numbers of people required access. A case in point is at the corner of Cardo V and the Decumanus Inferior, where you'll see two access points and counters with large amphorae for keeping dishes warm. This was one of the town's **Thermopolia**, the fast-food outlets of the ancient world. Next door for relaxed, discreet dining where, judging from the warren of private chambers within, more than just food and drink was on offer, there was the **Taberna di Priapo** *(Priapus's Tavern)*, complete with its waiting room at the back right. ⊠ *Insula IV (9 on official site map).*

Of course, no town would have been complete without its sports facilities, and Herculaneum was no exception. Just opposite the *thermopolium* on Cardo V is the entrance to the large **Palaestra**, where along with pedagogical activities, a variety of ball games and wrestling matches were staged. ✉ *Insula Orientalis (2 on official site map) II.*

★ On Cardo IV parallel to Cardo V, close to the Forum Baths, is the **Casa del Nettuno ed Anfitrite** *(House of Neptune and Amphitrite).* It takes its name from the mosaic that still sports its bright blue coloring and adorns the wall of the small, secluded *nymphaeum,* or shrine with fountains, at the back of the house. According to legend, in the time-honored fashion of the Olympians, Neptune (or Poseidon) saw Amphitrite dancing with the Nereids on the island of Naxos, carried her off, and married her. The adjacent wall, in similar mosaic style though less well preserved, has a hunting scene with a stag being pursued by a dog. Annexed to the same house is a remarkably preserved wine shop, where amphorae still rest on carbonized wooden shelves. ✉ *Insula IV.*

Stories of Roman licentiousness are belied by the **Terme del Foro** *(Forum Baths),* where there were separate sections for men and women. Here you see most of the architectural ingredients of *thermae* (baths). But besides the mandatory trio in the men's section (a round *frigidarium,* a cool swimming pool; a *tepidarium,* a semiheated pool; and a *calidarium,* or heated pool), there's also an *apodyterium,* or changing room, with partitioned shelves for depositing togas and a low podium to use as seating space while in line to use the facilities. For more attractive mosaics—particularly a spectacular rendition of Neptune—go around into the women's baths (with seemingly no frigidarium). The heating system in the tepidarium was also different (no hot air piped through or under, only braziers). Note the steam vents ingeniously built into the bath's benches and the small overhead cubbies in which bathers stored their togas. ✉ *Insula VI (26/27 on official site map).*

★ An outstanding example of carbonized remains is in the **Casa del Tramezzo di Legno** *(House of the Wooden Partition),* as it has been prosaically labeled by archaeologists. Following renovation work in the mid-1st century AD, the house was designed to have a frontage on three sides of Insula III and included a number of storerooms, shops, and second-floor habitations. This suggests that the owner was a wealthy *mercator,* a member of the up-and-coming merchant class that was starting to edge the patricians out of their privileged positions. The airy atrium has a lovely garden. Look closely at the *impluvium* (a channel to collect rainwater), and you'll see the original flooring below, which was later replaced with marble, perhaps after a change of owners. Next to the *impluvium* is an elegant marble table, or *cartibulum,* while behind is the *tablinum* (reception room), partially screened off by a bronze-studded wooden partition (the central part of which is missing) that would also have had hooks for hanging *lucernae* (lamps). On the Sede degli Augustali, in the "College of the *Augustales*"—freed slaves raised in the cult of the Emperor, constituting a sort of sect of religio-social climbers—are two large frescoes, one depicting Hercules on Olympus, another of Hercules fighting Acheleus, while in a small room alongside is the room of the guard whose skeleton was discovered still stretched out on his bed. ✉ *Insula III, 11–12.* ✉ *Corso Resina 6, Ercolano* ☎ *081/8575347* ⊕ *www.pompeiisites.org* 🎫 *€11 for Herculaneum only; €20 for big-lietto cumulativo ticket to 5 sites (Pompeii, Herculaneum, Boscoreale,*

Oplontis, and Stabiae) valid for 3 days ☉ Nov.–Mar., daily 8:30–5, ticket office closes at 3:30; Apr.–Oct., daily 8:30–7:30, ticket office closes at 6.

Fodor's Choice
★

Spectacular "virtual" re-creations of Herculaneum's streets and squares, computerized re-creations of the House of the Faun, even a vaporized steam bath standing in for the "burning cloud" of 79 AD: it is all here, in Herculaneum's brand-new 1st-century-meets-the-21st-century museum extravaganza, the **Museo Archeologico Virtuale (MAV)**. Opened in 2008, and a hundred yards up from the main archaeological site, which, in a virtual sense, partly restores to its original glory, this is an amazing new addition to the ancient site. First stop off at the ticket office for the headset audio tour and then descend, as in an excavation, to a floor below. Passing ancient faces that have now been given a name, the "percorso" path inserts you inside a re-creation of Herculaneum's first dig, replete with voices echoing from large terra-cotta vases.

Then get ready to experience, complete with mephitic effects, Herculaneum's Villa dei Papiri before and—even more dramatically—during the eruption. Then enter, courtesy of vaporized water, "the burning cloud" of 79 AD and finally emerge, at least virtually speaking, inside Pompeii's House of the Faun, both as it is now and, depending on a mere movement of your feet, as it was for two centuries BC. The next re-creation—complete with rippling grass and moving cart and oxen—is, again, Ercolano's Villa dei Papirii, particularly apposite given that the real site is currently closed for further excavation. Then comes a magical pre- and post-flooding view of Baia's "Nymphaeum," the now displaced statues arrayed as they were in days of Emperor Claudius who commissioned them. Another screen displays Capri's more-town-than-a-palace of the Villa Jovis that was Tiberius's residence atop the island.

Most spectacular of all, take a front row seat for "Day and Night in the Forum of Pompeii," with soldiers, litter-bearing slaves, and toga-clad figures moving spectrally to complete the spell. Down a corridor at the back you can make a vicarious visit to the "Lupari," brothels, their various pleasures illustrated in virtual and graphic frescoes along the walls. There are also holograms of jewelry of the earthquake fugitives and a touch-and-browse section of the Papyrii's 1,800 scrolls. "Wonder is the beginning of knowledge," said somebody and this museum does yeoman work in joining the two to impressive effect. ⊠ *Via IV Novembre 44, Ercolano* ☎ *081/19806511/2* ⊕ *www.museomav.com* 🖅 *€7.50* ☉ *Closed Mon.*

WHERE TO EAT AND STAY

¢
SOUTHERN
ITALIAN

✕ **La Fornacella.** Doing a brisk trade for both *stranieri* and locals—always a good sign—this ristorante-pizzeria is a 10-minute walk up from the excavations of Herculaneum on the roundabout near the Circumvesuviana station. Dishes and wines vary according to season but always draw on local recipes: pasta *e fagioli* (with beans) is a winter favorite, while richly garnished *schiaffoni* (flat tube pasta) with seafood is a summer stalwart. If sensitive to traffic noise, you're best avoiding the outside tables. ⊠ *Via IV Novembre 90–92, Ercolano* ☎ *081/7774861* 🍴 *AE, DC, MC, V* ☉ *Closed Mon.*

$ 🏨 **Hotel Ercolano.** Perfectly placed for a visit to the Herculaneum archaeological site across the road, this B&B offers vistas over the ancient site and the sea beyond. Inside is a pleasant rustic-style atmosphere, complete with a dining room that showcases the best wines of Campania on display. All in all, it's much quieter than Naples and is a good base for also exploring nearby Pompeii and Oplontis, let alone the newly opened MAV museum, which is a short walk uphill. **Pros:** nice location; many board plans available; free parking in town where parking is rare. **Cons:** guest rooms on smallish side. ✉ *Corso Resina 230, Ercolano* ☎ *081/7771357* ⊕ *www.hotelercolano.com* ⮑ *10 rooms* ⚬ *In-room: a/c; refrigerator; Wi-Fi. In-hotel: restaurant, parking (free)* ▭ *AE, DC, MC, V* ⦿| *BP, FAP.*

$$$–$$$$ 🏨 **Miglio d'Oro Park Hotel.** The grand Vesuvian villas lined up along "the
Fodor's Choice golden mile" are normally for visits but this rare example is one you can
★ actually stay in. The "park" here is to be taken literally—its entrance is presided over by an original statue of Hercules (Ercolano's mythical founder) rearing above a tiered fountain, behind which extends an orchard strewn with boulders that might have landed on the town in 79 AD. Reception in the hotel is courteous and friendly, with guest rooms furnished in a combination of whites, blacks, and grays, their spaciousness complemented by the sea view. There's a breakfast room (a former stable) with a volcanic floor and then, on the first floor, an exquisite restaurant. Some rooms are in the top price bracket but there are others for as little as €95. The place is a five-minute walk from the Herculaneum's site. For luxury and good taste, the hotel needs little advertisement, so book well ahead. **Pros:** friendly reception; spacious rooms; rare "villa" experience; cheaper rooms a nice find. **Cons:** can be superpricey. ✉ *Via Corso Resina 230* ☎ *081/7399999* ⊕ *www.migliodoroparkhotel. it* ⮑ *43 rooms, 7 suites* ⚬ *In-room: a/c, safe, refrigerator. In-hotel: restaurant, bar, pool, parking (free)* ▭ *AE, MC, V.*

SHOPPING

Donadio Manifattura Coralli (✉ *Piazzale L. Sapio, near Ercolano exit of Napoli–Salerno autostrada, Portici* ☎ *081/7752900* ⊕ *www.donadio.it*) is first and foremost a cameo factory; it also sells directly to the public. Local artisans can be observed making the cameos, an age-old tradition in which shells—now virtually all imported—are meticulously carved to produce mythological scenes in relief, exploiting the natural layering and contrasting colors of the raw material.

VESUVIUS

Fodor's Choice *16 km (10 mi) east of Naples, 8 km (5 mi) northeast of Herculaneum,*
★ *40 km (25 mi) northwest of Salerno.*

Vesuvius may have lost its plume of smoke, but it has lost none of its fascination—especially for those who live in the towns around the cone. They've now nicknamed it the "Sterminator." In centuries gone by, their predecessors would study the volcano for signs of impending destruction. *Napoli fa i peccati e la Torre li paga*, the residents of nearby Torre del Greco used to mutter—"Naples sins and the Torre suffers." When reports of depraved behavior circulated about Neapolitans across the

You'll be amazed at how Vesuvius looms over the entire region—even in Naples, ten miles away, it remains a totally commanding presence.

bay, chastisement was only to be expected. Today, the world continues to watch 'O Vesuvio with bated breath.

GETTING HERE

To arrive by car, take the A3 Napoli–Salerno highway exit "Torre del Greco" and follow Via E. De Nicola from the tollbooth. Follow signs for the Parco Nazionale del Vesuvio.

There's regular bus service up Vesuvius operated by **Vesuviana Mobilitá** (☎ 081/9634420 ⊕ www.vesuvianamobilita.it) (€10.60 return from Pompeii Piazza Anfiteatro, €9.60 from Ercolano Circumvesuviana station), although it's far quicker to take the trips up Vesuvius on minibuses run by **Vesuvio Express** (☎ 081/7393666 ⊕ www.vesuvioexpress. it) (€10 return from Ercolano Circumvesuviana station). Both services will take you up to the car park and the starting point of the path up to the cone's top.

A branch of the aptly named Circumvesuviana railway (☎ 800/053939 ⊕ www.vesuviana.it) serves the main archaeological sites at the foot of Vesuvius. Trains leave from the Porta Nolana-Corso Garibaldi station in Naples, stop at the main terminal at Piazza Garibaldi 10 blocks away to link up with the Naples *metropolitana,* and then head southeast for Sorrento (about two trains per hour; €1.80 to Ercolano and Torre Annunziata, and €2.40 to Pompei Scavi–Villa dei Misteri). Confusingly, the station called "Pompei-Santuario," which is the stop for the modern city, lies on a different line, which will leave you not at the main entrance to the archaeological site but just behind the Santuario, closer to the amphitheater.

EXPLORING

Although its destructive powers are undoubtedly diminished, Vesuvius's threat of an eruption is ever present. In bygone ages the task of protecting the local inhabitants fell to the martyred patron saint of Naples, San Gennaro, or St. Januarius, whose statue was often borne aloft through the streets of the city in an effort to placate the volcano's wrath. Volcanic activity is attentively monitored by the Osservatorio Vesuviano. Founded under Bourbon king Ferdinand II in the mid-19th century, it's the facility where the seismic scale was invented. The original observatory, conspicuous with its Pompeiian-red facade, has survived unscathed on the volcano's upper slopes and now serves as a conference center and small museum: the **Museo dell'Osservatorio Vesuviano** houses a mineralogical display, characteristic landscape gouaches, early seismographs, and information panels. Access during the week is restricted to scientific groups, associations, and schools. ⊠ *Via Osservatorio, Ercolano* ☎ *081/7777149 or 081/6108483* ⊕ *www.ov.ingv.it* 🔁 *Free* ☉ *Weekends 10–2.*

Seen from the other side of the Bay of Naples, Vesuvius appears to have two peaks: on the northern side is the steep face of Monte Somma, possibly part of the original crater wall in AD 79; to the south is the present-day cone of Vesuvius, which has actually formed within the ancient crater. The AD 79 cone would have been considerably higher, perhaps peaking at more than 6,000 feet. The upper slopes bear the visible scars left by 19th- and 20th-century eruptions, the most striking being the lava flow from 1944 lying to the left (north side) of the approach road from Ercolano on the way up.

There are two main ways to the top. **Vesuvio Express** (☎ *081/7393666* ⊕ *www.vesuvioexpress.it)* at €10 round-trip leaves from the Ercolono-Scavi station, following the main Torre del Greco road to an antiatmospheric car park from where, leaving the souvenir kiosks behind, you walk for some 15 minutes to the crater. More scenic by far (and also more popular) is the newer route that approaches the crater from the other side. Close to the Pompei-Scavi station, buses run by **Busvia del Vesuvio** (☎ *3409352616* ⊕ *www.busviadelvesuvio.com*) cost €18.50 and include guided tours of the crater. These buses leave from Camping Zeus (9:30–4:30 summer, 9:30–3:30 winter) and wend up through Pompeii's upper outskirts to the Vesuvius National Park. There you are transferred to a converted Unimog bus, which ascends the Strada Matrone. It has reopened after 20 years, with pinewood views and views over the bay and Vesuvian towns below. A footpath with a wooden bridge over blackish clefts left by recent lava flows takes you to the top. In this route nature in its raw beauty comes first, including lack of toilet facilities and occasional suspension of service during bad weather (when the terrain's high iron content can attract thunderbolts). Here you can find a crater-side kiosk selling Lacrimae Cristi, which, complete with commemorative stamp, comes to €5 a bottle. (Busvia del Vesuvio ☎ *mobile 3409352616* ⊕ *www.busviadelvesuvio* 🔁 *€18.50 includes guided tour of crater*).

■**TIP**➜ Bring binoculars for bird-watching and taking in the sweeping panorama across the bay.

OPLONTIS (TORRE ANNUNZIATA)

Fodor's Choice   *20 km (12 mi) southeast of Naples, 5 km (3 mi) west of Pompeii.*
★
Surrounded by the fairly drab 1960s urban landscape of Torre Annunziata, Oplontis justifies its reputation as one of the more mysterious archaeological sites to be unearthed in the 20th century. The villa complex has been imaginatively ascribed—from a mere inscription on an amphora—to Nero's second wife, Poppaea Sabina. Her family was well known among the landed gentry of neighboring Pompeii, although, after a kick in the stomach from her emperor husband, she died some 15 years before the villa was overwhelmed by the eruption of 79. As Roman villas go, Poppaea's Villa, or Villa A, as it's called by archaeologists, is way off the top end of the scale.

GETTING HERE

By car, take the A3 Napoli–Salerno highway to the "Torre Annunziata" exit. Follow Via Veneto west, then turn left onto Via Sepolcri for the excavations. By train take the Circumvesuviana line to Torre Annunziata, the town's modern name (€3.70 round-trip from Naples).

EXPLORING

What has so far been excavated so far of the **Villa of the Empress Poppaea** covers more than 7,000 square meters (75,000 square feet), and because the site is bound by a road to the west and a canal to the south, we are unlikely to ever gauge its full extent. Complete with porticoes, a large peristyle, *piscina* (pool), baths, and extensive gardens, besides the standard atria, triclinia, and a warren of cubicula, the villa is thought by some to have been a training school for young philosophers and orators. Certainly, for those overwhelmed by the throngs at Pompeii, a modern-day visit to the site of Oplontis offers a chance for contemplation and intellectual stimulation.

Access is easiest from the Circumvesuviana station of Torre Annunziata (about 600 feet away). Outside the station, turn left and then right downhill. The site is just after the crossroads down on the left. If coming by car, take the Torre Annunziata Sud turnoff from the Naples–Salerno autostrada, turn right, and then look for signs on the left for Oplontis at the first major crossroads. At the ticket office you can get a site map and a helpful information booklet. Unlike Herculaneum and Pompeii, no skeletons were found here, leading scholars to think that this villa had been abandoned after the earthquake of 62 AD and was undergoing restructural work pending sale to another owner. But if no skeletons, this villa has wall paintings so fresh that one could imagine the eye was playing tricks.

Now that many of the frescoed houses in Pompeii are closed for restoration or for limited viewing, you have to come here to appreciate the full gamut of Roman wall paintings. One highlight is found in Room 5, a sitting room once overlooking the sea, where a painted window depicts the sanctuary of Apollo, while off to the left a photogenic peacock perches next to a theatrical mask. Thanks to the 2nd Pompeiian style, the walls, via frescoed arches and columns, seem to open out onto a scene beyond as seen in the paintings in the triclinium (dining

Another of the bay area's archaeological treasures is the Villa of the Empress Poppaea, so vast it dwarfs the residences in Pompeii.

room; Room 6), the cubiculum (bedroom; Room 7), and the atrium's illusionistic architectural fittings of painted podiums, doors, and "compluvium" roof opening, plus a rain-catching "impluvium" beneath. At the back, through a cooling garden newly planted with bay trees as in antiquity, is an Olympic-size swimming pool. The adjacent guest rooms, or hospitalia, display murals of the 4th Pompeiian Style, dating them to 50 AD onward. With painted fruits and flowers, vegetation was guaranteed to flourish all year, while in the open viridarum (Room 16) guests could compare painted flora and the odd bird with the real thing. Room 21 is a Roman latrine, ancient fittings clearly on view.

Note that Oplontis is sometimes used as a theater venue between June and September, with productions featuring ancient Greek and Latin playwrights (in Italian); tickets can be bought at the Proloco in Torre Annunziata (close to the Oplontis site at Via Sepolcri 16). ⊠ *Via Sepolcri 1, Torre Annunziata* ☎ *081/8621755* ⊕ *www.pompeiisites.org* ✉ *€5.50 for Oplontis, Stabia, and Boscoreale; €20 for biglietto cumulativo pass to 5 sites (Pompeii, Herculaneum, Boscoreale, Oplontis, and Stabiae) valid for 3 days* ☉ *Nov.–Mar., daily 8:30–5, ticket office closes at 3:30; Apr.–Oct., daily 8:30–7:30, ticket office closes at 6. Closed Jan. 1, May 1, Dec. 25.*

POMPEII: CITY OF VESUVIUS

Mention Pompeii and most travelers will think of ancient Roman villas, prancing bronze fauns, writhing plaster casts of Vesuvius's victims, and the fabled days of the Emperors. Mention Pompeii to many southern

Italians, however, and they will immediately think of Pompei (to use the modern-day Italian spelling, not the ancient Latin), home to the Santuario della Madonna del Rosario, the 19th-century basilica in the center of the new town, with the archaeological ruins taking second place. Although millions of culture seekers worldwide head for ancient Pompeii every year, the same number of Italian pilgrims converge on Pompei's basilica as a token of faith—joining processions, making *ex-voto* offerings, or just honoring a vow. Wealthy Neapolitans come to make their donations to help the Church carry out its good deeds. New-car owners come to get their vehicles blessed—and given driving standards in these parts of the world, insurance coverage from on high is probably a sensible move.

Caught between the hammer and anvil of cultural and religious tourism, the modern town of Pompei has shaken off its rather complacent approach and is now endeavoring to polish up its act. In attempts to ease congestion, parts of the town have been made pedestrian-friendly and parking restrictions tightened. Departing from the rather sleazy reputation of previous years, several hotels have filled the sizable niche in the market for quality deals at affordable prices. As for recommendable restaurants, if you deviate from the archaeological site and make for the center of town, you will be spoiled for choice. The modern town may be a circus but the center ring is always the splendors and wonders of ancient Pompeii itself—*see our special photo feature, "Ancient Pompeii: Tomb of a Civilization," for a suggested tour of the fabulous site.*

GETTING HERE

To get to Pompeii by car, take the A3 Napoli–Salerno highway to the "Pompei" exit and follow signs for the nearby "Scavi" excavations. There are numerous guarded car parks near the Porta Marina, Piazza Essedra, and Anfiteatro entrances where you can leave your vehicle for a fee.

Pompeii has two central Circumvesuviana stations served by two separate train lines. The Naples–Sorrento train stops at "Pompei Scavi-Villa dei Misteri," 100 yards from the Porta Marina ticket office of the archaeological site, while the Naples–Poggiomarino train stops at Pompei Santuario, more convenient for the Santuario della Madonna del Rosario and the hotels and restaurants in the modern town center. A third FS (state) train station south of the town center is only convenient if arriving from Salerno or Rome.

VISITOR INFORMATION

The Pompeii offices of **Azienda Autonoma di Cura Soggiorno e Turismo** (✉ *Via Sacra 1, Pompeii* ☎ *081/8507255* ⊕ *www.pompeiturismo. it*) are open 8–3 in winter, 8–7 in summer, closed Sunday. The **Ufficio Informazione** (✉ *Piazza Porta Marina, Pompei* ☎ *081/8575347* ⊕ *www. pompeiisites.org*) outside the archaeological site is open 9–5 daily.

Continued on page 223

ANCIENT POMPEII
TOMB OF A
CIVILIZATION

The site of Pompeii, petrified memorial to Vesuvius's eruption on the morning of August 24, AD 79, is the largest, most accessible, and probably most famous of excavations anywhere.

A busy commercial center with a population of 10,000–20,000, ancient Pompeii covered about 160 acres on the seaward end of the fertile Sarno Plain. Today Pompeii is choked with both the dust of 25 centuries and more than 2 million visitors every year; only by escaping the hordes and lingering along its silent streets can you truly fall under the site's spell. On a quiet backstreet, all you need is a little imagination to sense the shadows palpably filling the dark corners, to hear the ancient pipe's falsetto and the tinny clash of cymbals, to envision a rain of rose petals gently covering a Roman senator's dinner guests. Come in the late afternoon when the site is nearly deserted and you will understand that the true pleasure of Pompeii is not in the seeing but in the feeling.

A FUNNY THING HAPPENS ON THE WAY TO THE FORUM

as you walk through Pompeii. Covered with dust and decay as it is, the city seems to come alive. Perhaps it's the familiar signs of life observed along the ancient streets: bakeries with large ovens just like those for making pizzas, tracks of cart wheels cut into the road surface, graffiti etched onto the plastered surfaces of street walls. Coming upon a *thermopolium* (snack bar), you imagine natives calling out, "Let's move on to the am-phitheater." But a glance up at Vesuvius, still brooding over the scene like an enormous headstone, reminds you that these folks—whether

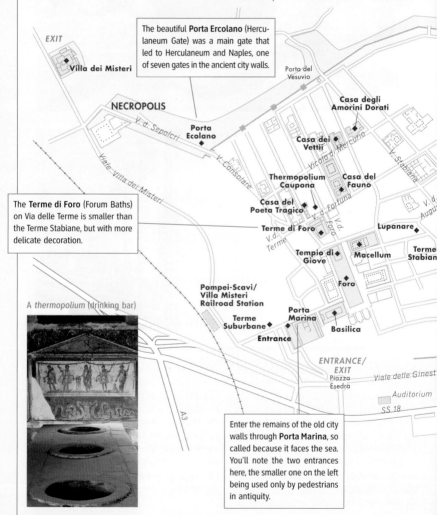

EXIT

Villa dei Misteri

The beautiful **Porta Ercolano** (Hercu-laneum Gate) was a main gate that led to Herculaneum and Naples, one of seven gates in the ancient city walls.

Porta del Vesuvio

NECROPOLIS

Casa degli Amorini Dorati

V. d. Sepolcri

Porta Ecolano

V. Consolare

Casa dei Vettii

Vicolo d. Mercurio

V. Stabiana

Viale Villa dei Misteri

Thermopolium Caupona

Casa del Fauno

Casa del Poeta Tragico

V. d. Fortuna

V. d. Foro

The **Terme di Foro** (Forum Baths) on Via delle Terme is smaller than the Terme Stabiane, but with more delicate decoration.

Terme di Foro

V.d. Terme

Lupanare

V. d. Augu

Tempio di Giove

Macellum

Terme Stabian

Foro

Pompei-Scavi/ Villa Misteri Railroad Station

A *thermopolium* (drinking bar)

Terme Suburbane

Porta Marina

Basilica

Entrance

ENTRANCE/ EXIT
Piazza Esedra

Viale delle Ginest

Auditorium

SS 18

A3

Enter the remains of the old city walls through **Porta Marina**, so called because it faces the sea. You'll note the two entrances here, the smaller one on the left being used only by pedestrians in antiquity.

imagined in your head or actually wearing a mantle of lava dust—have not taken a breath for centuries. The town was laid out in a grid pattern, with two main intersecting streets. The wealthiest took a

Pompeii's cemetery, or Necropolis

whole block for themselves; those less fortunate built a house and rented out the front rooms, facing the street, as shops. There were good numbers of *tabernae* (taverns) and *thermopolia* on almost every corner, and frequent shows at the amphitheater.

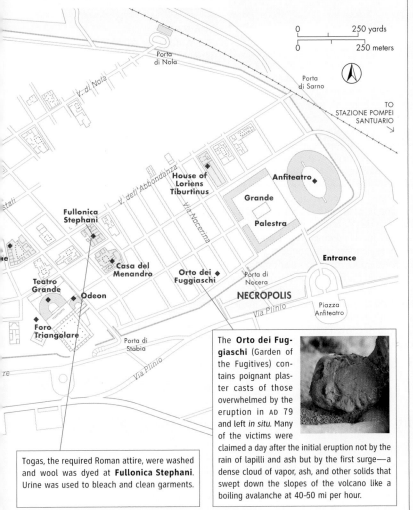

0 _____ 250 yards
0 _____ 250 meters

Porta di Nola

Porta di Sarno

TO STAZIONE POMPEI SANTUARIO

V. di Nola

V. dell'Abbondanza

Via Nocerina

House of Loriens Tiburtinus

Anfiteatro

Grande

Palestra

Fullonica Stephani

Entrance

Casa del Menandro

Orto dei Fuggiaschi

Porta di Nocera

NECROPOLIS

Via Plinio

Piazza Anfiteatro

Teatro Grande

Odeon

Foro Triangolare

Porta di Stabia

Via Plinio

The **Orto dei Fuggiaschi** (Garden of the Fugitives) contains poignant plaster casts of those overwhelmed by the eruption in AD 79 and left *in situ.* Many of the victims were claimed a day after the initial eruption not by the rain of lapilli and ash but by the first surge—a dense cloud of vapor, ash, and other solids that swept down the slopes of the volcano like a boiling avalanche at 40–50 mi per hour.

Togas, the required Roman attire, were washed and wool was dyed at **Fullonica Stephani**. Urine was used to bleach and clean garments.

PUBLIC LIFE IN ANCIENT POMPEII

Forum

THE CITY CENTER

As you enter the ruins at Porta Marina, make your way uphill to the **Foro** (Forum), which served as Pompeii's cultural, political, and religious center. You can still see some of the two stories of colonnades that used to line the square. Like the ancient Greek *agora* in Athens, the Forum was a busy shopping area, complete with public officials to apply proper standards of weights and measures. Fronted by an elegant three-column portico on the eastern side of the forum is the **Macellum**, the covered meat and fish market dating to the 2nd century BC; here vendors sold goods from their reserved spots in the central market. It was also in the Forum that elections were held, politicians let rhetoric fly, speeches and official announcements were made, and worshippers crowded around the **Tempio di Giove** (Temple of Jupiter), at the northern end of the forum.

Basilica

On the southwestern corner is the **Basilica**, the city's law court and the economic center. These rectangular aisled halls were the model for early Christian churches, which had a nave (central aisle) and two side aisles separated by rows of columns. Standing in the Basilica, you can recognize the continuity between Roman and Christian architecture.

THE GAMES

The **Anfiteatro** (Amphitheater) was the ultimate in entertainment for Pompeians and offered a gamut of experiences, but essentially this was for gladiators rather than wild animals. By Roman standards, Pompeii's amphitheater was quite

Amphitheater

small (seating 20,000). Built in about 80 BC, making it the oldest permanent amphitheater in the Roman world, it was oval and divided into four seating areas. There were two main entrances—at the north and south ends—and a narrow passage on the west called the Porta Libitinensis, through which the dead were probably dragged out. A wall painting found in a house near the theater (now in the Naples Museum) depicts the riot in the amphitheater in AD 59 when several citizens from the nearby town of Nocera were killed. After Nocerian appeals to Nero, shows were suspended for three years.

Fresco of Pyramus and Thisbe in the House of Loreius Tiburtinus

BATHS AND BROTHELS

In its day, Pompeii was celebrated as the Côte d'Azur, the seaside Brighton, the Fire Island of the ancient Roman empire. Evidence of a Sybaritic bent is everywhere—in the town's grandest villas, in its baths, and especially in its rowdiest *lupanaria* (brothels), murals still reveal a worship of hedonism. Satyrs, bacchantes, hermaphrodites, and acrobatic couples are pictured indulging in hanky-panky.

The first buildings to the left past the ticket turnstiles are the **Terme Suburbane** (Suburban Baths), built—by all accounts without permission—right up against the city walls. The baths have eyebrow-raising frescoes in the *apodyterium* (changing room) that strongly suggest that more than just bathing and massaging went on here. Reservations are required for entry.

On the walls of **Lupanare** (brothel) are scenes of erotic games in which clients could engage. The **Terme Stabiane** (Stabian Baths) had underground furnaces, the heat from which circulated beneath the floor, rose through flues in the walls, and escaped through chimneys. The water temperature could be set for cold, lukewarm, or hot. Bathers took a lukewarm bath to prepare themselves for the hot room. A tepid bath came next, and then a plunge into cold water to tone up the skin. A vigorous massage with oil was followed by rest, reading, horseplay, and conversation.

GRAFFITI

Thanks to those deep layers of pyroclastic deposits from Vesuvius that protected the site from natural wear and tear over the centuries, graffiti found in Pompeii provide unique insights into the sort of things that the locals found important 2,000 years ago. A good many were personal and lend a human dimension to the disaster that not even the sights can equal.

At the baths: "What is the use of having a Venus if she's made of marble?"

At the entrance to the front lavatory at a private house: "May I always and everywhere be as potent with women as I was here."

On the Viale ai Teatri: "A copper pot went missing from my shop. Anyone who returns it to me will be given 65 bronze coins."

In the Basilica: "A small problem gets larger if you ignore it."

PRIVATE LIFE IN ANCIENT POMPEII

The facades of houses in Pompeii were relatively plain and seldom hinted at the care and attention lavished on the private rooms within. When visitors arrived they passed the shops and entered an open peristyle, from which the occupants received air, sunlight, and rainwater, the latter caught by the *impluvium*, a rectangular-shaped receptacle under the sloped roof. In the back was a receiving room, the *tablinum*, and behind was another open area, the atrium. Life revolved around this uncovered inner courtyard, with rows of columns and perhaps a garden with a fountain. Only good friends ever saw this part of the house, which was surrounded by *cubicula* (bedrooms) and the *triclinium* (dining area). Interior floors and walls usually were covered with colorful marble tiles, mosaics, and frescoes.

House of Paquius Proculus

Several homes were captured in various states by the eruption of Vesuvius, each representing a different slice of Pompeiian life.

The **Casa del Fauno** (House of the Faun) displayed wonderful mosaics, now at the Museo Archeologico Nazionale in Naples. The **Casa del Poeta Tragico** (House of the Tragic Poet) is a typical middle-class house. On the floor is a mosaic of a chained dog and the inscription *cave canem* ("Beware of the dog"). The **Casa degli Amorini Dorati** (House of the Gilded Cupids) is an elegant, well-preserved home with original marble decorations in the garden. Many paintings and mosaics were executed at **Casa del Menandro** (House of Menander), a patrician's villa named for a fresco of the Greek playwright. Two blocks beyond the Stabian Baths you'll notice on the left the current digs at the **Casa dei Casti Amanti** (House of the Chaste Lovers). A team of plasterers and painters were at work here when Vesuvius erupted, redecorating one of the rooms and patching up the cracks in the bread oven near the entrance—possibly caused by tremors a matter of days before.

Small Garden
Triclinium
Owner's Quarters
Kitchen
Servant's Quarters
Secondary Atrium
Entrance
Garden
Main Peristyle
Impluvium
Atrium

CASA DEI VETTII

The **House of the Vettii** is the best example of a house owned by wealthy *mercatores* (merchants). It contains vivid murals—a magnificent *pinacoteca* (picture gallery) within the very heart of Pompeii. The scenes here— except for those in the two wings off the atrium—were all painted after the earthquake of AD 62. Once inside, cast an admiring glance at the delicate frieze around the wall of the *triclinium* (on the right of the peristyle garden as you enter from the atrium), depicting cupids engaged in various activities, such as selling oils and perfumes, working as goldsmiths and metalworkers, acting as wine merchants, or performing in chariot races. Another of the main attractions in the Casa dei Vettii is the small cubicle beyond the kitchen area (to the right of the atrium) with its faded erotic frescoes now protected by Perspex screens.

UNLOCKING THE VILLA DEI MISTERI

Villa dei Misteri

There is no more astounding, magnificently memorable evidence of Pompeii's devotion to the pleasures of the flesh than the frescoes on view at the **Villa dei Misteri** (Villa of the Mysteries), a palatial abode 400 yards outside the city gates, northwest of Porta Ercolano. Unearthed in 1909, this villa had more than 60 rooms painted with frescoes; the finest are in the *triclinium*. Painted in the most glowing Pompeiian reds and oranges, the panels relate the saga of a young bride (Ariadne) and her initiation into the mysteries of the cult of Dionysus, who was a god imported to Italy from Greece and then given the Latin name of Bacchus. The god of wine and debauchery also represented the triumph of the irrational—of all those mysterious forces that no official state religion could fully suppress.

Pompeii's best frescoes, painted in glowing reds and oranges, retain an amazing vibrancy.

The Villa of the Mysteries frescoes were painted circa 50 BC, most art historians believe, and represent the peak of the Second Style of Pompeiian wall painting. The triclinium frescoes are thought to have been painted by a local artist, although the theme may well have been copied from an earlier cycle of paintings from the Hellenistic period. In all there are 10 scenes, depicting children and matrons, musicians and satyrs, phalluses and gods. There are no inscriptions (such as are found on Greek vases), and after 2,000 years historians remain puzzled by many aspects of the triclinium cycle. Scholars endlessly debate the meaning of these frescoes, but anyone can tell they are the most beautiful paintings left to us by antiquity. In several ways, the eruption of Vesuvius was a blessing in disguise, for without it, these masterworks of art would have perished long ago.

PLANNING FOR YOUR DAY IN POMPEII

GETTING THERE

The archaeological site of Pompeii has its own stop (Pompei–Villa dei Misteri) on the Circumvesuviana line to Sorrento, close to the main entrance at the Porta Marina, which is the best place from which to start a tour. If, like many visitors every year, you get the wrong train from Naples (stopping at the other station "Pompei"), all is not lost. There's another entrance to the excavations at the far end of the site, just a seven-minute walk to the Amphitheater.

ADMISSION

Single tickets cost €11 and are valid for one full day. The site is open Apr.–Oct., daily 8:30–7:30 (last admission at 6), and Nov.–Mar., daily 8:30–5 (last admission at 3:30). For more information, call 081/8575347 or visit www.pompeiisites.org.

WHAT TO BRING

The only restaurant inside the site is both overpriced and busy, so it makes sense to bring along water and snacks. If you come so equipped, there are some shady, underused picnic tables outside the Porta di Nola, to the northeast of the site.

MAKING THE MOST OF YOUR TIME

Visiting Pompeii does have its frustrating aspects: many buildings are blocked off by locked gates, and enormous group tours tend to clog up more popular attractions. But the site is so big that it's easy to lose yourself amid the quiet side streets. To really see the site, you'll need four or five hours.

Three buildings within Pompeii—Terme Suburbane, Casa del Menandro, and Casa degli Amorini Dorati—are open for restricted viewing. Reservations must be made on-line at www.arethusa.net, where you can find information on opening times.

TOURS

To get the most out of Pompeii, rent an audio guide (€6.50 for one, €10 for two; you'll need to leave an ID card) and opt for one of the three itineraries (2 hours, 4 hours, or 6 hours). If hiring a guide, make sure the guide is registered for an English tour and standing inside the gate; agree beforehand on the length of the tour and the price, and prepare yourself for soundbites of English mixed with dollops of hearsay. For a higher quality (but more expensive) full-day tour, try Context Travel (⊕ www.contexttravel.com).

MODERN POMPEI

Caught between the hammer and anvil of cultural and religious tourism, the modern town of Pompei (to use the modern-day Italian spelling, not the ancient Latin) is now endeavoring to polish up its act. In attempts to ease congestion and improve air quality at street level, parts of the town have been pedestrianized and parking restrictions tightened. Several hotels have filled the sizable niche in the market for excellent deals at affordable prices. As for recommendable restaurants, if you deviate from the archaeological site and make for the center of town, you will be spoiled for choice.

IF YOU LIKE POMPEII

If you intend to visit other archaeological sites nearby during your trip, you should buy the *biglietto cumulativo* pass, a combination ticket with access to four area sites (Herculaneum, Pompeii, Oplontis, Boscoreale). It costs €20 and is valid for three days. Unlike many archaeological sites in the Mediterranean region, those around Naples are almost all well served by public transport; ask about transportation options at the helpful Porta Marina information kiosk.

WHERE TO EAT

$$$
SOUTHERN
ITALIAN
★

✕ **Il Principe.** This is the closest you'll get to experience the tastes of ancient Pompeii, though the wines (fortunately) will be quantum leaps better. At times the food is so artistically presented that it seems boorish to pick up a knife and fork. Try the *pasta vermiculata garo*, otherwise known as spaghetti with *garum pompeianum*, a fish-based sauce consumed widely in Roman times. Round off the meal with the *cassata di Oplontis* (a sweet made with ricotta cheese and honey), inspired by a famous still-life fresco found in a triclinium at the site of Oplontis. If you're overawed by the grandiose decor inside, opt for more informal outdoor dining. ✉ *Piazza B. Longo 8* ☎ *081/8505566* ⊕ *www.ilprincipe.com* ▭ *AE, DC, V* ⊗ *Closed Sun. dinner, Mon. (except lunch in summer), and 3 wks in Aug.*

WORD OF MOUTH

"We did not have a guide or the audio tour at Pompeii. Huge mistake. Even with the map, we had such a hard time, missed so much, many regrets…. We eavesdropped on a guide with a client, and wished we were with a guide."
—Giftnurse

$
SOUTHERN
ITALIAN
★

✕ **Ristorante dei Platani.** The simple, seasonal food at this family-run establishment a few minutes' walk from the Anfiteatro ticket office will take your mind off the kitschy faux frescoes inspired by the Villa dei Misteri. Locals and informed tourists alike are drawn to their classic stand-bys like *gnocchi alla sorrentina* (with tomato and mozzarella) and *frittura di paranza* (fried fish) as well as to their more inventive takes on local tradition—try the *fusilli con crema di ceci e frutti di mare* (with pureed chickpeas and seafood). Those who make it through to the *dolce* (desserts) should sample the delicate *delizia al limone* (lemon profiteroles) brought in daily from Minori on the Amalfi Coast. ✉ *Via Colle S. Bartolomeo 8* ☎ *081/8633973* ⊕ *www.ristorantedeiplatani.it* ▭ *AE, DC, MC, V* ⊗ *Closed Wed.*

$$
SOUTHERN
ITALIAN
★

✕ **Ristorante President.** The Gramaglia brother-and-sister team is well versed in top-level catering and makes sure that customers sigh with satisfaction after every course. For something different, try the *aragosta ubriacata* ("drunken" lobster cooked in white wine) accompanied by some imaginative side dishes, like *sfoglie di zucca in agrodolce* (sweet-and-sour pumpkin strips). Beautiful presentation, impeccable service, and excellent value all add up to a stellar meal. They also host decadent Roman inspired banquets with musical accompaniment, worth a try if you're spending the night in town. ✉ *Piazza Schettini 12* ☎ *081/8507245* ⊕ *www.ristorantepresident.com* ▭ *AE, DC, MC, V* ⊗ *Closed Mon. Nov.–Mar.*

WHERE TO STAY

¢

Camping Zeus. With Pompeii's legendary Villa of the Mysteries practically across the road and with an on-site bus to take you a winding way up through modern Pompeii's upper outskirts to the top of the volcano, this shady campsite includes very economically priced rooms for one to five people. Bargain-basement prices here range from 30 to 70 euros for rooms, 5 to 10 euros for campsites (prices are 10 euros higher in August). Parking is included in the price as is breakfast while

CLOSE UP

Pompeii Prep

Pompeii is impressive under any circumstances, but it comes alive if you do some preparation before your visit.

First, read up—there are piles of good books on the subject, including these engaging, jargon-free histories: *Pompeii: The Day a City Died* by Robert Etienne, *Pompeii: Public and Private Life* by Paul Zanker, *The Lost World of Pompeii* by Colin Amery, and most recently, *Pompeii: Life of a Roman Town* by Mary Beard. For accurate historical information woven into the pages of a thriller, pick up *Pompeii: A Novel* by Robert Harris.

Second, be sure to visit the Museo Archeologico Nazionale in Naples, where most of the finest art from Pompeii now resides, from the epic Alexander fresco (which once decorated the House of the Faun) to, in the Museum's "Gabinetto Secreto," the louche frescoes advertising services on offer in the Lupari brothels. The museum is a remarkable treasure trove—it's a rewarding place to visit even if Pompeii isn't in your plans.

---

other meals come by arrangement with the restaurant/pizzeria on-site. **Pros:** Very economical; nifty option for those visiting Vesuvius. **Cons:** bedrooms overlook car park. ⊠ *Via Villa dei Misteri* ☎ *0818615320* ⊕ *www.campingzeus.it* ⬎ *6 rooms* ⬙ *In-hotel: restaurant (nearby)* ⊟ *AE, DC, MC, V* ⦿ *BP*.

$ ☆ ⛨ **Hotel Amleto.** *Appassionati* and connoisseurs of historical styles of furnishings will find this hotel a real treat. Enjoy the Pompeiian-type mosaic in the reception room and the mesmerizing House-of-the-Vettii-type scene in the breakfast room before retiring to your quarters, either 19th-century Neapolitan in style or Venetian in taste. Convenient to say the least, this spot is near the archaeological site and close to Pompei's cathedral. As traffic noise may be a problem, ask for a quieter room on the upper floor. **Pros:** convenient location near sites and restaurants; excellent, attentive service. **Cons:** books up in high season; rooms facing street are noisy. ⊠ *Via B. Longo 10* ☎ *081/8631004* ⊕ *www. hotelamleto.it* ⬎ *26 rooms* ⬙ *In-room: a/c, refrigerator, Internet. In-hotel: bar, parking (free)* ⊟ *AE, D, MC, V* ⦿ *BP*.

$ ⛨ **Hotel Diana.** At the lower end of the price range, this small family-run hotel is a convenient base for budget travelers who wish to be in striking distance of Pompeii's ruins or the Sanctuary. It's a 3-minute walk from the train, a 10-minute walk from the Amphitheater entrance and close to the action in Pompeii's main square—yet seemingly miles away from the tourist throngs—and ideal for travelers without private transport. Clean and well-appointed rooms and an outgoing young staff make this place an attractive option. **Pros:** 10-minute walk to archaeological site; convenient location for strolling in evening; charming garden, quiet setting and very helpful staff; tours organized from hotel. **Cons:** no pool; a bit noisy due to tiled halls; smallish rooms. ⊠ *Vico Sant'Abbondio 12* ☎ *081/8631264* ⊕ *www.pompeihotel.com* ⬎ *22 rooms* ⬙ *In-room: a/c, Internet. In-hotel: parking (free)* ⊟ *AE, DC, MC, V* ⦿ *BP*.

WEST OF NAPLES: THE PHLEGREAN FIELDS

Extinct volcanoes, steaming fumaroles, bubbling mud, natural spasms, and immortal names, all steeped in millennia of history, are the basic ingredients of the Campi Flegrei, or Phlegrean Fields (from the ancient Greek word *phlegraios,* or burning). Pompeii and Herculaneum, to the east of Naples, may be the most celebrated archaeological sites in Campania, but back in the days of the emperors they were simple middle-class towns compared to the patrician settlements to the west of Naples. Here, at Baia, famed figures like Cicero, Julius Caesar, Claudius, Nero, and Hadrian built sumptuous leisure villas (*villae otiorum*) and ports for their gigantic pleasure barges; here St. Paul arrived at Puteoli (to use Pozzuoli's ancient Latin moniker) on board an Alexandrian ship; here the powerful came to consult the oracles of the Cumaean Sibyl; and here Virgil visited Lago d'Averno—the legendary entrance to the Underworld—to immortalize it in his *Aeneid.* Although several villas have now sunk beneath the sea, there are many archaeological sites still extant: the Flavian Amphitheater, which, if not as imposing aboveground as the Colosseum at Rome, is far better preserved in the galleries and cages below the arena in which wild beasts, gladiators, and stage props were kept in readiness; the ancient acropolis area of Puteoli now known as Rione Terra, the ruins of the Sibyl's cave in Cumae; and the ancient baths of Baia.

POZZUOLI

Fodor's Choice
★
8 km (5 mi) west of Naples.

Legendary spirits populate Pozzuoli. St. Paul stepped ashore at the harbor here in AD 61 en route to Rome: his own ship had been wrecked off Malta, and he was brought here on the *Castor and Pollux,* a grain ship from Alexandria that was carrying corn from Egypt to Italy. Not far from the harbor esplanade, San Gennaro, patron saint of Naples, earned his holy martyrdom by being thrown to the lions at an imperial gala staged in the town's enormous amphitheater, constructed by the Flavian emperors (the wild beasts were said to have torn the rags from Gennaro's body but to have left him unharmed—at which point he was taken to the Solfatara and decapitated). More recently, that latter-day goddess Sophia Loren was raised in a house still standing on a backstreet; later she set off to Naples and celluloid fame.

GETTING HERE

By car take the Tangenziale (bypass) from Naples toward Pozzuoli and get off at the Pozzuoli–Via Campana exit. At the roundabout, follow the signs for "Porto" to get to the port and the town center. There are subsequent signs for the "Anfiteatro" and Solfatara. The FS (state-run) Metropolitana Linea 2 from Naples (Piazza Garibaldi, Cavour, and Montesanto stations) stops at Pozzuoli–Solfatara near the Anfiteatro. Bus No. 152 departs Naples Piazza Garibaldi and ends at the Port in Pozzuoli.

VISITOR INFORMATION

The Pozzuoli office of **Azienda Autonoma di Cura Soggiorno e Turismo** (✉ *Via Campi Flegrei 3, Pozzuoli* ☎ *081/5262419* ⊕ *www.infocampiflegrei.it*) is open 8–3 in winter, 8–7 in summer, closed Sunday.

EXPLORING

Today Pozzuoli is a well-connected, busy town with about 80,000 inhabitants who are mainly employed by its fisheries, docks, and the tourism industry. Built on geologically unstable land, the area near the port was partially evacuated in the early 1980s due to a phenomenon known as *bradyseism,* or the rise and fall of the land surface. Since then it has been gradually recolonized and partially gentrified: many of the buildings in the Centro Storico have been given a face-lift, the main park (Villa Avellino) has become a mecca for open-air summer festivals, and the town's reputation as a center for gastronomy has been firmly established. Pozzuoli has also capitalized on its strategic position close to two of the islands in the Bay of Naples, Procida, and Ischia. One of its main selling points is its main arena—Puteoli was the only place in the empire to boast two amphitheaters—offering glimpses into the life of *panem et circenses* (bread and circuses) in classical times, when Puteoli was one of the busiest ports in the Mediterranean and easily eclipsed Neapolis (today's Naples).

★ The **Anfiteatro Flavio** (seating capacity, 40,000) is a short walk from the Pozzuoli Metropolitana railway station and about 15 minutes' walk down from the Solfatara. Despite the wear and tear of the millennia and the loss of some of the masonry to lime making in the Middle Ages, the site is one of the marvels of Roman architecture in the Campi Flegrei area. The foundation date is open to question. Like many sites in antiquity, the period from conception to completion could stretch over decades. It was probably built under Vespasian (AD 70–AD 79), given various inscriptions reading *"Colonia Flavia augusta Puteolana pecunia sua"* ("[built] by the Flavian colony of Puteoli with its own money"), although some maintain that work may have started under Nero (AD 54–AD 69) and merely completed later. As you approach the site, note the external part in *opus reticulatum* (volcanic stone masonry arranged in a net-shaped pattern) and *opus latericium* (horizontal bands of brick). When used together, they are called *opus mixtum*, a technique typical of the late 1st and early 2nd centuries, designed to reduce stress and minimize damage during seismic events.

Although we now get a fairly good idea of the horizontal ground plan in ancient times, comparison with the Colosseum in Rome shows that much of the superstructure has been lost (much of it removed in late Roman times as a cheap form of building material or to be converted in builder's lime), with the exterior once consisting of three stories surmounted by an *atticus* (decorative attic). Used in medieval times as ready-made terraces for vine growing, the original *cavea* (sitting area) would have had a portico above the top row of seats, decorated with a number of statues and supported by columns. At ground level there was an *ambulacrum* (covered walkway) along which spectators would have passed to reach the *vomitoria* (exits). Overhead would have risen a forest of poles supporting the velarium, a richly decorated awning

West of Naples:
The Phlegrean Fields

KEY

Ferry Lines

Golfo di Napoli

Golfo di Pozzuoli

CAMPI FLEGREI

Naples
Staz. Centrale
Miano
Capodimonte
Staz. Cumana
Mergellina
Castel Dell'ovo
Posillipo
Marechiaro
S. Paolo
Fuorigrotta
Agnano Terme
Mostra D'Oltremare
Bagnoli
Isola di Nisida
Torre Caracciolo
Quarto
Pianura
Lago Grapae
Astroni
Solfatara
Pozzuoli
Monte Nuovo
Monterusciello
Amphitheater
Lago d'Averno
Stazione Lucrino
Lago Lucrino
Baia
Lago del Fusaro
Stazione Fusaro
Lago Miseno
Bacoli
Capo Miseno
Monte de Procida
Torregaveta
Cumae
Antro della Sibilla
(Cave of the Cumaean Sybil)

A56
SS7

0   2 miles
0   2 km

The Amfiteatro Flavio is a marvel of ancient Roman architecture.

managed by naval personnel skilled at handling sails. After recent excavation you can now walk the massive elliptical arena, at 75 by 42 meters the third largest in the empire.

In classical times, entertainment here consisted mainly of *venationes* (animal hunts), often involving exotic animals like lions and tigers brought from far-flung corners of the Roman Empire through the port of Puteoli, public executions, and *munerae* (gladiator fights). The *fossa,* or large ditch in the middle of the arena, may well have contained the permanent stage setting, which could be raised when necessary to provide a scenic backdrop. ⊠ *Anfiteatro Grande, Via Terracciano 75* ☎ *081/5266007* 🔊 *€4, including admission to Cumae and Museo Archeologico dei Campi Flegrei, and site of Baia* ☉ *Daily 9–1 hr before sunset. Closed Tues., Jan. 1, May 1, and Dec. 25.*

WHERE TO EAT AND STAY

$

SOUTHERN
ITALIAN

★

✗ **Bobò.** Just across from the ferry terminal—with the somewhat unromantic parking lot in between—is this stylish but *simpatico* restaurant. There is a *menu degustazione* (€50) for the truly ravenous, and an ample à la carte menu of mainly fish. Exquisite antipasti, delicately garnished pasta, and *pesce* straight off the boats make this a favorite with the locals, so book ahead on the weekends and at dinner. A meal here is a fitting way to round out a day in the Campi Flegrei with some of the best the region has to offer. ⊠ *Via C. Colombo 20* ☎ *081/5262034* 🖧 *Reservations essential* ▭ *AE, DC, MC, V* ☉ *Closed Tues. and 2 wks in Aug. No dinner Sun.*

¢–$

SOUTHERN
ITALIAN

★

✗ **Ristorante Don Antonio.** Despite its unflattering location up a *vicolo* (alley) one block from the Pozzuoli waterfront, this restaurant has achieved cult status in Neapolitan circles for its fresh seafood and unbeatable prices. Unlike other eateries, which will happily serve well into the afternoon siesta or late at night, this spot rolls down the shutters as soon as the day's catch has been consumed. ⊠ *Vico Magazzini 20, off Piazza San Paolo* ☎ *081/5267941* ⚵ *Reservations not accepted* ⊟ *No credit cards* ⊗ *Closed Mon.*

$–$$ 🍽 **Hotel Terme Puteolane.** At the far end of Lungomare, Pozzuoli's equivalent of its swankier Naples namesake, this venue is also quieter and more manageable in terms of both price and distance. Climb the two flights of steps and beyond the slightly dilapidated classical facade, you are met by the twirling-moustachioed bust of Crescenzo D'Alicandro, the hotel's founder. Nephews once or twice removed man the reception with Pozzuolian style, grace, and charm. In the hotel's 1930s-style salon, one Sofia Scicolone a couple of decades later was elected Miss Bella Flegrea, going on to become first Miss Italia and eventually Hollywood diva, Sophia Loren. Beauty is still the hotel's business, thanks to the Centro d'Estetica on the premises (along with mud and/or thermal baths, along with private treatments under the aegis of the Italian health service). **Pros:** breakfast room with views of Ischia and, on a clear day, Capri; safe parking; much more economical than Naples equivalents. **Cons:** not for the disco-minded (as the receptionist said with a smile, "This is a serious hotel"). ⊠ *Corso Umberto I 195, Stazione Gerolomini* ☎ *081/5261303* ⬧ *termeputeolane@tiscali.it* ⬎ *27 rooms* ⚬ *In-room: a/c. In-hotel: bar, parking (free)* ⊟ *AE, DC, MC, V* 🍴 *BP.*

BAIA

12 km (7 mi) west of Naples, 4 km (2½ mi) west of Pozzuoli.

Now largely under the sea, ancient Baia was once the most opulent and fashionable resort area of the Roman Empire, the place where Sulla, Pompey, Cicero, Julius Caesar, Tiberius, and Nero built their holiday villas. Petronius's *Satyricon* is a satire on the corruption, intrigue, and wonderful licentiousness of Roman life at Baia. (Petronius was hired to arrange parties and entertainment for Nero, so he was in a position to know.) It was here that Cleopatra was staying when Julius Caesar was murdered on the Ides of March (March 15) in 44 BC; here that Emperor Claudius built a great villa for his third wife, Messalina (who is reputed to have spent her nights indulging herself at local brothels); and near here that Agrippina (Claudius's fourth wife and murderer) is believed to have been killed by henchmen sent by her son Nero in AD 59. Unfortunately, the Romans did not pursue the custom of writing official graffiti—"Here lived Crassus" would help—so it's difficult to assign these historical events to specific locations. Consequently, conjecture is the order of the day: Julius Caesar's villa is now thought to be at the top of the hill behind the archaeological site and not near the foot of the Aragonese castle, though we cannot be absolutely certain. We do know, however, that the Romans found this area staggeringly beautiful. A visit to the site can only confirm what Horace wrote in one of his epistles: *Nullus in orbe sinus Baiis praelucet amoenis* ("No bay on Earth outshines pleasing Baia").

Viewing Underwater Baia by Boat

From the small modern-day port of Baia you can board a boat with glass panels on its lower deck and view part of the *città sommersa,* the underwater city of ancient Baia.

The guided tour—usually in Italian, but given in English if arranged well in advance—lasts about 1¼ hours and is best undertaken in calm conditions, when you can get good glimpses of Roman columns, roads, villa walls, and mosaics. The fare (€10) also includes a brief talk about significant changes to the coastline over the last two millennia and the main underwater sights.

There are sailings Saturday at noon and 3 or Sunday at noon and 3 (depending on weather and water conditions); booking ahead is essential. For further information and bookings, contact **Baiasommersa** (☎ *349/4974183* ⊕ *www. baiasommersa.it*).

GETTING HERE

To arrive by car take the Tangenziale from Naples and exit at Pozzuoli–Arco Felice and follow the indications for Baia. By train, take the Cumana railway (trains leave every 20 minutes from Montesanto in Naples, travel time 30 minutes, nearest stop Fusaro) followed by a SEPSA bus for the last 3 km (2 mi). On Friday, weekends, and public holidays, take the City Sightseeing Campi Flegrei bus from Piazza della Repubblica in Pozzuoli (or from other sites in the area). Where the bus stops in the square outside the Baia station, cross the disused railway line on a footbridge. Continue upward for about five minutes until you reach the entrance to the site (limited parking is available). The same SEPSA bus also stops at the Museo in the castle. To arrive from Naples by bus, take the SEPSA Linea 1 from Piazza Garibaldi and ask to get off at either the Parco Archeologico or the Museo.

EXPLORING

★ Housed in the Castle of Baia, which commands a fine 360-degree view—eastward across the Bay of Pozzuoli and westward across the open Tyrrhenian—is the exquisite **Museo Archeologico dei Campi Flegrei.** Arrive by train at Fosaro (Baia station being closed at this writing), then take a SEPSA bus marked Monte di Procido, with the stop outside the castle plainly visible. Though its foundation dates to the late 15th century, when Naples was ruled by the House of Aragon and an invasion by Charles VIII of France looked imminent, the castle was radically transformed after the nearby eruption which threw up Monte Nuovo in a single night (so local legend has it) in 1538. Spanish viceroy Don Pedro de Toledo brought in a top Sienese military designer Giorgio Martini to take into account the new topography and extend the battlements to prevent outflanking manoevres. Indeed, its bastions bear a striking resemblance to the imposing Castel Sant'Elmo in Naples, built in the same period and most of all to Castello Aragonese in Ischia, a sort of castellar twin. After unification under the house of Savoy the castle went into decline. This is an ideal spot for museumphobes: spacious, uncluttered rooms display tastefully contextualized finds; there's a virtual absence of large tour groups; there's access to bastion terraces; and it only takes about an hour to see. That is, until recent municipal strictures forced the closure of much of the museum (at press time); it is hoped in the future that most rooms will welcome museumgoers again. Of the various exhibitions (many closed at this writing), the first on the suggested itinerary consists of plaster casts from the Roman period found at the Baia archaeological site. This gives valuable insights into the techniques used by the Romans to make copies from Greek originals in bronze from the classical and Hellenistic periods.

Pride of place in the museum goes to the *sacellum,* or small sanctuary, transported from nearby Misenum and tastefully displayed inside the Aragonese tower, the Torre Tenaglia. Standing about 20 feet high, the sacellum has been reconstructed, with two of its original six columns (the rest in steel) and a marble architrave with its dedicatory inscription to the husband-and-wife team of *Augustales* (imperial cult devotees), who commissioned restoration of the sanctuary in the 2nd century AD, this surmounted by a pediment depicting the beneficent couple. Behind the facade are the naked marble figures of Vespasian (left) and Titus (right) in a flattering heroic pose, at least from the neck downward.

Moving on to the upper floor of the tower, you come to the other *capolavoro,* or showpiece, of the museum, the reconstruction of Emperor Claudius's nymphaeum. Discovered in 1959 but only systematically excavated in the early 1980s, the original nymphaeum now lies together with much of the ancient site of Baia under 20 feet of water in the Bay of Pozzuoli. The sculptural elements salvaged from the seabed include a recognizable scene of a headless Odysseus plying Polyphemus (statue never found) with wine, suitably aided by Baios with a wineskin. The function of the nymphaeum is suggested by the marble supports for *klinai* (couches) set on the floor near the entrance: this must have been a showy triclinium, with its full complement of statues and fountains designed to ease the weight of imperial cares and provide due source for reflection and inspiration. (There is a beautiful virtual version of this nymphaeum, both before and after flooding, in the MAV museum in Herculaneum.) At the top of the castle Room 47 two giant caryatids announce the partial recreation of an Augustan temple, this replacing another temple from Republican times. Remains on display inside were only discovered in 1964 after Pozzuoli's Basilica of Proculus was struck by fire. ⊠ *Via Castello 39, Bacoli, loc. Baia* ☎ *081/5233797* 🖂 *€4, including Cumae, site at Baia, and Flavian amphitheater in Pozzuoli* ⊗ *Tues.–Sun. 9–1 hr before sunset. Closed Jan. 1, May 1, Dec. 25.*

★ At the ticket office for the **Parco Archeologico e Monumentale di Baia** you should receive a small map to the site while information panels in readable English are posted at strategic intervals. In antiquity this whole area was the Palatium Baianum (the Palace of Baia), dedicated to *otium*—the ancient form of *dolce far niente*—and the residence of emperors from Augustus to as late as Septimius Severus in the 3rd century AD. The first terrace, the aptly named Villa dell'Ambulatio, is one of the best levels from which to appreciate the topography of the site: the whole hillside down to the level of the modern road near the waterfront has been modeled into flat terraces, each sporting different architectural features.

While up on this terrace look for the exquisite stuccoed artistry, with its depictions of dolphins, swans, and cupids in the *balneum* (thermal bathing, Room 13), and admire the elaborate theatrical motifs in the floor mosaic in Room 14. Below the balneum and inviting further exploration is a nymphaeum shrine, which can be reached from the western side. Make sure you get down to the so-called Temple of Mercury, on the lowest level, which has held so much fascination for travelers from the 18th century onward. It has been variously interpreted as a frigidarium and as a *natatio* (swimming pool) and is the oldest example of a large dome (50 BC–27 BC), predating the cupola of the Pantheon in Rome. (Test the impressive echo in the interior.) A long walk down the steps, on the other side of the road from the upper entrance, is the newly restored sector with the showstopper being the **Temple of Diana** (3rd AD), in effect an ancient baths, the inner cavity of its dome rivaling some of those back in the Roman Forum for size. Note a logistic problem: tickets have to be purchased at the castle, quite a distance away. ⊠ *Parco Archeologico e Monumentale di Baia, Via Fusaro 37, Bacoli, loc. Baia* ☎ *081/8687592* ≙*€4 including Cumae, site at Museo Archeologico dei Campi Flegrei, and Flavian amphitheater in Pozzuoli* ☉ *Tues.–Sun. 9–1 hr before sunset. Closed Jan. 1, May 1, Dec. 25.*

WHERE TO EAT

¢–$ ✕ **Azienda Agrituristica Il Casolare.** Il Casolare offers the rare chance of
SOUTHERN   dining and lodging within a 10,000-year-old volcanic crater (thankfully
ITALIAN   extinct). This place is particularly known for its restaurant, perched on the inner slopes of the volcano, offering a view of the patchwork of farmed plots on the crater floor. Specializing in *cucina contadina napoletana* (Neapolitan rustic cuisine), the owner Tobia serves whatever is in season. The set price menu is about €30: expect a cornucopia of antipasti and some nouvelle vegetarian dishes like pasta *e cicerchia* (with vetchling). The inn's four *mini-appartmenti* are small but tastefully furnished, a perfect base for exploring the surrounding area (booking ahead for both restaurant and hotel is essential). Transfers can be arranged from the nearby railway station of Lucrino. ⊠ *Via P. Fabbris 12–14, Bacoli, loc. Coste dei Fondi di Baia* ☎ *081/5235193* ⊕ *www.datobia.it* ⊟ *No credit cards* ☉ *Closed Mon. No dinner Sun.* ⎮⊙⎮*EP.*

¢   ✕ **Down Town.** Unlike at other eateries in this area, you won't be pres-
MEDITERRANEAN   sured to have a *Satyricon*-style banquet at Down Town. Check the whiteboard inside for the day's specials, which often include exotic items (for Naples) like couscous, and always something for nonseafood eaters. Vaulted ceilings and wooden tables inset with tiles give the place a fairly spartan but distinctive feel. Refreshingly good local wines served by the glass pair perfectly with their fried appetizers and pizzas. The main entrance is right off the little port of Baia. Reservations are essential on weekends. ⊠ *Via Lucullo 39* ☎ *081/8687261* ⊕ *www.downtown.it* ⊟ *DC, MC, V* ☉ *Closed Wed. and lunchtime, except Sun.*

WHERE TO STAY

$ ⛨ **Batis B&B.** Right in front of the Temple of Venus this spot is entered through a well-equipped bar. Pleasant guest rooms were originally domestic quarters and now are named after the flora of the area (Juniper, Lavender, Broom, etc). Ask for "*lato mare*" for a view of the sea framed by the Tempio di Venere, or "*lato parco*" for views of the park with ancient Roman baths (the latter would be preferable for those worried about traffic noise). Signora Marinella, an excellent host, will also explain how the restaurant was once part of the 8th-century cistern while the cool and shady seating area outside was a vaulted oven (the stoke holes to prove it). Adding further to the archaeological ambience, the Piperno stone visible throughout completes the local feel, as do the regional wines and food products on tap in the restaurant, which are all strictly Flegreian. **Pros:** regionally true; high room standards; parking for disabled. **Cons:** noisy main road. ⊠ *Via Lucullo 101, Porto di Baia, Bacoli* ☏ *081/8688763* ⊕ *www.batis.it* ⤴ *12 rooms* ⚘ *In-room: a/c. In-hotel: restaurant, bar* ▭ *AE, DC, MC, V* ¶◎¶ *BP.*

$ 📷 **La Rada B&B.** For views like this many a five-star hotel would be envious: two rooms look directly out onto the bay of bays: two others, perfect for painters, frame, via some palm and fig trees, the world's largest Roman bath complex. This B&B is also beautifully furnished with wardrobes and other fittings brought down from Florence. To quote Signora Carmen, the courteous and welcoming live-in manager, there is also "grande silenzio." No breakfast room but there are nearby restaurants. Divers would love La Rada, as some diving shops are next door and there's Claudius's sunken palace just a short swim offshore. **Pros:** quiet; very much the personal touch; wonderful views. **Cons:** no computer connection or Wi-Fi; cash only. ⊠ *Via Violo di Baia 9, Porto di Baia, Bacoli* ☏ *081/8688880* ⊕ *www.laradadibaia.it* ⤴ *4 rooms* ⚘ *In-room: a/c, refrigerator* ▭ *No credit cards* ¶◎¶ *BP.*

CUMAE

Fodor's Choice
★

16 km (10 mi) west of Naples, 5 km (3 mi) north of Baia.

Being perhaps the oldest Greek colony on mainland Italy, Cumae overshadowed the Phlegrean Fields and Neapolis in the 7th and 6th centuries BC, since it was home to the **Antro della Sibilla,** the fabled Cave of the Cumaean Sibyl—one of the three greatest oracles of antiquity—who is said to have presided over the destinies of men. In about the 6th century BC the Greeks hollowed the cave (closed for restoration at time of writing) from the rock beneath the ridge leading up to the present ruins of Cumae's acropolis. Today you can walk—just as Virgil's Aeneas did—through a dark, massive 350-foot-long stone tunnel that opens into the vaulted Chamber of the Prophetic Voice, where the Sibyl delivered her oracles. Standing here in one of the most venerated sites of ancient times, the sense of the *numen*—of communication with invisible powers—is overwhelming. "This is the most romantic classical site in Italy," claimed famed travelogue writer H. V. Morton. "I would rather come here than to Pompeii."

GETTING HERE

If driving, take the Cumae Exit 13 of the Naples Tangenziale and proceed along Montenuovo Licola Patria, following signs for Cumae. At the first major intersection, take a left onto Via Arco Felice Vecchio, pass under the arch, and make a right at the next intersection and after around 400 yards turn left into the site. There is a free parking lot. There is no train station in Cumae, so to arrive from Naples, take the Cumana railway to Fusaro, then the SEPSA Miseno–Cumae bus to Cumae. SEPSA also runs buses to Cumae from Pozzuoli's station and Baia.

EXPLORING

Cumae was founded in the third quarter of the 8th century BC by Greek colonists. The name has legendary origins: Myth has it that Euboean mariners found a woman who had miscarried a baby on the beach here, and the fetus was washed out to sea by great breakers on the shore. Thinking this an omen from the gods of fertility, the mariners built an altar here and called their new settlement *kuema* (or "fetus" in Greek). Centuries later Virgil wrote his epic of the *Aeneid,* the story of the Trojan prince Aeneas's wanderings, partly to give Rome the historical legitimacy that Homer had given the Greeks. On his journey, Aeneas had to descend to the underworld to speak to his father, and to find his way in, he needed the guidance of the Cumaean Sibyl. Virgil did not dream up the Sibyl's Cave or the entrance to Hades—he must have actually stood both in her chamber and along the rim of Lake Avernus, as you yourself will stand. When he described the Sibyl's Cave in Book VI of the *Aeneid* as having *"centum ostia"*—a hundred mouths—and depicted the entrance to the underworld on Lake Avernus so vividly, *"spelunca alta . . . tuta lacu nigro nemorum tenebris"*—"a deep cave . . . protected by a lake of black water and the glooming forest"—it was because he was familiar with this awesome landscape. In Book VI of the *Aeneid,* Virgil describes how Aeneas, arriving at Cumae, sought Apollo's throne (remains of the Temple of Apollo can still be seen) and "the deep hidden abode of the dread Sibyl/An enormous cave . . ."

Although Cumae never achieved the status of Delphi, it was the most important oracular center in Magna Graecia, and the Sibyl would have been consulted on a whole range of matters. Governments consulted the Sibyl before mounting campaigns. Wealthy aristocrats came to channel their deceased relatives. Businessmen came to get their dreams interpreted or to seek favorable omens before entering into financial agreements or setting off on journeys. Love potions were a profitable source of revenue; women from Baia lined up for potions to slip into the wine of handsome charioteers who drove up and down the street in their gold-plated four-horsepower chariots. Still, it was the Sibyl's prophecies that ensured the crowds here, prophecies written on palm leaves and later collected into the corpus of the Sibylline books.

Allow at least two hours for this visit to soak up the ambience and study the ruins. Unlike in Greek and Roman times, when access to Cumae was through a network of underground passages, an aboveground bus service leaves the old Baia station at regular intervals. ✉ *Via Acropoli 1* ☎ *081/8543060* 💶 *€4, including museum and site at Baia and Flavian amphitheater in Pozzuoli* ☉ *Daily 9–1 hr before sunset.*

WHERE TO STAY

$–$$ 🏠 **Villa Giulia.** Built with characteristic yellow tuff walls and restored in
★   immaculate taste, this beautiful and historic stone farmhouse provides an excellent base for the Cumae area provided you have a car. The decor

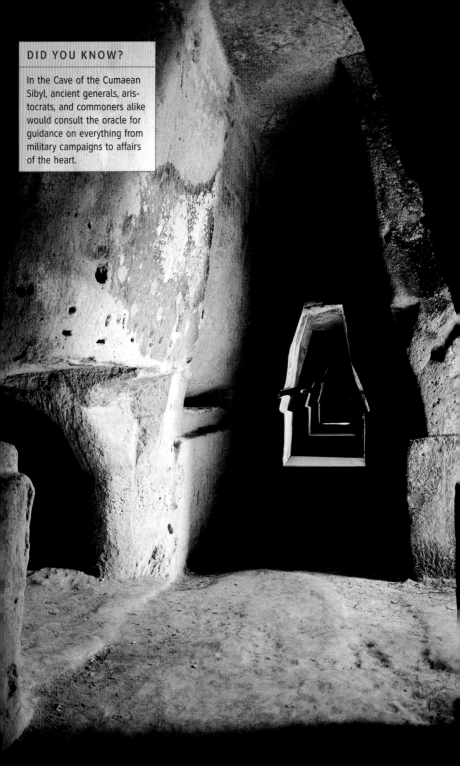

and atmosphere are those of a top-notch hotel, while the price is refreshingly accessible. Out of the way and off the main road, directions are clearly set out on the Web site. For an extra €30, try Giulia's inventive cuisine (evenings only) served under her leafy pergola. **Pros:** excellent food and service; absolutely charming surrounds and garden; pool, family-friendly; one room a honeymooner's dream come true. **Cons:** isolated, so car is essential. ✉ *Via Cumae–Licola 178* ☎ *081/8540163* ⊕ *www.villagiulia.info* ↝ *6 rooms* ⌂ *In-room: kitchen (some). In-hotel: restaurant, pool, Internet terminal, parking* ▭ *AE, DC, MC, V* ¡◎¡ *BP*.

Naples

WORD OF MOUTH

"We liked Naples very much from our first moments in the city. If there is a city whose people appear more filled with the sheer joy of life, I have not yet been there!"

—ekscrunchy

WELCOME TO NAPLES

TOP REASONS TO GO

★ **A Spaccanapoli Stroll:** For perfect people-watching, promenade through this historic district of Naples, whose packed streets, pungent aromas, and operatic hawking offer all the energy, chaos, and beauty that make this the most operatic of cities.

★ **A Baroque Extravaganza:** Gorge yourself on Naples's greatest moment in art history, the era of the baroque, by exploring the city's 17th-century churches, whose swirling gilt naves melt even the stoniest of hearts.

★ **Buried Pleasures:** All the excavated treasures from Pompeii and Herculaneum ended up in Naples's Museo Archeologico Nazionale, the finest treasure trove of ancient art.

★ **Festa di San Gennaro:** Everything in Naples is brought to a boil twice a year, on the first Saturday in May and on September 19, when "Il Miracolo," the Liquefaction of the Blood of San Gennaro, is celebrated at the city duomo.

Bay of Naples

1 Toledo and Quartieri Spagnoli. The central Toledo district has a concentration of monuments, including the sumptuous apartments of the Palazzo Reale and the broad open space of Piazza Plebiscito. Built by Viceroy Pedro di Toledo to bring some order to the city, the pedestrianized Via Toledo leads into the grid of Quartieri Spagnoli, a sort of NATO base of its time, where Spanish soldiers were deployed between campaigns to guard the palazzos of the ruling class.

2 The Lungomare. The area along the harbor west of Toledo consists of two quarters, Santa Lucia and Chiaia. Both areas are thin on culture and geared to *la dolce vita*: in Santa Lucia you can expect serenades from street musicians over dinner, while most locals head for their favorite trattoria up a side street in Chiaia.

GETTING ORIENTED

In Naples "up and down" is often as accurate a form of direction as "to and fro." From the bay, the city rises up steep hillsides, which you can ascend with the help of three funiculars, as well as strategically placed *ascensori* (elevators). Via Toledo, one of the major thoroughfares, serves as a north–south axis. Farther north, the long Corso Vittorio Emmanuele, a panoramic strip of road, runs up along the Vomero linking the sea-level southwest with the elevated northeast.

------- Funicular

=M= Metro stop

3 **Vomero.** Connected to the city below by three funiculars, the Vomero hill offers a peaceful contrast to the hustle downtown. The Certosa at San Martino, a monastery turned museum complex is a highlight, with magnificent works of art, wraparound views of Naples, and gardens fit for contemplation.

4 **Spaccanapoli.** For art and archaeology, this must be one of the most exquisitely packed neighborhoods on earth, and at the same time it teems with vibrant street life. The United Nations has dubbed the district an open-air museum—which in this case feels like an understatement.

NAPLES PLANNER

Beyond First Impressions

If you're arriving in Naples by train, don't expect to be instantly charmed.

Piazza Garibaldi, which is home to the Stazione Centrale, the main railroad terminal, is now a battered labyrinth—crowded, messy, and inhospitable, with the local bus station perched in the middle of a tangle of intersections.

Longtime home to street sharks and souvenir hawkers, the piazza is now also a meeting point for Eastern European guest workers, who have become a growing presence in the city.

When you make your way beyond Piazza Garibaldi, first impressions begin to mellow: Delightfully and unforgettably, Naples reveals itself as a cornucopia of elegant boulevards, treasure-stocked palaces, the world's greatest museum of classical antiquities, the stage-set neighborhood of Spaccanapoli, and scores of historic churches.

Naples becomes *Napoli la bella*, a city that centuries of romantics have deemed one of the most beautiful in the world.

Making the Most of Your Time

Three to four days will be enough to give you a taste of the city and see you through the main monuments, as well as factor in a breather to one of the islands in the bay. Always make a contingency plan for each day. Naples can be fraying on the nerves and tiring in terms of legwork, so head for one of the city parks (Villa Comunale, Floridiana, or Capodimonte) for well-earned *riposo* in between doses of *cultura*. You may need a rest after touring the Spaccanapoli district, which, following the original Greek street plan is wonderfully compact, with more culture packed into a square mile or two than anywhere else in the world.

Sightseeing days should begin no later than 9, as most churches are usually open only from 7:30 until noon or 12:30, reopening only after the afternoon siesta, from 4 or 4:30 until about 7. Most museums have extended hours, with a few even open in evenings. If you come to Naples by car, park it in a garage as fast as you can, agree on the cost in advance, and then forget it for the duration of your stay (otherwise, city driving is not for the fainthearted, theft is a constant risk, and parking a nightmare).

Finding a Place to Stay

If you want seafront accommodation in Naples, remember that rooms with a view come at a sizable premium, and there are likely to be three busy lanes of traffic between you and the shoreline (though they often come with, happily, double-paned windows to keep out any noise). In fact, to avoid sleep-disturbed nights, always ask for a *camera tranquilla* (quiet room) regardless of where you stay. Taking advantage of pedestrianization schemes, several competitively priced hotels close to Piazza Plebiscito and in the Chiaia area, now offer better public transport connections and more touring options within walking distance. Do resist the temptation to stay near Piazza Garibaldi by the Stazione Centrale just because it's a transport hub: the area is unsafe (and unpleasant) for evening strolls after 8:30 pm.

The Campania Artecard

The Campania Artecard is a big boon for museum lovers. This pass offers free or discounted admission to almost 50 museums and monuments over a three- or seven-consecutive-day period for the city or the whole region, as well as discounted services ranging from audio guides to theater tickets and car parks.

The benefits depend on the pass: A three-day pass gets you free admission to the first three sites you visit, then half price for the others, plus free transport—including the Alibus from the airport and the Metro del Mare around the bay. The main passes are: Naples historic center, €12 (access to all sites); Naples and Campi Flegrei, €16; Naples and Caserta, €20; Archeologia del golfo including Pompeii, Herculaneum, Caserta, and Paestum, €30; and Naples and Campi Flegrei, €20 (access to all sites); in addition, there are generous youth discounts.

As sites and discounts are frequently updated, check ⊕ *www.campaniartecard.it* for the latest information.

Cards are available at all the major participating museums and archaeological sites, at main city hotels, as well as at the airport and the station.

A Neapolitan Night Out on the Town

Long queues are common at the more popular spots as people endlessly haggle about being on the guest list or try to avoid paying in some other way. Be patient and enjoy the experience—many long-standing friendships have been formed in queues outside nightclubs in Naples.

But remember that planning a night out in Napoli is rather like planning a military campaign, with many phone calls made, appointments fixed, changed, not met, and plans B, C, and D coming into action.

Visitor Information

The numerous tourist offices in Naples aren't always open when they claim to be, but most are generally open from Monday to Saturday 8:30–8 and Sunday 8:30–2 except where noted.

There's an **EPT** (✉ *Stazione Centrale, Piazza Garibaldi* ☎ *081/268779*) (Ente Provinciale per il Turismo) office in Stazione Centrale, where the people are quite friendly and helpful; the main administrative center (with an atmosphere of baroque mothballs) is in **Piazza dei Martiri** (✉ *Piazza dei Martiri 58, Chiaia* ☎ *081/4107211*), and is open weekdays 8:30–2. There's also a branch at **Stazione Mergellina** (☎ *081/7612102*). The **AACST** (✉ *Piazza Gesù Nuovo, Spaccanapoli* ☎ *01/5523328*) specializes in information on old Naples but generally just gives out brochures. A second office, which is closed Sunday, is handily inside the Palazzo Reale.

6

CAMPANIA'S SEAFOOD BOUNTY

Fish and other sea creatures are mainstays of the Campanian diet, especially along the region's stunning coastline, and on the islands ringing the Bay of Naples.

The waters along Campania's shore are regarded as some of the cleanest in Italy. Evidence of that claim comes from the ubiquity of anchovies (*alici* or *acciuga*) that are said to only swim in pristine waters. Fishermen in some villages still go out at night in lighted fishing boats to attract and net anchovies, which are cooked fresh or cured with salt.

The Mediterranean Sea's bounty extends far beyond alici. Some of the most popular fish varieties are listed on the following page, but there are scores more waiting to be tasted. Gustatory explorers eating their way down the coastline might also encounter these sea creatures: *aguglie* (needle fish); *calamari* (squid); *cicale* (mantis shrimp); *mazzancolle* (a type of prawn); *orata* (seabream or daurade); *pesce spada* (swordfish); *seppia* (cuttlefish); *scorfano di fondale* (ocean perch); *scorfano rosso* (scorpion fish); and *scampi* (langoustines).

MENU DECODER

Campanian chefs know how to treat fresh fish, using simple preparations that showcase the fresh flavors of the region. These are some of the typical preparations.

- baked (*al forno*)
- baked in a paper pouch (*al cartoccio*)
- cured (*salato*)
- fried (*fritto*)
- grilled (*alla griglia*)
- marinated (*marinato*)
- poached (*affogato*)
- raw (*crudo*)
- roasted (*arrostito*)
- roasted in salt (*al sale*)
- smoked (*affumicato*)

ALICI OR ACCIUGHE (ANCHOVY)

Highly flavored, small fish that may be served fresh or cured. Grilled or fried anchovies have a milder taste than the cured fish, which can be quite pungent. Fried anchovies are a popular snack along the coast.

BACCALÀ (SALT COD)

Cod that has been dried and cured in salt. Before use, the dried baccalà fillet is soaked repeatedly in water to reduce saltiness and reconstitute the flesh. Common dishes include sautéed baccalà with potatoes, and baccalà baked in spicy tomato sauce.

BRANZINO (EUROPEAN SEA BASS)

A medium-size fish with lean, flaky white meat and a slightly sweet, mild flavor. May also be called *spigola*. It is often grilled and served with potatoes, or baked *al cartoccio*.

COZZE (MUSSELS)

Extremely popular in the region since Roman times, these fat yellow delights are more likely than not to be farmed, as natural resources have been severely depleted. They are often served with a side plate for the shells.

GALLINELLA (GURNARD)

A meaty white fish that may also be called *mazzole* or tub fish. Gallinella *all'acqua pazza* is cooked in "crazy water" (oil mixed with water and flavored with tomatoes and herbs). A related fish is *cappone gallinella* (red gurnard).

POLPO (OCTOPUS)

The firmly textured, gently flavored octopus may be boiled in simple soups, stewed (polpi *in cassuola*), or simply sautéed with garlic and olive oil, among myriad preparations. Polpetto is the term used for little octopi.

SARDE (SARDINES)

Sardines are considered *pesce azzurro*— small blue fish that swim near the surface of the sea—along with anchovy and *cecinelli* (smelt). These fish typically appear in seafood *fritto misto*, a mixture of small fried fish.

TOTANI (FLYING SQUID)

These squid closely resemble calamari, and likewise are a popular snack when cut into rings and deep-fried. May be stuffed with diced vegetables, fried as a snack, or boiled and served cold in salads.

TRIGLIA (RED MULLET)

Small bony fish with moderately fatty flesh and delicate flavor. Often featured in fish stews, and may also be served sautéed, baked, or roasted.

VONGOLE VERACI (STRIPED VENUS CLAMS)

These tiny, sweet clams are prized throughout Italy, where they play a starring role in spaghetti vongole.

Opposite page: A typical Amalfi meal.
top right: Fresh fish in Naples.
bottom left: Octopus, a staple in the Campania diet.

"Built like a great amphitheater around her beautiful bay, Naples is an eternally unfolding play acted by a million of the best actors in the world," Herbert Kubly observed in his *American in Italy*. "The comedy is broad, the tragedy violent. The curtain never rings down." Is it a sense of doom from living in the shadow of Vesuvius that makes some Neapolitans so volatile, so blind to everything but the pain or pleasure of the moment?

A huge zest for living and crowded conditions are the more probable causes. But whatever the reason, Naples remains the most vibrant city in Italy—a steaming, bubbling, reverberating minestrone in which each block is a small village, every street the setting for a Punch-and-Judy show, and everything seems to be a backdrop for an opera not yet composed.

It's said that northern Italians vacation here to remind themselves of the time when Italy was *molto Italiana*—*really* Italian. In this respect, Naples—Napoli in Italian—doesn't disappoint: Neapolitan rainbows of laundry wave in the wind over alleyways open-windowed with friendliness, mothers caress children, men break out into impromptu arias at sidewalk caffè, and street scenes offer Fellini-esque slices of life. Everywhere contrasting elements of faded gilt and romance, rust and calamity, grandeur and squalor form a pageant of pure *Italianità*—Italy at its most Italian.

As the historic capital of Campania, Naples has been perpetually and tumultuously in a state of flux. Neapolitans are instinctively the most hospitable of people, and they've often paid a price for being so, having unwittingly extended a warm welcome to wave after wave of invaders. Lombards, Goths, Normans, Swabians, Spanish viceroys and kings, and Napoleonic generals arrived in turn; most of them proved to be greedy and self-serving. Still, if these foreign rulers bled the populace dry with taxes, they left the impoverished city with a rich architectural inheritance.

Much of that inheritance is on display in the Spaccanapoli district, where the Piazza Gesù Nuovo and the surrounding blocks are a showplace for the city's most beloved churches and a showcase for the city's greatest attraction, the Neapolitan people. On the piazza, watch and rub elbows with them. Let their charm, gaiety, effervescence, and undiluted spontaneity pull you into their unique and glorious concept of life and living. You'll soon begin to sense that Neapolitans are possibly the happiest people in the world. In an hour or two you'll feel like part of the *famiglia* yourself.

Compared to most other great metropolises of the world, Naples has little tourist infrastructure, forcing you to become a native very quickly, as you'll find out if you spend some time wandering through the gridlike narrow streets of the old center. Lost? You'll be taken in hand (probably by way of mamma's house). Hungry? Can't think of the right word? A translation is shouted out over the din, and a single word is never sufficient when 10 will do—as you could have seen one September afternoon when an English couple asked for directions to the Church of Pio Monte della Misericordia. One passerby started explaining, but another man suddenly thought of a still shorter way and butted in. In no time 8 or 10 people were volubly offering their own directions. The arguing that ensued was not unfriendly; a torn racing form was the only casualty. The inquiring couple never learned the shortest—or, for that matter, any other—way to Pio Monte. But the sun was warm, the sky was blue, and there are plenty of other beautiful churches in Naples.

EXPLORING NAPLES

Updated by
Martin Wilmot
Bennett

Naples, a bustling city of a million people, can be a challenge for visitors because of its hilly terrain and its twisty, often congested streets. Though spread out, Naples invites walking; the bus system, funiculars, and subways are also options for dealing with weary legs.

The city of Naples stretches along the Bay of Naples from Piazza Garibaldi in the east to Mergellina in the west, with its back to the Vomero Hill. From Stazione Centrale, on Piazza Garibaldi, Corso Umberto I (known as the "Rettifilo") heads southwest to the monumental city center—commonly known as "Toledo"—around the piazzas Bovio, Municipio, and Trieste e Trento; here is the major urban set piece composed of the Palazzo Reale, Teatro San Carlo, and Galleria Umberto Primo.

To the north are the historic districts of old Naples, most notably Spaccanapoli, I Vergini, and La Sanità; to the south, the port. Farther west along the bay are the more fashionable neighborhoods of Santa Lucia and Chiaia, and finally the waterfront district of Mergellina. The residential area of Vomero sits on the steep hills rising above Chiaia and downtown.

At the center of it all is picturesque Spaccanapoli—the heart of the *centro storico* (historic center), called the Decumanus Inferior in Roman times. The entire quarter takes its name from its main street, a partly pedestrianized promenade referred to as Spaccanapoli. Rather confusingly, this street changes its name—Via Benedetto Croce and Via San Biagio dei Librai, among others—as it runs its way through the heart

Visited by Boccaccio and Giotto, massive Castel Nuovo sits near the shore of the Bay of Naples and once protected the heart of the medieval city.

of old Naples. The area is particularly suited to strolling. The slopes are manageable, and a gridlike street layout makes navigation extraordinarily simple. The *vicoli* (side streets) are seldom more than 100 meters long, and the high number of intersections means there is always a square on hand where you can take a coffee and watch life go by, a favorite Neapolitan activity.

Tying much of this geographic layout together is the "spine" of the city, Via Toledo—Naples's major north–south axis, which begins at Piazza Trieste e Trento and heads up all the way to Capodimonte. It's basically one straight road with four different names (five if you count the official name of Via Roma, which is how the locals refer to it).

Via Toledo links Piazza Trieste e Trento with Piazza Dante. Going farther north you get into Via Pessina for about 100 yards, which takes you up to the megajunction with the Museo Archeologico Nazionale.

North of that, you head up to the peak of Capodimonte by traveling along Via Santa Teresa degli Scalzi and then Corso Amedeo di Savoia.

To make things a bit more confusing, parts of Via Toledo are pedestrianized—that means no buses or scooters, thankfully—from just south of Piazza Carità (where Via Toledo/Roma intersects with Via Diaz) all the way to Piazza Trieste e Trento.

GETTING AROUND NAPLES

PUBLIC TRANSIT

Naples's rather old Metropolitana (subway system), also called Linea 2, provides fairly frequent service and can be the fastest way to get across the traffic-clogged city.

The other urban subway system, Metropolitana Collinare (or Linea 1), links the hill area of the Vomero and beyond with the National Archaeological Museum and Piazza Dante. Trains on both lines run from 5 am until 10:30 pm.

For standard public transportation, including the subways, buses, and funiculars, an UnicoNapoli costs €1.10 and is valid for 90 minutes as far as Pozzuoli to the west and Portici to the east; €3.10 buys a *biglietto giornaliero*, good for the whole day (€2.60 on weekends).

Bus service has become viable over the last few years, especially with the introduction of larger buses on the regular R1, R2, R3, and R4 routes. Electronic signs display wait times at many stops.

PARKING

If you come to Naples by car, find a garage, agree on the cost, and leave it there for the duration of your stay. (If you park on the street, you run the risk of theft.) **Garage Cava** (✉ *Via Mergellina 6* ☎ *081/660023*), **Grilli** (✉ *Via Ferraris 40, near Stazione Centrale* ☎ *081/264344*), and **Turistico** (✉ *Via de Gasperi 14, near port* ☎ *081/5525442*) are all centrally located, safe, and open 24 hours a day.

TAXIS

When taking a taxi in Naples, make sure that the meter is switched on at the start of your trip. Trips around the city are unlikely to cost less than €10 or more than €20. Set fares for various destinations within the city should be displayed in the taxi, as should extra charges for things like baggage and night service. For trips outside the city, negotiate your fare before getting in. Watch out for overcharging at three locations: the airport, the railway station, and the hydrofoil marina. And in peak summer weeks, don't forget that most cabs in Naples have no air-conditioning—which the city's buses and metro do have—and you can practically bake if caught in one during a half-hour traffic jam.

TOURS

Handily close to the port is the terminal for double-decker buses belonging to **City Sightseeing** (✉ *Piazza Municipio* ☎ *081/5517279* ⊕ *www.napoli.city-sightseeing.it*). For €22 you can take two or three different excursions, giving you reasonable coverage of the downtown sights and outlying attractions like the Museo di Capodimonte.

A welcome center in the old town, the **Centro di Accoglienza Turistica Museo Aperto Napoli** (✉ *Via Pietro Colletta 89* ☎ *081/5636062* ⊕ *www.museoapertonapoli.it*), offers €6 audio guides you can listen to as you wander around.

For in-depth tours of Naples, the **Comune di Napoli** (✉ *Piazza Municipio* ☎ *081/5422090* ⊕ *www.comune.napoli.it*) occasionally offers English-language guided tours. These tours are a great way to see monuments that are otherwise off-limits.

6

TOLEDO: THE MONUMENTAL CITY CENTER

Naples's setting on what is possibly the most beautiful bay in the world has long been a boon for its inhabitants—the expansive harbor has always brought great mercantile wealth to the city—and, intermittently, a curse. Throughout history, a who's who of Greek, Roman, Norman, Spanish, and French despots has quarreled over this gateway to Campania. Each set of conquerors recognized that the area around the city harbor—today occupied by the Molo Beverello hydrofoil terminal and the 1928 Stazione Marittima—functioned as a veritable welcome mat to the metropolis and consequently should be a fitting showcase of regal and royal authority. This had become imperative because of explosive population growth, which, by the mid-16th century, had made Naples the second-largest city in Europe, after Paris. With the mass migration of the rural population to the city, Naples had grown into a capricious, unplanned, disorderly, and untrammeled capital. Thus, the central aim of the ruling dynasties became the creation of a *Napoli nobilissima*—a "most noble" Naples.

The monuments they created remain prominent features of the city center: one of the most magnificent opera houses in Europe, a palace that rivals Versailles, an impregnable *castello* (castle), a majestic church modeled on Rome's Pantheon, and a 19th-century shopping galleria are landmarks that characterized the shifts among the ruling powers, from the French Angevins to the Spanish Habsburgs and Bourbons and, later, the postunification rise of the bourgeoisie and the regime of Mussolini. This historic sector is the much-put-upon Cinderella—as Naples is seen by many of her fans—but dressed up in her *principessa* finery, all ready to wow the spectators at the royal ball. In contrast to the intense intimacy of the Spaccanapoli district, the official center of Naples unrolls its majesty with great pomp along its spacious avenues and monumental piazzas.

TOP ATTRACTIONS

★ **Castel Nuovo** *(New Castle)*. Known to locals as Maschio Angioino in reference to its Angevin builders, this imposing building is now used more for marital than military purposes, its being partly a government registry office. Looming Angevin stonework is upstaged by the white four-tier triumphal entrance arch, ordered by Alfonso of Aragon after his entry into the city in 1443 to seize the throne from the increasingly unpopular and beleaguered Angevin Giovanna II. (She had promised Alfonso the throne on her death in return for some much needed protection, only to switch allegiances to a fellow Angevin prince.) Completed by Francesco Laurana and others, the arch on its first level shows the king riding a triumphal cart accompanied, Roman fashion, by a procession of followers. At the top, as if justifying Alfonso's claim to the throne, stands the Archangel Gabriel in the act of slaying a demon. Add four orders of Corinthian columns, rose reliefs, and putti, and you have self-promotion that was built to last. As you enter, admire on the arch's side walls Renaissance soldiers sporting the latest military fashion.

Across the courtyard within is Sala Grande, also known as the Sala dei Baroni. Alfonso's triumphal arch notwithstanding, his son King

Castel Nuovo **7**

Galleria
Umberto I **5**

Piazza
Plebiscito **1**

Palazzo Reale **3**

Palazzo
Zevallos **9**

San Francesco
di Paola **2**

Santa Brigida **6**

Sant' Anna dei
Lombardi **8**

Teatro
San Carlo **4**

SANTA
CHIARA

SPACCANAPOLI

Piazza
Carità

Piazza
G. Matteotti

Piazza
Bovio

TOLEDO

Piazza
Municipio

Piazza
Trieste et
Trento

Caffè
Gambrinus

Piazza
Plebiscito

Bacino Vittorio
Emanuele III

PIZZO-
FALCONE

Golfo di Napoli

SANTA
LUCIA

Largo
Bianchi
Nuovi

Piazza
Bovio

0   1/8 mi

0   1/8 km

Toledo

NAPOLI EVER AFTER: A GOOD WALK

In a day filled with monarchist grandeur, it's fitting to start out at **Caffè Gambrinus,** in the very center of Naples on Piazza Trieste e Trento, between Piazza del Plebiscito and Piazza Municipio. This ornate caffè was once the rendezvous for Italian dukes, prime ministers, and literati. Treat yourself to a cappuccino and a pastry as rich and velvety as the surroundings, then step outside into the grand **Piazza del Plebiscito,** which makes an imposing setting for **San Francesco di Paola,** the domed 19th-century church built by Ferdinand I.

From here head directly across the piazza to take in the facade of the **Palazzo Reale,** then enter the palace from Piazza Trieste e Trento, walk up the grand staircase of its Scalone d'Onore, and tour the spectacular 18th- and 19th-century salons of the Museo dell'Appartamento Reale. To visit the adjacent **Teatro San Carlo,** head back down to the piazza and make a right turn in the Piazza Trieste e Trento. Opera lovers will want to take a guided tour of the famous red-and-gold theater (these tours were suspended in fall 2010 but may restart in summer 2011). Across the way is the vast, elegant **Galleria Umberto I,** an ancestor of the shopping mall. Walk through it to Via Santa Brigida and tour the Church of **Santa Brigida.** Head back through the Galleria and then gently downhill on the Via San Carlo and the Via Vittorio Emanuele III; you'll come to the usually light-drenched Piazza Municipio, for years a sprawling building site for the Municipio metro station. To appreciate some of the technical difficulties faced by the subway engineers, peer down into the various layers of civilization

from Roman times on. Above the piazza rises the imposing fortress of the **Castel Nuovo.** From the outside, study its great sculpted triumphal arch of Alfonso of Aragon; inside, explore the museum and Hall of the Barons.

Head across Piazza Municipio to Via Medina until you reach the 20th-century complex at Piazza Matteotti. Then trip across the centuries by continuing up Via Monteoliveto to its pedestrianized piazza, where you can find both the quiet church of **Sant'Anna dei Lombardi** and the Tuscan-influenced rusticated facade of Palazzo Gravina.

Make a left leaving Sant'Anna dei Lombardi and head over to Piazza Carità for ice cream at La Scimmia, then take the 10 or so blocks down Via Toledo (the main thoroughfare of the area, often referred to as Via Roma) back to the Piazza Trieste e Trento; along the way, take in the 17th-century opulence of the **Palazzo Zevallos,** do some window-shopping, and pick up a hot, flaky *sfogliatella* pastry at Mary's by the entrance to Galleria Umberto. You'll arrive back at Piazza Trieste e Trento in time to seek out a leisurely lunch. (*See the "Where to Eat" section for a number of good options.*)

TIMING

Not including stops at the Palazzo Reale and Castel Nuovo museums, this walk will take about three hours. There's no escaping the crowds, but if you start early you may catch the spectacular Piazza del Plebiscito *senza gente* (without people).

Ferrante soon found himself waging a war at the Pope's bidding against Florence. In 1486 the local barons hatched a plot against him. King Ferrante reacted by inviting them here for a wedding banquet, which turned promptly into a mass arrest. (Ferrante is also said to have kept a crocodile in the castle as his special executioner.) In the stupendous 28-meter high vault is a luminous hole toward which spider 16 massive rather sinister arms of reinforcing piperno stone quarried from nearby Pozzuoli. You can also visit the Sala dell'Armeria, where a glass floor reveals recent excavations of a Roman baths from the Augustan period, and a collection of skeletons of 20- to 40-year-olds dating back to the Angevin period.

The next room on the left is the Cappella Palatina. Among the wall frescoes particularly noteworthy is Nicolo di Tomaso's painting of Robert Anjou, one of the first realistic portraits ever. Others, or bits of them anyway, are by various Giotteschi, as the followers of Giotto are known. Giotto's own work in the same chapel was destroyed in a 1456 earthquake and now only remains in Petrarch's poems.

Meanwhile, making up the loss somewhat, the castle's first floor hosts a small gallery with works by Luca Giordano (again), Caracciolo, Solimena, and Maria Preti, as well as a beautiful early Renaissance Adoration of the Magi that once adorned the altar of the Palatine chapel. The painting is by Marco Cardisco and the three Magi are none less than the three Aragonese kings Ferrante I, Ferrante II, and Charles V. ✉ *Piazza Municipio, Toledo* ☎ *081/7952003* 💶*€5* ⊗ *Mon.–Sat. 9–6* Ⓜ *Montesanto (in construction: Piazza Municipio).*

Galleria Umberto I. In 1885, in reaction to the devastating cholera epidemic of the previous year, authorities hastily implemented a massive urban renewal plan whose "clean-up" of Naples entailed the destruction of slum areas between Spaccanapoli and the Palazzo Reale. With facades on Via Toledo—the most animated street in Naples at the time—and across from the Teatro San Carlo, this galleria, built in 1887–90 according to a design by Emanuele Rocca, had a prestigious and important location from the start. As with its larger predecessor, the Galleria Vittorio Emanuele II in Milan, the Galleria Umberto Primo exalts the taste of the postunification commercial elite in a virtuoso display of late-19th-century technology clothed in traditional style. Here are the iron-ribbed glass barrel vault and 188-feet-high dome by Paolo Boubée, which represented the latest advance in modern form yet is layered over with the reassuring architectural ornament of the 14th century (another era when the bourgeoisie triumphed in Italy). The ground floor was designed to offer weatherproof shopping for the new rich of the day; professional studios, fashion ateliers, and newspaper offices occupied the three upper stories. A small underground theater, the Salone Margherita, was constructed near the Via Toledo entrance for chamber music concerts, but within a few months of opening it evolved into a legendary nightclub and a center of Naples's turn-of-the-20th-century nightlife.

As the favored hangout for American soldiers (and their Neapolitan fans), the gallery throbbed with life during the American liberation of

Italy in 1943–44. The locals used to come here for a leisurely Campari; today they occasionally visit for a quick caffè and to check out the pricey designer outlets. Light streaming through one of the upper-level loggias into the magnificent vastness of the arcade (with its sumptuous marble inlay) makes for a great scene. At Christmastime a huge crèche is set up, and the space becomes quite festive. ⊠ *Entrances on Via San Carlo, Via Toledo, Via Santa Brigida, Via Verdi, Toledo* Ⓜ *Montesanto (in construction: Piazza Municipio).*

Fodor's Choice
★   **Palazzo Reale.** Now entered from the Trieste and Trento Square, the Palazzo Reale, or Royal Palace is one of the showplaces of Naples. It was meant to be the apotheosis of Bourbon power in the city. Renovated and redecorated by successive rulers, once lorded over by a dim-witted king who liked to shoot his hunting guns at the birds in his tapestries, and filled with salons designed in the most deliciously lavish 18th-century Neapolitan taste, it remains a palatial pile. The Spanish viceroys commissioned it in 1600, ordering Swiss architect Domenico Fontana to build a suitable new residence for Philip III, should he chance to visit Naples (which he didn't); the immense complex was not completed until 1843 (by Gaetano Genovese). The palace saw its greatest moment of splendor in the 18th century, when Charles III of Bourbon became the first permanent resident; during that century Luigi Vanvitelli filled in half the arcades in the lower register of the facade to strengthen it, and Ferdinando Fuga created the State Wing after the accession of Ferdinand IV in 1759. Today this wing comprises the Museo dell'Appartamento Storico, or **Royal Apartments,** where visitors can get a taste of Bourbon glory.

To view these 30 rooms on the second floor, enter from Piazza Trieste e Trento and head toward the *Biglietteria* (ticket booth). You'll be channeled through the bookshop and past medieval archaeological remains toward the monumental Scalone d'Onore. Montesquieu, the French 18th-century writer, considered this to be the finest staircase in Europe, and it does set a tone for the glitter and grandeur to come. The first doors on the right open into the **Court Theater,** built by Ferdinando Fuga for Charles III, who in 1763 had created an opera company for private performances of comic opera. Damaged by World War II bombing, it was restored in the 1950s; note the resplendent royal box, which abandons the lure of monumentality for intimate luxury. Following are the suite of rooms around the courtyard that constitute the royal apartments. Through a series of antechambers, you eventually reach Room VI, the **Throne Room,** with wine red striped-silk walls and gilded stuccos representing the 12 provinces of the Kingdom of the Two Sicilies; the ponderous Empire-style throne in fact dates from after 1850.

The decoration picks up in the **Room of the Ambassadors** (Room VIII), where a pair of choice 18th-century Gobelin tapestries grace the light green walls while the ceiling painting honoring Spanish military victories is by local artist Belisario Corenzio and his school (1610–20). Room IX, with pale gold walls and a simple white vault, was the bedroom of Charles's queen, Maria Amalia of Saxony, and hides a small, brilliantly gold private oratory in the corner, with beautiful paintings by Francesco Liani of Parma (1760).

The **Great Captain's Room** (Room XI), small and square, has wonderful ceiling frescoes by Battistello Caracciolo (1610–16)—all velvet, fire, and smoke, they reveal the influence of the visit by Caravaggio to Naples—a jolly series by Federico Zuccari depicting 12 proverbs on small wood panels, along with, last but not least, a Titian portrait (circa 1543) of Pier Luigi Farnese. Room XII, the **Flemish Hall,** has a rather brash 19th-century gilded ceiling with 12 paintings representing the coats-of-arms of the kingdom's provinces and a large neo-Gothic centerpiece depicting the 12th-century Tancred and Constance.

Room XIII was **Joachim Murat's writing room** when he was king of Naples; he brought with him from France some regal furniture by the great French *ébeniste* (cabinetmaker) Weisweiller, originally commissioned by Marie Antoinette and completed through commissions of his own (including the desk and two dignified clocks) in 1812. The next few rooms combine ponderous 19th-century furnishings and rather better baroque paintings: Room XVII, in particular, has a good selection of paintings by followers of Caravaggio; Room XVIII has an intensely colorful Guercino depiction of the biblical Joseph dreaming; and Room XIX is full of still lifes from the important Neapolitan school. The huge Room XXII, painted in green and gold with kitschy faux tapestries, is known as the **Hercules Hall,** for in a moment of glory it once housed the *Hercules Farnese.* The authentic tapestries are from the Royal Factory of Naples (1783–89), but the things to look at here are the porcelain creations from Sèvres, including the Atlas with his starry globe and the huge green chrome vase (1812) opposite, painted by Louis Béranger.

The **Palatine Chapel,** redone by Gaetano Genovese in the 1830s, is, as chapels go, a disappointing affair, having been gussied up with an excess of gold, but it has a stunning Technicolor intarsia altar from the previous chapel (Dionisio Lazzari, 1678). Note the false-perspective panels, which almost propel the altar into the stratosphere of bad taste. Also here on a long-term loan is the famous *Presepio* (Nativity) scene of the Banco di Napoli—it may lack the spectacular setting of the *Presepio Cuciniello* in the Museo di San Martino but has even better sculpture, with pieces by important sculptors such as Giuseppe Sammartino, Francesco and Antonio Viva, Francesco Celebrano, and others. There are some pleasant 19th-century landscapes in the next few rooms, as well as Queen Maria Carolina's Ferris wheel–like reading lectern (which enabled her to do a 19th-century reader's version of channel surfing). Speaking of reading, another wing of the complex holds the **Biblioteca Nazionale Vittorio Emanuele III,** the largest library in southern Italy and one of the most important in the country. Begun, as with so many other Bourbon collections, with Farnese bits and pieces, it was enriched with the priceless papyri from Herculaneum found in 1752 and opened to the public in 1804. You can view these and a splendid selection of manuscripts and rare editions in the elegant rooms open to visitors. To use the library for scholarly research, you need to apply for a card. The library also has a lovely garden, which looks out on the Castel Nuovo. ⊠ *Piazza del Plebiscito, Toledo* ⊕ *www.palazzorealenapoli.it* ☏ *081/400547, 848/800288 schools and guided tours* ⊠ *€4* ☉ *Thurs.– Tues. 9–7* Ⓜ *Dante (in construction: Piazza Municipio).*

Across from the Palazzo Reale is the most famous coffeehouse in town, the Caffè Gambrinus (✉ *Piazza Trieste e Trento, near Piazza del Plebiscito* ☎ *081/417582*). Founded in 1850, this 19th-century jewel once functioned as a brilliant intellectual salon. The glory days are over, but the inside rooms, with amazing mirrored walls and gilded ceilings, make this an essential stop for any visitor to the city. To its credit, the caffè doesn't inflate prices to cash in on its fame.

★ **Palazzo Zevallos.** Tucked inside this beautifully restored palazzo, which houses the Banca Intesa San Paolo (one of Italy's major banks), is a small museum that's worth seeking out. Enter the bank through Cosimo Fanzago's gargoyled doorway and take the handsome elevator to the upper floor. The first room to the left holds the star attraction, Caravaggio's last work, *The Martyrdom of Saint Ursula*. Scholarship only found out in the 1970s that this work was actually painted by the great master for Marc-Antonio Doria, son of the Genovese Doge, in honor of his daughter, who had recently taken a vow as a nun under the same name. The saint here is, for dramatic effect, deprived of her usual retinue of a thousand followers. On the left, a face of pure spite, is the king of the Huns, who has just shot Ursula with an arrow after his proposal of marriage has been rejected. Opposite a map shows the city of Caravaggio's day, then like now, a chaotic warren of streets or so-called *vicoli*, perfect for getting lost in and, as such, tailor-made for a fugitive like Caravaggio (who, on the run from Rome where he had committed a murder, would have found more protection in Naples, a city which still respected the tradition of *omertà*, or honor killing. The bedroom's soft blue walls, with stuccoed poppy flowers and swans created as symbols of gentle sleep, contrasts with the painting's violence, only increasing its impact. There is a good bookshop on-site. ✉ *Via Toledo 185, Piazza Plebiscito* ☎ *00800/16052007* ⊕ *www.palazzozevallos.com* 💶 *€3* ⊘ *Mon.–Sat. 10–6.*

Piazza Plebiscito. After spending time as a car park, this square was restored in 1994 to one of Napoli Nobilissima's most majestic spaces, with a Doric semicircle of columns resembling Saint Peter's Square in Rome. It was originally built under the Napoleonic rule. When the Napoleonic regime fell, Ferdinand, new king of the Two Sicilies, ordered the addition of the Church of San Francesco di Paola. On the left as you approach the church is a statue of Ferdinand and on the right his father, Charles III, both clad in Roman togas. Around dusk the floodlights come on, to magical effect. The square is aired by a delightful sea breeze and on Sunday one corner becomes an improvised soccer stadium where local youth emulate their heroes.

★ **San Francesco di Paola.** Modeled after Rome's Pantheon, this circular basilica is the centerpiece of the Piazza del Plebiscito and remains one of the most frigidly voluptuous examples of the *Stile Empire*, or Neoclassical style, in Italy. Commissioned by Ferdinand I in 1817 to fulfill a vow he had made in order to enlist divine aid in being reinstated to the throne of the Kingdom of the Two Sicilies, it rose at one end of the vast parade ground built several years earlier by Joachim Murat. It

Continued on page 260

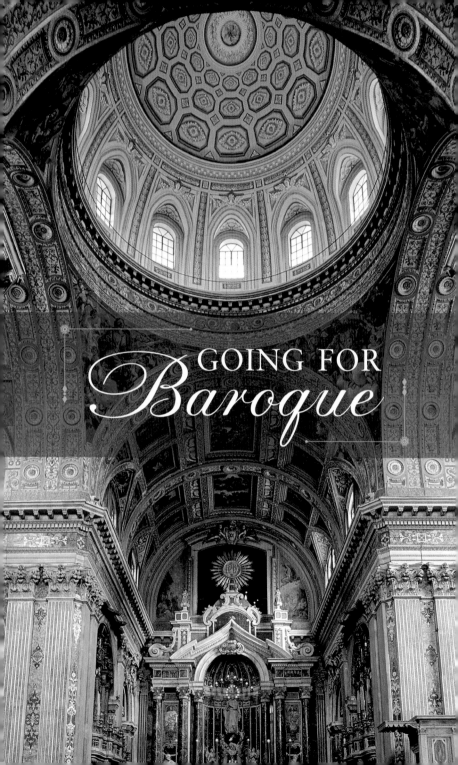

GOING FOR
Baroque

Even charitable observers would say that excess, fake opulence, and exaggeration are typical Neapolitan qualities. It's not surprising, then, that the baroque, an artistic style that revels in details added to swirls added to flourishes added to twists—a style that is playful, theatrical, dynamic, and seems permanently about to burst its bonds—should find one of its most spectacular showcases in Naples.

The very word "baroque" derives from a Portuguese word describing an impressive-looking but worthless type of pearl, and was originally used as an insult to describe the flagrantly emotional, floridly luxurious style that surfaced in Europe around 1600. Critics now use baroque to describe a style more than a period.

It's a style that found immediate favor in a city of volcanic passions. Like the city itself, the decorative scheme is diffuse and disjunc-tive, with little effort to organize everything into an easily understood scheme.

Contradictions still abound in Naples: plenty with want; grandeur with muddle; beauty with decay; the wide bay, lush countryside, and peaceful sky harboring the dense, chaotic city, sheltered by the ever-present threat of the slumbering Mount Vesuvius. In this context, the vivid, dramatic baroque style feels right at home.

NAPLES AND BAROQUE: A MATCH MADE FOR HEAVEN

At the beginning of the 17th century, thanks to the Counter-Reformation, the Catholic Church was busy making an overt appeal to its congregants, using emotion and motion to get its message across—and nowhere was this more blatant than in Naples, which, as the most populous city in Italy at the time, had more clerics (some 20,000) than even Rome. Baroque artists and architects, given an open invitation to indulge their illusionistic whims on church cupolas and the like, began arriving in Naples to strut their aesthetic stuff.

The most representative practitioner of Neapolitan baroque was **Cosimo Fanzago (1591–1678)**. A Lombard by birth, he traveled to Naples to study sculpture; even when decorating a church, he usually covered it head to toe with colored and inlaid marbles, as in his work at the Certosa di San Martino atop the Vomero hill.

Preceding Fanzago by two decades was **Caravaggio (1571–1610)**, who moved to Naples from Rome. This great painter took the city by storm, with an unflinching truthfulness and extroverted sensuality in his work. Experts will continue to argue to what degree Caravaggio was or wasn't a baroque painter, but certainly his use of chiaroscuro, a quality common in baroque art, can be seen dramatically in his Neapolitan paintings *The Flagellation of Christ* and *The Seven Acts of Mercy*.

(preceding page) The dome of Gesú Nuovo; (top) *St Bruno* by Cosimo Fanzago; (bottom) Caravaggio

BAROQUE TECHNIQUES: TRICKS OF THE TRADE

MEMENTO MORI. Lest all the sumptuous decoration should appeal too directly to the senses, the Church (as the major sponsor of the baroque) felt it was necessary to remind people of their ultimate message: *memento mori*—"remember that you will die." Don't be surprised if, in the midst of the most delicate and beautiful inlaid marble floor, you find leering skulls. In the tiny church of **Purgatorio ad Arco ❶** in Spaccanapoli, a winged skull by Fanzago awaits salvation.

DOMES: LOOK UP! If there was one thing baroque architects loved, it was a dome— Exhibit One being the **Duomo di San Gennaro ❷**. Domes offered space and height and

lots of opportunities to trompe your oeil. Even in the tightly packed old center of Naples, domes manage to make you feel as if you are in an enormous, heavenly space. This is in part due to their acoustic qualities, which reduce the city and its noisy inhabitants to swirling whispers and echoes.

MARVELOUS MARBLE. Making the most of the large quantities of marble quarries in Italy, baroque architects outdid their Renaissance predecessors. They used softer kinds of stone and developed intricate, interlaced patterns of

different colored marble, such as seen in the **Certosa di San Martino ❸**.

KEEPING IT (HYPER)REAL. Getting solid marble or stone to "move" was one of the skills of any baroque sculptor worth his chisel. Giuseppe Sammartino, who sculpted the **Veiled Christ ❹** in the Capella Sansevero, was so good at his craft that it was rumored (falsely) his boss had him blinded so he couldn't repeat his genius anywhere else. In Gesù Nuovo a dead Christ lies near the entrance in a glass case, often giving visitors cause to stop momentarily as they think they've stumbled across a real person. It is common to find saints' marble effigies still dressed in real period clothes.

OUT OF THE SHADOWS. Chiaroscuro ("light-dark") is the word most often used to describe baroque painting, with its mixture of bright shafts of light and thick shadows. Figures loom out of the dark while the main action is highlighted by dazzling beams of light—as in Rubino's *Apollo and Marsyas* ❺ at the Museo di Capodimonte.

TROMPE L'OEIL. Literally "tricking the eye," trompe l'oeil is an illusionist method of painting that consists, quite simply, of making things look like something they're not. Angels lean over balconies and

out of paintings, walls become windows, and skylights bestow views into heaven itself, as grandly displayed in Luca Giordano's *Triumph of Judith* ❻ at the Certosa di San Martino. There is something very baroque in trompe l'oeil's sense of trickery, of something being built upon nothing.

STAIRWAYS TO HEAVEN. The principles of movement and ascension naturally conveyed by a staircase made baroque architects drool with possibilities. Staircases can often be seen with winged banisters, as if those simply climbing the steps were on a journey into a higher realm. The staircase in the entrance of the Royal Palace in Naples splits and divides and splits again, its movement magnified

and reflected dizzyingly by the windows and mirrors surrounding it. At the Palazzo della Spagnola in the Sanità neighborhood, the M.C. Escher–esque staircase boasts steps wide enough to ride a horse up them—which is precisely what they were used for in the 17th century.

ON STAGE. If some of the more extravagant interiors of Neapolitan churches remind you of theater sets, you're not far off. Many designers crossed over into ecclesiastical work, usually having first been noticed in the theater. Many arches over altars are made from a reinforced form of papier-mâché, originally used in theatrical productions.

One of the most frigidly voluptuous examples of the Neoclassical style, the church of San Francesco di Paolo was designed to emulate Rome's Pantheon.

managed to transform Murat's inconveniently grandiose colonnade—whose architect was clearly inspired by the colonnades of St. Peter's in Rome—into a setting for restored Bourbon glory. The church also usefully fulfilled a prophecy by the 15th-century saint Ferrante d'Aragona, for whom it is named, that one day a large church and square would occupy the crowded site. Pietro Bianchi from Lugano in Switzerland won a competition and built a slightly smaller version of the Pantheon, with a beautiful coffered dome and a splendid set of 34 Corinthian columns in gray marble; but the overall lack of color (so different from the warm interior of the Pantheon) combined with the severe geometrical forms produces an almost defiantly cold space. To some, this only proves the ancients did sometimes know their own architecture better. Art historians find the spectacle of the church to be the ultimate in Neoclassical *grandezza*; others think this Roman temple is only fitting to honor Jupiter, not Christ. In any event, the main altar, done in gold, lapis lazuli, and other precious stones by Anselmo Caggiano (1641), was taken from the destroyed Church of the Santi Apostoli and provides some relief from the oppressive perfection of the setting. ⊠ *Piazza del Plebiscito, Toledo* ☎ *081/7645133* ⊗ *Mon.–Sat. 6:45–noon and 4:30–5:30, Sun. 8–noon* Ⓜ *Dante (in construction: Piazza Municipio).*

Sant'Anna dei Lombardi. Long favored by the Aragonese kings, this church, simple and rather anonymous from the outside, houses some of the most important ensembles of Renaissance sculpture in southern Italy. Begun with the adjacent convent of the Olivetani and its four cloisters in 1411, it was given a baroque makeover in the mid-17th century by Gennaro Sacco, although this is no longer so visible, as the bombs

CLOSE UP

Attenzione! How to Cross Naples' Streets

Long considered a threatened species, the Naples pedestrian is gradually being provided with a friendlier environment. Once Piazza Garabaldi has been negotiated, traffic in much of Naples is no more off-putting than in other Italian cities. (Accident rates involving pedestrians are higher in Rome.) In fact, large tracts of Naples are open to pedestrians only. That's the case for most of Via Toledo—called by Stendhal "the most beautiful street in the world" and by Sartre, less romantically, "a long hygienic clearing in this pox-ridden city." Leading off it is the fashionable Via Chiaia, a destination for posh shopping and the birthplace of the pizza Margherita. Piazza del Plebiscito, once reduced to a parking lot, is also now an ideal space to stroll through, touched by a pleasant sea breeze.

That being said, crossing major thoroughfares in Naples still takes some savvy. In a city where red traffic lights may be blithely ignored, especially by two-wheelers, walking across a busy avenue can be like a game of chess—if you hesitate, you capitulate. Some residents just forge out into the unceasing flow of traffic, knowing cars invariably slow down to let them cross. (A trick for the fainthearted: look for an elderly couple—when they cross, you *know* it will be safe.) Look both ways even on one-way streets, as there may be motorcyclists riding against the flow. Areas where you have to be particularly vigilant—and cross at the lights—are around the Archaeological Museum and on Via Marina outside the port, as well as the ever-challenging Piazza Garibaldi.

6

of 1943 rather radically altered the decoration and led to a modern restoration favoring the original *quattrocento* (15th-century) lines. The wonderful coffered wooden ceiling adds a bit of pomp. Inside the porch is the tomb of Domenico Fontana, one of the major architects of the late 16th century, who died in Naples after beginning the Palazzo Reale.

On either side of the original entrance door are two fine Renaissance tombs. The one on the left as you face the door belongs to the Ligorio family (whose descendant Pirro designed the Villa d'Este in Tivoli) and is a work by Giovanni da Nola (1524); the tomb on the right is a masterpiece by Giuseppe Santacroce (1532) done for the del Pozzo family. To the left of the Ligorio Altar (the corner chapel on the immediate right as you face the altar) is the Mastrogiudice Chapel, whose altar contains precious reliefs of the *Annunciation* and *Scenes from the Life of Jesus* (1489) by Benedetto da Maiano, a great name in Tuscan sculpture. On the other side of the entrance is the Piccolomini Chapel, with a *Crucifixion* by Giulio Mazzoni (circa 1550), a refined marble altar (circa 1475), a funerary monument to Maria d'Aragona by another prominent Florentine sculptor, Antonello Rossellino (circa 1475), and on the right, a rather sweet fresco of the Annunciation by an anonymous follower of Piero della Francesca.

The true surprises of the church, however, are to the right of the altar, in the presbytery and adjoining rooms. The chapel just to the right of the main altar, belonging to the Orefice family, is richly decorated in pre-baroque (1596–98) polychrome marbles and frescoes by Luis Rodriguez; from here you continue on through the Oratory of the Holy Sepulchre, with the tomb of Antonio D'Alessandro and his wife, to reach the church's showpiece: a potently realistic life-size group of eight terra-cotta figures by Guido Mazzoni (1492), which make up a Pietà; the faces are said to be modeled from people at the Aragonese court. ⊠ *Piazza Monteoliveto 15, Toledo* ☎ *081/5513333* ☉ *Tues.–Sat. 9–noon* Ⓜ *Dante (in construction: Toledo).*

Fodor'sChoice
★

Teatro San Carlo. La Scala in Milan is the famous one, but San Carlo is more beautiful, and Naples is, after all, the most operatic of cities. Built in eight months and 10 days in 1737 by Angelo Carasale for Charles III of Bourbon—and opened on the king's saint's name day—it burned down in 1816 and was rebuilt, with its facade of five rustic gray arches surmounted by an elegant loggia, in a mere nine months. This time the architect was Antonio Niccolini, working under the impetus of Domenico Barbaja, the Milanese director appointed by Joachim Murat in 1810. Barbaja, San Carlo's most legendary director, started out as a waiter in a tavern and enriched himself through a talent for gambling. Obviously wanting to remain part of the new regime, he bet the king that he could have the theater open within nine months. More important, he also managed in the same year to convince Gioacchino Rossini to come to Naples as conductor and house composer; Stendhal hailed Ferdinand's wise retaining of Barbaja and his prompt sponsorship of the theater as a "coup d'état" for the deep and immediate bond it created between the ruler and his opera-loving populace. This was further cemented by the many operas composed for the house, including Donizetti's *Lucia di Lammermoor* and Rossini's *La Donna del Lago.*

In the theater, nearly 200 boxes are arranged on six levels, and the huge stage (12,000 square feet) permits productions with horses, camels, and elephants and even boasts a removable backdrop that can lift to reveal the Palazzo Reale Gardens. Above the rich red-and-gold auditorium is a breathy ceiling fresco, by Giuseppe Cammarano, suitably representing Apollo presenting poets to Athena. At many performances, however, all eyes strayed to the sumptuous royal box, which seats 15 and is topped by a gigantic gilded crown. Check the San Carlo Web site, the local press (*Il Mattino, La Repubblica, Corriere della Sera*), or the *Qui Napoli* for information on performances, or pick up the annual program at the ticket office and get ready for a great evening of opera. Performance standards are among the highest in Europe at the San Carlo—even the great Enrico Caruso was hissed here—although some locals really come to study the fashion show in the auditorium, not the Verdi on stage. If you can't catch a performance, see if the 30-minute guided tours are back in action (they were cut in summer 2010 for lack of funding) to see the splendid theater—as Stendhal wrote: "The first impression one gets is of being suddenly transported to the palace of an oriental emperor. There is nothing in Europe to compare with it, or even give the faintest idea of what it is like." ⊠ *Via San Carlo 101–103, Toledo* ☎ *081/7972331 box office, 081/7972412* ⊕ *www. teatrosancarlo.it* Ⓜ *Piazza Municipio (in construction).*

Awash in gold and red velvet, the interior of the Teatro San Carlo, Naples's grand opera house, is almost more spectacular than its stage presentations.

WORTH NOTING

Santa Brigida. The Lucchesi fathers built this church around 1640 in honor of the Swedish queen and saint who visited her fellow queen, Naples's unsaintly Giovanna I, in 1372 and became one of the first persons to go on record as denouncing the loose morals and irrepressible sensuality of the Neapolitans. The height of the church's dome was limited to prevent its interfering with cannon fire from nearby Castel Nuovo, but Luca Giordano, the pioneer painter of the trompe l'oeil baroque dome, effectively opened it up with a spacious sky serving as the setting for an *Apotheosis of Saint Bridget* (1678), painted (and now in need of considerable restoration) in exchange for his tomb space, marked by a pavement inscription in the left transept. ⊠ *Via Santa Brigida 72, Toledo* ☎ *081/5523793* ⊙ *Daily 6:45–12:45 and 4:30–7:30* Ⓜ *Dante (in construction: Piazza Municipio).*

THE VOMERO TO THE LUNGOMARE

Neapolitans often say their town's glories are vertical—the white *guglia* (religious obelisk) of the historic quarter, the eight-story tenements of Spaccanapoli, and Vomero, the towering hill that overlooks the city center. Even longtime residents love to head up here to gaze in wonder at the entire city from the balcony belvedere of the Museo di San Martino. Before them, a rich spread of southern Italian amplitude fills the eye: hillsides dripping with luxuriant greenery interspersed with villainously ugly apartment houses, streets short and narrow—leading to an unspeakable as well as unsolvable traffic problem—countless church spires and domes, and far below, the reason it all works, the intensely blue Bay of Naples. To tie together the lower parts and upper reaches of the city, everyone uses the *funicolare*—the funicular system that runs on three separate routes up and down the Vomero.

Thanks to the funiculars, you can readily take in many of Naples's aristocratic pleasures and treasures on the same day: the chic Piazza dei Martiri sector; the gilded 19th-century Villa Pignatelli; three major landmarks that crown the Vomero hill—the Villa Floridiana, the Certosa di San Martino, and the Castel Sant'Elmo; down to the Lungomare, the grandest stretch of waterfront in Naples. In the 19th century Naples's waterfront harbored the picturesque quarter that was called Santa Lucia, a district dear to artists and musicians and known for its fishermen's cottages. The fishermen were swept away when an enormous landfill project extended the land out to what is now Via Nazario Sauro and Via Partenope, the address for some of Naples's finest hotels. Today, the waterfront promenade has lost much of its former color, but it still retains a uniquely Neapolitan charm.

TIMING

As always in Naples, it's best to start out early in the morning to fit most of your sightseeing in before the lunch break—and the midday heat. Aim to get to the San Martino complex atop the Vomero hill at opening time and allow at least three hours to take it in along with the Castel Sant'Elmo and an additional half hour for the Villa Floridiana. If you prefer a leisurely wander or wish to visit an exhibition at Castel Sant'Elmo, go straight to the Borgo from the Riviera di Chiaia following the seafront, and then swing back to Villa Pignatelli and the Aquarium.

TOP ATTRACTIONS

Aquarium. Originally named by the Greeks after the mermaid Parthenope (who slew herself after being rejected by Odysseus, at least in the poet Virgil's version), it's only fitting that Naples should have established one of Europe's first public aquariums in 1874. At the time—when, not so incidentally, the public imagination was being stirred by Jules Verne's Captain Nemo and Hans Christian Andersen's "Little Mermaid"—technological innovations came into place to funnel seawater directly from the bay into the aquarium tanks, which showcase some 300 species of fish and marine plants (undoubtedly better off here than in the somewhat polluted Bay of Naples, their natural habitat). Officially named the Stazione Zoologica, founded by the German scientist Anton Dohrn, and housed in a *Stile Liberty* (Art Nouveau) building designed by Adolf von Hildebrandt, the aquarium quickly became the wonder of Naples for children and art-exhausted adults. Today the ground floors contain the aquarium tanks—fishy "living rooms" decorated with rocks and plants of the region and illuminated by skylights. ✉ *Stazione Zoologica, Viale A. Dohrn, Chiaia* ☎ *081/5833263 for information and library visits* ⊕ *www.szn.it* 🎫 *€1.50* ⊗ *Mar.–Oct., Tues.–Sat. 9–6, Sun. 9:30–7:30; Nov.–Feb., Tues.–Sat. 9–5, Sun. 9–2* Ⓜ *Piazza Amedeo.*

Fodor's Choice
★ **Castel dell'Ovo.** The oldest castle in Naples, the Castel dell'Ovo sits on the most picturesque point of the bay, standing guard over the city it

protects. Occupying the isle of Megaris, it was originally the site of the Roman villa of Lucullus—proof, if you need it, that the ancient Romans knew a premium location when they saw one (for the same reason, some of the city's top hotels share the same site today). By the 12th century, it had become a fortress under the Normans; it was once the prison of Conradin and of Beatrice, daughter of Manfred, last of the Hohenstaufen rulers. The castle's gigantic rooms, rock tunnels, and belvederes over the bay are among Naples's most striking sights as well as a magical setting for the temporary contemporary-art exhibitions sponsored by the city council.

You enter the castle through its main entrance with its forbidding trio of cannons. On the right is a large picture of the castle in Renaissance times. Turn left and glimpse through the battlements the sleepy Borgo Marinaro below. An elevator on the left ascends to the castle top or you can also continue along the walkway overlooking the ramparts. The roof's Sala della Terrazze offers a postcard-come-true view of Ischia. Then, as the odd car honk drifts across from inland, use the tiled map to identify the sights of the city and maybe plot an itinerary for the rest of the day.

As for the egg of the castle's name, the poet Virgil, rather anachronistically, is supposed have hidden an egg in the walls. The egg, like the blood of San Gennaro, was believed to have protective powers, but only as long as it remained intact. If it broke, disaster would strike. The belief was taken so seriously that when in the 15th century there was an earthquake, followed by a Hungarian invasion, followed by a plague, Queen Giovanna I brought forth an intact egg, solemnly declaring it to be the Virgilian original, in order to quell the people's panic. ✉ *Santa Lucia waterfront, Via Partenope* ☎ *081/2400055* 🎫 *Free* ☉ *Weekdays 8–7:30; Sun. 8–2.*

Castel Sant'Elmo. Looming over all of Naples from its hilltop perch, this daunting, nearly impregnable castle has long landmarked the Vomero hill. Reachable by one of the three Funicolari lifts, the castle is entered using an elevator on the far left of the entrance yard. Replacing a smaller Angevin prototype, the building is almost as large as a small town. Under Viceroy Pedro di Toledo it was completely remodeled into the present six-pointed-star shape by Charles V's ace military architect Pier Luis Scribà. Small wonder the Castelan in charge here was given powers equal to that of a mayor. Guarding Naples's northern reaches, the castle was also regarded as impregnable, at least from the ground (but that could not stop lightning strikes from the air, one of which in 1587 ignited the gunpowder store and caused 150 deaths). It was also, once entered, a difficult place to escape from, its walls also including the scary "High Prison." Among its most famous inmates were philosopher Tommaso Campanella on a charge of heresy and the various leaders of the 1799 Naples Revolution. More happily these days the prison, or *Carcere alto di Castel Sant'Elmo,* hosts the recently opened **Museo di Novecento Napoli,** which traces Naples's artistic links to the first Futurists through to work of the 1980s. Walk the castle's six-starred parapets for the best views of Naples anywhere (the signs rightly proclaim: *Attenzione: 'E' pericoloso do sporgersi*, meaning "Do not lean over!"): the whole bay

The Vomero to the Lungomare

Aquarium **6**

Castel dell'Ovo **7**

Castel Sant'Elmo **2**

Certosa di San Martino **1**

Museo Diego Aragona
Pignatelli Cortes **5**

Palazzo delle Arti Napoli ... **4**

Palazzo Serra di Cassano ... **9**

Parco dei Poeti **11**

Pizzofalcone **8**

Santa Maria degli Angeli
a Pizzofalcone **10**

Villa Floridiana **3**

KEY

M Line 1 Metropolitana Collinare

M Line 2 Metropolitana FS

A GOOD WALK: VOMERO/LUNGOMARE

Begin at the main station of the Funicolare Centrale, on the tiny Piazza Duca d'Aosta, opposite the Via Toledo entrance to the Galleria Umberto I. After two hillside stops, get off at the end of the line, Stazione Fuga, near the top of the Vomero Hill. To get to the Castel Sant'Elmo/Certosa di San Martino complex, head out from the station, turning right across the pedestrianized Piazza Fuga toward the escalator, then left on Via Morghen. At the next junction, Via Scarlatti—the main thoroughfare of the neighborhood—turn right uphill and take the escalator (or steps), cutting twice across the snakelike Via Morghen, then follow the path around the left side of the Montesanto funicular until you run into the Via Tito Angelini. This street, lined with some of Naples's best Belle Epoque mansions, leads to the **Certosa di San Martino** past the adjoining **Castel Sant'Elmo**, which commands magnificent 360-degree vistas over city and sea to Vesuvius.

After viewing this enormous complex, backtrack to Via Scarlatti until you make a left on Via Bernini at Piazza Vanvitelli. This piazza, with no shortage of smart bars and trattorias, remains the center for the Vomero district, and is a gathering point for talented street performers.

Walk right onto Via Cimarosa for two blocks until you reach the entrance to the **Villa Floridiana**, today a museum filled with aristocratic knickknacks and surrounded by a once-regal park. After viewing the villa, make a right from the park entrance on Via Cimarosa for two blocks until you reach the Stazione Cimarosa of the Chiaia funicular, which will take you back down to the Lungomare area.

From the Amedeo funicular station walk down Via del Parco Margherita, past Piazza Amedeo, making a left onto Via Colonna. Stop at the rambling **Palazzo delle Arti Napoli** if there's an exhibit that catches your eye; otherwise take the first right turn down off Via Colonna onto the steps at the top of Via Bausan. The steps will take you down toward the Riviera di Chiaia (*chiaia* means "beach" in the Neapolitan dialect), where a final right turn brings you to the **Museo Diego Aragona Pignatelli Cortes**. From here cross the Riviera to the waterfront park of the Villa Comunale and its world-famous **Aquarium**.

Follow the Riviera past the Piazza della Vittoria onto Via Partenope to reach the spectacular **Castel dell'Ovo**. From here, a walk north on Via Chiatamone takes you to the Piazza dei Martiri, where you can join chic Neapolitans shopping the boutiques, bookstores, and antiques shops lining the streets that radiate off the piazza (particularly the designer-dense stretch between Via Carlo Poerio and Via dei Mille).

The area around Piazza dei Martiri is excellent for both snacking and more substantial meals. From here it's a relatively short walk back to one of the funiculars (the Centrale and Chiaia are roughly equidistant from the piazza), or you can catch any number of buses westward along the area's main artery, the Riviera di Chiaia.

6

there in a circuit of the eye on one side, the city spread out like a map, its every dome and turret clearly visible while to the east slumbers Vesuvius and its smaller parent, Mount Somma. Again, as at Castel dell'Ovo, there is an on-site map to direct your gaze. ⌂ *Largo San Martino, Vomero* ☎ *081/2294401*

⊕ *www.polomusealenapli.beniculturali.it* ⌂ *€3; Museo del Novecento Napoli, €5* ⊙ *Wed.–Mon. 8:30–7:30; Museo del Novecento Napoli, Wed.–Mon. 9–7* Ⓜ *Vanvitelli.*

Fodor's Choice   **Certosa di San Martino.** Atop a rocky promontory with a fabulous view of
★   the entire city, and with majestic salons that would please any monarch, the Certosa di San Martino is a monastery that seems more like a palace. In fact, by the 18th century Ferdinand IV was threatening to halt the order's government subsidy, so sumptuous was this *certosa,* or charter house, which had been started in 1325 under the royal patronage of Charles of Anjou. With the Carthusians' vast wealth and love of art, it was only a matter of time before dour Angevin Gothic was traded in for varicolored Neapolitan Baroque, thanks to the contributions of many 17th- and 18th-century sculptors and painters. Although the Angevin heritage can be seen in the pointed arches and cross-vaulted ceiling of the Certosa Church across the courtyard just opposite the ticket barrier, the church was overhauled from 1631 onward, partly as a response to Naples's deliverance from Vesuvius the same year.

The sacristy leads into the later Cappella del Tesoro, with Luca Giordano's ceiling fresco of Judith holding aloft Holofernes's head and the painting by Il Ribera (the *Pietà* over the altar is one of his masterpieces). The main baroque style note was set by Cosimo Fanzago (1591–1678), an architect, sculptor, and decorator who was as devout as he was mad. His polychrome marble work is at its finest here in the church, while he displays a gamut of sculptural skills in the **Chiostro Grande** (Great Cloister), also adding the curious small monks' graveyard, bounded by a marble balustrade topped with marble skulls. Fanzago's ceremonial portals at each corner of the cloister are among the most spectacular of all baroque creations—aswirl with Mannerist volutes and Michelangelo-esque ornament, they serve as mere frames for six life-size statues of Carthusian saints, who sit atop the doorways, judging all with deathless composure.

Not always open, the Museo dell'Opera, set in rooms around the Great Cloister, contains rooms with sociological-themed rooms. With the umbrella-type title "Images and Memories," they make up a chronological tour of the city, including one room featuring 13 gouaches of Vesuvius and another containing paintings of that frequent visitor to Naples, the Plague.

Just by the entrance to the monastery's terraced gardens is the **Quarto del Priore,** which was the residence of the only monk who had any contact with the outside world. It's an extravaganza, with a series of

Castel dell'Ovo provides impressive views of the bay, the city, and looming Vesuvius.

salons filled with frescoes, 18th-century majolica-tile floors, and paintings, plus extensive gardens where scenic *pergolati* (roofed balconies) overlook the bay—all in all, a domicile that might be called the very vestibule of heaven.

Entering from the Quarto del Priore side, you come upon two splendid gilded coaches, as if parked there after a not-so-recent performance of Cinderella. Then comes the **"Vessels of the King" museum**, beyond which lies three new rooms. The first two house Early Renaissance masterpieces. In one, Charles and Robert of Anjou feature as two of the wise men, while another painting by an unknown Catalan master depicts an adoration of the shepherds with angels perched in the rafters. Room 8 contains a wonderful statue by Pietro Bernini, Gian-Lorenzo's less famous father. The following rooms, in a further feast of Neapolitan baroque, contain works by Caracciolo, Vaccaro, Solimena, the tireless Luca Giordano, Lanfranco, and a bronze San Bruno from the aforementioned Fanzago. As diversion from painting, turn left from Room 16 to admire the library's majolica floor, the heavens tiled colorfully before your feet. Then comes the famed **Sezione Presepiale,** the world's greatest collection of Christmas cribs and a must for children of all ages. With its cohorts of angels pirouetting through an almost real-size sky plus a cast of hundreds of exquisitely costumed figures on the ground, pride of place must go to the *Presepe* (Nativity scene) of Michele Cucineniello. Equally amazing, in its way, though, is another crib that fits literally into an eggshell, while in another room stand 14 almost life-size figures that were originally on show in Naples's church of San Giovanni a Carbonara. ⊠ *Piazzale San Martino 5, Vomero*

📠 *081/2294589* ⊕ *museosanmartino.campaniabeniculturali.it* 📇 *€6 includes admission to Castel Sant'Elmo* ☾ *Thurs.–Tues. (Sezione Presepiale, Thurs.–Mon.) 8:30–7:30. Some rooms are often closed (Quarto del Priore) depending on staffing* Ⓜ *Vanvitelli.*

★ **Palazzo Serra di Cassano.** By the late 18th century, Via Monte di Dio had become one of Naples's poshest addresses. Lined with palazzi and villas, it was chosen by Prince Aloisio Serra di Cassano for his family palace, designed by Ferdinando Sanfelice, the most important architect of domestic architecture in Naples. In this city where spectacle and love of show have always been important, the appropriately gigantic double-flight staircase that Sanfelice built in the palace courtyard wouldn't have been out of place in a lavish 1950s MGM musical. When his son Gennaro was executed as one of the participants in the 1799 revolution, the prince closed the building down in protest, and it remained closed for 200 years. Today the Istituto Italiano per gli Studi Filosofici, an institute devoted to philosophy studies, occupies much of the palazzo; it offers a full calendar of courses and lectures throughout the year. ■ TIP➜ To view the staircase, ask the portiere (concierge) for permission ("Posso vedere lo Scalone?" should do the trick). ✉ *Via Monte di Dio 14, Pizzofalcone* 📠 *081/7642652* ⊕ *www.iisf.it* ☾ *Weekdays 8–1 and 3–7, Sat. 8–noon.*

WORTH NOTING

Museo Diego Aragona Pignatelli Cortes. Set behind what, except for the palm trees, would be a very English expanse of lawn, this salmon-pink building with its Athenian-style porch was built in 1826 for Ferdinand Acton, the son of English aristocrat Sir John Acton. In 1841 it was bought by the Rothschild family, who brought in Gaetano Genovese—he of the Palazzo Reale's sumptuous staircase—to design a "Style Rothschild" Salotto Rosso (a splendid red-velvet-and-gold salon), smoking room, and ballroom. The villa then passed to a distant ancestor of Spanish conquistador Hernando Cortes, and eventually to the Italian State in 1955. Using its old official name, the Villa Pignatelli, this museum also contains a sumptuous collection of porcelain and a *biblioteca-discoteca*—a collection of classical and operatic records. It also hosts part of Banco di Napoli's collection of paintings, including works by masters of Neapolitan baroque; another room containing 18th- and 19th-century landscapes. ✉ *Riviera di Chiaia 200* 📠 *081/76112356* 📇 *€2* ☾ *Wed.–Mon. 8:30–2* Ⓜ *Piazza Amedeo.*

Palazzo delle Arti Napoli. Occupying the enormous Palazzo Roccella, the Palazzo delle Arti di Napoli—or PAN, as it's conveniently called—acts as a temporary exhibition center for contemporary arts and as a permanent center for art research and documentation. Given the size of the building (6,000 square meters—roughly 60,000 square feet—on three floors), expect several exhibitions at any one time, featuring artists of international stature. There is also a fine Electa bookshop with works on contemporary artists, both international or Italian, as well as other books on Naples. ✉ *Via dei Mille 60, Chiaia* 📠 *081/7958605* ⊕ *www. palazzoartinapoli.net* 📇 *Free (except for certain exhibitions)* ☾ *Mon., Wed.–Sat. 9:30–7:30, Sun.10–2* Ⓜ *Piazza Amedeo.*

Parco dei Poeti. Behind the S. Maria di Piedigrotta church this little-visited park (part of what is officially called the Parco Vergiliano) can claim to be Naples's most bucolic spot. Opened in 1930 to celebrate the 2,000th anniversary of the death of Virgil—the greatest poet of the ancient Romans—this garden-hill contains not just the famed poet's supposed burial place but all the plants mentioned in his works, from the humble strawberry to the timber used in Troy's wooden horse. For a poetical botany lesson, as each specimen is accompanied by a Virgilian quote, it is best to bring an Italian-English dictionary. On the path up is also the tomb of the noted poet Leopardi, who died in the Naples cholera epidemic of 1837. The path ascends to the "Grotta grande," a mausoleum from the age of Augustus. For centuries this was regarded as the "Tomb of Virgil," and a must-see on the Grand Tour itinerary, but modern scholars have now come down on the side of such doubters as Plutarch and Boccaccio. ⊠ *Parco Vergiliano a Piedigrotta, Salita della Grotta 20, Mergellina* ☎ *081/669390* ◨ *Free* ☉ *9–5:30.*

Pizzofalcone *(Falcon's Beak).* In the 7th century BC, Pizzofalcone *was* Naples. The ancient Greeks had settled here because, legend says, the body of the siren Parthenope had been found washed ashore on the beach at the foot of the Pizzofalcone Hill, then known as Monte Echia. More than two millennia later, in the 18th century, the hill, mere feet from the bay and the Castel dell'Ovo, became a fashionable address as Naples's rich and titled sought to escape the congestion and heat of the city center. The rocky promontory soon became studded with baroque palaces and Rococo churches.

You can walk up to Pizzofalcone by taking Via G. Serra just to the right-hand colonnade of the Church of San Francesco di Paola, on Piazza del Plebiscito, to Pizzofalcone's main piazza, Santa Maria degli Angeli; or take the elevator during daylight hours (*never* the dark staircase) by the bridge on Via Chiaia. The leading sights are the palazzi along Via Monte di Dio—including Palazzo Serra di Cassano—and the churches of La Nunziatella and Santa Maria degli Angeli. Like other parts of Naples, Pizzofalcone harbors both palaces and slums; unlike other parts, it's off the beaten path, so don't stop to answer questions from seemingly innocuous strollers. ⊠ *Piazza Santa Maria degli Angeli, accessed via elevator at Ponte di Chiaia on Via Chiaia, Pizzofalcone.*

Santa Maria degli Angeli a Pizzofalcone. In 1590, the princess of Sulmona, Costanza Doria del Carretto, commissioned this church, not far from her palace on Pizzofalcone, for the Teatini, one of the orders founded during the Counter-Reformation. Below a dome painted by Giovani Beinaschi, the walls are embellished with paintings by Luca Giordano and Massimo Sanzione. Even more impressive, perhaps, are Caselli's wall-size canvases in the chapels left and right of the altar: a Nativity scene and the Adoration of the Magi. Behind the altar are the equally large scenes of Judith with the head of Holophernes and, opposite, the Judgment of Solomon. ⊠ *Piazza Santa Maria degli Angeli, Pizzofalcone* ☎ *081/7644974* ☉ *Daily 7:30–11:30 and 5:30–7.*

Villa Floridiana. Now a chiefly residential neighborhood, the Vomero Hill was once the patrician address of many of Naples's most extravagant estates. La Floridiana is the sole surviving 19th-century example, built in 1817 on order of Ferdinand I for Lucia Migliaccio, duchess of Floridia—their portraits are by the main entrance. Only nine shocking months after his first wife, the Habsburg Maria Carolina, died, when the court was still in mourning, Ferdinand secretly married Lucia, his longtime mistress. Scandal ensued, but the king and his new wife were too happy to worry, escaping high above the city and court gossip to this elegant little estate. Designed by architect Antonio Niccolini in Neoclassical style, the house is now occupied by the **Museo Nazionale della Ceramica Duca di Martina,** a museum devoted to the decorative arts of the 18th and 19th centuries. Countless display cases on the upper floor are filled with what Edith Wharton described as "all those fragile and elaborate trifles the irony of fate preserves when brick and marble crumble": Sèvres, Limoges, and Meissen porcelains, gold watches, ivory fans, glassware, enamels, majolica vases. Sadly, there are no period rooms left to see. Outside is a park designed in the English style by Degenhardt, who also laid out the park at Capodimonte. Too bad—graffiti defaces the Grecian Tempietto and the lawns are worn bare by aspiring soccer players. ⊠ *Via Cimarosa 77, Vomero* ☎ *081/5788418* 🖪 *€2.50* 🕙 *Museum Wed.–Mon. 8:30–2; park daily 8:30–1 hr before sunset* Ⓜ *Vanvitelli.*

NEED A BREAK?

Walking down the fashionable Via Scarlatti in the Vomero, a bustling pedestrian precinct, you'll come upon **Caffè Scarlatti** (⊠ *Via Scarlatti 106/108, Vomero* ☎ *081/3723027*), which produces a wide range of cakes and waist-threatening delicacies. If you need something more substantial, look at the *rosticceria* selection on the left.

SPACCANAPOLI: THE SOUL OF NAPLES

If your plan for Naples is just to do the sights, you'll see the city, but you'll miss its essence. To get that, you need to discover Spaccanapoli, the unforgettable neighborhood that is the heart of old Naples. A buzzing hive of daily chaos in a constantly re-created grid of ancient patterns, this densely populated neighborhood presents the city's most familiar face. This is the Naples of peeling facades and enough waving laundry to suggest a parade; of arguments in the streets (or are they gossiping? It's sometimes hard to tell) swelling to operatic proportions, often with onlookers adding their comments to supplement the lyrical principals; of small alleyways fragrant with freshly laid flowers at the many shrines to the Blessed Virgin. Here, where the cheapest pizzerias in town feed the locals like kings, the full raucous street carnival of Neapolitan popular culture is punctuated with improbable oases of spiritual calm. All the contradictions of Naples—splendor and squalor, palace and slum, triumph and tragedy—meet here and sing a full-throated chorale. The amazing thing is that it seems, somehow, more real in its conscious theatricality. And, paradoxically, it also seems impossible to remain stressed out in the midst of all this ricocheting vitality.

Spaccanapoli

KEY

 Line 1 Metropolitana Collinare

 Line 2 Metropolitana FS

Cappella Sansevero **4**

Chiesa dei Girolamini/Quadreria dei Girolamini **11**

Duomo di San Gennaro **13**

Gesù Nuovo **1**

Monte di Pietà **7**

Museo Diocesano **15**

Napoli Sotterranea **9**

Pio Monte della Misericordia **12**

San Domenico Maggiore ... **3**

San Giuseppe dei Ruffi **14**

San Gregorio Armeno **5**

San Lorenzo Maggiore **8**

San Paolo Maggiore **10**

Sant'Angelo a Nilo **6**

Santa Chiara **2**

Santi Apostoli **16**

But the Spacca is not simply picturesque. It also contains some of Naples's most important sights, including a striking conglomeration of churches—Lombard, Gothic, Renaissance, baroque, Rococo, and Neoclassical. Here are the majolica-adorned cloister of Santa Chiara; the sumptuous Church of the Gesù Nuovo; two opera-set piazzas; the city duomo (where the Festa di San Gennaro is celebrated every September); the Cappella Sansevero; the greatest painting in Naples—Caravaggio's *Seven Acts of Mercy* altarpiece—on view at the Church of Pio Monte; and Via Gregorio Armeno, where shops devoted to *Presepe* Nativity scene (crèche) wares make every day a rehearsal for Christmas. And even though this was the medieval center of the city, night owls will find that many of Naples's most cutting-edge clubs and bars are hidden among its nooks and alleys.

> **WORD OF MOUTH**
>
> "Cappella Sansevero will be a quick stop, as it's a small museum, but the Shrouded Christ is truly beautiful. If I ever get back to Naples, it would be the first thing I would go back to—I was awed."
> —cynstalker

This area is best explored by starting out at its heart, the Piazza Gesù Nuovo (approachable from all directions but easily reachable from Via Toledo by heading eastward from Piazza Carità through the pedestrianized Piazza Monteoliveto and then up Calata Trinità Maggiore), then heading east along the Spacca street to the Duomo, then back along Via dei Tribunali. The Via dei Tribunali is often referred to as part of the city's Decumano Maggiore, but as it's only one block over from the Spacca, the entire region is also commonly grouped under the name Spaccanapoli. Wherever you head, you'll find half of Naples's populace crowded at your elbow, all pursuing life *con gusto*.

TIMING

Because many churches open at 7:30 and close for the afternoon around 1, it's imperative to get an early start to fit in as many sights as possible before the midday break. Scaturchio in Piazza San Domenico is the perfect place for a postlunch espresso. Then fit in a bit of shopping by browsing around Piazza Dante, Port'Alba, and the Via Santa Maria di Costantinopoli for used books and antiques, or head over to the Via San Gregorio Armeno to pick out a manger figure to take back home—but remember that many shops close for three hours, from 1:30 to 4:30. By 4 many of the churches reopen. Plan on a good two hours to walk this route, plus a quarter to a half hour for each of the principal churches you decide to visit. However, Spaccanapoli is the most memorable part of Naples so take a full day, if you can, to explore its varied pleasures.

TOP ATTRACTIONS

Fodor's Choice **Cappella Sansevero.** Rightly one of the emblematic monuments of Naples
★ in the popular imagination, this dazzling masterpiece, the funerary chapel of the Sangro di Sansevero princes, combines noble swagger, overwhelming color, and a touch of the macabre—which is to say, it expresses Naples perfectly. The di Sangros were renowned military leaders as far back as the Dark Ages, and they boast no fewer than six saints in their family (who are portrayed in the chapel's painted

Continued on page 278

WALKING SPACCANAPOLI

Spaccanapoli is the informal designation given to the long, straight street running down the middle of Naples's *centro storico* (historic center). The name has also come to stand for the neighborhood surrounding the street, an area that's chaotic, vibrant, edgy, colorful, noisy, mysterious, and very beautiful. In other words, it's the essence of Naples. A walk along Spaccanapoli takes you past peeling palaces, artisans' workshops, many churches and street shrines, stores of all sorts, bars, and people young and old.

left, Via San Gregorio Armeno; top right, church of Gesú Nuovo; bottom right, a *presepe* shop window

A STROLL THROUGH THE HEART OF NAPLES

Santa Chiara

Frescoes, Santa Chiara

Morning is the best time to make this walk—many of the churches are closed in the afternoon. The route is a mile and a half long; done at a leisurely pace, with numerous stops along the way, it will take a full morning.

❶ **Start at Piazza Gesù Nuovo.** At this point Spaccanapoli goes by the name Via Benedetto Croce. The Guglia dell'Immacolata, an extravagant carved-stone spire honoring the Virgin Mary, stands in the middle of the district's largest square. The forbidding 15th-century facade of the church of **Gesù Nuovo** suits the building's original function as a fort; it was converted into the city's most extravagant baroque church by the Jesuits in the 18th century.

❷ **Cross the road and enter the church of Santa Chiara.** Originally built by Robert of Anjou in the early 1300s and reconstructed after a direct hit from a bomb in 1943, the church is light, airy, and spacious. Look for the traces of the Giotto frescoes behind the altar. A side

entrance leads to a delightful vine-laden cloister decorated with hundreds of majolica tiles, an unexpected outbreak of peace in noisy Naples.

❸ **Head east on Spaccanapoli.** You'll cross Via San Sebastiano, a street filled with music shops frequented by students from the nearby

Piazza Gesú Nuovo

conservatory; it can be a veritable symphony in the morning. **Palazzo Filomarino**, former home of philosopher Benedetto Croce and now the site of his library, is on the left as you continue. Next on your right is architect Cosimo Fanzago's **Palazzo Carafa della Spina**; coachmen once used the mouths of the gargoyles at the entrance to tamp out their torches.

❹ **Continue east to Piazza San Domenico Maggiore.** The rear of the church of San Domenico Maggiore, the Palazzo Corigliano (today part of the university), and another spire

Piazza San Domenico Maggiore

Chapel of San Gennaro

Capella Sansevero

Marionettes in a shop window.

contribute to one of Naples's most charming squares. Outdoor cafés (including Scaturchio, one of Naples's most celebrated pastry shops) give the piazza the feel of an open-air living room. Heading up the right-hand side of the piazza, swing right onto Via Francesco de Sanctis, where you find the fascinating **Cappella Sansevero**, the tomb-chapel of the Sangro di San Severo family.

5 Return to Spaccanapoli on Via Nilo. Where the two streets intersect you pass a statue of the Egyptian river god Nile reclining on a pedestal. (A few steps beyond, Spaccanapoli's street name changes to Via San Biagio dei Librai.) Several blocks down on the right is the ornate palazzo **Monte di Pietà**, and beyond it the storefront Ospedale delle Bambole (Doll Hospital).

6 Turn left (north) when you reach Via Duomo. The next main intersection is Via Tribunali, the other great thoroughfare of the district. Take a right to reach the **Pio Monte della Misericordia**, which contains one of the greatest 17th-century altarpieces in Europe, Caravaggio's *Seven Acts of Mercy*. Return to the Via Duomo to visit the **Duomo di San Gennaro** and its spectacular chapel.

7 Head west on Via dei Tribunali. After a short block you'll reach one of the street's many imposing churches, the gigantic **San Lorenzo Maggiore**. Its 18th-century facade hides a Gothic-era nave and—surprise—one of the most interesting archaeological sites in the city.

8 Turn left onto Via San Gregorio Armeno. This may be the most charming street in Naples. The towering campanile of the Rococo church of **San Gregorio Armeno** arches over the street, which is lined with *presepe* (crèche) stores.

9 Continue west along Via Tribunali. Stop to note the curious brass skulls outside the church of **Purgatorio ad Arco** on your right—touch them to bring good luck. At the end of Via Tribunali, turn right into Piazza Bellini and stop for a drink at one of the leafy square's many cafés.

roundels between the windows). The chapel was begun in 1590 by Giovan Francesco di Sangro, the result of a vow to be fulfilled if he were cured of a dire illness. He lived for another 14 years, which was good for the building campaign, but the present aspect of the chapel is due to his descendant Raimondo di Sangro, prince of Sansevero, who had it completely redone between 1749 and 1770. (His tomb and portrait are halfway down on the right.)

Soldier, necromancer, and anatomist, Prince Sansevero was, according to scholar Benedetto Croce, a sort of latter-day Doctor Faustus, popularly suspected of signing a pact with the devil so as to better plumb nature's secrets. Youthful portraits show this fascinating character with a pronounced pointy chin. Confident and sophisticated in his tastes, legendarily brilliant and an important mover in Naples's Enlightenment, this princely intellectual, mad scientist, and inventor was accused of just about everything then considered base: atheism, alchemy, and Freemasonry. The last two are likely: He seems to have been a Grand Master of the Freemasons, and his claim to be able to reproduce the miracle of San Gennaro's blood got him kicked out of the Fraternity of the Treasure of San Gennaro. He left a personal touch in the basement, where two glass cases house a pair of "anatomical machines," a small male and a dauntingly tall, seemingly pregnant, and glass-eyed female. Although fake, they look so real they gave rise to the rumor they were the prince's servants/human guinea-pigs who fell victim to his curiosity when he injected them while still alive with what is conjectured to be a mercury solution that hardened their arteries.

Prince Raimondo is generally credited with the design of the splendid marble-inlay floor; he hired Francesco Maria Russo to paint the ceiling with a *Glory of Paradise* (1749) and also hired a team of up-and-coming sculptors, whose contributions remain the focal point for most visits here: the showpiece is smack in the middle of the chapel, Giuseppe Sammartino's *Veiled Christ* (1753). The artist was only 33 years old when he sculpted this famous work, which was originally meant to be placed in the crypt. It was too good to leave down below; the audacious virtuosity of the clinging drapery showing the wounds underneath is one of the marvels of Neapolitan sculpture (the seemingly transparent marble veil had once been attributed to a chemical formula provided by the prince himself). A taste for the outré and extravagant had already been demonstrated by other statues in the chapel, especially Francesco Quierolo's *Disillusion,* to the right of the altar, with its chisel-defying net making a spectacular transition to empty space. This Genovese sculptor also did the female statue representing *Sincerity* on the right and the commemorative *Altar to St. Odorisio* between the two *Allegories.* Antonio Corradini, who came to Naples from the Veneto region via Rome, is responsible for the allegorical statue to the left of the altar, *Veiled Modesty* (1751), widely considered his masterpiece; he also sculpted the funerary monument and allegorical figure of *Decorum,* on the inside of the front wall to the right of the exit. Francesco Celebrano contributed the stunning funerary monument above the front door: the figure clambering out of a coffin while wielding a sword is not from a nightmare, but commemorates a real event. The family's Cecco di

Murder in the Cathedral?

Most of the frescoes of the San Gennaro chapel are by the Bolognese artist Domenichino, but his compatriot Guido Reni was originally engaged to paint the cycle, and thereby hangs a tale.

When he arrived in Naples, Reni found himself so harassed and threatened by jealous local artists, who were indignant that the commission had been given to an outsider, that he gave up the job and fled town. Ultimately he was replaced by the great Domenichino, who came to

Naples only after the viceroy himself guaranteed his protection.

Domenichino started painting under armed guard beginning in 1630 and had almost completed the work in 1641 when he died suddenly; poisoning was suspected. The committee charged with finding his replacement pointedly refused to consider a Neapolitan painter, instead selecting the Roman Giovanni Lanfranco, who bravely (and quickly) finished the dome. It was Lanfranco who painted the dome's frescoed vision of Paradise.

6

Sangro, believed dead in battle, had been set in a coffin, only to climb out again, much to the consternation of his enemies. ⊠ *Via Francesco de Sanctis 19, Spaccanapoli* ☎ *081/5518470* ⊕ *www.museosansevero. it* ☑€6 ☾ *Mon. and Wed.–Fri. 10–5:10, weekends 10–1:10.*

★ **Duomo di San Gennaro.** The shrine to the paterfamilias of Naples, San Gennaro, the city's cathedral is home to the saint's devotional chapel, among the most spectacular—in the show-biz sense of the word—in the city. With a colonnade leading to an apse bursting with light and baroque splendor, the Duomo's nave makes a fitting setting for the famous **Miracle of the Blood,** when the blood of the martyred San Gennaro liquefies (hopefully) in its silver ampule every September 19 before an audience of thousands massed in front of the Duomo's altar. *"San Genna, fa'o miracolo! Fa ampresso! Nun ce fa suffrì!"* yell the congregants during the ritual—"Saint Genna, do the miracle! Hurry up! You'll pay for it if you don't do it!" If St. Januarius (to use his ancient Latin name) doesn't cooperate, however, it's usually the city that winds up paying, or so the locals believe: eruptions of Vesuvius, cholera outbreaks, and defeats of the Naples soccer team have all been blamed on the saint when the *miracolo* has failed to occur.

The Duomo was first established by Charles II of Anjou, using imported French architects, on the site of a previous structure, the Cattedrale Stefania (AD 570), and next to an even earlier structure, the still-extant Basilica di Santa Restituta (4th century AD). Already restored in 1456 and 1484, it was largely redesigned in 1787 and 1837. The original facade collapsed in the earthquake of 1349, and the present pseudo-Gothic concoction is a modern (1877–1905) fake by Enrico Alvino and Giuseppe Pisanti, which, however, reemploys the doors—still majestic in spite of extensive damage—from the 1407 facade. The central door, by Antonio Baboccio, features a *Madonna and Child* by Tino da Camaino under its arch. Inside, the splendid nave welcomes all, with a gilt wooden ceiling (1621) and golden roundels painted above the pillars by Luca Giordano and his school depicting various saints. From the nave head to the right side of the church to see the chapel devoted to the city's patron saint.

The **Cappella del Tesoro di San Gennaro,** or Chapel of the Treasure of Saint Januarius, was built in 1608–37 by the Theatin architect Francesco Grimaldi to fulfill a desperate vow pronounced by city fathers during an outbreak of the plague (January 13, 1527), some 80 years earlier. The chapel honors San Gennaro (250–305), one of the earliest Christian martyrs; as bishop of Benevento, he was executed at Pozzuoli during the rule of Emperor Diocletian. The entrance to the chapel is marked by a heavy gilt-bronze baldachin gate (1668–86) by noted architect Cosimo Fanzago, who also designed the chapel's superb floor, and is flanked by statues of Sts. Peter and Paul by Giuliano Finelli. Inside, the elegant Greek-cross plan is decorated everywhere possible with gold, colored marble, bronze, and paint, but nothing could be too overdone for the home of San Gennaro's most famous DNA sample and the fabulous treasure of jeweled offerings bestowed by numerous sovereigns. The 40-odd *brocatello* columns, with their musty tones of dried roses, were sent from the quarries of Tortosa in Valencia, Spain. The high altar on the back wall (1689–90), designed by the painter Francesco Solimena, seems to swell as it tries to contain the opulence of the central relief, created in silver (circa 1692) by Giovan Domenico Vinaccia (who inserted into it a portrait of himself holding eyeglasses). Above the altar, against the wall, is a large bronze of St. Gennaro on his bishop's throne by one-time Bernini assistant Giuliano Finelli. Also behind the altar are two silvered niches donated by Charles II of Spain to house the reliquaries containing the blood of the saint (the right-hand one) and his skull. This latter reliquary consists of the famous gilded medieval bust done by three French artists (1305) set on a silver base from 1609, the actual repository of the precious vials of the saint's blood.

Note Il Ribera's *San Gennaro in the Furnace* (1647), on the right-hand wall—perhaps the most beautiful church painting in Naples. Dating from his early Neapolitan period, it clearly shows the influence of Velasquez in the figures on the left, and it's imbued with a Mediterranean luminosity that is rare in his work. The chapel, a veritable church-within-a-church, also has its own sacristy (sometimes closed), which contains a luxurious washbasin by Cosimo Fanzago. This room leads into a suite of rooms with frescoes by Giacomo Farelli and a splendid altarpiece by Massimo Stanzione; at the back are kept the 51 statues of the "co-patron" saints, displayed in the chapel proper in May and September and which accompany the reliquary of the blood on its annual procession to Santa Chiara.

The main altar sits in the resplendent apse redesigned in 1744 by Paolo Tosi and framed by two magnificent jasper columns found in a dig in 1705. A staircase on either side of the entrance to the presbytery (high altar area) descends to the Caraffa Chapel, better known as the **Succorpo di San Gennaro,** or, more simply, the crypt (1497–1506), a Renaissance masterpiece by Tommaso Malvito in the form of a rectangular room divided into three naves by rows of columns. Malvito also carved the imposing statue of Cardinal Oliviero Caraffa, who commissioned the chapel.

Coming back up into the nave and continuing in a counterclockwise direction, you find the Chapel of San Lorenzo, with highly restored frescoes by Lello da Orvieto (circa 1314–20). This chapel hides an elevator that ascends through one of the corner towers to the roof, which offers an intimate yet panoramic view of the historic quarter. Nearby is the tomb of Pope Innocent, sculpted in 1315 and redone in the 16th century by Tommaso Malvito. The sarcophagus to the left belongs to Andrea of Hungary, the unfortunate consort of Queen Joan I, who allegedly had him strangled in Aversa (at least the dogs at the foot of the deceased show a little sadness). Beyond the tombs of Pope Innocent XII and the late-Renaissance chapel of the Brancaccio family, a door leads to the Chapel of Santa Restituta. The **Cappella di Santa Restituta** is in fact the oldest church in Naples, dating from the 4th century AD and, according to tradition, built by order of the first Christian emperor, Constantine, on the site of a temple to Apollo. It was dedicated to Santa Restituta in the 8th century when the martyr's relics were transferred to the church. Newly opened after a long restoration, the Baptistery of S. Giovanni in Fonte is Europe's oldest (3rd century), its mosaics comparable to Ravenna's in quality. Kneeling in the dug-out pool, the newly baptized or "Catechumen" could look up and admire the same monogrammed cross and four winged corner figures, although the gospel scenes have suffered the ravages of time. Beside the church is the flashy but somewhat dry **Museo del Tesoro di San Gennaro** housing religious works by silversmiths over the centuries. ⊠ *Via Duomo 147, Spaccanapoli* ☎ *081/449097 Duomo, 081/294764 museum* ⊕ *www. museosangennaro.com* 🎫 *€6 (extra €1.50 for Baptistery)* ☉ *Daily 9–6; baptistery, 8:30–12:30, 2:30–6:30.*

★ **Gesù Nuovo.** *Opulenza* and *magnificenza* are the words that come to mind when describing this floridly baroque church, the centerpiece of the Piazza del Gesù Nuovo. Its formidable diamond-point facade is actually a remnant of the Renaissance palace of the Sanseverino princes (1470), destroyed to make way, in 1584–1601, for a generically stupendous exercise in the full-throated Jesuit style, albeit one with an unusual Greek-cross plan, masterminded by Jesuit architect Giuseppe Valeriani. Behind the entrance is Francesco Solimena's action-packed *Helidorus' Eviction from the Temple*. The dome originally also contained a masterwork by Lanfranco but the 1688 earthquake brought the work tumbling down; Lanfranco's figures of the Evangelists in the support arches give an idea of the scale and quality. The bulk of the interior decoration took more than 40 years and was completed only in the 18th century. You can find the familiar baroque sculptors (Naccherino, Finelli) and painters. The gracious *Visitation* above the altar in the second chapel on the right is by Massimo Stanzione, who also contributed the fine frescoes in the main nave: they're in the presbytery (behind and around the main altar). In the chapel to the left of the main altar is a frescoed vault by the young Francesco Solimena, who became a leading baroque painter, and on either side is a wonderful gallery of reliquary portraits, each placed in its own opera box. Like many

Beneath the city you can tour Napoli Sotterranea (Naples Underground), an extensive network of tunnels, caverns, and aqueducts.

churches in Naples, much of the interior was undergoing restoration at this writing. ✉ *Piazza Gesù Nuovo, Spaccanapoli* ☎ *081/5578111* 🕙 *Daily 7–12:30 and 4–7:30.*

★ **Monte di Pietà.** Lush and lavish, this baroque-era landmark is a must-see for anyone interested in Neapolitan decorative arts. As Spaccanapoli was home to both Naples's poorest and richest residents, the latter formed several charitable institutions, of which the Monte di Pietà was one of the most prominent. At the beginning of the 16th century, it constructed this palazzo (F. Cavagna, 1605), with a grand courtyard leading to the **Cappella della Pietà**, with gilt stuccoes and beautiful frescoes by Belisario Corenzio. Leading off the chapel are a number of salons, including the **Sala delle Cantoniere,** with inlaid marbles and precious intarsia woodwork. Since most Neapolitan residential palace interiors are private or have disappeared, this 17th-century enfilade of salons offers a rare glimpse of Naples at its most sumptuous. Concerts and theatrical performances are often held in the courtyard in summer. Today the palazzo is an office for the SanPaolo Banco di Napoli. ✉ *Via Biagio dei Librai 114, Spaccanapoli* ☎ *081/5517074* 🕙 *Sat. 9–7, Sun. 9–1* Ⓜ *Piazza Cavour (in construction: Duomo).*

★ **Museo Diocesano.** Situated opposite the Archbishop's palace, this museum incorporates the baroque church of Santa Maria Donnaregina Nuova. Started in 1617 and consecrated 50 years later for the Francescan nuns (les Clarisses) in the attached cloister, the church replaced the Gothic Donnaregina Vecchia, which was damaged by earthquake. In more modern times the building was used as legal offices before being closed completely, becoming prey to the occasional theft, not to mention bomb damage during the World War II. In September 2008, it was reborn as a museum. Instantly recognizable by the fresco of the Virgin above the entrance, the building houses the work, brilliantly restored, of late Gothic and Renaissance masters, and many of the main practitioners of the Neapolitan baroque.

On the ground floor, as suits the church's name, the artwork centers on the life of the Virgin Mary, beginning with the first chapel on the left and French painter Charles Mellin's beautiful depiction of the Immaculate Conception (1646), while on the other side of what was once the nave is an equally fine Madonna and Child by Massimo Stanzione. Also on the left is a space rich in Gothic and Renaissance statuary from the former church. You then take the elevator upstairs to where the nuns once attended Mass, concealed from the congregation by a special screen. The hundred works on show follow a theme of life as an imitation of Christ. There is also the rare chance see roof paintings close up, with state-of-the-art floodlights displaying the restoration to maximum effect.

⊠ *Largo Donnregina, Spaccanapoli* ☎ *081/5571365* ⊕ *www. museodiocesanonapoli.it* ⊡ *€8* ⊘ *Mon. and Wed.–Sat. 9:30–4:30, Sun. 9:30–2* Ⓜ *Piazza Cavour (in construction: Duomo).*

6

♻ **Napoli Sotterranea.** Naples has been compared to a multilayer cake.
Fodor's Choice Here, off left from the San Paolo Maggiore church, is not only the bot-
★ tom layer par excellence, but also, even deeper, the Greek and Roman quarries from which it was carved. Featured in the History Channel's "Cities of the Underworld," this is a tour you won't forget. After a descent into Naples's stomach (food storehouses), as it has been called, the first stop is the amphitheater where Nero famously performed three times with the strangely latticed stone—or *opus reticulatum*—wound up providing a Roman antiseismic device. Until 1999 part of a garage, here, or 6 feet below, stood Nero when an earthquake struck in midperformance and—so Suetonius relates—the Imperial entertainer forbade the 6,000 spectators to leave. All that rumbling, he insisted, was the gods applauding the brilliance of his performance. The arches forming the theater entrance are visible up above in Via Anticaglia. A second descent drops you 30 meters to what was originally part of the city system of quarries and aqueducts. Used from Greek times right up to the 1845 cholera epidemic, the aqueducts were only closed in 1942, when a section was reopened to provide an air-raid shelter big enough to sleep 3,000 people. A further descent takes you to the Greco-Roman quarry and what might be called the Genesis of the city: soft tufa stones were cut from here and then raised to the surface. Finally, prepare for a highly claustrophobic 1-km walk with only a candle to light your way. Efforts to dramatize the experience—amphoras lowered on ropes to draw water from cisterns, candles distributed to negotiate narrow passages as in pre-electric days, objects shifted to reveal secret passages—combined with excellent guiding in English make this particularly exciting for children. ■ TIP➜ Be prepared to go up and down a lot of steps, and handle a few narrow corridors—remember that temperatures in summertime will be much lower undergound than at street level, so bring a wrap. ⊠ *Piazza San Gaetano 68, Spaccanapoli* ☎ *081/296944*

CLOSE UP

Caravaggio's Seven Acts of Mercy

The most unforgettable painting in Naples, Michelangelo Merisi da Caravaggio's *Seven Acts of Mercy*—in Italian, the *Sette Opere della Misericordia*—takes pride of place in the Church of Pio Monte della Misericordia, as well as in nearly all of southern Italy, for emotional spectacle and unflinching truthfulness.

Painted in 1607, it combines the traditional seven acts of Christian charity in sometimes-abbreviated form in a tight, dynamic composition under the close, compassionate gaze of the Virgin (the original title was *Our Lady of Mercy*).

Borne by two of the most memorable angels ever painted, she flutters down with the Christ child into a torch-lighted street scene.

Illuminated in the artist's landmark chiaroscuro style (featuring pronounced contrasts of light, *chiaro,* and deep shadow, *scuro*), a man is being buried, a nude beggar is being clothed, and—this artist never pulled any punches—a starving prisoner is being suckled by a woman.

Caravaggio, as with most geniuses, was a difficult artist and personality. His romantic bad-boy reputation as the original bohemian, complete with angry, nihilistic, rebel-with-a-cause sneer and roistering and hippielike lifestyle, has dominated interpretations of his revolutionary oeuvre and tend to present him as an antireligious painter.

This is perhaps understandable—most of the documents pertaining to his life relate to his problems with the law and make for a good story indeed (he came to Naples after killing a man in a bar brawl in Rome, where his cardinal patrons could no longer protect him).

But in spite of (or perhaps because of) his personal life, Caravaggio painted some of the most moving religious art ever produced in the West, whittling away all the rhetoric to reveal the emotional core of the subject.

His genuine love of the popular classes and for the "real" life of the street found expression in his use of ordinary street folk as models.

If his art seems to surge directly from the gut, his famous "objectivity" of observation and reduced palette have clear antecedents in paintings from his home region in northern Italy.

The simplicity and warts-and-all depictions of his characters show a deeply original response to the Counter-Reformation writings on religious art by Carlo Borromeo, a future saint, also from Lombardy.

The *Seven Acts of Mercy*, the first altarpiece commissioned for the new church of the charitable institution, has been called "the most important religious painting of the 17th century" by the great 20th-century Italian art critics Roberto Longhi and Giuliano Argan, and if that may not be immediately obvious, it's nevertheless easy to imagine the impact this astonishing painting had on artists and connoisseurs in Naples.

Naples affected his style, too: he began to express visual relations purely in terms of dramatic light and shadow, which further exalted the contrasts of human experience.

⊕ *www.napolisotterranea.org* ☉ *Daily; tours weekdays at noon, 2, and 4, weekends at 10, noon, 2, 4, and 6; evening tour Thurs. at 9* 🎟 *€9.30* Ⓜ *Piazza Cavour.*

Fodor's Choice **Pio Monte della Misericordia.** One of the defining landmarks of Spac-
★ canapoli, this octagonal church was built around the corner from the Duomo (practically in front of its constantly used side door) for a charitable institution founded in 1601 by seven noblemen. The institution's aim was to carry out acts of Christian charity: feeding the hungry, clothing the poor, nursing the sick, sheltering pilgrims, visiting prisoners, ransoming Christian slaves, and burying the indigent dead—acts immortalized in the history of art by the famous altarpiece painted by Caravaggio (1571–1610) depicting the *Sette Opere della Misericordia* (or *Seven Acts of Mercy*) and now the celebrated focus of the church. In this haunting work the artist has brought the Virgin in palpable glory, unforgettably borne atop the shoulders of two angels, right down into the street—and not a rhetorical place, but a real street of Spaccanapoli (scholars have in fact suggested a couple of plausible identifications) populated by figures in whose spontaneous and passionate movements the people could see themselves given great dignity. Along with other paintings in the church, the sculptures by Andrea Falcone on its porch refer to this commitment. The original church was considered too small and destroyed in 1655 to make way for the new church, designed by Antonio Picchiatti in 1658–78.

The extraordinary expressiveness and efficiency of the Caravaggio altarpiece—the work was so revered that soon this institution's minutes decreed that all copies be forbidden, although this did not prevent the painting giving rise to a whole new chapter in Neapolitan art, with a school of fellow painters adopting Caravaggio's almost cinematic light and shade techniques—can be judged by comparison with the church's other paintings, commissioned from Neapolitan painters after Caravaggio hit the road again (to Malta) to stay one step ahead of the law. In particular, in the painting to the left of the altar, *St. Peter Rescuing Tabitha* (1612), Fabrizio Santafede is clearly struggling to modify his Technicolor formalist style to suggest the dramatic impact of the altarpiece—but the figures here merely occupy the space of the painting, rather than animate it. The painting to the right of the exit door is a beautiful work by one of the best of the Neapolitan Caravaggesques, Giovan Battista Carraciolo, who was 29 years old when the slightly older artist came to town. Depicting the *Liberation of St. Peter* (1615), the composition is almost shockingly spartan, nearly all dark brown with contained blocks of white, red, and flesh tones. For more paintings of the Neapolitan Seicento, head up the staircase to the church's small **Pinacoteca,** a museum of 17th- and 18th-century paintings. Immediately one is struck by the portraits of the high-faluting Carlo di Tocco wearing the Spanish Order of the Golden Fleece. With such a character around, small wonder the Neapolitan masses rebelled every now and then. A side room has an intense, remarkably modern-looking self-portrait of *Luca Fa Presto* (Superquick Luca), the noted painter Luca Giordano, here portrayed wearing glasses. Elsewhere, proving beauty is no monopoly of class, Francesco di Mura, the collection's donor, portrays his wife and former washerwoman turned lady in the latest silk fashions and fingering a lock of hair. ⊠ *Via dei Tribunali 253, Spaccanapoli* ☎ *081/446973* ⊕ *www.piomontedellamisericordia. it* ⊙ *Thurs.–Tues. 9–2:30* 🎟 *€5, including audio guide* Ⓜ *Piazza Cavour (in construction: Duomo).*

★ **San Gregorio Armeno.** Set on Via San Gregorio Armeno, the street that is lined with Naples's most adorable Presepe—or Nativity crèche scene–emporiums—and landmarked by a picturesque campanile, this convent is one of the oldest and most important in Naples. The nuns (often the daughters of Naples's richest families) who lived here must have been disappointed with heaven when they arrived—banquets here outrivaled those of the royal court, hallways were lined with paintings, and the church was filled with gilt stucco and semiprecious stones. Described as "a room of Paradise on Earth" by Carlo Celano and designed by Niccolò Taglicozzi Canle, the church has a highly detailed wooden ceiling, unique papier-mâché choir lofts, a shimmering organ, candlelit shrines, and important Luca Giordano frescoes of scenes of the life of St. Gregory, whose relics were brought to Naples in the 8th century from Byzantium. In the last chapel on the right are the remains of Saint Patricia, after whom the church is also sometimes known. An ampoule of her blood believed to have curative powers is kept by the nuns behind the altar and is occasionally brought out to be kissed by devoted worshippers. Notable also, like the ticket office of some celestial railway, is the brass grill behind which the nuns heard Mass. An arcade leads to the grand and pretty convent's cloister, where you can spot the nuns' gallery shielded by 18th-century jalousies. Other areas off the cloister, such as the Salottino della Badessa—generally not on view, as this is still a working convent—are preserved as magnificent 18th-century interiors. ⊠ *Piazzetta San Gregorio Armeno 1, Spaccanapoli* ☎ *081/5520186* ⊙ *Mon.–Sat. 9–noon, Sun. 9–1* Ⓜ *Dante.*

San Lorenzo Maggiore. One of the grandest medieval churches of the Decumano Maggiore, San Lorenzo features a very unmedieval facade of 18th-century splendor. Due to the effects and threats of earthquakes, the church was reinforced and reshaped along baroque lines in the 17th and 18th centuries, and remaining from this phase is the facade by Ferdinando Sanfelice (1742) based on the sweeping curves of Borromini's Filomarino altar in the Church of Santi Apostoli. Begun by Robert d'Anjou in 1265 on the site of a previous 6th-century church, the church's single, barnlike nave reflects the desire of the Franciscans for simple spaces with enough room to preach to large crowds. Numerous statues and paintings from the 14th century are indicative of San Lorenzo's importance during this period. In 1334, in fact, Boccaccio met and fell in love with his fabled Lady Fiammetta here, and in 1343 another great Italian poet, Petrarch, resided in the monastery next door. The transept is announced by a grandiose triumphal arch, while the main altar (1530) is the sculptor Giovanni da Nola's masterpiece; notice the fascinating historical views of Naples in the reliefs.

The apse was built by an unknown imported French architect of great caliber, who gives here a brilliant essay in the pure French Angevin style, complete with an ambulatory of nine side chapels that is covered by a magnificent web of cross arches. The most important monument in the church is found here: the tomb of Catherine of Austria (circa 1323), by Tino da Camaino, one of the first sculptors to introduce the Gothic style into Italy. The left transept contains the 14th-century funerary monument of Carlo di Durazzo and yet another Cosimo Fanzago masterpiece, the **Cappellone di Sant'Antonio**—*cappella* (or small chapel) being too diminutive a word, especially in this behemoth of a church. Outside the 17th-century cloister is the entrance to the **Greek and Roman** *scavi,* or excavations, under San Lorenzo, which are a good initiation to the ancient cities beneath the modern one. Near the area of the forum, these digs have revealed streets, markets, and workshops of another age.

Next door to the church is the **Museo dell'Opera di San Lorenzo,** installed in the 16th-century palazzo around the *torre campanaria* (belltower). In Room 1 ancient remains from the Greek agora beneath combine with modern maps to provide a fascinating picture of import and export trends in the 4th century BC. The museum also contains ceramics dug up from the Svevian period, many pieces from the early Middle Ages, large tracts of mosaics from the 6th century basilica, and helpful models of how the ancient Roman forum and nearby buildings must have looked. ⊠ *Via dei Tribunali 316, Spaccanapoli* ☎ *081/2110860* ⊕ *www.sanlorenzomaggiore.na.it* ✉ *Excavations and museum €9* ☉ *Museum, Mon.–Sat. 8–1 and 4–6:30, Sun. 9:30–1:30; church Mon.–Sat. 9–noon, Sun. closed to sightseers* Ⓜ *Dante.*

Fodor's Choice
★   **Santa Chiara.** Across from the Gesù Nuovo and offering a stark and telling contrast to the opulence of that church, Santa Chiara is the leading monument of Angevin Gothic in Naples. The fashionable church for the nobility in the 14th century, and a favorite Angevin church from the start, Santa Chiara was intended to be a great dynastic monument by Robert d'Anjou. His second wife, Sancia di Majorca, added the adjoining convent for the Poor Clares to a monastery of the Franciscan Minors so she could vicariously satisfy a lifelong desire for the cloistered seclusion of a convent; this was the first time the two sexes were combined in a single complex. Built in a Provençal Gothic style between 1310 and 1328 (probably by Guglielmo Primario) and dedicated in 1340, the church had its aspect radically altered, as did so many others, in the baroque period, when the original wooden roof was replaced with a vault dripping in stuccos. A six-day fire started by Allied bombs on August 4, 1943, put an end to all that, as well as to what might have been left of the important cycle of frescoes by Giotto and his Neapolitan workshop: Giorgio Vasari, writing in the mid-16th century, tells us that the paintings covered the entire church. The most important tomb in the church towers behind the altar. Sculpted by Giovanni and Pacio Bertini of Florence (1343–45), it is, fittingly, the tomb of the founding king: the great Robert d'Anjou, known as the Wise. To the right of the altar is the tomb of Carlo, duke of Calabria, a majestic composition by Tino da Camaino and assistants (1326–33), and answering it on the side wall is Tino's last work, the tomb of Carlo's wife, Marie de Valois.

Around the left side of the church is the **Chiostro delle Clarisse,** the most famous cloister in Naples. It's clear here that we are not dealing with any normal convent; complemented by real citrus trees, the benches

Unique in all the world, the majolica-decorated cloister at Santa Chiara also serves as a tranquil oasis in the midst of hectic Spaccanapoli.

and octagonal columns comprise a light-handed masterpiece of painted majolica designed by Domenico Antonio Vaccaro, with a delightful profusion of landscapes and light yellow and green floral motifs realized by Donato and Giuseppe Massa and their studio (1742). The elegant 14th-century porch around the garden features some fading frescoes. In the back corner the Museo dell'Opera, built on the visible remains of an old Roman baths establishment, contains interesting sculptural fragments from the damaged church, a pair of photographs illustrating the altar before and after the 1943 bombing, as well as objects illustrating life in the cloister. ✉ *Piazza Gesù Nuovo, Spaccanapoli* ☎ *081/7971231* ⊕ *www.santachiara.info* ✉ *Museum and cloister €5* ⊘ *Church: daily 7–12:30 and 4:30–6:30. Museum and cloister: Mon.–Sat. 9:30–5:30, Sun. 10–2:30* Ⓜ *Dante (in construction: Piazza Borsa-Università).*

WORTH NOTING

Chiesa dei Girolamini/Quadreria dei Girolamini. The Girolamini is another name for the Oratorians, followers of St. Philip Neri, to whom the splendid church I Girolamini is dedicated. Built in 1592–1619 by the Florentine architect Giovanni Antonio Dosio, the dome and gray-and-white facade were rebuilt after a design by Ferdinando Fuga (circa 1780) in the most elegant Neoclassical style. Hit by Allied bombs in 1943, the massive church has been undergoing restoration for many decades but in early 2010 the wraps came off and the public has finally been allowed to enter this once very powerful and rich cathedral-sized church, whose exterior is encircled by 12 massive granite columns from the island of Giglio.

Although some paintings in the nave remain under cover Luca Giordano's cinema-size mural above the portal is now on view. Christ, flail raised, chases the moneymakers from the temple, Giordano here including local sellers of doughnuts (*ciambelle*) and of caged birds while sheep stampede down

WORD OF MOUTH

"I really enjoyed the Basilica di Santa Chiara—it has a big garden in the interior with lovely tile details. Very peaceful in the middle of a busy city!" —orangetravel

the temple stairs. The pictures in the dome were badly damaged during the bombing, yet the ceiling has now been restored to original baroque glory, the occasional cherubic pink punctuating the gold, pride of place going to a gloriously framed *Saint Mary of the Nativity* to whom the church is dedicated. The facade outside features in the figures of Moses and Aaron, two works by Sammartino, the famous sculptor of the veiled Christ in the Cappella San Severo. Although the church's main entrance is on Via Tribunali, the elegant cloister and access to the **Quadreria** (museum) on the upper floor can only be entered around the corner on Via del Duomo. The collection includes paintings by Santafede, Pizzolino, an entire room filled with Riberas, and such masterworks as Luca Giordano's *Dead Christ* and Guido Reni's *Flight from Egypt*. Here, too, is one of the most gloriously decorated 18th-century libraries in Europe, the 60,000-volume **Biblioteca dei Girolamini**, now used by scholars. In fact, this area was an important nucleus of intellectual life in the Renaissance and baroque periods, thanks to the presence of this library. Directly across the street, note an inscription by Naples's profusely subtle philosopher, historian, and politician Benedetto Croce (1866–1952) that marks the house in which his illustrious predecessor, the philosopher Giambattista Vico, lived for nearly 20 years. ⊠ *Via Duomo 142, Spaccanapoli* ☎ *142/08129444* 🖃 *Free* ⊘ *Church, daily 9–noon and 4–7; Museum, Mon.–Sat. 9–12:50* Ⓜ *Piazza Cavour.*

San Domenico Maggiore. One of the largest churches of Spaccanapoli, this Dominican house of worship was originally constructed by Charles I of Anjou in 1238. Legend has it that a painting of the Crucifixion spoke to St. Thomas Aquinas when he was at prayer here. This early structure, however, was nearly gutted by a fire three centuries later and, in 1850, a neo-Gothic edifice rose in its place, complete with a nave of awe-inspiring dimensions. In the second chapel on the right (if you enter through the north door) are remnants of the earlier church—14th-century frescoes by Pietro Cavallini, a Roman predecessor of Giotto. Along the side chapels are also some noted funerary monuments, including those of the Carafa family, whose chapel, to the left of Cosimo Fanzago's 17th-century altar, is one of the most beautiful Renaissance-era set pieces in Naples. ⊠ *Piazza San Domenico Maggiore 8/a, Spaccanapoli* ☎ *081/459188* ⊘ *Mon.–Sat. 8:30–noon and 4–7, Sun. 9–1 and 4:30–7* Ⓜ *Dante.*

San Giuseppe dei Ruffi. Half a block up from the Duomo, this late-17th-century church, built by Dionisio Lazzari, features a dramatically baroque facade. Inside, look for the armored wooden figure of a winged Michael slaying a rather docile dragon on the nave's right end. Behind a gate rises the altar, layer after baroque layer, Lazzari's sumptuous gold and marble (1686) topped by the putti and the figures of Hope and Charity by Matteo Bottigliero (1733). If you arrive around 7:30, most mornings you'll hear the nuns beautifully singing early mass. ⊠ *Piazza San Giuseppe dei Ruffi 2, Spaccanapoli* ☉ *Mon.–Sat. 7:30–1 and 4–6, Sun. 7:30–10:30* Ⓜ *Piazza Cavour.*

San Paolo Maggiore. Like Santi Apostoli, this church was erected for the Theatin fathers in the late 16th century (1583–1603), the period of their order's rapid expansion. This was another instance where Francesco Grimaldi, the (ordained) house architect, erected a church on the ruins of an ancient Roman temple, then transformed it into a Christian basilica. Spoils from the temple survive in the present incarnation, especially the two monumental Corinthian columns on the facade holding up a piece of their architrave to form a portal over the entrance door. The cloaked torsos of the ancient gods, which used to lie under the statues of Peter and Paul, have been moved. An earthquake knocked down the original facade in 1688, and World War II, coupled with decades of neglect, did further damage to the marble facing along the aisle and to the ceiling, both of which have now been restored. ⊠ *Piazza San Gaetano, Spaccanapoli* ☏ *081/454048* ☉ *Weekdays 9–1 and 3–6, Sat. 9–1* Ⓜ *Dante.*

Sant'Angelo a Nilo. Originally built by Cardinal Brancaccio in the late 1300s, this church was redesigned in the 16th century by Arcangelo Guglielminelli. Inside the graciously beautiful interior is the earliest evidence of the Renaissance in Naples: the cardinal's funerary monument, sculpted by the famous Donatello and the almost-as-famous Michelozzo in 1426–27. The front of the sarcophagus bears Donatello's contribution, a beautiful bas-relief *Assumption of the Virgin;* upheld by angels, the Virgin seeming to float in air. ⊠ *Piazzetta Nilo, along Via San Biagio dei Librai, Spaccanapoli* ☏ *081/5516227* ☉ *Mon.–Sat. 9–1 and 4–6, Sun. 8:30–noon* Ⓜ *Dante.*

Santi Apostoli. This baroque church in a basic Latin-cross style with a single nave shares the piazza with a contemporary art school in a typically anarchic Neapolitan mix. Built (1610–49) by the ordained architect Francesco Grimaldi for the Theatin fathers above a previous church, itself built on the remains of a temple probably dedicated to Mercury, it's worth a quick peek inside for its coherent, intact baroque decorative scheme. There are excellent paintings on the inside of the entrance wall and on the ceiling by Giovanni Lanfranco (circa 1644), with a good number painted by his successors Francesco Solimena and Luca Giordano. For lovers of baroque architecture, there's an altar in the left transept by the great architect Francesco Borromini. Commissioned by Cardinal Ascanio Filomarino, this is the only work in Naples by this architect, whose freedom from formality so inspired the exuberance of the baroque in southern Italy, although its massive virile flourish of monochrome gray stone comes as a bit of a shock in the midst of this polychromed city. ⊠ *Largo Santi Apostoli 9, Spaccanapoli* ☏ *081/299375* ☉ *Mon.–Sat. 9–noon, Sun. 9–1* Ⓜ *Piazza Cavour.*

6

MUSEO ARCHEOLOGICO NAZIONALE TO PORTA CAPUANO

It's only fitting that the Museo Archeologico Nazionale—the single most important and remarkable museum of Greco-Roman antiquities in the world (in spite of itself, some observers say)—sits in the upper *decumanus,* or neighborhood, of ancient Neapolis, the district colonized by the ancient Greeks and Romans. Repository of many of the greatest surviving art treasures of antiquity—including most of the celebrated finds from Pompeii and Herculaneum—the museum has so many rooms it almost constitutes its own walking tour. As Naples's preeminent treasure trove, it deserves your undivided attention. Happily, it's open all day (its core collection, that is). But if two hours are your limit for gazing at ancient art, nearby you'll discover some of the lesser-known delights of medieval and Renaissance Naples, along with the city's lush botanical gardens (which are set in the neighborhood quarter known as Carlo III). Along the way you'll visit churches that are repositories for magnificent 15th- and 16th-century art and sculpture; the Museo Madre, the city's flagship museum of modern art; and the famed Porta Capuana, one of the historic gates to the city walls.

TOP ATTRACTIONS

Fodor'sChoice
★
Museo Archeologico Nazionale *(National Museum of Archaeology)*. Those who knew and loved this legendary museum once had the tendency upon hearing it mentioned to heave a sigh: for decades it had been famous not only for its unrivaled collections but also for its off-limit rooms, missing identification labels, poor lighting, billows of dust, suffocating heat in summer, and indifferent personnel—a state of affairs seen by some critics as an encapsulation of everything that was wrong with southern Italy in general.

But it was precisely because of this emblematic value that the National Ministry of Culture finally decided to lavish attention and funds on the museum in a complete reorganization. This process has been ongoing for some time and the museum now runs and looks befitting the world-class and legendary masterworks of antiquity that are on view here. Ticketing has been privatized and opening hours extended (for the center-core "masterpiece" collection, that is; other rooms are still subject to staffing shortages and can be closed on a rotating basis). Some of the "newer" rooms, covering archaeological discoveries in the Greco-Roman settlements and necropolises in and around Naples, have helpful informational panels in English. A fascinating display (free) of the finds unearthed during digs for the Naples metro has been set up in the Museo station close to the museum entrance.

Even if some rooms may be closed, this still leaves available the core of the museum, a nucleus of world-renowned archaeological finds that puts most other museums to shame. It includes the legendary Farnese collection of ancient sculpture, together with local sculptural finds, and almost all the good stuff—the best mosaics and paintings—from Pompeii and Herculaneum. The quality of these collections is unexcelled and, as far as the mosaic, painting, and bronze sections are concerned, unique in the world.

This museum was actually the end product of the kind of discovery that every archaeologist dreams about: in 1748, ancient Pompeii was uncovered. By 1750 a makeshift museum had been set up in the royal palace at Portici and Naples, with its exciting excavations, soon became an obligatory stop on travelers' Grand Tour itineraries. After a time the question of a fitting museum became an international issue, and given the precarious position of Portici (it lies under Vesuvius), a solution was deemed urgent, especially when the fabled Farnese collection of ancient sculpture arrived, shipped by the family from Rome, despite the strident complaints of the Pope and various other personages, including Goethe. Everything of great value was then moved to the new museum in Naples. First named the Royal Library of Naples and ultimately reorganized as a so-called National Museum it finally opened in 1801.

After buying your tickets (many study the sign indicating which rooms are open and which closed), head to the heart of the main floor: the Atrium of the Magistrates, which contains a dignified but discreet introduction to the sculpture collections, including a pair of Dacians from Trajan's Forum in the middle aisle. If you want to continue with marble sculpture, wend your way back to the door framed by two columns of antique Numidian yellow marble, and enter the Room of the Tyrannicides. It makes more sense, however, to start your visit on the top floor of the museum, which contains some of the works more demanding on the eye, and work your way down. Head for the stairs flanked at the base by two large reclining 2nd-century AD river deities.

Go up two flights of stairs to the first floor (that's by Italian accounting; the mezzanine only counts for half a floor—except when it comes to subsidies). To the right is the important collection of bronzes. The first room (CXV) presents a delightful collection of small decorative bronzes (Silenus heads, children's portraits, leopard antefixes) from the grandiose Villa of the Papiri in Herculaneum, while the adjoining room (CXIV) has a permanent exhibition on the papyrus scrolls, from where the villa got its name. The big room (CXVI) ahead contains statues from the villa that most museums would sell their souls to get as virtually all metal objects from antiquity, especially bronze statues, were melted down. Here you have a treasury of life-size masterpieces, with a splendid set of heads along the left wall illustrating the ancient themes of illustrious men—Hellenistic princes, philosophers, poets—and generic, ideal figures referring to aspects of civilized life: theatrical figures and athletes. In front of these sits the famous **Drunken Satyr**. The far wall has a celebrated set of five female **Dancers** (recently reinterpreted as water carriers and identified with the Danaids, who were condemned to draw water endlessly) in the stiff but expressive Severe style. The next room (CXVII) contains an impressive 1st-century BC copy of a lance-throwing Athena Promachos, which replicates the monumental statue that once decorated the Acropolis in Athens, and the justifiably renowned portrait head known as the Seneca, whose world-weary expression will still move you deeply.

Rooms CXVIII to CXXI shift the focus from Herculaneum to ancient Neapolis (Naples) and the first Greek settlement overlooking what is now Castel dell'Ovo, Palaeopolis. Exhibits include important finds from public buildings and necropolises during the Greco-Roman period with helpful information panels (in English). Back through the bronze galleries and to the right at the staircase, you come into the large Sala della Meridiana, gussied up with a series of huge 19th-century mediocrities detailing the family history of the fabulous Farnese. Beyond the famous Farnese Atlas, a pair of Trajan-era kneeling Persians in white and purple *pavonazzetto* marble drapery provides a suitable announcement of the celebrated collection of ancient frescoes beyond.

Room 1 (or CXVI; most rooms are numbered in both Arabic and Roman styles) starts off with some excellent 4th Style painted-stucco friezes from the House of Meleager in Pompeii but this is just an antechamber to the cream of the crop, spread around the rooms branching off from Room 2 (CXVIII). Handy English-language displays of information, on the left as you enter, give a good presentation of the so-called Four Styles of Roman painting as seen in Pompeii and Herculaneum, evidence of the "golden age" of Roman wall painting. The room to the right displays what's left of the 3rd Style paintings from the villa at Boscoreale; the next room (LXX) contains two versions of the *Three Graces* on the right. Room LXXII has a wonderful *Perseus Freeing Andromeda* from the House of the Dioscuri in Pompeii, plus the celebrated image of *Theseus and the Minotaur* next to the exit door. The last room (LXXIII) along the front facade houses a number of panels in the refined but cold antiquarian current of the 3rd Style, a reflection of Augustan classicism.

Room LXXXV starts the **Glass Collection**; in an adjacent room is the spectacular 100:1 scale model of Pompeii made in 1879. The main part of the glass and jewelry collection (Room LXXXVI) has some fine mosaic glass bowls that would grace any triclinium (banquet room) dining table. Stairs take you back down to the mezzanine, site of the **Mosaic Collection**. And what mosaics they are! The finest works are saved for the last two rooms: the world-renowned opus vermiculatum mosaics from the House of the Faun in Pompeii. The star piece here is the gigantic *Alexander and Darius at the Battle of Issus* on the far wall. Considered to be a copy of a famous painting by Philoxenos of Eretria done for King Cassander of Macedonia (end of the 4th century BC), this mosaic copy, which dates to 125 BC, would be, even if clumsily rendered, of priceless documentary value for our knowledge of the lost art of Greek painting; as it happens, the mosaic itself is a masterpiece.

Tucked in discreetly by the mosaic area is the **Gabinetto Segreto**, a unique collection of objects covering a gamut of sexually explicit themes, from phalluses in imaginative poses to Pan doing indescribable things to a nanny goat. After many years of closure due either to 19th-century prudery or 20th-century restoration, the Gabinetto can now be viewed (guided tours only, every 30 minutes, no children under

11) by prior request at the main ticket office. The information panels here are helpful, so you might like to browse at your own pace rather than hurry along with the hurried guided tour.

Once back on the ground floor, follow the signs to the **Gallery of the Great Masters** (Rooms II–VI), which contains mostly copies of works by Greek masters, but some of these copies are among the finest known, including the *Apollo Citharedos* and the *Doriphoros* of Polycleites in Bay II. Back into the Room of the Tyrannicides and to your right is the Gallery of Flora (Room VIII), with a beautifully intact *Artemis of Ephesus* in basalt and antique yellow marble, her fecundity underlined by her multiple breasts. In the middle of the gallery stands a voluptuous *Aphrodite Callipygos* ("of the beautiful buttocks"), originally found in the area of Nero's Domus Aurea in Rome.

The collections of ancient sculpture culminate in the **Gallery of the Farnese Bull** (Rooms XI–XV), whose monumentality is no less than the grandiose sculptures from the Baths of Caracalla deserve. The right end of the gallery is dominated by the awesomely powerful *Farnese Hercules*, a signed ("Glykon of Athens made this") copy of a 4th-century BC bronze by Lysippus. The left arm is a restoration, and the nearby set of legs was made by Guglielmo della Porta in the 16th century to complete the statue when it was first discovered; the originals, found afterward, were long judged inferior to these and were not reintegrated until much later. At the left end, the splendid *Farnese Bull*—the largest sculptural group to come down to us from antiquity—answers the Hercules in magnificence. Yes, it has been highly restored (this is well documented on the wall), but all in all, the restorers did a decent job. The strong composition, with its calm depiction of murder, still inspires awe, and numerous artists, from Michelangelo to Picasso, have been influenced by this sculpture.

As you enter the building, the ticket booth is on your left. To view the remarkable Farnese collection of ancient marble sculpture, take the right-hand corridor at the end of the entrance atrium and follow the signs. You might try the audio guide (€4; ID required), though for a collection of this magnitude it is woefully incomplete. ⊠ *Piazza Museo 19, Spaccanapoli* ☎ *081/440166* ⊕ *www.archeona.arti.beniculturali.it* 🎫 *€6.50, €10 for special exhibits* ⊙ *Wed.–Mon. 9–7:30*

★ **Museo Madre.** Don't be misled by the scaffolding across the street: Museo d'Arte Contemporanea Donnaregina or Madre for short, with 8,000 square meters of exhibition space and a host of young helpful attendants, is very much up and going—in fact one of Naples's most visited museums. The artworks on the first floor are mostly installed in situ by their creators, while on the second floor a "historic" gallery features works by such 20th-century luminaries as Rauschenberg, Oldenburg, Warhol, and Damien Hirst. For a complete contrast, the museum includes the Gothic church of Donnaregina across a courtyard. It also hosts temporary shows by major international artists (and is the only museum in Europe to stay open until 11 PM weekends). ⊠ *Via Settembrini 79, San Lorenzo* ☎ *081/19313016* ⊕ *www.museomadre.*

Museo Archeologico Nazionale to Capodimonte

Parco di Capodimonte

10

CAPODIMONTE

9

Parco di Capodimonte

Via Capodimonte

Via S. Antonio

Salita Moiariello

Salita Capodimonte

C.So Amedeo Di Savoia Duca D'Aosta

Via della Veterinaria

Piazza Carlo III

Orto Botanico

6

Corso Giuseppe Garibaldi

Salita Della Ricia

Salita Mirados

Piazza Sansevero

Via S. Antonio

Via Tenore

Via Foria

8

P. Della Sanità

LA SANITÀ

Via Della Sanità

Via Dei Cristallini

Piazza Miracoli

Via Piazzi

Emiciclo Capodimonte

Santa Teresa degli Scalzi

V. Arena Della Sanità

Via Vergini

Piazza Pagano

7

Via Antonio Villari

Via Crocelle

Via Cirillo

5

Via Cesare Rosaroll

4

Piazza de Nicola

Via Della Stella

Salita D. Stella

Piazza Cavour

M **Cavour**

Via Foria

2

Via Carbonara

3

Castel Capuano

Via Salvatore Rosa

Via E. Pessina

P. Museo Nazionale

1

M **Museo**

V.S. Maria di Costantinopoli

V. Duomo

V.S. Giuseppe D.R.

V. Donnaregina

Duomo

V. Dei Tribunale

Via Pietro Colletta

Via S. Giuseppi dei Nudi

SPACCANAPOLI

◆ Pio Monte d. Misericordia

Piazza Bellini

Piazza Miraglia

V. Dei Tribunale

V.S. Greg. Armeno

Via Nilo

Via Dei Librai

Via Vicaria Vic.

0   1/8 mi

Port'Alba

Cappella Sansevero ◆

Biagio

V. Grande Archivio V. D.

0   1/8 km

Dante

Piazza Dante

Piazza S. Domenico Maggiore

V.S.

Vico S. Severino

KEY

M ⇒ Line 1 Metropolitana Collinare

M ⇒ Line 2 Metropolitana FS

M

Via Toledo

Santa Marta

Via Sebastiano

Via B. Croce

SS. Marcellino e Festo

Piazza Gesù Nuovo

Catacombe di
San Gennaro **9**

Museo Archeologico
Nazionale **1**

Museo di Capodimonte **10**

Museo Madre **2**

Orto Botanico **6**

Palazzo della
Spagnola **7**

Porta Capuana **3**

San Giovanni a
Carbonara **5**

Santa Caterina
a Formiello **4**

Santa Maria
della Sanità **8**

it ⬚€7, *free Mon.* ⊘ *Mon., Wed., Thurs., Sun. 10–9, Fri. and Sat. 10 AM–midnight* Ⓜ *Piazza Cavour.*

★ **Orto Botanico.** Founded in 1807 by Joseph Bonaparte and Prince Joachim Murat as an oasis from hectic Naples, this is one of the largest of all Italian botanical gardens, comprising some 30 acres. One enters up staircases from busy Via Forio to a vast island of green tranquility. A grand parterre road, lined with towering trees, leads to an astonishing collection of cactii and succulents from around the world, all displayed in a semicircular "arable" environment built up of boulders and sand-pits. Nearby a dark and damp "fernery," very much in vogue during the 19th century, hides amid a holm oak forest. Farther back, 19th-century greenhouses and picturesque paths hold an important collection of tree, shrub, cactus, and floral specimens from all over the world. Next to the Orto Botanico, with a 1,200-foot facade dwarfing Piazza Carlo III, is one of the largest public buildings in Europe, the Albergo dei Poveri, built in the 18th and 19th centuries to house the city's destitute and homeless; it's now a UNESCO World Heritage Site awaiting an ambitious restoration scheme. ⊠ *Via Foria 223, Carlo III* ☏ *081/449759* ⊕ *www.ortobotanico.unina.it* ⬚ *Free* ⊘ *By appointment weekdays 9–2.*

★ **San Giovanni a Carbonara.** This often-overlooked church is an engaging complex of Renaissance architecture and sculpture. Its curious name is the result of its location during medieval times near the city trash dump, where refuse was burned (carbonized); this location is just outside the Capuana Gate of the old city walls. Its history starts in 1339, when the Neapolitan nobleman Gualtiero Galeota gave a few houses and a vegetable garden to a small convent of Augustinian monks who ministered to the poor neighborhood nearby.

To enter the church, go up the dramatic staircase in piperno stone with a double run of elliptical stairs—modeled after a 1707 design by Ferdinando Sanfelice (similar to other organ-curved stairways in Rome, such as the Spanish Steps). Upon entering the rectangular nave, the first thing you see is the monument of the Miroballo family, which is actually a chapel on the opposite wall, finished by Tommaso Malvito and his workshop in 1519 for the Marchese Bracigliano; the magnificent statues in the semicircular arch immediately set the tone for this surprising repository of first-class Renaissance sculpture.

To the right—beyond the skeletal main altar, which has been stripped of its 18th-century baroque additions—is the suitably royal (59-foot-tall), if not megalomaniacal, funerary monument of King Ladislas (who funded the original church) and Joan II, finished by Marco and Andrea da Firenze in 1428. Four monumental female statues of Virtues hold up the sarcophagi of Ladislas and his sister, as well as statues of the two monarchs seated on thrones, and, finally, an energetic armed Ladislas on horseback being blessed by a bishop (the king died excommunicate, but you can buy anything in Naples). A door underneath this monument leads to the **Ser Caracciolo del Sole** chapel, with its rare and beautiful original majolica pavement—the oldest (1427) produced in Italy, from a workshop in Campania, it shows the influence of Arab motifs and glazing technique.

6

The Salone della Meridiana, on the top floor of the Museo Archeologico, is one of the largest rooms in Europe.

Coming back out into the nave and immediately turning right at the altar, you enter another circular chapel, the **Caracciolo di Vico** chapel. This cohesive, sophisticated ensemble shows how Italian art history, first written by Tuscans with a regional agenda, tends to simplify the evolution of Renaissance art and architecture at the expense of other centers. The dating for the chapel is the object of debate; usually given as 1517, with the sculptural decor complete by 1557, the design (usually attributed to Tommaso Malvito) may go back to 1499 and thus precede the much more famous Tempietto in Rome, by Bramante, which it so resembles. In fact, the chapel's superlative quality has led some scholars to reject the traditional attribution and give it to Bramante himself or one of the Sangallos under the assumption that such a fine work should naturally be by someone quite famous.

Coming once again into the nave, see if the next door on the right is open (or ask the custodian): this leads to the small rectangular room of the **Old Sacristy,** commissioned by the Caracciolo di Sant'Erasmo. The walls are decorated with 18 colorful fresco panels depicting scenes from the Old and New testaments as well as saints and doctors of the Church, painted by Giorgio Vasari, disciple of Michelangelo and godfather of Renaissance art history. You can be thankful this great church is off the path of tour groups so you can absorb the ordered beauty of the decoration in peace. ⊠ *Via San Giovanni a Carbonara 5, Decumano Maggiore* ☎ *081/295873* ☉ *Mon.–Sat. 9:30–1* Ⓜ *Piazza Cavour.*

WORTH NOTING

Porta Capuana. This ceremonial gateway is one of Naples's finest landmarks of the Renaissance era. Ferdinand II of Aragon commissioned the Florentine sculptor and architect Giuliano da Maiano to build this once-white triumphal arch—perhaps in competition with the Arco di Trionfo found on the facade of the city's Castel Nuovo—in the late 15th century. As at Castel Nuovo, this arch is framed by two peperino stone towers, here nicknamed Honor and Virtue. Across Via Carbonara stands the medieval bulk of the **Castel Capuano,** once home to Angevin and Aragonese rulers until it was transformed in 1540 by the Spanish Viceroy into law courts, a function it still fulfills today. On Sunday this is a meetingplace for Naples's *extracommunitari* (immigrants), who chat in their native tongues—from Ukrainian and Polish to Twi and Igbo. ⊠ *Piazza San Francesco, Carlo III.*

Santa Caterina a Formiello. After a complete makeover completed in July 2008, this church is eminently visitable, the full explanations of its paintings and sculptures on display worthy of a good museum. The Formiello in the name refers to the *formali,* the nearby underground aquaduct, which, history relates, the Aragonese also used to capture the town from beneath. The church facade in dark piperno stone was designed for the Dominicans by Tuscan architect Romolo Balsimelli, a student of Brunelleschi.

The side chapels are as interesting for their relics as for their art. In the Orsini Chapel on the left are the elaborately framed remains of St. Helodorus and other Dominican saints, while the fourth chapel displays some 20 skulls of the martyrs of Otranto, brought to Naples by King Alfonso in 1490. The event referred to is the Ottoman sack of Otranto in 1480, when 813 Christians were executed for refusing to renounce their faith. (More martyrs' skulls occupy a much larger cabinet in Otranto's cathedral.) Depicted in the rather surrealistic altar painting is the headless Antonio Primaldo, whose body, through the strength of faith, stands upright to confound his Ottoman executioner.

In the fifth chapel a cycle of paintings by Giacomo del Po depicts the life and afterlife of Saint Catherine, while in the vault Luigi Garzi depicts the same saint in glory. Up in the rather faded dome painted by Paolo di Mattei, Catherine, together with the Madonna, implores the Trinity to watch over the city. Below are the tombs of the Spinelli family, feudal loyalty to the Aragonese cause being rewarded by something of a family Pantheon. The sumptuous altar is by Lorenzo Fontana. ⊠ *Via Carbonara, Decumano Maggiore* ☎ *081292316* ⊙ *Mon.–Sat. 8:30–8–1, Sun. 8:30–2* Ⓜ *Piazza Garibaldi.*

TOWN AND COUNTRY: LA SANITÀ TO CAPODIMONTE

The Parco di Capodimonte is the crowning point of the vast mountainous plain that slopes down through the city to the waterfront area. Nearly 5 km (3 mi) removed from the madding crowds in the *centro storico,* the sylvan and verdant mount of Capodimonte is enjoyed by locals and visitors alike as a favored escape from the overheated city center. With its picture-perfect views over the entire city and bay, the park was first founded in the 18th century as a hunting preserve by Charles of Bourbon. Before long, partly to house the famous Farnese collection that he had inherited from his mother, he com-

WORD OF MOUTH

"The Neopolitans' joy at just being alive spills over with enthusiasm and generosity. The personal warmth one can find in Naples can't be matched in any city in the world."   —Waldo

missioned a spectacular Palazzo Reale for the park. Today this palace is the Museo di Capodimonte, which contains among its treasures the city's greatest collection of old-master paintings. Here, rooms virtually wallpapered with Titians, Caravaggios, and Parmagianinos will be your reward for making the effort to reach this area of the city, accessible only by vehicles on wheels rather than rails.

If you're feeling intrepid—and not carrying anything of value—you might like to deviate into La Sanità, one of Naples's most densely populated and uncomfortably lawless neighborhoods, still studded with legendary palaces and gilded churches. In the district known as I Vergini (so-called after an inscription found on an ancient Greek tomb in the area relating to the women who had dedicated their virginity to the Greek goddess Eunostos), you can catch your breath at the haunted Catacombs of San Gaudioso. Alternatively, avoid the hassle at street level by taking a fascinating tour with Napoli Sotterranea (⊕ *www. napolisotterranea.org*) to the Cimitero delle Fontanelle.

TOP ATTRACTIONS

★ **Museo di Capodimonte.** The grandiose 18th-century Neoclassical Bourbon royal palace, in the vast Bosco di Capodimonte (Capodimonte Wood), which served as the royal hunting preserve and later as the site of the Capodimonte porcelain works, is a spectacular setting for Naples's finest collection of old-master paintings and decorative arts. Perched on top of a hill overlooking all of Naples and the bay, the palace was built in 1738 by Charles III of Bourbon as a hunting retreat, then expanded by Antonio Medrano—architect of the Teatro San Carlo— to become the repository of the fabled Farnese art collection Charles inherited from his mother, Elizabeth Farnese. For this art-loving king, however, collecting was not enough; to compete with his father-in-law, Frederick Augustus, the Elector of Saxony, who had founded the celebrated Meissen porcelain factory, Charles decided to set up his own royal factory, opposite the Capodimonte Palace, and before long, the "soft-paste" porcelain figurines of Pulcinello, biscuit vendors, and pretty nymphs were the choicest collectibles for Europe's rich. Fittingly, the most unique room in the palace is entirely crafted from porcelain (3,000 pieces of it)—**Queen Maria Amalia's Porcelain Parlor** (1757–59), built for the royal palace at Portici but relocated here.

But Capodimonte's greatest treasure is the excellent collection of paintings, well displayed in the **Galleria Nazionale** on the palace's first and second stories. Before you arrive at this remarkable collection, a magnificent staircase leads to the royal apartments, where you'll find beautiful antique furniture, most of it on the splashy scale so dear to the Bourbons, and a staggering collection of porcelain and majolica from the various royal residences.

It is with a string of portraits by Raphael and Titian of Farnese cardinals and popes, which the museum begins. An A-to-Z of the great Renaissance masters continues, with a Masaccio (Room 3); giant sketches by Michelangelo bequeathed by Cardinal Oduardo Farnese (Room 4); Masolino, Mantegna, and Giovanni Bellini (Room 5–8). Proceed via noted works by Lorenzo Lotto and del Piombo to a particularly sumptuous trove of Correggio and Parmigianino, as the Farnese family used their Parma roots to claim something of a lion's share on paintings from that region, including Parmegianino's famous *Antea* (1531). Room 17, by contrast, has two Breughels, *The Blind leading the Blind* and the black-hooded *Misanthrope*. This Renaissance Hall of Fame segues into the baroque into two or three roomfuls of favorite Farnese employees, including the Caracci brothers, then other rooms featuring Domenichino (a Caracci pupil) and Lanfranco, both active in Naples as well as Rome. Upstairs, Room 66 stars Simone Martini's *St. Louis Crowning King Robert* (1317). Once encrusted with jewels (though the gold remains), the picture, commissioned by King Robert d'Anjou, is famed for being maybe the first picture done for specifically political ends, namely to justify the dubious claim of the saint's younger brother to the Naples throne. Saint Louis, renouncing his own claim by becoming a Franciscan monk and later bishop of Toulouse, holds a crown above his sibling's head. Past more Titians, including the celebrated *Danaë* (1545), then a series of now fruity, now fishy still lifes, the rest of the floor is a Who's Who of the High Neapolitan baroque. A room to itself, the starting point is Caravaggio's *Flagellelation* (1607–10), while farther on are masterpieces by Ribera and Luca Giordano, aka *Luca fa presto* ("the fast worker"). In the dozen works displayed, Luca lives up to his nickname, somehow managing to match quantity with the very highest quality. In Room 103 there are more Giordanos, notably his picture of Saint Gennaro interceding for the victims of the 1656 Naples plague (which the artist himself would have witnessed, thus the gruesome realism of the greyish figures sprawled below).

On the top floor, a set of galleries features international contemporary art—including Andy Warhol's *Mount Vesuvius,* painted when the artist visited Naples in 1985—while the second floor holds extensive collections of 14th- to 19th-century Neapolitan painting and decorative arts, including plenty of dramatic renditions of Vesuvius in all its raging glory. When you've had your fill of these, take time to admire the genuine article from the vast and shady parkland outside, designed by Ferdinando Sanfelice and then adapted into the "natural" English style, which affords a sweeping view of the bay from a few outlooks. On weekends, you can rent bicycles (€3 per hour; ID required) by the Porta Piccola entrance to explore several circuits inside this large city park. You can get to the museum via Bus 24 from Piazza Municipio or Piazza Carità, or by Bus C57, R4, or C63 from outside the Archaeological Museum. ⊠ *Via Miano 2, Porta Piccola, Via Capodimonte, Capodimonte* ☎ *848/800288 for information and tickets for special exhibitions* ⌨ €7.50, after 2 pm €6.50 ⊗ Daily 8:30–7:30; ticket office closes at 6:30.

WORTH NOTING

Catacombe di San Gennaro. These catacombs—designed for Christian burial rather than as refuges—go at least as far back as the 2nd century AD. This was where St. Gennaro's body was brought from Pozzuoli in the 4th century, after which the catacombs became a key pilgrimage center. The 45-minute guided tour of the two-level site takes you down a series of vestibules with fine frescoed niche tombs. The imposing bulk of the early-20th-century church looms over the site (Madre del Buon Consiglio), apparently inspired by St. Peter's in Rome. ⊠ *Via Tondo di Capodimonte 13, next to Madonna del Buon Consiglio church, Capodimonte* ☎ *081/7441305* ⊕ *www.catacombedinapoli.it* ⌨ €8 (including Catacombe di Gaudioso plus reduction to Museo Diocesano within year, Tesoro di S. Gennaro within 3 days) ⊗ Guided tours Mon.–Sat., 10–5, Sun. 10–1.

Palazzo della Spagnolo. Built in 1738 for the Neapolitan aristocrat Marchese Moscati, this white and greenish palazzo is famed for its external "hawk-winged staircase," believed to follow the design of star architect Ferdinando Sanfelice and decorated with sumptuous stucco and ornately snug busts facing each other at each veering flight. The palace was at one point owned by a Spanish nobleman, Don Tommas Atienza, thus the name "della Spagnolo." In the left corner of the courtyard in the back, a nondescript metal door leads to a tunnel running all the way to Piazza Carlo III—another example of the Neapolitan underground. ⊠ *Via Vergini 19, Sanità* ⊗ Daily 7–7.

Santa Maria della Sanità. This baroque, Greek cross–shaped basilica, replete with majolica-tile dome, was commissioned by Dominican friars in the early 17th century. The church contains a small museum of 17th-century Counter-Reformation art—the most flagrantly devotional school of Catholic art—and includes no less than five Luca Giordano altarpieces. Elsewhere, the richly decorated elevated presbytery, complete with double staircase, provides the only note of color in the gray-and-white decoration. This also provides access to the noted Catacombe di San Gaudioso (daily, 10 to 1, hourly visits). ⊠ *Piazza Sanità 124, Sanità* ☎ *081/5441305* ⊕ *www.catacombedinapoli.it* ⊗ Mon.–Sat. 9:30–12:30 and 5–7:30, Sun. 9:30–12:30.

NEED A BREAK? In teeming Via dei Vergini, give in to temptation with a pastry from Pasticceria dei Vergini (⊠ *Via dei Vergini 66, Vergini* ☎ *081/455989*) to enjoy a truly calorie-bursting Neapolitan specialty. If you don't have a sweet tooth, pick up a sandwich from da Salvatore, a tiny snack bar next door.

WHERE TO EAT

Updated by Fiorella Squillante

Let's be honest: You really want a traditional Neapolitan dinner against the backdrop of Vesuvius with a great show of Neapolitan love songs to get you crying into your limoncello. There's no reason to feel guilty, because even the natives love to get into the spirit. But listening to

Neapolitan Folk Songs at Your Table

If you want to hear *canzoni napoletane*—the fabled Neapolitan folk songs—performed live, you can try to catch the city's top troupes, such as the Cantori di Posillipo and I Virtuosi di San Martino, in performances at venues like the Teatro Trianon. But an easier alternative is to head for one of the city's more traditional restaurants, such as La Bersagliera or Mimì alla Ferrovia, where most every night you can expect your meal to be interrupted by a *posteggiatore*. These singers aren't employed by the restaurants, but they're encouraged to come in, swan around the tables with a battered old guitar, and belt out classics such as "Santa Lucia," "O' Surdato Innamurato," "Torna a Surriento," and, inevitably, "Funiculì Funiculà."

These songs are the most famous of a vast repertoire that found international fame with the mass exodus of southern Italians to the United States in the early 20th century. "Funiculì Funiculà" was written by Peppino Turco and Luigi Denza in 1880 to herald the new funicular railway up Vesuvius. "O Sole Mio," by Giovanni Capurro and Eduardo di Capua, has often been mistakenly taken for the Italian national anthem. "Torna a Surriento" was composed by Ernesto de Curtis in 1903 to help remind the current Italian prime minister how wonderful he thought Sorrento was (and how many government subsidies he had promised the township).

The singers are more than happy to do requests, even inserting the name of your *innamorato* or *innamorata* into the song. When they've finished they'll stand discreetly by your table. Give them a few euros and you'll have friends for life (or at least for the night).

6

someone warble "Santa Lucia" while feasting on a pizza *Margherita* (with basil, mozzarella, and tomatoes) from a table overlooking the bay is just one example of the pleasures awaiting diners in Naples. From *vitello alla Principe di Napoli* (veal garnished with truffles) to sea bass in *acqua pazza*—that is to say, poached in water "maddened" with cherry tomatoes, parsley, garlic, *peperoncino*, and olive oil—to Neapolitan pastries like the light, fluffy, exotic *babà al Rhum,* the city expresses its gastronomic self in many ways. The *haute*-hungry should look elsewhere (particularly Ristorante Don Alfonso 1890 and the Torre del Saraceno, both just across the bay near Sorrento) and so should those in search of newer-than-now nouvelle flights of fantasy served on designer plates. Although these can be found, the cuisine in Naples is by and large earthy, pungent, and *buonissima,* as attested to by those signature dishes: *mozzarella in carrozza* (mozzarella cheese fried in a "carriage" of two slices of bread); *polpo alla luciana* (octopus stewed with garlic, chili peppers, and tomatoes); *risotto ai frutti di mare* (seafood risotto); and *spaghetti puttanesca* (streetwalker's spaghetti with black olives and capers in sea salt). In Naples it is still the old reliables that apply—the recipes time-tested by centuries of mammas who still manage to put meat on your bones and smiles on your faces.

This means pizzerias aplenty. As the birthplace of pizza, Naples prides itself on its vast selection of pizzerias, the most famous of which—Da

Michele (where Julia Roberts filmed her pizza scene in *Eat Pray Love*) or Sorbillo—deserve the encomium "incomparable." Many Neapolitans make lunch their big meal of the day, and then have a pizza for supper, with a late-night treat—*ogni tanto* (every now and then)—perhaps enjoying the light sea breezes out at Marechiaro accompanied by some of the Mediterranean's best produce, like at Da Cicciotto. Note that "pizzerias" in Naples does not simply mean the linoleum-floored, neon-lighted ones you'll find back in New York City—they range here from holes-in-the-wall to full-scale restaurants.

When it comes to *i secondi* (main dishes), you won't be disappointed by the *salsicce* (pork sausages), but the reason visitors to Naples want to eat seafood is a good one: geography. Naples's position, hugging a rich bay, has guaranteed that marine creatures feature prominently on local menus. Marinated seafood salad (*insalata di mare*) is a classic antipasto, as well as marinated anchovies (*alici*). Spaghetti *con le vongole veraci* (with clams, garlic, and a baby's fistful of chopped Italian parsley) is a popular and dependable standard, as are myriad variations on linguine or fresh pasta with mixed seafood (mussels, shrimp, clams, and so forth), usually "stained" with fresh cherry tomatoes. As for seafood Neapolitan style, the best—*spigola* (sea bass), *pesce spada* (swordfish), and, if you can find it, *San Pietro* (sort of a sole for grown-ups)—is grilled simply and ennobled with a splash of olive oil and a squeeze of lemon. When it's not on the menu—and many top delicacies are only available if you ask the waiter—go for the *pezzogna* (blue-spotted bream), as you can be almost sure it hasn't been fish-farmed. Fresh calamari, kissed lightly by a grill, can be exquisitely delicate, but the fried version, which can be uniquely satisfying, is, alas, too often done these days with frozen squid. Another good way to have fish is *all'acqua pazza* (literally, in crazy water), poached with cherry tomatoes, parsley, chili pepper and olive oil, a brew said to have been invented by returning fishermen using seawater to cook up a meal on the beach.

There isn't a surfeit of expensive, luxury restaurants in Naples: most Neapolitans will go out of town for a high-end restaurant meal, heading to gastronomic enclaves on the Sorrento peninsula or the Pozzuoli area, or opting for a feast at one of the private dining clubs that the Neapolitan aristocracy favors. That said, if you stay in town you're likely to be pleasantly surprised. Palazzo Petrucci in the old town opened to much fanfare in 2007 and offers palatal treats at reasonable prices—surrounded by late Renaissance elegance. Other new entries, Coco Loco and Radici, fill a quality niche in the more upmarket area of Chiaia, close to the waterfront and the Villa Comunale. Wherever you go, be prepared to deviate from the menu (locals rarely ask for one) and ask the waiter for the chef's special *piatto* (dish). At the lower end, service may be rough and ready, but then again, this is Naples, and you don't expect to be served by liveried waitstaff when your restaurant sits at the end of an alley. Note that many restaurants in Naples close for at least a week around August 15 to celebrate the Ferragosto holidays.

WHAT IT COSTS IN EUROS					o
	¢	$	$$	$$$	$$$$
AT DINNER	under €20	€20–€30	€30–€45	€45–€65	over €65

Prices are for a three-course meal (*primo, secondo,* and *dolce*), excluding wine.

CITY CENTER

Appropriately, the monumental city center environs feature Naples's most iconic restaurants.

$$ ✕ **Amici Miei.** A place favored by meat eaters who can't take another bite
SOUTHERN of sea bass, this small, dark, and cozy den is well loved for specials such
ITALIAN as tender carpaccio with fresh artichoke hearts, and a rice-and-arugula
★ dish featuring duck breast. There are also excellent pasta dishes, such as *orecchiette* with chickpeas or *alla barese* (with chewy green turnips), or that extravaganza, the *carnevale lasagne,* an especially rich concoction relied on to sustain revelers in the build up before Lent. Everyone finishes with a slice of chocolate and hazelnut *torta caprese.* ✉ *Via Monte di Dio 78, Chiaia* ☎ *081/7646063* ⌂ *Reservations essential* ▭ *AE, DC, MC, V* ◷ *Closed Mon. and July and Aug. No dinner Sun.* ✛ *D5.*

$$ ✕ **Brandi.** Forget that this historic place gave the world *pizza Margher-*
PIZZA *ita*—the classic combo of tomato sauce, mozzarella, and basil, named after King Umberto's queen. This is, hands down, one of the most picturesque restaurants in Italy. Set on a cobblestone alleyway just off chic Via Chiaia, it welcomes you with an enchanting wood-beam salon festooned with 19th-century memorabilia, saint shrines, gilded mirrors, and bouquets of flowers, beyond which you can see the kitchen and the *pizzaioli* (pizza makers) at work. That's the good news. Unfortunately, most of Naples stays away, considering the pizzas are far, far better elsewhere, and finding the service somewhat offhand. But there's no denying the decor is *delizioso* and if tourists like Chelsea Clinton, Bill Murray, and Gerard Depardieu have dined here, why not you? ✉ *Salita Sant'Anna di Palazzo 1, Piazza Municipio* ☎ *081/416928* ▭ *AE, DC, MC, V* ◷ *Closed Tues.* ✛ *D4.*

¢–$ ✕ **Cantina della Tofa.** Two blocks up one of the narrow alleys that lead off
NEAPOLITAN Via Toledo into the Quartieri Spagnoli, this small, welcoming restaurant
★ serves traditional Neapolitan fare that goes beyond standard pasta with seafood or tomatoes. Try the *vellutata di cicerchie,* a creamy soup made from beans that are a cross between chickpeas and fava beans, or a delicious mix of *contorni* (side dishes). ✉ *Vico Tofa 71, Piazza Municipio* ☎ *081/406840* ▭ *No credit cards* ◷ *Closed Sun. No dinner Mon.* ✛ *D3.*

$$ ✕ **Ciro a Santa Brigida.** Just off Via Toledo, Ciro has been an obligatory
NEAPOLITAN entry on any list of Neapolitan cooking (as opposed to cuisine) since 1932, when Toscanini and Pirandello used to eat here. Popular with business travelers, artists, and journalists, Ciro is famous for a wide variety of favorites, with an emphasis on rustic food, from very fine pizzas and justly famed versions of pasta *e fagioli* to the classic *sartù*—rice loaf first concocted by baroque-era nuns—and the splendid *pignatiello e vavella,* shellfish soup. The menu looks too large for all its items to be good, but the owners must be doing something right, as the place

6

is often packed with Neapolitan regulars. The old waiters are darling wherever you sit, but try to get a table upstairs, which has a more pleasant atmosphere. ⊠ *Via Santa Brigida 71, Toledo* ☎ *081/5524072* ⊕ *www.ciroasantabrigida.it* ⊟ *AE, DC, MC, V* ⊗ *Closed Sun. and last 2 wks in Aug.* ✛ *D4.*

$$ **✕ Trattoria San Ferdinando.** Almost the first doorway on the right as you
NEAPOLITAN go up Via Nardones from Piazza Trieste e Trento—ring the bell outside
★ to get let in—this cheerful trattoria is open in the evening only from Wednesday to Friday, with the fine intention of running a restaurant for the sheer pleasure of it. Try the excellent fish or the traditional (but cooked with a lighter modern touch) pasta dishes, especially those with *verdura,* fresh leaf vegetables, or those with potatoes and smoked mozzarella, *pasta e patate con la provola.* Close to the San Carlo Theater and aptly decorated with playbills and theatrical memorabilia both ancient and modern, this is an excellent place to stop after a visit to the opera. ⊠ *Via Nardones 117, Toledo* ☎ *081/421964* ⊟ *AE, DC, MC, V* ⊗ *Closed Sun. No dinner Sat.–Tues.* ✛ *D4.*

SPACCANAPOLI

Spaccanapoli is now one of *the* evening locations where *buona cucina* meets both low- and high-brow culture (what a change from 15 or 20 years ago, when it was a dark and dangerous part of town). The teeming alleyways and 17th-century palazzi house many inexpensive places to eat, which begin to fill up after 9 pm. For a classier restaurant, try Palazzo Petrucci on the main square of San Domenico Maggiore, at the very cultural heart of Spaccanapoli.

¢ **✕ Gino Sorbillo.** There are three restaurants called Sorbillo along Via
PIZZA dei Tribunali; this is the one with the crowds waiting outside. Order
★ the same thing the locals are here for: a basic Neapolitan pizza (try the unique pizza al pesto or the stunningly simple marinara—just tomatoes and oregano). They're cooked to perfection by the third generation of pizza makers who run the place. The pizzas are enormous, flopping over the edge of the plate onto the white marble tabletops. ⊠ *Via dei Tribunali 32, Spaccanapoli* ☎ *081/446643* ⊟ *AE, DC, MC, V* ⊗ *Closed Sun. (except Dec.) and 3 wks in Aug.* ✛ *E2.*

¢ **✕ I Decumani.** Every pizzeria along Via dei Tribunali is worth the long
PIZZA wait (all the good ones are jammed and you'll have to wait for a table)
★ and none more so than the Decumani, thanks to the superlative *pizzaioli* (pizza makers)—say hello to Gianni and Enzo for us—at work here. They turn out a wide array of pizzas and do them all to perfection. If you are not on a diet, try the *frittura* and you'll be pleasantly surprised with this mix of Neapolitan-style tempura: zucchini, eggplants, riceballs, and many other delicacies. ⊠ *Via dei Tribunali 58, Spaccanapoli* ☎ *081/5571309* ⊟ *No credit cards* ⊗ *Closed Mon. (except Dec.)* ✛ *E2.*

¢ **✕ La Campagnola.** This well-known trattoria–wine shop sees everyone
NEAPOLITAN from foodies to students and professors from the nearby university. The menu changes daily and there is always a good selection of pastas, meat, fish, and vegetable side dishes. Go for a plate of *pasta e fagioli* or octopus salad and fried anchovies with a carafe of a good local wine. ⊠ *Via Tribunali 47, Spaccanapoli* ☎ *081/459034* ⊟ *MC, V* ⊗ *Closed Sun. and Tues. No dinner Mon.* ✛ *E2.*

Continued on page 312

AN APPETITE FOR NAPLES

"But there's nothing to it!" cry food snobs when Neapolitan cuisine is mentioned among the higher rungs of the world's culinary ladder. And they might be right—after all, there are no secret spices or special skills needed in its preparation.

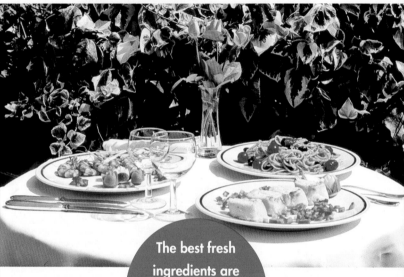

The best fresh ingredients are all you need when the local produce is this good

But indeed, simplicity is the key, and the best fresh ingredients are what Napoli has in spades. Long, fleshy, deep-red San Marzano tomatoes grow on the fertile slopes of Vesuvius. The olive groves of the Cilento provide fragrant oil. Buffalo chew the grass on the plains toward Caserta, north of Naples, producing milk that makes the best mozzarella cheese in the world. And Neapolitans have long used the fish-filled waters of the bay to their gastronomic advantage. Tiny fish are marinated, fried, and eaten whole, or used to flavor sauces. Swordfish are sliced up to make steaks. Clams, mussels, and octopus are ubiquitous, and usually enhanced with oil, lemon juice, garlic, and parsley, rather than masked with sauces.

With it all being so simple, you'd think you could replicate it at home. But it's never quite the same: perhaps it's that the water is different, or that you can never quite get the right variety of tomato. Or maybe it doesn't taste the same simply because you're not in Napoli anymore.

Classic Neapolitan dishes featuring the best of the sea and the field.

6

IN FOCUS THE SIMPLE GOODNESS OF NEAPOLITAN FOOD

PIZZA: THE CLASSIC MARGHERITA

Locally grown San Marzano tomatoes are a must.

The best pizza should come out with cheese bubbling and be ever-so-slightly charred around its edges.

Only buffalo-milk mozzarella or fior di latte cheese should be used.

The dough has to use the right kind of durum wheat flour and be left to rise for at least six hours.

Be prepared: ranging from the size of a plate to that of a Hummer wheel, Neapolitan pizza is pretty different from anything you might find elsewhere in Italy—not to mention what's served up at American pizza chains. The "purest" form is the marinara, topped with only tomatoes, garlic, oregano, and olive oil.

OTHER FAVORITES ARE . . .

■ **CAPRICCIOSA** (the "capricious"), made with whatever the chef has on hand.

■ **SICILIANA** with mozzarella and eggplant.

■ **DIAVOLA** with spicy salami.

■ **QUATTRO STAGIONE** ("four seasons"), made with produce from each one.

■ **SALSICCIA E FRIARIELLI** with sausage and a broccoli-like vegetable.

A PIZZA FIT FOR A QUEEN

Legend has it that during the patriotic fervor following Italian unification in the late 19th century, a Neapolitan chef decided to celebrate the arrival in the city of the new Italian queen Margherita by designing a pizza in her—and the country's—honor. He took red tomatoes, white mozzarella cheese, and a few leaves of fresh green basil—reflecting the three colors of the Italian flag—and gave birth to the modern pizza industry.

Margherita of Savoy

ONLY THE BEST

An association of Neapolitan pizza chefs has standardized the ingredients and methods that have to be used to make pizza certified DOC (*denominazione d'origine controllata*) or STG (*specialità tradizionale garantita*). See the illustration on the opposite page for the basic requirements.

Buffalo-milk mozzarella

FIRED UP!

The Neapolitan pizza must be made in a traditional wood-burning oven. Chunks of beech or maple are stacked up against the sides of the huge, tiled ovens, then shoved onto the slate base of the oven where they burn quickly at high temperatures. If you visit Pompeii, you will see how similar the old Roman bread-baking ovens are to the modern pizza oven. The *pizzaiolo* (pizza chef) then uses a long wooden paddle to put the pizza into the oven, where it cooks quickly.

A pizzaiolo at work

PIZZERIE

There are hundreds of restaurants that specialize in pizza in Naples, and the best of these make pizza and nothing else. As befits the original fast food, *pizzerie* tend to be simple, fairly basic places, with limited menu choices, and quick, occasionally brusque service: the less complicated your order, the happier the waiters.

Typical pizzeria in Naples

THE REAL THING

Naples takes its contribution to world cuisine seriously. The Associazione Verace Pizza Napoletana (www.pizzanapoletana.org) was founded in 1984 in order to share expertise, maintain quality levels, and provide courses for aspirant pizza chefs and pizza lovers. They also organize the annual Pizzafest—three days in September, dedicated to the consumption of pizza, when *maestri* from all over the region get together and cook off.

Simple, fresh toppings

6

IN FOCUS THE SIMPLE GOODNESS OF NEAPOLITAN FOOD

REMEMBRANCE OF THINGS PASTA . . .

Studded with clams, spaghetti con vongole is a top menu favorite.

While the most famous of Neapolitan foods can be eaten standing up, there is more to local cuisine than pizza. Don't even think about leaving without having tried these Napoli classics.

HOW SIMPLE IS NEAPOLITAN CUISINE?

Take a handful of tomatoes and squeeze them into a pan along with a drizzle of olive oil, a pinch of salt, and some fresh basil leaves. Leave them in just long enough to warm through. Boil some pasta for just as long as it needs. Put it all together, and you have pasta al pomodoro fresco, one of the most delicious dishes Italy has to offer. There really is nothing to it!

■ **SPAGHETTI CON LE VONGOLE:** spaghetti topped with different kinds of clams, from the tiny lupini to the big red fasullari, still in their shells.

■ **IMPEPATA DI COZZE:** mussels, thrown in a pot, heated up, and served with lots of fresh black pepper.

■ **BACCALÀ:** dried salt cod, fried and served with some fresh herbs. Once you try it, you'll understand why many Neapolitans regard it as the authentic taste of home.

■ **POLPETTINE AL RAGÙ:** meatballs in tomato sauce. Italian food's biggest export has never tasted as good as in Napoli.

■ **PESCE ALL'ACQUA PAZZA:** fish in "crazy water," with garlic, a few small tomatoes, then some of the water from the fish added to the hot oil. The bubbles are what make it "crazy."

■ **PARMIGIANA DI MELANZANE:** layers of eggplant, mozzarella, and tomato sauce baked in the oven.

■ **PASTA ALLA GENOVESE:** not from Genoa, as its name may suggest, but invented by a Neapolitan chef named Genovese. Onions are added to a ham bone and cooked for hours, then added to the pasta.

"POOR FOOD"

During the winter when the best fresh produce isn't so abundant, Neapolitans head for the store cupboard and soak large quantities of dried cannellini beans, chickpeas, and lentils. These are then made into hearty soups, to which any kind of pasta can be added. They're great as filling and warm dishes, but because *pasta fagioli*, *pasta ceci*, and *pasta lenticchie* are regarded as "poor food" (the kind of thing you make at home), they aren't often found on restaurant menus.

Baccalà alla vicentina, a traditional Italian codfish stew

LA FRITTURA

Forget all that stuff about the Mediterranean diet being so healthy. Lots of pizzerie and roadside stalls will offer you a selection of *frittura*—deep-fried balls of dough and seaweed, fried sliced eggplant, fried potato croquettes, fried zucchini flowers. Eat them with your fingers, and don't feel guilty.

Fried zucchini flowers

CAKE SEASON

Like everything else, cakes are seasonal. If you're visiting over Christmas, check out the teeth-challenging *rococò*, made of hazelnuts, or the softer *struffoli*, tiny balls of fried pastry doused in honey. Carnival time (mid-February to mid-March) is for *chiacchiere*—large, flat slices of light pastry sprinkled with icing sugar—while Easter sees rivalries for the best *pastiera*, a rich cake filled with ricotta, sifted grain, and orange or rose water. Around All Souls' Day (late October), cake shops fill up with *torrone* (soft or hard nougat). Two Napoli classics are, thankfully, available year-round: the large soft sponge *babà*, soaked in rum, and the *sfogliatella*, sweet and spicy ricotta cheese wrapped in short crust or puff pastry.

Divine pies and pasteria

LIMONCELLO

No serious meal is complete without a final *liquore*, and the local limoncello is the best of the lot. Made from the zest of lemons, lots of sugar, and pure alcohol, limoncello is very sweet, very strong, and must be served very cold.

Many brands of limoncello

U CAFFÈ

Whether to help you digest a big meal, give you a morning pickup, or accompany a cake, *u caffè* (to give coffee its name in the local dialect) is a Neapolitan rite. You can have it in its pure state, small and black with a teaspoonful of sugar, or order *nocciola* (with hazelnut syrup), *macchiato* (with a dash of frothy milk), or *corretto* (with a shot of liqueur) varieties. If you want to keep to local customs, never ask for a cappuccino after a meal. It's considered bad for digestion.

U caffè

¢–$ ✗ **La Cantina di Via Sapienza.** With
NEAPOLITAN a balanced array of mainly land-
based cuisine, owner-manager
Gaetano attracts students and
young professionals to this unpretentious eatery—mainly regulars
from the school of medicine round
the corner. It's busy and not big
enough (expect to share a table—
and if your fellow diners are not
shy, why should you be?), but the
prices can't be beat, and the daily

selection of a good dozen vegetable side plates merits a detour of its
own, even if you're not a vegetarian. ⊠ *Via Sapienza 40, Spaccanapoli*
☎ *081/459078* ▤ *No credit cards* ⊘ *Closed Sun. and Aug. No dinner*
✛ *E2.*

$ ✗ **La Vecchia Cantina.** On a rather dark side street in the tattier section
NEAPOLITAN of Spaccanapoli (the easiest access point is to head to Via Toledo 380),
this place is well worth seeking out for its combination of old-style Neapolitan hospitality and attention to the quality of its food and wine. The
place is run as a family affair, with Patrizia and Mimmo in the kitchen,
much like a typical Neapolitan household. The pasta with chickpeas
is a must, and *baccalà fritto* (fried salt cod) is a specialty. Backed up
with a selection of wines mainly from Campania, this place is a great
value. ⊠ *Via S. Nicola alla Carità 13–14, Spaccanapoli* ☎ *081/5520226*
▤ *MC, V* ⊘ *Closed 1 wk Aug. No dinner Sun.* ✛ *D3.*

¢–$ ✗ **Lombardi a Santa Chiara.** Right on Spaccanapoli opposite the Palazzo
PIZZA Croce, home to the philosopher and historian Benedetto Croce, this is
one of the city's most famous pizzerias, packed night after night. The
young crowd heads down into the more boisterous basement, while
the atmosphere upstairs is calmer and more congenial to conversation
at standard decibel levels. On the ground floor you can watch the *pizzaioli* working the pizza dough, manipulating each pie as if it were a
live creation. ⊠ *Via Benedetto Croce 59, Spaccanapoli* ☎ *081/5520780*
▤ *AE, MC, V* ⊘ *Closed last 3 wks in Aug.* ✛ *E2.*

$ ✗ **O' Munaciello.** Right on Piazza Gesù, this restaurant is a good place to
NEAPOLITAN sit outside, relax, and people-watch after a tour around Spaccanapoli.
It caters to diverse palates and budgets: pizzas are served here at lunchtime and there is a menu of small plates for €8. Alternatively, opt for
the single dish *linguine al coccio,* combining pasta with locally caught
fish. ⊠ *Piazza del Gesù Nuovo 26–27, Spaccanapoli* ☎ *081/5521144*
▤ *AE, DC, MC, V* ✛ *E2.*

$–$$ ✗ **Osteria da Carmela.** Conveniently close to the famous archaeologi-
ITALIAN cal museum, yet surprisingly off the tourist beat, this small eatery is
patronized by *professori* from the nearby Academy of Fine Arts and
theatergoers from the Teatro Bellini next door. A specialty here is the
blend of seafood with vegetables—try the *tubettoni con cozze e zucchini*
(tube-shape pasta with mussels and zucchini) or a *risotto mare e monti*
(garnished with prawns and mushrooms). The service is both swift and

obliging. ⊠ *Via Conte di Ruvo 11–12, Spaccanapoli* ☎ *081/5499738* ⊟ *AE, DC, MC, V* ☻ *No dinner Sun.* ✢ *E2.*

$$$
NEAPOLITAN
Fodor's Choice
★
✕**Palazzo Petrucci.** Nestled in a 17th-century mansion facing the grandeur of Piazza San Domenico Maggiore, Palazzo Petrucci doesn't lack for dramatic dining options. Choose between tables under the vaulted ceiling of the former stables, in the gallery where a glass partition lets you keep an eye on the kitchen, or in the cozy room overlooking the piazza, where the famous Guglia di San Domenico marble monument soars heavenward. Fortify yourself with a complimentary glass of prosecco before making the agonizing choice between the à la carte offerings and the *menu degustazione* (€45). A popular starter is *mille-feuille* of local mozzarella with raw prawns and vegetable sauce. The *paccheri all'impiedi* (large tube-shape pasta served standing up) in a rich ricotta and meat sauce is an interesting twist on an old regional favorite. The decor is elegantly minimal but the culinary delights found here are anything but. ⊠ *Piazza San Domenico Maggiore 4, Spaccanapoli* ☎ *081/5524068* ♧ *Reservations essential* ⊟ *AE, DC, MC, V* ☻ *Closed 3 wks in Aug. No dinner Sun., no lunch Mon.* ✢ *E2.*

$–$$
NEAPOLITAN
✕**Ristorante Bellini.** Worth visiting just to observe the waiters, who all seem to have just stepped off the stage of a Neapolitan comedy at the nearby Teatro Bellini, this spot claims a proud perch on the corner of the chicly bohemian Piazza Bellini. But if the neighborhood remains suave, this staple Neapolitan restaurant proudly retains its old-world feel. Good bets here include a fine (if rather small) pizza, and classic fish dishes such as linguine *al cartoccio* (baked in paper) or *all'astice* (a type of small lobster). Go up the narrow stairs to get to the spacious upper rooms, or squeeze in at one of the pavement tables in summer. ⊠ *Via Santa Maria di Costantinopoli 79, Spaccanapoli* ☎ *081/459774* ⊟ *DC, MC, V* ☻ *Closed 1 wk in Aug. No dinner Sun.* ✢ *E2.*

¢–$
NEAPOLITAN
★
✕**Timpani e Tempura.** A tiny shrine to local culinary culture with three small tables and bar-style counter, this place is worth the squeeze for its *timballi di maccheroni* (baked pasta cakes) and its unique *mangia-maccheroni*, spaghetti in broth with caciocavallo cheese, butter, basil, and pepper. High-quality wines by the glass make this a spot for a swift but excellent lunch. You can also buy cheese and salami to take home with you. ⊠ *Vico della Quercia 17, Spaccanapoli* ☎ *081/5512280* ⊟ *No credit cards* ☻ *Closed Aug. No dinner* ✢ *E2.*

THE PORT AND PIAZZA GARIBALDI

Forget waterfront restaurants and outdoor candlelighted terraces. This is an area noted for fine no-nonsense eating, with some of the city's most traditional restaurants offering excellent value for money. If returning to base after dark, stick to well-lighted main roads or ask one of the restaurant staff to order a taxi.

¢
PIZZA
Fodor's Choice
★
✕**Da Michele.** You have to love a place that has, for more than 130 years, offered only two types of pizza—marinara (with tomato, garlic, and oregano) and *margherita* (with tomato, mozzarella, and basil)—and a small selection of drinks, and still manages to attract long lines. The prices have something to do with it, but the pizza itself suffers no rivals, so even those waiting in line are good-humored; the boisterous, joyous atmosphere wafts out with the smell of yeast and wood smoke onto the

Where to Eat and Stay in Naples

A   **B**   **C**   **D**

TO
CAPODIMONTE

Via Materdei

Corso Amedeo di Savoia

Via Matteo Renato Imbrinani

Salita S. Raffaele

V. S. Teresa degli Scalzi

Via Gracinio

Vico Nocelle
Via S. Mandato

Via S. Giuseppi dei Nudi

Via U. Nutta

Via G. Orsi

V. Battistello Caraccidio

Via Salvator Rosa

Via Salvator Rosa

Via F. S. Carrera (Cavone)

□ La Controra

Via Salvator Tommasi

P.
Med D'oro

Santacroce

P.
Leonardo

Girolamo

Salita Pontecorvo

Megaron

P. Dante

Via Ventaglieri

Salita Tarsia

Vaco 'e Press

Via M. Fiore

Viale Michelangelo

Viale Raffaello

Corso Vitt. Emanuele

Via Tarsia

VOMERO

Via G.L. Bernini

Metropolitana Collinate

Montesanto Ⓜ

Stazione Cumana

Via Solimente

Via F. Cilea

FUNICOLARE DI MONTESANTO

Via Tito Angelini

Via Pasquale Scura

Via F. Girardi

La Vecchia Cantina

Via Roma

Trattoria Vanvitelli ■

Osteria Donna Teresa ■

Via A. Scarlatti

Via R. Morghen

FERROVIE CUMANA

La Cantina di Sica ■

Ambrosino ■

QUARTIERI SPAGNOLI

Via Cimarosa

Acunzo ■

Friggitoria Vomero ■

San Francesco al Monte □

Toledo

Via Luigia

FUNICOLARE DI CHIAIA

FUNICOLARE CENTRALE

Via E. De Dio

Il Convento ■

Via Roma

Via Toledo

Villa Floridiana

Sanfelice

Emanuele

Cantina della Tofa ■

Ciro a Santa Brigida ■

Via Filippo Palizzi

Grand Hotel Parker's
Corso Vittorio

L.u.i.s.e. ■

Ⓜ
Amadeo

Via del Parco

Trattoria S. Ferdinando ■

Margherita

Corso Vittorio Emanuele

P. Amedeo

L'Ebbrezza di Noè ■

P.
Trieste e Trento

Via Nardones

Via F. Crispi

V. Campiglione
G. Martucci

Via dei Mille

Brandi ■

Chiaja Hotel de Charme

Pinto
Storey

Majestic □

CHIAIA

Via Ascensione

Via G. Bausan

Coco Loco ■

Via
Chiaia

Pza. dei
Martiri

Cappella Vecchia

P. del Plebiscito

Trattoria dell'Oca ■

Via S. Pasquale a Chiaia

Via Carducci

La Focaccia ■

Palazzo
Alabardieri

11 □

Amici Miei ■

Via Solitaria

■ **Da Dora**
■ **'A Fenestella**
■ **Da Ciccotto**
■ **La Mescita**

Umberto ■

Via Carlo Poerio

Radici ■

Riviera di Chiaia

Via Morelli

Via Monte di Dio

PIZZOFALCONE

Tunnel Vittoria

Villa Comunale

P.
Vittoria
Parteno □

Via Chiatamone

SANTA LUCIA

Marino ■

Via San

□ **Ausonia**
■ **La Cantina di Triunfo**

Via Caracciolo

Grand
Hotel
Vesuvio

La Terrazza

Excelsior

← TO POSILLIPO

← TO MERGELLINA

B&B ■
Chiatamone

Via

Partenop

Golfo di Napoli

I Re di Napoli ■

Hotel Santa Lucia

Castel del Ovo

Trattoria Castel dell'Ovo ■

A   **B**   **C**   **D**

street. At almost all times there is a wait for a table, and now more than ever, since Julia Roberts filmed the pizza scene from *Eat, Pray, Love* right here. So step right up to get a number at the door and then hang outside until it's called. Note: The restaurant is off Corso Umberto, between Piazza Garibaldi and Piazza Nicola Amore. ⊠ *Via Sersale 1/3, Piazza Garibaldi* ☎ *081/5539204* ⊟ *No credit cards* ⊗ *Closed Sun. and 2 wks in Aug.* ✛ *G2.*

$–$$ ✕**La Taverna dell'Arte.** As its name suggests, this gracious trattoria on a
NEAPOLITAN small side street near Naples' main university is popular with actors, but it manages to remain welcomingly low-key. Warmed with touches of wood, it prides itself on its fresh interpretations of Neapolitan classics: excellent salami, mozzarella, and *frittura* (fried vegetables) among the appetizers, cabbage soup fragrant with good beef stock, and meat and fish grilled over wood. Typical Neapolitan desserts, such as babas and the familiar crunchy almond cookies called *quaresimali,* are served with homemade liqueurs. ⊠ *Rampe San Giovanni Maggiore 1/a, Port* ☎ *081/5527558* ⌂ *Reservations essential* ⊟ *MC, V* ⊗ *Closed Sun. and last 2 wks in Aug. No lunch* ✛ *F3.*

$$ ✕**Mimì alla Ferrovia.** Clients of this Neapolitan institution have included
NEAPOLITAN Fellini and that magnificent true-Neapolitan comic genius and aristo-
★ crat, Totò. Mimì manages to live up cheerfully to its history, proudly serving fine versions of everything from pasta *e fagioli* (with beans) to the sea bass *al presidente,* baked in a pastry crust and enjoyed by any number of Italian presidents on their visits to Naples. Not so much a place to see and be seen as a common ground where both the famous and the unknown can mingle, feast, and be of good cheer, Mimì's sober beige-and-green hues, accented with updated art deco features, pale yellow tablecloths, and retro bentwood chairs, pleasantly tone down the bustle. Given the fairly seedy neighborhood, splurge on a taxi there and back especially at night. ⊠ *Via A. D'Aragona 19/21, Piazza Garib-aldi* ☎ *081/289004* ⊕ *www.mimiallaferrovia.com* ⊟ *AE, DC, MC, V* ⊗ *Closed Sun. (except Dec.) and last 2 wks in Aug.* ✛ *G1.*

¢ ✕**Trianon.** Across the street from its archrival Da Michele—and without
PIZZA the lines outside—this is a classic pizzeria with a simple ambience in soothing tile and marble. More relaxed and upmarket than its rival, Tri-anon does the classics (Margherita, marinara) in an exemplary manner, but you can also feast on pizza with sausage and *friarielli* (Campanian broccoli), while the signature pizza Trianon comes with eight different toppings. ⊠ *Via P. Coletta 46, Piazza Garibaldi* ☎ *081/5539426* ⊟ *No credit cards* ✛ *G2.*

SANTA LUCIA AND CHIAIA

While Santa Lucia is a classic choice for both chic and touristy fish restaurants with that just-how-you-imagined-Naples sea view, the upscale area of Chiaia is a favorite with both locals and discerning expatriates and is likely to offer better value. If you are looking for an international cuisine, there is a wide choice in Via Bausan. Along this tiny road off the Riviera di Chiaia, you'll find Spanish, Mexican, Greek and French restaurants sometimes with some Neapolitan influences. You can have a proper meal or just snack on something to get a taste from different countries.

Caffè Gambrinus, across from the Palazzo Reale, is the most famous coffeehouse in town.

$$$
NEAPOLITAN
★

✕ **Coco Loco.** This place has taken the Naples dining scene by storm, thanks to the innovative cuisine of master chef Diego Nuzzo, a stylish ambience, and a quiet location off Via Filangieri, a 10-minute walk from the Palazzo Reale. If possible, take a table in the more-spacious outdoor section in the square, and then be pampered with subtle dishes like *insalata di aragosta e gamberi alla catalana* (lobster and prawn salad garnished with citrus). ⊠ *Piazzetta Rodinò 31, Chiaia* ☎ *081/415482* ▭ *AE, MC, V* ⊙ *Closed Sun. and 3 wks in Aug. No lunch July–Sept.* ✛ *C5.*

$$$
NEAPOLITAN
Fodor's Choice
★

✕ **Da Dora.** Despite its location up an unpromising-looking *vicolo* (alley) off the Riviera di Chiaia, this small restaurant has achieved cult status for its seafood platters. It's remarkable what owner-chef Giovanni can produce in his tiny kitchen. Start with the pasta dish linguine *alla Dora,* laden with local seafood and fresh tomatoes, and perhaps follow up with grilled *pezzogna* (blue-spotted bream). Like many restaurants on the seafront, Dora has its own guitarist, who is often robustly accompanied by the kitchen staff. ⊠ *Via Fernando Palasciano 30, Chiaia* ☎ *081/680519* ⚜ *Reservations essential* ▭ *AE, DC, MC, V* ⊙ *Closed Sun., 2 wks in Dec., and 2 wks in mid-Aug.* ✛ *B5.*

$$
PIZZA

✕ **I Re di Napoli.** With its inviting blue-and-green custom-tile interior and tables set along the seafront drive, this chic pizzeria is an essential hangout for Naples' gilded youth—so if you want better service and are not interested in fashion statements, go early evening and avoid peak times like weekends when Via Partenope is positively heaving. Thirty kinds of pizza plus a fine selection of salads and an ample buffet make the place a refreshing change from the more minimal *pizzerie*. The various stuffed pizzas named after kings are classics with a modern twist:

try the *Boccone di Re Ferdinando,* filled with *speck* (lean cured pork), *provola* cheese, and artichokes. ⊠ *Via Partenope 29/30, Santa Lucia* 🕾 *081/7647775* ▭ *MC, V* ✛ *D6.*

$$　╳ **Il Transatlantico.** Within the picturesque Borgo Marinaro harbor, in
NEAPOLITAN　the shadow of Castel dell'Ovo (foodies should note this was the site of the Roman villa of Lucullus, the moneyed aristocrat famous for his passion for luxurious dining) it is as if you were eating aboard a Transatlantic cruise ship. With the Bay of Naples setting and Vesuvius the backdrop, you can understand the nautical decor, blue tablecloths, and the menu abrim with fish delicacies. A best bet is the *schiaffoni* with *astice* and *pescatrice* (large flat tube pasta with lobster and angler fish), or one of the tasty pizzas, but leave room for the *dolce* of the day (great homemade tiramisu or pear cake with ricotta). If, after one too many limoncellos, you feel like crashing just head upstairs in this make-believe ocean liner and book one of the bright and airy guest rooms in this newly opened hotel. ⊠ *Via Luculliana 15, Borgo Marinaro, Santa Lucia* 🕾 *081/7648842* ▭ *AE, DC, MC, V* ☾ *Closed Tues. from Nov. to Apr.* ✛ *D6.*

$$$$　╳ **La Terrazza.** The Hotel Excelsior's Terrazza attracts A-list stars visiting
ITALIAN　the area with its Pompeian-red marble floorings and brown leather fur-
★　nishings (all aimed at highlighting the gold cutlery, *capisce?*). A breath-taking buffet counts as an appetizer (but would be a banquet in itself for mere mortals), while the à la carte menu creates a fusion of Italian regional culinary styles. Dress up, and expect to be impressed. ⊠ *Hotel Excelsior, Via Partenope 48, Santa Lucia* 🕾 *081/7640111* ▭ *AE, DC, MC, V* ✛ *D6.*

$　╳ **L'Ebbrezza di Noè.** A small bar leads into a larger dining area decorated
ITALIAN　in the style of a very elegant farmhouse. Owner Luca has an enthusi-
★　asm for what he does that is quite moving—as you sip a recommended wine you can sense that he hopes you like it as much as he does. The attention paid to the quality of the wine carries over to the food—here you can taste delicate *carpaccio di chianina* (thinly sliced Tuscan steak), rare cheeses such as the Sicilian *ragusano di razza modicana* and the local *caciocavallo podolico,* and a daily selection of hot dishes. ⊠ *Vico Vetriera a Chiaia 8b/9, Chiaia* 🕾 *081/400104* ▭ *AE, DC, MC, V* ☾ *Closed Mon. No lunch* ✛ *C4.*

¢–$　╳ **Marino.** Just around the corner from the Borgo Marinaro and the
PIZZA　Hotel Vesuvio, this famous pizzeria offers up its delights in a cool white-and-blue room. Try the house specialty, the Santa Anastasia, with cherry tomatoes and lots of premium mozzarella. A wide sidewalk and partial pedestrianization of Via Santa Lucia make this a pleasant outdoor venue in summer. ⊠ *Via Santa Lucia 118/120, Santa Lucia* 🕾 *081/7640280* ▭ *AE, MC, V* ☾ *Closed Mon. and 2 wks in Aug.* ✛ *D5.*

$$$　╳ **Radici.** Combining low-key elegance with well-tried combinations
NEAPOLITAN　of Mediterranean cuisine, Radici is one of Naples's best restaurants.
Fodor's Choice　Among a cluster of restaurants set on Naples's busy Riviera di Chiaia, it
★　affords views of the leafy gardens of the Villa Comunale but your atten-tion will be taken at once by the master of ceremonies, Agostino, as he steers you through the elaborate choices on offer. Dishes invariably taste as good as they sound, as this fine pasta favorite, *ravioli di ricotta di*

bufala profumata al limone e vongole veraci (ravioli filled with lemon-scented buffalo ricotta, served with clams). Or should it be the delicate *riso giallo sauté ai frutti di mare e crostacei, verdurine di stagione* (rice garnished with sea food and fresh greens)? With all the delights on offer here, you could easily be forgiven for indecision. Dessert? You can't go wrong with the cannolo filled with a mousse of lemon-flavored ricotta cheese. ⊠ *Riviera di Chiaia 268, Chiaia* ☎ *081/2481100* ⊟ *AE, MC, V* ☽ *No lunch except Sat. and Sun.* ✢ *C5.*

$ ✕ **Trattoria Castel dell'Ovo — Tabacchi.** If you're trying to keep to a budget
NEAPOLITAN   but want to enjoy the splash-out of a seafood feast side by side with the yachts of the Borgo Marinaro harbor, head to this *tabaccaio,* or former tobacco store. Although your eyes feast on all the pretty boats, the Lungomare hotels, the Castel dell'Ovo, and Vesuvius, your tongue can savor classic Neapolitan seafood spaghetti or an *impepata di cozze* (mussels with pepper and garlic). Or just opt for the special made with the fish of the day. ⊠ *Borgo Marinaro, Santa Lucia* ☎ *081/7646352* ☽ *Closed Thurs., and from October to March. No dinner Sun.* ✢ *D6.*

$–$$ ✕ **Trattoria dell'Oca.** The bright, clean, simple decor reflects this place's
NEAPOLITAN   lighter take on occasionally heavy Neapolitan food, also echoed in the younger crowds who pack this place on weekends. The soupy pasta *e piselli* (with peas) is a wonderful surprise for anyone who has bad memories of pea soup, while the penne *alla scarpariello* (pasta quills with fresh tomato, basil, and pecorino cheese) is a specialty to set the taste buds quivering. ⊠ *Via S. Teresa a Chiaia 11, Chiaia* ☎ *081/414865* ⊟ *AE, MC, V* ☽ *Closed Aug. and Sun. June–Sept. No dinner Sun. Oct.–May* ✢ *B5.*

$–$$ ✕ **Umberto.** Run by the Di Porzio family since 1916, Umberto is one of
NEAPOLITAN   the city's classic restaurants. It combines the classiness of the Chiaia
★   neighborhood and the friendliness of other parts of the city. Try the *tubettini 'do tre dita* ("three-finger" pasta with a mixture of seafood), which bears the nickname of the original Umberto. Owner Massimo and sister Lorella (Umberto's grandchildren) are both wine experts and oversee a fantastic cellar. Umberto is also one of the few restaurants in the city that caters to those who have a gluten allergy. ⊠ *Via Alabardieri 30–31, Chiaia* ☎ *081/418555* ⊕ *www.umberto.it* ⊟ *AE, DC, MC, V* ☽ *Closed Mon. and 3 wks in Aug.* ✢ *C5.*

MERGELLINA AND POSILLIPO

These ritzy bay-side suburbs feature some of the most popular restaurants in Naples. Several of these spots are found at the end of waterfront cul-de-sacs, so unless you have your own wheels, taxis will be the most convenient option.

$$–$$$ ✕ **'A Fenestella.** This restaurant is picturesquely perched over a beach in
NEAPOLITAN   Posillipo near the end of a long winding side road, and has long capitalized on its location. The landmark comes with its own legend: The story goes that in the 19th century any Juliet would promise herself simply by appearing at the window ("fenestella" in the local dialect) to the Romeo sailing in the boat below, thus inspiring the famous Neapolitan folk song. Today, the restaurant is blatantly traditional, with a comfortable decor and the usual suspects on the menu. (For more stylish food and people, and better value for money, head across the road

to Da Cicciotto.) ⊠ *Calata del Ponticello a Marechiaro 23, Posillipo* ☎ *081/7690020* ▤ *AE, MC, V* ⊙ *Closed Tues.* ✛ *A5.*

$$$
NEAPOLITAN
★

✕ **Da Cicciotto.** One of Naples's best-kept secrets, this chic and charming spot corrals more than a few members of the city's fashionable set—there's a fair chance you'll find a Neapolitan count or off-duty film star enjoying this jewel. A tiny stone terrace overlooks a pleasant anchorage, centered on an antique column, with seats and canopy exquisitely upholstered in blue-and-white matching-but-mixing fabrics. You can appreciate the outdoor setting at either lunch or dinner, and don't even bother with a menu—just start digging into the sublime antipasti and go with the waiter's suggestions. ■TIP➔ Cicciotto is at the end of the same long winding road that leads to the famed 'A Fenestella restaurant and shoreline, so phone for the restaurant's free shuttle service if starting out from the city center. ⊠ *Calata del Ponticello a Marechiaro 32, Posillipo* ☎ *081/5751165* ⌦ *Reservations essential* ▤ *AE, DC, MC, V* ✛ *A5.*

$$
NEAPOLITAN

✕ **La Cantina di Triunfo.** Founded by Carmine Triunfo in 1890 and now run by great-grandson Antonio (who looks after the wines) and his mother Tina (who looks after the kitchen), this place has recently made a successful bid to move upmarket. Well-prepared *cucina povera* ("poor people's food") still dominates, from the antipasto of hot peppers, salami, and cheese to the famous *vermicelli alle vongole fujute* (pasta with "escaped" clams, flavored with a dose of seawater). Dinners here are fixed price (€30), there's no written menu, and choice is limited to two dishes of the day. ⊠ *Riviera di Chiaia 64, Mergellina* ☎ *081/668101* ⌦ *Reservations essential* ▤ *DC, V* ⊙ *Closed Sun. and Aug. No lunch* ✛ *A5.*

$$
NEAPOLITAN
★

✕ **La Mescita.** Close to Cape Posillipo and a short walk from the Parco Virgiliano, this trattoria-cum-pizzeria is a good place for a wintertime plate of fresh seafood like *spaghetti ai ricci* (spaghetti with sea urchins) or a land-based *paccheri alla Genovese* (pasta garnished with an onion and meat sauce). Rather noisy outside tables—it's near the end of the C21, C31, 140 bus routes—make this more of a winter and evening venue, with pleasing alcoves inside for greater privacy. ⊠ *Discesa Coroglio 88, Posillipo* ☎ *081/5983375* ⌦ *Reservations essential* ▤ *AE, DC, MC, V* ⊙ *Closed Mon.* ✛ *A5.*

VOMERO

Sitting on top of the hill, the wealthy residential Vomero doesn't look like the first place you'd pick to eat out in. However, if you've been on a shopping spree on Via Scarlatti or taking in the Castel Sant'Elmo, you could do worse than stick around for a bite. Absence of tourists means that there are still a few stalwart places frequented by locals.

¢–$
PIZZA

✕ **Acunzo.** If you see a line of hungry-looking patrons near the top station of the Chiaia Funicular, you'll know you are close to Pizzeria Acunzo. To avoid anxious waits, many like to get here as soon as it opens for the busier evening session at 7:30. When ordering, note that few variations on the pizzas are permitted; but then owner Michele and his wife Caterina have been running the establishment since 1964 and have a tried-and-tested product. The house specialty, pizza Acunzo, comes replete with a daunting list of ingredients, but ends up being *fenomenale.* ✉ *Via Cimarosa 60–62, Vomero* ☎ *081/5785362* ⊟ *AE, MC, V* ☾ *Closed Sun. and 3 wks in Aug.* ⊕ *B3.*

$$ ✕**La Cantina di Sica.** This rustically elegant trattoria serves variants on
NEAPOLITAN traditional faves: the *tubettoni al pesce spada* (small pasta tubes with succulent pieces of swordfish), *peperoni imbottiti* (peppers stuffed with bread crumbs, olives, and capers), and the *parmigiana di melanzane* (layers of tomato, eggplant, and mozzarella baked in the oven) are all excellent. The kitchen's take on the traditional Neapolitan *pastiera* is as good as, if not better than, anybody's mamma ever made it. ✉ *Via Bernini 17, Vomero* ☎ *081/5567520* ☾ *AE, DC, MC, V* ☾ *Closed Mon. and 2 wks in Aug.* ⊕ *B3.*

¢ ✕**Osteria Donna Teresa.** Donna Teresa has managed to keep a piece of
NEAPOLITAN old-style Napoli alive on the otherwise modern and unspectacular Via Kerbaker. A tiny place, this restaurant is always full of clients who are treated like children (and that means being encouraged, if not actually forced, to eat everything on their plates). Patrons flock here at lunchtime, in particular for a fill of classic *pasta e fagioli* (with beans), *pasta e ceci* (with chickpeas), or solid helpings of fried anchovies or baccalà (salt cod). ✉ *Via Kerbaker 58, Vomero* ☎ *081/5567070* ⊟ *No credit cards* ☾ *Closed Sun. and Aug.* ⊕ *B3.*

$ ✕**Trattoria Vanvitelli.** A small low-key entrance on Piazza Vanvitelli opens
ITALIAN into a labyrinth of underground cellars and a large covered courtyard surrounded by palazzos. This bustling eatery suits both a wide range of palates and budgets: pizzas and several variants of *filletto* (fillet steak) are highly recommended. Portions are large, so be conservative when ordering. ✉ *Piazza Vanvitelli 9/c, Vomero* ☎ *081/5563015* ⊟ *AE, DC, MC, V* ⊕ *B3.*

FOOD ON THE GO

If you get caught up in the chaotic head-spinning atmosphere of downtown Napoli, you might not even be able to sit still for an hour to eat. If so, follow the locals and indulge in some of the delicious quick snacks that Neapolitans have dreamed up to assuage hunger in a short time and at a low price. Many of Naples' specialties can be consumed while standing up—a fantastic advantage if you've got little time or money.

¢ ✕**Ambrosino.** Once they opened for business, the owners of this grocery
NEAPOLITAN store quickly realized that people were eating the produce as soon as it was handed to them so they added a counter. Now you can take your pick from the pizzas and pasta dishes, or ask the owners to make up a *panino* (sandwich) by choosing the ingredients from the huge range of excellent cheeses, vegetables, and meats on display. A uniformly excellent quality of ingredients makes up for the rather spartan surroundings. ✉ *Via Scarlatti 49, Vomero* ☎ *081/3721170* ⊟ *AE, DC, MC, V* ☾ *Closed Sun. in July and Aug., and 3 wks in Aug.* ⊕ *B3.*

¢ ✕**Friggitoria Pizzeria Giuliano.** A favorite place of students from the adja-
PIZZA cent school of architecture, Giuliano has an old-style glass cabinet in which are kept *arancini* (balls of fried rice) the size of tennis balls, and deep-fried pizzas filled with mozzarella, tomato, prosciutto, or ricotta, that can fill that yawning void in your stomach—even if you have to

sit down on the steps in the square afterward to recover. ⊠ *Calata Trinità Maggiore 31–33, Spaccanapoli* ☎ *081/5510906* ▭ *No credit cards* ✛ *E3.*

¢ ✕ **Friggitoria Vomero.** Popular with kids heading home from school, this

NEAPOLITAN   spot also often draws guilty-looking adults attracted by its greasy brown

★   paper bags filled with deep-fried eggplant, zucchini, zucchini flowers, *zeppole* dough balls, or potato croquets—the Neapolitan versions of Proust's madeleines. Forget all that stuff about the Mediterranean diet being so healthy and indulge in some oil-drenched bliss. ⊠ *Via Cimarosa 44, Vomero* ☎ *081/5783130* ▭ *No credit cards* ⊘ *Closed Sun. and Aug.* ✛ *B3.*

¢ ✕ **La Focaccia.** While the flat, pan-cooked focaccia is enough to make

ITALIAN   pizza fundamentalists wince (coming as it does from Rome), this place makes mouthwatering slices of crunchy-bottomed snacks with a variety of toppings. Skip the predictable tomato variations and go for the delicious potato-and-rosemary focaccia with melted provola (smoked mozzarella). Washed down with a beer, this makes for a great speedy lunch or late-night snack. ⊠ *Vico Belledonne a Chaia 31, Chiaia* ☎ *081/412277* ▭ *No credit cards* ✛ *C5.*

¢ ✕ **L.u.i.s.e.** Elbow your way through the crowds at lunchtime, point to

NEAPOLITAN   what you want in the tempting glass counter, and pay for it at the cash desk. If you're lucky you'll get a seat, but if not you can still enjoy the usual *frittura* (fried dough balls and potato croquets stuffed with mozzarella), the tangy cheese pies (*sfoglino al formaggio*), the pizza *scarola* (an escarole pie with black olives), or slices of omelets stuffed with spinach, peppers, or onions. The immaculately liveried waiters aren't polite, but they are quick. ⊠ *Via Toledo 266–269, Toledo* ☎ *081/415367* ▭ *No credit cards* ✛ *D4.*

¢ ✕ **Vaco 'e Press.** Stoke up here before or after your visit to the Museo

NEAPOLITAN   Archeologico, a five-minute walk away. This busy eatery close to the metro station in Piazza Dante has a bewildering variety of hot meals, pizzas, vegetable pies and rolls, and even has seating at the back. As usual in this type of establishment, pay at the *cassa* before you eat. ⊠ *Piazza Dante 87, Spaccanapoli* ☎ *081/5499424* ▭ *No credit cards* ✛ *D2.*

CAFFÈ AND COFFEE

Naples is ground zero for coffee lovers. Espresso was invented here and is still considered by the Neapolitans to be an essential and priceless part of their cultural patrimony (the word *espresso,* by the way, should probably be understood here in its meaning "pressed out," rather than the more common interpretation of "quick"). For many cognoscenti, Naples has the best coffee in the world. Almost any bar you walk into, no matter how dingy or how close to the train station, is likely to serve up an espresso that would make any Malibu hot spot wilt in envy.

Even Italian bars (meaning coffee bars) are generally tied to, as English pubs once were with brewers, a coffee roaster–distributor. The sponsoring brand is indicated with a sign on the outside, so you can choose your bar by looking for the sign of your favorite brand. Brands tend to be highly regional; the most widely advertised Neapolitan brand is

Kimbo, but Moreno, Salimbene, and Tico are considered far superior by the cognoscenti. Some small, family-run caffè still roast their own.

You won't find any double low-fat mochas with extra vanilla here, though there are certain permitted variations: *corretto*, with a shot of grappa or the local moonshine thrown in; *al vetro*, in a glass; *macchiato*, "stained" with a burst of steamed milk; and, of course, cappuccino. On the whole, coffee is a Neapolitan sacred ritual with precise rules. Cappuccino, for instance, is essentially a breakfast beverage, accepted in the afternoon with a pastry but looked strangely at after a meal (they claim it's bad for the liver). Many Italians like to order a glass of water (*bicchiere d'acqua*) with their coffee as a chaser. As for flavor coffees, Neapolitans, like all Italians, stubbornly believe that you only add flavorings to coffee to hide imperfections in the original grind. Coffee is perhaps the one feature of life in which Neapolitans don't gild the lily. Why fix what works?

CHIAIA

This fashionable district offers a moveable feast of tempting coffeehouses.

If you want to taste a coffee made in Naples but with an international up-to-the-minute look, head to **Anèlo Caffè** (⊠ *Via C. Poerio 47, Chiaia* ☎ *081/7645764*) Sit at one of the minimalist-style tables, or stand at the bar, as you sip the blend (created in Naples in 1930) and scan the with-it Chiaia crowd. Lunch and dinner (try the spaghetti with codfish) are available but you can just come to check your e-mail (there's Wi-Fi) while having a good glass of wine and creative tapas. A fave with Via Chiaia shoppers is **Bar Guida** (⊠ *Via Dei Mille 46, Chiaia* ☎ *081/426570*), which offers you not only the luxury of being able to sit down, but also has a decent range of savory light meals. The most famous coffeehouse in town is the **Caffè Gambrinus** (⊠ *Via Chiaia 1/2, Chiaia* ☎ *081/417582*), catercorner to the Palazzo Reale across the Piazza Trieste e Trento. Founded in 1850, this 19th-century jewel functioned as a brilliant intellectual salon in its heyday but has unfortunately fallen into a Sunset Boulevard–type existence, relying on past glamour, at the mercy of tourists and their pitiless cameras, and with often-indifferent service. However, the opening and renovation of some of its long-closed inside rooms, replete with amazing mirrored walls and gilded ceilings, still makes it an essential stop for any visitor to the city. **La Caffetteria** (⊠ *Piazza dei Martiri 30, Chiaia* ☎ *081/7644243*) is a classic address in the chic Chiaia district, and it has a second space in Vomero. Both addresses sell their famous coffee-flavor chocolates in the shape of tiny coffeepots. You may find it more worthwhile to continue along the Via Chiaia shopping street with its fashionable clothes shops as far as **La Torteria** (⊠ *Via Filangieri 75, Chiaia* ☎ *081/405221*) not only for its excellent coffee but also for its selection of beautiful-looking cakes—concoctions of cream, chocolate, and fruit that look like Abstract Expressionist paintings with their swirls of color. Near the southern border of the Chiaia district is the Borgo Marinaro waterfront, where **Megaride** (⊠ *Via Borgo Marinaro 1, Santa Lucia* ☎ *081/7645300*), on the port under the shadow of the Castel dell'Ovo, provides a romantic outdoor setting for a coffee or aperitif.

SPACCANAPOLI

Piazza Bellini, in the historic Spaccanapoli area, also contains a gaggle of good and hip caffè, *and almost any of the pastry shops listed below will have excellent coffee.*

Between the famed archaeological museum and the Academy of Fine Arts, the **Caffè Liberty** (⊠ *Galleria Principe di Napoli 6, Spaccanapoli* ☎ *081/5640814*) is ensconced in a scenic 19th-century glass and cast-iron arcade, built when the Stile Liberty, or Art Nouveau, was all the rage. A surprisingly quiet spot to have breakfast, sandwich, or salad this wicker-chair literary coffee shop retains some of the charm of yesteryear, for it not only has a useful Wi-Fi hotspot but also has a bevy of lovely books to peruse.

Gran Caffè Aragonese (⊠ *Piazza San Domenico Maggiore 5, Spaccanapoli* ☎ *081/5528740*) offers a fine coffee in the heart of historic Spaccanapoli: Sit out on the Piazza San Domenico or inside in the elegant tearoom with its marble-top tables.

PASTRY AND GELATO SHOPS

On the whole, Neapolitan pastry tends to suffer from the excesses that mark most southern Italian desserts: Falstaffian enthusiasm rather than precision in technique, ricotta clogging up everything, sentimental glops of glaze, and effusive dousings of perfumed syrups (one local specialty, babà al rhum, often succumbs to this last vice). But the Neapolitan tradition of pastry is an old and venerable one, and the most classic local invention in matters of *pasticceria* (pastry making), the *sfogliatella,* is a true baroque masterpiece, with puff pastry cut on a bias and wrapped around a nugget of cinnamon-sugar ricotta to form a simple but intricate shell. These are best eaten hot, and they are easy to find in Naples this way. For a hot-out-of-the-oven morsel as soon as you get off the train, **Attanasio** (⊠ *Vico Ferrovia 2, Piazza Garibaldi* ☎ *081/285675*), hidden away off Piazza Garibaldi, is justifiably famous.

CHIAIA AND MERGELLINA

Both set near the Lungomare, the chic Chiaia quarter and the pretty residential district of Mergellina have places any Willy Wonka would love.

Connoisseurs will say the most refined pastry in town can be found at **Gran Caffè Cimmino** (⊠ *Via G. Filangieri 12/13, Chiaia* ☎ *081/418303*). Most of the city's many lawyers congregate here, to celebrate or commiserate with crisp, light cannoli; airy lemon eclairs; *choux* paste in the form of a mushroom laced with chocolate whipped cream; and delightful wild-strawberry tartlets. Among the good pastry shops in the upscale Chiaia neighborhood is **Moccia** (⊠ *Via San Pasquale a Chiaia 21, Chiaia* ☎ *081/411348*). This is often said to be the finest pasticceria in the city, and it has great babas (decorated, should you wish, with whipped cream and wild strawberries) and an out-of-this-world pound cake injected with just the right dose of intense lemon curd. All these addresses will have exemplary ice cream as well, but you may prefer a more informal setting. Just off Via Gramsci, a five-minute walk west of the Villa Comunale and the American Consulate, is the highly rated gelateria **Remy** (⊠ *Via F. Galiani 29/A, Mergellina* ☎ *081/667304*). If

Sfogliatelle are a classic Neapolitan pastry—gourmands point out that the trick in eating this multilayered wonder is to enjoy it while it is hot.

you're going to abandon your low-cholesterol diet, this is definitely the place to do it, preferably with a selection of their *semi-freddi* (a cross between ice cream and mousse).

SPACCANAPOLI/TOLEDO

The charming historic quarter and the bustling city center are both studded with spots custom-made for indulging your sweet tooth.

Cioccolateria Perzechella (✉ *Vico Pallonetto a S. Chiara 36, Spaccanapoli* ☎ *081/5510025*) looks set to challenge Gay Odin's supremacy in the chocolate world. How can it not, since owners Pina and Giulia have rather shamelessly devised the *Tre Re* ("three kings")—three hazelnuts stuck together with chocolate in honor of King Ferdinand II, revolutionary Masaniello, and Naples' unofficial saint, the soccer player Diego Maradona. They just may tip the scales with their *Torna a Surriento*—Sorrento orange peel dipped in dark chocolate.

A small alleyway leading off the side of the Gesù Nuovo toward Via Toledo hides a little-known jewel that is worth the detour: **Gallucci** (✉ *Via Cisterna dell'Olio 6, Spaccanapoli* ☎ *081/5513148*), founded in 1890, specializes in fruit-filled chocolates (the cherry and grape are memorable) and also produces a delightfully original local cult item, chestnuts filled with marsala. It also produces the most fantastically packaged Easter eggs, all with huge silver or gold bows, that you are ever likely to see.

Chocolate lovers will be relieved to know that **Gay Odin** (✉ *Via Toledo 214, Toledo* ☎ *081/400063* ⊕ *www.gay-odin.it*), Naples' most famous *cioccolateria*, has several stores around town, all recognizable by their inviting dark-wood Art Nouveau decor; try the signature chocolate forest cake (*foresta*) or their unusual "naked" chocolates (*nudi*), a suave mixture of chestnuts and walnuts, some with a whole coffee bean wrapped in the center. The branch store at Via B.Croce 61, in the Spacca, sells delicious gelato, too. The excellent **La Sfogliatella Mary** (⊠ *Galleria Umberto 66, Toledo* ☎ *081/402218*), just at the Via Toledo entrance to the Galleria Umberto, offers a broader array of pastries than the name suggests. The classic address for sfogliatelle is **Pintauro** (⊠ *Via Toledo 275, Toledo* ☎ *081/417339*). **Scaturchio** (⊠ *Piazza San Domenico Maggiore 19, Spaccanapoli* ☎ *081/5516944*) is the essential Neapolitan pastry shop. Although the coffee is top-of-the-line and the ice cream and

pastries quite good—including the specialty, the *ministeriale,* a pert chocolate cake whipped with rum-cream filling—it's the atmosphere that counts here (though not the luxe, it's a rather unprepossessing sort of place). In the heart of Spaccanapoli, it's where nuns, punks, businesspeople, and housewives commune on the good things they all have in common.

WHERE TO STAY

Updated by
Martin Wilmot
Bennett

For a long time, staying in Naples meant gritting your teeth and praying your credit card could stand the cost of one of the impressive seafront landmarks—or risking one of the gloomy little hostels crowded around the Piazza Garibaldi railway station. Fortunately, the options have greatly improved over recent years, with the addition of a great many new places to stay, from top-end hideaways to simple, family-run B&Bs and *pensioni*. Usually small and intimate, and often set in historic palazzi, these hotels are often marked by the personal touch, hospitality in the case of Naples rising to an art form. But whether you're in a five-star hotel or a more modest establishment, you may enjoy one of the greatest pleasures of all: Rooms with a view—and not just *any* view, but the lay-down-and-die panorama of the Bay of Naples and Vesuvius. Often best provided for in hotels along the waterside Lungomare, be sure to ask for a bay-side room if your hotel can provide one—though be warned that *"camere panoramiche"* often cost more than regular rooms.

Since Naples is not known for peace and quiet, it's good news that it features a bevy of hotels that deliver exactly that—most accommodations are cool and tranquil sanctums, with the emphasis on cool, for many of its hotels do offer some of the strongest air-conditioning around (when making reservations, be sure to inquire if there is a supplement for air-conditioning). Bear in mind that high seasons in Naples are really the "shoulder seasons" elsewhere—April to June and September to October—so be sure to book well in advance if visiting then.

WHAT IT COSTS IN EUROS					
	¢	$	$$	$$$	$$$$
FOR TWO PEOPLE	under €75	€75–€125	€125–€200	€200–€300	over €300

Prices are for two people in a standard double room in high season including tax and service.

LUNGOMARE AND SANTA LUCIA

This prominent stretch of seacoast, with an unsurpassed view of the Bay of Naples, naturally has the greatest concentration of luxury hotels in the city, although more reasonable lodging is available on the side streets.

$$ ★ **Chiaja Hotel de Charme.** No views, but there's plenty of atmosphere in these converted first-floor apartments that occupy a spruce 18th-century palazzo. In fact, part of this establishment includes a converted historic brothel. Above the fireplace in the cozy entrance hall, the distinguished-looking chap with the moustache in the painting is the Marchese Nicola Le Caldano Sasso III, original owner of the building, whose granddaughter Mimi now runs the place. Antiques, many of them original to the Marquis's home, give a personal touch to the elegant guest rooms (most have whirlpool baths and some are named after the Marchese's favorite relatives). Toward the back is a section that once was a converted historic brothel (with names after the ladies who once occupied them). The location is tops, a two-minute walk from Piazza Plebiscito and the Royal Palace and a stagger from the liveliest nightlife in town in the backstreets around Piazza dei Martiri. **Pros:** central location on bustling; pedestrians-only street. **Cons:** small rooms get hot in summer (a/c notwithstanding); on second floor of historic palazzo (elevator was recently renovated). ⊠ *Via Chiaia 216* ☎ *081/415555* ⊕ *www.hotelchiaia.it* ⇆ *27 rooms* ⚒ *In-room: safe, Internet. In-hotel: bar* ⊟ *AE, MC, V* ⦿ *BP* ✛ *D4.*

$$$$ **Excelsior.** A swarm of maharajahs, emperors, and Hollywood legends has stayed at this hotel, a grand-tradition outpost since 1909. The exterior is awash in elegant detail, while the interior is a symphony of soaring columns, gilded French doors, and Venetian chandeliers. Today the hotel caters to corporate chiefs, its ballrooms host company meetings, and the breakfast is delicious. Discreet but attentive service gives the hotel a personal touch—if you even want to hire a yacht, the concierge can oblige. After a day of sightseeing, repair to the peaceful piano bar, where the barman mixes the driest martini in town—ask for a Hemingway. Decorated with corporate-looking leather chairs and colored marbles, the restaurant La Terrazza serves first-rate food, and the terrace with sweeping views of the bay makes summer dining out a memorable event. **Pros:** great views from the breakfast room and the rooftop terrace; spacious rooms; new soundproofing keeps out traffic

Hotel Palazzo Decumani

Grand Hotel Vesuvio

Costantinopoli 104

noise. **Cons:** the busy road outside is a challenge to cross; decor feels a little dated. ⊠ *Via Partenope 48, Santa Lucia* ☎ *081/7640111* ⊕ *www. excelsior.it* ⤴ *123 rooms, 12 suites* ⚐ *In-hotel: 1 restaurant, bar, gym, Internet terminal, parking (paid)* ⊟ *AE, DC, MC, V* ⟨◯⟩ *BP* ⊹ *D6.*

$$$–$$$$
Fodor's Choice
★
🏨 **Grand Hotel Vesuvio.** You'd never guess from the modern exterior that this is the oldest of Naples' great seafront hotels—the place where Enrico Caruso died, Oscar Wilde escaped with lover Lord Alfred Douglas, and Bill Clinton charmed the waitresses. Fortunately, the spacious, soothing interior compensates for what's lacking on the outside. Guest rooms are done in luxurious, traditional style with antique accents, vibrantly colored walls, and gleaming bathrooms. The best ones overlook the bay. You can pamper yourself at the spa, where there are myriad special services (though they come at a price). The famous Caruso restaurant sits atop the hotel, affording wonderful views. **Pros:** luxurious atmosphere; historic setting; location directly opposite Borgo Marinaro. **Cons:** extra charge for health club and Internet use; reception staff can be snooty; not all rooms have great views. ⊠ *Via Partenope 45, Santa Lucia* ☎ *081/7640044* ⊕ *www.vesuvio.it* ⤴ *146 rooms, 17 suites* ⚐ *In-room: safe, refrigerator, Internet. In-hotel: restaurant, bar, gym, spa, Internet terminal, parking (paid)* ⊟ *AE, DC, MC, V* ⟨◯⟩ *BP* ⊹ *D6.*

$$$$
★
🏨 **Hotel Santa Lucia.** Neopolitan enchantment can be yours if you stay here, for right outside your window will be the port immortalized in the song "Santa Lucia," bobbing with hundreds of boats, lined with seafood restaurants, and backed by the medieval Castel dell'Ovo. Even if your room doesn't have this bay-side view, you're likely to be impressed by the hotel's luxurious, quietly understated polish. The lobby is aglow with antiques, chandeliers, and full-length portraits of Neapolitan aristocrats. The comfortable guest rooms are traditional, if somewhat bland (and some are small for the price), but some bathrooms are equipped with whirlpool bath. Just off the lobby, the restaurant Megaris is a good spot for luxe hotel dining. **Pros:** great views; close to the main port, so convenient for trips to the islands and along the coast. **Cons:** rooms disappointingly boxy; the entrance is on the busy Via Partenope. ⊠ *Via Partenope 46, Santa Lucia* ☎ *081/7640666* ⊕ *www.santalucia. it* ⤴ *95 rooms* ⚐ *In-room: Wi-Fi. In-hotel: restaurant, bar* ⊟ *AE, DC, MC, V* ⟨◯⟩ *BP* ⊹ *D6.*

$–$$
Fodor's Choice
★
🏨 **Il Transatlantico Napoli.** Enjoying perhaps the most enchanting setting in all of Naples, this new modestly priced hotel recently opened and has promptly zoomed to the top of most travelers' dream list of places to stay. Perched in one of the harbor buildings of the Borgo Marinaro toy-sized harbor, directly within the shadow of the fabled Castel del'Ovo medieval fortress, this hotel offers guest rooms that are fitted out in yacht style: all blue and white, with swab-the-decks gleaming wood trim, they stand no comparison directly out the windows to vistas over the harbor, the Lungomare, and even the grand panorama of Vesuvius at the end of the bay (a view folks paying $2,000 can't even enjoy at the luxury hotels just across the pier on the mainland). On top of all this is the superior restaurant (see our separate review) aboard. All in all, it's almost like having your own luxury yacht. **Pros:** fabulous location; gentle prices. **Cons:** rather cheap and ugly hotel furniture. ⊠ *Via Luculliana*

15, Santa Lucia ☎ *081/768842* ⊕ *www.transatlanticonapoli.com* ➾ *8 rooms* ♿ *In-room: a/c, safe, refrigerator, Internet. In-hotel: restaurant, bar, Internet terminal* ▤ *AE, MC, V* ✢ *E6.*

$$–$$$ 🏨 **Parteno.** Undoubtedly proud of their premier address—"No. 1" on
★ Naples's main waterfront street—welcoming owner Alex Ponzi has installed an exclusive and elegant bed-and-breakfast near the Villa Comunale, five minutes from Castel dell'Ovo and 15 from the hydrofoils to the bay islands. Named after flowers, the surprisingly quiet rooms are tastefully decorated with period etchings and gouache views of Naples. One looks onto the bay; the others face a side street, fortunately removed from the swirling traffic on the bay-side avenue. Breakfast (served in your bedroom if you wish) is the real treat here—one of a tempting range of specialty Neapolitan pastries will accompany your caffè. **Pros:** in the five-star neighborhood, without the five-star price; friendly, helpful staff. **Cons:** except for the "Azalea" room (with a twin balcony onto the bay and islands beyond), rooms are neither large nor light. ⊠ *Via Partenope 1, Santa Lucia* ☎ *081/2452095* ⊕ *www.parteno. it* ➾ *6 rooms* ♿ *In-room: a/c. In-hotel: room service, Wi-Fi hotspot* ▤ *AE, DC, MC, V* ⛨ *BP* ✢ *C5.*

PIAZZA GARIBALDI TO LA SANITÀ

Hardly the nicest or most interesting part of town to stay in, the Piazza Garibaldi area is noisy and edgy. It's handy if you have to get an early train in the morning, but otherwise you're better off putting some distance between you and the central station.

$ 🏨 **Alloggio del Conte.** Down from Piazza Garibaldi, then off from Corso Umberto, with a left turn at the Santa Maria della Scala church, and then a right turn, this B&B can be difficult to find. Once there, however, a warm Neapolitan welcome is assured. Simply furnished guest rooms go hand-in-hand with the economical price. Just up from the bustling markets selling anything from fresh fish to thirdhand shoes the B&B is well placed for the main station hub of Pizza Garibaldi. **Pros:** quiet; computer connection in hallway. **Cons:** dodgy TV; no breakfast or safe; a tendency for the otherwise very hospitable hosts to go occasionally AWOL. ⊠ *Via Salaiolo all'Orto del Conte 27, Piazza Garibaldi* ☎ *081/200322* ⊕ *www.alloggiodelconte.com* ➾ *12 rooms* ♿ *In-room: a/c. In-hotel: Internet* ▤ *AE, DC, MC, V* ⛨ *EP* ✢ *G2.*

$–$$ 🏨 **Del Real Orto Botanico.** Near Naples's noted botanical gardens, this 18th-century building has been turned into a spacious hotel, an eightminute taxi ride from the airport and a short bus ride from the bustling center of town. Front guest rooms are noisy if you leave the balcony window open, but they face the gorgeous tropical gardens of the Orto Botanico; a better bet may be the back, particularly on summer nights. All rooms are spacious, decorated in stylish, soothing greens and beiges but the real stunner is the fabulous roof terrace with views over the gardens and the Sanità right up to Capodimonte. **Pros:** near the Archaeological Museum; some rooms overlook the botanical gardens. **Cons:** pretty far from other attractions; noisy location. ⊠ *Via Foria 192, Carlo III* ☎ *081/4421528* ⊕ *www.hotelrealortobotanico.it* ➾ *36 rooms* ♿ *In-room: Internet. In-hotel: restaurant, bar* ▤ *AE, DC, MC, V* ⛨ *BP* ✢ *F1.*

$ ⌂**La Casa del Monacone.** It's not every day you can be a "guest" of a famed 17th-century church but this distinctive B&B was once part of the giant complex of Santa Maria della Sanità, the main landmark of the Rione Sanità quarter. Before visions of gilded frescoes pop into view, this church is Franciscan and this hotel's decor would please the spartan taste of their saints. Happily, the place is warmed up with modern majolica flooring, art photographs of Sanità street life, a "floorshow" of tiles decorated with lotto numbers, Presepe figures, and a beautiful terrace. Guest rooms, however, remain minimal modern. La Sanità can be a rough district but this church casts a peaceful halo and La Casa is genteelly located at the far west border of the quarter, on a scooter-strummed byway (double-pane windows cut down on all the noise). **Pros:** dynamic and friendly staff. **Cons:** Sanità quarter; small bathrooms; no intercom so need to call just before entering the hotel or enter via back of church. ⊠ *Via Sanità 124, Carlo III* ☎ *081/7441305* ⊕ *www.casadelmonacone.it* ⬏ *6 rooms* ♿ *In-hotel: Internet terminal (paid)* ⊟ *No credit cards* ◎*BP* ✢*D1*

SPACCANAPOLI AND PIAZZA MUNICIPIO

Spaccanapoli is Naples's most picturesque quarter, so if you're looking for classic Neapolitan atmosphere, this is the place to roost. The flip side of the coin is the nearby area around Piazza Municipio; it's the bustling heart of the modern city, and it has a collection of upscale, large-capacity business hotels, along with some delightful finds housed in historic buildings.

$$ ⌂**Caravaggio.** In a 17th-century palazzo on a tiny square behind the Duomo, this place takes its name from the painter of the amazing *Sette Opere della Misericordia* altarpiece, which can be seen in the chapel opposite. Spaccanapoli's first "modernist" hotel, it's atmospherically furnished with blocks of volcanic stone in the entrance hall, while the guest rooms (some of which include a Jacuzzi, others with hydromassage) are all refreshingly light and airy. **Pros:** fine location for sightseeing. **Cons:** in an old building with smallish rooms; just across Via Duomo from Spaccanapoli so a bit "on the wrong side of the tracks." ⊠*Piazza Riario Sforza 157, Spaccanapoli* ☎*081/2110066* ⊕*www. caravaggiohotel.it* ⬏*15 rooms* ♿*In-hotel: bar, Internet terminal* ⊟*AE, DC, MC, V* ◎*BP* ✢*F2.*

$$$ ⌂**Costantinopoli 104.** An oasis of what Italians call *Stile Liberty* (Art
Fodor'sChoice Nouveau style), with impressive colorful glass fittings, this calm and
★ elegant hotel is well placed between the Museo Archeologico Nazionale and Spaccanapoli. Each room is individually decorated. Ask for a room with a balcony in the warmer months and enjoy your breakfast alfresco, or opt for one of the garden rooms that open onto the small swimming pool. **Pros:** swimming pool (a rarity in Neapolitan hotels) and garden; pleasant service. **Cons:** can be difficult to find from street (look for the sign saying Villa Spinelli, the name of the original building). ⊠ *Via Costantinopoli 104, Spaccanapoli* ☎*081/5571035* ⊕*www.costantinopoli104.com* ⬏*19 rooms* ♿*In-room: safe, refrigerator, Internet. In-hotel: bar, pool, laundry service, parking (paid)* ⊟*AE, DC, MC, V* ◎*BP* ✢*E2.*

6

$–$$ 🖼 **Golden Hotel.** Opened in January 2010 this "techno-style" hotel is one of the most plugged-in in the city. The decor is minimal chic, with guest rooms done up in steel grays, night blacks, and rich purples. Lack of a view is compensated by large flat-screen TV (with foreign channels available) and Wi-Fi connection in every room. Downstairs is an equally chic breakfast room, replete with Lucite chairs, plus a sleek bar, so drinks or snacks are available around the clock. A five-minute stroll to Spaccanapoli, it is also just a short walk to the Molo Beverello and the Castel Nuovo/Via Toledo downtown quarter, making this in the middle of things while being out of the whirlwind. **Pros:** state-of-the-art tech facilities; polite and obliging multilingual staff; safe large enough to store a laptop. **Cons:** lack of views from rooms. ⊠ *Via dei Fiorentini 51, Spaccanapoli, Piazza Municipio* ☎ *081/2514192* 🛏 *15 rooms* 🕭 *In-room: a/c. In-hotel: bar, parking (paid)* ⊟ *AE, DC, MC, V* ⦿| *BP* ✛ *E4.*

$$–$$$ 🖼 **Hotel Palazzo Decumani.** Opened in 2008, the Decumani is a wel-
Fodor's Choice come addition to the small list of higher-end hotels in Spaccanapoli.
★ The design here is pleasingly contemporary—no heavy, ornate furnishings, but instead an emphasis on light and space (both in short supply in old Naples). The services and professional approach are on a par with the grander hotels on the seafront or the Corso Vittorio Emanuele. The Decumani is a great choice for comfortable lodgings in the heart of classic Napoli. **Pros:** well located for both transportation links and sightseeing; large rooms and bathrooms; soundproofed windows. **Cons:** the location on a side street can be hard to find—(follow signs from Corso Umberto). ⊠ *Piazzetta Fortunato Giustino 8, Spaccanapoli* ☎ *081/4201379* ⊕ *www.palazzodecumani.com* 🛏 *28 rooms* 🕭 *In-room: Wi-Fi. In-hotel: restaurant, bar* ⊟ *MC, V* ⦿| *BP* ✛ *F2.*

$$ 🖼 **Il Convento.** In a 17th-century palazzo tucked away in the (sometimes
★ dicey) Quartieri Spagnoli, Il Convento is close to Via Toledo. Guest rooms are small but elegant, with original architectural features such as arched or beamed ceilings. They are decorated in simple, modern Mediterranean style. Two junior suites have private roof gardens. **Pros:** close to cafés and shops; free Internet access; warm Neapolitan reception and pleasantly personal touch. **Cons:** church bells may wake you in the morning; on a busy street; tiny lobby. ⊠ *Via Speranzella 137/A, Toledo* ☎ *081/403977* ⊕ *www.hotelilconvento.com* 🛏 *12 rooms, 2 suites* 🕭 *In-room: refrigerator. In-hotel: bar, Internet terminal* ⊟ *AE, MC, V* ⦿| *BP* ✛ *D4.*

$$–$$$ 🖼 **Mediterraneo.** This large, modern, efficient business hotel is within walking distance of both the Teatro San Carlo and Spaccanapoli. The entire lobby area is dressed in nouveau Mediterranean colors, and the guest rooms are similarly attractive. A nice plus here is the beautiful roof garden. **Pros:** convenient to the port; attractive rooftop breakfast terrace. **Cons:** restaurant food is mediocre. ⊠ *Via Nuova Ponte di Tappia 25, Toledo* ☎ *081/7970001* ⊕ *www.mediterraneonapoli.com* 🛏 *256 rooms* 🕭 *In-room: Internet. In-hotel: restaurant, bar* ⊟ *DC, MC, V* ⦿| *BP* ✛ *E4.*

$ 🖼 **Megaron.** This very upmarket B&B looks down on Piazza Dante, where the statue of the poet rises sublimely above the traffic and seems to approve all the secondhand bookstalls here (the square is a bibliophile's paradise). Four of the hotel's very spacious rooms flank a narrow courtyard so they suffer from a lack of light but this is made up for by large flat-screen TVs (and a radiant breakfast area). One room over the street has plenty of light plus excellent soundproofing against noisy Via Toledo. The room called Karpathos has a spacious mezzanine-type interior (living room downstairs, sleeping area above) so highly suitable for families. **Pros:** polite staff; simply but tastefully furnished; good computer and TV facilities; hotel well placed for both Spaccanapoli and the historic center. **Cons:** no views in four rooms. ⊠ *Piazza Dante 89, Spaccanapoli, Piazza Municipio* ☎ *081/5446109* ⊕ *www.megaron.na.it* 🛏 *5 rooms* ♿ *In-room: a/c. In-hotel: Internet terminal (paid)* ⊟ *AE, DC, MC, V* ⦿⎮ *BP* ✛ *D2.*

$$ 🛏 **Mercure Napoli Angioino.** In the heart of town, right off Piazza Municipio in the shadows of the famed Castel Nuovo, and close to the Teatro San Carlo, this popular hotel with a sober yet luminous lobby and quiet, tastefully appointed guest rooms is a good choice if you're taking a boat from the nearby Molo Beverello. **Pros:** good location near the port and sights; newly renovated rooms. **Cons:** on a busy road; less character and charm than many Naples hotels. ⊠ *Via De Pretis 123, Toledo* ☎ *081/5529500* ⊕ *www.mercure.com* 🛏 *85 rooms* ♿ *In-room: a/c, refrigerator, Wi-Fi. In-hotel: restaurant, Internet terminal (paid)* ⊟ *AE, DC, MC, V* ⦿⎮ *BP* ✛ *E4.*

$-$$ 🛏 **Neapolis.** On a narrow alley off the humming Via Tribunali close to Piazza Bellini, this relatively new hotel looks out over the 13th-century Pietrasanta bell tower. A mix of modern and traditional style furnishings, with a terra-cotta floor, make this a good bet if you want to stay in the Spacca, Naples's fascinating medieval center. **Pros:** great location in the heart of the *centro storico.* **Cons:** difficult to find (follow signs from Via Tribunali); a closed window won't always keep out the roar of passing scooters. ⊠ *Via Francesco Del Giudice 13, Spaccanapoli* ☎ *081/4420815* 🖷 *081/4420819* ⊕ *www.hotelneapolis.com* 🛏 *24 rooms* ♿ *In-room: Internet. In-hotel: bar, parking (paid)* ⊟ *AE, DC, MC, V* ⦿⎮ *BP* ✛ *E2.*

$$ 🛏 **Palazzo Turchini.** Adjacent from the impressive *fontana di Nettuno,* ★ just a few minutes' walk from the Castel Nuovo, Palazzo Turchini is one of the more-attractive smaller hotels in the city center. Its location is an 18th-century building, and the elegant design mixes historical styles, as seen in the combination of marble floors and piperno stairs throughout the hotel. Guest rooms are small but surprisingly quiet (with soundproofing newly fitted) despite being on a busy street, and many offer views over the roofs and domes of the old town. **Pros:** good location for centro storico and the port; more intimate than neighboring business hotels. **Cons:** fee for Internet in room, but free Wi-Fi and Internet area. ⊠ *Via Medina 21, Toledo* ☎ *081/5510606* ⊕ *www.palazzoturchini.it* 🛏 *27 rooms* ♿ *In-room: safe, Internet. In-hotel: bar, Internet terminal (free), Wi-Fi hotspot* ⊟ *AE, DC, MC, V* ⦿⎮ *BP* ✛ *E4.*

$$ 🛏 **Toledo.** A centuries-old palazzo has been tastefully transformed into this boutique hotel, a two-minute walk up from Via Toledo, near Spaccanapoli and the Royal Palace. Guest rooms are furnished in a pleasing rustic style, while the leafy rooftop terrace provides a quintessentially

6

Neapolitan backdrop for your breakfast. **Pros:** convenient location for Via Toledo shopping; great views from the roof garden over Certosa di S. Martino. **Cons:** rooms are small; by foot, it's a steep walk up Via Montecalvario. ⊠ *Via Montecalvario 15, Toledo* ☎ *081/406800* ⊕ *www.hoteltoledo.com* ↪ *18 rooms* ⬧ *In-room: a/c, refrigerator, Wi-Fi. In-hotel: bar, Internet terminal (paid)* ☰ *AE, DC, MC, V* ⦿ *BP* ✛ *D3.*

CHIAIA, VOMERO, AND POSILLIPO

Chiaia is the ritziest residential neighborhood of Naples, studded with 19th-century mansions and an elegant shopping district bordering the Villa Comunale gardens by the water. Above Chiaia rises the Vomero hill, offering great vistas of the bay. The bay-side atmosphere continues at Mergellina, a transportation hub set at the far western end of the Riviera di Chiaia, and beyond at the suburban coastal district of Posillipo.

$ 🏨 **Ausonia.** The spic-and-span rooms of this hotel are decorated in a nautical motif, giving it a homey feel. In the courtyard of a building on the waterfront at Mergellina, this is quite handy if you're taking a boat from the Mergellina pier. On the other hand, perhaps this is why some guests have said they suffer from cabin fever after staying here a few nights—the constant presence of boats and windows like portholes may have you thinking you're onboard a ship. **Pros:** one of the few hotels in the Mergellina area; away from the hubbub of the center and convenient to the port. **Cons:** located inside a larger palazzo—make sure you have the address written down. ⊠ *Via Caracciolo 11, Mergellina,* ☎ *081/682278* ⊕ *www.hotelausonianapoli.com* ↪ *20 rooms* ⬧ *In-hotel: bar, Internet terminal (paid)* ☰ *AE, MC, V* ⦿ *BP* ✛ *A5.*

$ 🏨 **Cappella Vecchia 11.** One of the city's outstanding budget options lies
Fodor's Choice just a stone's throw from the Platinum Card square of Naples, Piazza dei
★ Martiri, now colonized by the likes of Cartier, Ferragamo, and Versace. Protected from the city hubbub by being set on a quiet, cobblestoned street (and in a building with an even quieter courtyard), this small B&B has six amply sized guest rooms decorated in a breezily modern way: Ikea colors, contemporary furnishings, and paintings by local mod artists. **Pros:** fabulous location off chic Martiri square; friendly staff. **Cons:** lack of room phones; prefers cash payment. ⊠ *Vicolo Santa Maria a Capella Vecchia 11, Chiaia* ☎ *081/2405117* ⊕ *www.cappellavecchia11. it* ⬧ *In-room: no phone. In-hotel: Internet terminal (free), Wi-Fi hotspot (paid)* ☰ *AE, MC, V* ⦿ *BP* ✛ *C5.*

$$$–$$$$ 🏨 **Grand Hotel Parker's.** Set midway up the Vomero hill, this land-
Fodor's Choice mark hotel (whose doors first opened in 1870) continues to serve up
★ a supremely elegant dose of old-style atmosphere. It welcomes visiting VIPs, ranging from rock stars to Russian leaders, who probably enjoy the hotel decor, an homage to the Neoclassical style, brought to Naples by Napoléon and his general Joachim Murat. Gilt-trimmed Empire bureaus, shimmering chandeliers, fluted pilasters, and ornate ceilings all glitter. A bit of a walk from its funicular stops, the hotel's perch offers fine views of the bay and distant Capri. Drink it all in from the superb rooftop-garden "George's" restaurant, which proffers regional specialties. **Pros:** the excellent restaurant; fabulous views. **Cons:** a very, very long walk or taxi ride from city center and seafront;

not quite as grand as it once was. ✉ *Corso Vittorio Emanuele 135, Vomero* ☎ *081/7612474* ⊕ *www.grandhotelparkers.com* ➭ *83 rooms* ⌂ *In-room: a/c, refrigerator, safe, Wi-Fi. In-hotel: restaurant, bar, parking (paid)* ☰ *AE, DC, MC, V* ⦿ *BP* ✢ *C4.*

¢   ⊞ **La Controra.** You get a unique experience here, at what is probably the cheapest place to stay in the city. Originally a monastery, but recently turned into what the owners modestly describe as a "backpackers' hostel," the Controra provides its own entertainment: it hosts film showings, art exhibitions, alternative conferences, and themed parties. There are only a few private rooms, but if you have a spirit of adventure and like meeting others, the kitsch retro-designed dorms here offer the perfect place to do so. **Pros:** the energetic, arty, funky vibe; international clientele. **Cons:** don't expect the facilities of a luxury hotel; location is slightly odd, higher up than the old town but lower than the Vomero; hidden behind a crumbling church. ✉ *Piazzetta Trinità alla Cesarea 231, Vomero La Sanità* ☎ *081/5494014* ⊕ *www.lacontrora.com* ➭ *3 rooms with shared bath, 4 dorms* ⌂ *In-room: no a/c, no TV, Wi-Fi* ☰ *DC, MC, V* ⦿ *BP* ✢ *C2.*

$$ ⊞ **Majestic.** Heralded by a huge blue mosaic "M," which covers almost the entire facade of this (otherwise unspectacular) building, the Majestic is perfectly located for the swish Via dei Mille shopping street, the buzzing Chiaia nightlife, and the new PAN contemporary art gallery. There's a spacious and welcoming lobby area, which makes for a great meeting place if you're in town to check up on friends or do business. Guest rooms are delightfully modern, with sleek windows, cool colors, and a lovely restful ambience in such a stressed-out city. Only a few of the rooms on the higher floors have sea views, however, so ask for one when you book. **Pros:** located in chic Chiaia; great for shopping. **Cons:** uninteresting 1950s building. ✉ *Plargo Vasto a Chiaia 68, Chiaia* ☎ *081/416500* ⊕ *www.majestic.com* ➭ *120 rooms* ⌂ *In-room: a/c, safe, refrigerator. In-hotel: restaurant, bar, Wi-Fi hotspot* ☰ *DC, MC, V* ⦿ *BP* ✢ *C5.*

$$$$ ⊞ **Palazzo Alabardieri.** Just off the chic Piazza dei Martiri, Palazzo Alabardieri is the most fashionable choice among the city's growing number of smaller luxury hotels. Past an elegant stone passageway, a glittering, chandeliered marble-floored lobby opens its welcoming arms with florid flowers, baroque mirrors, painted murals, and shot-silk fabrics. Its impressive size makes the place seem bigger than it actually is, yet the Alabardieri maintains a feeling of discretion and intimacy. The hotel prides itself on its comfortable guest rooms, especially its marble bathrooms. While not one of the city's super-duper luxury hotels, this does have the most luxurious location of them all, just feet from the very heart of fashionable Naples, the Piazza dei Martiri and its top selection of shops and restaurants. For some, there is simply no other hotel in Naples. **Pros:** impressive public salons; central yet quiet location (a rare combination); fancy Martiri boutiques a short stroll away; polite, pleasant staff. **Cons:** no sea view; difficult to reach by car but once reached, parking is free. ✉ *Via Alabardieri 38, Chiaia* ☎ *081/415278* ⊕ *www.palazzoalabardieri.it* ➭ *35 rooms* ⌂ *In-room: a/c, safe, refrig-*

Fodor's Choice
★

6

erator, Internet. In-hotel: bar, Internet terminal, parking (free), some pets allowed ☐ *AE, DC, MC, V* ⍓| *BP* ✛ *C3.*

$$$ 🏨 **Paradiso.** This impressive hotel on the hillside of Posillipo is famous for the views of the Bay of Naples from its rooms, its roof-garden restaurant, and its garden terrace. From your own flower-bedecked balcony you can also take in the immediate neighborhood, less enchantingly filled with apartment buildings. Although the hotel is at the western edge of the city, the nearby funicular takes you efficiently to the harbor port and transportation hub of Mergellina, at the end of the Riviera di Chiaia. **Pros:** sweeping view of the bay; posh Posillipo neighborhood is quieter and safer than city center. **Cons:** some rooms face inland, so ask for a *camera con vista*; a long walk up a steep hill or a taxi ride into the city center, although there is a regular funicular to take you to Mergellina. ☒ *Via Catullo 11, Posillipo* ☎ *081/2475111* ⊕ *www. bestwestern.it* ⌁ *74 rooms* ♿ *In-hotel: restaurant, bar, parking (paid)* ☐ *AE, DC, MC, V* ⍓| *BP* ✛ *A5.*

$$–$$$ 🏨 **Pinto Storey.** The name juxtaposes a 19th-century Englishman who
★   fell in love with Naples and a certain Signora Pinto who together went on to establish this hotel, which overflows with warmth and charm. Its late 19th-century (but fully renovated) style makes you feel like a character in a period movie, photographs of 1953 Naples complementing the atmosphere. The simple and airy guest rooms are on the fourth and fifth floors of an elegant building off the chic Piazza Amedeo. They are always in demand, so book far in advance. **Pros:** safe neighborhood; near public transportation: option of rooms without a/c with a €9-a-day reduction. **Cons:** not close to major sights; rickety elevator; only a few rooms have views. ☒ *Via G. Martucci 72, Chiaia* ☎ *081/681260* ⊕ *www.pintostorey.it* ⌁ *16 rooms* ♿ *In-room: a/c, safe, refrigerator, Internet. In-hotel: Internet terminal (paid)* ☐ *AE, MC, V* ⍓| *EP* ✛ *B4.*

$$–$$$ 🏨 **San Francesco al Monte.** This high-end hotel retains hints of its former life as a Franciscan monastery: The small lobby leads to narrow corridors lined with doors that look dauntingly cell-like, until you enter and find surprisingly spacious, simply decorated rooms, many with their own hot tubs, antique furnishings, majolica-tile floors, and stunning views of the city below and the bay beyond. The hotel's restaurant serves regional specialties, and the wine bar has a selection of smaller dishes. **Pros:** rooftop pool (June to September 15 only); several dining options; all guest rooms with seaviews and with Jacuzzi or hydromassage showers. **Cons:** breakfast provided but other meals paid for à la carte; isolated hillside location, with taxi needed if you can't wait for the C16 bus. ☒ *Corso Vittorio Emanuele 328, Vomero* ☎ *081/4239111* ⊕ *www.hotelsanfrancesco.it* ⌁ *45 rooms* ♿ *In-room: safe, refrigerator, Internet. In-hotel: restaurant, bar, pool, parking (paid)* ☐ *AE, DC, MC, V* ⍓| *BP* ✛ *D3.*

NIGHTLIFE AND THE ARTS

THE ARTS

Updated
by Fiorella
Squillante

Lively and energetic yet also chaotic and often difficult to follow, the cultural scene in Naples reflects the city's charming yet frustrating character. Schedules of events are published in daily newspapers, particularly *Il Mattino, La Repubblica,* and *Corriere della Sera,* and the free sheet *City* and listings magazine *Zero 81,* though they can't be relied on to cover everything that is happening, or frequent last-minute changes of program or venue. The best source of information is word of mouth (ask the receptionists in your hotel what's going on this evening) or by keeping your eyes peeled for the theater and concert posters that wallpaper much of the city center. Information and ticket sales are provided by the following ticket agencies:

Box Office (✉ *Galleria Umberto I 17, Piazza Municipio* ☎ *081/5519188* ⊕ *www.boxofficenapoli.it*). **Concerteria** (✉ *Via Schipa 23, Chiaia* ☎ *081/7611221* ⊕ *www.concerteria.it*). **FNAC** (✉ *Via Luca Giordano 59, Vomero* ☎ *081/2201000* ⊕ *www.fnac.it*).

CONCERT HALLS AND THEATERS

In addition to the world-famous Teatro San Carlo, Naples has several other leading concert halls and theaters. Each theater generally plans its entire season—which usually runs October through May—in advance with a printed schedule.

CHIAIA

The cognoscenti inhabit this district and love to patronize these spots for their after-hours entertainment.

Teatro delle Palme (✉ *Via Vetriera 12, Chiaia* ☎ *081/418134*) is a rather ugly postwar-plywood, auditorium-cum-movie theater, which regularly hosts chamber music concerts presented by the Associazione Alessandro Scarlatti. The **Teatro Politeama** (✉ *Via Monte di Dio 80, Chiaia* ☎ *081/7645001*) could almost be considered an off-Broadway playhouse, considering its challenging bill of fare, which includes much contemporary dance. The Teatro San Carlo company uses it for contemporary works, which they don't dare perform in their hallowed temple.

Fodor'sChoice
★

For a satisfying Neapolitan "soul" experience, catch a local singer like Lina Sastri or Lara Sansone warbling at the **Teatro Sannazzaro** (✉ *Via Chiaia 157, Chiaia* ☎ *081/418824*) ; traditional Neapolitan plays by Edoardo di Filippo are also often presented here, and they also program shows by younger Italian bands and singers. For those with a knowledge of Italian, the **TAM Tunnel** (✉ *Gradini Nobili 1, Chiaia* ☎ *081/682814*) has a solid program of cabaret and stand-up.

SPACCANAPOLI

The Old Naples quarter is home to two of the city's favorite theaters.

Teatro Bellini (✉ *Via Conte di Ruvo 14, Spaccanapoli* ☎ *081/5491266*) is a gilded Belle Epoque theater that presents plays and concerts of a more traditional flavor.

Fodor'sChoice
★

Teatro Trianon (✉ *Piazza Calenda 9, Spaccanapoli* ☎ *081/2258285*) is a refurbished cinema opened in 2003 to provide a "home for Neapolitan song," mixing showings of classic Neapolitan movies with local

6

comedies and frequent concerts by traditional Neapolitan musicians (not to be missed if you want to feel tearful while singing along to "Turna a Surriento").

TOLEDO   The center city district is home to many of Naples's most important halls and theaters.

The **Augusteo** (⊠ *Piazza Augusteo, Toledo/Piazza Municipio* ☎ *081/414243*) is a large, centrally located theater off Via Toledo that usually presents commercial Italian theater and concerts. **Galleria Toledo** (⊠ *Via Montecalvario 36, Toledo* ☎ *081/425824*) attracts the hip set with high-quality fringe and avant-garde theater presentations. **Teatro Mercadante** (⊠ *Piazza Municipio, Toledo/Piazza Municipio* ☎ *081/5513396*), a Belle Epoque theater with an ultramodern foyer, hosts touring productions of invariably high quality. **Teatro Nuovo** (⊠ *Via Montecalvario 16, Toledo* ☎ *081/425958*) is a top venue for the avant-garde.

FILM

Neapolitans take their cinema seriously: The city has many cinema and video stores and rental outlets, and several cinemas even run their own "cineforums" one day a week to cater to more discerning cinemagoers. From the end of June to mid-September, open-air cinemas come into their own, and provide film aficionados with a chance to catch up on movies they missed during the year. Remember, however, that your favorite movie star will be speaking fluent Italian on the big screen—the dubbers still have a stranglehold on the industry.

The city's love fest with the movies reaches its high point every year with the Napoli Film Festival, usually presented every June at different locations across the city—the 2008 festival found a home in the impressive surroundings of the Castel Sant'Elmo and the nearby **America Hall** (⊠ *Via Tito Angelini 21, Vomero* ☎ *081/5788982*). Moviegoers should also look out for the **Warner Village Metropolitan** (⊠ *Via Chiaia 149, Chiaia* ☎ *081/5511247*), a city-center multiplex in the American style, with as much popcorn as you can eat. **Modernissimo** (⊠ *Via Cisterna dell'Olio, 59, Spaccanapoli* ☎ *081/5800254*) is an Italian style multiplex cinema in the historical center.

OPERA AND CLASSICAL MUSIC

Naples features a reasonable calendar of classical and chamber music concerts; check the newspaper listings and street posters for information about concerts frequently held in the historic churches of the city.

CHIAIA   This wealthy residential district loves its classical music concerts.

The **Associazione Alessandro Scarlatti** (⊠ *Piazza dei Martiri 58, Chiaia* ☎ *081/406011*) organizes a series of chamber music concerts at various venues across the city, including the auditorium of the Castel Sant'Elmo and the Villa Pignatelli—check their Web site for details. **Villa Pignatelli** (⊠ *Riviera di Chiaia 200, Chiaia* ☎ *081/76123561*) is the former residence of the 19th-century Rothschilds and makes a fitting venue for concerts that are often held in the summer here.

PIAZZA MUNI-   The very hub of the city is home to the famous San Carlo theater, heart
CIPIO/TOLEDO   of Naples's performing-arts scene.

Fodor's Choice
★

Opera is a serious business in Naples. Not the music, that is, but the costumes, the stage design, the players, the politics. Anyone who aspires to anything absolutely has to be present at the season's major openings, where what's happening on the stage and in the pit are secondary to the news of who is there, who they're with, and what they're wearing. Given this, it's hardly surprising that the city's famous San Carlo company does not offer a particularly challenging repertoire but spends time endlessly redressing the classics. All this takes place in the historic **Teatro San Carlo** (✉ *Via San Carlo 101–103, Piazza Municipio* ☎ *081/7972412 box office, 081/7972331* 🌐 *www.teatrosancarlo.it*), the luxury liner of opera houses in southern Italy. In 2008 the concert hall underwent a massive renovation, with everything from the seats to the gold inlay on the ceiling frescoes being replaced, and the statue of the mermaid Parthenope (missing since 1969) being restored to its position on the building's facade. The program, however, remains traditional, although the choice of Benjamin Britten's comparatively obscure opera *Peter Grimes* (directed by English conductor Jeffrey Tate, who follows in the illustrious footsteps of former conductors Riccardo Muti and Claudio Abbado) to open the new house in January 2009 hints at a newfound adventurousness. The company is usually of very high quality—and if they're not on form, the audience lets them know. Although rotten vegetables are terribly passé, catcalls and boos are perfectly acceptable.

For the opera and ballet season (generally December through June), many seats are presold by subscription but there are usually some seats available if you go to the box office several days before the performance (unless a superstar is performing). If you are under 30, you can buy an unsold ticket one hour before the curtain rises for €15. Otherwise, for some opera performances, tickets can only be bought five days before the performance, but at other times you can buy tickets weeks in advance. You can book ahead using a credit card on the theater's Web site. Unlike many leading opera companies in the United States, the San Carlo does not operate on a revolving repertory schedule: each opera or ballet is usually scheduled for a minirun, generally over a 10-day period.

Prices vary due to both seat location and date. The front rows of the stalls, known as *poltronissime*, might cost as much as €200 for a performance on the first night of an opera, while up in the sixth tier, the Balconata VI, you would pay a fifth of that price, or much less if you go on a later night. Prices are always highest at first nights with the best opera divas, then fall off as top performers are sometimes substituted after a few nights. If you get a box seat, keep in mind that there are as many as six people sharing a box, so it's worth getting there early to get a front seat. Some people tip the *maschere* (ushers), and this is especially appreciated if they have fixed you up with a better seat than the one you were allocated originally (maybe a season ticket holder didn't show up). Ballet and concert performances are up to 50% less expensive than operas. One way of getting into the San Carlo for much less is to go on a guided tour (weekends only, 2 to 3:30). At €6.50, you soak up some of its magnificence, which might be preferable to paying 50 times as much and sitting through five hours of the Ring cycle. For complete information, contact the **box office,** which is open Monday to Saturday 10 to 7, Sunday 10 to 3:30 and one hour before performances.

SPACCANAPOLI Many historic churches in this open-air-museum of a neighborhood often host concerts.

The **Centro di Musica Antica Pietà de' Turchini** (⊠ *Via Santa Caterina da Siena 38, Spaccanapoli* ☎ *081/402395*), based in the early-baroque church of Santa Caterina da Siena, offers an excellent season of early music that runs from October to early May. Even if madrigals aren't your thing, it's worth visiting just for the location. **Villa Pignatelli** (⊠ Riviera di Chiaia, 200, *Chiaia* ☎ *081 7612356*)is one of the historical locations where concerts are often held in summer.

NIGHTLIFE

Nightlife in Naples begins well after the sun has gone down. If you're going to a club, don't even think about turning up before 11, as more than likely it'll still be empty, and don't plan on going to bed much before 3. Yet if you're willing to stay up late enough, and prepared to hang around outside places—with the rest of the *perdi-tempo* ("time wasters")—where there's sometimes more going on in the street than in the clubs themselves, Naples offers distractions for night owls of all persuasions. The designer-clad young and not so young hang out in the area around Chiaia and Mergellina; a more artsy poststudent crowd congregates around Piazza Bellini; the rawer, punkier edge prefers to hang around on Piazza Dante or Piazza San Domenico. Clubs tend to open and close or change name, style, or ownership with bewildering rapidity, so be sure to check locally before planning a night out. The best way to find out what's going on is to keep your eyes on the flyers that cover Spaccanapoli or check the monthly publication *Zero 81.*

Many dance clubs issue a drink card (prices vary, €15 is average) at the door that must be returned when you leave, stamped to show you've consumed at least one drink. After the first or second drink, other drinks usually run less (about €5).

SPACCANAPOLI With just one step you can hurtle through the centuries here in this historic quarter, as you step pass 18th-century palaces on the way to 21st-century discos.

Arty and funky describe the scene at **Aret' 'a Palm** (⊠ *Piazza S. Maria La Nova 14, Spaccanapoli* ☎ *339/8486949*) with a dark-wood interior, marble-top bar, and red plush seats that suggest Paris far more than the Mediterranean. Nearby Piazza Bellini is somewhat more relaxed than the club-studded alleyways of Spaccanapoli, and you might even be able to sit down at a proper table. **Caffè Intramoenia** (⊠ *Piazza Bellini 70, Spaccanapoli* ☎ *081/290988* ⊕ *www.intramoenia.it*) is the granddaddy of the bars here—set up as a bookshop in the late 1980s, it still has its own small publishing house and a variety of the attractive titles are on sale. Seats in the heated veranda are at a premium in winter, though many patrons sit outside year-round. **Kestè** (⊠ *Largo S. Giovanni Maggiore 26, Spaccanapoli* ☎ *081/5513984* ⊕ *www.keste.it*) nestles in the small square in front of the Orientale University. Cool chrome furnishings contrast with the old arched ceiling inside but try to bag one of the few tables out in the beautiful square. A DJ spins tunes, and there's live jazz on the tiny stage on weekends. Just around the corner from the Superfly bar, **Kinky Klub** (⊠ *Vicolo della Quercia 26, Spaccanapoli* ☎ *081/5521571* ⊕ *www.kinkyjam. com*) is actually a reggae bar. The place fills up quickly so that in summer the whole scene spills out onto the street.

If Piazza Bellini is too packed, head around the corner to **Perditempo** (⊠ *Via San Pietro a Maiella 8, Spaccanapoli* ☎ *081/444958* ⊕ *www. perditempo.org*), which advertises *libri, vini e vinili* ("books, wine, and vinyl"). Set up as a used book

6

and record store, it is now a place to enjoy a glass or two and peruse their stock. Inside there is always a great variety of music but from 7 pm there's no more room inside so you'll be joining a crowd of *perditempo* ("time wasters") outside the bar in the street. The same team here is ready to inaugurate a bigger music-bar in Piazza Dante (at No. 44) sometime in 2011 that promises to be a certain success. **Rising Mutiny** (⊠ *Via Bellini 15, Spaccanapoli* ☎ *3358790428*) hosts live acts, from Italian singer-songwriters to U.S. indie-rockers, in a large hall with eclectic furnishings.

Via Cisterna dell'Olio hosts the tiny but agreeably funky **Superfly** (⊠ *Via Cisterna Dell'Olio 12, Spaccanapoli* ☎ *347/1272178*), where a DJ stands next to the bartender and regularly changed photographic exhibitions line the walls. Choose to play board games while having a drink at **Volver** (⊠ *Via Bellini, 56, Spaccanapoli* ☎ *081/0606630* ⊕ *www. volvercafe.it*), a lounge that hosts live music, tango (classes are given, too), and other events.

CHIAIA Naples's dressiest crowds congregate here at some of the city's better nightspots.

Miles (⊠ *Via S. Pasquale 47, Chiaia* ☎ *081/405000*) is named after "Davis," though its music policy has shifted from cool jazz to hard techno, which nevertheless manages to get the slightly older crowd here moving. Jazz fans should seek out the **Otto Jazz Club** (⊠ *Salita Cariati 23, Chiaia* ☎ *081/5524373*), a staple of the city's trad jazz scene. Between Vico dei Sospiri and Vico Belledonne you'll find a lounge-bar that lives up to every expectation at the **Pescheria Mattiucci** (⊠ *Vico Belledonne a Chiaia 27, Chiaia*).On Tuesday, Thursday, and Friday this little fish-shop becomes a trendy spot to take an aperitif. If you want to experience superb Neapolitan sushi and cold wine while sitting on a buoy stool, go early, or for a full fish lunch, come to this pescheria for lunch.

The bar entitled simply **66** (✉ *Via Bisignano 58, Chiaia* ☎ *081/415024*) describes itself as a "fusion bar." Some prefer it as a chic place to have an aperitif (help yourself to the snacks beautifully laid out on the bar). You can also come here to dine and listen to the chilled-out DJ in one of rooms upstairs. **S'move** (✉ *Vico dei Sospiri 10, Chiaia* ☎ *081/7645813* ⊕ *www.smove-lab.net*) is somewhere between a bar and a club, with its high-tech bar leading into an oriental-style room complete with scatter cushions if you want to arrange yourself artfully on the floor to the chill-out sound track. It fills around midnight with a young crowd that wears its clothes so that the designer labels show. A large space that hosts a wide range of artistic and musical events, **Trip** (✉ *Via Martucci 64, Chiaia* ☎ *081/19568994* ⊕ *www.cra.na.it*) has a full calendar every month packed with an array of surprising events and themed evenings.

ENOTECAS AND WINE BARS

If you can't face any chaotic nightlife after the all-too-chaotic daylife of Naples, there's the civilized option of the *enoteca*, not exactly a wine bar, but a place where you can stop for a drink or meet up with friends without having to shout over the music or hang around on the street outside for hours, and have something more substantial to eat than peanuts and pretzels. The **Enoteca Belledonne** (✉ *Vico Belledonne a Chiaia 18, Chiaia* ☎ *081/403162* ⊕ *www.enotecabelledonne.com*) is something of an institution among inhabitants of Chiaia. Between 8 and 9 in the evening it seems like the whole neighborhood has descended into the tiny space for an *aperitivo*. The small tables and low stools are notably uncomfortable, but the cozy atmosphere and the pleasure of being surrounded by glass-fronted cabinets full of wine bottles with beautiful labels more than makes up for it. A particularly quiet and refined option in Chiaia is **L'ebbrezza di Noè** (✉ *Vico Vetriera a Chaia 9, Chiaia* ☎ *081/400104* ⊕ *www.lebbrezzadinoe.com*). A small bar leads into a larger dining area decorated in the style of what seems to be a very elegant farmhouse. The attention paid to the quality of the wine is backed up by that of the food—more than just a "prop," here you can taste delicate slices of Tuscan steak *carpaccio di chianina* or rare cheeses such as the Sicilian *ragusano di razza modicani*.

SHOPPING

Updated
by Fiorella
Squillante

Naples is a fascinating and largely underrated city for shopping. From the delightful *Presepe* (Nativity scene) shops that transform Via San Gregorio Armeno into a perpetual Christmas morning to its noted leather-goods emporia, the city's rich history of skilled workmanship means it abounds in unique souvenirs and gifts, including some of the world's best ties (**Marinella**), crèche figures (**Ferrigno**), masks (**Nel Regno di Pulcinella**), shoes (**Mario Valentino**), and intarsia tabletops (**Domenico Russo**). At the other end of the price scale are world-famous, dirt-cheap bootleg CDs of Italian and Neapolitan music for you to check out. A sense of adventure is once again the key, especially in the open markets, which are worth a visit just as a social experience—bargaining here is an art and a necessity (watch your wallet and leave the expensive extra camera lenses at the hotel).

Shops are generally open from around 9:30 in the morning to 1:30, when they close for lunch, reopening around 4:30 and staying open until 7:30 or 8. Most stores are closed Sunday, but certain higher-volume addresses have procured a license allowing them to open on Sunday morning. Sales run twice a year, from mid-January to mid-March for the fall–winter collections and from mid-July to early September for the spring–summer collections, with half-price discounts common.

MARKETS

Shopping in an outdoor market is an essential Neapolitan experience; do prepare yourself against pickpockets (relax—just don't wear your tiara). Food markets are all over town, offering a Technicolor feast for the eyes as well as free street theater. The **Mercatino della Pignasecca** (✉ *Spaccanapoli*), several blocks west of Piazza Carità off Via Toledo, is open every day 8–2 and is the best place in the city for fish, fruit, and vegetables. For low price and surprisingly high-quality clothing and linen, go to the **Mercatino di Antignano** (✉ *Piazza degli Artisti, Vomero*), open daily 8–1.Great bargains can be found at the **Mercatino di Posillipo** (✉ *Viale Virgilio, Posillipo*) which takes place once a week, on Thursday mornings. In Chiaia, the **Bancarelle di San Pasquale** (✉ *Via San Pasquale, Chiaia*) takes place every morning, with a smaller but higher quality selection of shoes, bags, and clothing.

Clothes merit a special mention. Neapolitans are the world masters of the used-clothing trade and also specialize in, well, let's call them unofficial brand-name knockoffs, sometimes of excellent quality. If you trust your eye, you can have a field day: you might find excellent shoes made by the same factories that turn out top brands, quality leather purses, or secondhand cashmere at the price of discount-store cotton. Of course, quite often you have to wade through a lot of dismal stock of no interest in order to get to the good stuff, but that's part of the fun. Over the last few years, a large number of Chinese merchants have moved in, lowering prices, but also some of the quality of the clothes on offer. The best stomping ground is the **Mercato di Porta Capuana** (✉ *Porta Capuana/Piazza Leone Piazza Garibaldi*), which is open Monday–Saturday 8–1:30 PM and has a good collection of jeans, shoes, and a surprising number of untagged name-brand items at half price. (✉ *Via S. Antonio AbatePiazza Garibaldi*) open daily 8–2. The **Mercatino di Poggioreale** (✉ *Via Nuova Poggioreale, Piazza Garibaldi*) requires a longish walk from Piazza Garibaldi but rewards with a vast selection of shoes of all styles and sizes at uniformly low prices.

SHOPPING DISTRICTS

Most of the luxury shops in Naples are along a crescent that descends the Via Toledo to Piazza Trieste e Trento and then continues along Via Chiaia to Via Filangieri and on to Piazza Amedeo, as well as continuing south toward Piazza dei Martiri and the Riviera di Chiaia. Within this area, the Via Chiaia probably has the greatest concentration and variety of shops (and caffè–pastry shop Cimmino, on the corner of Via Filangieri and Via Chiaia, makes for an excellent rest stop along this route). The area around Piazza Vanvitelli, and Via Scarlatti in particular, in the Vomero also has a nice selection of shops outside the tourist zone. This area can be conveniently reached by funiculars from Piazza Amedeo, Via Toledo, or Montesanto. Secondhand book dealers tend to collect in the area between Piazza Dante, Via Port'Alba, and Via Santa Maria di Constantinopoli. Antique shops can also be found in the latter. The charming shops specializing in Presepi (Nativity scenes) are in Spaccanapoli, on the Via San Gregorio Armeno. Via San Sebastiano, close to the Conservatory, is the kingdom of musical instruments.

SPECIALTY STORES

ART GALLERIES

With the opening of four new museums dedicated to contemporary art, the gallery scene in Naples has been kick-started back into life, following a slump after the death of Lucio Amelio, the gallery owner who brought international superstars like Andy Warhol and Joseph Beuys to the city, and who was instrumental in creating the Arte Povera and Transavanguardia movements. Along with established galleries, a number of more modish spaces have opened, often showing local artistic talent.

CHIAIA There is a nice concentration of noted art galleries in the posh district of Chiaia. **Changing Role** (⊠ *Via Chiatamone 26, Santa Lucia* ☎ *081/19575958* ⊕ *www.changingrole.com*) works frequently with photographers and designers to produce distinctly modish, energetic work. **Galleria Lia Rumma** (⊠ *Via Vannella Gaetani 14, Chiaia* ☎ *081/7643619* ⊕ *www.gallerialiarumma.it*) has a status-heavy array of artists, including Cindy Sherman, Anselm Kiefer, and Vanessa Beecroft, along with famed Neapolitan photographer Mimmo Jodice. **Galleria Scognamiglio** (⊠ *Via M. D'ayala, Chiaia* ☎ *081/400871* ⊕ *www. mimmoscognamiglio.com*) has built a fine reputation and shows work by international luminaries, including Antony Gormley and local mainstay Mimmo Paladino. **Studio Trisorio** (⊠ *Riviera di Chiaia 215, Chiaia* ☎ *081/414306* ⊕ *www.studiotrisorio.com*) shows artists of the world-class caliber of Rebecca Horn and William Eggleston.

SPACCANAPOLI In the area of Spaccanapoli, the contemporary art scene is growing stronger and stronger thanks to the following art galleries. At the **Fondazione Morra Greco** (⊠ *Largo Avellino 17, Spaccanapoli* ☎ *081/210690* ⊕ *www.fondazionemorragreco.com*) influential collector Maurizio Morra Greco has put his private collection on display, and also holds frequent shows by emerging artists. **Palazzo Bagnara** (⊠ *Piazza Dante 89, Spaccanapoli* ☎ *081/5641655* ⊕ *www.fondazionemorra.org*) is the headquarters of the Fondazione Morra, whose founder Giuseppe Morra has been one of the leading patrons promoting visual poetry, Actionism, and Conceptual art in Naples since the 1960s. **Raucci Santamaria** (⊠ *Corso Amedeo di Savoia 190, Spaccanapoli* ☎ *081/7443645* ⊕ *www.raucciesantamaria.com*), which showcases such international artists as Mat Colishaw, Ugo Rondinone, and Tim Rollins.

BOOKS AND PRINTS

CHIAIA The largest cluster of bookstores, ranging from mass-market to super-elegant antiquarian shops, is the chic Chiaia district. **Arethusa** (✉ *Riviera di Chiaia 202/b, Chiaia* ☎ *081/411551*) specializes in collectible posters and has an excellent selection of both rare and inexpensive book editions.

Fodor'sChoice For antique prints, postcards, watercolors, photographs, engravings
★ and some books, the most famous shop in town is **Bowinkel** (✉ *Piazza dei Martiri 24, Chiaia* ☎ *081/7644344*) where the lucky collector can often pick up pricey treasures, many of which are delectable views of 19th-century Naples.

Fodor'sChoice Everyone usually begins with the largest bookstore in town, **La Feltrinelli**
★ (✉ *Piazza dei Martiri, Chiaia* ☎ *081/2405411*), with two floors stuffed with an extensive range of books, CDs, and DVDs, plus an inviting coffee bar on the lower ground floor and a space for daily meetings and book launches. Besides the mother branch on Piazza dei Martiri, **Feltrinelli** (✉ *Via Tommaso D'Aquino 70, Piazza Municipio* ☎ *081/5521436*) has a branch that has a much larger selection of English-language books.

SPACCANAPOLI Historians and book lovers always flock to the old town district of the Spacca and it doesn't fail to deliver some top bookstore choices. If you're an art-history student and pictures are what matter, **Alpha** (✉ *Via Sant'Anna dei Lombardi 10, Spaccanapoli* ☎ *081/5525013*) has a great selection of cut-rate art books. **Colonnese** (✉ *Via San Pietro a Maiella 32/33, Spaccanapoli* ☎ *081/459858*), near Via Port'Alba, has a wide assortment of antique books, postcards, and magical objets d'art. **Libreria Guida** (✉ *Via Port'Alba 20/23, Spaccanapoli* ☎ *081/446377*) has a wide selection of local interest books in English and Italian and an expert staff.

VOMERO **FNAC** (✉ *Via Luca Giordano 59, Vomero* ☎ *081/2201000*) is the Neapolitan branch of the French chain, and has a huge basement brimming with books and CDs, as well as a coffee bar and meeting space.

CLOTHING AND ACCESSORIES

CHIAIA Fashionistas and supermodels flock to the caffè and fancy hotels of this district, and it is also, needless to say, address to many of the poshest boutiques in town. Neapolitans are famous for their attention to style, and Chiaia proves it. Begin at tiny and elegant Via Calabritto, a veritable "shopping mall" jammed with the likes of Gucci, Mario Valentino, Prada, and Giorgio Armani.

Livio de Simone (✉ *Via Domenico Morelli 15, Chiaia* ☎ *081/7643827*) is a Neapolitan designer famous for his bright, printed-textile designs, and who has a range of less traditional clothing.

Up near the top of the price scale, **Emporio Armani** (✉ *Piazza dei Martiri 64, Chiaia* ☎ *081/425816*) has a shop right on *elegantissime* Piazza dei MartiriAlthough based in Florence,**Salvatore Ferragamo** (✉ *Piazza dei Martiri 54/60, Chiaia* ☎ *081/*) is also beloved by Neapolitans who appreciate centuries of fine Italian taste and craftsmanship. The French **Hermès** (✉ *Via Filangieri 53/57, Chiaia* ☎ *081/4207054*) has accessories that only seem to get chicer and chicer. **Furla** (✉ *Via Filangieri 58, Chiaia*

Bringing smiles to even the stoniest hearts, the Doll Hospital in Spaccanapoli is a Neapolitan institution.

☎ 081/412190) offers a range of accessories from scarves to bags to shoes at surprisingly accessible prices.

A number of local, and almost as exclusive, shops are also worthy of notice.

Fodor's Choice Since 1865 **Tramontano** (⊠ *Via Chiaia 143, Chiaia* ☎ 081/414837) has ★ crafted some of the finest leather luggage, bags, shoes, belts, and wallets. Among those who have paid a call to this atelier are Claudia Cardinale, Woody Allen, and Tom Cruise. Italian and international designer brands at reasonable prices can be found at **Jossa** (⊠ *Via Carlo Poerio 43, Chiaia* ☎ 081/7649835). If your credit card is crying in pain, head for **Lo Stock** (⊠ *Via Fiorelli 7, Chiaia* ☎ 081/2405253), a large basement in which designer-label end-of-lines can be found at hugely reduced prices.

Naples is a surprisingly good city for male fashion and tends to spoil its male clotheshorses (many would use the word peacocks). If you feel like indulging in a custom-made suit or shirt, try the world-famous **Mariano Rubinacci** (⊠ *Via Filangieri 26, Chiaia* ☎ 081415793), where men's suits have been created since the 19th century. Opening his doors in 1887 as a hat designer and soon bringing in customers like Enrico Caruso, **Eddy Monetti** (⊠ *Via dei Mille 45 Chiaia* ☎ 081/427716) has been one of the landmark Neapolitan names in sartorial splendor for men (women can now find his fashions on Via S. Caterina). Widely considered by globe-trotting VIPs to be the finest ties in the world, **Marinella** (⊠ *Riviera di Chiaia 287, Chiaia* ☎ 081/2451182) is where Maurizio Marinella, grandson of the founder, Eugenio, cuts made-to-measure ties for the world's royalty and other sensitive necks. **Argenio** (⊠ *Via Filangieri 15,*

Chiaia ☎ *081/418035*) is another famous and exclusive address for men's accessories.

PIAZZA MUNI-
CIPIO/TOLEDO
Italy wouldn't be Italy without shoes, and many shoe stores can be found along Via Toledo (higher-priced options can be found in the many shoe stores on Via Chiaia).

Barbaro (✉ *Galleria Umberto I 3/7, Piazza Municipio* ☎ *081/414940*) has a stylish choice of name designers. International chains are present, of course. A good selection of affordable clothes can be found at **Benetton** (✉ *Via Toledo 253, Piazza Municipio* ☎ *081/4238711*), which continues to represent easy Italian chic to most of the world.

SPACCANAPOLI
Melinoi (✉ *Via Benedetto Croce 34, Spaccanapoli* ☎ *081/5521204*) is particularly known for its originality. It also stocks clothes and accessories by a number of French designers, with an eye for uniqueness of style.

CRAFTS AND GIFTS

The classic handicraft of Naples is the Presepe—or Nativity crèche scene—with elaborate sets and terra-cotta figurines and elements of still life. The tradition goes back to the medieval period, but its acknowledged golden age arrived in the 18th century. The tradition is alive and flourishing; although the sets and figurines retain their 18th-century aspect, the craftsmen keep their creativity up-to-date with famous renditions of current political figures and other celebrities. The scenes are appropriately completed with a profusion of domestic animals and food of all sorts, meticulously rendered. A number of the smaller articles make great Christmas tree ornaments, if you don't feel up to adopting an entire Bethlehem-on-the-bay Nativity scene.

6

SPACCANAPOLI
Shops cluster along the Via San Gregorio Armeno in Spaccanapoli, and they're all worth a glance, but the most famous is **Ferrigno** (✉ *Via San Gregorio Armeno 10, Spaccanapoli* ☎ *081/5523148*). *Maestro* Giuseppe Ferrigno himself died in 2008 but the family business continues, still faithfully using 18th-century techniques. While it only opened in 1996, **La Scarabattola** (✉ *Via Tribunali 50, Spaccanapoli* ☎ *081/291735*) has already created a Nativity scene for the Spanish royal family. The Scuotto family creates a wide array of Neapolitan *Presepi* in both classic and their own contemporary style and will be happy to fashion one for you. If you're seriously bitten by the Presepe-collecting bug, you can find rare antique Nativity figures at **Marisa Catello** (✉ *Via Santa Maria Costantinopoli 124, Spaccanapoli* ☎ *081/444169*). The **Ospedale delle Bambole** (✉ *Via San Biagio dei Librai 81, Spaccanapoli* ☎ *081/203067*)—a tiny storefront operation—is a world-famous "hospital" for dolls, a wonderful photo op, and a great place to take kids. **Nel Regno di Pulcinella** (✉ *Vico San Domenico Maggiore 9, Spaccanapoli* ☎ *081/5514171*) is the workshop of famous Pulcinella maker Lello Esposito. This shop, a converted 16th-century stable, also offers some wonderful model volcanoes and the traditional good-luck symbol of the city, a red horn.

Music lovers can get a prestigious mandolin at **Liuteria Calace** (✉ *Vico San Domenico Maggiore 9, Spaccanapoli* ☎ *081/5515983*). **Egraphe** (✉ *Piazza L. Miraglia 391, Spaccanapoli* ☎ *081/446266* is a tiny hole-in-the-wall crammed with notebooks of every style and size, different kinds of handmade papers, and unusual pens and pencils.

DECORATION AND ANTIQUES

In the *centro antico* antiquarians or simple *robivecchi* (secondhand shops) are found not only along the streets of Costantinopoli and San Sebastiano but along Via Tribunali and other streets of Spaccanapoli.

CHIAIA If you're interested in original antiques, several prestigious dealers are clustered along Via Carlo Poerio and Via Domenico Morelli up to Piazza dei Martiri, where one of the largest expositions is at the **Galleria Navarra** (⊠ *Piazza dei Martiri 3* ☏ *081/764359*).

Domenico Russo e Figli (⊠ *Via Bisignano 51, Chiaia* ☏ *081/7648387*) continues the centuries-old Neapolitan tradition of marble-inlay work, creating precious tables and console tops.

JEWELRY

The densest selection of goldsmiths' and jewelers' shops is located around the old jewelry-makers' quarter, Via degli Orefici (Street of the Goldsmiths), between Corso Umberto and Via Marina, but the area is noisy and frenetic.

SPACCANAPOLI Dealers in this quarter offer good choice and competitive prices. Near the center of the Spacca you'll find the upscale **Gioielleria Caso** (⊠ *Piazza San Domenico Maggiore 16, Spaccanapoli* ☏ *081/5516733*), which has antique jewelry, silver and great coral works.

PIAZZA MUNI- Naples has also long been famous for its coral and cameos, and although
CIPIO/TOLEDO the raw material now comes most often from the Far East, it is Nea-
politan technique and inspiration that transform the shells and coral into works of art. A number of touristy shops are along the Sorrento coast and Torre del Greco, where coral fishing and manufacture started and the first official factory was opened in 1805. When in Naples, however, visit **Ascione** (⊠ *Piazzetta Matilde Serao 19, Piazza Municipio* ☏ *081/4211111*), a century-old family firm which has a showroom-cum-gallery hidden away in a wing of the Galleria Umberto, including pictures of traditional methods of working coral.

Brinkmann (⊠ *Piazza Municipio 21, Piazza Municipio* ☏ *081/5520555*) is noted for its exquisite collection of watches that incorporate rare coins. For antique wonders or eclectic creations in gold, precious stones, and silver, make yourself at home on one of the velvet chairs inside **Leonardo Gaito** (⊠ *Via Toledo 278, Toledo* ☏ *081/421104*) and get ready to be regaled with some fabulous Neapolitan-style jewels.

CHIAIA **Ventrella** (⊠ *Via Carlo Poerio 11, Chiaia* ☏ *081/7643173*) is a posh salon showing original designs by the most exclusive contemporary workshop. **Bulgari** (⊠ *Via Filangieri 40, Chiaia* ☏ *081/400856*) showcases internationally famous jewelry. Almost directly opposite Bulgari is its rival for high-end jewelry, **Damiani** (⊠ *Via Filangieri 15, Chiaia* ☏ *081/405043*). More unusual jewelry (including silver charms by Pomellato) can be found at **DoDo** (⊠ *Via Filangieri 58, Chiaia* ☏ *081/418245*).

ITALIAN VOCABULARY

ENGLISH	ITALIAN	PRONOUNCIATION

BASICS

Yes/no	Sí/no	see/no
Please	Per favore	pear fa-**vo**-ray
Yes, please	Sí, grazie	see **grah**-tsee-ay
Thank you	Grazie	**grah**-tsee-ay
You're welcome	Prego	**pray**-go
Excuse me, sorry	Scusi	**skoo**-zee
Sorry!	Mi dispiace!	mee dis-spee-**ah**-chay
Good morning/afternoon	Buongiorno	bwohn-**jor**-no
Good evening	Buona sera	**bwoh**-na **say**-ra
Good-bye	Arrivederci	a-ree-vah-**dare**-chee
Mr. (Sir)	Signore	see-**nyo**-ray
Mrs. (Ma'am)	Signora	see-**nyo**-ra
Miss	Signorina	see-nyo-**ree**-na
Pleased to meet you	Piacere	pee-ah-**chair**-ray
How are you?	Come sta?	**ko**-may **stah**
Very well, thanks	Bene, grazie	**ben**-ay **grah**-tsee-ay
Hello (phone)	Pronto?	**proan**-to

NUMBERS

one	uno	**oo**-no
two	due	**doo**-ay
three	tre	tray
four	quattro	**kwah**-tro
five	cinque	**cheen**-kway
six	sei	say
seven	sette	**set**-ay
eight	otto	**oh**-to
nine	nove	**no**-vay
ten	dieci	dee-**eh**-chee
eleven	undici	**oon**-dee-chee
twelve	dodici	**doe**-dee-cee

thirteen	tredici	**tray**-dee-chee
fourteen	quattordici	kwa-**tore**-dee-chee
fifteen	quindici	**kwin**-dee-chee
sixteen	sedici	**say**-dee-chee
seventeen	diciassete	dee-cha-**set**-ay
eighteen	diciotto	dee-**cho**-to
nineteen	diciannove	dee-cha-**no**-vay
twenty	venti	**vain**-tee
twenty-one	ventuno	vain-**too**-no
twenty-two	ventidue	vain-tee-**doo**-ay
thirty	trenta	**train**-ta
forty	quaranta	kwa-**rahn**-ta
fifty	cinquanta	cheen-**kwahn**-ta
sixty	sessanta	seh-**sahn**-ta
seventy	settanta	seh-**tahn**-ta
eighty	ottanta	o-**tahn**-ta
ninety	novanta	no-**vahn**-ta
one hundred	cento	**chen**-to
one thousand	mille	**mee**-lay
ten thousand	diecimila	dee-eh-chee-**mee**-la

USEFUL PHRASES

Do you speak English?	Parla inglese?	**par**-la een-**glay**-zay
I don't speak Italian ee-tal-**yah**-no	Non parlo italiano	non **par**-lo
I don't understand	Non capisco	non ka-**peess**-ko
Can you please repeat?	Può ripetere?	pwo ree-**pet**-ay-ray
Slowly!	Lentamente!	**len**-ta-men-tay
I don't know	Non lo so	non lo **so**
I'm American	Sono americano(a)	**so**-no a-may-ree-**kah**-no(a)
I'm British	Sono inglese	so-no een-**glay**-zay
What's your name?	Come si chiama?	**ko**-may see kee-**ah**-ma

My name is . . .	Mi chiamo . . .	mee kee-**ah**-mo
What time is it?	Che ore sono?	kay **o**-ray **so**-no
How?	Come?	**ko**-may
When?	Quando?	**kwan**-doe
Yesterday/today/ tomorrow	Ieri/oggi/domani	**yer**-ee/**o**-jee/do-**mah**-nee
This morning/	Stamattina/Oggi	sta-ma-**tee**-na/**o**-jee
afternoon	pomeriggio	po-mer-**ee**-jo
Tonight	Stasera	sta-**ser**-a
What?	Che cosa?	kay **ko**-za
What is it?	Chee cos'é?	kay ko-**zay**
Why?	Perché?	pear-**kay**
Who?	Chi?	kee
Where is . . .	Dov'è . . .	doe-**veh**
the bus stop?	la fermata dell'autobus?	la fer-**mah**-tadel ow-toe-**booss**
the train station?	la stazione?	la sta-tsee-**oh**-nay
the subway?	la metropolitana?	la may-tro-po-lee-**tah**-na
the terminal?	il terminale?	eel ter-mee-**nah**-lay
the post office?	l'ufficio postale?	loo-**fee**-cho po-**stah**-lay
the bank?	la banca?	la **bahn**-ka
the . . . hotel?	l'hotel . . .?	lo-**tel**
the store?	il negozio?	eel nay-**go**-tsee-o
the cashier?	la cassa?	la **kah**-sa
the . . . museum?	il museo . . .?	eel moo-**zay**-o
the hospital?	l'ospedale?	lo-spay-**dah**-lay
the first-aid station?	il pronto soccorso?	eel **pron**-to so-**kor**-so
the elevator?	l'ascensore?	la-shen-**so**-ray
a telephone?	un telefono?	oon tay-**lay**-fo-no
the restrooms?	Dov'è il bagno?	do-**vay** eel **bahn**-yo
Here/there	Qui/là	kwee/la
Left/right	A sinistra/a destra	a see-**neess**-tra/a **des**-tra
Straight ahead	Avanti dritto	a-**vahn**-tee **dree**-to
Is it near/far?	È vicino/lontano?	ay vee-**chee**-no/lon-**tah**-no
I'd like . . .	Vorrei . . .	vo-**ray**
a room	una camera	**oo**-na **kah**-may-ra
the key	la chiave	la kee-**ah**-vay

a newspaper	un giornale	oon jor-**nah**-lay
a stamp	un francobollo	oon frahn-ko-**bo**-lo
I'd like to buy . . .	Vorrei comprare . . .	vo-**ray** kom-**prah**-ray
How much is it?	Quanto costa?	**kwahn**-toe **coast**-a
It's expensive/cheap	È caro/economico	ay **car**-o/ay-ko-**no**-mee-ko
A little/a lot	Poco/tanto	**po**-ko/**tahn**-to
More/less	Più/meno	pee-**oo**/**may**-no
Enough/too (much)	Abbastanza/troppo	a-bas-**tahn**-sa/**tro**-po
I am sick	Sto male	sto **mah**-lay
Call a doctor	Chiama un dottore	kee-**ah**-mah oon doe-**toe**-ray
Help!	Aiuto!	a-**yoo**-toe
Stop!	Alt!	ahlt
Fire!	Al fuoco!	ahl **fwo**-ko
Caution/Look out!	Attenzione!	a-ten-**syon**-ay

DINING OUT

A bottle of . . .	Una bottiglia di . . .	**oo**-na bo-**tee**-lee-ahdee
A cup of . . .	Una tazza di . . .	**oo**-na **tah**-tsa dee
A glass of . . .	Un bicchiere di . . .	oon bee-key-**air**-ay dee
Bill/check	Il conto	eel **cone**-toe
Bread	Il pane	eel **pah**-nay
Breakfast	La prima colazione	la **pree**-ma ko-la-**tsee**-oh-nay
Cocktail/aperitif	L'aperitivo	la-pay-ree-**tee**-vo
Dinner	La cena	la **chen**-a
Fixed-price menu	Menù a prezzo fisso	may-**noo** a **pret**-so **fee**-so
Fork	La forchetta	la for-**ket**-a
I am diabetic	Ho il diabete	o eel dee-a-**bay**-tay
I am vegetarian	Sono vegetariano/a	**so**-no vay-jay-ta-ree-**ah**-no/a
I'd like . . .	Vorrei . . .	vo-**ray**
I'd like to order	Vorrei ordinare	vo-**ray** or-dee-**nah**-ray

Is service included?	Il servizio è incluso?	eel ser-**vee**-tzee-o ay een-**kloo**-zo
It's good/bad	È buono/cattivo	ay **bwo**-no/ka-**tee**-vo
It's hot/cold	È caldo/freddo	ay **kahl**-doe/**fred**-o
Knife	Il coltello	eel kol-**tel**-o
Lunch	Il pranzo	eel **prahnt**-so
Menu	Il menù	eel may-**noo**
Napkin	Il tovagliolo	eel toe-va-lee-**oh**-lo
Please give me . . .	Mi dia . . .	mee **dee**-a
Salt	Il sale	eel **sah**-lay
Spoon	Il cucchiaio	eel koo-kee-**ah**-yo
Sugar	Lo zucchero	lo **tsoo**-ker-o
Waiter/Waitress	Cameriere/cameriera	ka-mare-**yer**-ay/ ka-mare-**yer**-a
Wine list	La lista dei vini	la **lee**-sta **day**-ee **vee**-nee

Travel Smart Amalfi Coast, Capri & Naples

GETTING HERE AND AROUND

■ AIR TRAVEL

Air travel to Italy is frequent and virtually problem-free, except for airport- or airline-related union strikes that may cause delays. Alitalia, Italy's national flag carrier, has the most nonstop flights to Rome and Milan, from which you can fly on to Naples.

Flying time to Milan or Rome is approximately 8–8½ hours from New York, 10–11 hours from Chicago, 11½ hours from Dallas (via New York), and 11½ hours from Los Angeles. Flights from Rome to Naples are around 30 minutes and from Milan to Naples, about 1 hour.

Confirm flights within Italy the day before travel. Labor strikes are frequent and can affect not only air travel, but also the local trains that serve the airport. Your airline will have information about strikes directly affecting its flight schedule. If you are taking a train to get to the airport, check with the local tourist agency or rail station about upcoming strikes.

Airline Security Issues Transportation Security Administration (⊕ www.tsa.gov) has answers for almost every question that might come up. A helpful Web site for information (location, phone numbers, local transportation, etc.) about all of the airports in Italy is ⊕ www.travel-library.com/airports/europe/italy.

AIRPORTS

The major gateways to Italy include Rome's Aeroporto Leonardo da Vinci (FCO), better known as Fiumicino, and Milan's Aeroporto Malpensa (MXP). Most flights to Naples from North America and Australia make connections at Fiumicino and Malpensa or another European airport, though a number of budget airlines offer direct flights to Naples from European destinations. You can also take the FS airport train to Termini, Rome's main station, to connect with a train to Naples. It will take about 30 minutes to get from Fiumicino to Termini.

Just outside Naples, **Aeroporto Capodichino** (NAP) serves the Campania region. It handles domestic and international flights, including several flights daily between Naples and Rome (flight time 30 minutes). The airport is run by GESAC, part of BAA (British Airports Authority), the majority stakeholder.

Although it was completely renovated in 2009, being so close to Naples's city center—a 10-minute drive at nonpeak travel times—Capodichino Airport has little room for expansion. There are skeletal facilities at the airport, so no Internet center, no fitness center, and no airport hotels: On short stopovers—especially if you have to leave early the next morning before road traffic builds up—you're better off staying in the city center. The nearest thing to an airport hotel is the Holiday Inn (shuttle service every hour to the airport): in the *Centro Direzionale* (Business District) close to the industrial eastern suburbs, this is not the sort of place for evening strolls by the Mediterranean.

Airport Information Aeroporto Capodichino (⊠ *Viale Umberto Maddalena, 5 km [3 mi] north of Naples* ☎ *081/7896111* ⊕ *www.gesac.it*). **Aeroporto Leonardo da Vinci-Fiumicino** (*Fiumicino* ⊠ *35 km ([20 mi]) southwest of Rome* ☎ *06/65951* ⊕ *www.adr.it*). **Aeroporto Malpensa** (⊠ *45 km [28 mi] north of Milan* ☎ *02/74852200* ⊕ *www.sea-aeroportimilano.it*).

FLIGHTS

When flying internationally, you must usually choose among a domestic carrier, the national flag carrier of the country, and a foreign carrier from a third country. You may, for example, choose to fly Alitalia to Italy—as the national flag carrier, it has the greatest number of nonstops. However, domestic and international carriers, such as Meridiana, Air Italy, EasyJet, and Air Berlin may have direct connections between Naples and destinations in other European countries and slightly cheaper flights within Italy.

Until a few years ago, no international carrier made a transatlantic flight to Naples, but Meridiana now connects New York's JFK Airport to Naples's Aeroporto Capodichino once or twice a week from late June to early September (it also flies to Palermo). Alitalia (operating with Air One) offers an extensive schedule of daily flights connecting Naples with the major international hubs of Rome and Milan, as well as Bologna, Catania, Genoa, Palermo, Trieste, Turin, and Venice. It also offers nonstop flights to Italy from the United States as part of a transatlantic joint venture with Air France-KLM and Delta. Alitalia has direct flights to Boston, Chicago, Los Angeles, Miami, and New York City. For further information about schedules, special fare promotions visit ⊕ *www.alitalia.com* or *www.alitaliausa.com*.

Domestic connections to Naples are also handled by other carriers, such as Easy-Jet (Milan Malpensa and Venice), Air Italy, (Catania, Milan Bergamo, Olbia, Palermo, Turin, and Verona), Meridiana (Cagliari, Milan Linate, Olbia, and Venice) and Lufthansa (Milan Linate). For connections from abroad, Alitalia also offers direct flights from Athens, Vueling offers a daily flight from Barcelona, and Air Berlin competes with Lufthansa on direct flights from German airports. Several other carriers link major European cities with Naples—for instance, British Airways offers a direct route from London-Gatwick, Iberia connects Madrid and Naples, and Transavia serves connections from Amsterdam and Copenhagen. Other connections are offered between Naples and Dublin (Aer Lingus), and Budapest and Prague (WizzAir).

Airline Contacts Aer Lingus
(📞 02/43458326 ⊕ www.aerlingus.com).**Air Berlin** (📞 199/400737 within Italy ⊕ www.airberlin.com). **Air Italy** (📞 895/5895589 within Italy ⊕ www.airitaly.it). **Alitalia** (📞 06/2222 within Italy ⊕ www.alitalia.com 📞 1800/2235730 within U.S.). **British Airways**

(📞 800/247–9297 ⊕ www.britishairways.com). **EasyJet** (📞 848/887766 ⊕ www.easyjet.com). **Meridiana** (📞 892/928 within Italy ⊕ www.meridiana.it). **Transavia** (📞 899009901 ⊕ www.transavia.com).**Vueling** (📞 899/234555 within Italy ⊕ www.vueling.com). **Wizz Air** (📞 199/259100 within Italy ⊕ www.wizzair.com).

▮ BOAT TRAVEL

As one of the great harbors of the world, Naples offers a wide array of boat, ferry (*traghetti*), and hydrofoil (*aliscafo*) services between the city, the islands of the bay, the Sorrentine peninsula, and other Mediterranean destinations. The main station is at the Molo Beverello—the port harbor of Naples opposite the Castel Nuovo (and near the Montesanto and future Piazza Municipio metro stops)—along the waterfront of Piazza Municipio. Here, hydrofoils and ferries run by Caremar, Linee Lauro, SNAV, and Alilauro connect Naples with Sorrento, Capri, Ischia, and Procida. More hydrofoils depart for Capri, Ischia, and Procida, as well as the farther-flung islands of Ponza and Ventotene to the northwest and the Aeolian islands off Sicily's northern coast, from the Mergellina harbor (a short walk from the Mergellina train station) at the far western end of the Riviera di Chiaia; the trip to Ischia and Procida is shorter and cheaper if you use the ferry that departs from Pozzuoli harbor (the nearest metro station is on the Cumana line at Pozzuoli). Next to the Molo Beverello is the Stazione Marittima (Molo Angioino), where larger ferries make trips to Ponza, the Aeolian Islands, Sicily, and Sardinia.

In 2002, Campania unveiled its exciting and extensive new Metro del Mare public transport system. This ambitious new network is headquartered at the Molo Beverello port in downtown Naples. From this major harbor hub, and sailing north as far as the Phlegrean Fields and as south as Salerno, a web of ferries and fast jet boats connect the top ports of call, including Bacoli, Pozzuoli, Naples (Molo Beverello), Torre Annunziata, Sorrento, Positano, and Amalfi. There are six lines of the Metro del Mare, with some running only on weekends (e.g., MM4, which runs from Naples to Sapri in the Cilento south of Maiori) and others running on a daily basis (e.g., MM1, which goes four times daily from Sorrento to Monte di Procida, stopping at Castellammare, Torre del Greco, Portici, Napoli Mergellina, Pozzuoli, and Bacoli). If you want to go directly from Naples to Positano, you will have to pay more a ticket on one of the three daily express boats. Note that the Metro del Mare service runs from Easter time through October only. Check the local papers (*Il Mattino* or *La Repubblica*) for timetables or go to ⊕ *www. metrodelmare.net*. Prices are highly competitive and make this the cheapest way to get around by sea. One-way fares vary from as little as €2 (Naples to Pozzuoli) to €12 (Naples to Salerno). Better, if you purchase a three-day Campania Artecard (*see the Planner section in Chapter 6*), you also get a three-day travel card and two free Metro del Mare tickets.

Hydrofoil service is generally twice as fast as ferries and almost double the price. The service is considerably more frequent in summer. *For specific information about boat, ferry, and hydrofoil travel between Naples and other destinations on the Bay of Naples and the Amalfi Coast, see the "Getting Here" and "Getting Around" sections near the beginning of each regional chapter.* Car ferries operate to the islands of the Bay of Naples, but advance reservations are best.

FARES AND SCHEDULES

The most comprehensive coverage of ferry, hydrofoil, and boat services and schedules is found in the local paper *Il Mattino*, which features a *Per chi Parte* ("For Those Departing") section every day. *Qui Napoli*, the helpful monthly English-language periodical for visitors to Naples, as well as the handy events booklet, *Le Pagine dell' Ozio*, also lists ferry and hydrofoil

schedules. As there are substantial seasonal variations, double-check departure times and days, especially when traveling further afield on low-frequency services. Alternatively, consult the excellent Web site, ⊕ *www.campaniatrasporti.it* for a helpful overview of most public transport lines in Campania.

Boat Information Alilauro (☎ *081/7614909* ⊕ *www.alilauro.it*). **Caremar** (☎ *081/5513882* ⊕ *www.caremar.it*). **Linee Lauro** (☎ *081/5522838* ⊕ *www.lineelauro.it*). **Metro del Mare** (☎ *199/446644* ⊕ *www. metrodelmare.net*). **Navigazione Libera del Golfo** (☎ *081/5527209* ⊕ *www.navlib.it*). **Siremar** (☎ *081/5800340* ⊕ *www.siremar.it*). **SNAV** (☎ *081/7612348* ⊕ *www.snavali.com*). **Tirrenia** (☎ *8408/99000 or 081/7201111* ⊕ *www. tirrenia.it*).

▎BUS TRAVEL

Campania's bus network is extensive and in some areas buses can be more direct (and, therefore, faster) than local trains, so it's a good idea to compare bus and train schedules. Bus services outside cities are organized on a regional level, and often by private companies. Campania has three main bus companies, listed below. ANM handles buses within Naples, CTP usually handles medium- and long-distance routes out of Naples, while SITA services longer trips, including the Amalfi Coast. Taking buses from Naples requires both research and patience, since there's no central bus station as such: different bus lines leave from different city squares, with the situation being compounded by regular traffic reorganization in Piazza Garibaldi to accommodate the ongoing metro construction. Once you've tracked down the schedule and departure point, you'll find the service fairly reliable and uniform. All buses—as indeed all public transport—are no-smoking.

CUTTING COSTS

For bus services within the region of Campania you should buy a **Unicocampania** ticket. For bus trips to Benevento, for example, where bus connections are better than train, you should buy a Fascia 6 ticket (€4.30, valid 180 minutes). This will cover combined use of other buses, funiculars, trains, trams, and trolley buses on an outward journey. Note that if you purchase a three-day **Artecard**, you get free transport within the region, regardless of the *Fascia*. Children up to 1 meter (just over 3 feet) tall travel free.

Discount Passes Artecard (☎ 800/600601 toll-free in Italy ⊕ www.campaniartecard.it). **Unicocampania** (☎ 081/5513109 ⊕ www. unicocampania.it).

PAYING

Tickets are not sold onboard buses so you must purchase them in advance (cash only) by machine (often no change given), at newsstands, or at tobacconists. Remember to time-stamp your ticket after you board as conductors sometimes do spot checks. Keep in mind that many ticket sellers close for several hours at midday, so it's always wise to stock up on bus tickets when you have the chance.

Bus Information ANM (✉ Via G.B. Marino 1, Napoli ☎ 800/639525 toll-free in Italy ⊕ www.anm.it). **CTP** (✉ Via Sannio 19, Napoli ☎ 081/7001111 ⊕ www.ctpn.it). **SITA** (✉ Varco Immacolata, inside Molo Beverello port, Napoli ☎ 199/730749 ⊕ www.sitabus.it).

▌CAR TRAVEL

Combine the cost of gasoline (as much as €1.40 per liter, or $6 per gallon, at this writing), the weak and ever changeable dollar, the gridlock traffic in and around Naples, parking fees, and driving standards in southern Italy, and you get some good reasons for not traveling by car in Campania. For recidivist motorists and those who need to reach isolated locations, there's an extensive network of *autostrade* (toll highways), complemented by equally well-maintained but free *superstrade* (expressways). The ticket you're issued on entering an autostrada must be returned when you exit and pay the toll; on some shorter highways, like the *Tangenziale* around Naples, the flat-rate toll €0.80 is paid on exiting; the Naples–Salerno toll €1.60 is paid on entry. Viacard cards, on sale for €25, €50, or €75 at many autostrada locations, allow you to pay for tolls in advance, although if you're just using the car on local autostrade within Campania you may find yourself with substantial surplus credit on your card at the end of your trip. It is easier to simply use your credit card. At special lanes, identifiable by the blue sign, you simply slip the card into a designated slot at many autostrada locations, make paying tolls easier and faster. Here are some important signage words to know. A *raccordo* is a ring road surrounding a city, while a *tangenziale* bypasses a city entirely. An *uscita* is an "exit." *Strade regionale* and *strade provinciale* (regional and provincial highways, denoted by *S, SS, SR,* or *SP* numbers) may be single-lane roads, as are all secondary roads; directions and turnoffs aren't always clearly marked.

Your driver's license may not be recognized outside your home country. An International Driver's Permit is a good idea; it's available from the American or Canadian automobile association, and, in the United Kingdom, from the Automobile Association or Royal Automobile Club. These international permits are universally recognized, and having one in your wallet may save you a problem with the local authorities.

If you want to hire a driver, this service can usually be arranged through hotels or travel agents. Agree on a flat daily rate beforehand, which will include the driver, car, and gasoline. In most cases you would be expected to pay extra for the driver's meals, as well as any parking fees incurred.

AUTO CLUBS

There are two major automobile clubs operative in Italy: ACI (Automobile Club d'Italia), which also provides breakdown assistance coverage; subscription to the TCI (Touring Club Italiano) provides motorists with maps and logistical assistance when planning journeys and holidays, besides taking an active interest in Italian heritage preservation. For an annual surcharge of €20, the TCI will also provide breakdown assistance.

In Italy Automobile Club D'Italia (☎ 081/7253811 ⊕ www.aci.it). Touring Club Italiano (☎ 081/4203489 ⊕ www.touringclub.it).

In the U.S. American Automobile Association (AAA ☎ 315/797-5000 ⊕ www.aaa.com) ; most contact with the organization is through state and regional members.

GASOLINE

Gas stations are along the main highways. Those on autostrade are open 24 hours. Otherwise, gas stations are generally open Monday through Saturday from 7 am to 7 pm with a break at lunchtime. Many stations also have self-service pumps, which usually accept bills of €5, €10, or €20. Gas stations on autostrade offer motorists the choice of self-service or full-service gasoline (more expensive per liter, no tip required). Credit cards are widely accepted, especially at major stations along main roads. Gas, so-called *benzina verde* (unleaded fuel known as "green gasoline"), costs about €1.30–€1.40 per liter. Confusingly, the Italian word *gasolio* means diesel fuel. It costs about €1.20 per liter (if you are renting a car, ask about the fuel type before you leave the agency).

PARKING

Parking space is at a premium in Naples and most towns, but especially in the *centri storici* (historic centers), which are filled with narrow streets and restricted circulation zones. It's often a good idea (if not the only option) to park your car in a designated (preferably attended) lot. The *parcometro*, the Italian version of metered parking in which you purchase prepaid tickets (from a newsstand or tobacconist's) that you scratch to indicate time and date of arrival and leave on the dashboard, is common both in Naples

and in many of the surrounding towns. You will also find coin-only parking ticket machines at regular intervals. Watch the display panel at the front of the machine, which gives you the expiration time as you insert the coins. If driving to the more popular venues in Naples at night, you may be encouraged to park by a *parcheggiatore abusivo* (unlicensed parking attendant) who will expect a tip (about €1). Bear in mind that this will not stop your car from being clamped or towed away, and such practices are really just fueling the submerged economy.

A red sign with a horizontal white stripe through it means do not enter; a blue circular sign with a red slash or an X means no parking, as do the signs "Vietato Sostare, Divieto di Sosta" and "Non Parcheggiare." Wheel clamping is increasingly common in Naples, making parking offenses potentially costly and time-consuming. ■TIP➔ If you have baggage in the car, always park your car in an attended car park or garage.

RENTALS

Most American chains have affiliates in Italy, but the rates are usually lower if you book a car before you leave home. To rent a car in Italy, generally you must be at least 23 years old. Additional drivers must be identified in the contract and must qualify with the age limits. There may be an additional daily fee for more than one driver. Upon rental, all companies require credit cards as a warranty; to rent bigger cars (2,000 cc or more), you must often show two credit cards. There are no special restrictions on senior-citizen drivers. Book car seats, required for children under age 3, in advance (the cost is generally about €50 for the duration of the rental). Most rentals are standard transmissions. You must request an automatic and often pay a higher rate. A satellite navigation system will cost around €10 per day, and is an extremely useful investment.

All rental agencies operating in Italy require that you buy a collision-damage waiver and a theft-protection policy, but those costs will already be included in the rates you are quoted. Be aware that coverage may be denied if the named driver on the rental contract is not the driver at the time of the incident. Also ask your rental company about other included coverage when you reserve the car and/or pick it up.

Hiring a car with a driver can come in handy, particularly if you plan to do some wine tasting or drive along the Amalfi Coast. Ask at your hotel for recommended drivers, or inquire at the local tourist office.

RENTAL CARS

Renting a car in Italy is helpful when exploring the off-the-beaten-track countryside, but not necessary, as the bus system throughout Campania is excellent and far-flung. Signage on country roads is usually pretty good, but be prepared for fast and impatient fellow drivers. Major car-rental companies have boxy "utility" cars and Fiats in various sizes that are always in good condition.

Your driver's license may not be recognized outside your home country. You may not be able to rent a car without an International Driving Permit (IDP), which can be used only in conjunction with a valid driver's license and which translates your license into 10 languages. Check the AAA Web site for more info as well as for IDPs ($15) themselves.

LOCAL AGENCIES

Major Agencies Alamo (☎ 877/222–9075 ⊕ www.alamo.com). **Auto Europe** (☎ 888/223–5555 ⊕ www.autoeuropa.it). **Avis** (☎ 800/331–1212 ⊕ www.avis.com). **Budget** (☎ 800/527–0700 ⊕ www.budget. com). **Hertz** (☎ 800/654–3131 ⊕ www.hertz. com). **National** (☎ 877/222–9058 ⊕ www. nationalcar.com). **Nova** (☎ 866/668–2227 ⊕ www.novacarhire.com).

Car and Driver Due Golfi Car Service (☎ 339/830–7748 in Italy ⊕ www.duegolficarservice.com).

ROAD CONDITIONS

Autostrade are well maintained, as are most interregional highways. The condition of provincial (county) roads varies, but road maintenance at this level is generally decent in Campania. Street and road signs are often challenging—a satellite navigator or good map and patience are essential. When stopping to ask locals for directions, it's usually pointless to refer to maps as there is no widespread map-reading culture in southern Italy. Just say the name of your destination and listen carefully or watch for hand gestures. In general, driving standards are poor: some drive fast and are impatient with those who don't, while others dawdle along oblivious to those behind them. Widespread nonuse of direction indicators means you have to do a lot of guesswork while motoring.

ROADSIDE EMERGENCIES

In the event of a breakdown, if you're on a major highway or autostrada, you should stay in your car and wait for assistance. It can be extremely dangerous to walk by the roadside. If you have to abandon your vehicle, make sure you use the reflective triangle and wear the orange jacket that every vehicle in Italy should contain.

In the event of an accident that goes beyond a mild bump or scratch, make sure the emergency services are notified as soon as possible—this is where mobile phones really come in handy. If you have rented the car, there should be an emergency number on the rental contract or on the key ring.

Emergency Services ACI Emergency Service offers 24-hour road service. Dial ☎ 803116 from any phone to reach the ACI dispatch operator.

RULES OF THE ROAD

Driving is on the right. Regulations are similar to those in the United States, except that a right turn is not permitted on a red light. Daytime use of headlights is now obligatory on all roads outside urban areas, and seat belts must be worn at all times—despite high noncompliance rates in Campania. In most Italian towns the use of the horn is forbidden; a large sign, "Zona di Silenzio," indicates where. Elsewhere, according to the Italian Highway Code, horns can only be used in situations where there is "immediate and real danger." Some drivers interpret this as covering every sharp bend on the Amalfi Coast, although an alternative noise-free technique is to slow down and keep a foot hovering over the brake pedal. In winter you'll often be required to have snow chains, especially when traveling south on the main autostrada from Salerno to Reggio Calabria, and in upland areas within the region. Speed limits are 130 kph (80 mph) on autostrade, 110 kph (70 mph) on *superstrade,* and 90 kph (55 mph) on state and provincial roads, unless otherwise marked. If your mobile phone rings while driving, you should either ignore it or pull over and stop when it's safe to do so—stiff sanctions have been introduced to reduce the use of handheld mobile phones while driving. Fines for driving after drinking are heavy, including the suspension of license and the additional possibility of six months' imprisonment.

▌ TRAIN TRAVEL

The fastest trains in Italy are the Alta Velocità (AV) and Freccia Rossa (Red Arrow), operating between Rome and Naples (70 minutes), and also running the length of the peninsula, including Naples–Milan via Rome, Florence, and Bologna. A close second come the Eurostar (ES) trains (1 hour 45 minutes); seat reservations are included in the fare of the AV and ES. Some Eurostars (the ETR 460 trains) have little aisle and luggage space (although there's a space near the door where you can put large bags). To avoid having to squeeze through narrow aisles, board at your car (look for the number on the reservation ticket). Car numbers are displayed on their exterior. Next-fastest trains are the Intercity (IC) trains, for which you pay a supplement and for which seat reservations may be required.

Interregionale trains usually make more stops and are a little slower. *Regionale* and *locale* trains are the slowest; many serve commuters.

Note that Naples has four main-line stations: Stazione Centrale, Piazza Garibaldi, Napoli Mergellina, and Napoli Campi Flegrei. Stazione Central (ground level) and Piazza Garibaldi (lower level) are in the same building; for Piazza Garibaldi, take the escalator down to the level below Napoli Centrale (follow signs to the *Metropolitana*). Some trains to Rome leave from the classy station of Mergellina, four stops away from Piazza Garibaldi on the Metropolitana. As many as four trains— of varying speed and cost—connect Roma Termini and Napoli Centrale every hour (Alta Velocità: 1 hour 10 minutes, €44, second class; Eurostar: 1 hour 45 minutes, €34, second class; Intercity: about 2 hours 10 minutes, €20.50, second class); fewer departures on Sunday and after 5 pm.

There is a refreshment service on all long-distance trains, with mobile carts and a cafeteria or dining car. Tap water on trains is not drinkable. There's no smoking on any public transport in Italy, though you will find diehards puffing away near the luggage compartments between carriages. When traveling in the Naples area, potential confusion can arise in Pompeii, as the main-line station is a good 20-minute walk from the archaeological site. For the site, you need to take the Circumvesuviana network from Naples to Sorrento and get off at Pompei Scavi (35 minutes).

CLASSES

Most Italian trains have first and second classes. On local trains the higher first-class fare gets you little more than a clean doily on the headrest of your seat, but on long-distance trains you get wider seats, more legroom, and better ventilation and lighting (the Alta Velocità even offers a complimentary drink and snack). At peak travel times, first-class train travel is worth the difference. Remember always try to make seat reservations in advance, for either class, as you can easily run into long ticket lines at the station just when you're hoping to board a train. The self-service machines in major stations can save a lot of time. One advantage of traveling first class is that the cars are almost always not crowded—or, at the very least, less crowded than the second-class compartments. A first-class ticket, in Italian, is *prima classe*; second is *seconda classe*.

CUTTING COSTS

To save money, look into rail passes. But be aware that if you don't plan to cover many miles, you may come out ahead by buying individual tickets.

If Italy is your only destination in Europe, consider purchasing a Eurail Italy pass, which allows unlimited travel on the entire Italian Rail network for a set number of travel days within two months: $255 for 4 days of travel in first class ($207 second class); 8 days of travel ($366 first class, $297 second class); and 10 days of travel ($421 first class, $341 second class). Prices are further reduced for groups of two to five people traveling together. More information can be found at ⊕ *www.raileurope.com*.

Once in Italy, inquire about the Carta Verde (Green Card) if you're under 26 (€40 for one year), which entitles you to a 10% discount on all first- and second-class tickets in Italy, and up to 25% discount on international lines. Those under 26 should also inquire about discount travel fares under the Billet International Jeune (BIJ) and Euro Domino Junior schemes. Also in Italy, you can purchase the Carta Argento (Silver Card) (€30 for one year, free for over 75s), if you are over 60, which also allows a 15% discount on all first- and second-class rail travel. For further information, check out the Ferrovie dello Stato (FS) Web site (⊕ *www. trenitalia.com*). Toddlers under 4 travel free on trains, though they have no right to a seat, while children under 12 travel for half the fare, but must be accompanied by an adult.

If you plan to take many trains, consider a Cartaviaggio (Travel Card) or Cartafreccia (Arrow Card). The travel points you collect can be converted to free train tickets.

Italy is one of 21 countries in which you can use Eurail Passes, which provide unlimited first-class travel in all of the participating countries. If you plan to rack up the miles, get a standard pass. Train travel is available for 15 days (from $648) up to 3 months ($1,816). You can also receive discounted fares on some ferry lines. In addition to standard Eurail Passes, ask about special rail-pass plans. Among these are the Eurail Youthpass (for those under age 26), Eurail Saverpass and Eurail Saver Flexipass (which give a discount for two or more people traveling together), Eurail Flexipass (which allows a certain number of travel days within a set period), and the EurailDrive Pass, which combines travel by train and rental car. Whichever pass you choose, remember that you must purchase your Eurailpass before you leave for Europe. You can get further information and order tickets at the Rail Europe Web site (⊕ *www.raileurope.com*).

Many travelers assume that rail passes guarantee them seats on the trains they wish to ride. Not so. You need to book seats ahead even if you're using a rail pass. Seat reservations are required on some European trains, particularly high-speed trains, and are a good idea on trains that may be crowded—particularly in summer on popular routes. You'll also need a reservation if you purchase sleeping accommodations. Trains going from the north of Italy via Naples through to Reggio Calabria in the toe of Italy will be particularly tightly packed, especially around weekends and public holidays. If traveling on a Saturday evening or Sunday, it may be worth finding out about important soccer matches and steering well clear of local fans by upgrading to first class or changing your schedule.

If you're on a tight schedule or just want to avoid unpleasant surprises, double-check beforehand whether there's a strike (*sciopero*) planned for the day you're traveling. On average, industrial action is usually planned for 24-hour periods on Friday or Monday, and only limited service may be provided while the strike lasts.

FARES AND SCHEDULES

Trains can be very crowded; it's often a good idea to make a reservation. To avoid long lines at station windows, you can buy tickets with seat reservations up to two months in advance at travel agencies displaying the Trenitalia emblem. The self-service machines in major stations will also save you time. Tickets can be purchased at the last minute, but seat reservations can be made at agencies (or the train station) in advance on Eurostar and Alta Velocità trains; your ticket includes a free seat reservation: if you board without a ticket, you will have to pay a surcharge of €50 on application to train staff.

Except on Eurostar and Alta Velocità trains, and Inter City trains with booking, where your ticket is only valid for one train on one day, all tickets must be date-stamped in the small yellow or red machines near the tracks before you board. Once stamped, your ticket is valid for six hours if your destination is within 200 km (124 mi), for 24 hours for destinations beyond that. You can get on and off at will at stops in between for the duration of the ticket's validity. If you forget to stamp your ticket in the machine, or you didn't buy a ticket, you are liable to a hefty €50 fine, over and above the fare to your destination. Don't wait for the conductor to find out that you're without a valid ticket (unless the train is overcrowded and walking becomes impossible), as he might charge you a much heavier fine. You can buy train tickets for nearby destinations (within a 200-km [124-mi] range) at tobacconists and at ticket machines in stations.

PAYING

In most cases you can pay for train tickets with any of the major credit cards, though ticket office staff at smaller stations (like Mergellina in Naples) may still raise eyebrows at plastic. Only euros are accepted in cash payment, though at Napoli Centrale station there's a handy exchange bureau—and a bank in the same forecourt—where you can change currency.

Information and Passes Eurailpasses are available through travel agents and **Rail Europe** (☎ 800/622–8600 ⊕ www.raileurope.com).

Information The main train station in Campania is Naples's **Stazione Centrale** (✉ *Piazza Garibaldi* ☎ *199/892021 within Italy* ⊕ *www.trenitalia.com*). The Ferrovia Circumvesuviana leaves for points east from the **Stazione Circumvesuviana** (✉ *Corso Garibaldi 387* ☎ *081/7722444* ⊕ *www.vesuviana.it*) ; all trains also stop on the lower level of Stazione Centrale. Destinations include Ercolano (Herculaneum), Pompei Scavi–Villa dei Misteri (Pompeii), and Sorrento. Note that there are two Circumvesuviana stations in the town of Pompeii, served by different lines. For the archaeological site, take the Sorrento line. SEPSA manages two railway lines that leave from the **Stazione Cumana** (✉ *Piazzetta Montesanto, near Montesanto Metro station* ☎ *081/7354111* ⊕ *www.sepsa.it*). Both end at Torregaveta, at the west end of the Bay of Naples; the Cumana line goes along the coast and stops at Pozzuoli and Lucrino (near Baia), among other places. **Salerno's train station** (✉ *Piazza V. Veneto* ☎ *199/892021 within Italy* ⊕ *www.trenitalia.com*) is a stop on the Milan–Reggio Calabria line.

Other Resources Trenitalia (☎ *199/892021 within Italy* ⊕ *www.trenitalia.com*).

ESSENTIALS

■ ACCOMMODATIONS

Campania has a varied and abundant number of hotels, bed-and-breakfasts, *agriturismi (farm stays)*, and rental properties. Throughout the cities and the countryside you can find very sophisticated, luxurious palaces and villas as well as rustic farmhouses and small hotels. Six-hundred-year-old palazzi and converted monasteries have been restored as luxurious hotels, while retaining the original atmosphere. At the other end of the spectrum, boutique hotels inhabit historic buildings using chic Italian design for the interiors. Increasingly, the famed Italian wineries are creating rooms and apartments for three-day to weeklong stays.

The lodgings we list are the cream of the crop in each price category. We always list the facilities that are available, but we don't specify whether they cost extra; when pricing accommodations, always ask what's included and what costs extra (air-conditioning often incurs an extra charge). Properties are assigned price categories based on the range between their least- and most-expensive standard double room at high season (excluding holidays).

Note that this region of Italy has many resort hotels and in peak-season months (usually June to September), some of them require either half- or full-board arrangements, whereby your (increased) room tab includes one or two meals provided by the hotel restaurant. Board plans, which are usually an option offered in addition to the basic room plan, are generally only available with a minimum two- or three-night stay and are, of course, more expensive than the basic room rate, running from €10 to €50 per meal. Note that the hotel price charts in this book reflect basic room rates only. Inquire about board plans when making your reserva-

tions; details and prices are often stated on hotel Web sites.

Useful terms to know when booking a room are *aria condizionata* (air-conditioning), *bagno in stanza* (private bath), *letto matrimoniale* (double bed), *letti singoli* (twin beds), *letti singoli uniti* (twin beds pushed together). Italy does not really have queen- or king-size beds, although some beds, particularly in four- and five-star accommodations, can be larger than standard. Phrases that could come in handy include: *Vi prego di fornire informazioni riguardo il vostro albergo/pensione. Vorrei una camera doppia/camera matrimoniale con bagno in camera.* (Please supply me with information regarding your hotel/pensione. I would like a room with two single beds/a double bed with private bath); *Una camera sul piano alto con vista* (A room on a high floor with a view); *Una camera al piano basso* (A room on a low floor); *Una camera silenziosa* (A quiet room).

Hotels with the designation BP (for Breakfast Plan) at the end of their listing include breakfast in their rates; offerings can vary from coffee and a roll to an elaborate buffet. Those designated EP (European Plan) have no meals included; MAP (Modified American Plan) means you get breakfast and one meal; FAP (Full American Plan) includes all meals.

APARTMENT AND HOUSE RENTALS

More and more travelers are turning away from the three-countries-in-two-weeks style of touring and choosing to spend a week in one city or a month in the countryside. Renting an apartment, a farmhouse, or a villa can be economical depending on the number of people in your group and your budget. All are readily available throughout Italy. The rental agent may meet you at the property for the initial check-in or the owner may be present, while the rental agent only handles the online reservation and financial arrangements.

Issues to keep in mind when renting an apartment in a city or town are the neighborhood (street noise and ambience), the availability of an elevator or number of stairs, the furnishings (including pots and pans and linens), and the cost of utilities (ask if they are included in the rental rate). Inquiries about countryside properties should also include how isolated the property is. (Ask about accessibility to the nearest town.)

Contacts At Home Abroad (☎ *212/421-9165* ⊕ *www.athomeabroadinc.com*). **Barclay International Group** (☎ *516/364-0064* or *800/845-6636* ⊕ *www.barclayweb.com*). **Drawbridge to Europe** (☎ *541/482-7778* or *888/268-1148* ⊕ *www.drawbridgetoeurope. com*). **Home Away** (☎ *512/493-0382* ⊕ *www.homeaway.com*). **Interhome** (*800/882-6864* ⊕ *www.interhome.us*). **RentaVilla** (☎ *877/250-4366* ⊕ *www. rentavilla.com*). **Villas & Apartments Abroad** (☎ *212/213-6435* ⊕ *www.vaanyc. com*). **Villas International** (☎ *415/499-9490* or *800/221-2260* ⊕ *www.villasintl. com*). **Villas of Distinction** (☎ *800/289-0900* ⊕ *www.villasofdistinction.com*).

BED-AND-BREAKFASTS

Increasing numbers of southern Italians, especially Neapolitans, are following the long-tried British formula of bed-and-breakfast. Although these may represent substantial cost savings, be aware that quality varies. When booking, try to find out exactly what's on offer: It could be a cramped room in a faceless suburb with overly inquisitive hosts, or you could strike it lucky with a room with an 18th-century frescoed ceiling in a quiet city-center location. For further information, contact the local tourist information office or one of the agencies below.

Reservation Services Bed & Breakfast. com (☎ *512/322-2710* or *800/462-2632* ⊕ *www.bedandbreakfast.com*) also sends out an online newsletter. **Bed & Breakfast Inns Online** (☎ *310/280-4363* or *800/215-7365* ⊕ *www.bbonline.com*). **BnB Finder.com** (☎ *212/432-7693* or *888/547-8226* ⊕ *www.bnbfinder.com*). **Rent a Bed** (☎ *081/417721* ⊕ *www.rentabed.it*).

FARM HOLIDAYS AND AGRITOURISM

Rural accommodations in the *agriturismo* (agritourism) category are increasingly popular with both Italians and visitors to Italy. A little surfing on the Internet can pay dividends: just call up a search engine and key in the words, say, "agriturismo" and "Campania," and see what gives. Although technologically literate, few farms in the Naples area accept credit cards, so remember to load up with cash before your stay.

Information Agriturist (☎ *06/6852337* ⊕ *www.agriturist.it*). **Italy Farm Holidays** (☎ *914/631-7880* ⊕ *www.italyfarmholidays. com*). **Turismo Verde** (☎ *06/3240111* ⊕ *www. turismoverde.it*).

HOME EXCHANGES

With a direct home exchange you stay in someone else's home while they stay in yours. Some outfits also deal with vacation homes, so you're not actually staying in someone's full-time residence, just their vacant weekend place.

Italians have historically not been as enthusiastic about home exchanges as others have been; however, there are many great villas and apartments in Italy owned by foreigners, such as Americans, who use the home exchange services.

Exchange Clubs Home Exchange.com (☎ *310/798-3864* or *800/877-8723* ⊕ *www. homeexchange.com*) ; membership from $9.95 a month. **HomeLink International** (☎ *800/638-3841* ⊕ *www.homelink.org*) ; $115 yearly for membership **Intervac U.S.** (☎ *800/756-4663* ⊕ *www.intervacus.com*) ; $100 for membership.

LOCAL DO'S AND TABOOS

GREETINGS

Upon meeting and leave-taking, both friends and strangers wish each other good day or good evening (*buongiorno, buonasera*); *ciao* isn't used between strangers. Italians who are friends greet each other with a kiss, usually first on the left cheek, then on the right. When you meet a new person, shake hands.

SIGHTSEEING

Italy is full of churches, and many of them contain significant works of art. They are also places of worship, however, so be sure to dress appropriately. Shorts, tank tops, and sleeveless garments are taboo in most churches throughout the country. Some churches provide scarves at the entrance, but to be safe carry a sweater or other item of clothing to wrap around your bare shoulders before entering.

You should never bring food into a church, and do not sip from your water bottle while inside. If you have a cell phone, turn it off. And avoid entering a church when a service is in progress, especially if it is a private affair such as a wedding or baptism.

OUT ON THE TOWN

Table manners in Italy are formal; rarely do Italians share food from their plates. In a restaurant, be formal and polite with your waiter—don't call across the room for attention.

When you've finished your meal and are ready to go, ask for the check (*il conto*); unless it's well past closing time, or there is a waiting list, no waiter will put a bill on your table until you've requested it.

Wine, beer, and other alcoholic drinks are almost always consumed along with food. Public drunkenness is very much looked down on.

Smoking has been banned in all public establishments, much as it has in much of the United States, although you may spot some people flouting the law.

Flowers, chocolates, or a bottle of wine are appropriate hostess gifts when invited to dinner at the home of an Italian.

DOING BUSINESS

Showing up on time for business appointments is the norm and expected in Italy, although there is some flexibility with this in Naples. There are more business lunches than business dinners, and even business lunches aren't common, as Italians view mealtimes as periods of pleasure and relaxation.

Business cards are used throughout Italy, and business suits are the norm for both men and women. To be on the safe side, it is best not to use first names or a familiar form of address until invited to do so.

Business gifts are not the norm, but if one is given it is usually small and symbolic of your home location or type of business.

LANGUAGE

One of the best ways to make connections with the locals is to learn a little of the language. You need not strive for fluency; even just mastering a few basic words and terms is bound to make chatting with the locals more rewarding. "Please" is *per favore*, "thank you" is *grazie*, and "you're welcome" is *prego*.

In larger cities such as Naples, Venice, Rome, and Florence, language is not a big problem. Most hotels have English speakers at their reception desks, and if not, they can always find someone who speaks at least a little English.

You may have trouble communicating in the countryside, but a phrase book and expressive gestures will go a long way. A phrase book and language-tape set can help get you started before you go. *Fodor's Italian for Travelers* (available at bookstores everywhere) is excellent.

■ COMMUNICATIONS

INTERNET

Getting online in and around Naples isn't difficult: free Wi-Fi is available in many places, and there are many public Internet stations and Internet cafés. Prices differ from place to place, so spend some time to find the best deal. Bear in mind that you are required by law to show a photo ID before logging on. Some hotels in Campania have in-room modem lines and have implemented Wi-Fi systems but, as with phones, using the hotel's line is relatively expensive. Always check rates before logging on. You might need an adapter for your computer for the European-style plugs. As always, if you're traveling with a laptop, carry a spare battery and an adapter. Never connect your computer to any socket before asking about surge protection. IBM sells a pea-size modem tester that plugs into a telephone jack to check whether the line is safe to use.

Contact Cybercafes (⊕ *www.cybercafes.com*) lists more than 4,000 Internet cafés worldwide.

PHONES

The good news is that you can now make a direct-dial telephone call from virtually any point on Earth. The bad news? You can't always do so cheaply. Calling from a hotel is almost always the most expensive option; hotels usually add huge surcharges to all calls, particularly international ones. In Naples, you can phone from call centers, many of which are found around Stazione Centrale. Calling cards usually keep costs to a minimum, but only if you purchase them locally. And then there are mobile phones; as expensive as mobile phone calls can be, they are still usually a much cheaper option than calling from your hotel.

When calling Italy from the United States, begin by entering 011 (begin with 00 in other countries), followed by Italy's country code, 39. Note that Italian telephone numbers do not have a standard number of digits (they can range anywhere from four to eight). The area code for Naples

is 081. Essentially, the region from Naples to the islands (Capri, Ischia, Procida) and around the Bay of Naples to Sorrento uses the area code 081; the region along the Amalfi Coast from Positano to Salerno uses the area code 089. For example, a call from New York City to Naples would be dialed as 011 + 39 + 081 + phone number. From the United Kingdom, dial 00 + 39 + 081 + phone number. When dialing an Italian number from abroad, you do not drop the initial 0 from the local area code. The same goes for when you're in Italy. When dialing numbers within Italy, you must always use the area code (e.g., 081 for Naples) even if the number you're calling is just down the road. When dialing from Italy overseas, the country code is 001 for the United States and Canada, 0061 for Australia, 0064 for New Zealand, and 0044 for the United Kingdom.

Mobile phone numbers can be easily recognized; they begin with the digit 3, and run up to about 10 numbers. The first three numbers indicate the service provider (for example, 347 is a Vodafone prefix, 339 is TIM) and are followed by another six or seven digits. Both Vodafone and TIM have good network coverage throughout the Naples area.

CALLING WITHIN ITALY

With the advent of mobile phones, public pay phones are becoming increasingly scarce, although they can be found at train and subway stations, main post offices, and in some bars. In rural areas, town squares usually have a pay phone. Pay phones require a *sceda telefonica* (prepaid phone card). You buy the card (values vary) at Telecom centers, post offices, and tobacconists. Break off the corner of the card, and insert it in the slot on the phone. When you dial, the card's value appears in the window. After you hang up, the card is returned so you can use it until its value runs out.

For all calls within Italy, whether local or long-distance, dial the area code followed by the number. Rates for long-distance calls vary according to the time of day;

it's cheaper to call before 9 am and after 7 or 8 pm. Italy uses the prefix "800" for toll-free or "green" numbers.

CALLING OUTSIDE ITALY

Hotels tend to charge handsomely for long-distance and international calls, so it's best to make calls to the rest of Europe and the United States using a prepaid card. Calling cards on sale for €5 at major newsstands and tobacconists offer up to 380 minutes' worth of calls. Of course, you need to dial either a local Naples number or a toll-free number first in order to gain access. These numbers are given on the card together with the PIN code.

Alternatively, call from public phones using a *scheda telefonica* (see above). These can be purchased from newsstands and tobacconists. You can make collect calls from any phone by dialing 170, which will also get you an English-speaking operator. Calling cards purchased in the United States usually offer terrible rates. Buy a local card when you arrive in Naples. Alternatively, you can call AT&T Direct from Italy using the number below.

The country code for the United States is 1 (dial 00 + 1 + U.S. area code and number).

Access Codes AT&T Direct (☎ *800/172–444*).

MOBILE PHONES

If you have a triband phone (some countries use different frequencies from those used in the United States) and your service provider uses the world-standard GSM network (as do T-Mobile, Cingular, and Verizon), you can probably use your phone abroad. Roaming fees can be steep, however: 99¢ a minute is considered reasonable. And overseas you normally pay the toll charges for incoming calls. It's almost always cheaper to send a text message than to make a call, because text messages have a low set fee (often less than 5¢).

If you just want to make local calls, consider buying a new SIM card (note that your provider may have to unlock your phone for you to use a different SIM card)

and a prepaid service plan in the destination. You'll then have a local number and can make local calls at local rates. If your trip is extensive, you could also simply buy a new cell phone in your destination, as the initial cost will be offset over time.

■TIP→ If you travel internationally frequently, save one of your old mobile phones or buy a cheap one on the Internet; ask your cell phone company to unlock it for you, and take it with you as a travel phone, buying a new SIM card with pay-as-you-go service in each destination.

The cost of cell phones is dropping; you can purchase a cell phone with a prepaid calling card (no monthly service plan) in Italy for less than €50. Inexpensive cell phones are dual band and will not allow you to call the United States, but using an international calling card and the cell phone solves that problem in an inexpensive manner. Most medium to large towns have stores dedicated to selling cell phones. You will need to present your passport to purchase the SIM card that goes with the phone.

Rental cell phones are available from some tour operators in Naples and the Amalfi Coast. Most rental contracts require a refundable deposit that covers the cost of the cell phone (€75–€150) and then set up a monthly service plan that is automatically charged to your credit card. Frequently, rental cell phones will be triple band and allow you to call the United States. Be sure to check the rate schedule before you rent a cell phone and commence calling to prevent a nasty surprise when you receive your credit-card bill two or three months later.

■TIP→ Beware of cell phone (and PDA) thieves. Keep your phone or PDA in a secure pocket or purse. Do not lay it on the bar when you stop for an espresso. Do not zip it into the outside pocket of your backpack in the city or public transport. Do not leave it in your hotel room. If you are using a phone with a monthly service plan, notify your provider immediately if it is lost or stolen.

Contacts Cellular Abroad (☎ 800/287–5072 ⊕ www.cellularabroad.com) rents and sells GMS phones and sells SIM cards that work in many countries. **Mobal** (☎ 888/888–9162 ⊕ www.mobal.com) rents mobiles and sells GSM phones (starting at $49) that will operate in 170 countries. Per-call rates vary throughout the world.

▍ CUSTOMS AND DUTIES

You're always allowed to bring goods of a certain value back home without having to pay any duty or import tax. But there's a limit on the amount of tobacco and liquor you can bring back duty-free, and some countries have separate limits for perfumes; for exact figures, check with your customs department. The values of so-called duty-free goods are included in these amounts. When you shop abroad, save all your receipts, as customs inspectors may ask to see them as well as the items you purchased. If the total value of your goods is more than the duty-free limit, you'll have to pay a tax (most often a flat percentage) on the value of everything beyond that limit.

Travelers from the United States should experience little difficulty clearing customs at any airport in Italy. For returning to the United States, clearing customs is sometimes more difficult. U.S. residents are normally entitled to a duty-free exemption of $800 on items accompanying them. As a general rule, mature cheeses like Parmesan—especially if they're vacuum-packed—are fine, but soft cheeses are not. Condiments such as oil, vinegar, honey, jelly, and jam, are generally admissible. You cannot bring back any of that delicious prosciutto or salami or any other meat product. Fresh mushrooms, truffles, or fresh fruits and vegetables are also forbidden. There are also restrictions on the amount of alcohol allowed in duty-free. Export of antiques and antiquities is best avoided unless you have access to specialist advice; you must have documents such as export permits and receipts when importing such items into the United States. In any case, to avoid unpleasant surprises—and such regulations change with the arrival of every health scare—check with the relevant authorities listed below.

Of goods obtained anywhere outside the EU or goods purchased in a duty-free shop within an EU country, the allowances are: (1) 200 cigarettes or 100 cigarillos or 50 cigars or 250 grams of tobacco; (2) 4 liters of still table wine or 1 liter of spirits over 22% volume or 2 liters of spirits under 22% volume or 2 liters of fortified and sparkling wines; and (3) 60 milliliters of perfume and 250 milliliters of toilet water.

Of goods obtained (duty and tax paid) within another EU country, the guidance levels are: (1) 3,200 cigarettes or 400 cigarillos or 200 cigars or 3 kilograms of tobacco; (2) 90 liters of still table wine plus (3) 10 liters of spirits over 22% volume plus 20 liters of spirits under 22% volume plus 90 liters of sparkling wines plus 110 liters of beer.

To bring pets into Italy, the animal has to have a certificate of health and origin from a recognized public authority in your country, and may also need a certificate that it's free of infectious diseases. For cats and dogs the health certificate must include a declaration of an anti-rabies vaccination at least 20 days and no more than 11 months after issuing the certificate. Similar rules apply to exporting pets from Italy to the United States.

Information in Italy Italian Customs (*Dipartimento delle Dogane e Imposte Indirette* ✉ *Via A. de Gasperi 20, Naples* ☎ *081/7803036 or 081/5521759* ⊕ *www.agenziadogane.it*).

U.S. Information U.S. Customs and Border Protection (⊕ *www.cbp.gov*).

▍ EATING OUT

Though pizza, mozzarella, and pasta with seafood are the flagship dishes in the Naples region, regional cuisine in Campania is both varied and distinctive.

This is reflected by the choice of eateries, especially in Naples and Sorrento: meals range from on-the-hoof two-euro pizzas at kiosks, to earthy *osterie* serving *cucina povera* (land-based cuisine with a good dose of vegetables), and upscale restaurants where service, location, and *piatti* (dishes) should be worth the higher price tag. Italian restaurateurs have become sensitive to those with special dietary requirements, though vegetarians may still have a rough ride, especially as bacon or kindred pork products may be used to flavor many land dishes but never appear as an item on the menu.

MEALS AND MEALTIMES

Breakfast (*la colazione*) is usually served from 7 to 10:30, lunch (*il pranzo*) from 12:30 to 2:30, dinner (*la cena*) from 7:30 pm until midnight. Although it's not usually necessary to reserve a table, remember that you'll find restaurants deserted before 8 in the evening and packed by 9:30, while lunch can extend until as late as 5 pm on Sunday. Menus often seem to be an optional extra in many restaurants, and even if one exists it often bears little relation to what is actually on offer that day. Tune in carefully as the waiter reels off a list of what's good today—following their advice often pays off. A full-scale meal consists of a selection of antipasti followed by a *primo* (pasta or rice), then a *secondo* (meat or fish), rounded off with *frutta o dolci* (fruit or dessert). And unless you want to shock the locals, *never* order a cappuccino after dinner—but a regular espresso is a perfectly acceptable way to finish a meal. A good compromise—if you like your coffee with a dash of milk—is to ask for a *caffè macchiato*.

In general, Neapolitans have moved away from the classic *abbuffata* (Satyricon-style blowout) toward healthier two-course, or even one-course, meals. You should not feel guilty about skipping the main course, especially if you've already had a rich antipasto and primo.

Enoteche (wine bars) are open also in the morning and late afternoon for a snack at the counter. An enoteca menu is often limited to a selection of cheese, cured meats, salads, and desserts, but if there's a kitchen you'll also find soups, pastas, and main courses, too. Most pizzerias are open all day, closing around midnight–1 am, or later in summer and on weekends. Most bars and caffè are open nonstop from 7 am until 8 pm; a few stay open until midnight or so. They can usually fix you up with *un toast* (a toasted sandwich) if every other option is closed.

Not too long ago, *ristoranti* tended to be more elegant and expensive than *trattorie* and *osterie,* which serve traditional, home-style fare in an atmosphere to match. But the distinction has blurred considerably, and an osteria in the center of town might be far fancier (and pricier) than a ristorante across the street. In any sit-down establishment, be it a ristorante, osteria, or trattoria, you are generally expected to order at least a two-course meal, such as: a *primo* (first course) and a *secondo* (main course) or a *contorno* (vegetable side dish); an *antipasto* (starter, often a *crostini,* similar to bruschetta, with a variety of toppings) followed by either a primo or secondo; or a secondo and a *dolce* (dessert).

The typical pizzeria fare in Naples includes *fritti* (deep-fried finger food), such as *crocchè* (fried mashed potatoes) and *arancini* (rice balls stuffed with mozzarella).

The handiest and least expensive places for a quick snack between sights are probably bars, caffè, and *friggitorie* (small stalls selling fritti and small handheld pizzas) spots.

Bars are primarily places to get a coffee and a bite to eat, rather than drinking establishments. Most bars have a selection of *panini* (sandwiches) warmed up on the griddle (*piastra*) and *tramezzini* (sandwiches made of untoasted white bread triangles). Most bars offer beer and a variety of alcohol as well as wines by the glass (sometimes good but more often mediocre). A café (*caffè* in Italian) is like a bar but usually with more tables. Pizza at a *caffè* should be avoided—it's usually heated in a microwave.

If you place your order at the counter, ask if you can sit down: some places charge for table service, others do not. In self-service bars and *caffè* it's good manners to clean your table before you leave. Note that in some places you have to pay a cashier, then place your order and show your *scontrino* (receipt) at the counter. Menus are posted outside most restaurants (in English in tourist areas); if not, you might step inside and ask to take a look at the menu (but don't ask for a table unless you intend to stay). Italians take their food as it is listed on the menu, seldom if ever making special requests such as "dressing on the side" or "hold the olive oil." If you have special dietary needs, however, make them known; they can usually be accommodated. Although mineral water makes its way to almost every table, you can order a carafe of tap water (*acqua dal rubinetto*).

Wiping your bowl clean with a piece of bread (*fare la scarpetta*) is usually considered a sign of appreciation, not bad manners. Spaghetti should be eaten with a fork, although a little help from a spoon won't horrify locals the way cutting spaghetti into little pieces might. Order your espresso (Neapolitans don't usually drink cappuccino after breakfast time) after dessert, not with it. Don't ask for a doggy bag.

Unless otherwise noted, the restaurants listed in this guide are open daily for lunch and dinner.

PAYING

As indicated on *il conto*—the restaurant check—prices for goods and services in Italy include tax. Most restaurants have a cover charge per person, usually listed at the top of the check as *coperto* or *pane*. It should be a modest charge (around €2 per person), except at the most expensive restaurants. Some restaurants add an additional service charge (*servizio*), a percentage of the total bill, but this must be clearly stated on the menu. If *servizio* is included at the bottom of the check, no tip is necessary. Otherwise, a few extra euros left on the table are appreciated. Remember that there's no line to write a tip on the credit card receipt; you will be presented with a slip that includes only the cost of the meal. Although the vast majority of eateries now accept major credit cards, tips are still left in cash. Visa and MasterCard are more widely accepted than American Express.

The price of fish dishes is often given by weight (before cooking), so the price you see on the menu is for 100 grams or a kilo of fish, not for the whole dish. An average fish portion is about 350 grams. When it comes to smaller *caffè* and pizzerias, you sometimes place your order and then show your *scontrino* (receipt) when you move to the counter. Like the rest of Italy, there's a two-tier pricing system in many *caffè*, one for drinks consumed at the counter, and another if you sit down. If there's waiter service in a *caffè*, you should sit down and patiently wait for service, and resist the temptation to pay first (counter prices), pick up your drink, and walk to the table.

When you leave a dining establishment, take your meal bill or receipt with you; although not a common experience, the Italian finance (tax) police can approach you within 100 yards of the establishment at which you've eaten and ask for a receipt. If you don't have one, they can fine you and will fine the business owner for not providing the receipt. The measure is intended to prevent tax evasion; it's not necessary to show receipts when leaving Italy.

RESERVATIONS AND DRESS

Regardless of where you are, it's a good idea to make a reservation if you can. We only mention them specifically when reservations are essential (there's no other way you'll ever get a table) or when they are not accepted. For popular restaurants, book as far ahead as you can (a week or two in advance), and reconfirm as soon as you arrive. (Large parties should always call ahead to check the reservations policy.)

We mention dress only when men are required to wear a jacket or a jacket and tie. But unless they're dining outside or at an oceanfront resort, Italian men never wear shorts or running shoes in a restaurant. The same applies to women: no casual shorts, running shoes, or plastic sandals when going out to dinner. Shorts are acceptable in pizzerias and caffè.

WINES, BEER, AND SPIRITS

Almost all eateries now proudly include a range of local wines from Campania. In terms of grape varieties, Aglianico is the undisputed king of reds, while Fiano, Falanghina, and Greco di Tufo contend for the white crown. Refreshingly, there's a fairly low markup on bottled wines, and a liter of house wine rarely costs more than €8–€10. At the end of your meal you may well be offered some of the house liqueur, probably *limoncello* (a lemon-based liqueur with varying proportions of sugar) or *nocillo* (from green walnuts).

In general, the southern Italians have a relaxed attitude to alcohol consumption. In many homes, a bottle of wine on the dining table is a necessary accompaniment to any meal, like salt and olive oil. All bars and caffè are licensed to serve alcohol, and even takeaway pizzas can be enjoyed with a beer in a city park.

■ ELECTRICITY

The electrical current in Italy is 220 volts, 50 cycles alternating current (AC); wall outlets take Continental-type plugs, with two or three round prongs.

Consider making a small investment in a universal adapter, which has several types of plugs in one lightweight, compact unit. Most laptops and mobile-phone chargers are dual voltage (i.e., they operate equally well on 110 and 220 volts), so require only an adapter. These days the same is true of small appliances such as hair

dryers. Always check labels and manufacturer instructions to be sure. Don't use 110-volt outlets marked "For Shavers Only" for high-wattage appliances such as hair dryers. Adaptors can be found at some *ferramente* (hardware stores) in Naples and the Amalfi Coast. Ask for "*un adatattore per una presa americana.*"

Contacts Steve Kropla's Help for World Travelers (⊕ www.kropla.com) has information on electrical and telephone plugs around the world. **Walkabout Travel Gear** (⊕ www.walkabouttravelgear.com) has a good coverage of electricity under "adapters" in their product index.

■ EMERGENCIES

No matter where you are in Italy, dial 113 for all emergencies, or find somebody (your concierge, a passerby) who will call for you, as not all 113 operators speak English; the Italian word to use to draw people's attention in an emergency is "*Aiuto!*" (Help!, pronounced "ah-YOU-toh"). "*Pronto soccorso*" means "first aid" and when said to an operator will get you an *ambulanza* (ambulance). If you just need a doctor, you should ask for *un medico*; most hotels will be able to refer you to a local doctor. Don't forget to ask the doctor for *una ricevuta* (an invoice) to show to your insurance company in order to get a reimbursement. Other useful Italian words to use in an emergency are "*Fuoco!*" (Fire!, pronounced "fuh-WOE-co"), and "*Ladro!*" (Thief!, pronounced "LAH-droh").

Italy has a national police force (*carabinieri*) as well as local police (*polizia*). Both are armed and have the power to arrest and investigate crimes. Always report the loss of your passport to either the carabinieri or the police, as well as to your embassy. When reporting a crime, you'll be asked to fill out *una denuncia* (official report); keep a copy for your insurance company. Local traffic officers are known as *vigili* (though their official name is *polizia municipale*)—they are responsible for, among other things, giving out parking tickets and clamping cars (note that there are also private firms licensed to do this). Should you find yourself involved in a minor car accident in town, you should contact the vigili.

Pharmacies are generally open weekdays 8:30–1 and 4–8, and Saturday 9–1. Local pharmacies rotate covering the off-hours in shifts: On the door of every pharmacy is a list of which pharmacies in the vicinity will be open late. In the major towns and cities of Campania, you can always find a pharmacy open at any time of day or night.

Foreign Embassies U.S. Consulate Naples (✉ *Piazza della Repubblica, at west end of Villa Comunale, Naples* ☎ *081/583–8111* ⊕ *naples.usconsulate.gov*). **U.S. Embassy** (✉ *Via Veneto 119/A, Rome* ☎ *06/46741* ⊕ *www.usembassy.it*).

General Emergency Contacts Emergencies (☎ *113*). **Police** (☎ *112*). **Naples' Main Police Station** (✉ *Via Medina 75* ☎ *081/7941111* ✉ *Foreigners' office (Questura): Via Ferraris 131* ☎ *081/6064111*) has an *ufficio stranieri* (foreigners' office) that usually has an English speaker on staff and can help with passport problems.

Ambulance (☎ *081/7520696 or 081/7528282*). **Medical emergency** (☎ *081/7613406, 081/2547215 after 8 pm*), ask for an English-speaking nurse. **Car breakdowns and emergencies** (☎ *803, 116*).

▮ HOURS OF OPERATION

Before you travel, check ahead for public holidays, especially April 25, May 1, and June 2, when public offices and most shops are closed. When holidays fall on a Sunday, it is business as usual on Monday.

Banks are open weekdays 8:30 to 1:15 and 2:45 to 3:45.

Post offices are open weekdays 8:30 am to 2 pm and Saturday from 9 am to 1 pm; central and main district post offices stay open until 6 pm weekdays, 9 to 1 on Saturday.

Gas stations open about 7 am and close at about 8 pm. In sleepy country areas away from major roads they will close for lunch between 1 and 4 pm, and on Sunday, so make sure you fill up beforehand. Services open around the clock can be found on autostrade and the tangenziale around Naples, and there are about 20 *benzinai notturni* (night-shift gas-stations) operating in various parts of Naples. Details can be found in local newspapers.

The major museums in Naples, such as Museo Archeologico Nazionale, Museo di Capodimonte, Palazzo Reale, and San Martino, are open through to the evening, although you may find some rooms closed due to lack of staff. Many smaller private museums are only open from 9 am to 1 or 2 pm. The opening times of archaeological sites are subject to seasonal variations, with most sites closing an hour before sunset, and preventing access as much as two hours before. When this book refers to summer hours, it means approximately Easter to October; winter hours run from November to Easter. Most museums are closed one day a week, often Monday or Wednesday. Always check locally.

Most churches are open from early morning until noon or 12:30, when they close for three hours or more; they open again in the afternoon, closing about 7 pm or later. Be as discreet as possible when services are in progress.

Pharmacies are generally open weekdays from 8:30 to 1 and from 4 to 8, and Saturday mornings 9 to 1. Local pharmacies cover the off-hours in shifts: On the door of every pharmacy is a list of pharmacies that will be open in the vicinity on Saturday afternoon, Sunday, or 24 hours.

If the *farmacia* (pharmacy) in Naples's Stazione Centrale is closed, it will post the address of one that's open; the newspaper *Il Mattino* also prints a list of pharmacies that are open nights and weekends.

Most shops are open Monday–Saturday 10–1 and 3:30 or 4–7:30 or 8. Clothing shops are generally closed Monday mornings but open regular afternoon hours, except from July to early September when they close Saturday afternoons and open on Monday mornings. Some bookstores and fashion and tourist-oriented shops are open all day, as well as Sunday. Large chain supermarkets such as Standa and COOP do not close for lunch and are usually open Sunday. *Alimentari* (grocers) and *panifici* (bakeries) open as early as 8 am every day except Sunday, but are (generally) closed on Thursday afternoons and Sunday—though you can find larger supermarkets and out-of-town malls open at all times except Sunday afternoons. Barbers and hairdressers, with some exceptions, are closed Sunday and Monday. On Sunday the *pasticcerie* (cake shops) do a roaring trade, as most southern Italians like to round off their luncheon ritual with calorie-rich *pasticcini* (little pastries). Most shops in downtown Naples will close for two to four weeks in August. They observe extended hours for the three weeks leading up to Christmas and many close from December 25 to January 6.

HOLIDAYS

If you can avoid it, don't travel through Italy in August, when much of the population is on vacation. Most cities are deserted (except for foreign tourists) and many restaurants and shops are closed. Resort towns burst with Italians on holiday.

National holidays include January 1 (New Year's Day); January 6 (Epiphany); Easter Sunday and Monday; April 25 (Liberation Day); May 1 (Labor Day or May Day); June 2 (Founding of the Italian Republic); August 15 (Assumption of Mary, also known as Ferragosto); November 1 (All Saints' Day); December 8 (Immaculate Conception); and December 25 and 26 (Christmas Day and St. Stephen's Day). During these holidays many shops and restaurants are closed, while decisions about whether to open major museums

and archaeological sites like Pompeii and Herculaneum are usually made at the 11th hour.

The feast days of patron saints are observed locally in various towns and villages; some of the more famous *feste* are: San Costanzo, Capri, May 14; San Antonio, Anacapri, June 13; Sant'Andrea, Amalfi, June 25–30; San Pietro, Positano, June 29; Sant'Anna, Ischia, July 26; and San Pantaleone, Ravello, July 27. In Naples, two annual celebrations are held at the Duomo on the first Sunday in May and on September 19 to celebrate the Festa di San Gennaro, or the Liquefaction of the Blood of San Gennaro. *For information on these and other holidays, see also "On the Calendar" in the front of this book.*

▌ MAIL

The Italian mail system has made great progress in speed and reliability, although it can still be slow, so allow up to 10 days for mail to and from the United States and Canada, about a week to and from the United Kingdom.

Standing in line at the *ufficio postale* (post office) in Naples to draw pensions, pay bills, or send registered mail is a major local pastime, and best avoided. You should be able to buy postage stamps at tobacconists without having to line up in post offices. If you still need to go, they are open weekdays 8:30 am to 2 pm and Saturday 8:30 am to 1 pm; central and main district post offices are usually open 8:30–6 weekdays, 9–1 on Saturday.

Airmail letters and postcards (lightweight stationery) to the United States and Canada cost €0.85 for the first 20 grams and €1.85 up to 100 grams. Always stick the blue airmail tag on your mail, or write "airmail" in big, clear characters to the side of the address. Postcards and letters in Italy cost €0.60 for the first 20 grams and €1.50 up to 100 grams, while the same categories to other EU countries cost €0.65 and €1.70. Delivery within Italy should take two to three days. To send urgent letters and papers to the United States and elsewhere, consider the *Paccocelere Internazionale* system, which is similar to a courier system, but not necessarily cheaper. This service is offered at several major post offices in Naples and in town post offices throughout the area.

Correspondence can be addressed to you in care of the Italian post office. Letters should be addressed to your name, "c/o Ufficio Postale Centrale," followed by "Fermo Posta" on the next line, and the name of the city (preceded by its postal code) on the next. You can collect it at the central post office by showing your passport or photo-bearing ID and paying a small fee. American Express also has a general-delivery service. There's no charge for cardholders, holders of American Express traveler's checks, or anyone who booked a vacation with American Express.

SHIPPING PACKAGES

You can ship parcels via air or surface. Air takes up to two weeks, and surface anywhere up to three months to most countries. If you have purchased antiques, ceramics, or other objects, ask if the vendor will do the shipping for you; in most cases, this is a possibility. If so, ask if the article will be insured against breakage. When shipping a package out of Italy, it is virtually impossible to find an overnight delivery option—the fastest delivery time is 48 to 72 hours.

▌ MONEY

The days when Italy's high-quality attractions came with a comparatively low Mediterranean price tag are long gone. Italy's prices are in line with those in the rest of Europe, with costs in its main cities comparable to those in other major capitals, such as Paris and Madrid. As in most countries, prices vary from region to region and are a bit lower in the countryside than in the cities. Good value for money can still be had in many places in Campania, especially in Naples and on the Amalfi Coast.

Prices throughout this guide are given for adults. Substantially reduced fees are almost always available for children, students, and senior citizens from the European Union; be sure to bring EU passports to receive discounts.

■TIP➡ Banks never have every foreign currency on hand, and it may take as long as a week to order. If you're planning to exchange funds before leaving home, don't wait until the last minute.

ATMS AND BANKS

Your own bank will probably charge a fee for using ATMs abroad; the foreign bank you use may also charge a fee. Nevertheless, you'll usually get a better rate of exchange at an ATM than you will at a currency-exchange office or even when changing money in a bank. And extracting funds as you need them is a safer option than carrying around a large amount of cash. Check with your bank to confirm that you have an international PIN (*codice segreto*) that will be recognized in Italy, to find out your maximum daily withdrawal allowance, and to learn what the bank fee is for withdrawing money.

■TIP➡ Be aware that PINs beginning with a 0 (zero) tend to be rejected in Italy.

Fairly common in cities and towns as well as in airports and train stations, ATMs are the easiest way to get euros in Italy. Don't, however, count on finding ATMs in tinier towns and rural areas. Italian ATMs are reliable, and are commonly attached to a bank—you won't find one, for example, in a supermarket. Do check with your bank to confirm you have an international PIN number, to find out your maximum daily withdrawal allowance, and to learn what the bank fee is for withdrawing money. The word for ATM in Italian is *bancomat*, for PIN, *codice segreto*.

CREDIT CARDS

Throughout this guide, the following abbreviations are used: AE, American Express; DC, Diners Club; MC, MasterCard; and V, Visa.

It's a good idea to inform your credit-card company before you travel, especially if you're going abroad and don't travel internationally very often. Otherwise, the credit-card company might put a hold on your card owing to unusual activity—not a good thing halfway through your trip. Record all your credit-card numbers—as well as the phone numbers to call if your cards are lost or stolen—in a safe place, so you're prepared should something go wrong. Both MasterCard and Visa have general numbers you can call (collect if you're abroad) if your card is lost, but you're better off calling the number of your issuing bank, since MasterCard and Visa generally just transfer you to your bank; your bank's number is usually printed on your card.

If you plan to use your credit card for cash advances, you'll need to apply for a PIN at least two weeks before your trip. Although it's usually cheaper (and safer) to use a credit card abroad for large purchases (so you can cancel payments or be reimbursed if there's a problem), note that some credit-card companies *and* the banks that issue them add substantial percentages to all foreign transactions, whether they're in a foreign currency or not. Check on these fees before leaving home, so there won't be any surprises when you get the bill.

■TIP→ Before you charge something, ask the merchant whether he or she plans to do a dynamic currency conversion (DCC). In such a transaction the credit-card processor (shop, restaurant, or hotel, not Visa or MasterCard) converts the currency and charges you in dollars. In most cases you'll pay the merchant a 3% fee for this service in addition to any credit-card company and issuing-bank foreign-transaction surcharges.

Dynamic currency conversion programs are becoming increasingly widespread. Merchants who participate in them are supposed to ask whether you want to be charged in dollars or the local currency, but they don't always do so. And even if they do offer you a choice, they may well avoid mentioning the additional surcharges. The good news is that you *do* have a choice. And if this practice really gets your goat, you can avoid it entirely thanks to American Express; with its cards, DCC simply isn't an option.

MasterCard and Visa are preferred by Italian merchants, so don't expect American Express to be accepted everywhere, even in tourist spots; Travelers Checks are also seldom accepted. Credit cards aren't accepted everywhere; if you want to pay with a credit card in a small shop, hotel, or restaurant, it's a good idea to make your intentions known early on. In general, use cash, not credit cards, for purchases below €20. Southern Italy is still very much a cash-based society, and many shops and smaller *trattorie* have yet to see the benefits of handling plastic.

Reporting Lost Cards American Express (☎ 800/528–4800 in U.S., 336/393–1111 collect from abroad ⊕ www.americanexpress. com). **Diners Club** (☎ 800/234–6377 in U.S., 303/799–1504 collect from abroad ⊕ www. dinersclub.com). **MasterCard** (☎ 800/627– 8372 in U.S., 636/722–7111 collect from abroad ⊕ www.mastercard.com). **Visa** (☎ 800/847–2911 in U.S., 800/819–014 collect from abroad ⊕ www.visa.com).

CURRENCY AND EXCHANGE

The unit of currency in Italy is the euro, currently adopted in 16 countries of the European Union (the only EU Member States not to adopt the euro were Britain, Denmark, and Sweden). Italian banks no longer accept the lira—the currency used prior to 2002—but if you have some left over from a previous visit it can be changed at the **Banca D'Italia** (⊠ *Via M Cervantes 71* ☎ *081/7975111*), in the center of Naples, until the year 2012. The euro is printed in bills of 500 (practically impossible to change outside of banks), 200, 100, 50, 20, 10, and 5. Coins are €2, €1, 50 cents, 20 cents, 10 cents, 5 cents, 2 cents, and 1 cent (although Neapolitans tend to ignore these last two). All coins have one side that has the value of the euro on it and the other side with each country's unique symbol. Notes have principal architectural styles from antiquity onward on one side and the map and the flag of Europe on the other and are the same for all countries. ■TIP→ When changing money, make sure you ask for small denomination notes, preferably of 50 euros and below, as retailers in Naples and the surrounding area are notoriously bereft of small change.

The euro continues to fluctuate considerably against other currencies. At the time of this writing the exchange rate was about €0.77 to the U.S. dollar.

■TIP→ Even if a currency-exchange booth has a sign promising no commission, rest assured that there's some kind of huge, hidden fee. As for rates, you're almost always better off getting foreign currency at an ATM or exchanging money at a bank.

▌PACKING

The weather is considerably milder in Italy than in the north and central United States or Great Britain.

In summer, stick with clothing that is as light as possible, although a sweater may be necessary for cool evenings, especially in the Lattari Mountains along the Amalfi Coast (even during the hot months). Sunglasses, a hat, and sunblock are essential, now more than ever due to global warming, which often sends the temperature soaring to 95°F or more in the middle of summer. But, contrary to myth, the sun does not shine all day, every day on Campania: brief summer thunderstorms are common in Naples, while typhoon-like storms occasionally arrive along the Amalfi Coast, so an umbrella will definitely come in handy. In winter bring a medium-weight coat and a raincoat; winters in Naples can be both humid *and* cold. Even in Naples, central heating may not be up to your standards, and interiors can be chilly and damp; take wools or flannel rather than sheer fabrics. Bring sturdy shoes for winter, and comfortable walking shoes in any season.

For sightseeing, pack a pair of binoculars; they will help you get a good look at Naples' wondrous painted ceilings and domes. If you stay in budget hotels, take your own shampoo and soap; many such hotels do not provide it, or allot only one tiny bar per room.

▌PASSPORTS AND VISAS

U.S. citizens need only a valid passport to enter Italy for stays of up to 90 days. Ensure that the passport is valid for six months after the date of arrival. Children are required to have their own passport or be included in the passport of the parent with whom they are traveling.

PASSPORTS
■TIP→ Before your trip, make two copies of your passport's data page (one for someone at home and another for you to carry separately). Or scan the page and e-mail it to someone at home and/or yourself.

VISAS
When staying for 90 days or less, U.S. citizens are not required to obtain a visa prior to traveling to Italy. If you plan to travel or live in Italy or the European Union for longer than 90 days, you must acquire a valid visa from the Italian consulate serving your state *before you leave the United States*. Plan ahead because the process of obtaining a visa will take at least 30 days and the Italian government does not accept visa applications submitted by visa expediters.

U.S. Passport Information U.S. Department of State (☎ 877/487–2778 ⊕ *www.travel.state. gov/passport*).

U.S. Passport Expediters A. Briggs Passport & Visa Expeditors

(☎ 800/806–0581 or 202/338–0111 ⊕ www. abriggs.com). **American Passport Express** (☎ 800/455–5166 or 603/559–9888 ⊕ www. americanpassport.com). **Passport Express** (☎ 800/362–8196 or 401/272–4612 ⊕ www. passportexpress.com). **Travel Document Systems** (☎ 800/874–5100 ⊕ www. traveldocs.com). **Travel the World Visas** (☎ 866/886–8472 ⊕ www.world-visa.com).

▮ RESTROOMS

Public restrooms are rather rare in Naples; the locals seem to make do with well-timed pit stops and rely on the local bar. Although private businesses can refuse to make their toilets available to the passing public, some bars will allow you to use the restroom if you ask politely. Alternatively, it's not uncommon to pay for a little something—a euro for a mineral water or coffee—to get access to the facilities. Standards of cleanliness and comfort vary greatly. In downtown Naples, restaurants, hotel lobbies, department stores such as Coin, and McDonald's restaurants tend to have the cleanest restrooms. Pubs and bars rank among the worst and, for these, it may help to have your own small supply of tissues. There are bathrooms in most museums and in all airports and train stations. In major train stations you'll also find well-kept pay toilets for around €0.50. There are also bathrooms at highway rest stops and gas stations: a small tip to the cleaning person is always appreciated. There are no bathrooms in churches, post offices, public beaches, although some stops on the Naples metro have one.

The Bathroom Diaries (⊕ www. thebathroomdiaries.com) is flush with unsanitized info on restrooms the world over—each one located, reviewed, and rated.

▮ SAFETY

Naples, like any modern metropolis, has had certain problems with crime. Although great inroads have been made since the 1990s and the city today is as safe as many other big urban centers in Europe, you should continue to be vigilant, especially around the main rail station of Piazza Garibaldi where petty theft is common. In Italy, in general, violent crimes are rare.

▮ TIP→ Distribute your cash, credit cards, IDs, and other valuables between a deep front pocket, an inside jacket or vest pocket, and a hidden money pouch. Don't reach for the money pouch once you're in public.

LOCAL SCAMS

The areas round Piazza Garibaldi and near the port in Naples are infamous for a variety of scams. Avoid getting involved in the three-card monte around the station, and never buy any goods from an unlicensed street vendor—you may discover on returning to your hotel or cruise ship that the package with the digital camera you bought at an unbeatable price near the port actually contains little more than wooden chocks. Besides, under current Italian law, any purchase—except at a newsstand or tobacconist's—has to be accompanied by a proper receipt. Without one, both purchaser and vendor are liable to a fine, so you're putting yourself at risk by buying bootleg goods.

Be especially vigilant if traveling on public transport, especially crowded buses, as pickpockets can materialize from seemingly nowhere in large numbers. Dress down rather than up to attract less attention, and never wear gold jewelry.

Both in town and out on the highway, one scam is the *cavallo di ritorno*. Car owners lose their cars by some ruse—usually they're told they have a problem at the back or under the chassis; once they get out, and the car is driven off. The owner is then traced and contacted by an intermediary, who will stipulate the ransom for the car (as much as €1,500–€2,500). You do need to stop if you're flagged down by the police; otherwise act with due caution.

The difficulties encountered by women traveling alone in Italy are often overstated. Younger women have to put up with much male attention, but it's rarely dangerous. Ignoring whistling and questions is the best way to get rid of unwanted attention. Fortunately, the vast majority of locals are extremely protective both of foreign visitors and women. As a general rule, in urban areas you're fine walking at street level when the shops are open (until about 8:30 pm). At other times, especially around the seedier parts of Naples, taking a taxi is a sound investment.

▮ TAXES

Value-added tax (IVA or V.A.T.) is 20% on clothing and luxury goods. On most consumer goods, it's already included in the amount shown on the price tag, whereas on services it may not be.

At hotels, the service charge and the 10% IVA, or value-added tax, are included in the rate except in five-star deluxe establishments, where the IVA (10%) may be a separate item added to the bill at departure. If your purchases in a single store total more than €155 you may be entitled to a refund of the V.A.T.

When making a purchase, ask for a V.A.T. refund form and find out whether the merchant gives refunds—not all stores do, nor are they required to. Have the form stamped like any customs form by customs officials when you leave the country or, if you're visiting several European Union countries, when you leave the EU. After you're through passport control, take the form to a refund-service counter for an on-the-spot refund (which is usually the quickest and easiest option), or mail it to the address on the form (or on the envelope with it) after you arrive home. You receive the total refund stated on the form, but the processing time can be long, especially if you request a credit-card adjustment.

Global Refund is a Europe-wide service with 225,000 affiliated stores and more than 700 refund counters at major airports and border crossings. Its refund form, called a Tax Free Check, is the most common across the European continent. The service issues refunds in the form of cash, check, or credit-card adjustment.

V.A.T. Refunds Global Blue (☎ 800/321–11111 ⊕ www.global-blue.com).

▮ TIPPING

In tourist areas like Capri and the Amalfi Coast, a 10% to 15% service charge may appear on your check; this must be clearly written on the menu in order to be applied. If service is added to the bill, it's not necessary to leave an additional tip. If service is not included, leave a cash tip of a couple of euros per person. Usually there will not be a line item on your credit-card slip for a tip—but even if there is, tip in cash. Tip checkroom attendants €1 per person and restroom attendants €0.50 (more in expensive hotels and restaurants). A service charge is added at caffè for table service, so it is not necessary to leave additionally gratuity. At a hotel bar tip €1 for a round or two of drinks. At a caffè, tip €0.10 per coffee.

Italians rarely tip taxi drivers, and at most round up to the nearest euro. That said, a euro or two is appreciated, particularly if the driver helps with luggage. Service-station attendants are tipped only for special services; give them €1 for checking your tires. Railway and airport porters charge a fixed rate per bag. Tip an additional €0.50 per person, more if the porter is helpful. Give a barber €1 and a hairdresser's assistant €2–€4 for a shampoo or cut, depending on the type of establishment.

On large group sightseeing tours, tip guides about €5 per person for a half-day group tour, more if they are especially knowledgeable. In monasteries and other sights where admission is free, a contribution (€1–€2) is expected.

In hotels leave the chambermaid about €1 per day, or about €5 a week in a moderately priced hotel; tip a minimum of €1 for valet or room service. Double these amounts in an expensive hotel. In expensive hotels tip doormen €0.50 for calling a cab and €1.50 for carrying bags to the check-in desk and bellhops €1.50–€2.50 for carrying your bags to the room.

▌ TOURS

Guided tours are a good option when you don't want to do it all yourself. You travel along with a group (sometimes large, sometimes small), stay in prebooked hotels, eat with your fellow travelers (the cost of meals sometimes included in the price of your tour, sometimes not), and follow a schedule. But not all guided tours are an if-it's-Tuesday-this-must-be-Belgium experience. A knowledgeable guide can take you places that you might never discover on your own, and you may be pushed to see more than you would have otherwise. Tours aren't for everyone, but they can be just the thing for trips to places where making travel arrangements is difficult or time-consuming (particularly when you don't speak the language). Whenever you book a guided tour, find out what's included and what isn't. A "land-only" tour includes all your travel (by bus, in most cases) in the destination, but not necessarily your flights to and from or even within it. Also, in most cases prices in tour brochures don't include fees and taxes. And remember that you'll be expected to tip your guide (in cash) at the end of the tour.

Also keep in mind that the province of Naples has tour guides licensed by the government. Some are eminently qualified in relevant fields such as architecture and art history, but most, especially those that linger outside Pompeii have simply managed to pass the test (or purchase the license!). Few local guides have their own Web sites, though all reputable agencies do. Check online before you leave home. Tourist offices and hotel concierges also can provide the names of knowledgeable local guides and the rates for certain services. Before you hire a local guide, ask about their background and qualifications and make sure you agree on a price, content, and scheduling. Tipping is appreciated, but not obligatory, for local guides.

Recommended Generalists Abercrombie & Kent (☎ 800/554-7016 ⊕ www.abercrombiekent.com). **Andante** (☎ 888/331-3476 ⊕ www.andantetravels.co.uk). **Context Travel** (☎ 800/691-6036, 06/97625204 within Italy ⊕ www.contexttravel.com). **Tauck** (☎ 800/788-7885 ⊕ www.tauck.com). **Travcoa** (☎ 800/788-7885 ⊕ www.travcoa.com).

Biking and Hiking Tour Contacts Backroads (☎ 800/462-2848 ⊕ www.backroads.com). **Butterfield & Robinson** (☎ 866/551-9090 ⊕ www.butterfield.com). **Ciclismo Classico** (☎ 800/866-7314 ⊕ www.ciclismoclassico.com).

Culinary Tour Contact Epiculinary (☎ 888/380-9010 ⊕ www.epiculinary.com). **Italian Connection** (☎ 800/462-7911 ⊕ www.italian-connection.com). **Vesuvius Vs Pompeii** (☎ 328/6238668 within Italy ⊕ www.vesuviusvspompeii.com).

Volunteer Programs Road Scholar (☎ 800/454-5768 ⊕ www.roadscholar.org).

Wine Tour Contacts Cellar Tours (☎ 310/928-7559 ⊕ www.cellartours.com).

▌ VISITOR INFORMATION

Italian Government Tourist Board (ENIT ☎ 212/245-5618 in New York ⊕ www.italiantourism.com ☎ 310/820-1898 in Los Angeles ☎ 312/644-0996 in Chicago ☎ 416/925-4882 in Toronto).

Ente Provinciale per il Turismo (EPT) (☎ 081/268-779 Stazione Centrale ☎ 081/410-7211 Piazza dei Martiri ☎ 081/761-2102 Stazione Mergellina ⊕ www.enit.it). The official site of the local region (⊕ www.regione.campania.it) also provides some coverage.

Ufficio Informazioni Turistiche (☎ 081/551-2701 Piazza del Gesù, 7 ☎ 081/402-394 Via San Carlo 9 ⊕ www.inaples.it).

▌ ONLINE TRAVEL TOOLS

The site for Trenitalia (the national rail), ⊕ *www.trenitalia.com* is a good source for train information and journey planning, although you can only purchase tickets online with an Italian credit card. The national train service is ⊕ *www.ferroviedellostato.it*. On a local level ⊕ *www.campaniatrasporti.it* provides an easily downloadable overview of local transport networks. The local bus service has a Web site (⊕ www.anm.it) while the Circumvesuviana Web site (⊕ www.vesuviana.it) and Ferrovia Cumana/Circumflegrea Web site (⊕ www.sepsa.it) have public transport information for getting around the bay. The train site for Naples is ⊕ *www.metro.na.it*. The SITA site (Italian only) has schedules for bus travel in Campania, ⊕ *www.sitabus.it*. The website for the municipality of Naples is ⊕ *www.communenapoli.it*. A handy site for Capri is ⊕ *www.capri.net*; Ischia has its official Web site at ⊕ *www.ischia.com* while ⊕ *www.ravellotime.it* is the best-maintained site of the Amalfi Coast. Many hotels now have online reservation facilities and several restaurants have thoughtfully posted menus to whet the appetites of Internet surfers. Where known, Web sites have been included at the end of individual listings.

INDEX

A

'A Fenestella ✕ , 319–320
A' Paranza ✕ , 77
Abbazia di San Michele, 160–161
Acqua Pazza ✕ , 94
Acunzo ✕ , 320–321
Agritourism, 365
Air travel, 12, 355–356
Al Convento ✕ , 94–95
Al Grottino ✕ , 133
Al Teatro ✕ , 69
Albergo della Regina Isabella ▣ , 153–154
Albergo Il Monastero ▣ , 150
Albergo l'Approdo ▣ , 151
Albergo Sant'Andrea ▣ , 71
Alloggio del Conte ▣ , 330
Alfonso a Mare ✕ , 55
Amalfi, 42–43, 62–78
Amalfi Coast, 10, 24–96
beaches, 28–29, 53, 59
dining, 35, 37–38, 44–45, 52, 55, 58, 69–71, 77, 86–87, 94–95
exploring, 31–44, 55, 56, 58, 59–61, 64–69, 76–77, 80–86, 93–94, 96
festivals and seasonal events, 51, 53, 74–75, 92
itineraries, 26
lodging, 26, 47–51, 55, 58–59, 61–62, 71–74, 77–78, 83, 87–90, 95, 96
nightlife and the arts, 51, 53, 75, 92
outdoor activities and sports, 53–54
price categories, 26
shopping, 54, 75, 92–93, 95, 96
transportation, 27, 31, 33, 42–43, 55, 56, 59, 63–64, 76, 79, 93, 95
visitor information, 33, 64, 79
Amalfi drive, 17, 39–44
Ambrosino ✕ , 321
Ambulance service, 373
Amici Miei ✕ , 305
Anacapri, 126–133
Anhelo Caffè ✕ , 323
Anfiteatro, 218
Anfiteatro Flavio, 226–227
Antico Francischiello du Pep-pino ✕ , 189–190
Antiques shops, 348
Antro della Sibilla, 233

Apartment and house rentals, 364–365
Aquarium, 264
Arco Naturale, 108
Arsenale della Republica, 64–65
Art galleries and museums
Capri, 113
Naples, 265, 269–270, 272, 282–283, 286–287, 290, 295, 297, 300–302, 344
Sorrento, 177
ATMs, 375
Atrani, 75–78
Auditorium Niemeyer, 81
Aurora (Amalfi) ▣ , 71
Aurora (Capri) ✕ , 133
Ausonia ▣ , 334
Auto clubs, 358–359
Azienda Agricola Seliano ▣ , 96
Azienda Agrituristica Il Casolare ✕ , 232

B

Bacco ✕ , 58
Bagni di Tiberio beach, 125
Baia, 229–233
Banks, 375
business hours, 373
Bar Guida ✕ , 323
Bar Internazionale ✕ , 37
Bar Villa Comunale ✕ , 177
Barbarossa ✕ , 135
Baroque art and architecture, 18, 257–259
Bar-Pasticceria La Zagara ✕ , 35
Bar-Ristorante Bagno Teresa ✕ , 156
Basilica (Paestum), 96
Basilica (Pompeii), 218
Basilica di Sant'Antonino, 174
Batis B&B ▣ , 232–233
Bay of Naples, 10, 194–236
dining, 208, 223, 228–229, 232
guided tours, 211, 222, 230
lodging, 196, 209, 223–224, 229, 232–233, 234, 236
price categories, 196
shopping, 209
transportation, 197, 202, 210, 212, 214, 222, 225, 230, 233–234
visitor information, 202, 214, 226
when to tour, 196

Beaches, 19
Amalfi Coast, 28–29, 53, 59
Capri, 125
Bed and breakfasts, 365
Bellevue Syrene ▣ , 182
Belvedere ▣ , 61–62
Belvedere of Infinity, 17, 83
Biancamaria ▣ , 138, 140
Biblioteca Comunale Popolare Luigi Bladier, 113
Biblioteca dei Girolamini, 290
Biblioteca Nazionale Vittorio Emanuele III, 253
Bicycling
Procida, 159
tours, 380
Blue Grotto, 123, 128–129
Boat tours
Baia, 230
Marina del Cantone, 192
Positano, 53–54
Boat travel, 356–357
Amalfi Coast, 27
Bay of Naples, 197
Capri, 107, 119–124
Ischia, 147
Procida, 159
Sorrento and the Sorrentine Peninsula, 169
Bobò ✕ , 228
Book shops
Capri, 143
Naples, 345
Bowinkel (shop), 345
Brandi ✕ , 305
Buca di Bacco ▣ , 47
Bus travel, 357–358
Amalfi Coast, 27, 43
Bay of Naples, 197
Capri, 107
Ischia, 147
Naples, 247
Procida, 159
Sorrento and the Sorrentine Peninsula, 169
Business hours, 373–374

C

Caesar Augustus ▣ , 140
Caffè Gambrinus ✕ , 255, 323
Caffè Liberty ✕ , 324
Caffè Scarlatti ✕ , 272
Campania, 12–21, 242–243
Camping, 223–224
Camping Zeus ▣ , 223–224
Cantina della Tofa ✕ , 305

Cantine di Marisa Cuomo, *56*
Capella di Santa Restituta, *281*
Cappella del Tesoro di San Gennaro, *280*
Cappella Sansevero, *274, 278–279*
Cappella Vecchia 11 ⟨T⟩, *334*
Capri, *10, 17, 98–144*
beaches, 125
dining, 133–135
exploring, 108–133
itineraries, 100
lodging, 101, 136–140
nightlife and the arts, 140–142
outdoor activities and sports, 101, 102–103, 110–111, 119–124, 127, 142–143
price categories, 101
shopping, 143–144
transportation, 100, 102, 107
visitor information, 106
when to tour, 100
Capri Palace ⟨T⟩, *140*
Capri Town, *108–126*
Capri's ✕, *133*
Car travel and rentals, *13, 358–361*
Amalfi Coast, 27, 42, 44
Bay of Naples, 197
emergency services, 360
gasoline, 359
Ischia, 147
parking, 168, 247, 359
Sorrento and the Sorrentine Peninsula, 168
Caravaggio, *284*
Caravaggio ⟨T⟩, *331*
Carracioli di Vico chapel, *298*
Caruso ✕, *87*
Casa Albertina ⟨T⟩, *47*
Casa degli Amorini Dorati, *220*
Casa dei Casti Amanti, *220*
Casa dei Cervi, *205–206*
Casa dei Vettii, *220*
Casa del Fauno, *220*
Casa del Menandro, *220*
Casa del Nettuno ed Anfitrite, *207*
Casa del Poeta Tragico, *220*
Casa del Tramezzo di Legno, *207–208*
Casa di Tasso, *178*
Casa Rossa, *128*
Casamicciola, *151–152*
Castel Capuano, *299*
Castel dell'Ovo, *264–265*
Castel Nuovo, *248, 251*
Castel Sant' Elmo, *265, 268*
Castello Aragonese, *149*

Castello Barbarossa, *131*
Castles
Capri, 131
Ischia, 149
Naples, 248, 251, 264–265, 268, 299
Catacombe di San Gennaro, *302*
Catacombs, *302*
Cattedrale dell'Assunta, *149*
Certosa di San Giacomo, *108, 113*
Certosa di San Martino, *268–270*
Cetara, *29, 42–43, 93–95*
Cetus ⟨T⟩, *95*
Changing money, *375–377*
Chez Black ✕, *37*
Chiaja Hotel de Charme ⟨T⟩, *327*
Chiesa dei Girolamini/Quadreria dei Girolamini, *289–290*
Chiesa di Sant'Andrea, *115*
Children, attractions for, *264, 283, 286*
Chiostro delle Clarisse, *288–289*
Chiostro Grande (Capri), *113*
Chiostro Grande (Naples), *268*
Chiostro Piccolo, *113*
Churches
Amalfi, 65–66
Atrani, 77
Capri, 113, 115, 125–126, 129–130, 131, 133
Conca dei Marini, 61
hours, 373
Ischia, 149, 155
Naples, 16, 253, 255, 260–262, 263, 271, 297–298, 299, 302
Naples (Spaccanapoli), 16, 274, 278–282, 286–291
Positano, 35–36
Procida, 161
Ravello, 81–82, 86
Sant'Agata sui Due Golfi, 189
Sorrento, 174, 177
Cioccolateria Perzechella ✕, *325*
Ciro a Santa Brigida ✕, *305–306*
Climate, *12*
Clothing shops
Capri, 144
Naples, 345–347
Coco Loco ✕, *317*
Cocumella ⟨T⟩, *188*
Cocumella monastery, *187*
Coffee houses, *20, 322–324*

Conca dei Marini, *29, 31, 40–41, 59–62*
Convento di San Francesco, *174*
Convento di Santa Rosa, *60–61*
Convents
Amalfi, 69
Conca dei Marini, 60–61
Procida, 161
Sorrento, 174
Corricella, *161–162*
Costantinopoli 104 ⟨T⟩, *331*
Court Theater, *252*
Covo dei Saraceni ⟨T⟩, *47–48*
Craft shops, *347–348*
Credit cards, *7, 376*
Cuisine, *18, 20*
Campania, 242–243
Naples, 307–311
Culinary lessons
Positano, 51
Ravello, 92
tours, 380
Cumae, *233–236*
Cumpa' Cosimo ✕, *86*
Currency, *375–377*
Customs, *369*

D

Da Adolfo ✕, *37*
Da Cicciotto ✕, *320*
Da Dora ✕, *317*
Da Emilia ✕, *180*
Da Gelsomina ✕, *135*
Da Gemma ✕, *69*
Da Gennaro ✕, *148*
Da Michele ✕, *313, 316*
Da Salvatore ✕, *86*
Dance clubs
Capri, 141
Naples, 340–342
Positano, 51
Davide ✕, *177–178*
Del Corso ⟨T⟩, *182*
Del Real Orto Botanico ⟨T⟩, *330*
Dining, *7, 13, 369–372.* ⇨ *See also under specific cities and towns*
cuisine, 18, 20, 242–243, 307–311
price categories, 26, 101, 167, 196, 305
tipping, 379
Discount passes, *241*
Don Alfonso 1890 ⟨T⟩, *190–191*
Down Town ✕, *232*
Duomo (Ravello), *81–82*
Duomo dei SS Filippo e Giacomo, *174, 177*

Duomo di San Gennaro, 279–281
Duomo di Sant' Andrea, 65–66
Duties, 369

E

Edode ✕ , 133–134
Electricity, 372
Embassies, 373
Emergencies, 372–373
road service, 360
Eolo ✕ , 69–70
Ercolano (Herculaneum), 202–209
Esedra Maiolicata, 178
Etiquette, 366
Excelsior (Naples) ⊡ , 327, 329
Excelsior (Sorrento) ⊡ , 182–183
Ex-convent of Santa Margherita Nuova, 161

F

Farm holidays, 365
Ferry service
Bay of Naples, 197
Capri, 107
Procida, 159
Sorrento and the Sorrentine Peninsula, 169
Festivals and seasonal events
Amalfi Coast, 51, 53, 74–75, 92
Ischia, 148, 150, 154
Sorrento, 185
Figli di Papà ✕ , 86
Film
festivals, 150, 154
Ischia Ponte, 150
Lacco Ameno, 154
Naples, 338
Forio, 155–158
Foro Romano, 96
Friggitoria Pizzeria Giuliano ✕ , 321–322
Friggitoria Vomero ✕ , 322
Fullonica Stephani, 217
Furore, 56, 58–59
Furore Inn ⊡ , 58–59

G

Galleria Umberto I, 251–252
Gallucci ✕ , 325
Gardens, 19
Amalfi Coast, 35
Capri, 118, 125
Ischia, 156
Naples, 297
Gas station hours, 373

Gasoline, 359
Gay Odin ✕ , 325–326
Gelati shops, 21, 324–326
Gesù Nuovo, 281–282
Giardini Caffè Calice ✕ , 86
Giardini di Augusto, 118, 125
Giardini Poseidon Terme, 157
Gift shops, 347–348
Gino Sorbillo ✕ , 306
Golden Hotel ⊡ , 332
Graal ⊡ , 87
Graffiti, 219
Gran Caffè Aragonese ✕ , 324
Gran Caffè Cimmino ✕ , 324
Grand Hotel Convento di Amalfi ⊡ , 71–72
Grand Hotel Parco dei Principi ⊡ , 188
Grand Hotel Parker's ⊡ , 334–335
Grand Hotel Vesuvio ⊡ , 329
Graziella ✕ , 162
Great Captain's Room, 253
Greek ruins and artifacts, 16, 19
Bay of Naples, 198–199
Cumae, 233–236
Herculaneum, 202–209
Ischia, 149, 152–153
Naples, 283, 286, 288, 292–295
Paestum, 95, 96
Grotta Azzurra, 123, 128–129
Grotta dello Smeraldo, 61
Grotta di Matermania, 125
Grottoes
Capri, 123, 125, 128–129
Conca dei Marini, 61
Guided tours, 380
Bay of Naples, 211, 222, 230
Naples, 247
Sorrento and the Sorrentine Peninsula, 167, 192

H

Harbor of Santa Maria della Neve, 59
Herculaneum, 202–209
Hercules Hall, 253
Hiking
Capri, 101
Ischia, 101
Positano, 54
tours, 380
Holidays, 374
Home exchanges, 365
Hotel Amalfi ⊡ , 72
Hotel Amleto ⊡ , 224
Hotel Astoria ⊡ , 183

Hotel Diana ⊡ , 224
Hotel Ercolano ⊡ , 209
Hotel Floridiana ⊡ , 72
Hotel La Villarosa Terme ⊡ , 148
Hotel Palazzo Decumani ⊡ , 332
Hotel Santa Lucia ⊡ , 329
Hotel Semiramis ⊡ , 157
Hotel Terme Puteolane ⊡ , 229
Hotels. ⇨ See Lodging
House rentals, 364–365
Household decoration shops, 348
House of Telephus, 205
Houses, historic
Capri, 118, 126, 128
Herculaneum, 205–206, 207–208
Naples, 271–272
Pompeii, 220, 221
Ravello, 84–85

I

I Decumani ✕ , 306
I Faraglioni, 113
I Re di Napoli ✕ , 317–318
Il Buco ✕ , 180
Il Convento ⊡ , 332
Il Convento di San Paolo al Deserto, 189
Il Cucciolo ✕ , 135
Il Gatto Bianco ⊡ , 136
Il Gattopardo ⊡ , 157
Il Melograno ✕ , 156–157
Il Principe ✕ , 223
Il Saraceno ⊡ , 62
Il Tari ✕ , 70
Il Transatlantico ✕ , 318
Il Transatlantico Napoli ⊡ , 329–330
Internet, 367
Ischia, 10, 98–101, 144–158
dining, 148, 149–150, 151, 156–157
exploring, 146–149, 151, 152–153, 155–156
festivals and seasonal events, 148, 150, 154
itineraries, 100
lodging, 101, 148, 151–152, 153–154, 157
nightlife and the arts, 148, 150–151, 154
outdoor activities and sports, 101, 150, 154–155, 157
price categories, 101
shopping, 158

transportation, 100, 146, 147,
    149, 152, 155
visitor information, 146
when to tour, 100
Ischia Ponte, 148–151
Ischia Porto, 146, 148
Italian vocabulary, 349–353

J

J.K. Place ⛉ , *136*
Jewelry shops
Capri, 143
Naples, 348
Joachim Murat's writing room,
    253

L

L.u.i.s.e. ✕ , *322*
La Basilica ✕ , *180–181*
La Caffeteria ✕ , *323*
La Cambusa ✕ , *38*
La Campagnola ✕ , *306*
La Cantina di Triunfo ✕ , *320*
La Cantina di Sica ✕ , *321*
La Cantina di Via Sapienza
    ✕ , *312*
La Canzone del Mare, 115
La Canzone del Mare ✕ , *134*
La Capannina ✕ , *134*
La Caravella ✕ , *70*
La Casa del Monacone ⛉ ,
    331
La Casa sul Mare ⛉ , *162*
La Colombaia, 156
La Conchiglia ✕ , *162*
La Controra ⛉ , *335*
La Favorita ⛉ , *183–184*
La Favorita–O' Parrucchino
    ✕ , *181*
La Feltrinelli (shop), *345*
La Fenice ⛉ , *48*
La Focaccia ✕ , *322*
La Fontelina ✕ , *134*
La Fornacella ✕ , *208*
La Guarrancino ✕ , *38*
La Lanterna ✕ , *181*
La Mescita ✕ , *320*
La Mortella, 156
La Palma ⛉ , *136–137*
La Pergola ✕ , *38*
La Piazzetta, 17, 113–114
La Rada B&B ⛉ , *233*
La Rondinella ✕ , *135*
La Scalinatella ⛉ , *137*
La Sfogliatella Mary ✕ , *326*
La Taverna dell'Arte ✕ , *316*
La Terrazza ✕ , *318*
La Tonnara ⛉ , *162*
La Vecchia Cantina ✕ , *312*

Lacco Ameno, 152–155
Language, 13, 349–353, 366
Le Arcate ✕ , *77*
Le Grottelle ✕ , *134–135*
Le Sirenuse ⛉ , *48–49*
L'Ebbrezza di Noè ✕ , *318*
Li Galli, 191–192
Libraries
Capri, 113
Naples, 253, 290
Lido Capo di Conca, 59
Lo Smeraldino ✕ , *70*
Lodging, 7, 13, 364–365. ⇨ *See*
    also specific cities and towns
meal plans, 7, 364
price categories, 26, 101, 167,
    196, 327
taxes, 379
tipping, 379–380
Lombardi à Santa Chiara ✕ ,
    312
Luna Convento, 69
Luna Convento ⛉ , *72–73*
Lupanare, 219

M

Maccus ✕ , *70–71*
Macellum, 218
Mail and shipping, 374–375
Majestic ⛉ , *335*
Maria Grazia ✕ , *192*
Marina del Cantone, 186,
    191–192
Marina del Corricella, 161
Marina di Furore, 56, 58
Marina di Praia, 55
Marina Grande (Capri), *125*
Marina Grande (Sorrento),
    178
Marina Grande Sancio
    Cattolico, 160
Marina Piccola, 114–115
Marina Riviera ⛉ , *73*
Marino ✕ , *318*
Markets, 343
Meal plans, 7, 364
Mediterraneo ⛉ , *332*
Megaride ✕ , *323*
Megaron ✕ , *332–333*
Mercure Napoli Angioino ⛉ ,
    333
Mezzatorre Resort & Spa ⛉ ,
    154
Miglio d'Oro Park Hotel ⛉ ,
    209
Mimì alla Ferrovia ✕ , *316*
Miracle of the Blood, 279
Miramalfi ⛉ , *73*
Moccia ✕ , *324*

Monasteries
Capri, 108, 113
Naples, 268–270
Ravello, 85
Sant'Agata sui Due Golfi, 189
Sant'Agnello, 187
Monastero di Santa Chiara, 85
Money matters, 22, 375–377
Monte di Pietà, 282
Monte Solaro, 129
Mount Vesuvius, 16, 201–212
Murat, Joachim, 253
Museo Archeologico dei Campi
    Flegrei, 230–231
Museo Archeologico di
    Pithecusae, 152–153
Museo Archeologico
    Nazionale, 16, 292–295
Museo Archeologico Virtuale
    (MAV), *208*
Museo Bottega della Tarsia
    Lignea, 178
Museo Civico (Amalfi), *66, 68*
Museo Correale di Terranova,
    177
Museo del Corallo (Ravello), *85*
Museo del Duomo, 82
Museo del Mare Ischia, 149
Museo del Tesoro di San
    Gennaro, 281
Museo della Carta, 69
Museo dell'Opera di San
    Lorenzo, 288
Museo dell'Osservatorio Vesu-
    viano, 211
Museo di Capodimonte,
    300–302
Museo di Novecento Napoli,
    265, 268
Museo Diefenbach, 113
Museo Diego Aragona
    Pignatelli Cortes, 270
Museo Diocesano, 282–283
Museo e Scavi Santa Restituta,
    153
Museo Madre, 295, 297
Museo Nazionale (Paestum), *96*
Museo Nazionale della Ceram-
    ica Duca di Martina, 272
Museums. ⇨ *See also* Art
    galleries and museums
in Amalfi, 66, 68, 69
archaeology, 16, 96, 152–153,
    208, 230–231, 288,
    292–295
in Baia, 230–231
business hours, 373
in Capri, 113, 128
ceramics, 272

coral, 85
decorative arts, 82, 177, 178,
   270, 272, 282, 286–287,
   300–302
fisherman, 149
in Forio, 156
in Herculaneum, 208
history, 66, 68, 156
intarsia, 178
in Ischia, 149
in Lacco Ameno, 152–153
in Naples, 16, 265, 268,
   269–270, 272, 281, 282–283,
   286–287, 288, 290, 292–295,
   297, 300–302
in Paestum, 96
papermaking, 69
in Ravello, 82, 85
in Sorrento, 177, 178
in Vesuvius, 211
volcanoes, 211
Music
Capri, 141
Ischia, 148, 150–151, 154
Naples, 303, 337–340
Ravello, 92
Sorrento, 185

N

Naples, 10, 238–348
Baroque art and architecture,
   18, 257–259
children, attractions for, 264,
   283, 286
cuisine, 307–311
dining, 255, 272, 302–326
discount passes, 241
exploring, 245–302
guided tours, 247
itineraries, 250, 267, 275–277
La Sanità to Capodimonte,
   299–302
lodging, 240, 326–336
Lungomare, 263–272
Napoli Sotterranea, 283, 286
nightlife and the arts, 241, 303,
   337–342
Pizzofalcone, 271
price categories, 305, 327
safety, 261, 378–379
shopping, 342–348
Spaccanapoli, 16, 272–291
Toledo, 248–255, 260–263
transportation, 247, 261
visitor information, 241
Vomero, 263–272
Napoli Sotterranea, 283, 286
Neapolis 🖭 , 333

O

O' Capurale ✕ , 38, 44
O' Munaciello ✕ , 312
Old Sacristy, 298
Onda Verde 🖭 , 55
Opera, 338–340
Oplontis (Torre Annunziata),
   212–213
Orto Botanico, 297
Orto dei Fuggiaschi, 217
Osteria da Carmela ✕ ,
   312–313
Osteria del Buonconvento ✕ ,
   181
Osteria Donna Teresa ✕ , 321

P

Packing, 12, 377
Paestum, 17, 78–79, 95–96
Palaces
Naples, 252–253, 255, 270,
   300–302
Positano, 35
Procida, 161
Ravello, 82–83, 84–85
Sorrento, 178
Palaestra, 206–207
Palatine Chapel, 253
Palazzo a Mare, 125
Palazzo Alabardieri 🖭 ,
   335–336
Palazzo Correale, 178
Palazzo d'Avales, 161
Palazzo della Spagnola, 302
Palazzo delle Arti Napoli, 270
Palazzo Ferraioli 🖭 , 77–78
Palazzo Murat, 35
Palazzo Murat 🖭 , 49
Palazzo Petrucci ✕ , 313
Palazzo Reale, 252–253
Palazzo Sasso 🖭 , 88
Palazzo Serra di Cassano, 270
Palazzo Turchini 🖭 , 333
Palazzo Veniero, 178
Palazzo Zevallos, 255
Palumbo 🖭 , 88
Paper mills, 68–69
Paradiso 🖭 , 336
**Parco Archeologico e Monu-
   mentvale di Baia,** 231–232
Parco dei Poeti, 271
Parco dei Principi, 187–188
Parking, 359
Naples, 247
Sorrento, 168
Parks
Capri, 131
Naples, 271

Sant'Agnello, 187–188
Sorrento, 177
Parsifal 🖭 , 89
Parteno 🖭 , 330
Passports, 377–378
Pasta, 310–311
Pasticerria dei Vergini ✕ , 302
Pastry shops, 324–326
Pensione Maria Luisa 🖭 , 49
Perfume shops, 143–144
Pharmacies, 373
Philosophical Park, 131
Phlegrean Fields, 225–236
Piazza della Vittoria (Sor-
   rento), 178–179
Piazza Flavio Gioia (Amalfi), 69
Piazza Fontana Moresco
   (Ravello), 85
Piazza Plebiscito (Naples), 255
Piazza Tasso (Sorrento), 179
Piccolo Paradiso 🖭 , 73–74
Pinacoteca, 286–287
Pintauro ✕ , 326
Pinto Storey 🖭 , 336
Pio Monte della Misericordia,
   16, 286–287
Pizza, 308–309
Pizzofalcone, 271
Plane travel. ⇨ See Air travel
Pompeii, 213–224
Porta Capuano, 299
Porta Ercolano, 216
Porta Marina, 216
Poseidon 🖭 , 49
Positano, 17, 29, 31–38,
   40–41, 44–54
Post office hours, 373
Pozzuoli, 225–229
Praiano, 55
Price categories
Amalfi Coast, 26
Bay of Naples, 196
Capri, 101
dining, 26, 101, 167, 196, 305
lodging, 26, 101, 167, 196, 327
Naples, 305, 327
Sorrento and the Sorrentine
   Peninsula, 167
Procida, 10, 98–101, 158–162
dining, 162
exploring, 161–162
itineraries, 100
lodging, 101, 162
outdoor activities and sports,
   101
price catagories, 101
transportation, 100, 159, 161
visitor information, 160
when to tour, 100

Public transportation, *247*
Punta Tragara, *115–116*
Punta Tragara ⊡ , *137*
Pupetto ✕ , *44*

Q

Quarto del Priore, *268–269*
Quisisana ⊡ , *137-138*

R

Radici ✕ , *318–319*
Rail passes, *362–363*
Ravello, *17, 78–93*
Ravello Music Festival, *92*
Relais Palazzo Starace ⊡ ,
    184–185
Remy ✕ , *324–325*
Restaurants. ⇨ *See* Dining
Restrooms, *378*
Ristorante Bellini ✕ , *313*
Ristorante Calise Capriccio
    ✕ , *151*
Ristorante Cocò Gelo ✕ ,
    149–150
Ristorante dei Platani ✕ , *223*
Ristorante Don Antonio ✕ ,
    228–229
Ristorante il Ritrovo ✕ , *44–45*
Ristorante Museo Caruso ✕ ,
    180–181
Ristorante President ✕ , *223*
Road conditions, *360*
Roman ruins and artifacts,
    16, 19
Baia, *229–233*
Bay of Naples, *198–199*
Capri, *116, 118, 125*
Herculaneum, *202–209*
Naples, *283, 286, 288,
    292–295*
Oplontis, *212–213*
Pompeii, *213–224*
Pozzuoli, *225–229*
Room of the Ambassadors, *252*
Rua Nova Mercatorum
    (Amalfi), *68*
Rufolo ⊡ , *89*
Rules of the road, *360–361*

S

Safety, *261, 378–379*
Salto di Tiberio, *116*
San Costanzo, *125*
San Domenico Maggiore, *290*
San Francesco, *85*
San Francesco al Monte ⊡ ,
    336
San Francesco di Paola, *255,
    260*

San Giacomo, *113*
San Giovanni a Carbonara,
    297–298
San Giovanni del Toro, *82*
San Giuseppe dei Ruffi,
    290–291
San Gregorio Armeno, *287*
San Lorenzo Maggiore, *287–288*
San Michele, *131, 133*
San Pancrazio, *60*
San Paolo Maggiore, *291*
San Pietro (Cetara)✕, *95*
San Pietro (Positano) ⊡ , *50*
San Salvatore de Bireto, *77*
Santa Brigida, *263*
Santa Caterina ⊡ , *74*
Santa Caterina a Formiello, *299*
Santa Chiara, *288–289*
Santa Croce, *29*
Santa Croce ✕ , *45*
Santa Margherita Nuova, *161*
Santa Maria a Cetrella,
    129–130
Santa Maria a Gradillo, *86*
Santa Maria Assunta, *35–36*
Santa Maria degli Angeli a
    Pizzofalcone, *271*
Santa Maria della Sanità, *302*
Santa Maria delle Grazie, *189*
Santa Maria Maddalena, *77*
Sant'Agnello, *186–187*
Sant'Agata ✕ , *191*
Sant'Agata sui Due Golfi,
    188–191
Sant'Angelo a Nilo, *291*
Sant'Anna dei Lombardi,
    260–262
Sant'Antonio di Padova, *61*
Santi Apostoli, *291*
Santissima Annunziata, *85*
Santo Stefano, *125–126*
Santuario del Soccorso, *155*
Saraceno D'Oro ✕ , *45*
Scaturchio ✕ , *326*
Scoglio delle Sirene, *114*
Sedile Dominova (Sorrento),
    177
Ser Caracciolo del Sole, *297*
Sezione Presepiale, *269–270*
Shipping services, *374–375*
Shopping. ⇨ *See also specific
    cities and towns*
business hours, *374*
taxes, *379*
Soccer, *20–21*
Sorrento and the Sorrentine
    Peninsula, *10, 16, 164–192*
dining, *168, 177–178, 180–
    181, 189–191, 192*

exploring, *166, 174–178,
    187–188, 189, 191–192*
festivals and seasonal events,
    185
guided tours, *167, 192*
itineraries, *166*
lodging, *167, 182–185, 188,
    191*
nightlife and the arts, *185*
price categories, *167*
shopping, *185–186*
transportation, *166, 168–169,
    173, 187, 189, 191*
visitor information, *173*
when to tour, *167*
Spaggia Grande, *36*
Spas, *151, 154–155, 157*
Sphinx Parapet, *130*
Stabilimenti, *142–143*
Stella Maris ✕ , *71*
Succorpo di San Gennaro,
    280–281
Swimming, *142–143*
Symbols, *7*

T

Taberna di Priapo, *206*
Taverna del Capitano ✕ , *192*
Taxes, *379*
Taxis, *247*
Teatro San Carlo, *262,
    339–340*
Teatro Sannazzaro, *337*
Teatro Trianon, *337–338*
Telephones, *367–369*
Tempio della Pace, *96*
Tempio di Cerere, *96*
Tempio di Giove, *218*
Tempio di Nettuno, *96*
Temple of Diana, *232*
Terme del Foro (Herculaneum),
    207
Terme di Foro (Pompeii), *216*
Terme Manzi ⊡ , *151–152*
Terme Stabiane, *219*
Terme Suburbane (Hercula-
    neum), *205*
Terme Suburbane (Pompeii),
    219
Terra Murata, *160–161*
Terrace of M. Nonius Balbus,
    204–205
Theater, *337–338*
Theater buildings, *262*
Thermal baths, *151, 154–155,
    157*
Thermopolia, *206*
Timing the visit, *12, 19*
Timpani e Tempura ✕ , *313*

Tipping, *379–380*
Toledo, *248–255, 260–263*
Toledo 🍽, *333–334*
Torello, *92*
Toro 🍽, *89*
Torre Annunziata, *212–213*
Tours, *380*
Bay of Naples, 211, 222, 230
Naples, 247
Sorrento and the Sorrentine
    Peninsula, 167, 192
Traffic, *261*
Train travel, *361–363*
Amalfi Coast, 27
Bay of Naples, 197
Naples, 247
Sorrento and the Sorrentine
    Peninsula, 169
Tramontano (shop), *346*
Transportation, *12, 355–363*
Trattoria Castel dell'Ovo-
    Tabacchi ✕, *319*
Trattoria dell'Oca ✕, *319*
Trattoria San Ferdinando ✕,
    306
Trattoria Vanvitelli ✕, *321*
Trianon ✕, *316*

U

Umberto ✕, *319*

V

Vaco 'e Press ✕, *322*
Valle dei Mulini, *68–69*
Value-added tax (V.A.T.), *379*
Vascello, *160*
"Vessels of the King" museum,
    269
Vesuvius and environs, *16,
    201–212*
Via Krupp, *118, 125*
Via Positanesi d'America, *36–37*
Villa Amore 🍽, *89*
Villa Antonio 🍽, *150*
Villa Cimbrone, *17, 82–83*
Villa Cimbrone 🍽, *90*
Villa Comunale, *177*
Villa dei Misteri, *221*
Villa dei Papiri, *204*
Villa Episcopio, *85*
Villa Flavio Gioia 🍽, *51*
Villa Floridiana, *271–272*
Villa Giulia 🍽, *234, 236*
Villa Jovis, *116, 118*
Villa Krupp 🍽, *138*
Villa Lysis, *118*
Villa Malaparte, *126*
Villa Maria 🍽, *90*
Villa of the Empress Poppaea,
    212–213
Villa Rufolo, *84–85*

Villa San Michele, *17, 130–131*
Villa Sarah 🍽, *138*
Visas, *377–378*
Visitor information, *380*
Amalfi Coast, 33, 64, 79
Bay of Naples, 202, 214, 226
Capri, 106
Ischia, 146
Naples, 241
Procida, 160
Sorrento and the Sorrentine
    Peninsula, 173
Vittoria ✕, *86–87*
Vocabulary, *349–353*
Volcanoes, *16, 201–212*
Volunteer programs, *380*

W

Walking, *21*
*Capri, 101, 102–103, 110–111,
    127*
Naples, 250, 267, 275–277
Weather, *12*
Web sites, *381*
When to tour, *12, 19*
Wine, *372*
Amalfi Coast, 56
Campania, 170–171
Naples, 342
tours, 380

PHOTO CREDITS

1, Robert I. C. Fisher. 2–3, Demetrio Carrasco/age fotostock. 5, capripalace.com. Chapter 1: Experience the Amalfi Coast, Capri & Naples: 8–9, Chris Sargent/Shutterstock. 10, Allerina & Glen/Flickr. 11 (left), Alfio Ferlito/Shutterstock. 11 (right), iStockphoto. 14, Campania Tourism. 15 (left), ollirg/Shutterstock. 15 (right) and 16 (left), iStockphoto. 16 (top center), Public Domain. 16 (top right), Khirman Vladimir/Shutterstock. 16 (bottom right), Vacclav/Shutterstock. 17 (top left), Capri Tourism. 17 (bottom left), Campania Tourism. 17 (top center), Robert I. C. Fisher. 17 (bottom center), Floriano Rescigno/iStockphoto. 17 (right), Tina Lorien/iStockphoto. 18, Public Domain. 19 (left and right), Campania Tourism. 20, Jan Greune/age fotostock. 21, Maurizio Grimaldi/age fotostock. 22, Gina Sanders/Shutterstock. Chapter 2: The Amalfi Coast: 23, Robert I. C. Fisher. 24, Floriano Rescigno/iStockphoto. 25, ary6/Shutterstock. 27, Vladimir Khirman/iStockphoto. 28, Arialdo Rescigno/iStockphoto. 29 (top), Irina Korshunova/iStockphoto. 29 (bottom), Andrew Jalbert/Shutterstock. 30, Robert I. C. Fisher. 34, Bruce Bi/age fotostock. 39, José Fuste Raga/age fotostock. 40 (top), Khirman Vladimir/Shutterstock. 40 (bottom), george green/Shutterstock. 41 (left), Robert I. C. Fisher. 41 (center), ollirg/Shutterstock. 41 (right), Robert I. C. Fisher. 42 (top), Alfio Ferlito/Shutterstock. 42 (bottom), Khirman Vladimir/Shutterstock. 43 (left), Robert I. C. Fisher. 43 (center), Allerina & Glen/Flickr. 43 (right), ollirg/Shutterstock. 45–50, Robert I. C. Fisher. 57, Atlantide S.N.C./age fotostock. 60, Danilo Donadoni/age fotostock. 67, Demetrio Carrasco/age fotostock. 68, Atlantide S.N.C./age fotostock. 76, Bruno Morandi/age fotostock. 84, Richard T. Nowitz/age fotostock. 91, Jensens/wikipedia.org. 94, Wojtek Buss/age fotostock. Chapter 3: Capri, Ischia, and Procida: 97, Matz Sjöberg / age fotostock. 98 (top and bottom), Capri Tourism. 99, Vladimir Khirman/iStockphoto. 102, Malgorzata Kistryn/Shutterstock. 103 (top), Elena Uspenskaya/Shutterstock. 103 (bottom), Vacclav/Shutterstock. 104, Matz Sjöberg/age fotostock. 106, Massimo Rivenci/Alamy. 112, FAN/Alamy. 115, Danita Delimont/Alamy. 117, Juneisy Hawkins/iStockphoto. 119, Ken Gillham/age fotostock. 120 (top), Danilo Donadoni/age fotostock. 120 (bottom), Kiedrowski, R/age fotostock. 121 (top), deepblue-photographer/Shutterstock. 121 (bottom left), De Agostini Picture Library/ Fototeca ENIT. 121 (bottom right), caprirelaxboats.com/salsa/it. 122 (top), capripalace.com. 122 (bottom left), Capri Tourism. 122 (bottom right), Colin Sinclair/age fotostock. 123 (top), SCPhotos/Alamy. 123 (bottom), caprirelaxboats.com/salsa/it. 124, Barbara Positano/barbarapositano.it. 128, Capri Tourism. 132, scanpress/Alamy. 139, Demetrio Carrasco/age fotostock. 146, Paola Ghirotti/Fototeca ENIT. 153, Adam Eastland/Alamy. 158, Maurizio Grimaldi/age fotostock. 160, CuboImages srl/Alamy. Chapter 4: Sorrento and the Sorrentine Peninsula: 163, Robert I. C. Fisher. 164, Danilo Ascione/iStockphoto. 165 (top), Khirman Vladimir/Shutterstock. 165 (bottom), iStockphoto. 170, Atlantide S.N.C./age fotostock. 171 (top), Campania Tourism. 171 (bottom), iStockphoto. 172, keepwaddling1/Flickr. 175, Adam Eastland/Alamy. 179, John Mole Photography/Alamy. 180–90, Robert I. C. Fisher. Chapter 5: The Bay of Naples: 193, Danilo Donadoni/age fotostock. 194 (top), Pierdelune/Shutterstock. 194 (bottom), iStockphoto. 195, Paola Ghirotti/Fototeca ENIT. 198, Castello aragonese by Ferdinando Marfella www.flickr.com/photos/fotofm/1268328710/ Attribution-ShareAlike License. 199 (top), Angela Sorrentino/iStockphoto. 199 (bottom), Angela Sorrentino/iStockphoto.200, DEA PICTURE LIBRARY/age fotostock. 205, Demetrio Carrasco/age fotostock. 210, DEA/S AMANTINI/age fotostock. 213, GARDEL Bertrand/age fotostock. 215 (top), The Print Collector / age fotostock. 215 (bottom), SuperStock/age fotostock. 216, kated/Shutterstock. 217 (top), skyfish/Shutterstock. 217 (bottom), Walter Rawlings / age fotostock. 218 (top), Vito Arcomano/Fototeca ENIT. 218 (bottom left), Boris Stroujko/Shutterstock. 218 (right), Alastair Johnson/iStockphoto. 219, Doug Scott/age fotostock. 220, Katie Hamlin. 221, Demetrio Carrasco/Agency Jon Arnold Images/age fotostock. 228, Danilo Donadoni/age fotostock. 235, DEA/S VANNINI/age fotostock. Chapter 6: Naples: 237, Atlantide S.N.C./age fotostock. 238, wikipedia.org. 239 (top), Fabiuccio/wikipedia.org. 239 (bottom), Khirman Vladimir/Shutterstock. 241 (top), Dino/Shutterstock. 241 (bottom), Knud Nielsen/Shutterstock. 242, Robert I. C. Fisher. 243 (top), gallimaufry/Shutterstock. 243 (bottom), Dave Gordon/Shutterstock. 244, Tony French/Alamy. 246, Demetrio Carrasco/age fotostock. 254, Kiedrowski, R/age fotostock. 256, Doug Scott/age fotostock. 257 (top), Public Domain. 257 (bottom), wikipedia.org. 258 (top left), CuboImages srl/Alamy. 258 (bottom left), Neil Setchfield/Alamy. 258 (right), Sylvain Grandadam/age fotostock. 259 (top), Doug Scott/age fotostock. 259 (bottom left and right), Public Domain. 260, Khirman Vladimir/Shutterstock. 263, Sylvain Grandadam/age fotostock. 269, De Agostini Picture Library/Fototeca ENIT. 275 (left), AEP/Alamy. 275 (top and bottom right), Robert I. C. Fisher. 276 (top left), Lalupa/wikipedia.org. 276 (top right), Marisa Allegra Williams/iStockphoto. 276 (bottom), Tibor Bognar/Alamy. 277 (top left), Peter Horree/Alamy. 277 (top center), Vittorio Sciosia/Alamy. 279(top right), Doug Scott/age fotostock. 277 (bottom), Robert I. C. Fisher. 282, Ethel Davies/age fotostock. 285, CuboImages srl/Alamy. 289, vittorio sciosia/age fotostock. 298, Paolo Gallo/Alamy. 307, Robert I. C. Fisher. 308, Campania Tourism. 309 (top), Mary Evans Picture Library/Alamy. 309 (second from